The Rhetoric of Curse
in Galatians

Emory Studies in Early Christianity

General Editor
Vernon K. Robbins

Associate Editor
David B. Gowler, Chowan College

Cover Design by Gina M. Tansley
(adapted from Rick A. Robbins, *Mixed Media 1981*)

The cover design introduces an environment for disciplined creativity. The seven squares superimposed over one another represent multiple arenas for programmatic research, analysis, and interpretation. The area in the center, common to all the arenas, is like the area that provides the unity for a volume in the series. The small square in the center of the squares denotes a paragraph, page, or other unit of text. The two lines that extend out from the small square, perpendicular to one another, create an opening to territory not covered by any of the multiple squares. These lines have the potential to create yet another square of the same or different size that would be a new arena for research, analysis, and interpretation.

The Rhetoric of Curse in Galatians
Paul Confronts Another Gospel

by
Kjell Arne Morland

SCHOLARS PRESS
Atlanta, Georgia

EMORY STUDIES
IN EARLY CHRISTIANITY

The Rhetoric of Curse in Galatians
Paul Confronts Another Gospel

by
Kjell Arne Morland

Grateful acknowledgment is given to the Office of the Secretary of
the University, the Graduate School of Arts and Sciences, Emory
College, and the Department of Religion
and
to the Norwegian Research Council for Science and Humanities
(NAVF) in support of this volume.

Library of Congress Cataloging in Publication Data
Morland, Kjell Arne.
    The rhetoric of curse in Galatians : Paul confronts another Gospel
/ by Kjell Arne Morland.
    p.   cm.—(Emory studies in early Christianity ; 5)
    Includes bibliographical references and indexes.
    ISBN 1-55540-923-7
    1. Bible. N. T. Galatians I, 6–12—Language, Style. 2. Bible.
N.T. Galatians III, 8–14—Language, Style. 3. Blessing and cursing
in the Bible. 4. Bible. N.T. —Relation to the Old Testament.
I. Title. II. Series: Emory studies in early Christianity ; vol. 5.
BS2685.2.M676 1995   93-39947
                                                 CIP

Published by Scholars Press
for
Emory University

Previous titles in the series published by Peter Lang Publishing

Publication of this volume
was made possible with a gift
by Isabella Lewis
in honor of Clay Lewis

ACKNOWLEDGMENTS

The text from the Revised Standard Version of the Bible, copyright © 1946, 1952, 1971 by the Division of Christian Education of the National Council of the Churches of Christ in the USA, is used by permission.

The text from the Revised Standard Version Apocrypha, copyright © 1957 by the Division of Christian Education of the National Council of Churches of Christ in the USA, is used by permission.

The text from *The Dead Sea Scrolls in English*, edited by Geza Vermes, third edition, revised and augmented, copyright © 1987, is reproduced by permission of Penguin Books Ltd.

The text from *The Old Testament Pseudepigrapha I-II*, edited by James H. Charlesworth, copyright © 1983, 1985, is used by permission from Doubleday, a division of Bantam, Doubleday, Dell Publishing Group, Inc.

The text from *Loeb Classical Library* is reprinted by permission of the publishers and the Loeb Classical Library for the following works: Philo I-X; Josephus I-X; *ad C. Herennium*; Aristotle, *The 'Art' of Rhetoric*; and Cicero, *De Inventione*.

TABLE OF CONTENTS

vii

PART II: THE RHETORICAL HORIZON

Chapter 7 Methodological Considerations

Chapter 8 The Rhetoric of Galatians

PART III: ANATHEMA AND CURSE IN GALATIANS

Chapter 9 The Anathemas of Gal 1:8–9 in Context

Chapter 10 The Curses of Gal 3:10, 13 in Context

Chapter 11 Final Summary and Conclusion

EDITORIAL FOREWORD

Volumes in *Emory Studies in Early Christianity* contribute in various ways to the interdisciplinary dialogue that has developed in New Testament studies during the last two decades. The present volume by Kjell Arne Morland is in many ways a continuation of conversations begun in earlier volumes in this series concerning the nature and function of Pauline rhetoric. In part, it challenges assumptions made in the previous studies; in other ways, it reinforces some of their approaches and conclusions. This debate and dialogue, in our opinion, is an important one, not only in Pauline studies but in study of the entire New Testament.

The second volume in this series, by H. Wayne Merritt (1993), investigates classical and Hellenistic literature for the purpose of establishing a closer alliance between rhetoric and ethics in Pauline scholarship. Paul's defense of his apostleship utilized conventional language that established a moral vision understandable to a wide cross-section of ancient Mediterranean society. Jan Botha's volume (1994) merges linguistic, literary, rhetorical, and social-scientific criticisms to produce a multiple reading of Roman 13. He argues that a "responsible" (i.e., "ethical") reading cannot take place without an interdisciplinary approach to the text. Botha's volume provides an additional critical voice in the dialogue in Pauline studies—one which makes very clear the importance of one's ideological approach to these texts.

Kjell Arne Morland's volume continues this dialogue from a rather different ideological perspective. He combines a comprehensive survey of Israelite and Jewish tradition, rhetorical strategies of analysis and interpretation gleaned from Greco-Roman treatises, and semantic field analysis to interpret the meaning and dynamics of curse in Paul's epistle to the Galatians. Thus, it presents a distinctive interdisciplinary approach to an aspect of Pauline discourse that has intrigued, puzzled, or troubled interpreters for centuries.

One of the special purposes of the present volume is to nurture greater dialogue between Norwegian and American scholarship in Pauline studies. Morland speaks out of a context where Ernst Baasland has emphasized rhetorical analysis of New Testament epistles, Peder Borgen has shown scholars how to advance interpretation of New Testament texts with the rich resources that lie in the literature of Philo of Alexandria, and David Hellholm has highlighted the enthymematic nature of literature in antiquity. Merging insights gleaned from these rich traditions of interpretation in Norway with his own special interests and insights, Morland addresses the social and cultural dynamics of Paul's use of curse language in his epistle to the Galatians. The result is a systematic, interdisciplinary analysis and interpretation that is grounded in careful attention to language, traditional society and culture, and religious belief and commitment.

One of the notable ways in which Morland's volume differs from Merritt's and Botha's volumes in this series lies in the prominence it gives to Martin Luther's interpretation of Pauline discourse. With this emphasis, the volume enters a well-advanced dialogue in American scholarship on Paul. Many American scholars consciously attempt to free Pauline discourse from Augustinian and Lutheran interpretations. Others, in contrast, welcome both Augustinian and Lutheran interpretation into Pauline commentary. As Morland's volume speaks out of a social and cultural location that maintains a deep relationship with the modes of thinking and interpretation of Martin Luther, it brings its own particular voice to the conversation.

We offer this volume with the conviction that dialogue, even vigorous dialogue, is an important mode for advancement of biblical interpretation. In our view no tradition of interpretation, no matter what its potential for dominance may be, should be allowed to establish itself outside a context of energetic dialogue, debate, and review. From this perspective, the present volume represents a significant voice in the kind of international conversation characteristic of biblical scholarship at its richest moments in history.

Finally, the editors wish to express their sincere gratitude to the board of the Norwegian Research Council for Science and Humanities (NAVF), who made substantial resources available for the English styling and technical preparation and printing of this volume.

Vernon K. Robbins, *Emory University*
General Editor

David B. Gowler, *Chowan College*
Associate Editor

October 21, 1995

ABBREVIATIONS

Abbreviations follow the style of *Catholic Biblical Quarterly*, found, for example, in *CBQ* 46 (1984):393–408. Additional or divergent abbreviations are as follows:

Internal Abbreviations

cf.   = Compare
ch(s).   = References to chapter(s)
sec(s). = References to section(s) within a chapter

References to primary sources

Philo's writings
  Abr   = De Abrahamo
  Agric = De Agricultura
  Cher = De Cherubim
  Conf = De Confusione Linguarum
  Congr = De Congressu Eruditionis Gratia
  Decal = De Decalogo
  Deter = Quod Deterius Potiori insidiari soleat
  Fuga = De Fuga et Inventione
  Heres = Quis Rerum Divinarum Heres sit
  Leg   = Legum Allegoriae
  Migr = De Migratione Abrahami
  Mos   = De Vita Mosis
  Mut   = De Mutatione Nominum
  Post = De Posteritate Caini
  Praem = De Praemiis et Poenis
  Prob = De Providentia
  Quaest. in Exod. = Quaestiones in Exodum
  Sobr = De Sobrietate
  Somn = De Somniis
  Spec = De Specialibus Legibus
  Virt = De Virtutibus

Josephus' writings
  (Jos.) Ant = Antiquitates Judaicae
  (Jos.) Ap   = Contra Apionem
  (Jos.) Bell = De bello Judaico
  (Jos.) Vita = Vita Josephi

Qumran writings
  11QTem(ple) = Temple Scroll from Cave 11

Pseudepigrapha
  Prop. = Vitae Prophetarum

Rhetorical handbooks
  ad Alexan. = Rhetoric to Alexander
  ad Herenn. = Rhetoric to Herennium
  (Cic.) Inv. = Cicero, *De Inventione*
  (Arist.) Rhet. = Aristotle, *"Art" of Rhetoric*
  (Hermog.) Prog. = Hermogenes, *Progymnasmata*
  (Hermog.) Stat. = Hermogenes, *On Stases*

References to secondary sources and works of reference

  FS   = Festschrift (= Studies in Honor of)
  JSPseud = Journal for the Study of the Pseudepigrapha
  UTB = Uni-Taschenbücher

For abbreviations of other sources and works of reference, see Bibliography:301-304.

Citations from translations

When other references are not given, Biblical and Apocryphal quotations are from the RSV, texts from Pseudepigrapha are quoted from OTP, texts from Qumran are quoted from DSSE, and texts from Philo and Josephus are from LCL. For Rabbinic, Roman-Hellenistic, and Early Christian texts, cf. the Bibliography:302-304.

Theological abbreviation

  dtr-SH = the deuteronomistic scheme of history, cf. the presentation in sec. 3.2.1.

PREFACE

A number of people and institutions deserve my deepest gratitude for helping and encouraging me during this project.

The project was started in 1986 when I was accepted as a doctoral student by the dr. art. program at the University of Trondheim. Most of the work was completed while I worked as a research assistant for the Free Faculty of Theology in Oslo (1986-1990) with a teaching load each semester. The work was completed with the support of a grant from the Norwegian Research Council for Science and Humanities (NAVF), which made it possible for me to work in Tübingen, Germany, in the Fall of 1990. Thus, I benefitted from a double institutional connection, where colleagues gave advice in seminars in both places. In addition, I was given the opportunity to work abroad some months in excellent library conditions. I am very thankful for all of these opportunities.

My deepest gratitude goes to the Free Faculty of Theology in Oslo, who paid my salary the entire time and provided inspiring collegial fellowship, and to my main supervisor there, prof. dr. theol. Ernst Baasland, whose creative supervision has been most inspiring. I am also thankful to the University of Trondheim for the program I have attended there, and to my second supervisor there, prof. dr. theol. Peder Borgen, for his careful and comprehensive response to my work.

I also wish to express my gratitude to my wife Astrid, who has supported my work in an excellent manner, without letting me forget my family duties.

I am grateful to Hilde Hasselgård who read through most of my manuscript at an early stage and corrected its most disturbing errors. My gratitude extends further to David Gowler and Douglas Low, who adapted the manuscript to an American publishing format, and to N. Clayton Croy and Sarah Melcher who compiled and verified the indexes of authors and passages. Last, and with great importance, I wish to thank Vernon Robbins not only for the kindness with which he accepted this volume for publication in *Emory Studies in Early Christianity* but also for the skill and diligence with which he worked through the manuscript to bring its style closer to an American idiom of expression.

Varmbo
October 25, 1995

Kjell Arne Morland

CHAPTER 1

1.0: INTRODUCTION: TASK AND METHODS

1.1: Curse in Galatians

In our modern, western culture, concepts such as blessing and curse seem to have lost much of their content. Normally, curses are associated with swearing and the use of profane language, but in certain situations they may be viewed as justifiable expressions of deep emotion. Our predispositions against the ancient concept of curse place it at the fringes of the New Testament message. We lack adequate categories for ascribing to curses any real importance, and this is a handicap for modern research.

It is not difficult to find tribal societies even today where curses play an important role in social interaction. Curses are used in many cultures to enforce law and morality (Little:183); they are regarded as an effective force when spoken, charged with energy. Moreover, a curse is a baneful substance which may spread to its surroundings, especially through physical contact (Crawley:368–70). We may briefly present two typical examples:

> E. E. Evans-Pritchard has studied the religion of the Nuers in southern Egypt. In this culture curses are regarded as powerful sanctions of accepted norms of behavior, because failure to conform may bring about the negative consequence of the curse (17–18). If a curse is uttered with due cause from the right person, it will sooner or later cause misfortune, disease, or even death (165–68). If one has suffered injustice, it is not even necessary to utter the curse; it is enough to think it or feel it. The curse has its own psychological power, but it is God who makes it operative (170–73).
> C. A. Kratz has studied curses among the Okiek in Kenya. Also here formal curses are considered effective according to the kind of relationship that exists between the curser and the victim. They cause an array of misfortunes, notably death. Curses often end with a statement about their consequence (639–42). Once spoken, the curse will take effect. Therefore they are rarely used; Kratz only heard about ten formal curses over several years. A formal oath is especially dangerous, since it puts two parties under the curse: It is bound to hit one of them, since both cannot have right on their side. Kratz never heard of any such oath in actual use (644, 648–49).

These studies suggest that we might have reason to question our own predispositions toward the concept of curse. This volume is an attempt to give more attention to the importance of curses in the early church. Such an attempt may open up new avenues for understanding the central message of the New Testament.

I am not aware of any monograph from our century that is primarily occupied with the concept of curse in the New Testament. Two works may be mentioned, however, where this notion is interpreted together with related concepts.

L. Brun published a monograph in 1932 where he investigated blessing and curse in the early church: *Segen und Fluch im Urchristentum.* He investigated the curse both terminologically and phenomenologically, and he showed that it was present in a relatively broad spectrum of the New Testament.[1] His conclusion is that curses in the New Testament are remnants of older ways of thinking, which in principle have been overcome (6, 134). The blessing rather than the curse, in his view, was the most important in early Christianity.[2]

W. Doskocil published a monograph in 1958 where he investigated the ban in the early church: *Der Bann in der Urkirche.* In this study the concept of curse was taken to have a more important function, namely as a means in the early church to implement church discipline in a fluid, formative period before fixed procedures for excommunication had been established (1, 202). Since the main interest was in finding preliminary stages of excommunication, however, texts such as Matt 18:15–18 and 1 Cor 5 became more interesting than texts containing curse terms (27, 59, 194–95, 197–98). He also distinguished the concept of curse from the concept of expulsion in a manner that caused him to de-emphasize the importance of the curse (4, 9, 194–99, 202).

A fresh understanding of the curse motif in the New Testament requires both a new gathering of information and more careful reflection on curse itself than the studies of Brun and Doskocil. There are several reasons why I find the letter to the Galatians to be the most proper object of investigation:

a) It is natural as a point of departure to concentrate on the twenty seven curse-terms that appear in the New Testament:

---

[1] In addition to texts with curse terminology which will be referred to below, Brun also treats woe formulas (84–89) and some implicit curse formulas (cf. 100–105 for Acts 8:20–21; 13:10–11; 18:6; 23:3). He discusses miracles of judgment such as the cursing of the fig tree (Mark 11:12–14, 20 par), the signs accompanying the death of Jesus, the blinding of Bar-Jesus (Acts 13:6–12), the deaths of Judas, Ananias, Sapphira, Herod (Acts 1:18; 5:1–11; 12:20–23), and the visions of seals, trumpets, and bowls in Rev 6; 8–9; 16 (74–81). He discusses the curse ceremony of 1 Cor 5, together with many texts ordering the expulsion of sinners and false teachers (93–100, 106–09). He also discusses several texts that connect persecution, curse and reviling (111–15), oaths as self-imprecations (129–33), and texts with other motives.

[2] The blessing in the New Testament has also been treated in monographs after Brun. Schenk 1967 tried to demonstrate that even the concept of blessing has lost its original connotations in the New Testament, but he has been rightly refuted by Westermann 1968. A concentration on the concept of blessing by Paul is found in Thuruthumaly 1981.

Gospels/Acts: Matt 25:41 (καταράσθαι); 26:74 (καταθεματίζειν); Mark 11:21 (καταράσθαι); 14:71 (ἀναθεματίζειν); Luke 6:28 (καταράσθαι); Acts 23:12, 14, 21 (ἀνάθεμα/-τίζειν 4x); John 7:49 (ἐπάρατος);

Paul: Rom 3:14 (ἀρά); 9:3 (ἀνάθεμα); 12:14 (καταράσθαι); 1 Cor 12:3 (ἀνάθεμα); 16:22 (ἀνάθεμα); Gal 1:8-9 (ἀνάθεμα 2x); 3:10, 13 (κατάρα/ ἐπικατάρατος 5x).

Other: Heb 6:8 (κατάρα); Jas 3:9-10 (κατάρα/-σθαι 2x); 2 Pet 2:14 (κατάρα); Rev 22:3 (κατάθεμα).

b) Paul is the author who uses curse terms most frequently. In three of his main letters he uses curse terms twelve times, nearly half of the occurrences in the New Testament. Therefore, a concentration on Paul seems natural.[3]

c) We find more than half of Paul's curse terms in Galatians, and both ἀνάθεμα (2x in 1:8-9) and κατάρα/ἐπικατάρατος (5x in 3:10, 13) appear in important passages in the letter, both as part of the *exordium* and at the start of the main argumentation.

d) By concentrating on Galatians, we will have the benefit of the relation of the curses to a quite specific situation, which may provide significant information concerning their function.

Before presenting the method and the goal for this volume, (cf. sec. 1.4), I will give a survey of previous research. First, I will present the main features of research on curse in the Hebrew Bible to demonstrate that we have quite another starting point today than when Brun made his investigation (cf. sec. 1.2). Then, I will present the main features of research on the specific curses in Galatians to demonstrate that a new investigation of the curses is long overdue (cf. sec. 1.3).

1.2: A survey of research on the concept of curse in the Hebrew Bible

During this century, our understanding of curse has changed from an older basic consensus around the 1920's to a new, different consensus during the 1960's. Brun builds his work on the old consensus, represented by Pedersen, Mowinckel, and Hempel (Brun:5).

The fundamental study was J. Pedersen's 1914 study: *Der Eid bei den Semiten*. Pedersen, who worked within the framework of the History of Religions School, was especially interested in comparing curses in the

---

[3]Also the blessing terminology points in this direction. If we put aside the doxological use of εὐλογεῖν (which has no equivalent in the realm of curse), we find that Paul is responsible for 9 of its 25 occurrences, namely in Gal (3x), 1 Cor (1x), Rom (3x) and Eph (2x). It is only Hebrews that uses the term more frequently (7x); cf. the discussion and table in Schenk:33-35.

Hebrew Bible with curses in Assyrian texts. In Assyrian texts, he found the emphasis of curse, on one hand, to be magical: the curse as a ban, as an evil substance which occupies man, destroys him from the inside and causes physical as well as moral evil. On the other hand, the emphasis is on the consequences of the curse, which take away from man all his fortune and honor (1914:71–72). Pedersen considered the magical aspect of curse to be the most important: curse as a real power, as a poisonous substance in the soul (1914:88–91).[4] He connected this magical curse with the אלה-stem in the Hebrew Bible (1914:78–83).

Mowinckel supplemented this study with a historical focus by outlining the development of curse throughout Israelite history. He argued for a cultic *Sitz im Leben* for blessing and curse.[5] In the course of history, cultic practice transformed the concept of curse so that the magical curse was transformed into prayer tamed by new religious and ethical motivations.[6] Hempel described the transformation in a rather different way: as a tremendous struggle between religion and magic in a context where belief in one God was very slowly winning out. During this process, the different functions were more or less simultaneously present.[7]

A common picture arises from these studies: The origins of curse are magical. Cultic life provided a way of taming the concepts, and in the end belief in Yahweh almost overcame it. On this basis, we can understand why L. Brun treated curses in the New Testament as remnants of old thoughts, which in principle had been overcome. Although this overly simplistic model of development must be regarded as outdated, these studies are still valuable collections of sources containing evidence and observations about curses.

In the following decades many efforts have been made to trace more precisely the *Sitz im Leben* of the legitimate curse in Israel. Attempts were

---

[4]Pedersen developed this further in his later work: He connected this aspect of curse especially to sin. Sin and curse are closely intertwined: they both destroy a human soul from within (1926:411–52). In addition, curse could be imposed from without, namely by illegitimate curses and witchcraft from one's enemies (441–43, 446–51).

[5]Mowinckel:13–33 (blessing in cult); 68–82 (curse in cult); 97–107 (combination of blessing and curse in cult, at the new year festival with covenant renewal).

[6]Mowinckel:131–35. First there was a development from a magical word over a legal use in cult until the conviction that God alone could bless and curse; the Jew could only pray to him. Second there was a combination between the blessing and curse and religious/ethical motivation.

[7]Hempel:109–10. He preferred the picture of three circles (95): The outer circle is *folk religion*, where magical thought is deeply rooted. The next is *cult religion*, which systematizes and regulates blessing and cursing for the benefit of the people. The inner circle is *ethical/prophetic religion*, which loosens itself totally from magical/cultic concepts and prepares the way for New Testament teaching. He uses material from all religions around the Mediterranean, and from many centuries, to demonstrate how deeply rooted magic always has been in those religions (22–47).

made to trace it in the effectiveness of the spoken word in folk belief[8] or in a juridical setting.[9]   Other scholars developed the cultic setting from Mowinckel and argued that the combination of curse and blessing originated from the feast of covenant renewal.[10]   When the new consensus emerged around the 1960's, it was due to four important factors.

First, many scholars began to emphasize the connection between the legitimate curse and covenantal curses, an insight which was reinforced by the discovery of connections both in form and content with curses in ancient vassal-treaties.[11]

Second, J. Scharbert brought in new perspectives by investigating curse from the angle of terminology (1958a).   Then the interpretation of the אלה-stem became radically changed. He discovered that it was a juridical term, a conditional curse uttered to guarantee property, laws, treaties, and oaths (5; cf. TWAT 1:280). The קלל-stem, in contrast, had a much wider semantic field than curse; it mainly designated the treating of another person with disrespect and abuse (13–14).[12]   Therefore the ארר-stem, in Scharbert's view, was the main stem for the curse, and he argued that it mainly had social emphasis aiming at expulsion from the community (5–8; cf. *TWAT* 1:440–41).[13]

Third, this shift called forth the importance of an old distinction by Pedersen. Pedersen compared Hebrew Bible material not only with material from Assyrian texts, but also with Arabic texts. There he found the emphasis of curse to be social.   The term *al-laan* designates expulsion from human society, that is, from the nomadic clan (1914:65–66). Pedersen identified the

---

[8]Cf. Blank:73–83. The simple curse formula and the composite curse for the most part reveal curse as a profane wish, while freely composed curses bear witness to a development of curse into imprecatory prayer.

[9]Cf. Westermann 1960:140–42. He proposed that the form of curse indicates that the magical curse became part of the juridical setting, accompanying the pronouncement of a sentence.

[10]Cf. Alt:314, 324–30 and von Rad 1938:17–36 for Deut 27–28; Reventlow 1961: 142–61 for Lev 26; Reventlow 1962a:4–44, 157–68; 1962b:83–90 for curse and blessing in Ezekiel and Amos.

[11]Cf. Noth:132–37; Fensham 1962 and 1963; Hillers.   For Deut 28 especially, cf. further Frankena:144–50; Weinfeld 1965 and 1972:116–29.

[12]He holds that the noun always designated curse (11). Cf. also his *TWAT* 7:42–47.

[13]This terminological approach was also taken up by Brichto 1963. His scope was narrower than Scharbert's: He investigated whether or not the various terms are to be interpreted as oral imprecations, and whether they are connected to magic as an automatic self-fulfilling word (cf. the conclusions and summary, pp. 205–18). In spite of this, his results correspond roughly with Scharbert's with regard to אלה and קלל, but he concludes that the ארר-stem denotes the power to bind with a spell or to impose a ban (70–71, 114–15, 176–77, 199).

social expulsion from society with the ארר-stem in the Hebrew Bible (1914:78–83). When Scharbert investigated curse and blessing within a broader sociological context, he found it to be a major expression for the concept of solidarity (cf. 1958b).[14]

The fourth factor is the classical study of W. Schottroff: *Der altisraelitische Fluchspruch*, published in 1969. Schottroff analyzed the ארור-formula carefully, with an emphasis on form-critical method. He argued for the original form and *Sitz im Leben*, as well as for the process in which secondary elements were added. He also referred back to Pedersen's distinction between Assyrian and Arabic concepts of curse and asked whether it is possible that the Israelites had one concept of curse during their nomadic life, which was modified after the settlement in the land of Canaan (10–16). He shows convincingly that the analogous material from neighboring nations concentrates on secondary elements in the curse formula (97–105, 152–61). The original form ארור אתה, however, is without parallel in the Ancient Near East (68–73). In the last chapter, he tried to trace the *Gattungsgeschichte* of the curse formula throughout the era of the Hebrew Bible, and we may summarize his results in three main steps (231–33):

> a) The origin of the ארור-formula is to be found in nomadic life in the desert. It is a formula of social exclusion from the family or clan and is used by the head of the family/clan as a means of private jurisdiction. A person is received in the clan via the blessing formula and excluded by means of the curse formula, to be surrendered to the magical, evil powers of the outside sphere of misfortune (163–210).[15]
> b) With this as a foundation, he explained the changes which took place when Israel settled in the land. The curse became a juridical guarantee of oaths, treaties, and laws, and was used in this respect also in the cult, a cultic use that is clearly a secondary development. The consequences of the curse were modified from total exclusion to loss of fortune, fertility, and wealth (211–20).
> c) In due time the curse/blessing motifs became theological leitmotifs in Israelite history writing. The Yahwist used the curse motif (especially in the primal history) in a manner that suited very well the conditions within the great empire of David/Solomon (143–50, 202–5). The deuteronomistic writers combined the curse/blessing with Yahweh's covenant with the people, in order to explain the catastrophe of 587 BCE. In this way the concept became one of the most important for Jewish interpretation of their own history. The main text for this combination is Deut 27f, where we have eighteen of the thirty nine Hebrew Bible ארור-formulas (25, 220–28).

---

[14]In this study, Scharbert compares Hebrew Bible material with concepts of solidarity in Ancient Near Eastern cultures and in nomadic cultures (1958b:24-109) in order to identify which Hebrew Bible motifs of curse and blessing correspond with these cultures, and which motifs were unique to Israel (110—274, especially the summary 249—74).

[15]He argues that at least Gen 3:14(17); 4:11; (9:25; Jos 9:23) show some traces from this use (206).

In this way Scharbert and Schottroff have given a new basis for understanding the curse. It is not that curse as an effective power has been tamed within the Hebrew Bible. It is rather that the oldest texts bear witness to curse in private jurisdiction in tribal times; then several texts demonstrate curse as a guarantee of oaths, treaties, and laws in the nation after the settlement, while other later texts use the concept in theological reflection on the national identity and history of the Jewish people. Scholars such as O. H. Steck and K. Baltzer have demonstrated that this deuteronomistic theology also has been received on a broad scale in intertestamental literature.[16]

We have, therefore, every reason to believe that first century Christians still perceived curses as an effective and real power. The new element that may be important for them concerns the covenantal context of curses and their use as leitmotifs for Jewish identity.

1.3: A survey of research on the curses in Galatians

This general background provides a basic context for approaching the specific curses in Gal 1:8-9 and 3:10, 13. The exegetical challenge of these passages is that Paul seems to imply unspoken presuppositions in each instance. In Gal 1:9 he issues a double anathema, but he does not state explicitly what consequences he perceives it to have. In Gal 3:10 he issues a curse on those who rely on works of the law. He claims that they are hit by the curse of Deut 27:26, but he does not state explicitly the reason for it. In 3:13 he states that Christ redeemed us from the curse of the law by being a curse for us, but he does not explain how a curse on Jesus could have this effect. It is obvious that the curses in 3:10, 13 are parts of the same line of argumentation, but Paul does not explicitly reveal the logic behind this connection. And finally, if there is a connection between the anathemas of 1:8-9 and the curses in 3:10, 13, it certainly has to be implied, since we find no explicit statements about it. As we briefly review the most prominent solutions to these challenges, we will see that scholars incorrectly tend to treat these curses as minor arguments which have little or no bearing on the main argumentation in the letter.

1.3.1: The anathemas of Gal 1:8-9

With regard to the anathemas of 1:8-9, there is no consensus whether they should be interpreted as effective curses, as a prayer to God for their execution, as a means of excommunication, or as severe parenesis. This

---

[16]Steck 1967 has investigated the influence of the deuteronomistic scheme of history, while Baltzer 1971 has investigated the influence of the covenant formula.

uncertainty corresponds to an uncertainty about the tradition-history of the anathema-concept.

One major trend in research has been to trace a juridical background for the anathemas:

> In the first half of our century, it was common to explain the anathemas against the background of the practice of ban in the synagogue. Scholars argued that this practice had two degrees, and the most severe was denoted חרם.[17] In other words, anathema was considered to be a form of excommunication.[18] Recent research has demonstrated, however, that it is impossible to trace a second degree of the ban, a חרם ban, in the sources before the middle of the third century CE.[19]

A common approach is to connect the legal form of the anathemas with 1 Cor 16:22 and Christian "sacred laws,"[20] which are claimed to be a part of the eucharistic liturgy (Bornkamm),[21] and whose form may be compared with *ius talionis*-clauses such as 1 Cor 3:17 and 14:38 (Käsemann 1954:248–51). According to Käsemann, these anathemas were a part of the prophetic leadership of these congregations, where the prophet, guided by the Holy Spirit, made eschatological judgments with formulas taken from the Hebrew Bible. The intention was not to judge, but rather to exhort in a powerful way, because the guilty had the opportunity to repent and thus to escape the judgment (1954:249–50, 256–58).[22]

A rather recent alternative is to trace the legal background in Hebrew Bible legislation against false teachers in Deut 13, where we also find the casuistic form, the term ἀνάθεμα, and other similar phrases (Sandnes:70–73). A parenetic aim also seems to be the consequence as well, since Paul declares a law in a solemn way rather than uttering a curse.

The major alternative trend, however, is to regard the anathema as a curse. In the commentaries we often find a brief description of the use of ἀνάθεμα/חרם in the Hebrew Bible and a claim that it is not possible to discern the term ἀνάθεμα from the other curse terms at the time of Paul.

> Gal 1:8–9 is, therefore, frequently interpreted as an effective curse, but without further reflections on the implied consequences underlying such a curse in

---

[17]*Str-B* IV:293–329 argued that the practice of ban in ancient synagogues had two degrees, and the most severe form was denoted חרם. But *Str-B* itself did not interpret ἀνάθεμα nor ἀποσυνάγωγος on this basis (IV:331; III:446). Before *Str-B* this connection was defended by Döller 1913:13–14. Since ἀνάθεμα in the LXX is a translation of חרם, however, this link influenced many scholars.

[18]Döller:13–14; Bornhäuser 1932. For a recent publication, cf. Roetzel 1972:143–44.

[19]Hunzinger 1954:5–7, 66, cf. also his *TRE* 5:163–64. Hunzinger is followed by Forkman:92.

[20]A broad discussion is found in Klauck:351–63. Cf. among others: Becker 12–13; Bligh:91; Barrett 1968:397–98; Wiefel:226–29; Stuhlmacher 1968:69; Conzelmann:300; U. B. Müller:197–212; Synofzik:38; C. Wolff:229; Behnisch:247–48.

[21]The eucharistic allusions in 1 Cor 16 are the holy kiss, the μαράνα θά, and the blessing.

[22]For a broader presentation and a critical discussion of this theory, cf. below sec. 9.4a.

the Galatian situation.[23]

Some scholars tend to weaken the curses, however, either by interpreting them as Paul's prayer to God (Mussner:60–61; Burton:28) or as a solemn declaration of the limit beyond which no Christian must pass (Ebeling:81). They may even be transformed into a rhetorical means of frightening the judge by threats, which Quintilian recommends as a measure to be used when a judge is influenced by prejudice (H. D. Betz 1979:45–46).[24]

In conclusion, Paul's silence about the intention of his anathemas has caused much confusion in modern research. Also, most scholars who regard them as more than severe parenesis have not pursued the question of their intended effects in Galatia. One does not take the curse seriously if one claims uncritically that Paul is issuing a curse and then proceeds to the next verse without further reflection.

1.3.2: The curses of Gal 3:10, 13
a: Specific interpretations of 3:10

Gal 3:10 consists of an assertion that "all who rely on works of the law are under a curse" and a citation of Deut 27:26 that proves the assertion. We miss one premise in this argument, however, and scholars have implied it in various ways (cf. Stanley:481–86):

> The traditional interpretation is quantitative, where Paul's implicit presupposition is anthropological: Nobody is able to fulfill the whole law. Most scholars take this presupposition as a fundamental maxim about humanity's inability to keep the law (e. g., Mussner:224–25; Becker:36; Oepke:105; Hübner 1984a:19) or as a statement of an empirical fact (e. g., Noth; Wilckens 1974:92, 94). It may also be disputed whether 3:10 issues a curse or not. It may be a threat toward the Galatian Christians rather than a realized curse, a threat pointing to potential dangers associated with a life under the law (Stanley:497–501).
>
> Some scholars have tried to interpret Paul qualitatively in light of 3:11–12, where the emphasis seems to be on humanity's use of the law as a means of salvation. It is possible to interpret these verses as if it is the act of fulfilling the law itself that leads to a way of life that deserves the curse. In various ways this is interpreted as the typical Jewish behavior, namely to try to merit salvation by law-observance (e. g., Schlier 1965:132–35; H. D. Betz 1979:146; Fuller:32–35).[25]
>
> It is also possible to emphasize special words in the citation of the Hebrew Bible. E. P. Sanders, for example, states that Paul cites Deut 27:26 in Gal 3:10

---

[23]The broadest discussion is found in Hunzinger 1954:11–21. Discussions also by Becker:11–13; H. D. Betz 1979:50–54. Cf. also Behm:354–55; Burton:28; Brun:105; Mussner:60–61; Schottroff:27; Behnisch:241–42; Bruce:83.

[24]For a critique, cf. Kennedy:148. Kiss has even gone so far as to distinguish the term ἀνάθεμα, which only denotes that something is prohibited and withdrawn from human jurisdiction, from the annihilation that very often followed this kind of judgment. He tries to prove that this distinction is present in Josh 7.

[25]It is also possible to take 3:10 in the quantitative sense, but to find the qualitative emphasis in 3:11–12, cf. Bruce:159–60; Räisänen 1983:94–96; Luz:149–50.

because it is the only passage in the LXX in which νόμος is connected with a curse. Paul's only point is to stress that the law is connected with a curse (1983:21–22, 47).[26] G. Howard, in contrast, emphasizes the word πᾶς: The point of the citation is not to demand obedience, but rather to reveal the general, suppressing force of the law on both Jews and Gentiles (60–62).

In summary, there seems to be more of a consensus in interpretation of this verse, since most scholars lean toward the quantitative interpretation. It is difficult, however, to explain how Paul can imply a fundamental maxim about man's inability to keep the law which violently counters Jewish theology.[27]

b: Specific background of Gal 3:13

In 3:13 the problem is how to perceive the logic that a curse on Christ may be taken to redeem from the curse of the law. Paul may imply a logic taken from Christian tradition, from Jewish traditions, or invented on the spur of the moment.

The possible roots in Christian tradition may lie in traditions about substitution: Jesus took the curse on our behalf and thus opened a new way of salvation (e. g., Brun:71–72; Kuhn:35; Räisänen 1983:250; Oepke:108–9). It may be asserted that the death of Christ was meritorious since Jesus was free of sin (cf. 2 Cor 5:21; e. g., S. Kim:274–78; H. D. Betz 1979:151; Mussner:233–34), or because he had perfectly fulfilled righteousness (e. g., Schlier 1965:139–40; Thuruthumaly:118–19).

The possible roots in Jewish tradition are more numerous:

> It is possible that Paul takes up an important argument from Jewish anti-Christian polemic, pointing to the impossibility of regarding a cursed man as the Messiah (e. g., Jeremias:134–35). Paul picks up this argument, turns it around, and makes it suit his own theology.
> N. A. Dahl and M. Wilcox have argued that Paul advances a Jewish-Christian tradition that interprets the atonement in the light of the *Akedah*, that is, the binding of Isaac in Gen 22. God is said to remember the *Akedah* and therefore to rescue the descendants of Isaac on various occasions (Dahl 1974:151–53). Certain phrases in Gal 3:13–14 seem to have parallel expressions in Gen 22, and therefore Paul may have interpreted the death of Christ as God's deliverance of Israel as an adequate reward for the *Akedah* (Dahl 1974:153–54).[28]

---

[26]Cf. also Hays 1983:206–207. The reason for this is not stated explicitly and must be understood from the broader context: The law fails, because it is contrary to God's plan of salvation since it excludes the Gentiles.

[27]Hübner 1973:224–25 claims some support for it in Judaism, but he is rightly criticized by Sanders 1983:28–29 (cf. also his 1978:109–22). Also, the qualitative interpretation counters Jewish ways of thinking, cf. Sanders 1977:426–28.

[28]A broader argumentation with other links is found by Wilcox:94–99, who is followed by Cosgrove 1978:151.

H. Merklein has rather sought an analogy in the cultic sacrifice of animals from Lev 4–5 and 16–17. The expression γίνομαι κατάρα implies an identity between Christ and the curse which he finds to be similar to the identity between the sinner and the dying sacrificial animal in the cult (26–31).

There also exist other possibilities, some of which I will present below. Further, it may be that Paul alludes to Isa 53:5,[29] to the scapegoat ritual,[30] or to the punishment of the sinners in Num 25:1–5.[31]

Paul may also have invented the argument for this very occasion. Some have argued that when the curse of Deut 21:23 fell upon Jesus, the law was proved to be wrong in one particular instance, and must consequently be totally invalid (e. g., Schweitzer:207; Burton:173–74). Other scholars argue that Paul considers the vindication of Christ after his death to be the event which revealed the failure of the law, since it led to the crucifixion of Christ (e. g., Beker:261; S. Kim:273–74).[32]

Thus, with regard to the curse of 3:13b, scholarly opinion differs more than in any of the other Galatian curses. Most proposals share a common weakness, however: They are not developed out of the context, but rather asserted to be minor arguments that Paul would have picked up and introduced only here. One should ask if closer attention to the context reveals a logic that would be natural for the first readers of the letter to grasp.

1.3.3: The curses in context
a: Connections between 3:10 and 3:13

It is obvious that the curses in Gal 3 are connected to each other, since 3:10 presents a curse from the law, and 3:13a states that Christ redeemed from the curse of the law. A more accurate description of this logic is difficult to find, however:

The connection may be perceived as a simple one. F. F. Bruce, for example, emphasizes that the identical form of the curses demonstrates that Paul uses the rab-

---

[29]Cf. O. Betz 1990a:205–6: The ἐπικατάρατος phrase corresponds to מקולל in Hebrew (cf. 11QTemple 64:12), a term which Paul may have connected with מחולל in Isa 53:5.

[30]Schwartz:260–63: Just as the scapegoat of Lev 16 was sent into the wilderness carrying the curse on its back, so also Jesus was sent (cf. Gal 4:4 with the term ἀποστέλλειν) into the curse. Schwartz is followed by Hamerton-Kelly 1990a:114. Also Lightfoot:139 pointed to these connections.

[31]Hanson:6; Bruce:164; Hamerton-Kelly 1990a:110; Caneday:200–201. The Palestinian Talmud combines this text with Deut 21:23 when it is said that apostates are to be hanged upon the tree to turn away the anger of the Lord. Thus the crucifixion from Deut 21:23 may imply a context of taking away the wrath of God, which also may fit in with the death of Jesus.

[32]Klein 1918:62–67 (who is followed by Schoeps:179–80) argues that the dual significance of the Hebrew word תלי that lies behind the phrase "hangs on a tree" includes the resurrection: Paul, as John in his Gospel, may consider תלי to designate both "hanged" and "elevated."

binical exegetical principle *gezerah shawah* ("equal category"):   when two texts share a common term, each may throw light on the other (165–66).

J. D. G. Dunn states more specifically that the connection is to be sought in covenant traditions. Paul wants to break down the distinction between Jews and Gentiles by using covenantal curses in a new way: In Gal 3:10 the Jews are cursed because they have chosen a false set of priorities (1985:534),[33] and in 3:13 Jesus put himself demonstratively in the place of a Gentile by putting himself outside the covenant blessing. Thus Jesus abolished the disqualification of the Gentiles by himself being disqualified (1985:536–37).

T. L. Donaldson instead draws on Jewish traditions about the inclusion of the Gentiles in the era of restoration (99–100). The curse in 3:10 then describes the plight of Israel as a "representative sample" for the whole of humankind. In 3:13–14 Paul describes the eschatological liberation of Israel from that plight, with Christ as the representative individual of Israel, going from curse to blessing (102–106).

R. G. Hamerton-Kelly, on the other hand, emphasizes the religious violence that zealot Jews exercise because of the law. They are cursed in 3:10 because they do not live according to the real intention of the law, which is the love of one's neighbor. When this violent interpretation of the law also caused the death of Jesus according to 3:13, then the real nature of Mosaic life is revealed, the law is exposed, and it is clear to everyone how undesirable it will be to adopt the Mosaic life (1990a:110–12, 116–17).[34]

It is not obvious that these curses only affect Jews, however. For example, G. Howard argues that both 3:10 and 3:13 speak about the curse on entire humankind (58–62).[35] It may even be argued that the curses are ambiguous prophecies of the work of Christ (Bring).[36]

It is obvious that the curses in 3:10, 13 must be interpreted in light of each other, but the great variety of recent attempts to do this demonstrates that it is difficult to do it precisely. The question is whether it will be possible to argue for an interpretation that is more probable than others.

b: *Connections between 1:8–9 and 3:10, 13*

Since Paul gives no explicit indication of a possible connection between the anathemas and the curse section, scholars have mostly taken it for granted

---

[33]They have been focusing on the requirements that mark out Israel per se, putting "too much weight on physical and national factors, on outward and visible enactments, and giv[ing] too little weight to the Spirit, to faith and love from the heart" (1985:534).

[34]A similar reasoning is also found in Burton:163–75: He sees Jewish life as one of legalism rather than religious violence. Such life does not correspond to the intention of God, hence the curse in 3:10; and it became exposed and condemned when it led to the crucifixion of Christ, cf. 3:13.

[35]The point is that the law oppresses all people including Gentiles, since it denies them participation in salvation. Therefore Christ also liberates them from the curse of the law, so that they may be included on equal footing with Jews. Also such commentaries as those of Oepke (107) and Schlier (1965:136–37) defend an inclusive interpretation of the curses.

[36]The curse of Deut 27:26 in 3:10 is a prophecy about Christ as the only one who can fulfill its claim, and Deut 21:23 is a prophecy of the death of Christ which abolishes the curse of the law and transforms it into a blessing (Bring cf. Gal 3:10, 13).

that no such relation exists. I have been able to detect only two very general attempts to make such a connection explicit.

H. D. Betz states that the curse of 3:10 has to be connected to the anathemas. In both places Paul's opponents are included in the curses, and the logic is simply that exclusion from the blessing equals curse (1979:144).[37] M. Behnisch has discussed this connection more closely. He states that the curses of Gal 3 describe the era of evil and curse from which Christians have been liberated. Then the anathemas in 1:8–9 threaten those who seduce Christians into apostasy, with the result that they will fall back into the same sphere of curse again (251–52).

It is notable that Paul presents curses both at the opening of this letter and at the opening of his argumentative section in chapter 3. If curses were perceived as a strong means of interaction by the Galatian readers, the curses would inevitably have to be connected with each other.

1.4: Methodological guidelines

The above survey of research has demonstrated that we, on one hand, have reasonably good information about the use of curse in the Hebrew Bible. On the other hand, opinions vary considerably with regard to the interpretation of the Galatian curses. An attempt to contribute to a clarification in this field, however, has to be founded on more secure ground than only this new consensus about curse in the Hebrew Bible. The argumentation has to be sharpened with insights into the syntactic, semantic, and pragmatic aspects of the Galatian curses.[38]

I have pointed to a tendency in research to de-emphasize the function of the curses in the argumentation as a whole, that is, in their broader context. It is important to improve the discussion of the syntactic context of the curses.

I also have pointed to a tendency in research to choose very specific explanations for the curses, with the effect that their argumentative force must have been difficult for their first audience to grasp. It is important to

---

[37]Betz is more eager to relate Gal 1:8–9 to the conditional blessing in 6:16 at the end of the letter. Galatians thus becomes an example of a "magical letter" framed by a conditional curse and a conditional blessing. The letter is perceived to be a carrier of curse and blessing, a form which is known from ancient epistolography (H. D. Betz 1979:25). He admits that no proper investigation of this form exists, however, and he is not able to give any example of a magical letter that resembles Galatians.

[38]For this distinction, cf. Hellholm:19–27; Iser:89; Egger:75–76. Although the distinction is not precise in all aspects (cf. the critique by J. Lyons:114–19), it is useful for my purpose of roughly distinguishing between different approaches to the text.

investigate the semantic dimensions of Paul's curses more thoroughly, in order to have a more complete understanding of the type of curse he is transmitting.

Finally, I have exhibited the tendency to omit discussion of the effect of the anathema in 1:8–9. If curses are perceived to be a forceful means of interaction, it is important to discuss their pragmatic function more precisely. Therefore, my discussion will proceed on the basis of four methodological guidelines.

1.4.1: The method of rhetorical criticism

I will give priority to an analysis of the argumentation of Gal 1–3 on a syntactic level. It will be important to analyze the argumentation in light of accepted conventions of persuasion during the Hellenistic period. This means that I will not take up the historical challenge to identify the opponents of Paul and then to mirror Paul's argumentation against their possible claims. Such an approach is widespread and easily justified: since the claims of the opponents are known both to Paul and to the Galatians, the letter certainly plays upon them in various contexts. The problem for us, however, is that the letter itself does not reveal these claims explicitly. One therefore runs the risk of circular reasoning if one approaches Paul's argumentation from this theoretical perspective.

I find it more fruitful to join the new trend of using the method of rhetorical criticism, that is, to compare the argumentation of Paul with rules for accepted argumentation as witnessed by the handbooks of ancient rhetoric.[39] They bear witness to the fact that rhetoric was an acknowledged and widespread method of persuasion in antiquity. In some way or other the authors of the New Testament were also influenced by this art.

This method will be my main entrance into the text. It has only been applied to New Testament texts for a decade or two, however, so research is still in a formative stage. This means that I will not only take up an acknowledged method such as the one presented by G. A. Kennedy,[40] but I also want to contribute to the methodological discussion by emphasizing other aspects of rhetorical theory that have unfortunately not been given due attention in present discussion. As I will argue in chapters 7 and 8, I seek to

---

[39]Cf. briefly for the fruitfulness of this method on the syntactic level: Berger 1984a:42–53; Egger:85. For its employment on Galatians, cf. the review of scholars below in sec. 7.2.2. Cf. further Lategan:172–77; Stanley:487–88 for a combination of rhetoric with a reader perspective on Galatians.

[40]Kennedy:33–38. His methodological guidelines have been adopted and extended by Wuellner 1987:455–58.

underscore *invention* and *style* more than a discussion of *species* and *arrangement*.

1.4.2: The method of "semantic field analysis"

On the semantic level it is especially the relationship between curse terms in the text and the various concepts of curse that I will investigate. We have seen that curses may belong to different contexts and may have different effects and meanings. What type of curse is it that Paul refers to in Galatians? I find the method of "semantic field analysis" an appropriate tool for identifying the conventional language of Paul at this point.

The notion of "semantic fields" stems from linguistic research and its insight that the meaning of a term is closely related to its place in the system of language.[41] For our purpose we may press this insight somewhat further: if it is true that a specific meaning of the curse term is connected to its presence in a specific semantic field, then we may expect it to have the same meaning if we find it in other texts with the same (or similar) field.[42] If such connections are regularly found in texts, then we may follow K. Berger in regarding them as part of conventional language.[43] When authors want to articulate a certain theme for their readers, they must use conventional language familiar to all who are involved.

This insight that terms have to be interpreted in their context is not a new one, so why introduce a new method? I find it fruitful to do so, because this method is a helpful way to adhere to an important aspect of semantic investigation. For our purpose it is unnecessary to do this analysis at a methodologically advanced level. It is enough to choose a very simple version of the method, such as its adaptation by Berger. He states that a semantic field analysis has to be carried out to a large extent as concordance work, where we must investigate the actual occurrences of composites, synonyms, antonyms, forms, affinities, and associations (1984a:138, 144–59;

---

[41]Cf. J. Lyons:230–69 for an introduction both to the structuralist background of the theory and its different approaches to the meaning of a term both in its paradigmatic and its syntagmatic relations. For further approaches, cf. Vassilyev. Berger 1984a:138–41 takes this as a necessary correction of the lexical method which theologians have used to argue for the meaning of terms. Cf. also Mitchell:6–7 who wants to investigate the concept of blessing in the Hebrew Bible from this perspective.

[42]Cf. for this diachronic aspect J. Lyons:252–58. Although there may be differences among the fields, they may be regarded as covering the same "conceptual field" (253).

[43]Cf. Berger 1984a:139–40. This conventional language consists of "semantic fields" which are regularly repeated connections of words which may be found together in many texts. These fields will always change because of special needs in the actual situations, but the main features will survive. Therefore a semantic field will have a certain constancy throughout many texts, and this makes it conventional language.

further Egger:112, 115). Berger not only emphasizes the lexemes of the text, but also its form(s), since the form also is important for its conventional shape (1984a:137, 147–51). I find this simplified version of the method a fruitful one for our purpose, since it enables me to handle about 300 curse texts in a productive way within a reasonable amount of space.

1.4.3: A distinction from "Speech Act Theory"

On the pragmatic level I will give primary attention to the function of the curses in relation to their effects among the audience. Also for this purpose the method of rhetorical criticism is very fruitful (Berger 1984a:89–90; Egger:137). Rhetoric is an art of persuasion, and when one has recognized the overall structure of a text, one has also revealed the kind of persuasion toward which it aims.

I also find it useful to draw on a basic distinction from Speech Act Theory for this purpose. This theory has described an important aspect of many human utterances, namely that they have a certain persuasive force aiming at specific effects. The title of J. L. Austin's pioneering work is revealing: *How to Do Things with Words*.[44]

According to Austin, every utterance involves meaning, illocutionary force, and intended effects (94–103).[45] He classifies some utterances as performatives, since they are distinguished from descriptive utterances by an emphasis on their illocutionary force rather than on their meaning (145–46, further 116–18). Austin gives an example: "Shoot her!" Here we may distinguish three elements (101–2):

   a) The meaning (= locution) of this utterance is that it refers to the act of shooting a specific person.
   b) Its force (= illocution) is that it urges, advises, orders, and so forth a particular person to do it.

---

[44]Austin analyzed both performatives in institutional settings and illocutionary utterances more generally, and his insights may further be employed on the illocutionary force of large text-units (cf. Hellholm:52–61). The reception of his theory has therefore been utilized in several directions, cf. the survey by H. C. White 1988.

In this study I will apply speech act theory to the curse in Galatians, especially using the concept of performative utterances in an institutional setting. I will not (as e. g., in the reception theory of Iser:89–101) seek to uncover the illocutionary force of all different parts of Galatians. Although it would be an interesting task, it would go far beyond the limits of this work.

For references to speech act theory as fruitful for semantics in general, cf. J. Lyons:725–45, and for New Testament exegesis in general, cf. Egger:135–40.

[45]Austin's terms are "locutionary," "illocutionary," and "perlocutionary" acts involved in the utterance, and he connects these terms with meaning, force, and effects respectively (121).

c) Its effect (= perlocution) may be that it persuades this other person actually to perform the deed, but the possibility exists, of course, that the persuasion will fail.

There can be no doubt that curses belong to this class of performatives. We have seen that curses clearly imply expectations of their being effective words.[46] Curses are powerful words, but not necessarily because their roots are magic. If spoken legitimately, they create a new reality whose content is determined by conventional expectations (Austin:26–32).

This simple distinction is fruitful enough for our purpose. It is helpful for the purpose of underscoring an aspect which often is overlooked by New Testament scholars. Most scholars are content simply to explain the "meaning" of the curses. If they press the question further, they tend to go directly to the intended effects. The illocutionary force is more important, however. Paul cannot predict the effects on the readers in Galatia. He can, on the other hand, predict the illocutionary force of the curses, that is, the way they put a severe choice before the Galatian Christians!

1.4.4: Some reader perspectives

As supplementary aspects, I will occasionally draw on some reader-oriented perspectives. When defining the rhetorical situation of Paul's letter to the Galatians in sec. 8.1, I have found it fruitful to employ the notion of "implied readers," "implied opponents," and "implied author."[47] We often face "silent points" in Paul's argument, which are implications in a text that

---

[46]Cf. the discussion above in sec. 1.2. Mitchell 1987 draws on Speech Act Theory for the interpretation of blessing in the Hebrew Bible (7–8, 173–76). For its application in cultural anthropological research in Africa, cf. Finnigan 1969 and Ray 1973. They do not consider curses, but they do refer briefly to the fruitfulness of the approach to this concept, cf. Finnigan:550 and Ray:24. In his lexical article, Little:184 clearly applies it to the act of cursing.

[47]For discussions of various models of readers, cf. Fowler 1985, 1991 and Iser:50–67. Also Stanley:487–88, 496–97 chooses a reader perspective on Gal 3. I realize that my term *implied opponents* is not congruent with the terms *implied reader* and *implied author*, because an *implied opponent* is not a participant in the "narrative communication situation" (cf. Rimmon-Kenan:86–105). So I admit that the use of the term is idiosyncratic, but it is a helpful way of distinguishing the opponents reflected in the text from the actual, historical opponents, whoever they were.

I find it difficult to take my departure in the "real readers" in Galatia, since we know nothing about them. This does not mean that I follow McKnight, for example, in his insistence that Biblical texts should be interpreted primarily against the horizon of the modern reader (174, 221, 241–50; esp. 246–47, where he takes Galatians as an example). The first reader of a text is an important entity, so I will talk about the "implied first reader." This means that I must stick to explanations of the content in light of conventions from the first century CE, and that I will construct this "implied first reader" accordingly.

are left for the audience to fill. They may take the form of unstated premises, of unstated connections between arguments, of ambiguous expressions, and so on. When facing such "silent points," I find it fruitful to supplement the above methods by drawing on some of the basic insights in the Reception Aesthetic of W. Iser. His basic insight is that these points are not present by chance, but because authors are aware that they have to play upon the creativity of their audiences in order to involve them.[48] When an author says everything, the text is boring and dead. When the audience is given the chance to associate and imply meanings on their own, however, they will read with expectations, since they are drawn actively into the message.[49] Rhetorical conventions will explain most of these "silent points," but so will fundamental strategies such as Deviation, the tension between Theme and Horizon, the tension between Anticipation and Retrospection, and the Foreground-Background tension (Iser:145-69, 177-83).

1.4.5: Structure

This study thus employs one main method, namely rhetorical criticism. It is supplemented primarily by a simple version of semantic field analysis of Jewish curse texts and an important distinction from Speech Act Theory. I will also occasionally incorporate certain aspects from reader-oriented methods and, of course, common exegetical methods.

It is the "semantic field analysis" of Jewish curse texts that causes difficulties for the task of structuring this volume. I regard it as important to consider material as broadly as possible for comparison. We must have a considerable number of texts and also have texts from different contexts, in order to ensure that we identify accepted conventions. I prefer sources that may be dated prior to or contemporary with Paul (see the discussion in sec. 2.1). Although the analysis is to some extent dependent on the exegesis in chapters 9-10, the analysis is so extensive that it will be presented in an earlier section (part I). It should be possible for a reader to start reading in chapter 7 and then return to the semantic analysis when its results are drawn into the exegesis.

Since my primary method is rhetorical criticism, and since I want to contribute to the methodological discussion, I have found it necessary to

---

[48]According to Iser:257-67 "silent points" in a text are a necessary presupposition for the interaction between text and reader: "Der Kommunikationsprozess wird also nicht durch einen Code, sondern durch die Dialektik von Zeigen und Verschweigen in Gang gesetzt und reguliert" (265). Cf. also Berger 1984a:93.

[49]Cf. Iser:267: "Die Leerstellen . . . ziehen dadurch den Leser zur Koordination der Perspektiven in den Text hinein: sie bewirken die kontrollierte Betätigung des Lesers im Text."

profile my own rhetorical approach in a part II on its own. The aspects from Speech Act Theory and reader-oriented methods, however, are easy to integrate into the exegesis of part III.

Therefore, the structure of this volume is:

Part I: I will establish the Jewish horizon for Paul's use of curses on a semantic level. I will seek to identify conventional features which may reveal what type of curse he draws on, using a simple version of semantic field analysis.

Part II: I will establish the Galatian horizon for Paul's use of curses in the argumentation of the letter. I will seek to profile a way of employing the method of rhetorical criticism which is most fruitful in this respect.

Part III: I will turn to the passages of Gal 1:6-12 and 3:8-14 for a detailed exegesis with extensive contact with secondary literature. In this way I hope to interpret the curses in the most obvious and conventional way and give due attention both to their semantic, syntactic, and pragmatic aspects.

We all know that Paul presented his first audience with a severe choice in his letter. In the course of this study, I hope to demonstrate that the concept of curse plays a crucial role in this Galatian choice.

CHAPTER 2

2.0: CURSE AND ANATHEMA: A SEMANTIC FIELD ANALYSIS

2.1: Methodological considerations

As argued above (cf. sec. 1.4), the main method for selecting the most relevant Jewish curse texts for a productive comparative analysis with Galatians will be a simple semantic field analysis like the one presented by K. Berger. This study will employ the analysis with an important restriction, a specific procedure, and a view to specific sources. The important restriction will be to focus primarily on texts containing curse terminology, although there are many texts that contain curses or curse motifs without using the terms present in Galatians. Following the guidelines of this restriction yields about 310 different texts, which is a broad and representative resource for the present investigation.

The specific procedure will be to begin with the Galatian passages that contain curse terminology, namely Gal 1:6–9 and 3:8–14. The investigation identifies the major semantic elements in these texts and confirms the conclusions through analysis of the other curse texts in the Pauline corpus. A comparison of the Pauline semantic field with the semantic fields of Jewish curse texts follows, and this will bring to light the traditions that correspond to Paul's use of curses.

Since it is not possible in this study to present an equally detailed analysis of all the Jewish texts, I will present an abridged analysis in two appendixes. In appendix 2 all the texts are cited with markers for the semantic elements I have identified. For the sake of a practical overview, these findings are tabulated in columns in appendix 1.[1]

The investigation separates the ἀρά-stem and the ἀνάθεμα-stem in order to identify the distinctive features connected to each of the stems before they are compared with each other. We cannot exclude the possibility that some connotations may relate to one of the stems but not to the other. There are three reasons to take this precaution:

> a) ἀνάθεμα in the LXX always translates חרם, never other curse terms, and ἀρά never translates חרם.

---

[1] I am aware that at places other scholars would assign different values to certain semantic features. Although space forbids me to discuss these divergences, I am convinced that they are too few to make a substantive difference in the outcome of the analysis.

b) While curse terms are common in Jewish intertestamental literature, חרם very seldom appears.

c) The stems occur in separate contexts in Galatians: ἀνάθεμα in 1:8–9 and ἀρά in 3:10, 13.

With regard to Jewish sources, it is important to have a considerable number of texts, as well as to have texts from different contexts, in order to ensure that we identify accepted conventions. I give preference to sources that may be dated prior to or contemporary with Paul. This means that I consider texts within the Hebrew Bible, the Apocrypha, the oldest Pseudepigapha, Qumran, Philo, and Josephus.[2] These texts contain approximately 520 curse terms in 260 contexts, and חרם/ἀνάθεμα approximately 90 times in 50 contexts. The curses may be classified in five main groups: Curses related to Deut 27–30, to Genesis and Numbers, to divine laws, to social relations, and to a miscellaneous group of the remaining curses.

(a) The most extensive text is Deut 27–30. In these chapters we find 31 occurrences of curse terms as sanctions of the treaty. This is about 6% of the total number of terms — no other text contains nearly as many occurrences as these chapters.

Deut 27–30 has a broad history of reception. In some way or other 53 texts relate to these chapters. Half of them relate explicitly to Deut 27–30, while the other half have implicit connections which show that they are part of their history of reception.[3]

(b) Also, curses from Genesis and Numbers have a broad history of reception, yielding 56 texts in this investigation. It is especially the curses from the primal history (Gen 3, 4, 9), the curse formula of Gen 12:3, and the Balaam episode with which the later tradition deals.

(c) The group curses related to divine laws comprise 50 texts with curses on actions that violate divine commandments but which do not relate to Pentateuchal curse texts.

(d) The group curses related to social relations comprise 57 texts with both legitimate and illegitimate curses concerning human relations.

(e) The remaining 41 texts contain other curse terms.

An exhibit of the distribution of curse and ban terms looks as follows:[4]

---

[2]I will utilize Rabbinica and the Targums only occasionally, because it is difficult to determine the age of the traditions found there.

[3]These 54 texts, of course, represent only a part of the Deut 27–30-related texts, since many other texts relate to these chapters without curse terminology. These texts also relate to other Hebrew Bible texts and traditions. They will be referred to as "Deut 27–30-texts," however, since it is the correspondence in the use of the curse terminology that is of interest in this study.

Some texts that include deuteronomistic features will also be subsumed under other headings. In cases of doubt I have mostly chosen the alternative classification, in order to avoid overemphasizing their deuteronomistic features. Thus I will later note how covenantal influence is found in many more texts than those subsumed under this heading.

[4]I have followed these guidelines concerning which texts to include: The ban-terms are חרם in Hebrew and ἀνάθεμα in Greek. As Hebrew curse terms I have included references with ארר, אלה, and קלל (piel/noun) (I do not want at this early stage to discuss

Table: Distribution of Jewish curse/ban terms in numbers:

Curse terms:	Tot	HB	Oth.	Apo	Pse	Phi	Qum	Jos
Deut 27–30 curses	145	62	83	2	28	27	21	5
Gen/Num curses	158	34	124	2	37	75	–	10
Curse and divine laws	72	23	49	6	18	12	9	4
Curse and social rel.	88	55	33	8	5	–	3	17
Other curse terms	59	23	36	5	6	13	2	10
Total	522	197	325	23	94	127	35	46
חרם/ἀνάθεμα terms	92	72	20	4	9	–	7	–

It is difficult to draw any conclusions from a table like this, since our Jewish material is fragmentary in the sense that it reflects only certain contemporary Jewish traditions from the time of Paul. Some observations may, however, be valuable for our use of the material. The last three groups of curses contain only about half as many curse terms as the first two. This means that when we compare the groups to each other, terminological occurrences in the latter ones must be given double weight. The groups are about the same size, however, when we compare the number of texts included.

The most striking feature in this table appears in the חרם/ἀνάθεμα texts. These terms occur very infrequently outside the Hebrew Bible (only 20 times = 3%) compared to the frequent use of curse terms in the same traditions (325 times = 53%). Since a body of 20 texts is not very extensive, I find it advisable to treat the חרם/ἀνάθεμα texts after I have investigated the broader use of curse. The character of these few texts may be easier to describe against the background of the much more frequent curse motif. Therefore our semantic analysis will start with Gal 3 and its curse motif.

Once again, I wish to underscore that I am using a simple approach to analyze the semantic field. As a quantitative method, its results can never be

---

which of the קלל-references refer to cursing, cf. the discussion of Scharbert 1958a:8–14 and Brichto:118–99). In addition, those texts with קבב and זעם which Scharbert 1958a:14–15 and Brichto:200–203 discuss are included. As Greek curse terms I have only included ἀρά and κατάρα, but also other terms if they translate some of the Hebrew texts above.

Many of the older Pseudepigrapha do not exist in Hebrew or Greek, however. They are such important witnesses in the Jewish tradition that they have to be considered in spite of this fact. Therefore references without a discussion of terminology will also be made to *Adam and Eve (Vita)*, *2 Apoc. Bar.*, *Bib. Ant.*, parts of *1 Enoch*, *2 Enoch*, *Jubilees*, and *Mart. Isa.*

more than a hint toward the traditions that probably are most significant. The analysis is only a provisional tool for sorting out those Jewish texts that seem to deserve special attention for interpreting Galatians. The primary merit of the method is that it enables one to deal with a broad amount of material, but its weakness is that it is very abstract and paradigmatic.

The emphasis, therefore, will lie in the qualitative presentation of these texts and the attempt to argue for thematic connections between them (see chapters 3–6). Space and time do not allow a complete exegesis of the texts, but I hope to be able to demonstrate enough connections between them to make it probable that they belong to a common horizon of conventional expectations.[5]

It is also important to underscore the one-dimensional character of such an analysis. It only compares occurrences of formal elements, phrases, and terms when they are present rather indisputably in a text, and it will not presuppose a deeper interpretation. The exception is, of course, the Galatian passages, where the semantic analysis will at least partially presuppose the conclusions reached in chapters 9–10.

2.2: *The Semantic field of Gal 3:8–14*

2.2.1: *Pauline semantic field*
a: Texts
The main Pauline ἀρά text is Gal 3:10, 13, which exists in the broader context of 3:8–14:

> [8]And the scripture, foreseeing that God would justify the Gentiles by faith, preached the gospel beforehand to Abraham, saying, "In you shall all the nations be blessed." [9]So then, those who are men of faith are blessed with Abraham who had faith. [10]For all who rely on works of the law are under a curse; for it is written, "Cursed be every one who does not abide by all things written in the book of the law, and do them." [11]Now it is evident that no man is justified before God by the law; for "He who through faith is righteous shall live"; [12]but the law does not rest on faith, for "He who does them shall live by them." [13]Christ redeemed us from the curse of the law, having become a curse for us — for it is written, "Cursed be every one who hangs on a tree" — [14]that in Christ Jesus the blessing of Abraham might come upon the Gentiles, that we might receive the promise of the Spirit through faith."

---

[5]I can build on previous research in the same traditions which has sought for semantic conventions in a similar way: Steck 1967 traced texts with the deuteronomistic scheme of history, Baltzer 1971 traced texts with the Covenant Formulary, Hartman 1980 briefly sketched the semantic field of covenant texts and also identified texts similar to *1 Enoch* 1–5 by such a method (1979).

The remaining curse texts by Paul are in Romans:

> Rom 3:13-14: "Their throat is an open grave, they use their tongues to deceive." "The venom of asps is under their lips." "Their mouth is full of curses and bitterness."
> Rom 12:14: Bless those who persecute you; bless and do not curse them.

b: Context

It is undisputed among scholars that the section concerning the curses includes at least 3:10-14. But since Gal 3:8-9 contains a blessing, it is natural to include also these verses in the semantic analysis. I am aware that it may be somewhat controversial to extend the context in this fashion, but I will provide a rationale for this through grammatical, structural, and rhetorical arguments in chapter 10.

c: Structure and forms

It has been observed that semantic fields are often transmitted within specific forms (Berger 1984a:147-51). In Gal 3:8-14 we may ask if it is transmitted within a larger structure and within smaller forms. In fact, a larger structure becomes visible when we observe how the curse is connected with its antonym (= blessing) in the text:

In Gal 3:8-10 curse and blessing seem to be composed in opposition: In 3:8-9 we find an assertion that someone is blessed (3:9), which has been proved by a Hebrew Bible citation defining the blessed (3:8). In a similar way 3:10 contains an assertion that someone is cursed (3:10a), which also is proved by a Hebrew Bible citation (3:10b). In this way 3:8-10 seems to present curse and blessing in antithesis.[6] This is a rather unusual connection to make, but I will establish the case for it in section 10.1 below.

Gal 3:13-14 connects curse and blessing differently: Paul states that Christ became a curse ($\gamma\varepsilon\nu\acute{o}\mu\varepsilon\nu o\varsigma$ . . . $\kappa\alpha\tau\acute{\alpha}\rho\alpha$) so that the blessing might come upon the Gentiles ($\acute{i}\nu\alpha$ $\varepsilon\grave{i}\varsigma$ $\tau\grave{\alpha}$ $\acute{\varepsilon}\theta\nu\eta$ $\acute{\eta}$ $\varepsilon\grave{v}\lambda o\gamma\acute{i}\alpha$ . . . $\gamma\acute{\varepsilon}\nu\eta\tau\alpha\iota$). Thus Paul indicates a sequence of curse and blessing; the blessing succeeds the curse.[7]

---

[6]This *e contrario*-structure has been underscored by several commentaries, cf. Sieffert:152; Burton:163; Oepke:105; Ridderbos:122; Rohde:140.

Since it is most common among scholars to see 3:6-9 as an Abraham-section of its own, however, I am aware that this identification of a structural element may cause some objections. I will not forget the fact that Paul chooses his proof-texts from quite different traditions; the Abraham-tradition in 3:8 and the Deut 27-30-tradition in 3:10b.

[7]One may ask if a sequence is implied also in 3:8-10: In the Hebrew Bible the Abraham-blessing is followed temporarily by the curses of the mosaic covenant. I will return to this observation below in chapter 10. In the semantic analysis, however, I will restrict the discussion to observing what is explicitly present in the text: There we find a sequence only in 3:13-14 and not in 3:9-10, where both the blessed and the cursed are juxtaposed in the present tense.

Thus the structure of Gal 3:8–14 seems to consist in a double connection of curse and blessing: On the one hand the relation is described as an antithesis (either/or), and on the other hand it is described as a sequence (from/to).

The curse terms are also transmitted within smaller forms: Both curses contain a combination of expression(s) with the noun κατάρα and a citation from the Hebrew Bible with the adjective ἐπικατάρατος, which may be tabulated as follows:

ὅσοι γὰρ ἐξ ἔργων νόμου εἰσὶν
ὑπὸ κατάραν εἰσίν·

γέγραπται γὰρ ὅτι
Ἐπικατάρατος πᾶς ὃς
(+Deut 27:26)

Χριστὸς ἡμᾶς ἐξηγόρασεν
ἐκ τῆς κατάρας τοῦ νόμου
γενόμενος ὑπὲρ ἡμῶν κατάρα,

ὅτι γέγραπται,
Ἐπικατάρατος πᾶς ὁ
(+Deut 21:23)

The most important formal element is the form of the Hebrew Bible citations, both because it appears twice, and because Deut 21:23, which does not share this form in the Hebrew Bible, has been adapted to fit it in Galatians. It is a legal form characterized by ἐπικατάρατος followed by a curse condition.

The other three phrases differ from each other, and may be identified as follows:

a) Paul writes about "all who . . . are under a curse (ὑπὸ κατάραν εἰσίν)."

b) He also states that someone has been redeemed "from the curse of the law (ἐκ τῆς κατάρας τοῦ νόμου)."

c) Lastly he states that Christ has "become a curse (γενόμενος . . . κατάρα)."

The remaining Pauline (κατ)άρά texts may be tabulated as follows:

Rom 3:14: ὧν τὸ στόμα ἀρᾶς . . . .
Rom 12:14: εὐλογεῖτε τοὺς διώκοντας, εὐλογεῖτε καὶ μὴ καταρᾶσθε.
The curses in Romans refer to illegitimate cursing, that is, curse in another setting than in Gal 3. This type of curse is denied Christians in Rom 12:14 and is compared to bitterness, deception, and polluted organs of speech in Rom 3:14. These texts do not contain the form of the curses. I therefore conclude that these texts cannot supply us with additional features for the semantic field of Gal 3:8–14.[8]

---

[8]Their relation to the Galatian curses will be discussed further in sec. 9.3.2a below.

·d: *Affiliated terms and themes*

A semantic field does not only consist in forms, but primarily in composites, synonyms, antonyms, affinities, and terms more loosely associated with the field (Berger 1984a:144–47). Since Gal 3:8–14 does not contain any synonyms or composites besides κατάρα and ἐπικατάρατος, and since the antonym "blessing" has been identified above, we may now catalogue terms either closely or more loosely affiliated with the field.

I find it necessary to collect related terms in the text under common headings, which I will denote as themes. It may be that Paul occasionally chooses certain terms to express himself when he could have chosen other synonyms or related expressions. We must keep an eye on Paul's actual terms, however. Therefore, the few texts that use identical expressions will receive special attention.

In Gal 3 curse is related to themes of law keeping and law breaking, blessing is related to a Jew/Gentile theme, and themes of righteousness, life, and Spirit occur in this context of curse and blessing.

Related to the curse, we find a theme of law keeping in the assertion 3:10a: "rely on works of the law (ἐξ ἔργον νόμου)." Other expressions are "do them" (ποιεῖν αὐτά, cf. 3:10, 12) and "by the law" (ἐν νόμῳ, cf. 3:11).

The quotation from Deut 27:26 contains the theme of law breaking. It focuses on the general attitude of not keeping the whole law: "not abide by all things written."

Related to the blessing, we find a Jew/Gentile theme, with an emphasis on their equality of status in the blessing. It is denoted by the terms *Abraham* (cf. 3:8, 9, 14) and *Gentiles* (ἔθνη, cf. 3:8(2x) and 3:14). The text is primarily concerned with this theme, because it opens by stating that "In you (= Abraham) shall all the nations be blessed" (3:8b), and closes by stating that "the blessing of Abraham might come upon the Gentiles" (3:14a).

We also find three other relevant themes in the text: In 3:11 the law keeping theme is contrasted with the theme of righteousness. It is done both by the verb *to justify* (δικαιοῦν; cf. also 3:8), and the noun *righteous* (δίκαιος). In 3:11–12 we also find a theme of life, denoted with the verb *to live* (ζῆν). Finally, Gal 3:14 relates to a theme of Spirit by mentioning the promise of the Spirit (ἐπαγγελίαν τοῦ πνεύματος).

There are two themes in the text which will not be pursued in the semantic comparison: We have many phrases pointing to the theme of Gospel/Christ. Gal 3:13 contains the expression "Christ redeemed us (Χριστὸς ἡμᾶς ἐξηγόρασεν)" by having become a curse "for us (ὑπὲρ ἡμῶν)." In 3:14 this is followed by the expression "in Christ Jesus (ἐν Χριστῷ Ἰησοῦ)," while 3:8 states that the Scripture preached the Gospel beforehand (προευαγγελίζεσθαι). Such expressions are clearly Christian and belong to Paul's innovation, which one cannot expect to find in Jewish texts. Both in 3:11 and 3:12 the law keeping theme is contrasted with the theme of faith (ἐκ πίστεως; cf. also 3:8–9). This we also find in 3:14 (διὰ πίστεως) and 3:9 (πιστός). Even though this theme is found in some Jewish texts, it is only present once in our curse texts and is therefore not considered in this presentation.

2.2.2: *Correspondences with the Jewish material*

I intend to search for a Jewish background for the curses of Gal 3:8–14 by first concentrating on the structure of Gal 3:8–14 and then focusing on the additional elements in the curses of 3:10 and 3:13–14 respectively.

The structure of Gal 3:8–12 according to blessing and curse is double: Paul presents them in antithesis (abbreviation: CU/BL), but then places them in a sequence (abbreviation: CU-BL). The presentation of texts in chapter 3 will therefore be devoted to Jewish texts that share this double structure.

The important semantic features of Gal 3:10 are the two minor forms and two affiliated themes: The form of Deut 27:26 is ἐπικατάρατος with the curse condition (abbreviation: F). I will also look for similar constructions, such as curse with curse reason (abbreviation: f*) or other connections (abbreviation: f). The curse is also found in the expression ὑπὸ κατάραν (abbreviation: HK). The affiliated themes related to the curse are the themes of law breaking (abbreviation: LB) and law keeping (abbreviation: LK). We have seen that Gal 3:8–10 also contains curse and blessing in antithesis (abbreviation: CU/BL).

The tables in appendix 1 demonstrate that it is only the form of the curse which is a semantic element that enables one to differentiate between curse traditions. The theme of law breaking and the curse blessing antithesis are found so frequently throughout all traditions that they may be classified as conventional for curse texts on a broad scale. Since the theme of law keeping and the expression ὑπὸ κατάραν are found so infrequently, I will not present them until chapter 10. Thus the presentation of curse texts in chapter 4 will concentrate on texts with a form similar to Gal 3:10. I will also provide a presentation of texts with curse and blessing in antithesis, however, since the frequency of these texts is important for the interpretation of Gal 3:8–10.

The important semantic features of Gal 3:13 are two minor forms and some affiliated themes: Curse is present in the expressions κατάρα τοῦ νόμου (abbreviation: KN) and γίνομαι κατάρα (abbreviation: GK). We also found the themes of Jew/Gentile, especially with an emphasis on Blessing for Gentiles (abbreviation: BG), of righteousness (abbreviation: RI), life (abbreviation: L), and Spirit (abbreviation: S). In addition, we have seen that Gal 3:13–14 contains curse and blessing in sequence (abbreviation: CU-BL).

The tables of appendix 1 demonstrate that most elements are important for sorting out relevant traditions influencing Paul's concept of curse. Yet when it comes to the affiliated themes: Terms for righteousness appear occasionally throughout most groups, while terms for life and Spirit are highly infrequent. These features will thus not be treated especially in the general presentation below, but we will return to them briefly in the exegesis in chapter 10.

2.3: The semantic field of Gal 1:6–9

2.3.1: Pauline semantic field

a: Texts

The anathemas of Galatians are found in Gal 1:8–9, in the broader context of 1:6–9:

> ⁶I am astonished that you are so quickly deserting him who called you in the grace of Christ and turning to a different gospel — ⁷not that there is another gospel, but there are some who trouble you and want to pervert the gospel of Christ. ⁸But even if we, or an angel from heaven, should preach to you a gospel contrary to that which we preached to you, let him be accursed. ⁹As we have said before, so now I say again, If any one is preaching to you a gospel contrary to that which you received, let him be accursed.

The remaining anathemas by Paul are as follows:

> *1 Cor 12:3*: Therefore I want you to understand that no one speaking by the Spirit of God ever says "Jesus be cursed!" and no one can say "Jesus is Lord" except by the Holy Spirit.
> *1 Cor 16:22*: If any one has no love for the Lord, let him be accursed. Our Lord, come!
> *Rom 9:3*: For I could wish that I myself were accursed and cut off from Christ for the sake of my brethren, my kinsmen by race.

b: Context.

Few if any scholars dispute that the anathema-section at least includes the verses 1:6–9. The question is whether it ends with 1:9, or whether 1:10 or possibly also 1:11–12 should be included. In chapter 9 I will argue that the section 1:10–12 is loosely related to the curse section as a transition between this section and the narrative, and we may therefore exclude these verses from the semantic analysis. We may do this safely also because their semantic elements are not important for our purpose.⁹

c: Structure and forms

We also should investigate whether the anathemas are transmitted both within a conventional structure and minor forms. The structure of 1:6–9 is a double one: The formal curses are connected to a section of accusations con-

---

⁹Gal 1:10 contains terms of persuasion: "Seeking the favor of men ($\dot{\alpha}\nu\theta\rho\dot{\omega}\pi o\nu\varsigma$ $\pi\epsilon\dot{\iota}\theta\omega$), or of God?" and "trying to please men ($\dot{\alpha}\nu\theta\rho\dot{\omega}\pi o\iota\varsigma$ $\dot{\alpha}\rho\dot{\epsilon}\sigma\kappa\epsilon\iota\nu$)." Such phrases do not belong to the semantic field of Jewish curse texts.

The verses also contain terms connected to the theme of Gospel/Christ: In 1:10 Paul calls himself "a servant of Christ ($X\rho\iota\sigma\tauo\hat{\upsilon}$ $\deltao\hat{\upsilon}\lambda o\varsigma$)." In 1:11–12 the expression "the gospel which was preached by me ($\epsilon\dot{\upsilon}\alpha\gamma\gamma\epsilon\lambda\iota\sigma\theta\dot{\epsilon}\nu$ $\dot{\upsilon}\pi'$ $\dot{\epsilon}\muo\hat{\upsilon}$)" is followed by four phrases that define the Gospel more precisely.

cerning the present situation in Galatia. We may therefore ask if it is common to place anathemas within a context of present accusations.

The double curse has a form that corresponds to 1 Cor 16:22, and may be tabulated as follows:

ἐὰν ἡμεῖς ἢ ἄγγελος ἐξ οὐρανοῦ εὐαγγελίζηται
  παρ' ὃ εὐηγγελισάμεθα ὑμῖν,   ἀνάθεμα ἔστω.
εἴ τις ὑμᾶς εὐαγγελίζεται
  παρ' ὃ παρελάβετε,   ἀνάθεμα ἔστω.

1 Cor 16:22: εἴ τις οὐ φιλεῖ τὸν κύριον,   ἤτω ἀνάθεμα

All of these clauses are modelled as casuistic laws with the crime defined in the protasis, and the penalty prescribed in the apodosis. The penalty, however, is distinctive since it consists in a curse. More precisely we find the following common elements:

a) The conditional form with εἰ/ἐὰν.
b) The expression ἀνάθεμα εἶναι appears explicitly, in the form of an imperative.
c) The protases include a reference to 2nd person plural.

The remaining two Pauline anathemas have the following form:

1 Cor 12:3: ἀνάθεμα Ἰησοῦς
Rom 9:3:   ηὐχόμην γὰρ ἀνάθεμα εἶναι αὐτὸς ἐγὼ (+purpose)

The clause in 1 Cor 12:3 describes Jesus as ἀνάθεμα, and Rom 9:3 portrays Paul as ἀνάθεμα in a hypothetical wish. We find no legal form as in the other clauses, but again we find the expression ἀνάθεμα (εἶναι). This means that we have to consider this expression as a semantic element of its own.

d: Affiliated terms and themes

In Gal 1:6–9 we find neither composites nor synonyms of the curse terms. Antonyms are not emphasized either.[10] We therefore have to search for the affiliated terms. It will be useful, once again, for the analysis to subsume related terms under common themes, while we also keep an eye on the actual phrases of Paul. We find that the anathema is connected to a self-curse against angels and against seducers generally. In addition we find a theme of apostasy.

The conditional clauses of 1:8–9 reveal a triple connection of the anathema:

---

[10]We do find a grace-wish both in Gal 1:3 and 1 Cor 16:23, and Rom 9:5 blesses Christ (or God). But I consider these connections too indefinite to give them any weight in the semantic field.

First, it occurs as a *self-imprecation*, since Paul hypothetically includes himself in 1:8a (cf. the same in Rom 9:3).

Second, it is issued to "*an angel from heaven* (ἄγγελος ἐξ οὐρανοῦ)" (1:8b).

Third, it is issued to *seducers* who are "preaching to you a gospel contrary to (εὐαγγελίζεσθαι παρ' ὃ)" (1:8-9) the one preached and received earlier in Galatia. This latter theme also appears in 1:7, this time with the description that there are "some who trouble (ταράσσειν) you and want to pervert the gospel of Christ (μεταστρέφειν τὸ εὐαγγέλιον . . .)."

A related theme is that of *apostasy* (1:6). Paul fears that the opponents' activity will cause the Galatians to desert the one who called them (μετατίθεσθαι ἀπό) and turn to a different gospel (εἰς ἕτερον εὐαγγέλιον). This theme is also found in two other ἀνάθεμα texts: The curse in 1 Cor 16:22 is issued against those who do not love the Lord (οὐ φιλεῖ τὸν κύριον), and in Rom 9:3 we find the expression "cut off from Christ (ἀπὸ τοῦ Χριστοῦ)." A related theme appears in 1 Cor 12:2, namely the theme of idolatry: Paul describes how the Corinthians "were led astray to dumb idols, however you may have been moved (πρὸς τὰ εἴδωλα τὰ ἄφωνα ὡς ἂν ἤγεσθε ἀπαγόμενοι)."

In contrast to these themes, the two conditional clauses also contain the theme of *Gospel/Christ*. The true Gospel has been preached to (εὐαγγελίζεσθαι) and received by (παραλαμβάνειν) the Galatians. In 1:7 it is called the Gospel of Christ (τό εὐαγγέλιον τοῦ Χριστοῦ), and in 1:6 expressed with "him who called you (τοῦ καλέσαντος ὑμᾶς) in the grace of Christ (ἐν χάριτι [Χριστοῦ])." This theme, however, is Christian, and therefore to be expected as Paul's innovation, and not as part of the Jewish semantic field.

2.3.2: *Correspondences with the Jewish material*

The important semantic features of Gal 1:6-9 are present in structure, minor forms, and affiliated themes. The structure includes two elements, both present accusations and curse/anathema (abbreviation: AC+CU). The form is casuistic with εἴ/ἐὰν and a reference to the second person plural (abbreviation: f*). Anathemas in other legal forms will also be noted (abbreviation: f), as will expressions similar to ἀνάθεμα εἶναι (abbreviation: AE). The affinities include texts that relate anathemas to the same objects as Gal 1:8-9 (abbreviation: OBJ), either self-imprecations, curses on angelic beings, or curses on seducers. We will also consider the themes of apostasy and idolatry (abbreviation: AP).

When we turn to the tables of appendix 1, we find that these elements appear more frequently in curse texts than in ἀνάθεμα texts. This makes it necessary in chapter 6 first to devote attention to the connection between curse and חרם/ἀνάθεμα generally, before we turn to texts selected on the basis of their semantic field.

To conclude: The semantic field analysis of this chapter seems to indicate that the conventional concept of curse that Paul employs in Galatians seems to contain the following main features:

a) Curse and blessing both in antithesis and sequence (cf. chapter 3).

b) Curses with a form like Gal 3:10 (cf. chapter 4).

c) Expressions like γίνομαι κατάρα and κατάρα τοῦ νόμου, and an emphasis on blessing for Gentiles (cf. chapter 5).

d) Curse and ἀνάθεμα texts with form and structure like 1:8-9: the expression ἀνάθεμα εἶναι; curses on seducers, on angelic beings, and in self-imprecations; and the theme of apostasy (cf. chapter 6).

CHAPTER 3

3.0: CURSE, BLESSING, AND COVENANT

3.1: Introduction

In chapter two we found that Gal 3:8–14 presents curse and blessing both in antithesis and in sequence. The tables in Appendix One reveal that this double structure is present in fifteen Jewish curse texts or larger sections (cf. the columns CU/BL and CU-BL). Thirteen of them belong to the Deut 27–30 tradition: Deut 27–30; Isa 65; Jer 17, 24; Malachi; *Jub.* 1, 20–23; *1 Enoch* 5; *1 Enoch* 102; *T. Levi; T. Naph;* in Philo, *Praem.* 126–72; in Qumran, 1QS ii and CD i; in Josephus, *Ant.* 4:302-307. In most of these texts we also find other important elements of the semantic field from Gal 3:8–14:

> I have found ninety curses in total with a similar form to Gal 3:10. Twenty nine of them, i.e., one third, are present in these thirteen texts.
> I have found twenty two texts in total with the expressions κατάρα τοῦ νόμου and γίνομαι κάταρα. Eight of them are present in these thirteen texts.
> I have found twenty four texts in total that refer to blessing for Gentiles. seven of them are present in these thirteen texts.
> I have found seven texts in total that contain the theme of life, three of them are in these thirteen texts.

Therefore, these thirteen Deut 27–30 texts share a much broader part of the semantic field of Gal 3 than the double structure, and it is appropriate to devote a chapter to a presentation of them alone.[1]

In all of these texts related to Deut 27–30 we find a double emphasis: On the one hand they define the blessed and the cursed in antithesis on the basis of their obedience or disobedience toward the law; on the other hand they contain a view of history that has been referred to as *the deuteronomistic scheme of history* or as *the SER pattern* (Sin-Exile-Return). This pattern includes a prediction that the period of covenantal curses on the nation will be succeeded by penitence and blessing for Israel.

Three of the thirteen are covenant texts, that is, they contain curses and blessings that sanction law codes. Therefore section 3.2 will contain a dis-

---

[1]The two texts with the double structure that do not belong to the Deut 27—30 tradition are *Tob* 13 and Philo, *Migr* 113—118. *Tob* 13 will be postponed until the presentation of all Gen 12 texts in chapter 5, but I will argue that this text also draws on Deut 27–30. *Migr* 113–118 will also be postponed. It will be treated in sec. 4.2.2c, since the antithesis differs considerably from Gal 3: It presents an antithesis between the *act* of cursing and the *act* of blessing.

cussion of these three texts — Deut 27–30, *Praem* 126–72 by Philo, and *Ant.* 4:302–24 by Josephus. The remaining texts include covenantal parenesis that draws on the same patterns of curse and blessing. These patterns are brief and subsidiary in some Hebrew Bible prophets, but they are central in texts such as *Jubilees*, *1 Enoch*, Qumran scrolls such as 1QS and CD, and *T. 12 Patr.* We will discuss these texts in sec. 3.3, before we conclude in sec. 3.4.

3.2: Covenant texts with curse and blessing in antithesis and sequence

Three of the Hebrew Bible law codes conclude with sections that may be classified as covenantal texts.[2] Since Exod 23 and Lev 26 do not contain curse terminology, we will concentrate on Deut 27–30. Interpreters have argued convincingly that the custom of concluding a covenant with blessing and curse derives from ancient vassal treaties.[3] When the motif was transported from this political sphere into the covenantal relationship between Yahweh and Israel, a powerful and major motive was the parenetic need to exhort covenantal obedience. This aim is clear both in Deut 27–30 and in the succeeding texts expounding it.

3.2.1: Deut 27–30

The primary curse text in Judaism is Deut 27–30. It contains 6% of the total curse terms I have collected, and it is the text that later tradition most frequently transmitted. Scholars agree that the history of the literary formation of Deuteronomy is very complex. For our purpose it will suffice to read chapters 27–30 as an end-product that addresses the Jewish nation in or just after the exile.[4]

---

[2]Exod 23:20–33 concludes the Book of the Covenant (Exod 20:22 – 23:19) with brief warnings against the disobedient and a longer description of the blessings that will be poured out on the obedient nation. Lev 26 concludes the Code of Holiness (Lev 17:1 – 26:2) with a description of the blessings of the obedient nation and a long list of curses if the nation is disobedient. Deut 27–30 closes both the Deuteronomic law corpus (Deut 12–26) and the Pentateuch as a whole in a similar fashion.

[3]The classical study is McCarthy 1978. Some of his predecessors are mentioned above in sec. 1.2. Cf. also Weinfeld *TDOT* 1:266–70 and de Vaux:147–50.

Hittite and Akkadian treaties are found in *ANET*:201–206, 531–41. The similarities are especially striking between Deut 28 and the Akkadian treaty of Esarhaddon. Both McCarthy:206–76 and Baltzer:1–93 find reflections from such treaties also in other Hebrew Bible texts.

[4]While large parts of the law corpus may be pre-exilic, the present shape is commonly regarded to stem from the deuteronomic redaction in or just after the exile. Cf. the reviews by Preuss:1–61 and McBride *TRE* 8:536–39.

It is primarily chapter 28 that presents *blessing and curse in antithesis*, but reflections are found also in 27:11-13 and 30:15-20.[5]

Deut 28 is devoted to blessings on the obedient in 28:1-14 and curses on the disobedient in 28:15-68.[6]

The condition for *the blessings* of 28:1-14 is covenantal obedience, cf. 28:1: "And if you obey the voice of the Lord your God, being careful to do all his commandments" (Cf. also 28:13-14). The text has both an individual and collective emphasis (Plöger:193-94). The idea is not that Israel will merit the blessing if obedient; it is rather that covenantal obedience will uphold a relationship where Yahweh may continue to bestow blessings.[7]

The major part of chapter 28 consists of *curses on the disobedient* (28:15-68). The section is introduced in this way: "But if you will not obey the voice of the Lord your God, or be careful to do all his commandments and his statutes which I command you this day, then all these *curses* shall come upon you and overtake you. *Cursed* shall you be in the city, and *cursed* shall you be in the field . . . ." (28:15-16, cf. also 28:45, 58).[8] While these formulas of 28:16-19 denote individual misfortune, the rest of the chapter describes curses within the context of Yahweh's punishment on the nation.

Curse and blessing in sequence are present in 29:22-30:10, where the whole *deuteronomistic scheme of history* (=dtr-SH) is spelled out. After the description of Israel's sin and curse (29:22-28), there is a promise that the people one day will repent (30:1-2.10) and that Yahweh then will renew them in the land (30:3-9). In this text, as in its parallel in Deut 4, curse and blessing are historicized into successive events of history, which is a new element compared to earlier treaty texts.[9]

---

[5]The antithesis is presented briefly in 27:11-13, but in the following it is only the curses that are displayed. This list of 12 אָרוּר-formulas that correspond to Gal 3:10 will be presented in sec. 4.1.2a below.

In 30:15-20 we find the powerful choice between life and death, good and evil, curse and blessing. This choice, which is posed to the reader, is a choice which depends on obedience versus apostasy (cf. 30:16-17). It corresponds to a similar choice in 11:26-29 and thus forms a bracket around the whole law corpus, a feature underscoring the parenetic aim of Deuteronomy.

Both Deut 27 (cf. McCarthy:194-99) and Deut 29-30 (cf., for an analysis of the covenant form, McCarthy:190-94, 199-202 and Lohfink 1962:36-45) are generally regarded as units that have been combined with chapter 28 at a later stage.

[6]For an analysis of the rhetoric of chapter 28, cf. McCarthy:175-82. He regards the chapter mainly as a unity, cf. also Hillers:30-42. It is common, however, to regard it as a result of a complex literary development, cf. Preuss:153-58 for an overview, and Plöger:130-92 for an example.

[7]Cf. Noth:137-44; Mitchell:43. Plöger:194-213, on the other hand, argues that the blessing is also merited according to a "Tun-Ergehen-Zusammenhang." These blessings are not secondary elements in the text without emphasis, cf. Reventlow 1961:142-44.

[8]Cf. sec. 4.1.2a below for a comment on these אָרוּר-formulas.

[9]Cf. Mayes 1979:70, 156, 368 and Baltzer:34, 36, 154-55. Steck (1967:139-43) claims that these chapters are a later development of the dtr-SH as illustrated by Jeremiah and 2 Kings 17. McCarthy:191 regards it as a new adaptation of the covenant formulary.

The condition for this era of blessing to come is that "[you] return (שׁוּב) to the Lord your God, you and your children, and obey his voice in all that I command you this day, with all your heart and with all your soul" (30:2, cf. 30:8, 10 and 4:29–30). The dtr-SH is thus an indirect admonition for Jews to repent and keep the covenant.[10]

As a lesson to the exiled or newly freed Israelites, the goal of the book of Deuteronomy is to reestablish the new Israel on a covenantal basis in the shadow of the exile (Preuss:182, 197–98). Deuteronomy is more than a law code, since there are strong features of *parenesis* throughout the whole book.[11] Parenetic emphasis on loyalty to the covenant is an attribute of Deut 27–30. In addition, the chapters that historicize curse and blessing (Deut 4 and 29–30) offer hope for a nation that experienced the covenantal curses after 587 BCE, a hope for future blessing if they repent and live according to Deut 30:11–14 (H. W. Wolff 1961:180–86; McCarthy:203–205). The following sections will demonstrate that later Jewish readers also found this message in these chapters.

3.2.2: *Philo, Praem 79–172*

Philo has expounded the Pentateuch in the sequence of treatises that we denote as *The Exposition of the Laws of Moses*, where the aim is to emphasize the supreme role of the Jewish law (Borgen 1984b:233–41). As in the Hebrew Bible itself, Philo ends his presentation with a covenant text that expounds Deut 27–30/Lev 26 — namely *Praem* 79–172. Blessing and curse in antithesis govern the sections on blessings (cf. 79–126) and curses (cf. 127–162), while the last section is dominated by the dtr-SH (cf. 163–72).

When Philo presents curse and blessing in antithesis (cf. 79–126 versus 127–162), he primarily underscores the content of the blessings versus the curses. He has, however, several expressions that also reveal his parenetic aim. In the section on *blessings*, Philo underscores that the law should be

---

[10]We find different expressions for this deuteronomistic scheme: Some scholars denote it as the SER pattern (Sin-Exile-Return; de Jonge 1975:83–84; Hollander/de Jonge:39–40). This expression is somewhat misleading, because the important element of a future conversion to the covenant is missing. It is therefore more appropriate to denote it a pattern of sin-punishment-(repentance)-salvation (Nickelsburg 1981:78). In this study, however, I will follow Steck and refer to it with the more neutral dtr-SH. Steck 1967 refers to it in German as dtrGB = dtr. Geschichtsbild.

[11]Cf. the discussion in Preuss:93–94, 99–100 (for Deut 5–11), and 127–32 (for Deut 12–26): The law code also resembles a constitution for Israel, "the divinely authorized social order that Israel must implement to secure its collective political existence as the people of God," cf. McBride 1987:233. McBride demonstrates how the constitutional traits are present in Deut 12–26 (239–43).

fulfilled in *actual deeds* with terms resembling Paul's emphasis on ἔργα νόμου in Galatians:

> He opens the section by amplifying Deut 28:1 in this way: "If, he says, you keep the divine commandment in obedience to his ordinances and accept his precepts, *not merely to hear them, but to carry them out by your life and conduct* (ἀλλὰ διὰ τῶν τοῦ βίου πράξεων ἐπιτελῆτε)" (79).
>
> He later states that one must "add thereto deeds (ἔργων) which follow in their company, deeds shown in the whole conduct of our lives (ἐν τοῖς τοῦ βίου πᾶσιν)" (82).
>
> He concludes the section in this way in 126: "These are the blessings invoked upon good men, men who fulfil the laws by their deeds (τοὺς νόμους ἔργοις ἐπιτελούντων) . . . ."[12]

In the section on curses Philo uses various expressions that denote the cursed as lawbreakers and apostates.[13] In 153–57, however, Philo mentions the *laws of the Sabbath* and *the sabbatical Year* as especially neglected. This feature is briefly mentioned in Lev 26:43, and Philo elaborates it further: These laws are important because they are appointed also by nature (153) to secure rest for both humans and the land (155–56). With respect to Galatians, we may note that Philo thus emphasizes the neglect of laws that distinguish Israel *per se* from the Gentiles.[14]

Philo briefly alludes to the dtr-SH in the above sections,[15] but, more importantly, he concludes the whole treatise in 150–72 *by this historicization of curse and blessing* (cf. 150–57 for the period of curse; 157–58, 169–72 for a description of the future era of restoration; and R. Williamson:22–25).

---

[12]Cf. also 98: ". . . those who follow God and always and everywhere (ἀεὶ καὶ πανταχοῦ) cleave to His commandments and so fasten them to every part of life (ἑκάστῳ τῶν τοῦ βίου πᾶσιν) . . . ." Further 119: ". . . those who take pains to cultivate virtue and set the holy laws before them to guide them in all they do or say (κατὰ τὸν βίον λόγων καὶ ἔργων) in their private or in their public capacity." Additional emphasis on law obedience is found in 101 (φυλάσσειν) and 110–11 (κοσμουμένων τοῖς νόμοις); cf. also 104 and 122.

[13]They are denoted as lawbreakers (ἐκνόμοις 126 [cf. also 111]; παρανομία 142), transgressors (ἀθέσμοι 126), impious (ἀσεβεία; 129, 142 [cf. also 105]), "those who set at nought the holy laws" (ἀλογοῦντας νόμων ἱερῶν; 138), those who "go crookedly away from the straight paths which lead to truth" (148).

In 162 they are given this concluding description: "I have now described without any reservation the curses and penalties which they will deservedly suffer who disregard the holy laws of justice and piety, who have been seduced by the polytheistic creeds which finally lead to atheism and have forgotten the teaching of their race and of their fathers, in which they were trained from the earliest years . . . ."

[14]Cf. also *Migr* 89–93 for explicit references to Jews who disregarded Sabbath, calendar observance, ritual laws, and circumcision.

[15]In the blessing part, Philo concludes each description of a blessing with some verses referring to the future era of restoration for Israel, cf. 95–97, 106–107, 114, 117, 123–25 and the presentation by R. Williamson:20–21.

The emphasis is on describing the conditions for the new era to come (cf. 159–61, 163–68). Here we find notable amplifications versus the Hebrew Bible texts:

> In 159–61 Philo draws on an ambiguity in Isa 54:1. This promise of children for the barren woman (which also Paul refers to in Gal 4:27!) is taken to refer both to the future gathering of the nation to the land and also allegorically (ἀλληγορεῖται) to the return of virtues to the barren soul. Thus the text has a double message, both a promise and a reference to the conditions that must be met for the promise to be realized.[16]
> In 163–64, 167 Philo is especially interested in the necessary "whole-hearted conversion," the "full confession and acknowledgement of all their sin" and "the reformation working" as a necessary condition for the new era to break through.

This text demonstrates that a Jew in Alexandria at the time of Paul could read Deut 27–30 in a manner similar to our reading above. Philo's exposition sharpens *the parenetic feature* of Deut 27–30. He hones the positive claim for obedience, and he focuses on laws that mark out Israel as a nation of its own as examples of disobedience. The section including dtr-SH emphasizes the necessary condition of penitence. So the aim of the treatise seems to be an exhortation for Jews to follow the Law in order to prepare for the turning of the ages,[17] with the curse/blessing motif as an important element.

3.2.3: Josephus, Ant 4:302–14

Josephus also gives an account of the Pentateuch in *Ant* 1–4 and renders a paraphrase of Deut 27–30 in *Ant* 4:302–14. Compared to Philo's treatise, the section is very brief:

> Josephus only briefly refers to *curse and blessing in antithesis* in 302, 306–7, with phrases that define the obedient as blessed and the disobedient as cursed.
> Moses gave curses "upon such as should not live in accordance with the laws (μὴ κατὰ τοὺς νόμους ζησομένους) but should transgress (παραβησομένους) the ordinances that were therein" (302).
> The blessings, on the other hand, were "upon such as were zealous for the worship of God and for the observance of the laws (τοῖς περὶ τὴν θρησκείαν τοῦ θεοῦ καὶ τὴν νόμων φυλακὴν σπουδάσασιν) and were not disobedient to the words of Moses" (306).

---

[16]It is not necessary (pace Fischer:187–213) to play these interpretations off against each other to state that Philo's interest is only on the ethical level. I agree with Borgen 1992:342–44 that both the literal and allegorical sense must be seen together: Philo defends a universalism through particularism. Thus he can interpret the texts as containing a universal ethical message while dealing with Israel's national salvation. Cf. also R. Williamson:155–63 for the relation between literal and allegorical interpretation.

[17]Cf. *Praem* 4 where Philo states that Moses "called on them to make a practical exhibition of what they had learned."

> Also the paraphrase of dtr-SH in 312–14 is very brief, and reveals that Josephus understood the shift between blessing and curse as a recurring pattern of history. Note, for example, 314: "'Howbeit,' said he, 'God who created you will restore those cities to your citizens and the temple too; yet will they be lost not once, but often.'"

It is clear that the curse and blessing motif is not so important for Josephus in exhorting covenantal obedience. A major reason for this may be that he writes for a pagan audience around 90 CE (Attridge:210) and thus does not address Jews for inner exhortation. The parenetic aim is clear enough, however,[18] and at one point he even sharpens the claim for obedience: Josephus connects Deut 27–30 with Deut 13 in a powerful way:[19]

> ... he made them swear to observe the laws and that, taking strict account of the mind of God, they would verily in no whit transgress them, neither through favouritism to kin (cf. Deut 13:6), nor yielding to fear, nor in the belief that any other motive whatsoever could be more imperative than the observance of the laws; nay more, that should any person of their blood essay to confound and dissolve the constitution that was based on those laws (cf. Deut 13:6), should any city do the like (cf. Deut 13:12), they would rise in their defence, as a nation and as individuals, and, when victorious, would uproot that place from its very foundations, aye and leave not the very ground beneath those miscreants' feet, were that possible . . . (309–10).

In Deut 27–30 it is God who executes the curses, but Josephus urges his contemporaries to exterminate lawbreakers. The connection makes clear that the covenantal curses motivate such inner jurisdiction. We therefore once again find that the parenetic aim of Deut 27–30 has been perpetuated and even sharpened in a later exposition of the text.

3.3: *Covenantal parenesis with curse and blessing in antithesis and sequence*

When we turn from treaty texts to texts with covenantal parenesis, we find that the well-arranged structure of Deut 27–30 is split up and even scattered throughout larger portions of a text. It is clear, however, that it is the same cluster of motifs that is drawn upon to serve a parenetic aim.

---

[18]*Ant* 1:14 demonstrates that the necessity of conforming to God's will is the main lesson that is emphasized in the work as a whole, cf. Attridge:217. When Josephus paraphrases Deuteronomy in *Ant* 4:176–331, he uses the Greek term πολιτεία (constitution) to describe the importance of the laws (cf. 184, 193, 198 and 302, 310, 312). The emphasis is thus on describing Deuteronomy as the eminent constitution of the Jews, cf. McBride 1987:229–31.

[19]Cf. also sec. 6.3.6b below for this connection between Deut 27–30 and 13.

3.3.1: Reflections in the Hebrew Bible prophets

The motifs of curse and blessing are present in many places in the prophetic books of the Hebrew Bible.[20] Our interest concerns those texts that
use curse and blessing both in antithesis and in historical sequence, however,
and thus we are led to Jeremiah, Trito-Isaiah, and, above all, to Malachi.

In Jeremiah we find *curse and blessing in antithesis* most clearly in
17:5-8.[21] We also find the dtr-SH *in nuce* in several texts that are marked by
deuteronomistic phraseology:[22] compare the frequent references to Yahweh's
judgment on Israel with curse terminology (24:9; 25:17-18; 26:6; 29:18;
42:18; 44:8, 12, 22).[23] The pattern is especially clear in 24:5-7: The exiles
from Judah are promised that God will set God's "eyes upon them for good"
and "bring them back to this land" (24:6), "for they shall return to me with
their whole heart" (24:7b). In this chapter we also find the antithesis in the
vision of good versus bad figs: The good figs correspond to the penitent
exiled Jews (cf. 24:5, 7), while the bad figs signify the curse upon Zedekiah
and his followers.

The reference to Trito-Isaiah is more questionable and may be briefly
mentioned before moving ahead. In Isa 65, an early post-exilic prophecy,[24]
there appear to be reflections of *curse and blessing in antithesis* in 65:8-16a[25]

---

[20]Our approach only leads to a small selection of these reflections. Among other
approaches that lead to other texts, we may briefly mention the following: Hillers 1964
compares the content of ancient treaty curses and Hebrew Bible oracles, and he finds
many similarities also with Isa 1-39 and Hosea (cf. 77-78). With a similar method
Fensham 1963 finds curses in Isa 1-39 and Amos. Reventlow 1962a:4-44 and 1962b:83-
90 emphasizes traditional elements from Lev 26 in Ezekiel and Amos.

[21]The descriptions are general: "Cursed is the man who trusts in man and makes flesh
his arm, whose heart turns away from the Lord" (17:5), and "blessed is the man who
trusts in the Lord" (17:7). The curse has the form of an ארור-formula and will be commented upon further in sec. 4.1.2c below.

[22]The deuteronomistic phraseology is mainly found in the so-called prose-sections of
Jeremiah, cf. Stulman for a review of research (7-48) and a detailed analysis of
terminological correspondences both in the TM and the LXX (49-146). It is debated
whether this correspondence is due to deuteronomistic redaction, cf. Thompson 1980:33-
50. There exists the possibility that Jeremiah knew a Proto-Deuteronomy, cf. Holladay
1989:53-63.

[23]Cf. Holladay 1986:659-60 for a discussion of whether or not these lists of curses
may stem from Jeremiah. For connections with dtr-SH in the prose-sections, cf. Steck
1967:72-74, 137-39. For other connections with curses from vassal treaties in these sections, cf. Weinfeld 1972:138-46.

[24]Cf. Westermann 1969:295-96 for a dating of Trito-Isaiah in the period just after
537 BCE. Cf. Sekine:165-78 for a discussion of possible redaction of earlier traditions in
the chapter, and Pauritsch:171-94 for 65:2-23 as a unity.

[25]The prophet contrasts him who shall leave his name for a curse (65:15a, cf. 65:11-
12 for his sins) with him who blesses himself by the God of truth (65:16a, cf. 65:8-10).
Cf. Westermann 1969:406 for a connection to Deut 27-28. We find no curse term in
65:15a, but the synonym root שבע is present.

and an allusion to the dtr-SH in 65:16b-25.[26] In contrast with Deuteronomy and Jeremiah, this text does not treat the nation as a whole, but distinguishes between the obedient and the sinners within Israel (Wehmeier:224).

Curse and blessing in antithesis and sequence play the most important role in Malachi. While this feature is found as minor elements in Jeremiah and Isaiah, it dominates two of the six disputations of Malachi.[27]

> The second disputation (1:6-2:9) is dominated by *curse and blessing in antithesis*. Following a speech condemning the priests (1:6-14), we find a speech of punishment (2:1-9; Glazier-McDonald:47). It opens with a conditioned curse if the priests will not listen (2:1-2; cf. also 2:8-9 and the curse in 1:14). This curse finds its antithesis in the covenant of life and peace with Levi, to which Levi once was obedient (2:5-7).[28]
>
> In the fifth disputation (3:6-12) we find the dtr-SH (Steck 1967:144n): The people are addressed as sinners (cf. 3:8) who are "cursed with a curse" (3:9). If they bring in the full tithes, however, then Yahweh may send the blessing again (3:10-11) and ". . . all nations will call you blessed, for you will be a land of delight" (3:12). Here we find the full scheme of sin-curse-conversion-blessing. The emphasis in 3:6-12 is clearly upon exhorting conversion. Note, for example, the main theme of the dispute: "'Return to me, and I will return to you,' says the Lord of hosts. But you say, 'How shall we return?'" (3:7).[29]

Malachi was written in the middle of the 5th century BCE just before the reforms of Nehemiah, in a period when covenantal obedience was threatened. The aim was to recall the people to moral and religious earnestness in this situation (Glazier-McDonald:14-18). The text primarily emphasizes ritual laws (cf. the sins in the above presented sections: 1:7-8, 12-14; 3:8) and prohibitions against mixed marriages (cf. 2:10-11).[30] Malachi thus underscores obedience to laws that distinguish Israel as a nation *per se*, a feature

---

[26]The troubles of the past (65:16b) are contrasted with the era of salvation (65:17-25), cf. Westermann 1969:407. Also Sekine:173-74 takes 65:16b to introduce a new section. It may be argued, however, that 65:16b should be seen as a conclusion to 65:8(11)-16. If this is the case, the juxtaposition with 65:17-23 makes it a transitory statement, cf. Pauritsch:182.

In the new era the people will be the offspring of the blessed of the Lord (65:23b), and none will be accursed with a short life (65:20b).

[27]For the covenant theme in Malachi as a whole, cf. McKenzie/Wallace. The denotation of the sections as disputations is taken from Smith:299-300.

[28]Cf. McKenzie/Wallace:550-51 for an identification of the covenant of Levi with the Deut 27-30 tradition.

[29]Tångberg:138-41 argues that this text corresponds to the "Gattung der prophetischen Mahnrede," which has an exhortation to conversion as its most prominent feature. Glazier-McDonald:183-84 refers to the clear deuteronomistic background for the שוב-exhortation.

[30]It is debated whether 2:10-11 refers to mixed marriages or to apostasy from Yahweh. Cf. Glazier-McDonald:113-20 for a discussion and a plausible solution: The unit refers to both problems, because the result of mixed marriages was syncretism.

that is also present in Philo. For this purpose the double motif of curse and blessing serves a major role.

3.3.2: The Book of Jubilees (1; 20-23)

In the book of Jubilees, the author has inserted the double motif of curse and blessing at vital places in his recounting of Genesis and the first twelve chapters of Exodus. We find it in the opening chapter 1 and in chapters 20–23, which conclude the Abraham section.

> *Curse and blessing in antithesis* is found in the closing sections of the Abraham-stories (19:10–22:30). It is clearest in Abraham's farewell testimony of *Jub.* 20:6–10. There it is stated that those who do not guard themselves "from all fornication and impurity . . . will be cursed like Sodom" (20:6). On the contrary those who "worship the Most High God . . . will become a blessing upon the earth" (20:9–10). This antithesis is also present in 21:21–24 and 22:11–23, sections which contain only blessing terminology.[31]
>
> The dtr-SH is found in chapter 1 and in the conclusion to the Abraham-story, 23:16–32. Following sections that predict sins and punishment of the people (1:8–14 and 23:16–25), we find reference to repentance (1:15a, 22–23a; 23:26) and to the future era of blessing (1:15b-18, 23b-25 and 23:27–31). These sections stand out in this work as the only extensive treatments of eschatology.[32] With respect to Galatians we may note that the future era of restoration will bestow both an inner circumcision, a new Spirit, and a renewed obedience (cf. 1:23).

The Book of Jubilees was probably written in Palestine by a pious, conservative, and zealous Jew in the period around the Maccabean revolts.[33] The author strongly exhorts strict obedience in a number of ways, probably because he anticipates an age of increasing blessings in his own time as a result.[34] It may even seem as if the situation behind this book, by writing it and making it known, would prepare one for the turn of the eras.[35] We may

---

[31]The curse/blessing pattern of *Jub.* 22:11–23 is presented by Hartman 1979:74–75, and the covenant form of *Jub.* 21 is presented in Baltzer:137–41.

[32]Cf. Wintermute in *OTP* 2:38. For this reason, the chapters have sometimes been regarded as later additions to the book, cf. Davenport:10–18 and the discussion in Sanders 1977:386–87.

For discussions of these chapters, cf. Steck 1967:159–62 for chapter 1, Nickelsburg 1981:76–78 for chapter 23, and Davenport:19–46 for both.

[33]Cf. Wintermute in *OTP* 2:44–45. He dates the book after the Maccabean Wars, while Nickelsburg 1981:78–79 prefers a dating just before.

[34]Cf. *OTP* 2:38. For Jubilees representing Judaism as covenantal nomism, cf. Sanders 1977:362–83.

[35]The descriptions of the turning point emphasizes that "children will begin to search the law, and to search the commandments and to return to the way of righteousness" (23:26). Therefore it is only a part of Israel (= children, cf. 23:16) that will begin to repent. This may be a reference to the historical situation behind the book, cf. Steck 1967:160, 162. It at least refers to advocates of strict adherence to the Torah in the author's generation, cf. Davenport:41.

note that the book as a whole[36] and the above presented sections in particular
— more clearly than in Philo — underscore laws that separate Jews from
Gentiles.

In addition to general sins and idolatry, the curse/blessing sections point
to the following sins: The people "will err concerning new moons, sabbaths,
festivals, jubilees, and ordinances" (1:14, cf. 1:10; 23:19). They will also
forsake "my sacred place, which I sanctified for myself among them, and my
tabernacle and my sanctuary" (1:10) and "pollute the holy of holies" (23:21).
They underscore the commandment of circumcision (20:3), the prohibitions
against fornication (20:3-4), the prohibitions against mixed marriages (20:4;
22:20), the prohibition against blood (21:6, 18-20), laws for acceptable
sacrifices (21:7-17), and prohibitions against eating with Gentiles (22:16).
Once again, therefore, we find that Jewish tradition has taken up the double
curse/blessing motif as a major means of exhorting covenantal obedience.

3.3.3: *1 Enoch (1-11; 91-104)*

In the composite work *1 Enoch*[37] we find the double motif of curse and
blessing in the opening Book of the Watchers (cf. chs. 1-11) and in the concluding Epistle of Enoch (cf. chs. 91-107).

> The Book of the Watchers opens with *curse and blessing in antithesis* in chap-
> ters 1-5.[38] The special feature of this text is that it immediately presents us with the
> day of judgment: "The blessing of Enoch; with which he blessed the elect and the
> righteous who would be present on the day of tribulation at (the time of) the removal
> of all the ungodly ones" (1:1). On this day blessing is promised to the righteous and
> elect (1:8; 5:7-10) and curse to the wicked ones (5:4-7).
>
> This antithesis is succeeded by an outline of history which contains *curse and
> blessing in sequence*. The text opens with the curse on the Watchers (cf. ἀνάθεμα
> in 6:4, 6) and closes with the blessing at the turn of the ages (cf. 10:18; 11:1). This
> section does not contain dtr-SH as we have seen it in other texts, since the emphasis
> is not on Jewish history, but on universal history and the fate of the Watchers.
> Nevertheless we find a development from curse to blessing; an emphasis on the sins

---

[36]Cf. *OTP* 2:48 and Sanders 1977:364-65. The book ends with laws concerning
Passover and Sabbath (chs. 49-50), and there is a recurring emphasis on the solar calendar
throughout the book, cf. *OTP* 2:38-39. This emphasis is found also in the Abraham-
section taken as a whole: It opens with an expansion where Abraham fights against
idolatry (*Jub.* 11-12). Sections are inserted into the narrative which claim that the laws of
tithe (13:25-27), circumcision (15:25-34), the feasts of Booths (16:20-31), and first fruits
(22:1-9) stem from this time.

[37]For *1 Enoch* as a compilation of different tractates, cf. Isaac in *OTP* 1:6-8 and
Uhlig's text-edition (466-70). For the complex text-history, cf. Uhlig:470-91. When
Greek fragments exist, I have referred to their curse terms, since these fragments are con-
sidered to be among the best witnesses to the text.

[38]An extensive analysis of these chapters is given in Hartman 1979. Pages 22-38 give
an overview of contacts between this text and Deut 27-30.

of the Watchers, and an ending that recounts a universal restoration quite in line with dtr-SH.[39]

The concluding Epistle of Enoch is introduced by the Apocalypse of Weeks, which predicts the future history through punishment to restoration according to dtr-SH (93:1–10; 91:11–17).[40] This view of history is also expressed as a problem, however. In 103:9–15 the righteous man complains that he has been given over to the covenantal curses without experiencing the promised blessings.[41] The author accepts this description; note, for example, 102:5: "[I]ndeed the time you happened to be in existence was (a time of) sinners, a time of *curse*, and a time of plague." His solution is the promise that they have a blessed heavenly existence awaiting them (104:1–6).

In this epistle also the main emphasis is on *curse and blessing in antithesis*. The chapters 94–102 are dominated by several *woes unto the sinners* (94:6 – 95:7; 96:4–8; 97:7 – 99:2; 99:11–16; 100:7–9), where we also find reference to the sinners being given over to a great curse (cf. 97:10; 98:4; 102:3).[42] As a contrast we find *exhortations unto the righteous* (96:1–3; 97:1–6; 99:3–10), which assure them of their elected status.

The parenetic purpose of this section is indicated by the fact that it is introduced as a choice in a similar way to that of Deut 30:15–20: "Do not walk in the evil way, or in the way of death! Do not draw near to them lest you be destroyed! But seek for yourselves and choose righteousness and the elect life! Walk in the way of peace so that you shall have life and be worthy!" (94:3–4; cf. similar motifs also in 104:10–13; 108).

Scholars agree that the first and last sections of *1 Enoch* stem from Palestine during the 2nd and 1st century BCE.[43] Their authors, as well as their compilation as a whole, witness the importance of the double curse/blessing motif for exhorting covenantal obedience. Now the whole work is bracketed within deuteronomistically inspired covenantal exhortations, and the necessity for obedience and punishment for disobedience are constant themes in the book as a whole.[44]

It is difficult to determine what sort of covenantal obedience this work stresses. It seems, however, that this compilation also refers to Jews who abandoned their Jewish identity and adopted a Hellenistic way of life. In contrast to Jubilees, however, this feature is only implicitly present in the text.

---

[39]Also Nickelsburg 1977:391–95 has related this structure to dtr-SH texts such as Isa 65; *Jub.* 23 and the apocalypses of *1 Enoch* 85–90; 91–93.

[40]The original order of the Apocalypse attested by the Aramaic fragments situates 93:1–10 before 91:11–17, cf. Nickelsburg 1981:145 and *OTP* 1:72. Steck 1967:153–56 demonstrates the dtr-SH both for this section and the Animal-Visions in chapters 85–90.

[41]For this section and Deut 27–30, cf. Hartman 1979:152b; Nickelsburg 1981:148 and Steck 1967:255n.

[42]For the general connection between curse and woe, cf. Schottroff:112–20. Steck 1967:156–57 has pointed to connections also to the dtr-SH in these chapters, while Coughenour has emphasized wisdom elements from the related teaching of the Two Ways.

[43]Cf. *OTP* 1:6–8; Uhlig's text edition 506, 709 and Nickelsburg 1981:150–51.

[44]For *1 Enoch* representing Judaism as covenantal nomism, cf. Sanders 1977:346–62.

In *1 Enoch* 1-5 the wicked ones are only described in general terms as covenant breakers:

> But as for you, you have not been longsuffering and you have not done the commandments of the Lord (κατὰ τὰς ἐντολὰς αὐτοῦ), but you have transgressed (ἀπέστητε) and spoken slanderously grave and harsh words with your impure mouths against his greatness (5:4).

If we also take into consideration the sins of the Watchers in chapters 7-8, however, we may follow Hartman's proposal that the description of the sinners "reflects the horror our author and his readers felt over against fellow-Jews who went far in their acceptance of and compromises with Hellenism" (1979:137-38, citation 138).

In contrast to chapters 1-5, many descriptions of the accursed sins occur in chapters 94-102. The sins are both social and religious (Sanders 1977:352-55; Nickelsburg 1981:147). Some social sins point to a Hellenistic way of life: They eat the best bread and drink wine in large bowls (96:5); they have jewelry, ornaments, clothing, honor, and edibles (98:2); and they devour blood (98:11). Some religious sins point to Jews who have abandoned their Jewish life: They have forsaken the fountain of life (96:6); they do not listen to the wise (98:9); they alter the words of truth and pervert the eternal law (99:2); and reject the foundations and the eternal inheritance of the fathers (99:14).

3.3.4: Qumran

In the Qumran scrolls curse and blessing in antithesis and sequence open both The Rule of the Community, which regulates the monastic society at Qumran, and the Damascus Document, which regulates the lay town communities.[45] These features are most prominent in the former writing, but we may start with the latter, because it leads us to some main characteristics of the sect.

a: Damascus Document (CD i-iv)

The Damascus Document is incompletely preserved in several manuscripts, of which many are not yet published.[46] For our purpose we may concentrate on the opening columns of Mss A₁, which may be denoted as a summons to repentance, and thus has a strong feature of exhortation:[47]

---

[45]Cf. Vermes in *DSSE* 1-18 for the connection between these writings and the different branches of the sect. According to Stegemann:410 only a minor part of the sect may have lived in Qumran.

[46]For a discussion of the textual and redactory problems, cf. Schürer 1986:389-96.

[47]Cf. Baltzer:112-117 for the "covenant formulary" in Mss A₁, and Steck 1967:166 for dtr-SH.

The *antithesis* in ii.4–7 contains neither curse nor blessing terminology. The text promises forgiveness to those "who turn from transgression" but destruction to those "who depart from the way and abhor the Precept."

The dtr-SH is clearly present in the opening section. In col. i its perspective does not go beyond the period of covenantal curses (cf. i.17). The perspective is broader in col. iii:[48] After a new recounting of Israel's history with the recurring apostasy (iii.1–12), the text describes the turning point in iii.13–20.

The description of the turning point contains a clear reference to the self-understanding of the sectarian group. We may note some important aspects:

> The sect understands itself as "the remnant which held fast to the commandments of God" (iii.13). The text states that God "built them a sure house in Israel whose like had never existed from former times till now. Those who hold fast to it are destined to live forever and all the glory of Adam shall be theirs" (iii.19–20). It seems clear that the sect saw itself as the obedient remnant of Israel that prepared for the turning of the eras.[49]
>
> The text states that God made a Covenant with the sect, "revealing to them the hidden things in which all Israel had gone astray. He unfolded before them His holy Sabbaths and his glorious feasts . . ." (iii.14). In this way the sect did not claim obedience only to the Jewish law, but to the law as understood in a new, revelatory way (Sanders 1977:240–42, 313–14; *DSSE*:38–40). Therefore the sect not only demanded observance of the law, but also obedience to its own re-interpretation of it, with emphasis on ritual laws (*DSSE*:46–51).[50] This text contains a much stricter form of covenantal obedience than the other texts we have presented.

b: Rule of the Community (1QS i–iv)

The Rule of the Community contains *blessing and curse in antithesis* in the liturgy of ii.1–18. This part of the text contains one blessing and two curses modelled on the liturgical pattern of Deut 27:14–26:[51]

> A *blessing* upon the sectarians, modelled on Num 6:24–26 (cf. ii.2–4), addresses the sectarians, emphasizing their perfect obedience (ii.2) and their special wisdom and knowledge (ii.3; Sanders 1977:314).[52]
>
> The *first curse* is for those who belong to Belial, according to the darkness of their works (ii.7). It is modelled partly as a contrast to Num 6:24–26 (cf. ii.5–9).

---

for obedient sectarians (vii.4–9) and an extensive curse on lawbreakers mingled with elements from dtr-SH (vii.10 - viii.20), cf. Baltzer:116–17.

For CD i–iv as a summons to repentance, cf. Lichtenberger:148–49, 153–54.

[48]Cf. Lichtenberger:149–53 for a discussion of CD ii.14 - iii.20.

[49]Cf. 1QSa i.1–6 and Sanders 1977:243–55, 300–03. This is in contrast to *DSSE*:1–2, where Vermes argues that the sect saw itself as the true Israel.

[50]For the emphasis on the solar calendar, cf. the interpretation of 1QS ix–x in Weise:3–57.

[51]Cf. the similar opening (Deut 27:14 and 1QS ii.4b) and the similar amen from the people (Deut 27:15–26 and 1QS ii.10, 18). The text is commented on by Weise:81–112 and Lichtenberger:106–13.

[52]Weise:82–93, 99–101 has shown that rabbinical Judaism also interpreted Num 6:24–26 in a way similar to the expansions of the blessing and first curse in this liturgy.

This group contains Gentiles and non-sectarian Jews (Sanders 1977:243–44), but they are sharply distinguished from the blessed group. There is no attempt to call them back to obedience. Instead, the curse is intended to bring down the punishment on the men of Belial (Weise:98–99; Lichtenberger:112–13).

The *second curse* addresses the apostates of the sect and is modelled on Deut 27:15 and 29:17–20 (cf. ii.11–18 and Weise:104–09). It opens: "Cursed be the man who enters this Covenant while walking among the idols of his heart, who sets up before himself his stumbling-block of sin so that he may backslide" (ii.11–12).

The blessing and first curse divide humanity into two groups; the second curse hits those sectarians who commit secret apostasy. The holy character of the sect makes such inner cleansing necessary (Lichtenberger:107–108; Weise:110).

This ceremony of blessing and curse was both a liturgy of initiation (cf. i.18) and an annual ceremony within the sect (cf. ii.19; Weise:68–70; *DSSE*:48–49). In this way it functioned very much like Deut 27–30 as an obligation to total law obedience. As part of a liturgy, however, curse and blessing also created spheres of evil and fortune, and thus protected the holy character of the group.

The dtr-SH is found in the sections preceding and following this antithesis.

The annual ceremony was to be opened with a confession of Israel's and one's own sins according to the dtr-SH (i.22 – ii.1; Steck 1967:120–21).[53]

A teaching of the Two Ways (iii.13 – iv.26), which is a variation of the covenant form, follows the description of the ceremony. Within this teaching, there are blessings and curses in iv.6b–8, 12–14 and an eschatological section in iv.15–26.[54] This teaching has its special features, because it does not describe history with the Jewish nation in the center. Corresponding to the emphasis on the individual conversion to the sect (Sanders 1977:256–70, 320), a teaching of the power of the two Spirits in the world replaces the national history. With respect to Galatians, we may note that the future era of restoration will include a cleansing by the Holy Spirit (iv.21).

Both of the scrolls discussed above stem from about 100 BCE (Schürer 1986:384, 396), and the liturgy of 1QSii was probably celebrated annually also during the time of Paul. Thus these documents demonstrate just how earnestly the double motif of curse and blessing was taken by other Jews at the time of Paul, namely, by sectarians who in a special way saw it as their task to prepare for the turning of the ages by strict obedience to the law.

3.3.5: The Testaments of the Twelve Patriarchs (T. Naph. and T. Levi)

When we turn to the *T. 12 Patr.*, we find that scholars differ considerably in their opinion with regard to both the textual traditions and the

---

[53]Weise:75–82 emphasizes the traditional Jewish character of the confession.

[54]Cf. Baltzer:99–109 for "covenant formulary" in this section. For a discussion of the content in iv.6–26, cf. Lichtenberger:136–41.

Jewish elements in the testaments. I find these discussions inconclusive for our purpose. I intend to investigate the *Greek texts* and not bother about the question of whether or not they could have Aramaic or Hebrew originals.[55] We may also read them as *Christian documents*, illustrating how easily a Jewish concept of blessing and curse could be taken over by a Christian author.[56]

Like Jubilees, the Testaments are examples of the Deut 27–30 tradition being incorporated in a Genesis setting. They are modelled on Jacob's last words in Gen 49 and contain many exhortations both to avoid sins and to strive after virtue (de Jonge 1980:518–19). In seven out of the twelve Testaments we clearly find both the antithesis and the dtr-SH of Deut 27–30. Curse terminology is present in this context only in *T. Naph.* and *T. Levi.*[57]

> In the *Testament of Naphtali* we find *blessing and curse in antithesis* as a conclusion in 8:4–6 (Baltzer:161). On the one hand it is stated that "If you achieve the good, my children, men and angels will bless you" and on the other hand that "The one who does not do the good, men and angels will curse."
>
> The dtr-SH is present in several places, especially in chapters 3–4 (Hartman 1979:54–56). We find references to Israel's sin and exile (4:1–2; 5:8; 6:4–7), the turning point when they "return and acknowledge the Lord your God" (4:3), and a description of the future era of restoration with a universal perspective (4:5b; 6:9–10; 8:2–3).

---

[55]Cf. de Jonge 1980:508–17 for arguments against relating the Greek texts to Hebrew fragments. A broad presentation of this problem is found in Hollander/de Jonge:2–8, 10–29. Cf. also Kee in *OTP* 1:775–77.

[56]The extant texts are preserved only in a Christian form, cf. de Jonge 1980:516–17, 521–24 (cf. also his 1975:117–28). The verses of an indisputably Christian origin are very few, however, (Kee 1978:268, cf. also his *OTP* 1:777–78). See also Jervell:41–61 who argues that only small phrases may be interpolated. Therefore I find it possible to chose a specific strategy for our purpose: We may content ourselves with presenting the use of curse and blessing in the testaments. Since this feature is wholly understandable within a Jewish setting, we may take it as a witness of how the Jewish concept survives also in these documents, and how easily it could be taken over by a Christian author. We present Jewish texts as a possible context for Paul's Christian innovation, and then it is notable that there are examples of a similar Christian adaptation!

[57]Cf. Steck 1967:149–53; de Jonge 1975:83–86 and Hollander/de Jonge:39–40, 51–56 for a discussion of the dtr-SH elements. Elements from "covenant formulary" are discussed by Baltzer:155–61.
We also find a structure similar to Deut 27–30 in five other testaments. Especially *T. Asher* has this structure: Here we find a broad description of the two ways, the good and evil, in 1:3 – 5:4, which ends in a description of the dtr-SH in chapter 7. The structure is also clear in *T. Judah* 20–24: A description of the choice between "the spirit of truth and the spirit of error" (20:1) is followed by a reference to dtr-SH in chapters 23–24. In *T. Iss.* 4–5; *T. Zeb.* 5:1–2; and *T. Dan* 5:1–3 it is only the blessing part of the choice that is emphasized, but the sections are all followed by references to dtr-SH in *T. Iss.* 6; *T. Zeb.* 9:5–9; and *T. Dan* 5:5–13.

The *Testament of Levi* both opens and closes with *curse and blessing in antithesis*: It closes with a choice similar to Deut 30:15-20: "And now, my children, you have heard everything. Choose for yourselves light or darkness, the law of the Lord or the works of Beliar" (19:1). In 4:6 we find it connected to the attitude toward Christ: "Because those who bless him shall be blessed, and those who curse him shall be destroyed."[58]

The dtr-SH is then found in chapter 10 and in the apocalypse of chapters 14–18: Three times it is stated that Israel shall be a curse among the nations because of its sins (10:4; 14:4; 16:5). Here again, the era of blessing is proclaimed with universal consequences also for non-Jews (cf. especially 18:9-10). It is stated that "the spirit of holiness shall be upon them" (18:11) without restricting it to Israel. Cf. also *T. Jud.* 24:2 for the outpouring of Spirit as a blessing.

It has been debated whether or not the Testaments exhort covenantal obedience. The reference to the Law in *T. Naph.* 8:4-6 is very general. This has been understood by scholars to conform to a typical trend in the testaments to equate the law with natural law and make its application universal, with an openness toward Hellenistic virtues and a downplay of Jewish ritual laws.[59] *T. Levi* balances this picture to a certain extent. The sins that are emphasized here are on one hand sins against Christ,[60] but on the other hand, they include disrespect of offering-laws (14:5, cf. 9:7, 11–14) and mixed marriages (14:6, cf. 9:10). We may also note that Levi is concerned about the rite of circumcision (6:3-6). This testament therefore bears witness to the fact that *T. 12 Patr.* also emphasize typically Jewish laws.[61] This does not cause a dualism between Jews and Gentiles, however; a "covenantal nomism" with an emphasis on separation from the Gentiles is not present in *T. 12 Patr.* (Hollander/de Jonge:47).

---

[58]This is, of course, a Christian innovation of the Jewish antithesis, which lets the curse hit obedient Jews, cf. de Jonge 1975:50-51.

It is possible, however, to regard the reference to Christ in 4:4b as an interpolation and to change the pronoun in the formula. Charles *APOT* 2:307 proposes that one should read "thee" instead of "him" as in Jub 31:17 (cf. also *OTP* 1:789 where only 4:4b is regarded as a Christian interpolation). Then the whole chapter will refer to the central position of Levi, who is given blessing and the light of knowledge (4:1-4), so that other men will be treated according to how they relate to him and his instruction: "Because those who bless you shall be blessed, and those who curse you shall be destroyed" (4:5-6). In this way the section becomes a traditional Jewish one with an emphasis on obedience toward the law. This may indicate that the Christian author/interpolator did not need to change much to let a possible Jewish tradition serve his own purpose.

[59]Cf. Kee in *OTP* 1:779-80 and 1978 for a theory of Stoic influence. Cf. also Hollander/de Jonge:41-47 for the general character of the parenesis.

[60]Cf. de Jonge 1986:200-03 who regards this as the dominating aspect in *T. Levi*.

[61]Cf. Slingerland for a broad argumentation that the Jewish law is important in both *T. Levi* and *T. 12 Patr.* as a whole. Also Jervell:39, 47–54 argues that the Christian interpolator may have given the Jewish law (as taught by Christ) a central position. De Jonge 1975:39-40, on the contrary, argues that the Jewish elements in chapter 9 are fragments of a Jewish source without emphasis in its present form.

3.4: Summary

We have now briefly examined some important Jewish texts that, in a way similar to Gal 3:8–14, comprise curse and blessing both in antithesis and sequence. The survey has provided a basis for a rather safe conclusion: *Whenever we face a text with curse and blessing both in antithesis and sequence, we may suspect that it reflects conventional language dependent on the Deut 27–30 tradition.* The texts presented above attest to this as a widely employed pattern in Jewish literature:

a) It is employed in texts that survey the mosaic laws (cf. Philo and Josephus), in covenantal liturgy (cf. 1QS ii), and in texts marked by covenantal parenesis (cf. Mal, *Jub.*, *1 Enoch*, and CD).

b) It is employed rather consistently throughout the centuries: We found it in texts from the exile and early post-exilic times (cf. Deut, Isa, and Mal), in texts from the 2nd and 1st century BCE (cf. *Jub.*, *1 Enoch*, CD, and 1QS), and in texts from the 1st century CE (cf. Philo and Josephus).

c) It is employed in rather different Jewish contexts: Most of the texts belong to environments that promote covenantal nomism with an emphasis on laws that mark Israel out from the Gentiles (cf. Mal, *Jub.*, to a certain extent also *1 Enoch* in a Palestinian context, and Philo in the Diaspora). This is especially notable with respect to Galatians, which also focuses on this type of law (circumcision in Gal 5:1–12, kosher laws in 2:11–14, and calendar observance in 4:11). It is also found in stricter environments such as the sectarian Qumran, and in contexts with a more open outlook for Hellenism (cf. *T. 12 Patr.* and Josephus). The double pattern has even been reworked by Christians, as illustrated by *T. 12 Patr.*

d) The liturgical context of 1QS ii is interesting. It seems probable that Deut 27–30 was used not only in sectarian liturgy, but also belonged to the prescribed texts of the liturgy in the Temple and Synagogues (Steck 1967:133–34).[62]   If so, we have even more reason to regard this deuteronomistic pattern as part of conventional language.

We will now turn to the remaining semantic elements from Gal 3, to see whether they substantiate this conclusion or whether they point in other directions.

---

[62]Baltzer:84–89, 167–69 also notes the constancy in the covenant formula, and from the basis of Deut 31:9–13; Neh 8:1; *mSota* vii.8 and 1QS i-ii argues for a liturgical transmittance. Hartman 1979:96–120 compares some of these texts (*1 Enoch* 1–5; Philo; *Jub.*; 1QS i-ii) with liturgical elements from the feasts of Weeks and the first and tenth of Tishri, and he found several similarities.

CHAPTER 4

4.0: CURSES ON LAWBREAKERS

We have examined texts containing curse and blessing in antithesis and in sequence, so we now turn to texts that share features with Gal 3:8–10. As noted in section 2.2.2 above, we will concentrate on two elements: Section 4.1 will treat texts with a form similar to Gal 3:10, and section 4.2 will discuss texts with antithesis.

4.1: Curses with a form similar to Gal 3:10

4.1.1: Introduction

In Gal 3:10 Paul cites Deut 27:26. The form of this quotation seems to have been important to him, since in Gal 3:13 he incorporates and adapts Deut 21:23 into it.

Deut 27:26 contains an ארור/ἐπικαράρατος formula including a curse condition within a relative clause. In the Hebrew Bible we also find curse conditions as participial phrases, which also will be included as clauses with the same form as Gal 3:10 (=F in the tables). If the formulas are connected to curse reasons or if they only address a subject with second/third person pronouns, nomens or proper names without relation to condition or reason, they will be tabulated as similar to Deut 27:26 (f* if curse reason, otherwise f).[1]

Within the Jewish texts that I have investigated, I have found ninety-one such formulas. If we turn to the tables of appendix one, we find the same form as Gal 3:10 mainly in the Deut 27–30 tradition (31F), but also among curses in social relations and other curses which are related to the deuteronomistic History-Work or to Jeremiah (7F), and among the Gen 12 texts. It is therefore natural to begin with deuteronomistically inspired texts (cf. secs. 4.1.2 and 4.1.3). We also see a form similar to Gal 3:10 in texts elaborating on the curses from primal history, and these texts will be dealt with in a section of its own (cf. sec. 4.1.4). Lastly, a section will be devoted to curses related to divine laws (cf. sec. 4.1.5), while the three Gen 12 formulas will be postponed until the next chapter (cf. sec. 5.2.2).

---

[1]Cf. Schottroff:74–92 and H. P. Müller:150–59 for the distinction between curse conditions (Fluchbedingungen) and curse reasons (Fluchbegründungen). For the distinction between various subjects, cf. Schottroff:53.

The ארור formula is part of a covenantal setting in Deut 27, and we will see that the parenetic aspect also dominates this semantic feature. The formula seems to stem from a juridical context, however,[2] and this origin gives special emphasis to the formula that survives also in later traditions.

4.1.2: Curses from the Deut 27–30 tradition

a: Deut 27–28

The curses in the so-called Dodecalogue in Deut 27:15–26 have a juridical form, and they are connected both to a cultic setting and to a covenantal context.

The juridical form of Deut 27:15–26 is often emphasized by scholars.[3] On one hand, the form we find in the ארור series resembles מות־יומת clauses with participial definition of the crime, and, on the other hand, it resembles Hebrew Bible laws with a protasis in the form of a relative clause (Schottroff 1969:94). As far as the content, we find many similarities between these curses, מות־יומת clauses, and prohibitives as, for example, in the Decalogue.[4] While the Decalogue seems to function as a set of general norms, it is the מות־יומת and ארור clauses that seem to transform them into practicable jurisdiction (Schottroff:125).[5] The מות־יומת clauses do so by ordering the death penalty for the offender,[6] while the ארור series of Deut 27 instead leaves the punishment to Yahweh.

In Deut 27 the twelve ארור formulas are part of a liturgy, where each curse is answered by the people with an "Amen."[7] The cultic setting makes

---

[2]For a probable *Sitz im Leben* in the nomadic clan, cf. Schottroff:199–210 and the presentation of his work above in sec. 1.2. See also Scharbert *TWAT* 1:440–41; Wagner:36–39. For the possibility that the formula was used in jurisdiction in the period after the settlement, cf. Schottroff:220–24; Wallis.

[3]Whether we shall denote the ארור form as apodictic (as Alt:313–14), as casuistic (as Schottroff:95–97), or as simply belonging to a common juridical form (as Wagner:51–69), is a question which will not be taken up here. For a survey of positions, cf. also Liedke:101–10.

[4]Cf. table by Alt:320. We may also note that Deut 27:15–26 seems to have been shaped as a contrast to the Decalogue of Deut 5. Thus the law corpus Deut 12–26 is bracketed within the related series of the Decalogue and the Dodecalogue, cf. Schulz:66–68; Mayes 1979:345–46 and Preuss:152. According to Gese 1967:129–38, both Deut 27:16–25 and the Decalogue are constructed as a series of five pairs of laws.

[5]Schulz:6–61 argued that the מות־יומת clauses originate in prohibitives, while Bellefontaine argued for a similar connection for the ארור clauses.

[6]Cf. Schottroff:120–28 for a discussion of this civil rather than cultic setting of these laws.

[7]The cultic setting is emphasized by Alt:322–30; McCarthy:197–99. Schulz:68–71, on the other hand, argues that the dodecalogue is shaped with a view of this covenantal context. Deut 27:15, 26, at least, are commonly regarded to be redactory remarks added to the older tradition, since they have another syntactic structure, cf. Preuss:152 and Wag-

the curse series more effective than a series of death clauses as a sanction of the covenant: When curses are uttered, they are effective without involving a juridical process, and they also hit crimes committed in secret (cf. 27:15, 24). Whoever violates the curses will immediately fall into the sphere of misfortune that is created by the curse itself, and Yahweh will exclude that person from the community (Schottroff:125, 129; Preuss:152-53).

The covenantal setting gives the curses a strong parenetical aim, since the people obligate themselves to obedience toward the law by accepting each curse with an "Amen." This parenetical aim is also emphasized by the concluding 27:26, which seems too general for practical jurisdiction: "Cursed be he who does not confirm the words of this law by doing them." This aspect is also carried further in Deut 28:16-19.[8]

b: Citations of Deut 27-28 (Jub. 4:4-5; 33:11-12 and Leg 3:107-8; Post 84; [Praem 141])

One way of drawing on Deut 27-28 is to cite curses as authoritative statements, like Paul does in Gal 3. This feature we find in *Jubilees* and in Philo's writings.

Jubilees twice draws on curses from Deut 27 narratives utilizing Genesis. Both times the author has recounted a crime, and he introduces a curse as a sanction against it.

Jub. 4:1-4 recounts the murder of Abel, and in 4:5 Deut 27:24 is cited as a judgment of the crime: "And therefore it is written in the heavenly tablets, 'Cursed is one who strikes his fellow with malice. And all who have seen and heard shall say "so be it."'"

In *Jub.* 33:1-9 we find the account of Reuben's sin with Bilhah (cf. Gen 35:21-22). It is followed by a reference both to the מות־יומת clause of Lev 20:11 (cf. 33:10-11) and to the curse of Deut 27:20 (cf. 33:12): "And again it is written a second time: 'Let anyone who lies with his father's wife be cursed because he has uncovered his father's shame.' And all the holy ones of the Lord said, 'So be it, so be it.'"

The laws on "the heavenly tablets" or "eternal laws" are a special feature of *Jubilees*. They are frequently referred to, and when they are cited, they are always — with one exception — taken from the Dodecalogue of Deut

---

ner:33.

[8]In Deut 28:16-19 we find six curses without curse condition as in 27:15-26. They contain second person pronouns and descriptions of curse as misfortune in agricultural life, cf. the discussion of content by Schottroff:59-68, who noted that the curses are probably deuteronomistic shapings (224-28). The redactory 28:15, however, adds a condition to the curses. It takes up the theme of Deut 27:26 and relates the curses to those who "will not obey . . . or be careful to do all his commandments."

27 and מֹות־יּומַת laws (cf. also 2:25 and 30:9).[9] They contain ritual and sexual laws especially, that is, laws that single out a special Jewish way of life.[10] The emphasis of these eternal laws is therefore parenetical to exhort "covenantal nomism," which we found to be a mark also of the rest of *Jubilees*.[11]

The curses involve punishment executed by God. In 4:4 God makes Cain "a fugitive on the earth." In 33:10-14 there is (perhaps due to the מֹות־יּומַת clause?) an additional reference to a present, human jurisdiction with execution, killing, and stoning of the offender (33:13).

Philo cites curses from Deut 27 twice in treatises belonging to his allegorical interpretation of Genesis:[12]

> In *Leg* 3:107-108 Philo applies curses from Deut 27 to the vice of pleasure. He states that pleasure deserves to be cursed according to Deut 27:17, because: "it shifts ($\mu\varepsilon\tau\alpha\theta\varepsilon\tilde{\iota}\sigma\alpha$ as in Gal 1:6) the standards of the soul and renders it a lover of passion instead of a lover of virtue": "Accursed," says Moses in the curses, "is he who removes his neighbour's landmarks."
>
> Philo continues by referring to Deut 27:18, 24: "'Cursed again is he who causes a blind man to go astray in the way,' and 'he that smiteth his neighbour craftily.' And these also are acts of pleasure."
>
> In *Post* 83-84 it becomes clear that Philo refers to Jewish apostates by means of such expressions. Again he draws on Deut 27:17: "For if you delight in the witness borne to (the goodness of) everything that may present itself, you will desire to twist everything and turn it round, shifting ($\mu\varepsilon\tau\alpha\tau\iota\theta\acute{\varepsilon}\varsigma$ as in Gal 1) the boundaries fixed for things by nature. Moses, full of indignation at such people, pronounces a curse on them saying, 'Cursed is he that shifteth ($\mu\varepsilon\tau\alpha\tau\iota\theta\acute{\varepsilon}\varsigma$) his neighbour's boundaries.'"

In this context, Philo interprets the curses in Deut 27:15-26 in an allegorical sense:[13] In *Leg* 3:107-108 Philo actualizes the curses on pleasure ($\dot{\eta}\delta o\nu\acute{\eta}$) because he sees it as the passion par excellence ($\tau\grave{o}$ $\pi\acute{\alpha}\theta o\varsigma$ in 107), the utterly godless one ($\dot{\eta}$ $\dot{\alpha}\theta\varepsilon\omega\tau\acute{\alpha}\tau\eta$ in 108). The discussion therefore refers to Jews who, out of attraction for Egyptian ideals, at least changed their understanding of certain Jewish commandments. In *Post* 83-84 the curse hits

---

[9]The exception is 3:10-11 with the law of purification after childbirth.

[10]Cf. the laws concerning Sabbath (2:25-33); birth purification (3:8-14); covering shame (3:30-31); eating blood (6:10-14); feast of weeks (6:17-31); 364-days-per-year calendar (6:32-35); tithe (13:25-27; 32:10-15); circumcision (15:25-32); feast of Booths (16:28-31); mixed marriages (30:7-17); passover (49:1-23). In all these laws it is stated explicitly that they are given for Israel alone, so that they shall not live like the Gentiles.

[11]Cf. the discussion above in sec. 3.3.2.

[12]We may also briefly note that Deut 28:16-19 is expounded in *Praem* 141-42. Here we find six curses with a similar form as Gal 3:10, but we neither find curse condition nor curse reason. The concluding phrase emphasizes the parenetical scope of the section: "For these are the wages of impiety and disobedience."

[13]Cf. R. Williamson:144-75 for a discussion of Philo's allegorical method.

the apostates themselves, not only their pleasure. Philo concludes in *Post* 88: "Thus the man who removes the boundaries of the good and beautiful both is accursed and is pronounced to be so with justice."[14]

Philo's aim is parenetical: He uses allegory in order to deduce principles for a Jewish obedient life in a Diaspora situation where Jews were tempted to live a Hellenistic life (Borgen 1984b:243). We may also note, however, that there is a certain juridical flavor in Philo's use of the curses: Both in *Leg* 3:107–108 and *Post* 84 he first describes the crime and then refers to the curses as effective judgments hitting those who commit it.[15]

c: Curses in analogy to Deut 27–28 (Jer 11:3; 17:5; Mal 1:14; 2 Enoch 52 and Bib. Ant. 26:5)

Another way of drawing on the curse from Deut 27–28 is to construct new אָרוּר clauses in analogy to them. This feature we find in Jeremiah, Malachi, *2 Enoch*, and *Bib. Ant.*

In Jeremiah we find such curses in Jer 11:3–4 and 17:5–8.

> Jer 11:3–4 is constructed as an analogy to Deut 27:15–26 (Holladay 1986:350):[16] "Cursed be the man who does not heed the words of this covenant which I commanded your fathers when I brought them out of the land of Egypt, from the iron furnace, saying, 'Listen to my voice, and do all that I command you. So shall you be my people, and I will be your God.'"
> The curse and blessing in Jer 17:5–8 emphasize the contrast between the man who turns away from and the man who trusts in the Lord: "Cursed is the man who trusts in man and makes flesh his arm, whose heart turns away from the Lord. He is like a shrub in the desert . . . . Blessed is the man who trusts in the Lord, whose trust is the Lord. He is like a tree planted by water . . . ."

Both curses are commonly regarded as deuteronomistically influenced.[17] While the latter curse is parenetic in a way that is not juridically practicable,[18] the former is both a covenantal exhortation that will recall the nation to the Sinaitic treaty (Thompson 1980:343–44) and also part of Yahweh's judgment on Israel (Holladay 1986:352–53).[19]

---

[14]It is clear that Philo refers to an altering of the mosaic law, cf. *Post* 99, where he describes the right behavior as to "have kept to the limits laid down by the men of old, which they laid down in the cause of virtue." Cf. also that Philo expounds Deut 30:11–14 in *Post* 85, and that he refers to the chosen state of Israel in 91–92.

[15]Cf. *Leg* 3:111–199 where Philo expounds the effects of the curse on pleasure.

[16]As in Deut 27:26, the curse exhorts total obedience. The exhortation is to do *all* commandments, and it is followed by a promise of blessing corresponding to Deut 28:1–2, 9.

[17]For deuteronomistic influence, cf. Schottroff:133–34, 228–30. For Jeremianic origin, cf. Holladay 1986:349–53, 489–93.

[18]For the un-juridical features, cf. Schottroff:92–93 as well as for connections with parenetic wisdom tradition (93, 130–33).

[19]Holladay denotes the whole section as a pronouncement of curse and translates the

In Mal 1:14 we find a curse analogous to Deut 27 within a setting of Yahweh's jurisdiction over Israel. Following the accusation of false offerings (1:12-13) and preceding the judgment of the priests (2:1-9) we find this curse: "Cursed be the cheat who has a male in his flock, and vows it, and yet sacrifices to the Lord what is blemished." The covenantal setting of this second disputation has been presented above (cf. sec. 3.3.1c). Here we may underscore that the curse is also connected to divine judgment (cf. 2:2-3).

It is in *2 Enoch* 52 that we find the most extensive antithesis of blessing and curse outside Deut 27-30, with seven pairs of blessings and curses.[20] It occurs in the middle of the ethical instructions (chs. 39-68). Although there are no explicit connections to Deut 27-30, the section is dominated by curses and blessings like these chapters, and it also occurs in a similar farewell setting.

In this chapter there is no emphasis on "covenantal nomism" which separates Jews and Gentiles. The ethical content of the curses corresponds to the trend of *2 Enoch* of making the ethic general and humane (*OTP* 1:97).

> The first three curses concentrate on the reverence for God and for humans as being in the image of God: "Cursed is he who opens his heart to insults, and to slander against his neighbor" (52:2); "Cursed is he who opens his lips for cursing and blasphemy, before the face of the Lord" (52:4); "Cursed is he who insults the creatures of the Lord" (52:6).
> The last two curses (52:11-14) concentrate the ethical instruction on a peaceful way of life: "Cursed is he who strikes down those who are in peace" (52:12); "Cursed is he who speaks peace, but there is no peace in his heart" (52:14).
> Also the curse in 52:8 seems to be connected to general love for neighbor: "Cursed . . . who looks to obliterate the works of others."

This general aspect of the parenesis is not seen as a contrast to obedience to the Torah, however, as the curse in 52:10 illustrates: "Cursed is he who destroys the rules and restrictions of his fathers." Thus there seems to be a trend similar to the one in *T. 12 Patr.*:[21] The universal aspect of the Jewish law is emphasized without any open polemic against the law itself. A certain aspect of divine jurisdiction is present in this chapter also. According to the

---

curse in the present tense: "Cursed *is* the man . . . ." An accusation in 11:6-8 is followed by an assertion that Israel has broken the covenant and by a judgment on the nation (11:10-11).

[20]*2 Enoch* is a writing with several unsolved questions: Scholars disagree whether it is Jewish or not, and whether it dates from the turn of the century or from medieval times. In addition it is preserved in manuscripts of varying lengths. According to *OTP* 1:96-97, it could date from the turn of the era, and be written in any place where Jewish, Greek, Egyptian, and other Near Eastern ideas mingled, and could thus be a writing from a Jewish fringe sect.

[21]For *T. 12 Patr.*, cf. above sec. 3.3.5.

concluding verse of the chapter, "all this will make itself known in the scales in the book on the great judgment day" (52:15).

Bib. Ant. 26:5 also contains a curse analogous to Deut 27:15–26. It occurs in a major expansion of the book of Judges, which in *Bib. Ant.* 25–28 has been expanded with some chapters on Kenaz and the extermination of 6110 sinners from the people.[22]

> The punishment of the sinners is described as a juridical procedure which is a mixture of human jurisdiction and Yahweh's own intervention.[23] It is noteworthy that curses play a dominant role in the process:
> Kenaz refers to Deut 29:17–20 as the juridical basis for the judgment on the sinners: "Did not Moses the friend of the Lord speak about these people, saying, 'Lest there be among you a root bearing poison and bitterness?'"(25:5).
> The scene closes with Kenaz issuing a curse on these (and future) sinners, before executing the death-sentence: "And now cursed be the man who would plot to do such things among you, brothers." And all the people answered, "Amen, amen." And when this had been said, he burned all those men in the fire and everything that had been found with them except the precious stones.

The last curse is analogous to Deut 27:15–26. It functions both as a basis for the judgment and as a curse intended to exhort the readers of the book. The whole scene has a non-historical flavor and seems to have been constructed to serve the author's parenetical aim (Nickelsburg 1980:54–55). Corresponding to the main emphasis in the work, the sins that are punished in chapters 25–26 mainly refer to idolatry (Murphy 1988a:280; cf 25:6–13). The author sees idolatry as the most urgent crime, because an idolatrous Israel is like all other nations and thus counters the purpose of Israel's election (Murphy 1988a:275–76, 279–80, 284).

This writing is important because it may stem from an environment of synagogues in Palestine at the end of the first century CE.[24] It demonstrates also that these circles could draw on the juridical features of curses from Deut 27–30 in order to recall Israel to its true identity at a time when it was under attack.[25]

---

[22]The author of *Bib. Ant.* gives the most attention to the Book of Judges (1/3 of the work) in his retelling of the Hebrew Bible. Kenaz becomes a leader second in importance only to Moses, cf. Nickelsburg 1980:49–50. Kenaz is mentioned in Judg 3:9, 11 as the father of Othniel. Elsewhere in Jewish tradition he is only a name except for Josephus' *Ant* 5:182–184.

[23]Cf., for the intervention from God, the casting of lots to find the sinners (25:3), the oracle ordering the sinners to confess (25:6), and the oracle prescribing the punishment (26:1–4). This feature of dependency upon God's instruction is important in the book, cf. Murphy 1988c, especially pp. 2–4.

[24]*OTP* 2:299–300, 302. Schürer 1986:328–29 considers a date in the first century CE as most probable.

[25]Cf. Murphy 1988a:284–87. In *Bib. Ant.* the emphasis on dtr-SH is more upon the hope than upon the repentance, cf. Murphy:1988b.

d: Liturgical curses corresponding to Deut 27–28 (1QS ii; 4Q 280–82,
286–87; 1QM xiii.1–6)

We may lastly consider some examples from Qumran for curses corresponding to Deut 27–28 within a cultic setting. The great liturgy of 1QS ii has been treated above with its ארור clause opening the second curse (cf. sec. 3.3.4b). We also find some curses of Satan and his lot in 4Q 280–82 and 286–87, which are part of a cultic setting as 1QS ii.[26] Those who follow Satan are cursed in this way:

> Cursed be those who practi<se their wicked designs> and <es>tablish in their heart your (evil) devices, plotting against the Covenant of God . . . (4Q 280–82).
> <Cursed be a>ll those who practi<se> their <wicked designs> and establish <in their heart> your (evil) devices, <plotting against Go>d'<s Covenant> . . . to exchange the judgmen<ts> . . . (4Q 286–87).

Both 1QS ii and these latter fragments demonstrate that curses in the ארור form are employed as a form of "sacred law" in Qumran, to call down the judgment of God on sinners. Thus the parenetical aim recedes more into the background.[27] In a liturgical context curse is as an effective power that creates a sphere of evil and makes this the most important aspect of the context. A further example of such liturgical curses is found in 1QM xiii.1–6.[28]

4.1.3: Curses from the deuteronomistic History and Jeremiah

a: Hebrew Bible curses

In the deuteronomistic History and Jeremiah we find four texts containing curses with the same form as Gal 3:10. These curses do not serve a parenetical aim, but they secure oaths and laws in quite specific situations of warfare (Schottroff:40–43, 80–83, 211–17), with Jer 20:14–15 as an excep-

---

[26]The texts are presented in Milik:126–37 and commented on in Lichtenberger:113–15. For the connections with 1QS ii, see the parallel expressions between 1QS ii:5–9 and 4Q 280–82 and the responsorium "Amen, amen" twice in 4Q 286–87. Cf. also Milik and Lichtenberger.

[27]It may also be argued that these curses from the ceremony of initiation form the basis for the rules of expulsion from the sect. Cf. CD xx.3–8 (col. viii in *DSSE*) where expulsion is ordered with a basis in a ceremony of curses. Cf. also Lichtenberger:116–18 who refers to 1QS vii.19–21. See also Forkman:52–63, 72–74 for 1QS ii as a basis for more detailed regulations concerning both entry and expulsion, although he modifies the importance of the covenant-motif with regard to the rules for expulsion (74–78).

[28]1QM xiii.1–6 seems to resemble 1QS ii both by its liturgical setting and structure, cf. Weise:102–3. It is placed, however, within the Holy Warfare at the turn of the era. The section contains a blessing for the God of Israel and for "all those who <serve> Him in righteousness" (xiii.2– 3), and a curse for Satan and "all the spirits of his company for their ungodly purpose and . . . for all their service of uncleanness" (xiii.4–5).

tion.[29]   Their function is to reinforce the duty to attend Holy Wars (Judg 5:23–24; Jer 48:10), to control the army in a battle (1 Sam 14:24, 28), to punish Gentile enemies (Josh 9:23), and to assure that a banned city or tribe remains so (Josh 6:26; Judg 21:18).

There are two reports that the prohibition is violated, and then a juridical procedure follows the curses: The curse of 1 Sam 14:24, 28 is taken as the basis for a death sentence on Jonathan (cf. 1 Sam 14:36–44).   The curse of Josh 6:26 seems to be fulfilled by divine intervention when 1 Kings 16:34 reports that the rebuilder of Jericho lost two of his sons.[30]

b: Curses in later traditions

It is notable that when two of these texts are expounded in succeeding literature, the authors insert covenantal language, and thus bring them in closer connection with covenantal curses:

> In *Ant* 6:126–28 Josephus retells 1 Sam 14, and he inserts covenantal phrases into the text: According to Josephus, when Saul summons Jonathan, he asks "wherein he had gone astray and of what wrong or unholy act in all his life he was conscious" (126).   Jonathan acknowledges the death sentence with a reference to Saul's piety (cf. 127).   The people prayed for Jonathan, however, that God would grant him absolution "from his sin" (128).
>
> 4QTest 21–24 interprets the curse on the rebuilder of Jericho as a foreshadowing of the history of the sect.[31]   Josh 6:26 has been fulfilled by the coming of an accursed man who has set up "a wall and towers to make it a stronghold of ungodliness" and has "committed an abomination in the land."   Now the text does not concern the actual rebuilding of Jericho, but covenantal apostasy in Israel (Lübbe).   Like in Philo, we also here face an interpretation that emphasizes a hidden meaning in the text: The curse of Josh 6 is now understood as a prophetic reference to a current enemy of the sect.   Josh 6 has reported directly what is happening in the end of the days.[32]

Thus, even if these curses were connected to a context of their own in the Hebrew Bible, later readers have connected them to covenantal traditions.

---

[29]Jer 20:14–15 is singular among the curse texts.   Here a curse with the form of Gal 3:10 is issued on the day of Jeremiah's birth and on the man who brought the message about it to his father.   These verses probably illustrate an extraordinary use of curse to emphasize the depth of Jeremiah's personal despair, cf. Scharbert 1958a:7 and his *TWAT* 1:443.   These curses are extremely difficult to interpret, and scholars often tend to correct the text, cf. the different proposals of Holladay 1986:560–66 and Lundblom.

[30]This is so even if 1 Kings 16:34 refers to a foundation sacrifice of children rather than a sudden death.   For a discussion, cf. Schottroff:150–52.

[31]The text is briefly commented on in Lichtenberger:106.   It is common to identify the accursed man with Simon the Maccabee, cf., for example, Burgmann.

[32]For this hermeneutical principle, cf. Stegemann:411–12; *DSSE*:39–40; Lichtenberger:154–56.   The sect thus not only re-interpreted the Torah as argued above in sec. 3.3.4a, but also the prophetic books of the Hebrew Bible.

4.1.4: Curses from the primal history

a: Hebrew Bible curses

Curses in the primal history with a form similar form to Gal 3:10 occur in Gen 3:14, 17; 4:11; and 9:25. They belong to the Yahwistic interpretation of history, picturing the negative background for the blessings of Gen 12:2-3.[33] These curse sections reveal human sin in three fundamental relationships: In Gen 2–3 sin occurs in the relationship between man and wife, in Gen 4 in the relationship between brother and brother, and in Gen 9 in the relationship between parents and children (Westermann 1974:661).

No parenetical emphasis is explicitly present in these curses. Curse reasons connect them to their specific situations.[34] They are components in an imitation of juridical procedures: In Gen 3–4 Yahweh judges with curses, and in Gen 9 Noah, as the head of the family, delivers Canaan over to divine judgment.[35] When succeeding literature presents the primal curses, however, it adds covenantal terminology to the context.

b: Curses from the primal history in Philo

Philo devotes almost a whole treatise to the exposition of the curses in Gen 3, namely most of the third treatise in *Legum Allegorica*:[36]

> The *curse upon the serpent* in Gen 3:14 provides a basis for discussing pleasure in *Leg* 3:65–199. By drawing on an ambiguous meaning in the text, Philo lets the serpent represent pleasure, because: "What a serpent does to a man, that pleasure does to the soul" (76). He takes the curse of Gen 3:14 to reveal several aspects of the evil pleasure:
>   a) The serpent is not allowed to defend itself (65–75), because pleasure is evil in origin.

---

[33]Cf. the references above in sec. 5.2.2. For the proposal of Rendtorff that the curse of Gen 8:21–22 marks the end of the curse section, cf. the critique by Steck 1971:526–42.

[34]In 9:25 the curse reason is not part of the curse itself, but it is presented by the narrator in 9:24.

[35]For the juridical features, cf. Westermann 1964:47–58 and Schottroff:79–80, 85–89, 206. According to Schottroff:58–59, Gen 3:14 and 4:11 — with their preposition *min* — have preserved the original meaning of curse as excommunication.

The Canaan curse in Gen 9:25 is puzzling: Although it is Ham who showed disrespect to his father, Noah, it is Ham's son that is cursed. The ancient concept of solidarity in curse and blessing makes this difference unimportant: Since the family lived in solidarity, a curse on Canaan would imply a curse on his father Ham also. The author may have chosen to emphasize Canaan, however, because he as a patriarch embodied the people of the Canaanites, cf. Scharbert 1958b:139–41; Westermann 1974:648, 658. Cf. Westermann 1964:644–61 for a sound discussion of 9:18–27 as a whole.

[36]For the method of allegory and parenetical scope of this treatise, cf. above sec. 4.1.2b.

b) The serpent is cursed from all the cattle (108, 111–12), because pleasure is to be distinguished from neutral sense perception.

c) The serpent is cursed also beyond all the wild beasts, because pleasure is at the bottom of all passions (113).

The curse *on Adam* from Gen 3:17 Philo interprets allegorically in *Leg* 3:246–53. This curse does not hit Adam himself, since he is neutral mind (246). It hits the earth, which is the "doings of which the whole soul . . . is the means and occasion . . . when he allows wickedness to regulate them in each case." (247). Philo interprets *Eve* as sense perception. Therefore, when the curse of Gen 3:17 accuses Adam of having listened to his wife, it means that superior Mind should not listen to Sense-perception (222–23).

Thus, Philo takes the judgments from Gen 3 and universalizes their ethical relevance. By relating curse to pleasure, sense perception, and "doings," Philo manages to establish the curses for his readers as exhortations toward covenantal obedience. He then treats the Gen 3 curses similarly to the Deut 27 curses. He even combines these two types of curses: The Deut 27–28 curses, which occur in *Leg* 3:107–8 (cf. sec. 4.1.2b above), occur in the middle of the exposition of Gen 3:14! The same allegorical method is utilized on the curse on Cain (cf. *Agric* 20–25; *Deter* 96ff) and the curse on Canaan (Cf. *Sobr* 30–51).[37]

c: *Curses from primal history in other traditions (Adam and Eve, Apoc. 24–26; Jub. 7–10; Bib. Ant. 3:9–10)*

The Gen 3 curses are recorded also in *Adam and Eve, Apoc.* 24–26. Again we find clearly covenantal expressions introducing and concluding the curses: The curse on Adam begins and ends with the phrases: "Because you transgressed my commandment (παρήκουσας τὴν ἐντολήν μου) . . . because you did not keep my commandment (τὴν ἐντολήν μου οὐκ ἐφύλαξας)" (24:1, 4). The serpent is accursed because it "lead astray (πλανήσῃς) the careless of heart" (26:1).

---

[37]Turning to the curse on Cain in Gen 4:11, we find that Philo also here draws on allegorical meanings within a covenantal setting: In *Agric* 20–25 he contrasts the soul-husbandry of Noah with Cain who worked on the ground. The latter is cursed because he gave attention to his earthly body and its pleasures rather than the soul with its virtues (cf. 22, 25 and R. Williamson:153–54 for the whole passage). This curse is expounded thoroughly in *Deter* 96ff. Now Philo takes Cain to represent "love of self" (cf. 32) with the consequence that he gives attention to the senses (cf. 98–99), and therefore "God cannot but curse the godless and impious (ἄθεον οὖν καὶ ἀσεβῆ) Cain" (103).

Turning to the curse on Canaan in Gen 9:25, Philo treats it in *Sobr* 30–51. He explains the curse on Canaan by explaining the difference between rest and motion (34–43). Ham "is a name for vice (κακία) in quiescent state and the grandson Canaan for the same when it passes into active movement" (44). Then it is Canaan who is cursed, because he represents active sin (cf. 46). In this way Philo manages to transform even this puzzling curse into a strong covenantal exhortation.

This work probably represents Pharisaic Judaism of the first century CE (*OTP* 2:252). It is clear that the author wants his readers to be reminded of their own covenantal obligations when they read these curses from the primal history. He gains this effect by inserting covenantal phrases into the Hebrew Bible text.

The curse on Canaan in Gen 9:25 is taken up in *Jubilees*. The author recounts the biblical curse in 7:7-13, but he also gives his own explanation for the curse on Canaan instead of Ham. In 9:14-15 he expands the Hebrew Bible text with a reference to an oath between Noah and his sons, alluding to a covenantal ceremony:[38]   It is when Canaan has broken this oath with covenantal features (cf. 10:29-34) that he is accused of sedition and cursed (cf. 10:30).[39]   Thus the curse on him instead of Ham becomes more understandable, and also this curse can be taken to exhort covenantal obedience.

We may also briefly consider the way *Bib. Ant.* 3:9-10 expounds the curse of Gen 8:21, although this curse does not have a form similar to Gal 3:10. This context reveals that the dtr-SH may be connected with a curse from the primal history, giving it a parenetical feature.[40]   When Yahweh in Gen 8:21 promises never again to curse the earth, the author of *Bib. Ant.* continues: "But when those inhabiting the earth sin, I will judge them by famine or by the sword or by fire or by death" (3:9). In the appointed time, however, the era of restoration will come with another earth and another heaven (3:10).

4.1.5: *Curse and divine laws*

The group of curses connected to divine laws also contains some curses with a form resembling Gal 3:10. The curse of Gen 49:7 occurs in an oracle containing features that imitate juridical language (Schottroff:85-87). The curse is directed toward the tribes of Simeon and Levi by metonymically cursing their anger and wrath. The reason is given in Gen 49:6: "for in their anger they slay men, and in their wantonness they hamstring oxen."[41] When 4 Macc 2:18-20 takes up this curse, however, it becomes part of a parenetical setting by an allegorical technique resembling Philo: Here it is stated that

---

[38]Cf. K. Berger's text-edition (377) for references to Deut 27 and 1QS i-ii.

[39]Cf. K. Berger's text-edition (384) for this report as a unique explanation in Jubilees and texts dependent on this book.

[40]For dtr-SH in *Bib. Ant.* 3:9-10 and also in 12:4; 13:10; 19:2-5, cf. Steck 1967: 174-75.

[41]For a discussion of content and redaction, cf. Schottroff:134-41.

the rage is accursed in order to indicate that reason has the ability to control anger. Therefore God gave the Law to the intellect (2:23).

The remaining curses stem from the wisdom tradition where covenantal language is clearly present:

> Ps 119 opens with a blessing on "those whose way is blameless, who walk in the law of the Lord . . . those who keep his testimonies, who seek him with their whole heart" (119:1-2). The accursed ones, however, are presented in 119:21 as those "who wander from thy commandments."[42]
>
> In Wis 3:12-13 we find that with regard to the ungodly "who disregarded the righteous man, and rebelled against the Lord" (3:10), their "offspring are accursed" (3:12). As a contrast it is stated in 3:13: "For blessed is the barren woman who is undefiled, who has not entered into a sinful union."[43]
>
> In Wis 14:7-9 Noah's ark "by which righteousness comes" is blessed (14:7), and the idol and its maker are cursed (14:8), for "equally hateful to God are the ungodly man and his ungodliness" (14:9).[44]

4.1.6: Conclusion

When we turned to the semantic features of the form of Gal 3:10, the picture was more complex than in the previous chapter. Although most texts with the same form were found in the Deut 27-30 tradition, we also tabulated many other texts with the same or similar form. This complexity was present in the Hebrew Bible: Although most forms were found in Deut 27-28, Jeremiah, and Malachi (15F and 6f), we also found several curses in the context of warfare (5F and 2f*) and in the primal history (3f* and f). With respect to the interpretation of Galatians, however, it is more important to see how the form was perceived by later readers of the texts. Then it was remarkable to see how covenantal exhortation also became part of the exposition of these other curse texts. It therefore seems safe to conclude that *when we meet the form of Gal 3:10, it is natural to ask if it is part of covenantal exhortation influenced by Deut 27-30.*

Our survey also revealed another feature which may be important with respect to Galatians. It is probable that the ארור formula originated in *jurisdiction*. We have noted how most curses with a form identical or similar to Gal 3:10 in the Hebrew Bible have some connection with juridical procedure,

---

[42]In this text ארור is connected to a participial curse condition. It is not tabulated as a curse with the same form of Gal 3:10, however, since ארור is connected attributively to the preceding phrase.

[43]According to Schmitt:54-65, this contrast forms a transition between two related sections: Wis 3-4 addresses the problems of how the righteous can suffer (3:1-12), be childless (3:13 - 4:6), or experience a sudden death (4:7-19). These problems are caused by a rigorous "Tun-Ergehen"-theology, but may also be related to covenantal expectations according to Deut 27-30.

[44]This antithesis is found within a large section about the origin and folly of idolatry, cf. Schmitt:112-13, 117.

either as sanctions of the covenant (cf. Deut 27–28; Jeremiah; and Malachi), as sanctions in a setting of warfare (cf. dtr-History-Work and Jeremiah), or in Yahweh's jurisdiction in the primal period (cf. Gen 3–4). This juridical aspect has even survived in the succeeding Deut 27–30 tradition:

> a) In *Jub.* and *2 Enoch* curses are cited as belonging to heavenly laws.
> b) Philo takes them as judgments that hit pleasure and the life of Jewish apostates.
> c) *Bib. Ant.* even lets such curses play a dominant role in a procedure against apostates that includes human punishment.
> d) The sect of Qumran draws on such curses as a part of "sacred law" in a cultic setting in order to call down the judgment of God upon non-sectarians.

This feature gives curses in such a formal pattern a special emphasis which we may note with regard to the interpretation of Galatians: They normally involve more than parenesis or neutral argumentation; they are also perceived as judgments that are succeeded by divine (and/or human) punishment.

4.2: Curse texts with antithesis

4.2.1: Introduction

In Jewish curse texts we also find many texts with curse and blessing in antithesis (=CU/BL in the tables). The tables of appendix 1 review seventy-seven such units. Twenty eight of these texts have been presented in the sections above. Nine texts contain the Gen 12 formula, and we may once again postpone the discussion of them to chapter 5. At this point we will consider thirty texts, namely five texts from the Deut 27–30 tradition, nine texts from wisdom traditions, six texts from the Balaam tradition, and ten texts from other contexts.

The remaining ten texts contain an antithesis between the act of cursing and that of blessing. This perspective differs from that of Gal 3 and is closer to the antithesis of Rom 12:14 (cf. also Rom 3:14). We can therefore deal with them rather briefly for our purpose:

> Four of them attack illegitimate curses in a private sphere (cf. Prov 27:14; 30:11; Pss 62:5; 109:18, 28), two of them refer to the practice of uttering a blessing to counter the effect of a curse (cf. Judg 17:2; 1QS vii.1), two of them state that people will curse those that close their eyes for the needy (Prov 11:26; 28:27), one text accuses pagan gods of not being able to curse or bless (Ep. Jer. 66), and the last one refers to a certain Jesus son of Ananias who resisted both cursing and blessing (*Bell* 6:307).

4.2.2: Texts briefly considered

a: Antitheses in the Deut 27–30 tradition

The remaining references to curse and blessing in antithesis in the Deut 27–30-tradition consist mainly in brief references to the curse liturgy of Deut 27 in Josh 8:34 and by Philo in *Fuga* 73 and *Heres* 177–78. Two of these texts deserve a broader presentation, however:

The deuteronomic law corpus Deut 12–26 is not only succeeded by a treaty text in Deut 27–30, but it is also preceded by a brief one. With a choice similar to Deut 30:15–20 and a form similar to Gal 1:8–9, Deut 11:26–29 opens in this way:

> "Behold, I set before you this day a blessing and a curse: the blessing, if you obey the commandments of the Lord your God, which I command you this day, and the curse, if you do not obey the commandments of the Lord your God, but turn aside from the way which I command you this day, to go after other gods which you have not known" (11:26–28).

Josephus employs the antithesis in *in a speech of exhortation* in *Bell* 5:401 (cf. 5:375: παραίνειν). The antithesis opens the second part of the speech (399–415), where Josephus accuses his audience of being lawbreakers (cf. 397, 402):

> But as for you, what have you done that is blessed by the lawgiver, what deed that he has cursed have you left undone? How much more impious are you than those who have been defeated in the past (401)?

The covenantal context is clear, since the third part of the speech is a final appeal to repentance (cf. "confess and repent" in 416).[45]

b: Antitheses in wisdom traditions

Since Deuteronomy reveals clear correspondences to wisdom literature,[46] it is not surprising that we find curse and blessing in antithesis also in wisdom traditions.[47] We find it both in small proverbs with antithetical parallelism and in longer didactic poems. The aim is exhortative as in all wisdom traditions. Three wisdom texts have been treated above since they also have the form of Gal 3:10 (cf. sec. 4.1.5). Now we will turn to those with only antithesis, and we find that covenantal terminology is present rather explicitly:

---

[45]Although Michel 1984:959–62 analyses this speech from other perspectives, he also states that deuteronomistic elements are present, cf. pp. 970–71.

[46]Cf. Weinfeld 1972:257–319, especially pp. 258–59 for Deut 30:11–14 and pp. 276–79 for Deut 27:15–26.

[47]Cf. Mitchell:44–52 for a broader wisdom-context for the Hebrew Bible texts.

In Sir 3:9 we find the antithesis in connection with family solidarity: "For a father's blessing strengthens the houses of the children, but a mother's curse uproots their foundations." The perspective is enriched in Sir 3:16, however, where a break of family solidarity is compared to blasphemy: "Whoever forsakes his father is like a blasphemer, and whoever angers his mother is cursed by the Lord." To break off from one's family is thus equal to apostasy from Yahweh, and thus this text has a covenantal setting.[48]

Sir 33:12 seems to reflect Genesis texts. In a section of divinely ordained diversities in nature (cf. 33:7–15), Sirach claims that the Lord appointed different ways for different people: He seems to allude to the blessings of Noah and Abraham with their offspring when he states that "some of them he blessed and exalted" (cf. Gen 9:1; 12:2–3), while he seems to allude to the curse on Canaan and the Canaanites when he states that "some of them he cursed and brought low" (cf. Gen 9:25).[49] Also here the perspective is broadened with respect to covenantal obedience, when this contrast is followed by an antithesis similar to Deut 30:15: "Good is the opposite of evil, and life the opposite of death; so the sinner is the opposite of the godly."

In Prov 3:33 and Ps 37:21–22 the wicked one is cursed and the righteous blessed. This covenantal setting is carried further by Qumran in 4QPs 37.iii.9–13. The blessing on the righteous in Ps 37:21–22 is interpreted to be fulfilled with the sect, "the congregation of the Poor." The curses are directed toward their enemies, "the violent . . . the wicked of Israel."[50]

In Prov 24:23–25 a curse is spoken against those who acquit a wicked man, and a blessing for those who rebuke him.

In Sir 28:13–26 the man with an evil tongue is cursed (28:13), and the man who is protected from it is blessed (28:19). The link to covenantal exhortations is most explicit in 28:23, where it is stated that "those who forsake the Lord will fall into its power."

Ps. Sol. 4 addresses the profaner whose "heart is far from the Lord, provoking the God of Israel by lawbreaking" (4:1). The psalm issues many curses on the law-breaker (4:14–22), while it blesses "those who fear God in their innocence" (4:23). Cf. also *Ps. Sol.* 3:9–12 where the sinner curses his life (3:9), while "those who fear the Lord shall rise up to eternal life" (3:12).[51]

c: Antitheses in the Balaam tradition

The seven texts from the Balaam tradition comprise fourteen antitheses between curse and blessing. Most of them juxtapose Balaam's attempt to curse the Jewish nation with the result that he in fact blessed them (cf. Num 23:11; 24:10; 22:6; Josh 24:9–10; Philo *Conf* 159; *Mos* 1:283, 292; Jos. *Ant* 4:118). Thus also this tradition mainly emphasizes the act of cursing versus the act of blessing, which is a different use of the antithesis from the one in

---

[48] It is presupposed that one breaks off from a family where one has been given pious education. For family solidarity in wisdom literature, cf. Scharbert 1958b:235–41.

[49] Cf. *New Oxford Annotated Apocrypha* for these references.

[50]Cf. Lichtenberger:157. We thus find a new example of eschatological interpretation of a Hebrew Bible text, cf. the discussion above in sec. 4.1.3b.

[51]The covenantal features of *Pss. Sol.* also include the use of dtr-SH in Psalms 2; 8; 9; 17, cf. Steck 1967:170–71.

Galatians. This is so also in *Migr* 113, 117, where Balaam is judged to be an utterer of curses, since this was his intention behind the blessings.

Although these texts do not contain covenantal expressions, we find another link that is notable: The Gen 12:3 formula is cited in Num 24:9 (cf. *Mos* 1:291) and reflected in Num 22:12. Thus the emphasis on the curse-blessing-antithesis in this tradition seems to be caused by a Yahwistic re-interpretation of the Balaam episode: The unsuccessful attempt of Balaam to curse Israel is taken to demonstrate the truth of the promise in Gen 12:2–3.[52] We will return to this re-shaping below in sec. 5.2.

d: Antitheses in other texts

Among the remaining texts, those attached to the Yahwistic source do not use the antithesis within a covenantal setting: Gen 27:12–13 speaks of curse and blessing from a father in connection with Jacob's cheating of Isaac, while Jos. *Ant* 1:142 briefly refers to Noah's curse on Canaan and his blessing of the other sons.

In traditions later than Deuteronomy, however, it is possible to discern covenantal language:

Three texts are found in *1 Enoch* (27:1–2; 41:8; 59:1–2). The accursed are "those who speak with their mouth unbecoming words against the Lord" (27:2, cf. 5:4). Further, the blessing is equaled with "light to the righteous" and the curse with "darkness to the sinners" (41:8, cf. 5:6–7). Although these references are brief, a reader would connect them to the curse-blessing motif in chs. 1–11 and 90–104,[53] and thus they are embedded in a covenantal context.

The remaining five texts occur in Philo, and the covenantal context is even clearer here:

In *Conf* 196 he states that God appraises noble life but curses impiety. In *Congr* 56–57 he contrasts the "enjoyment of virtue" with "the life of the bad, a life of damnation and bloodguiltiness, the victim of every curse." In *Decal* 87 he states that the consciousness makes peace with those who listen to it, but those who do not are given over to a miserable and accursed life. In *Post* 80–81 he praises the one as happy who strives after "ends that are good," while he subsumes those who strive after their opposites under the curse. In *Prob* 137 he praises freedom to be glorious, but slavery to be execrable. The freedom has been defined above as following God (cf. 19–22).

---

[52]Cf. Schottroff:202–205 and especially Moore:109, 119–21. Moore seeks to explain the role of Balaam by comparing it to roles of diviners and exorcists in the Ancient East, and thus the Yahwistic re-interpretation of Balaam as a blesser is easier to perceive.

[53]Cf. the presentation above in sec. 3.3.3.

4.2.3: Summary

The semantic feature of curse and blessing in antithesis only proved more complex to handle than the features that have been been presented in ch. 3 and in sec. 4.1, namely the double motif of curse and blessing and the form of Gal 3:10. It turned out that curse and blessing in antithesis only is present also in wisdom traditions and Balaam traditions in later Jewish texts, so it is difficult to regard it as a feature resulting mainly from deuteronomistic influence. Covenantal terminology occurs so frequently in later texts of this kind, however, that our findings here do not speak against the conclusions that have been reached in secs. 3.4 and 4.1.6, namely that the semantic features exhibit covenantal language that reflects the Deut 27–30 tradition.

One conclusion may be noted with regard to Galatians: *Curse and blessing in antithesis occur so frequently in curse texts that whenever we meet it in a text we should attempt to regard this span of text as a coherent unit.* This observation may be a corrective to the widespread custom of interpreting Gal 3:6–9 as a section on Abraham that does not include the curse in 3:10.

CHAPTER 5

5.0: CURSE AND BLESSING IN HISTORY

We have examined texts containing the structure of Gal 3:8-14 and texts with similarities to the semantic field of 3:8-10. We now turn to texts that share important semantic features with 3:13-14. As argued above (sec. 2.2.2) we will concentrate on the following elements: texts with expressions similar to κατάρα τοῦ νόμου and γίνομαι κατάρα (sec. 5.1), texts with blessing for Gentiles (sec. 5.2), and texts with curse and blessing in sequence (sec. 5.3).

5.1: Curse texts with expressions similar to κατάρα τοῦ νόμου and γίνομαι κατάρα

5.1.1: Introduction

The tables of Appendix One demonstrate that expressions like κατάρα τοῦ νόμου (=KN in the tables) and γίνομαι κατάρα (=GK in the tables) occur almost exclusively in the Deut 27-30 tradition. These features confirm that an emphasis on this tradition is important for Paul's use of curse in Galatians.

5.1.2: Expressions similar to κατάρα τοῦ νόμου

In Gal 3:13 we find the expression κατάρα τοῦ νόμου. With this subjective genitive, the law is identified as the source of the curse. In Jewish curse texts we find eight texts that tie law and curse together in a similar way, all of them in the Deut 27-30 tradition:

> Deut 29:20-29 uses phrases such as "the curses of the covenant (αἱ ἀραὶ τῆς διαθήκης ταύτης) written in this book of the law (ἐν τῷ βιβλίῳ τοῦ νόμου τούτου)" (Deut 29:21; cf. also 29:20, 27). In this chapter צלה is even used as a synonym for covenant, cf. 29:12, 14 (MT 11, 13); "covenant" is even replaced by "curse" in 29:19 (MT: 18).[1] This is an amplification of the close link between covenant and curse in Deut 27-28.
> In 2 Chr 34:24-28 we find this phrase (34:24): "all the curses that are written in the book which was read before the king of Judah."[2]
> In the confession of sins in Dan 9 and Bar 1:15 - 3:8 these expressions occur: "the curse and oath which are written in the law of Moses" (Dan 9:11) and "the

---

[1]Cf. Brichto:28-31 for a discussion of *covenant* and *curse* as *hendiadys* in this text. Cf. also von Rad 1966:180.

[2]The Chronist refers to the tradition of the oracle from Huldah recorded in 2 Kings 22:15-20. See sec. 5.1.3 below for more discussion.

curse which the Lord declared through Moses his servant" (Bar 1:20).[3]

In Qumran there are references to the covenantal curses with phrases such as "the curses of the Covenant" (אלות הגות הברית) (1QS ii.16) and "the curses of His Covenant" (אלות בריתו) (CD i.17). Cf. also אלות ה(ברית) in 1QS v.12 and CD xv.2–3.

Therefore, it seems clear that, in Jewish texts, expressions similar to κατάρα τοῦ νόμου refer to the covenantal curses of Deut 27–30.

5.1.3: Expressions similar to γίνομαι κατάρα

In Gal 3:13 the expression γίνομαι κατάρα denotes Jesus as a curse in a metonymic way. J. Scharbert has proposed that a study of similar metonymic phrases in the Hebrew Bible may be fruitful for the Pauline exegesis (Scharbert 1958a:17, further pp. 5, 11). All but one of these expressions are found in traditions influenced by the dtr-SH.

In the Deut 27–30 tradition we find the following expressions that denote the Jewish nation as a curse:

> Among the prophets, Jeremiah most frequently uses such expressions. He repeatedly warns his fellow countrymen that Yahweh will make them a curse, viz. let them be/become a curse: ἔσονται . . . εἰς κατάραν (Jer 24:9; cf. 42:18 [LXX: 49:18]; 44:12 [LXX: 51:12]); γένησθε εἰς κατάραν (Jer 44:8 [LXX: 51:8; cf. also 44:22]); δώσω εἰς κατάραν (Jer 26:6 [LXX 33:6]); נתן לקללה (Jer 25:18; cf. 29:18).[4]
>
> Another prophetic reference occurs in Zech 8:13, where the prophet states that Israel has "been a byword of cursing (קללה . . . היה/ἦτε ἐν κατάρῃ) among the nations."[5]
>
> There is an oracle from the prophetess Huldah in 2 Kings 22:15–20. It is addressed to king Josiah after his repentance when he found the book of the law.[6] She refers to the curses of Deuteronomy in this way (22:19): ". . . when you heard . . . that they should become a desolation and a curse (τοῦ εἶναι . . . εἰς κατάραν)."
>
> In Baruch's confession of sins, this expression occurs in 3:8: "we are today in our exile . . . to be reproached and cursed (εἰς ἀράν)."

---

[3]Cf. Steck 1967:110–22 for dtr-SH in Jewish confessions of sin. For dtr-SH in Dan 9 and Bar 1:15 – 3:8, cf. *ibid* 113–16. Dtr-SH also structures Baruch as a whole, cf. *ibid* 130–32, 164–65.

The aim of such confessions of sin is to strengthen covenantal obedience, cf. *ibid* 123–24. They may be seen in connection with Lev 26:40 which demands the people to confess their own sins and those of their ancestors as part of the return to the law, cf. Scharbert 1958b:232–33, 247.

[4]For a discussion of deuteronomistic influence in such phrases, cf. above sec. 3.3.1a.

[5]For connections to dtr-SH in Zech 7–8 and also in 1:2–6, cf. Steck 1967:143–44. Although it is possible for the such versions as RSV to see the reference to Israel as a byword of cursing (cf. Wehmeier:99; Mitchell:59–60), it is also possible to see it as a metonymic description of Israel as a curse (cf. Schreiner:4).

[6]For the connection between Deuteronomy and the reform of Josiah, cf. Preuss:1–12. For this section as a deuteronomistic oration, cf. Weinfeld 1972:3, 25–26.

In Jubilees we find the statement "they will be a blessing and not a curse" (Jub. 1:16); cf. also "make your name a curse" (Jub. 20:6);

In T. Levi we find the statement "you will be . . . a curse (ἔσεσθε . . . εἰς κατάραν)" (T. Levi 10:4; 16:5).

It seems clear that all but four phrases similar to γίνομαι κατάρα in Jewish tradition refer to the curse that will fall upon disobedient Israel within the framework of dtr-SH. A related, national expression is found in an oracle against Edom in Jer 49:13 (LXX: 30:7) where it is stated that "Bozrah shall become a horror, a taunt, a waste, and a curse (εἰς κατάρασιν ἔσῃ)."

Three times, however, individual lawbreakers are denoted metonymically as a curse:

1 Enoch 5:6 uses this phrase for sinners: "make your names an eternal execration (ἔσται . . . εἰς κατάραν αἰώνιον)."

In Num 5:27 the ordeal ceremony concerning an adulterous woman includes the expression "make you an execration (לאלה . . . היה/ἔσται . . . εἰς ἀράν)" (cf. also 5:21).

The Hebrew text of Deut 21:23 also seems to use curse in this way when the hanged corpse of a man who has committed a capital crime is denoted as קללת אלהים. Since Paul cites this very passage in Gal 3:13, we will concentrate especially on the various Jewish interpretations of it below in sec. 10.4.2.

5.1.4: Summary

We have found that both the expression κατάρα τοῦ νόμου and the expression γίνομαι κατάρα in Gal 3:13 correspond to deuteronomistic phrases. Expressions like the "curse of the law" are found only in these traditions. Also the metonymic use of curse is a typical deuteronomistic device, with Num 5:21–27 as the only exception.

Once again, therefore, we have been led to the Deut 27–30 texts in our search for a suitable background for Gal 3, to texts that mostly aim at exhorting covenantal obedience in various ways. They refer to the "curse of the law" as a constant threat to Israel in their history, and most of them identify the disobedient and punished Israel with the curse.

5.2: Curse texts with blessing for Gentiles

5.2.1: Introduction

The tables of Appendix One show that the Gen 12:3 formula is almost the only text that refers to blessing for Gentiles with explicit use of the blessing term (=BG in the tables). These texts are important not only because of this feature, but also because they contain the antithesis of blessing and curse (cf. sec. 4.2.1), some curses with the form of Gal 3:10 (cf. sec. 4.1.1), and even one text with curse and blessing both in antithesis and sequence (cf. sec.

3.1). It is therefore natural to start with these texts in sec. 5.2.2.

The Gen 12:3 formula is also connected, however, to a promise of blessing for the Gentiles:

> Formula (12:3a): "I will bless those who bless you, and him who curses you I will curse;
> Promise (12:3b): and by you all the families of the earth shall bless themselves."

Paul cites this promise in Gal 3:8. Therefore, it is important for us to consider this promise in an excursus (cf. 5.2.3). Then we will turn to the Deut 27–30 tradition (cf. 5.2.4) and the remaining texts with blessing for Gentiles (cf. 5.2.5).[7]

5.2.2: Texts with the Gen 12:3 formula

The Gen 12:3 formula represents a reshaping of curse and blessing in the Yahwistic source of the Pentateuch. It has a more original form in Gen 27:29 and Num 24:9, where it is a formula of protection in the ארור form. In Gen 12:3 it has been adopted into an oracle from Yahweh which corresponds to the Yahwist's use of blessing and curse.[8] Gen 12:1–4a seems to be an important transitory unit between the primal history and the tribal period, emphasizing the promise that Israel will be a mediator of blessing to all humankind.[9] The Balaam pericope illustrates the truth of this formula in a paradigmatic way. Note Num 24:9, where the Yahwistic writer shows that the blessing bestowed on Israel is so strong that it is impossible for any human such as Balaam to destroy it.[10]

---

[7]Some will object because I consistently have postponed the discussion of the Gen-12 texts until now. This simplification is easy to defend in chapter 3, where I postponed only one text; it is more questionable in sec. 4.1.1, where three texts with the same form as Gal 3:10 were postponed. It also might give rise to many questions in sec. 4.2.1, where the treatment of nine texts with antithesis was postponed: Could it be that we after all face a curse tradition with so many semantic similarities to Gal 3 that it should be regarded as equal to the Deut 27–30 tradition?

Some observations speak against an equality of status: The form of Gal 3:10 is with one exception (Tob 13) not taken up in any later exposition of the formula, and is thus not a part of the conventional language in this tradition. The antithesis between curse and blessing is employed rather nakedly, without such qualifications that we find both in Gal 3 and the Deut 27–30 tradition. I therefore rather see the Gen 12 tradition as a tradition which has so close similarities to the Deut 27–30 tradition that it easily may be combined with it, as witnessed by Tob 13 (cf. the discussion below in sec. 5.2.4).

[8]Cf. H. W. Wolff 1964:358–59; Schottroff:37–40; Westermann 1981:174–75.

[9]This function of Gen 12:1–4a is a standard view in research, cf., for example, Scharbert 1958b:160–80; H. W. Wolff 1964:351–61; Wehmeier:199–203; Steck 1971:550–54; Ruprecht 1979a:183–85.

[10]Cf. the discussion above in sec. 4.2.2c.

The formula occurs ten times outside the Yahwistic source in the literature I have investigated. It is present with slight variations in Tob 13:12; *Jub.* 12:23; 25:22; 26:24; 31:17, 20; *T. Levi* 4:6; Philo *Migr* 1, 109; *Mos* 1:291.

For our purpose we may underscore two features in these texts that converge with the Deut 27–30 tradition. On one hand the formula is placed in an eschatological context, but on the other hand the antithesis of curse and blessing can be perceived in covenantal categories.

It is noteworthy that most texts outside Genesis/Numbers relate it to the Gentile nations[11] in *the future era of restoration*:[12]

> Tob 13:12 cites the formula in a section describing the new Jerusalem (13:9–18), to which the nations will come from afar (13:11) and partake in the blessing (13:14).[13]
>
> In *Jubilees* the future relevance is indicated clearly twice: In 25:22 the formula is placed in a section treating the "great day of peace" (25:20), when it is said that the "seed stand for all ages" and "his sanctuary be built in all ages" (25:21).[14] In 31:20 it is introduced in this way: "And on the day when you sit on your righteous throne of honor, there will be great peace . . . ."[15]
>
> *T. Levi* 4:6 occurs in a section describing the "judgment on the sons of men" (4:1), a setting which is present whether or not we regard the rest as a Christian shaping of the tradition.[16]
>
> Philo places the formula in an eschatological setting in *Mos* 1:291.[17] In the Hebrew text, Balaam's oracle promises victory for Israel in a setting with a view to the settlement in the land (Num 24:7–9). According to Philo it is a prediction of the future savior king: "There shall come forth from you one day a man, and he shall rule over many nations, and his kingdom spreading every day shall be exalted on high."[18]

---

[11]The formula is connected with the promise to the Gentiles in Gen 12:3, a connection also found in *Jub.* 12:23; *Migr* 1. Also in later traditions we find it mostly in a context that speaks about the nations, cf. Gen 27:29; Num 24:9; Tob 13:11f; *Jub.* 26:23–24; *Migr* 1:290–91. Some additions make this even more explicit: Tob 13:12 adds πάντες to the formula. *Jubilees* speaks about "all flesh" (25:22) and "all your enemies," "any nation" (31:17), "all who hate you and afflict you" (31:20).

[12]Ruprecht 1979b has demonstrated that the phrases of Gen 12:2–3 are chosen with a view to their fulfillment in the Davidic-Solomonic kingdom (cf. pp. 454–57 for the formula especially). After the judgment on the nation, it is not surprising that these verses were transposed to the era of restoration.

[13]For dtr-SH in Tob 13, cf. below sec. 5.2.4b and Steck 1967:147–49.

[14]Cf. K. Berger:451 for the eschatological perspective.

[15]Cf. Davenport:57–66 for the eschatological features both of the Judah blessing 31:18–20, and as an implicit meaning in the Levi blessing 31:11–17, where we also find a Gen 12:3 formula.

[16]Cf. the discussion of *T. Levi* 4 above in sec. 3.3.5.

[17]The Gen 12 formula is not carried over to the era of restoration in *Migr* 109–17, but with regards to the promise in *Migr* 125–26, however, this has been done (cf. below sec. 5.2.3).

[18]Cf. Borgen 1992:344–46, 351–54 for this passage. Philo also takes up Num 24:9 in another eschatological passage, cf. *Praem* 95 and the treatment in Borgen 1992:354–60.

We may also note that the contents of the antithesis in some texts are taken to correspond to *covenantal obedience*.   The formula itself demands that Gentiles must bless Israel in order to partake in the blessing and warns those who curse Israel that they will be cursed.   This demand is most probably taken to denote an act of solidarity versus enmity toward Israel.[19]

> In *Jubilees* this aspect of solidarity is developed further with regard to its negative connotation: As synonymous expressions to "curse" Israel, we find the expressions "hate" and "afflict you" (31:20), and the expressions "your enemies" (31:17) and he who "curses you falsely" (25:22).[20]
> In *Tob* 13:12 the relationships are denoted as "to love" versus "to hate" Jerusalem.   Also these expressions may be taken to refer to those who are allies of or enemies of Israel.[21]   It may also be taken as pointing to covenantal obedience among the Gentiles, however, since 13:11 describes a fellowship between Jews and Gentiles in the worship of Yahweh (Gross:50):   "Many nations will come from afar to the name of the Lord God, bearing gifts in their hands, gifts for the King of heaven."
> Philo connects the formula most closely to covenantal obedience by means of his allegorical method in *Migr* 109-117.   He emphasizes that the formula teaches the people to "shew honour to the righteous man . . . for encomiums are due to him who praises the good man and blame again to him who blames him" (110).

We have found two features in the Gen 12:3 formula that make these texts converge with the Deut 27-30 tradition.   It was quite conventional to relate the formula to the future era of blessing, and two texts connect their antithesis to covenantal obedience.

5.2.3: Excursus: Texts with promise of blessing

The Gen 12:3 promise that follows the formula is connected to the formula also in *Jub* 12:23 and *Migr* 1.   In addition we find it ten times in the literature I have investigated.   It is repeated four times in Genesis (Gen 18:18; 22:18; 26:4; 28:14).   It is also present in Jer 4:2; Ps 72:17; Sir 44:21; *Jub.* 20:10 and Philo *Migr* 118.122.

Also in this promise it is easy to recognize the same features that converge with the Deut 27-30 tradition.   Similar to the Gen 12:3 formula, this promise is mostly related to the *era of restoration* in traditions outside Genesis:

Borgen observes that already the LXX makes additions which transform the oracle into a prediction for the future savior king: "There shall come forth . . . a man, and he shall rule over many nations."

[19]Cf. Schottroff:209-10.   It may be formulas from the nomadic setting that have been transformed into a formula of solidarity/enmity with the nation.   See also Scharbert 1958b:175; Schreiner:5; Wehmeier:159-60; Mitchell:29-30, 128-29.

[20]This negative emphasis corresponds to the tendency of *Jubilees* to see the conflict between Israel and the nations as the conflict between good and evil, cf. Wintermute in *OTP* 2:48.   According to Davenport:63, 66, the author of *Jubilees* does not consider it

In Jer 4:2 the promise is part of an oracle of penance, promising blessing for the nations if the people will repent and return to the Lord (cf. Deut 30:2).[22]

Ps 72 clearly depicts the king of Israel in an eschatological manner, with descriptions that transcend the historic reality (Kraus:661-62). When, for example, Deut 11:24 promises Israel supremacy from the Euphrates to the western Sea, Ps 72:8 states: "May he have dominion from sea to sea, and from the River to the ends of the earth!"[23] It is thus the future ideal king that will be a universal source of blessing (cf. 72:17). Also Sir 44:21 relates the promise to a description of worldwide domain identical to Ps 72:8.

Philo interprets the promise in *Migr* 118-126. His exposition has some similarities to the eschatological closing section of *Praem*, which is presented below (sec. 5.2.4a).[24] He interprets the promise in his usual allegorical way: He takes it both to signify the healing power of the righteous mind in the soul (119, 124), the blessing that a righteous man can mediate to his society (120-25), and lastly also the role of Israel in the new era (126).[25]

The promise of blessing is also found in Gen 12:2 where Abraham is denoted as a blessing in a metonymic way: "You will be a blessing (היה ברכה)." Abraham is promised to become so full of blessing that it will influence his surroundings.[26] We will comment on this expression since we traced metonymous expressions of curse above (cf. sec. 5.1.3). It is significant that in addition to two references to individuals as a blessing (cf. Ps 21:7; 37:26 and further Prov 10:7), the Hebrew Bible refers to Israel and proselytes as a blessing in the future era of restoration:[27]

> Isa 19:24: "In that day Israel will be the third with Egypt and Assyria, a blessing in the midst of the earth."
> Zech 8:13: "And as you have been a byword of cursing among the nations, O house of Judah and house of Israel, so will I save you and you shall be a blessing."

---

possible that any nation should bless Israel and obtain blessing.

[21]Cf. Thompson 1977 and 1979 for this political aspect of love versus hate, which has its background in the ancient vassal treaties.

[22]Cf. Schreiner:14-29 for this and other reflections from Gen 12:3 in prophetic texts.

[23]Cf. Zech 9:10 for this expression in an indisputably eschatological context.

[24]Philo focuses upon the great influence on society that a righteous man has (*Migr* 120-21, cf. *Praem* 125, 172). He speaks about how the smallest spark of virtue may light up a great pile (*Migr* 123), cf. *Praem* 171 and the parable of the root and the new growths in *Praem* 172. The parable of the barren woman who becomes fertile is found both in *Migr* 123 and *Praem* 158-61, 168.

[25]The expressions in 126 are not explicit, but clear enough: Israel is "covered with a dark shadow, it may be, by men's missings of the due season but revealed again by due season that ever follows in God's steps." This turn of the era will come as surprisingly as when the barren Sarah got her son.

[26]Cf. Westermann 1981:173-74. Scharbert 1958a:25-26 takes the expression rather to denote that Abraham will become part of widespread blessing formulas. Ruprecht 1979a:180-82 includes both interpretations.

[27]Cf. the discussion by Scharbert 1958a:25. Cf. Wehmeier:218-22; Mitchell:52-61 for a presentation of the blessing theme by the prophets.

Ezek 34:26: "And I will make them and the places round about my hill a blessing."

The Gen 12:3 promise is also connected to *covenantal obedience*, even more explicitly than the formula itself:[28]

On one hand six of the texts emphasize covenantal obedience as a condition for Jews: Abraham's obedience is described as a condition for the promise (cf. Gen 22:18; 26:5; Sir 44:20), Israel's obedience is demanded (cf. Jer 4:1; *Jub.* 20:9; Gen 18:19), and Philo relates the promise to the righteous man (cf. *Migr* 120-22).

On the other hand there are expressions that demand solidarity from Gentiles. In Gen 12:3 it is debated whether the expression נברכו should be translated with passive ("be blessed"), reflexive ("bless themselves"), or middle ("acquire blessing") meaning.[29] The former alternative does not indicate any demands for Gentiles, while the latter two do. These alternatives probably do not exclude each other, since they may be present in a form that does not clearly distinguish among the meanings.[30]

The LXX has a passive translation in all occurrences but Jer 4:2, while Ps 72:17 takes up the reflexive meaning.[31] In contrast, *Jub.* 20:10 clearly required an active formulation: When the nations desire Israel, they will bless the sons of Israel in the name of Abraham, in order to receive the blessing.

5.2.4: Texts from the Deut 27-30 tradition

In the previous sections we have noted how the Abraham tradition contains features that converge with the emphasis of the Deut 27-30 tradition. In this section we will see that also some Deut 27-30 texts contain elements similar to the Abraham tradition, and further that these traditions have also been explicitly combined.

a: Blessing for Gentiles in the Deut 27-30 tradition

Although only one text from the Deut 27-30 tradition (cf. *Jub.* 20:10) connects the blessing term to the Gentiles, we find seven texts that include

---

[28]Cf. the concept of blessing as presented by Scharbert 1958b:268: Blessing is a sphere of fortune, a relationship between God and humankind, which is dependent upon both the redemption and the election of the patriarchs, and the human response of confession/obedience to God.

[29]Cf. a short survey of the debate by Mitchell:31-33.

[30]Cf. a combination of passive and reflexive by H. P. Müller 1969:53; Ruprecht 1979a:182-83; Westermann 1981:176. It is also worth considering if it should be taken as a middle, cf. Schreiner:6-7; Wehmeier:177-79; Mitchell:31-33.

[31]For a discussion of the *hithpael* in Ps 72:17 and Jer 4:2, cf. Wehmeier:180-82.

Gentiles into the description of the era of restoration. Some of them even picture the Gentiles as obedient to the covenant:

In Zech 8:20-23 the Gentiles are depicted on a pilgrimage to Jerusalem, saying "Let us go at once to entreat the favor of the Lord, and to seek the Lord of hosts" (8:21). Israel's unique position will be widely acknowledged: "In those days ten men from the nations of every tongue shall take hold of the robe of a Jew, saying, 'Let us go with you, for we have heard that God is with you'" (8:23). It is notable that the Gentiles take hold of the robe of the Jews, since these robes contained tassels which were to remind them of God's covenant (cf. Num 15:37-41).[32]

In *1 Enoch* 10:21 we find this description in the era of restoration: "And all the children of the people will become righteous, and all nations shall worship and bless me; and they will all prostrate themselves to me."[33]

In *Praem* 171-72, Philo ends the tractate and his description of the era of restoration by referring to the new relationship between Israel and the nations. The Gentiles will acknowledge the noble birth of the Jews and will observe that "from them shines out the glory which for a little while was quenched." The result is that virtue will spring forth in human life and "nations grow into a great population."[34]

In *Jub.* 20:6-10 the connection to the era of restoration is not so obvious, but we find a universal hope for Gentiles if they bless the Jews: "And you (=the Jews) will become a blessing upon the earth, and all of the nations of the earth will desire you, and they will bless your sons in my name, so that they might be blessed just as I am" (20:10).[35]

In the *T. 12 Patr.*, the era of blessing is promised for Jews and Gentiles alike.[36] Here we find no indications that the Gentiles are viewed as proselytes. The new era will give "mercy on all who are far and near" (*T. Naph.* 4:5b), and God will appear both "to save the race of Israel, and to assemble the righteous from among the nations" (*T. Naph.* 8:3; cf. also *T. Levi* 18:9-10; *T. Jud.* 24:3-6; *T. Zeb.* 9:8; *T. Asher* 7:3). As the texts now stand, they bear witness to how smoothly a Christian theology could adopt a universal perspective of salvation into dtr-SH.[37]

We may also review Ezek 16:53-63, although blessing is not described as universal, but only for two Gentile nations. In this text the fate of Israel is equaled with the fate of Sodom and Samaria in a way that resembles dtr-SH: For all these

---

[32]Cf. Petersen:319-20 for this feature as describing Gentiles as law-observant. Cf. H. W. Wolff 1964:372 for a connection with Gen 12:3 in this section.

[33]Cf. also *1 Enoch* 90:30 which asserts that Gentiles will obey the Jews, and 91:14 which asserts that "all people shall direct their sight to the path of uprightness."

[34]There is something vague about this description in *Praem* 171-72. It is clear, though, that Philo is to be interpreted here in the way I propose, cf. that *Praem* 152 describes the proselytes of his own time as obedient to the Law and also his description in *Mos* 2:44: "I believe that each nation would abandon its peculiar ways, and, throwing overboard their ancestral customs, turn to honouring our laws alone. For, when the brightness of their shining is accompanied by national prosperity, it will darken the light of the others as the risen sun darkens the stars." R. Williamson:25-26 also takes this latter passage as a qualification of the future hope in *Praem*.

[35]Cf. also above sec. 5.2.3 and below sec. 5.2.4b for this verse which includes the Gen 12:3 promise.

[36]Cf. de Jonge 1986 for a presentation of the material from the perspective that they are Christian texts. Cf. also Hollander/de Jonge:64-67.

[37]For *T. 12 Patr.* as Christian texts, cf. the discussion above in sec. 3.3.5.

nations we find a description of their sins (cf. 16:46–47, 58), their punishment (16:56–58), and their future restoration (cf. 16:53, 55, 61).[38]

Therefore, some Deut 27–30 texts also include the Gentiles in the future era of blessing, although the blessing term is not present. This tradition and the Abraham tradition have so many converging elements that it is not surprising to find them connected in Jewish tradition.

b: Combinations of Gen 12:3 and Deut 27–30 traditions

Already in Deut 27–20 itself the promise of blessing for Israel is connected to the Abraham promise. The clearest reference is found in Deut 30:20 where the blessing is described as a life in the land "which the Lord swore to your fathers, to Abraham, to Isaac, and to Jacob, to give them."

Such references to the promise are also found in some other Deut 27–30 texts: Jer 11:5 refers to "the oath which I swore to your fathers, to give them a land," Bar 2:34 states about the new era that "I will bring them again into the land which I swore to give to their fathers, to Abraham and to Isaac and to Jacob," and CD i.4 and iv.9 refer to the "Covenant of the forefathers."

When it comes to the blessing for the Gentiles, the traditions have been connected in two important places:

In Tobit 13 the Gen 12:3 formula has been put into the frame of dtr-SH.[39] The dtr-SH contains the description of the sins and punishment of Israel (13:3–5), and the repentance and restoration (13:5–10). It is followed by a description of the glorious new Jerusalem (13:11–18) which includes the Gen 12:3 formula in 13:12.

In *Jub.* 20:10 the Gen 12:3 promise has been put into a section with the antithesis of curse and blessing (20:6–10).[40] Secondly the author uses Deut 27–30 elements in vital places in his work, and he cites the Gen 12:3 formula five times.[41] Thirdly we noted that the Abraham section of the book (*Jub.* 11–23) has been expanded with several blessings related to Deut 27–30 (cf. 20:6–10; 21:21–24; 22:11–23) and concludes with a section of dtr-SH (cf. 23:16–25). We thus see that both the Abraham and the Deut 27–30 traditions are important in this work, and that they have been clearly connected to each other.

---

[38]Cf. Zimmerli:365–71 for these verses. Although he regards 16:44–58 and 16:59–63 as additions to chapter 16, he states that the end-product should be treated as a unit, cf. pp. 341–42.

[39]Cf. Steck 1967:147–49; Gross:48–49 for dtr-SH in Tob 13.

[40]Cf. above secs. 3.3.2 and 5.2.4a.

[41]In addition to their places in the Hebrew Bible story (12:23 and 26:24), he makes it conclude with blessings to Jacob (25:15–22), Levi (31:15–17), and Judah (31:18–20), which are all expansions of the Hebrew Bible text.

5.2.5: *Blessing for Gentiles in other texts*

Four other texts that discuss blessing of Gentiles easily fit into the picture outlined above: The dtr-SH apparently influenced Isa 24–25; Ezek 17; and *3 Apoc. Bar.* 4; and the Gen 12:3 formula is actualized by *Bib. Ant.* 18.

Isa 24–25 initiates the apocalypse of Isaiah, which is generally regarded as a later addition to the book.[42] This may explain why we find a structure that resembles dtr-SH, although the setting is not national, but universal. It opens by stating that a curse devours the earth because "they have transgressed the laws, violated the statutes, broken the everlasting covenant" (24:5–6),[43] and it continues by stating that "on this mountain the Lord of hosts will make for all people a feast of fat things" (25:6; cf. also 24:21–23 which pictures redemption in more nationalistic categories).

In Ezek 17:11–24 Zedekiah is accused of breaking an oath with the king of Babylon (cf. 17:16–18). This section is supplied with covenantal themes in two ways:[44] On one hand the breach of oath is equated with a breach of the covenantal oath with Yahweh (cf. 17:19) and with treason against Yahweh (cf. 17:20). On the other hand the description of the punishment is succeeded by a description of the new era of blessing for Israel: Israel as a huge cedar will give shelter for all kinds of beasts and birds (cf. 17:23), that is, will bring blessing also to Gentiles.[45]

As for *3 Apoc. Bar.* 4:15, we face a discussion similar to that of *T. 12 Patr.*: Opinions differ as to whether the text is Jewish with Christian interpolations, or whether it must be regarded as a Christian work in its entirety.[46] The sequence of curse and blessing is found in a clearly Christian verse: With regard to the cursed sprig from the garden of Eden, "its curse will become a blessing, and its fruit will become the blood of God . . ." (4:15a). If a Jewish tradition could be discerned behind the text, it would be dtr-SH, since the curse is described as a present punishment (cf. 4:16), and the blessing is promised for all people with regard to the new era: ". . . just as the race of men have been condemned through it . . . (they) will receive a calling and entrance into Paradise" (4:15b).

In some Balaam texts, Balaam is regarded as an example of the truth of the Gen 12:3 formula. In *Bib. Ant.* 18:6 Yahweh warns Balaam: "But if you curse them, who will be there to bless you?" Although Balaam was compelled by Yahweh to bless Israel, it was counted as a curse. As a man who cursed Israel, he thus perished according to Gen 12:3 (*Bib. Ant.* 18:12, cf. also Philo in *Migr* 113–15).

5.2.6: *Summary*

We have seen that the element of blessing of the Gentiles is found as conventional language in texts connected to the Abraham tradition. It is not found explicitly in the Deut 27–30 tradition, however, and we may ask whether our previous conclusions can be challenged by this finding.

---

[42]Cf. the discussion of redaction and a date in the 5th century BCE by Wildberger:892–911. Although there may be a complex history of redaction, he recommends that the chapters should be read as a unit (905).

[43]Cf. Wildberger:921–22 for influences from treaty texts on this expression.

[44]Cf. Zimmerli:384–90 for the text.

[45]Although these verses probably have been added to the chapter at a later stage, we follow Zimmerli:341–42, 388 in reading the end-product as a unit.

[46]Cf. the overview of positions in *OTP* 1:655–56. For *T. 12 Patr.*, cf. sec. 3.3.5.

In my view they cannot. It is clear in Gal 3 that Paul combines citations from Deuteronomy (3:10, 13) with a citation from Gen 12 (3:8). It is therefore quite possible that Paul has combined curse and blessing according to the Deut 27–30 tradition with blessing for Gentiles according to Gen 12. We have seen that such a combination both would correspond to converging elements in the two traditions, and that they also have been explicitly combined in Jewish texts before him. Although such a combination is too rare to be denoted as conventional, a combination in itself probably would not go counter to conventional expectations.

5.3: Curse texts with curse and blessing in sequence

The last semantic feature corresponding to Gal 3 that we will consider briefly is found in texts with curse and blessing only in sequence (=CU-BL in the tables). Again we seem to face a semantic element that appears to be conventional in the Deut 27–30 tradition, and where the other occurrences seem to have been influenced by it.

Among the Deut 27–30 texts, Zech 8:12–13; Dan 9; and Baruch 1–3 have been treated above in sec. 5.1, and Ezek 16:53–63 in sec. 5.2.4a. We are left with Lam 3:65–66, where the author prays that the curses will turn against the enemies of Israel in the era of restoration (cf. Deut 30:7).

The four Balaam texts all refer to the Balaam episode as an instance when Yahweh "turned the curse into a blessing." We may note that this expression is found for the first time in Deut 23:5, repeated in Neh 13:2, and used by Philo in *Deter* 71; *Migr* 115. Since the expression stems from Deuteronomy, it seems probable that it reflects deuteronomistic theology.[47] It seems to refer to the Balaam episode in a manner that makes it a prototype of what Yahweh will be able to do also in the era of restoration.

We are left with four texts where the influence from dtr-SH is either obvious, as in *Bib. Ant.* 3:9–10 (cf. sec. 4.1.4c above), or has been suggested, as in Isa 24–25; Ezek 17:13–21; and *3 Apoc. Bar.* 4 (cf. sec. 5.2.5 above).

To conclude: When curse and blessing occur in sequence, the results are clearer than in texts with antithesis only (cf. sec. 4.2 above). This semantic feature supports the conclusion in chapter 3 that the main semantic features of Gal 3 lead us to the covenantal curse tradition. In addition, we have more firmly established that curse and blessing in sequence belong to the conventional language of the Deut 27–30 tradition.

---

[47]Cf. Moore:109, 121–22 for this as a deuteronomistic reinterpretation of the Balaam tradition. Cf. also the discussion above in sec. 4.2.2c.

CHAPTER 6

6.0: חרם/ἀνάθεμα

6.1: Problems and limitation of task

In Gal 1:8-9 Paul employs the term ἀνάθεμα. This expression causes problems for a modern interpreter, because with it we are treading on even more uncertain ground than with the concept of curse. There are unsolved problems with terminology, the sources, and the Hebrew Bible context.

As for the *terminological problem*, the Greek term ἀνάθεμα is a positive term, denoting a dedicated offering.[1] The LXX, it seems, has given ἀνάθεμα its negative sense by connecting it exclusively to the translation of the root חרם in about thirty-five out of its eighty occurrences.[2]

Concerning *intertestamental sources*, we have access only to twenty terminological occurrences in seventeen texts from the literature investigated. This is a small amount compared to about 325 occurrences of curse terms in the same traditions. The negative use of ἀνάθεμα is not found in the writings of Philo and Josephus, both in Greek. It thus seems to be a Hebrew feature, found in Qumran, in the Hebrew fragments to Sirach,[3] and in writings with a Hebrew original such as 1 Macc, *1 Enoch, 2 Apoc. Bar.*, and *Bib. Ant.*[4]

Also the *Israelite origin* of the concept of חרם is a much more open question than the origin of the concept of curse. Very few Hebrew Bible texts are older than Deuteronomy, and we lack specific settings for חרם both

---

[1]This normal Greek use of ἀνάθεμα is found once in the New Testament (Luke 21:5). Philo uses ἀνάθεμα solely in this positive sense (*Migr* 98 [2x]; *Heres* 200; *Mutat* 220; *Decal* 133; *Spec* 1:66; *Spec* 2:32, 37, 115 [2x]; *Spec* 4:69; *Fuga* 42 [2x]; *Somn* 1:243 [2x], 251, 253; *Legat* 151, 157, 280, 297, 319, 335; *Deter* 20; *Plant* 126). It is also found in 4 of the 5 references of the Apocrypha (2 Macc 2:13; 9:16; 3 Macc 3:17; Jdt 16:19).

[2]This Greek term has not been sufficient, however: חרם is translated just as often with ἐξολεθρεύειν (=exterminate), a term which is also found frequently elsewhere in the Hebrew Bible as a translation of other stems (cf. Lohfink *TDOT* 5:182). Thus the LXX translates חרם with Greek terms for both dedication and extermination, without indicating clearly the reasons for the choices.

[3]The חרם texts in Sirach will be cited according to Sauer's German translation, since he translates the Hebrew fragments when they are preserved.

[4]1 Macc is preserved in Greek, but composed in Hebrew, cf. Goldstein:14-16. *1 Enoch* is preserved in Aramaic and Ethiopic, *2 Apoc. Bar.* in Syriac, *Bib. Ant.* in Latin, but all these writings were probably (at least partially) written in Hebrew, cf. *OTP* 1:6, 615-16; 2:298.

in wars and in punishments.[5]

It is outside the scope of this monograph to try to resolve these uncertainties. The terminological problem makes it necessary at the outset to include all texts containing חרם and ἀνάθεμα in a negative sense. The source problem makes it necessary to a certain extent also to draw on New Testament and Rabbinic literature.

With respect to Galatians we may then concentrate on two tasks: Since we want to trace connections between the anathemas of Gal 1 and the curses of Gal 3, we may present the development of חרם into curse in a diachronical section (cf. sec. 6.2). We also want to trace a specific background for Gal 1:6–9, and therefore we also have to concentrate on those Jewish texts that share features with Paul's semantic field (cf. sec. 6.3). Then I will briefly summarize my findings from part I of this volume (cf. sec. 6.4).

6.2: The development of חרם/ἀνάθεμα into curse

6.2.1: The Hebrew Bible development

Lohfink distinguishes three contexts for חרם in the Hebrew Bible:[6] Most frequently the stem occurs in contexts of *war and extermination*. Secondly we find it in contexts of *the sacred*, denoting something removed from the sphere of the profane and set apart for Yahweh. This use corresponds to the Greek term ἀνάθεμα, which mainly denotes a dedicated offering. The third context is that of *punishment and the first commandment*.

In pre-deuteronomistic traditions חרם refers both to a punishment (Exod 22:19) and to wars of extermination (cf. old traditions behind Num 21; Josh 10–11). It is unclear whether the חרם punishment involved more than the death sentence, and it is probable that חרם as the total annihilation of enemies during war was practiced only in a few instances.[7]

It is the deuteronomistic theory of חרם that occupies the most space in the Hebrew Bible, namely in about fifty out of eighty occurrences of the term. According to Lohfink:

---

[5]Cf. Lohfink *TDOT* 5:188 for deliberately vague definitions and for a list of unsolved questions. See also Welten:159, 161.

[6]N. Lohfink *TDOT* 5:183–85. See also Brekelmans:635–39. Brekelmans has written a monograph on חרם in Dutch which I have not been able to consult: *De 'cherem' in het Oude Testament* (Nijmegen 1959).

[7]Cf. Lohfink *TDOT* 5:193–95 and Brekelmans:637–38. Cf. also Lohfink (189–93) for ancient parallels to wars of extermination, especially to the Moabite Mesha inscription.

The most recent study of Yahweh-Wars has been made by Kang 1989. He surveys the features of divine wars in Mesopotamia, Anatolia, Syro-Palestine, and Egypt (11–110). He finds that the oldest Jewish wars with such features are found during the time of David (193–224). The various traits of Yahweh-War features at earlier stages he finds to be due mainly to dtr-redaction (114–92).

the Deuteronomistic historian frames a synthesis of the occupation according to which all the nations dwelling in the promised land were exterminated at Yahweh's command. The verb חרם becomes a catchword, losing its specific meaning and becoming a general term for radical destruction. [The חרם theory served] to systematize various ancient traditions concerning the occupation; at the same time, however, it performed certain specific functions for the readers of the time of Josiah. It was important to undergird their sense of religious and national identity (*TDOT* 5:195–97).[8]

The exilic revision of the theory pressed these points further. Israel's failure to fulfill the extermination became an explanation for the judgment on Israel, but it was also emphasized that חרם should protect Israel from seduction into idolatry (*TDOT* 5:197–98; cf. Deut 7:2, 25–26; 20:18).

This deuteronomistic fiction about חרם makes it difficult to trace the origins of the concept, but for our purpose this fiction is noteworthy: The deuteronomistic writers have transformed the concept both of curse and חרם, using both concepts as a means to secure the identity of the Jewish nation and the covenantal obedience of its people.

In post-exilic law we find חרם both as a dedicated offering (Lev 27:21, 28; Num 18:14; Ezek 44:29) and as a severe punishment (Lev 27:29; Ezra 10:7–8). The former context does not concern us here, and the latter will be discussed below in sec. 6.3.5.

In post-exilic prophecy we find חרם frequently in oracles against foreign nations (Isa 34:2, 5; 37:11; Jer 50:21, 26; 51:3; Dan 11:44), probably denoting extermination under the influence of deuteronomistic usage (Lohfink *TDOT* 5:198). We also find it as descriptions of Yahweh's actions against Israel, however (cf. Isa 43:28; Jer 25:9; Zech 14:11 and Mal 3:23). These references substantiate that a closer connection between חרם and curse emerged in texts written later than the deuteronomistic texts (Hunzinger 1954:12):

Isa 43:28 uses חרם as a parallel to reviling.

Jer 25:9 parallels חרם with horror, hissing, and reproach, in the same way as it parallels curse terms elsewhere with such expressions (cf. sec. 5.1.3 above).

Zech 14:11 states that the new era will put an end to חרם in Jerusalem. Zech 8:13 similarly states that curse will be replaced by blessing (cf. sec. 5.1.3 above).

Mal 3:23 threatens with חרם on the nation. Mal 3:9 similarly threatens with curse (cf. sec. 3.3.1c above).

6.2.2: חרם *as curse in texts outside the Hebrew Bible*

In nine of the seventeen חרם texts outside the Hebrew Bible we find that the term is connected to extermination in a setting of warfare:

---

[8]The importance of this deuteronomistic reshaping is also noted by Brekelmans:638 and Welten:160–61.

1 Macc 5:5 refers to the destruction of the sons of Baean.

1QM ix.6–7; xvii:5 uses the term with reference to the eschatological battle.

The law of warfare from Deut 20 is also restated in 11QTemple 62 (cf. line 14 for חרם).

Bib. Ant. 20–48 expands the books of Joshua and Judges. Thus 21:3; 26:2; 29:3 refer to the ban on the spoils, more specifically to prohibited Gentile property which is connected to idolatrous practice (cf. 21:1; 25:9–12; 29:3).

This connection with war is probably also present in the Hebrew fragments to Sirach in the expression גוי חרם which refers to a Gentile nation that has been destroyed for its sins (16:9) or to Joshua's extermination of enemy nations (46:6).[9]

Five intertestamental texts, however, bear witness to an even closer relation of חרם to the concept of curse:[10]

Sir 39:30 states that God has created some entities that are ready and biding their proper time: "the teeth of wild beasts, and scorpions and vipers, and the sword that punishes the ungodly with destruction." The allusions to Lev 26:21–25 seem clear:[11]   The sword is that which "shall execute vengeance for the covenant" (Lev 26:25), and thus there is a connection between the *hiphil* form of חרם and covenantal curses.

2 Apoc. Bar. 62:3 refers to "the חרם of Jezebel, and the idolatry which Israel practiced at that time." The text appears to use חרם synonymously with curse here, both because Jezebel is described with a curse term in 2 Kings 9:34 (Hunzinger 1954:14) and because the book as a whole reflects a deuteronomistic concept of curse in several places.[12]

1 Enoch 6:4–6 recounts that the Watchers bound one another by an oath in order to make sure that no one withdrew from their conspiracy: "Let us all swear an oath and bind everyone among us by a curse (ἀναθεματίσωμεν πάντες ἀλλήλους) not to abandon this suggestion but to do the deed" (6:4, cf. 6:5–6). It is widely attested that oaths can take the form of self-imprecatory formulas,[13] and in this text ἀνάθεμα clearly indicates this type of curse.[14]

The synonymity between curse and anathema in this context is also illustrated in the Greek Syncellos fragment to *1 Enoch*. The text is not easy to fit into the text of *1 Enoch*, but it relates thematically to the text of chapter

---

[9]Hunzinger 1954:12, on the other hand, takes these references to bear witness to חרם as a curse.

[10]Cf. Hunzinger 1954:12–15 who has drawn on the above references to the Hebrew Sirach; CD ix.1; *1 Enoch* 6; *2 Apoc. Bar.* 62:3 and the curse table of Megara.

[11]Cf. Sauer's text edition p. 602 for translation and allusion.

[12]Cf. Steck 1967:180–84 and Murphy 1985:117–20 for dtr-SH in *2 Apoc. Bar.*, and Murphy *ibid* 120–26 for the antithesis.

[13]Cf. Horst 1957:373–84; Lehmann:74–80; J. Pedersen 1914:108–18, 155–58; Brichto:70–76.

[14]Cf. Black:116–17 and Uhlig's text edition p. 518.

6: "Und wegen des Berges aber, auf dem sie schwuren und sich gegenseitig durch Verwünschungen (ἀνεθεμάτισαν) verpflichteten . . . nur der Fluch (εἰς κατάραν) soll auf ihn herabkommen."[15] We see that the relationship between anathema and curse which we found implicitly in *1 Enoch* 6 is explicitly stated here.

1 Enoch 95:4 refers to the illegitimate use of ἀνάθεμα by those who persecute the righteous: "Woe unto you who pronounce anathemas so that they may be neutralized!" The phrase is difficult to interpret, but according to Black:

> the reference seems to be to the practice of "anathematising" or "cursing," probably to the accompaniment of magical formulae, incantations and spells. The "woe" is on "sinners" who issue such anathemas with the intention of "loosing" them, i.e. "undoing" the spell. Because of their sins, however, there will be no "remedies" available to them to undo their curse or spell (Black:297).

Thus this reference to curse seems to function in the private sphere as a means of protection.[16]

The evidence of these texts is strengthened by texts from a pagan curse table, from the New Testament, and from Rabbinic literature:

> On a pagan curse table from Megara dating from the 1st or 2nd century CE, ἀνάθεμα is clearly used as an equivalent to curse. It is highly probable that this text has been influenced by Jewish usage,[17] so that it can be taken as evidence for the use of ἀνάθεμα as curse among Jews, at least as perceived by a Gentile.
> In the New Testament we often find ἀνάθεμα and oaths combined. In Acts 23:12, 14, 21 Luke reports that forty men have bound themselves by an oath (ἀνεθεμάτισαν; 23:12, 21), an oath which they refer to in this way: "We have strictly bound ourselves by an oath (ἀναθέματι ἀνεθεματίσαμεν ἑαυτούς) to taste no food till we have killed Paul" (23:14). Mark 14:71 utilizes the term in an oath of innocence. When Peter is accused of being a disciple of Jesus, he begins to invoke a curse on himself and to swear (ἤρξατο ἀναθεματίζειν καὶ ὀμνύναι), "I do not know this man of whom you speak." The parallel expression in Matt 26:74 is καταθεματίζειν καὶ ὀμνύειν. Thus half of the eleven New Testament references to ἀνάθεμα and its compounds seem to use it synonymously with curse in oaths.[18]
> In the Talmud we find some texts about the Jewish ban that connect חרם and curse: In *bMoᶜed Qat.* 16a we find that the ban as חרם is pronounced according to

---

[15]Translation by Uhlig:754; text by Black's text edition p. 26.

[16]The text may be read in other ways, however: The texts of Eth II read "that you do *not* loose," and this has caused Uhlig (cf. text edition p. 718) to translate it as: "Wehe euch, die ihr Verfluchungen ausstosst, die nicht zu lösen sind." Either way, the reference is to illegitimate curses in the private sphere.

[17]The table was introduced by Deissmann 1901:342. In his 1924:74 he points to the possibility of Jewish influence. Hofmann:428 refers to the word *abraikois* in the table in line 12. Cf. also Hunzinger 1954:14–15.

[18]Cf. Hunzinger 1954:15–16. In addition we find hypothetical self-imprecations in Rom 9:3 and Gal 1:8 which will be considered in chapter 9 below.

the ארור text Judg 5:23. We also find a reference in *bMoᶜed Qat.* 17a to the etymology of *shammetha*, the normal ban: Rab interpreted it as "death is there." Resh Lakish, on the other hand, interpreted it from the letter value of חרם, which is 248: "just as when it (the *cheræm*) enters, it penetrates the two hundred and forty eight joints (on one's body)." When it enters a body, it is according to Josh 6:17: "And the city shall be *Cheræm*." We see that the effects of חרם are described as a curse (cf. Horbury:35–36).

To conclude: This brief diachronic survey of the development of חרם/ἀνάθεμα into curse has justified a reading of Gal 1:8–9 as including curses by Paul. A deuteronomistic influence is therefore also to be expected in the language of Gal 1:6–9 if our conclusions in chapters 3–5 above are correct. Since Paul has chosen the term ἀνάθεμα, however, we will also look for חרם/ἀνάθεμα texts especially related to this semantic field.

6.3: חרם/ἀνάθεμα and the semantic field of Gal 1:8–9

6.3.1: Introduction

The tables in Appendix One reveal that features from the semantic field of Gal 1:8–9 are only occasionally found in Jewish חרם/ἀνάθεμα texts. Only Deut 13 contains חרם/ἀνάθεμα in an "if-you" law like Gal 1:8–9. This law treats the seducer like Gal 1:8–9, and it also includes the theme of apostasy, as Paul does. There are so many similarities that we will devote an entire section to this text and its reception in later traditions (cf. sec. 6.3.6). Before we turn to this text, however, we will take up the other semantic features in the field in due order (cf. secs. 6.3.2; 6.3.5).

6.3.2: Texts including present accusations (Josh 6–7; Isa 43:27–28; Jer 25:8–9)

The feature of placing an anathema in a context of present accusations is only found in three חרם/ἀνάθεμα texts, none of which are outside the Hebrew Bible. Thus it cannot be regarded as a conventional feature of these texts.

In Jewish curse texts, however, we often find that curses are embedded in a context of current accusations. Although we find about half of these texts in the Deut 27–30 tradition, it is also present so often in other traditions that it must be regarded as conventional for curse texts of most types. Thus we have yet another argument for regarding the anathema in Gal 1:8–9 as equal to a curse. It is noteworthy, however, that all three חרם/ἀνάθεμα texts with this structure seem to have been influenced by deuteronomistic features:

> The Achan episode of Josh 6–7 connects a judgment that Israel is חרם (cf. 7:12) to these accusations: "Israel has sinned; they have transgressed my covenant which I commanded them; they have taken some of the devoted things; they have

stolen, and lied, and put them among their own stuff" (7:11). This Ai-Achan episode is prominent in the ban texts: It is referred to also in Josh 22:20; and 1 Chr 2:7, and we find a total of sixteen ban terms connected to it. It has been reworked by the deuteronomists and has been adopted into a classic example of the dtr-SH (Begg).[19] In this way Achan's sin is seen as an example of Israel's recurring sins in history: Israel is said to have "transgressed my covenant" (צבר ברית) (7:11). Joshua 7 then presents the first example of Israel breaking the covenant in the land and experiencing death as its consequence (Butler:85).[20]

The prophetic texts also reveal such influence: In Isa 43:28 Yahweh leaves "Jacob to utter destruction" because of current sins (cf. 43:27), but continues to promise that God will pour out the blessing in the future (cf. 44:3). We clearly recognize elements from dtr-SH, namely sin, punishment, and restoration. In Jer 25:8-9 the Lord accuses Israel of disobedience (cf. 25:8) and parallels the punishment of utter destruction with expressions frequently found in the deuteronomistically influenced parts of the book: "and make them a horror, a hissing, and an everlasting reproach" (25:9).[21]

6.3.3: Texts with expressions similar to ἀνάθεμα εἶναι (Deut 7:25-26; Josh 6-7)

The expression ἀνάθεμα εἶναι is unambiguously present in only two חרם/ἀνάθεμα texts, but also we will comment on some additional texts with related expressions (cf. Lohfink *TDOT* 5:186, 187). This time we face a semantic element in the curse texts that is a typical feature of the Deut 27-30 tradition (cf. above sec. 5.1.3). It is therefore noteworthy that the two clear references in the חרם/ἀνάθεμα texts also reveal deuteronomistic influence.

Deut 7:26 exhorts Jews to avoid images of pagan gods: "And you shall not bring an abominable thing into your house, and become accursed like it (ἔσῃ ἀνάθεμα/חרם היה), you shall utterly detest and abhor it, for it is an accursed thing." It is the idolator who will become חרם according to this admonition, a judgment in accordance with the emphasis in Deuteronomy on the protection of the first commandment.[22]

In Josh 7:11-12 the people of Israel are placed under the ban: "Israel has sinned . . . . Therefore the people of Israel cannot stand before their enemies; they turn their backs before their enemies, because they have become a thing for destruction (ὅτι ἐγενήθησαν ἀνάθεμα/כי היה לחרם)."

---

[19]For deuteronomistic reworking of Joshua, cf. also Butler:xx-xxi, xxiv-xxvi.

[20]The main expression for the sin is found in Josh 7:1; 22:20; and 1 Chr 2:7: "The people of Israel broke faith (מצל)." This term appears only in exilic/postexilic language and denotes a break in a trust relationship between people or between Yahweh and the people (cf. Butler:83 and Knierim:920-22).

[21]For similar expressions, cf. above secs. 5.1.3 and 3.3.1a.

[22]Cf. Mayes 1981:24-39 for the relationship between these verses and other texts that emphasize prohibition against idolatry, namely Deut 4:1-40; 6:10-19; 7:4-15* and 8:1-20*. The reference to this text in 11QTemple 2:10-11 demonstrates that it was considered important also in Qumran.

This expression is found in the Ai-Achan episode of Josh 7-8. A similar expression in Josh 6:18 prepares the ground for it: "lest . . . you take any of the devoted things and make the camp of Israel a thing for destruction (שׂים לחרם)." We have commented on the deuteronomistic influence on this pericope in the section above.

The other expressions similar to ἀνάθεμα εἶναι mostly denote whole nations as חרם, a feature resembling the metonymous use of curse (cf. above sec. 5.1.3):

Isa 43:28 states that God has "delivered Jacob to utter destruction (נתן לחרם)." The influence from dtr-SH in this text has been presented in the section above.
Isa 34:5 refers to the people of Edom as ". . . the people I have doomed (וצל־צם חרמי)."
Sir 16:9 and 46:6 refer to Gentile nations as "a nation devoted to destruction (גוי חרם)."

In two texts individual lawbreakers are denoted as חרם:

Lev 27:29 refers to a sentenced man being חרם: "Any devoted (כל־חרם)."
1 Kings 20:42 refers to king Benhadad from Damascus as ". . . the man whom I had devoted to destruction (את־איש־חרמי)."

To conclude: The semantic element of expressions like ἀνάθεμα εἶναι seems to cover conventional language from the Deut 27-30 tradition. Both the occurrences among curse texts and the two clear חרם/ἀνάθεμα texts bring us to this tradition or to texts influenced by it. Although some texts with related expressions reveal a more ambiguous picture, the overall tendency is clear enough.

6.3.4: *Texts with curse in self-imprecations, curse on angelic beings, curse on seducers, and theme of apostasy (1 Enoch 6; Deut 13; 20)*

When we investigate the objects of the curses, whether they are directed against angelic beings, against seducers, or are parts of self-imprecations, we seem to face, if not deuteronomistic devices, at least features not uncommon to deuteronomistic texts.

Curse in self-imprecations is found in mostly two types of texts: Every oath implies a self-imprecation. Therefore this feature is conventional in texts with oaths. Among those texts that explicitly speak about self-imprecation, however, we find an emphasis in the Deut 27-30 tradition: When people obligate themselves to the covenant with an *Amen* formula, this obligation includes acceptance of the curses of the covenant as valid for themselves (cf. Deut 27:15-26; *Bib. Ant.* 26:5; *Jub.* 4:4; 33:12; 1QS ii.10.18; cf. also the related expressions in Neh 10:30 and CD xv.1-3). The only anathema text with this feature is found within a deuteronomistically influenced context: In *1 Enoch* 6 (cf. also the fragment of Syncellos) the watchers bind one another by an oath.[23]

· *1 Enoch* 6 is also the only anathema text with a *curse on angelic beings*, since the Watchers are presented as "children of heaven (οἱ ἄγγελοι υἱοὶ οὐρανοῦ)" (6:2). Elsewhere I have only found such a device in Qumran, where Satan and his lot are cursed in 1QM xiii.4–5 and 4Q 280–82; 286–87. Thus this feature cannot be regarded as belonging to conventional language, but we may note that when found, it is connected to deuteronomistically inspired traditions: In Qumran we find it in liturgical curses inspired by Deut 27, and *1 Enoch* 6 is embedded in a deuteronomistic context.

We face a similar picture when we investigate the *curse on seducers*. Among the חרם/ἀνάθεμα texts it is found only in the laws of Deut 13 and 20, which are recapitulated in the Temple Scroll. Among the Deut 27–30 texts we find this feature in Mal 2:8 and *T. Levi* 14:4, where the priests are accused of leading the people astray, and in CD i.14–16 where the "Scoffer" is accused of causing Israel to abolish the way of righteousness. Elsewhere this feature is found in texts that elaborate on the seduction of Eve by the serpent: It is indicated already in Gen 3:13 (cf. also Philo *Leg* 3:66) that the serpent beguiled Eve, but the terms for seduction are made more explicit in *Adam and Eve, Apoc.* 26, and by Philo in *Leg* 3:107. In *3 Apoc. Bar.* 4:8–9 the tree is accused of causing Adam to stray. We note an important distinction from the deuteronomistic texts, however: These latter texts do not depict present seducers as in Gal 1:8–9.

In 4QTest 23–24 there is a reference to seduction by a present enemy of the Qumran sect, however, but we have noted that this text is influenced by treaty-motives.[24]

Also the *theme of apostasy and idolatry* is found mainly in deuteronomistic texts. While such terms are scattered elsewhere, we find it in eighteen texts from the Deut 27–30 tradition. Among the חרם/ἀνάθεμα texts, we find six out of ten occurrences in laws of Deuteronomy.

6.3.5: חרם/ἀνάθεμα *in legal texts (Exod 22:19; Lev 27:29; Ezra 10:8; CD ix.1)*
When we turn to anathema within a legal form similar to Gal 1:8–9, we must once again start with the observation that among the curse texts, this feature is found most frequently in the Deut 27–30 tradition (cf. sec. 4.1 above for curses attached to curse conditions and curse reasons). In addition

---

[23]The text is presented above in sec. 6.2.2. For the deuteronomistically influenced context of *1 Enoch* 1–5, see sec. 3.3.3.
[24]Cf. Lübbe and above sec. 4.1.3b.

half of the חרם/ἀνάθεμα references are found in laws of Deuteronomy, which will be presented in the next section. It is noteworthy that we can trace a deuteronomistic influence also in the remaining texts:

In Exod 22:19 and Lev 27:29, we find חרם (*hophal*) related to death sentence formulas of מֹות־יוּמת:

> Exod 22:17-19: [17]You shall not permit a sorceress to live. [18]Whoever lies with a beast shall be put to death (מֹות־יוּמת). [19]Whoever sacrifices to any god, save to the Lord only, shall be utterly destroyed (חרם).
>
> Lev 27:29: No one devoted (חרם), who is to be utterly destroyed (חרם) from among men, shall be ransomed; he shall be put to death (מֹות־יוּמת).

Exod 22:18-19 places a חרם sentence after a מֹות־יוּמת sentence, and in Lev 27:29 the חרם of the protasis is prescribed as a death sentence in the apodosis. It is noteworthy that the ארוּר series of Deut 27 also had close connections to מֹות־יוּמת clauses (cf. sec. 4.1.2a). This means that the חרם laws already at an early stage seem to belong to the same cluster of legislation as the curse series of Deut 27.[25]

A deuteronomistic influence on these laws seems to be present in Ezra 10:8, which is often said to reflect a milder execution of חרם (*hophal*) than what is prescribed in the pentateuchal laws:

> . . . if any one did not come within three days, by order of the officials and the elders all his property should be forfeited (חרם), and he himself banned (בדל) from the congregation of the exiles.

Here we find חרם in a casuistic law. The issue at stake is the sin of mixed marriages that is seen as unfaithfulness against Yahweh (cf. 9:2, 4; 10:2, 10) and connected to seduction for idolatry (cf. 9:11-12 with reference to Deut 7:3-4).

The death sentence is not prescribed, however. According to W. Horbury this may be explained as an influence from the laws concerning admission to the temple congregation in Deut 23:2-9 (17, 19-20). He finds it likely that when Deut 29:20 prescribes for the sinner that the Lord "would single him out (בדל)," post-exilic readers would recall the practice of exclusion from the temple congregation (cf. קהל both in Deut 23 and Ezra 10:8). Ezra 10:8 then demonstrates a combination of the curse on the sinner from Deut 29:20, the exclusion from Deut 23, and the death penalty on the idolater from Exod 22: The death penalty is substituted by curse and excommunication, which was thought to prepare for Yahweh's own judgment (Hor-

---

[25]It is beyond the limit of this work to discuss whether or not the bans are changes of old death sentence formulas. Schulz:40-42, 58-59 argues for this, while Schwienhorst-Schönberger:318 sees an intended climactic structure in Exod 22:17-19.

bury:30).[26]

Thus we find that חרם in death sentence formulas has been influenced by texts from Deuteronomy, an influence which transformed the death sentence into curse and excommunication.

In Qumran, CD ix.1 seems to imply that the law of Lev 27:29 is upheld, probably under the influence outlined above. According to C. Rabin the verse may be translated as follows:

> As for every case of devoting, namely that a man be devoted so that he ceases to be a living man, he is to be put to death by the ordinances of the gentiles
> (כל אדם אשר יחרים אדם מאדם בחוקי הגוים להמית הוא).[27]

Rabin interprets the first clause as the implied meaning of the text, and he takes the *hiphil* חרם to be a passive similar to the one found in Lev 27:29. Thus the law prescribes that the person who is חרם according to Lev 27:29 shall not be put to death by the sect, but shall be handed over to the Gentiles for execution.[28] Thus some form of excommunication from the sect seems to be implied, but with the obvious purpose of causing the death of the law-breaker.

It is a general view among scholars that the custom of ban or excommunication was practiced only in sectarian contexts before 70 CE.[29] Horbury, however, has collected evidence for this as a continuous practice of ban in the period of the second temple also for the Jewish community as a whole. Some of the more important references will demonstrate the change

---

[26]Also H. G. M. Williamson:154–55 argues that Ezra 10:8 portrays a milder practice of death penalty. Cf. also Blidstein who compares it to the Greek penalty of ἀτιμία, a severe banishment that would cause the individual to suffer civic death.

[27]Translation from Rabin's text edition, p. 44.

[28]Cf. Rabin's text edition, p. 44. Most commentators take the *hiphil* in its most natural sense, however, and then the relation to Lev 27:29 is not so clear. We will present a few examples among many:

According to Derrett 1983 the law concerns those who "afflict with חרם any human being." It is thus a prohibition against cursing a fellow Jew as if he were a Canaanite. Such a person should be put to death according to the Noachide laws.

It is also possible to connect the reference to Gentile laws or customs to the protasis: Hunzinger 1954:12–13 asserts that the law prohibits vengeance upon fellow Jews according to Gentile custom, while Lohse (cf. text edition, p. 289) maintains that it prohibits sectarians to let a Gentile Jury issue the death penalty upon a fellow Jew according to pagan laws.

I find Rabin's objection to these types of interpretations worth considering: They "overlook that the sect would hardly have added to the biblical death penalties" (44).

Yet another possibility is to take חרם in the same sense as in Micah 7:2 = "entrap," cf. the proposal by Wacholder:166–67. This proposal would completely remove the text from our חרם texts.

[29]Cf. Forkman:102–105 who restricts the ban to pharisaic circles before 70 CE, but also investigates excommunication in Qumran. See also Hunzinger *TRE* 5:161–64.

of the death sentence (cf. Horbury:22–30 for the following):[30]

> Josephus refers to Jews who have been expelled (ἐκβεβλῆσθαι) for eating what is common, for sabbath breaking, or some similar sin (*Ant* 11:340, 346–47). According to Exod 31:14 a sabbath breaker should suffer the כרת penalty.
>
> In 3 Maccabees Jewish apostates are first shunned (2:33: ἐβδελύσσοντο) and later punished with death (7:12–15).
>
> Philo states in *Spec* 1:60 that Moses banishes (ἐλαύνει) the diviners listed in Deut 18:10–11, but according to Lev 20:6, 27 they are sentenced to death.
>
> The Damascus Document does not inflict stoning on the sabbath breaker as Num 15:35–36 does, but seven years under watch, cf. CD xii:3–6.
>
> Targum Pseudo-Jonathan turns the punishment of חרם in Deut 7:2 into a reference to ban: "you shall make an end of them with the Lord's *shammeta.*"

In addition to these and other texts, Horbury also argues that a certain terminology extends over the whole period, which may be just traces of a richer vocabulary.

To sum up: Jewish tradition considers the laws of Exod 22:19 and Lev 27:29 to prescribe the death sentence for grave apostasy from the first commandment. The texts discussed above seem to belong to the same cluster of legislation as the curse series of Deut 27. As the tradition developed, however, additional deuteronomistic influence seems to have caused a change from death sentence to curse and excommunication, as illustrated by Ezra 10:8 and other texts.

6.3.6: The law against seducers in Deut 13

Gal 1:8–9 contains the anathema in an *if-you* law. This feature is also found primarily in the Deut 27–30 tradition: Both Deut 11:28 and 28:15–16 contain curses in similar clauses, and it is also present in Jer 26:6 and Mal 2:2. The Malachi reference should be noted, because it is closely attached to a curse in the form of Gal 3:10 (cf. Mal 1:14). Also Jeremiah and Deuteronomy contain curses in the latter form (cf. Jer 11:3; 17:5–6 and Deut 27). This seems to indicate that deuteronomistic curses can be employed in both types of formats. They are usually found in the form of Gal 3:10, but occasionally also in a form similar to Gal 1:8–9.

The law in Deut 13 deserves special attention, however, since it is the only חרם/ἀνάθεμα text that employs the *if-you* form. In addition it includes a curse upon seducers and the theme of apostasy, so it seems to be closest to the semantic field of Gal 1:6–9 among these texts.[31]

---

[30]For a similar position, cf. Schürer 1979:431–33.

[31]We may briefly pass over the Law of Warfare in Deut 20, both because it is connected to the concept of warfare which is of minor importance to us, and because this law does not have the casuistic form that we are looking for. Deut 20:16–18 seems to be a secondary insertion (cf. Rofé:28–30) into the laws for warfare which has an apodictic form and prescribes חרם for enemy cities within Israel itself: ". . . you shall utterly

a: Deut 13 in the Hebrew Bible

In Deut 13 we find three laws against seducers clearly embedded in the casuistic form that includes a *you* element as Gal 1:8–9. The *if-you* laws are regarded as a development of the casuistic laws in the direction of parenesis, and they are a special feature of Deuteronomy (Liedke:29–30). Although we find some of them in the "Book of the Covenant" (Exod 21:13–14; 22:24–26 and 23:4–5), it is Deuteronomy that contains almost all the casuistic laws of this type.[32]

The three laws of Deut 13 all concern analogous forms of seduction and may be tabulated as follows:[33]

Deut 13:2–6:
Conditional clause: If a prophet arises among you, or a dreamer of dreams . . . .
Accusation: . . . and if he says, "Let us go after other gods (θεοῖς ἑτέροις) . . . ."
Punishment: . . . shall be put to death (ἀποθανεῖται),
Accusation: because he has taught rebellion against the Lord your God (πλανῆσαι σε ἀπὸ κυρίου τοῦ θεοῦ)."

Deut 13:7–11:
Conditional clause: If your brother, the son of your mother . . .
Accusation: . . . entices you secretly, saying (λάθρᾳ λέγων), "Let us go and serve other Gods . . . ."
Punishment: . . . you shall kill him (ἀποκτεῖναι αὐτόν) . . . you shall stone him to death with stones (λιθοβολήσουσιν αὐτὸν ἐν λίθοις, καὶ ἀποθανεῖται),
Accusation: because he sought to draw you away from the Lord your God (ἀποστῆσαί σε ἀπὸ κυρίου τοῦ θεόν).

Deut 13:13–18:
Conditional clause: If you hear in one of your cities . . . that certain base fellows (ἄνδρες παράνομοι)
Accusation: have gone out among you and have drawn away (ἀπέστησαν) the inhabitants of the city, saying, "Let us go and serve other gods . . . ."
Punishment: . . . you shall surely put the inhabitants of that city to the sword (ἀναιρῶν ἀνελεῖς . . . ἐν φώνῳ μαχαίρας), destroying it utterly (ἀναθέματι ἀναθεματιεῖτε).

---

destroy them . . . that they may not teach you to do according to all their abominable practices which they have done in the service of their gods, and so to sin against the Lord your God" (Deut 20:17–18). We may note the presence of seduction and apostasy in the text.

[32]The address to second person is found mostly in the protasis denoting the subject of the typical case (Deut 23:21: "When *you* make a vow to the Lord your God . . . .") and in the apodosis denoting the subject of the solution (Deut 23:21: ". . . *you* shall not be slack to pay it."). Casuistic laws of this kind are found in Deut 12:20–21; 13:2–19; 14:24; 15:7, 12–18; 17:2–20; 18:9, 21; 19:1–2, 8–9; 20:1, 10–12, 19; 21:10–14; 22:6–8; 23:10–11, 22–26; 24:10–13, 19–22; 26:1–2, cf. Liedke:21–22. For our purpose it is not important to distinguish between real laws and imitations as Liedke does.

[33]Horst 1930:16–40 emphasizes the analogy between the three laws to such a degree that he argues that the first example was derived from the third, and the second from the first.

The law is special, because it is the only Pentateuchal law that prescribes the death penalty for the mere incitement to sin.[34] We recognize a climactic structure: The seducer may be a prophet (13:1-5) or could be even from the family or a close friend (13:6-11); men may even seduce an entire Jewish city (13:12-18). The sanction is described as death (13:6), even death by stoning (13:10-11), or even death by חרם as in warfare (13:15-17).[35] The chapter is regarded mainly as a deuteronomistic shaping (Preuss:134), and therefore functions as a law obligating the new nation to take action against false teachers.

On a semantic level we find many links between Deut 13 and Gal 1:8-9:

> Deut 13 is not only in the *if-you* form, but as in Deut 15:12, 16 and 17:2, the second person element denotes those who experience the crime in their midst (cf. 13:2: "arises among you"). This corresponds to the second person feature of Galatians (cf. 1:8: "should preach to you a Gospel").
>
> Deut 13 first concentrates on the act of seduction of the prophet or prophetic dreamer (13:2). In a similar way Gal 1:8 focuses the possible seduction from commissioned preachers such as Paul, his co-workers, and an angel.
>
> In Deut 13 the crime is one of πλανᾶν ἀπὸ κυρίου τοῦ θεοῦ (13:6), of ζήτειν ἀποστῆσαι[36] ἀπὸ κυρίου τοῦ θεοῦ (13:11), and of ἀφιστάναι πάντας (13:14). These expressions correspond to Gal 1:6: μετατίθεσθε ἀπὸ τοῦ καλέσαντος ὑμᾶς.
>
> In Deut 13 the apostasy is described as one of serving θεοῖς ἑτέροις (13:3, 7, 14), an expression which corresponds to Gal 1:6: εἰς ἕτερον εὐαγγέλιον.
>
> MT describes the seducers in 13:13 by the difficult בני־בליצל.[37] By the New Testament era it was understood as the "children of Belial." But the LXX translates it as παράνομοι, thus depicting them as apostates from the law. The preposition παρά is also found in Gal 1:8-9: παρ' ὃ εὐηγγελισάμεθα/παρελάβετε.

When we bear in mind both the fact that Deut 13 is the only Pentateuchal law with a death sentence on seducers, and the many semantic similarities between this law and Gal 1:6-9, we have good reason to ask whether Paul may have chosen the term ἀνάθεμα because he wanted to allude to this law. Deut 13 prescribes the death sentence, however, and not חרם as a curse. We have seen, on the other hand, that the death sentence was often practiced as excommunication accompanied by curses by the time of Paul.

---

[34]It seems to be a reflection from the warnings against inciting treason in ancient vassal treaties, cf. Weinfeld 1972:91-100. Cf. Weinfeld also for the mingling of vassal loyalty commands and ordinary law covenants in the Hebrew Bible (146-57). Thus incitement to break the first commandment is equaled with incitement to treason against the national unity of the people (100). Horst 1930:17-18 also emphasizes this unity of religious and national concern.

[35]Cf. Schwienhorst-Schönberger:318-20 for this climactic structure, which may be inspired by Exod 22:17-19 (presented above).

[36]The Hebrew נדח (*hiphil*) designates an act of seduction only in Deut 13, 2 Kings 17:21, and 2 Chr 21:11.

[37]For the original meaning, cf. the discussion by Mayes 1979:236.

Therefore the difference between death sentence and anathema as curses would probably be perceived as unimportant for a Jew at the time of Paul.

b: Deut 13 in later traditions

The law of Deut 13 is taken up both in Qumran and in Rabbinic literature:

It is recounted in the Temple Scroll of Qumran: Among the three laws that use the חרם term, 11QTemple 2:10–11 takes up the prohibition against idols from Deut 7:25–26, col. 62:13–16 takes up the law of Holy Warfare of Deut 20:16–18, and col. 54–55 takes up Deut 13. The latter law is not rendered unconsciously, because the three analogous cases of Deut 13 are combined with the analogous law against idolators from Deut 17:2–7.

> The law is also found in the Mishnah:[38] In *mSanh.* 7 and 10 the laws of Deut 13 are upheld in all their seriousness. In 7:1 four types of death penalty are distinguished: Stoning, burning, beheading and strangling. It is discussed whether stoning or burning is the most severe punishment, cf. 9:3. Deut 13:1–12 is found among the crimes that are to be punished by stoning, cf. 7:4a. Deut 13:13–18 is present among the crimes that are punished by beheading, cf. 9:1b and 10:4–6. This latter crime was considered very serious, and the inhabitants of the apostate city had no share in the world to come (10:4).

A. Strobel has argued that this interest in Deut 13 corresponds to a broad stream of traditions that concerns jurisdiction against seducers. Working independently, O. Betz has made similar observations. We may briefly note the most important evidence to which they refer and reinforce it with references from Philo and Josephus:[39]

Strobel takes his departure in the fine distinctions within Deut 13 that are found in *mSanh.* 7: The text distinguishes between the מסית (7:10a–d, cf. Deut 13:7) and the מדיח (7:10e, cf. Deut 13:6, 11), a distinction better explained in *bSanh.* 67a and *ySanh.* 25d, 5ff. Such fine distinctions, which he supplies with other rabbinic references, make it probable that if the distinctions were not significant, at least the law itself was important at the turn of the era.[40]

Strobel also finds the importance of the law attested in Qumran. Besides the columns 11QTemple 54–55, we also find a reference in CD 12:2–3: "Every man who preaches apostasy (דבר סרה, cf. Deut 13:7) under the dominion of the spirits of Satan shall be judged according to the law relating

---

[38]Neusner:104–11, 173 argues that these texts originate in the time of Usha, about 140–170 CE.

[39]Cf. Strobel:81–86. References to O. Betz 1982 will be made in the notes.

[40]O. Betz 1982:571–80 discusses broadly also *bSanh.* 43a, where Deut 13 is connected to the death of Jesus.

to those possessed by a ghost or familiar spirit."[41] He is to be sentenced according to the law of Lev 20:27, which is a מֹות־יוּמַת sentence.

Strobel also sees the relevance of Deut 13 and the charge of seduction in the New Testament itself and in early Christian traditions (86–92):[42] Some Gospel passages, for example, reveal that Jesus was accused of seduction (e.g., Matt 27:63: "that impostor [πλάνος]"; Luke 23:5: "He stirs up [ἀνασείει] the people"; and John 7:12: "he is leading the people astray [πλανᾷ]").

Philo refers to Deut 13:1–11 in *Spec* 1:315–18. The killing of the prophet or deceiver seems to take the form of lynching: ". . . and we must send round a report[43] of his proposals to all the lovers of piety, who will rush with a speed which brooks no delay to take vengeance on the unholy man, and deem it a religious duty to seek his death" (316).[44]

Josephus also refers to those who "essay to confound and dissolve (συγχεῖν καὶ καταλύειν) the constitution" (*Ant* 4:309–10). Even if it should be any person of their blood (cf. Deut 13:7) or a city (cf. Deut 13:13), they should be uprooted when possible. It is noteworthy that Josephus connects Deut 13 to his exposition of Deut 27–30.[45] He thus bears witness to the fact that this law has been connected to the covenantal curses also in Jewish tradition.

We thus find that the law against seducers from Deut 13 has been taken up in the first century BCE (cf. Qumran), at the time of Paul (cf. Philo), in the last part of the first century CE (cf. Josephus and implicitly also the Gospels), and in the middle of the second century CE (cf. Mishnah). Therefore we have reason to expect it to be known by Paul and some of his addressees, especially if we accept that it may have played a part in the process against Jesus.

---

[41]Cf. also O. Betz 1982:594–95 for this reference.

[42]In addition to the Gospel passages, he refers, for example, to Acts 5:37 and Stephen in Acts 6, to Justin *Dial* 69:7 and 108:1, and the Christian interpolation in *T. Levi* 16:3–4. O. Betz 1982:596–97 asserts that Deut 13 lies behind the advice of Caiaphas in John 11:47–48.

[43]Philo uses the prescription to seek the report of Deut 13:14 in a very unusual way, cf. Colson's text edition VII:617.

[44]Cf. also the actions to be taken against apostates in *Spec* 1:54–55, which is connected (wrongly?) to Deut 13 in Colson's text edition VII:616–18.

[45]Cf. the presentation of the whole context above in sec. 3.2.3. O. Betz 1982:585–87 also refers to Josephus' descriptions of false prophets, which in some places reveal Deut 13-expressions (cf. *Ant* 20:97–99, 169–72; *Bell* 2:258–63). Betz reconstructs the reference to the death of Jesus in *Ant* 18:63–64 in a way that may also reflect Deut 13 (582–84).

6.4: Summary of chapters 2-6

The task of the first part of this book was to investigate whether Paul's use of curse in Galatians included conventional language belonging to specific parts of Jewish curse traditions. The perspective has not been historic-genetic in order to argue for specific intertestamental texts that may have had an influence on Paul. It has been much more general, in order to discover conventional concepts that may have been familiar to large groups of Jews. The semantic elements analyzed in chapter 2 seemed to correspond mainly to elements found in covenantal curses, which I have denoted as the Deut 27-30 tradition.

> This correspondence is unambiguous in texts that include curse and blessing both in antithesis and in sequence (cf. ch. 3), and in texts with expressions like γίνομαι κατάρα and κατάρα τοῦ νόμου (cf. sec. 5.1).
>
> It is also very clear in texts with the form of Gal 3:10, especially in texts succeeding the Hebrew Bible itself (cf. sec. 4.1), and in texts with curse and blessing only in sequence (cf. sec. 5.3).
>
> It was clear enough in texts with features corresponding to Gal 1:6-9 (cf. sec. 6.3).
>
> Texts with curse and blessing only in antithesis revealed a more ambiguous picture, but they at least demonstrated that this feature is conventional within curse texts (cf. sec. 4.2).

We noted two other traditions that also have to be given due attention in our exegesis of Paul:

> The feature of blessing of the Gentiles is only implicitly present in the Deut 27-30 tradition, but belongs to the conventional language of the Abraham tradition, especially the Gen 12:3 texts (cf. sec. 5.2).
>
> We also noted that the law of Deut 13 seems to be especially close to the semantic field of Gal 1 (cf. sec. 6.3.6).

This may indicate that Paul alludes to deuteronomistic traditions in both curse sections, but that he combines it with Deut 13 in Gal 1 and with the Abraham tradition in Gal 3. It will now be up to the exegesis of chapters 9 and 10 to test the fruitfulness of these findings.

CHAPTER 7

7.0: METHODOLOGICAL CONSIDERATIONS

When we turn to Paul's letter to the Galatians, we face a scholarly debate that has centered around two types of issues: One has discussed the historical questions of its addressees, its date, and the identification of Paul's opponents (cf. sec. 7.1). Modern scholarship has also examined possible connections between Galatians and ancient epistolography and Hellenistic rhetoric (cf. sec. 7.2). The following brief discussion will state the reason why I will emphasize the rhetorical approach rather than the former ones.

7.1: The historical questions

The scholarly debate concerning the addressees, the date of Galatians, and Paul's opponents has not yet generated anything resembling a consensus. Knowing this, and also knowing that it may be possible to analyze the logic of the letter without involving any historical reconstructions, we may regard these specific ventures as having no bearing on the subject at hand.

7.1.1: The quest for the real readers

With regard to the addressees and date of the letter, it will have little impact on our argument whether the Galatian churches were situated in the North[1] or in the South,[2] and correspondingly whether Paul wrote the letter as late as his third journey,[3] or as early as the Apostolic Council.[4] Although

---

[1] For a presentation of this *North theory*, cf. Mussner:3-9. This would mean that Paul used a territorial designation, addressing churches in the north of the province Galatia, where the inhabitants descended from Gallic blood.

[2] For the *South theory*, cf. Zahn:9-21; Burton:xxi-xliv; and Bruce:3-18. This would mean that Paul rather used the name of the Province Galatia, so that he addressed himself to the churches in the South, for instance in the cities of Pisidian Antioch, Iconium, Lystra, and Derbe.

[3] It is common within the *North theory* to date the letter to Paul's stay in Ephesus, cf. Hübner *TRE* 12:11. A detailed argumentation for such dating is found in Suhl:3068-82. Mussner:9-11, however, represents those who would rather date the letter to the Macedonian journey. He refers to the detailed argumentation by Borse 1972, who compares Galatians to the Corinthian correspondence and Romans. Cf. also Lightfoot:40-56 for a broader argumentation.

[4] Among the defenders of the *South theory*, Bruce:43-56 argues for a dating before the Apostolic Council, and Zahn:18-20; Burton:xliv-liii argue for the more widespread dating after it.

most modern scholars seem to opt for the former alternative,[5] there are also those who emphasize important topographical and archaeological data which support the latter.[6] Our interest, however, is not connected to those parts of the letter where a dating might be important for an interpretation (cf. 2:1–14 and 4:13–15). Further, we know practically nothing about the churches and the real readers of the letter, whether they are situated in the North or in the South.

This question may be of some relevance for our perception of the *implied reader* of the letter, however, since connections to Jewish synagogues and schools of rhetoric were more prevalent in the South than in the North. The possibility of a location of the churches in the North should therefore be a constant reminder for us to stick to the most conventional traditions in our explanation of the logic. We should not demand too much of the implied reader. Some familiarity with the most widespread Jewish traditions and rhetorical conventions, however, should also be expected to be found among Christians in the North.

7.1.2: *The quest for the real opponents*

With regard to the quest for the opponents of Paul in Galatia, our problem is that we only have access to their theology through the letter of Paul. Thus we face a methodological problem: How can we know which parts of the letter may allude to charges of the opponents? How are we to avoid the pitfalls of undue selectivity, of over-interpretation, of mishandling polemics and of wrongly identifying particular words and phrases as direct echoes of their vocabulary?[7] Surveys of the research in this area demonstrate these problems clearly.[8]

Today we do not find advocates of a *two-front theory* who claim that Gal 3–4 is directed against opponents from normative Judaism and the parenesis of Gal 5–6 against persons advocating some form of syncretism or enthusiastic religiousness.[9] Some recent scholars, however, present modified

---

[5]Cf. the overview in Rohde:6–7.

[6]Cf. Bruce:3–18. He draws on the archaeological works of Ramsay from the 1880s and 1890s, which show that no main road — that was natural for Paul to choose — leads through ethnic Galatia in the north (9, 12). More recent and broad discussions are found in Hemer:277–307 (with emphasis on usage in inscriptions, etc.) and Riesner:236–45 (with emphasis on geographical data).

[7]Cf. Barclay 1987:79–83 for a presentation of the research in light of these pitfalls. For a discussion of sound criteria to use in this respect, cf. 1987:84–86 and Berger 1980. For a rejection of the whole method, cf. G. Lyons:79–82, 96–105.

[8]Instructive surveys of the research history up to 1970 are found in Eckert:1–18 and Hawkins:1–68. Cf. also Brinsmead:9–22; Mussner:11–24; C. -N. Kim:8–23. For a survey of Pauline opponents generally, see Ellis 1975a.

[9]It was Lütgert 1919 who advocated this theory, although some commentators before

two-front theories. These theories explain Gal 5–6 not as directed against a group of opponents in Galatia, but rather as directed against internal problems caused by some sort of spiritual enthusiasm with which the churches had to cope.[10]

Another possible connection between Gal 3–4 and Gal 5–6 would be to argue that the Jewish opponents of Paul advocated a theology that caused both types of problems. Choosing a one-front theory, several scholars have argued that the opponents were influenced by *syncretistic Judaism* in a form that may cover aspects from all parts of the letter. The more extreme position claims that the opponents were Jewish-Christian Gnostics,[11] but recent research has tended to portray them as sectarian Jews representing apocalyptic, Qumranic, mystic, or some other form of non-conformist Judaism.[12]

Most scholars, however, tend to reject the identification of the opponents as a fringe sect of Judaism. It has been common to regard them as advocating an attitude similar to Pharisaism, with an emphasis on the claim for total obedience toward the Torah,[13] or to refrain from any precise identification.[14] There is a recent tendency, however, in the wake of E. P.

---

similar position is Ropes 1929, who also offers a brief commentary on the epistle in this light (28–42).

[10]Jewett:209–12 argues that the Galatians seem to share the typical Hellenistic misunderstanding about the Spirit, namely that earthly behavior should be irrelevant. H. D. Betz 1974:146–55; 1979:8–9 finds evidence of an early spiritual enthusiasm in Galatia, which after a period was running into problems with the flesh. For a critique, cf. G. Lyons:99–104.

[11]Cf. Schmithals 1956b. This proposal was not new in research, cf. Ellis 1975a:264–78. Cf. the critique from Vielhauer:120–21 and the answer from Schmithals 1983:29–30. For a similar position, cf. Marxsen:49–56. Cf. also the critique of Berger 1980:392–93 that he relies on sources that are too recent.

[12]Cf. the suggestion by Crownfield 1945:492–93 concerning syncretistic Christians that stemmed from Jewish mystery cults. Cf. further Schlier 1965:19–24 who refers to apocalypticism, Qumran, and pre-gnostic traits; Köster:191–94 who speaks about a pre-gnostic cosmic interpretation of the covenant; Ellis 1975a and 1975b who refers to parallels in apocalyptic Judaism and Qumran. For a critique of such a position, cf. Eckert:15–17.

A more complete survey of various positions is found in Hawkins:42–68. He devotes most of his dissertation to a critique of such views, cf. the discussion of antinomism (121–51), the term πνευματικοί (152–80) and στοιχεῖα τοῦ κόσμου (181–250). We may also point to two recent monographs: Gunther 1973 treats Pauline opponents generally, and Brinsmead 1982 treats the Galatian opponents especially.

[13]This is the early consensus from patristic times up through the Reformation, cf. Bruce:20–22. Among the older commentaries, cf. Lightfoot:27–30, 305–11; Sieffert:14 and Burton:liii–lvii (Eckert:8 lists 34 commentators between 1821 and 1962 with this position!). From recent research, cf. Eckert:224–28, 233–36 and Bruce:31–32.

[14]Cf. Mussner:25; Becker:3–4; Borse 1984:17–24; Hawkins:343–52.

Sanders' description of Judaism as *covenantal nomism*, to interpret the opponents in more national categories. Their claim for circumcision, food laws, and calendar observance could be motivated out of a concern for national and cultural identity rather than a concern for strict obedience.[15]

A major uncertainty in the research, however, causes problems also for this last position: Which sections of the letter should one emphasize in order to identify their teaching more accurately?

> Should one emphasize the opposition between Paul and Peter, letting the opponents represent a Petrine Christianity that was in sharp opposition to Pauline Christianity?[16]
> Should one emphasize a connection between 2:11–14 and 6:12–13, letting the opponents (as Peter) represent a tactical modification (not a theological concern) in order to avoid persecution?[17]
> Should one emphasize 3:1–5, identifying the problem as concerning the question of how a life in the Spirit should be carried out? Then the opponents may have claimed that obedience to the law would increase manifestations of the Spirit and would prepare for the coming of the kingdom.[18]
> Should one rather mirror expressions from 1:10 and 5:11, stating that the opponents may have claimed that Paul also preached circumcision, and that they now would give the necessary supplement to his Gospel?[19]
> Or should one take the present tense of οἱ περιτεμνόμενοι in 6:13 as an indication that the opponents were Gentiles, perhaps Gentile converts in Galatia who decided to adopt Judaism in order to ensure their part in the promises?[20]

---

[15]Cf. Sanders 1977 for the general view of Judaism as *covenantal nomism*, and Gordon 1987; Dunn 1988b for its application to Galatians.

[16]So the influential position of Baur 1866:280–87 and the Tübingen School. For a short presentation of the theory, cf. Eckert:4–8.

[17]So Suhl:3083–88. Then Paul's argumentation in 3:6 – 5:1 may be regarded as a preliminary preparation for the real confrontation from 5:2 onward (3132).

[18]So Cosgrove 1988:27–28, 38–45, 103–18.

[19]So Howard:8–19. From other angles also Tyson 1968; Dahl 1973:50–51; and Lull 1980:9, 31–33, 103–4, who state that the opponents would fulfill what Paul had begun. The latter two refer to the story about the conversion of King Izates of Adiabene (Jos. *Ant* 20:34–48) as an illuminating parallel. Cf. also Borgen 1983a:68–69 for this reference.

Borgen 1980 and 1982 has improved this theory by referring to the Jewish distinction between bodily and ethical circumcision: The opponents could claim that Paul preached ethical circumcision (cf. the parenesis of ch. 5), and that they wanted to fulfill this by its natural consequence: bodily circumcision. He draws mainly on Philo in *Migr* 86–92 and *Quest in Exod* II:2 for this distinction, but refers also to 1QS v.5–6 and 1QpHab xi.13 in Qumran. Cf. also his 1985:235–44 where he also mirrors 2:1–10 and 4:21–31 in this perspective.

[20]So Munck 1954:79–83, 124–26. He builds on Hirsch 1930 (cf. also Michaelis 1931) for this interpretation. These latter scholars, however, propose that the opponents came from Syrian Antioch, and represented a Gentile, legalistic mission. These and other variations of the Gentile theory are presented in Hawkins:21–31. Cf. G. Lyons:79 for a recent advocacy of the theory.

The above survey of attempts to identify the opponents of Paul in Galatia has demonstrated the difficulties involved in this approach. I find it unnecessary to enter this debate: In order to uncover the implied logic of the letter, it should be enough *to identify the opponents as they are explicitly referred to in the letter itself*. A historical reconstruction of the controversy may be postponed until after the analysis of the letter itself has been carried out.

7.2: *Comparisons with epistolography and rhetoric*

In recent decades, scholarly attention has been drawn to Galatians as a pièce of literature that can be analyzed on its own terms. Many parts of its logic may be uncovered without presupposing any historical reconstruction of the situation that "caused" it. Comparisons have been made with ancient epistolography and ancient rhetoric in this respect.

7.2.1: *Galatians in light of ancient epistolography*
Letter writing was carried out in specific forms in antiquity, but we only have two epistolary handbooks at our disposal today, namely *pseudo-Demetrius* (from the 2nd century BCE to 3rd century CE), and *pseudo-Libanius* (from the 4th to 6th century CE). We have, however, many letters and some other references to theories about them.[21] It seems that an elementary education in letter writing was part of the secondary stage of education, and the constancy of different patterns reveals widespread familiarity with epistolary conventions.[22]

It is especially N. A. Dahl and G. W. Hansen who have investigated Galatians in the light of these conventions.[23] They found many features in Galatians that correspond to *letters of rebuke*: The most specific element is the opening phrase θαυμάζω (Gal 1:6).[24] Other similarities are statements

---

[21]Cf. Malherbe 1977 for a diachronical survey of ancient epistolary theorists and for editions of the main texts. See also Stowers 1986 for a survey and a collection of many typical letters.

[22]Cf. Malherbe 1977:12–14; Stowers:32–33.

[23]Cf. Smiga:6–56 for an extensive survey of 20th century research of Paul's letters in light of epistolography, with an emphasis on the importance of an SBL seminar inspired by the work of N. A. Dahl and R. W. Funk.

[24]Cf. Dahl 1973:12–20. In appendix 1 (102–105) he has tabled his collection of 40 Greek and 14 Latin letters, where θαυμάζειν/*mirare* is placed as an opening formula in 38 letters. This formal use of the term was well established before the middle of the third century (16). Hansen:33–43 has cited 12 letters of this type and compared them with Galatians. For handbook references, cf. *papyrus Bononiensis* VI.4 and *ps.Libanius* 64 in Malherbe 1977:45–46, 72–73.

Cf. for this custom also Berger 1984c:1340; Smiga:127–28; Stowers:22, 87, 139; J. L. White 1986:201, 208, 210 with examples (42, 176) and further references (210, note 95).

about change of mind (cf. Gal 1:6), references to prior instructions (cf. 1:9a), complaints of foolishness (cf. 3:1, 3), expressions of distress (cf. 4:11, 20), and rebuke and irony, often in the form of questions (cf. 3:3b-4; 4:9).[25] In such letters, it is also common to find a pleading section introduced by παρακαλεῖν or other formulas (cf. Gal 4:12).[26]

Galatians also contains other formulas that may be epistolary, but such conventions only seem to be present clearly in the transitional parts of the letter: 1:1-9; 3:1-5; 4:8-20; 5:2-12; 6:11-18.[27] They thus ought to be kept in mind for the interpretation of Gal 1:8-9, but they do not seem to give much help for the interpretation of the argument of 3:8-14.[28] Therefore rhetorical handbooks may be of more relevance for our purpose.

7.2.2: Rhetorical handbooks and Galatians

Ancient handbooks in rhetoric were composed in Greek from the 4th century BCE and in Latin from the 1st century BCE.[29] In these books rhetoric is taught as an art of persuasion for public speeches. Scholars often assume that an introduction to rhetoric was part of secondary education, and that it was widespread knowledge in Hellenistic culture.[30] On these grounds there is a growing awareness among New Testament scholars of their importance.[31]

It is important to note that the handbooks contain conventions at different levels concerning Invention, Arrangement and Style for the composition of a speech (*ad Herenn.* I.ii.3).[32] Invention concerns identification of the cause of

---

[25]Cf. Dahl 1973:20-34 and Hansen:33-44. See also Berger 1984c:1345-46.

[26]Cf. Dahl 1973:86-87 and Hansen:44-47. See also Bjerkelund:177-78; J. L. White 1984:1744, 1748 (note 55); Smiga:121-26, 142-47.

[27]Cf. Dahl 1973:79-81 and Hansen:30-32. See also J. L. White 1984:1740-41, 1746.

[28]Smiga:171-82 has tried to utilize the I-you axis of letter conventions to understand the section 3:1 - 4:7. He discovers a triple division (3:6-14, 15-29 and 4:1-7), but when he proceeds further, we see that he implies more than epistolary conventions. Also the proposal by Cosgrove 1988:26-31, to take 3:1-5 as the central part of the argumentation, seems unsatisfactorily proved by epistolary conventions.

[29]For a brief diachronical survey and presentation of the most important books, cf. Vickers:12-52. For brief introductions to ancient rhetoric, cf. Kennedy:12-33 and Vickers:52-82. A broad and very useful presentation is found in Martin.

[30]Cf. Vickers:11-12; Stowers:32-33; Kennedy:9-10.

[31]A brief survey of the use of rhetoric in New Testament exegesis from the Church Fathers onward is found in Siegert:5-15. Cf. further Watson for a useful bibliography.

[32]"*Invention* is the devising of matter, true or plausible, that would make the case convincing. *Arrangement* is the ordering and distribution of the matter, making clear the place to which each thing is to be assigned. *Style* is the adaptation of suitable words and sentences to the matter devised" (*ad Herenn.* I.ii.3). In addition the handbooks contain advice for Memory and Delivery, levels which do not apply here.

the speech, whether the argument is Epideictic, Deliberative, or Judicial (*ad Herenn.* I.ii.2).[33] Arrangement concerns advice for the Introduction, Statement of Facts, Division, Proof, Refutation, and Conclusion (*ad Herenn.* I.iii.4). Recent research on Galatians has concentrated on which type of the three causes (γένη, *genus*) it represents and on its arrangement (τάξις, *dispositio*) according to the different parts of a speech.

The recent debate was inaugurated by H. D. Betz in his famous commentary, where he classifies the letter according to the judicial *genus* as an "apologetic letter."[34] This classification has influenced many scholars,[35] but it has also been questioned.[36] Alternatively it has been proposed that the letter is deliberative,[37] or of a mixed genre.[38]

---

[33] "The *epideictic* kind is devoted to the praise or censure of some particular person. The *deliberative* consists in the discussion of policy and embraces persuasion and dissuasion. The *judicial* is based on legal controversy, and comprises criminal prosecution or civil suit, and defence" (*ad Herenn.* I.ii.2).

[34] H. D. Betz 1975, cf. also his 1979 commentary. He states that it has the following structure: *Prescript* (1:1–5), *exordium* (1:6–11), *narratio* (1:12 – 2:14), *propositio* (2:15–21), *probatio* (3:1 – 4:31), *parenesis* (5:1 – 6:10), and *postscript/peroratio* (6:11–18).

[35] Cf., for example, Brinsmead:37–87; Hester 1984:223–24; Lüdemann:46–48; Barrett 1985:32, 50; Sandnes:52. Cf. also Hübner *TRE* 12:5–6, who argues for a different structure (1984b). Also J. Hall:334, 347–51 regards the letter as judicial, but without strict theories about the arrangement.

[36] Cf. the critique that the genre "apologetic letter" is difficult to uphold by Aune:324; Hansen:25–27: The only clear example is Plato *Ep.* 7, which only has a threefold structure: *Exordium, narratio* (which also functions as an *argumentatio*), and a short *peroratio*. It may also be questioned whether the letters often referred to are real letters. Another problem is the fact that Betz is unable to explain the presence of parenesis in Galatians, cf. his 1975:375–76.

[37] Cf. especially Kennedy:144–52. Other scholars have taken up this proposal and have shown that the structure of Galatians with *exordium, narratio, argumentatio*, and *peroratio* also conforms with this type of rhetoric. Cf. Vouga 1988 who refers to a speech from Demosthenes with this kind of structure, and Smit 1989 who refers to early rhetorical handbooks. Cf. further G. Lyons:112–21, 170–76; R. G. Hall 1987; Stanley:491.

Also here the main problem is the presence of parenesis in the letter, cf. Vouga:292 who only finds topical exhortations (not general parenesis) in the speech of Demosthenes, and Smit:8–9 who must regard the parenesis as a later addition to a deliberative speech.

[38] Aune:325–26 has found traces of both deliberative and epideictic rhetoric in the letter. Hansen:57–60 states that the letter is judicial up to 4:11, but switches over to deliberative rhetoric from 4:12 onward.

Berger has gone even further: Although he accepts Betz's classification of the letter as apologetic (cf. his 1984b:110 and 1984c:1290, 1347), he finds both judicial argumentation (cf. Gal 1–4 in his 1984c:1282–85, 1291, 1294), deliberative sections (cf. Gal 1:6–9; 3:1–5; 4:8–21 and chapters 5–6 in his 1984b:93–100, 181, 194, 198), and epideictic types of argumentation (cf. Gal 1–2; 3:1–18; 4:13–16, 21–31 in his 1984b:101–05, 268, 271, 280). Cf. also Mack:67–68 for such complexity.

In this approach, then, there is a diversity of opinions among scholars. The present contribution enters this debate from a different perspective, however, since we find conventions that illuminate the argumentation of the letter more directly. It should be possible to utilize other parts of the ancient handbooks that previous scholars have ignored, and I therefore have to make some methodological observations before I can start the analysis itself.

7.3: Methodological considerations for rhetorical criticism

7.3.1: The question of sources

It is important to utilize those handbooks as sources that most reliably reflect Hellenistic rhetoric at the turn of the century. Therefore the anonymous *ad Herennium* and Cicero's *De Inventione* (1st century BCE) will be preferred: Although they were written in Latin, they reflect Greek sources, they contain personal input, and they are prior to the special Roman development of rhetoric.[39] We will also utilize the most important ancient Greek handbooks, such as Aristotle (4th century BCE), and the anonymous *ad Alexandrum* (3rd century BCE). Although Hermogenes (2nd century CE) is later than Paul, we will also consult his works, since he taught in Tarsus[40] and for this reason may represent traditions known during the time of Paul at this important center of rhetoric.

The first problem with these sources is that they are *Hellenistic and not Jewish*. This problem is of minor importance since the process of Hellenization had influenced Judaism deeply by the turn of the century. Even in Judea this influence was pervasive, and in Jerusalem people could attain rhetorical education (Hengel 1989:19–26, 35–37; 1991:57–61). Since we lack any Jewish handbooks of this kind, we will use the ones presented above with some caution.

The second problem concerns the *gap in educational and sociological level* between the well-educated aristocracy and the skills of the middle class (Hengel 1989:54). We know that rhetoric was the basis for any career at the advanced level of education (Marrou:287–303).[41] It is unclear, however, whether the handbooks also reflect rhetoric as practiced in daily life by people from the "middle class." Even for this level the handbooks may be

---

[39]Cf. Smit:6 for the same judgment, and H. Caplan's text edition to *ad Herennium*, pp. vii–xxxiv for a discussion of both handbooks.

[40]Cf. Nadeau's text edition p. 363.

[41]Marrou denotes rhetoric as "die Krone des Studiums," and states that it is "der egentliche Gegenstand des griechischen Hochschulunterrichts" (288). It was so pervasive that "sie entwickelt, sie bereichert sich, überflügelt alle Nachbargebiete, dringt in alles ein . . . Sogar der Astronom und der Arzt, sie werden Vortragskünstler!" (289).

illuminating, however.   On one hand they would have some acquaintance with rhetoric as practiced by well-educated lawyers and orators.   On the other hand many of the rhetorical techniques in the handbooks are conceptualizations of universal patterns of persuasion that may be found in any culture (Kennedy:10–11).[42] We will therefore use these handbooks, but we will concentrate on conventional modes of persuasion rather than on refinements and precise classification.

Both Paul and the Galatians should be acquainted with rhetoric at such a modified level.   Greek education was of course pervasive in South Galatia, and the territory of the North could not be untouched by this fact.   For Paul, it is not critical whether he was brought up in Jerusalem and/or in the rhetorical center Tarsus.[43] Hengel documents many indications of rhetorical education in Jerusalem (1991:57–61), and states (60):[44]

> Whether Paul had such instruction may be left an open question.   However, it is beyond question that synagogue preaching in Greek, which sought to preach Jewish faith as true "philosophy" in the middle and upper classes in the city, presupposed a certain basic practical training in oratory, if it was really to hold and convince the audience.   As the pilgrims from the Diaspora usually did not come from the proletariat and also had some interest in education, I would prefer to assume that there was a concern for an equivalent oratorical level in the leading synagogues of the Hellenists in Jerusalem.   Would this have been a matter of indifference to so ambitious a young scholar and rising teacher and preacher as Paul?

7.3.2: *The question of methodology*

When it comes to the actual use of these handbooks for comparison, I will seek to contribute to a modification of the current debate in three important respects:

First, I will *interpret Galatians not as a speech, but as a letter.*   The rhetorical handbooks were written for speeches in public life that were connected to special settings in feasts, politics, and courts.   Paul, on the other hand, addresses Christian churches as their apostle (cf. Mack:35, 49).   In addition we noted above the several epistolographic features similar to letters of rebuke.   I therefore consider it to be a mistake to look for a letter com-

---

[42]Kennedy states: "The Greeks gave names to rhetorical techniques, many of which are found all over the world.   They organized these techniques into a system which could be taught and learned.   What we mean by classical rhetorical theory is this structured system which describes the universal phenomenon of rhetoric in Greek terms" (11). Cf. further Siegert:23–84 for a demonstration that many rhetorical features also are present in the LXX.

[43]For a discussion of Paul's upbringing and schooling see van Unnik 1973b (especially 272–301 where he discusses Acts 23:3) and Hengel 1991:18–39.   For Tarsus as a center of rhetoric, cf. the references in Hengel 1991:1–3 (with note 11).

[44]Cf. further Melanchton's judgment about Galatians, cited in Classen:1 that ". . . der Galaterbrief einen mittleren, der Umgangssprache näheren Ausdruck bevorzugt."

posed strictly in the form of one of the three *genera* of ancient rhetoric. I also find it a mistake to look for a strict arrangement in Galatians according to rules from rhetorical handbooks. The Greek epistolary theorist Demetrius states: "There should be a certain degree of freedom in the structure of a letter. It is absurd to build up periods, as if you were writing not a letter but a speech for the law courts" (*De Elocutione* 229; cf. Malherbe 1977:21).[45] We also have to take into account the judgment of E. Norden and other classicists that Paul does not seem to be a school rhetor (493–507).[46] This means that the recent discussion about Galatians concerning *genus* and arrangement is too superficial. One does not utilize the most fruitful potentials of the rhetorical handbooks by such an approach.

Second, I will *primarily seek for modes of argumentation* in the handbooks. We may underscore the fact that most definitions of rhetoric emphasize rhetoric as an art of persuasion. Aristotle noted, for example: "Rhetoric then, may be defined as the faculty of discovering the possible means of persuasion in reference to any subject whatever" (*Rhet.* I.ii.1).[47] Thus the most important feature in rhetoric is not formal rules regarding types or arrangement, but models for persuasion. These means of persuasion we find primarily in the sections concerning the Invention of a speech and concerning its appropriate Style.[48]

Third, I will *use the handbooks as sources of comparison*, not as patterns to be imposed from outside on Paul's way of arguing. It is important to

---

[45]It seems though that rules for certain types of speeches were adapted for use in corresponding letter types (cf. Stowers:34, 166): Epideictic rhetoric corresponds to letters of blame or praise, deliberative to letters of admonitions or advice, and judicial to accusing or apologetic letters (cf. Malherbe 1977:31–39 for these types of letters according to *ps.Demetrius*). In addition the mixed letter was known (cf. Malherbe 1977:67, 77 for this type in the handbook of *ps.Libanius*).

[46]Norden observes that Paul does not exhibit confidence with Greek literature, which was important in the schools; he also observes that his mode of argumentation and style is not a refined one, and he cites similar judgments by Fathers from the Early Church. He concludes: "Aber das Angeführte genügt, um daraus mit Sicherheit zu schliessen, dass der Apostel trotz seiner souveränen Verachtung der schönen Form, dennoch oft genug von den . . . geläufigen Mitteln zierlicher griechischer Rhetorik Gebrauch gemacht hat, freilich . . . nicht von solchen, die er sich aus der Lektüre von griechischen Schriftstellern angeeignet hat, sondern vielmehr von solchen, die in der damaligen "asianischen" Sophistik geläufig waren" (506–7).

[47]Cf. also Cic. *Inv.* I.v.6: "The end is to persuade by speech"; *ad Herenn.* I.ii.2: "The task of the public speaker is . . . to secure as far as possible the agreement of his hearers." A review of definitions is given in Martin:2–3.

[48]Cf. Classen:32. He takes Melanchton as a model for research that emphasizes rhetoric in minor arguments rather than in the overall Arrangement (16–29).

start in the Pauline text itself and then to ask if there may be something in these handbooks that might shed light on his way of stating an argument and the connections between them (similar Hansen:55–57). The objective is not to explain Paul's own purpose in detail, but to seek conventional patterns that may guide his audience in their perception of the letter.

To conclude: The contribution of this volume is to shift the discussion from an emphasis on *genus* and Arrangement to an interest in Invention and Style. I also want to facilitate an interest in the most widespread and simple rhetorical conventions, rather than focus on the subtle refinements present in the handbooks.

CHAPTER 8

8.0: THE RHETORIC OF GALATIANS

8.1: The Rhetorical Situation

A decisive point in any rhetorical analysis is the identification of the rhetorical situation.[1] It is not necessary to grasp the truth of the situation as it really was. It is enough to identify the kernel of the problem as Paul perceives it. After all, the letter is his response to a situation, and therefore its rhetoric is determined by his perception of the current challenge.[2] Therefore we may analyze briefly the picture of the *implied readers*, the *implied opponents*, and the way the *implied author* interacts with these groups.[3]

The implied readers of Galatians mainly come from a Gentile background (4:8-9) and are the result of the Pauline mission (cf. 1:8-9 and 4:13-15). They have been taught the main content of the Gospel (3:1), have been converted and baptized (3:26-27; 4:9a), have received the Spirit (3:2, 5; 6:1), and have also become familiar with the biography of Paul (1:13). Their present situation, however, is described in many ways as on the verge of apostasy: They are deserting Christ by turning to a different Gospel (1:6); they seem to have experienced everything in vain (3:4; 4:11); they are about to turn back to and to submit to slavery (4:9; 5:1); to fall away from grace (5:4b); and to stop obeying the truth (5:7). This causes them to be addressed twice as "foolish" (3:1, 3). The situation is turbulent (cf. 5:15 for the metaphor that they bite and devour one another).

The crux of this situation is that they are on the verge of circumcising themselves (5:2-3; 6:12-13), a problem that more generally is denoted as one of desire to be under law (4:21) and a desire to be justified by the law (5:4a). The problem also seems to concern calendar observance of some kind (4:10).

---

[1]Kennedy:33-38 presents methodological steps in this order: Determination of the Rhetorical Unit; identification of the Rhetorical Situation, which also includes the theories of *stasis* and *genus*; identification of the Arrangement of Material. The first step causes no problems when one focuses on the whole letter as we do.

[2]Cf. also Stanley:488, 496 for an emphasis on Paul's perception of the problem as the important question.

[3]For the distinction between the *implied reader/author* and the *real reader/author*, see, for example, Fowler and Iser:50-67. I should also re-emphasize that I realize that the term *implied opponents* is imprecise. These implied opponents are not part of the narrative communication situation, as are the implied reader and the implied author. Yet the term is helpful in order to distinguish my focus from a strictly historical reconstruction of the real readers.

The pressure toward circumcision is caused by the *implied opponents* who are explicitly referred to in 1:6–9; 3:1; 4:17; 5:7–8, 10, 12 and 6:12–13.[4] Paul denotes their preaching as "a different gospel" (1:6) and "a gospel contrary to that which you received" (1:9), but he does not identify its content. He depicts their activity as trouble (cf. 1:7 and 5:10), bewitchment (cf. 3:1), persuasion (cf. 5:8), and a cause of dissension (cf. 5:12). They seek to prevent the Galatians from obeying the truth (cf. 5:7), they "want to pervert the gospel of Christ" (1:7), and they "want to shut you out, that you may make much of them" (4:17). They are accused of not keeping the law, of wanting "to make a good showing in the flesh," and of seeking to avoid persecution (6:12–13). In Paul's judgment they deserve to receive a curse (cf. 1:9), to bear their judgment (cf. 5:10), and to mutilate themselves (cf. 5:12).

Also here we only find one concrete reference: They *preach circumcision*. Paul refers to this aspect three times: It is so typical of them that Paul in 5:13a characterizes them as "those who receive circumcision (οἱ περι-τεμνόμενοι)."[5] Paul further states that "they desire to have you circumcised" (6:13b), and that they pursue this goal to such an extent that they "compel you to be circumcised" (6:12b).

The implied author (narrator) interacts with the "implied addressees" (narratees) by underscoring the seriousness of the situation (cf. 1:6–7a; 3:1, 3–4; 4:9, 11). He is perplexed about them and does not know exactly what to do (cf. 4:20). The letter is written in travail (cf. 4:19) and with the fear that it may cause enmity between him and his audience (cf. 4:16). Thus the narrator's concrete warnings concern the possible acceptance of circumcision (twice in 5:2–3), which is generalized into a warning against a desire to be justified by the law (cf. 5:4). The narrator rather exhorts them to become like himself (cf. 4:12) and to stand fast in freedom (cf. 5:1). He reveals that he has a certain hope that they will follow his advice (cf. 5:10).

---

[4]In these sections, and only here, Paul explicitly refers to certain people whom he distinguishes from the Galatians. He uses imprecise descriptions, cf. the pronouns τίς/τινές, ὅστις, ὅσοι, οὗτοι or 3rd person plural expressions of the verb.

[5]I take the present participle as a "timeless" participle, as a description of the opponents from the center of their activity, cf. Zahn:279–80; Sieffert:339; Mussner:412–13; Rohde:274. See also Lightfoot:222–23: "the circumcision party." Bruce:270 takes it "as middle voice with causative significance ('causing to be circumcised')."

The most natural reading is to interpret the present as referring to those being circumcised. To argue that the opponents were Gentiles by birth from this phrase (cf. Hirsch; Munck:79–81) is probably to stress it too much. Cf. Hawkins:90–108 who rejects it in the light of the letter as a whole, in spite of admitting it as the most natural reading. According to Richardson:84–97 the phrase may at least be open to the possibility that there were Gentile Christians among the opponents.

He interacts with the *implied opponents* by accusing them of perverting the Gospel of Christ (cf. 1:7b), of bewitching the Galatians (cf. 3:1), and of persuading them to depart from the truth (cf. 5:7-8). It is not enough to accuse, however, he also finds it necessary to curse them (cf. 1:8f; 5:10b). Again, the only concrete item with which he directly interacts is their claim for circumcision (cf. 6:12-13). This interaction is so important that he performs it with large letters by his own hand (cf. 6:11).

All the above observations converge at one important point: The rite of circumcision.[6] The kernel of the rhetorical situation may be formulated in this way: The *implied readers* are about to accept the rite of circumcision, and the *implied opponents* have posed this as a claim for them, while Paul as the *implied author* strongly wants to interact in a way that prevents the rite from being accepted.

8.2: The Genus of Galatians

Although I have argued that the quest for the *genus* of Galatians is not of decisive importance, it is natural to include some brief comments on this point also. As for the kernel of the rhetorical situation, it seems to demand *both deliberative and judicial rhetoric.* The *implied readers* had to make a choice in the future about the necessity of circumcision, a situation which calls for deliberative rhetoric.[7] On the other hand, the *implied author* regards this as a question of whether or not one conforms to the will of God, that is, a question of interpreting the will of God as revealed in scripture.[8]

---

[6]Cf. for the same judgment Eckert:32 who refers to this as "die einzig ganz präzise Angabe des Vorhabens der mit Paulus konkurrierenden Prediger in Galatien." See also C. -N. Kim:44-53; Barclay 1988:45-46; Hansen:170.

We will not pursue the question of possible motivations behind this claim from the opponents. A brief survey of aspects and literature should suffice:

The widespread practice of circumcising proselytes is documented by McEleney:320-24; O. Betz *TRE* 5:717. Under certain circumstances one could dispense with the rite, cf. references by McEleney:328-33; Borgen 1983a:68-69. See especially the famous example of the conversion of King Izates in Jos. *Ant* 20:38-46.

In Rabbinic literature, circumcision is regarded as the sign of the covenant, cf. the references in *Str-B* IV:31-40; McEleney:333-34; O. Betz *TRE* 5:718-19. In Josephus we find attested motivations as obedience (*Ant* 20:44-45) and concern for national identity (*Ant* 1:192), cf. McEleney:333. In Philo and Qumran we find a concern for circumcision as the outer sign of an inner ethical conversion (cf. *Migr* 92; *Quest in Exod* II.2; 1QS v.5f; 1QpHab xi.13), cf. Borgen 1980:86-88; 1983a:66-68.

[7]Cf. the definition of Aristotle: The deliberative kind concerns "the future, for the speaker, whether he exhorts or dissuades, always advises about things to come" (*Rhet.* I.iii.4).

[8]Cf. the definition by Aristotle that "the end of the forensic speaker is the just or the unjust (τὸ δίκαιον καὶ τὸ ἄδικον)" (*Rhet.* I.iii.5).

I find it too restrictive to choose only one of these *genera* for the letter as a whole. Paul writes a letter and not a speech. He is free to pick and chose those perspectives he finds most suitable. Any question about the Mosaic Torah would include both judicial and deliberative perspectives, since it will always be a question of identifying the will of God in order to observe it. In addition it is important to note that a merger of both deliberative and judicial argumentation occurs in the handbooks.[9]

I will not devote much attention to the deliberative argumentation, since it seems to be dominant from 4:12 onward (Hansen:57-60). This feature is found especially in 5:1-12, which conforms to a deliberative dissuasion (*dissuasio*) in the sense that it dissuades concerning a future choice (*ad Herenn.* I.ii.2; Dahl 1973:91-92).[10] There are close connections between this section and the conclusion in 6:12-18;[11] thus also the conclusion of the letter is marked by dissuasive elements.[12] The general parenesis in 5:13 - 6:10, which stands between these sections, is also deliberative.[13] If the last part of Galatians is mainly deliberative, what about the first part? We should not too quickly assume that it is marked by judicial rhetoric only. Some observations about argumentation in general will precede our discussion of judicial argumentation in particular.

---

[9]Although Aristotle tries to distinguish the *genera* from each other (cf. Arist. *Rhet.* I.iii.5), we find fluid transitions in most other handbooks, cf. the documentation by Martin:169-75. The early *ad Alexandrum* includes a discussion of the lawful (νόμιμος) in deliberative speeches, that is, whether or not the action conforms to written laws (cf. 1421b, 25; 1422a, 3-4; cf. also the late Hermog. *Stat.* 76:4, 12-14). Cicero states in *Inv.* I.x.14 that a deliberative argument generally includes one or more judicial *stases.*

[10]The content of such advice ought to be an item that *necesse est*, that is a matter necessary for being whole and free, cf. Martin:168 who refers to Cicero *Part.* 24,83-84. This corresponds with Gal 5:1 which regards circumcision as a matter of freedom or slavery. According to Cic. *Inv.* II.lii.158; lvi.168-69, deliberative advice should be motivated by references to advantage (*utilitas*), which should underscore the benefits of the action, cf. 5:2: "Christ will be of no advantage to you (ὑμᾶς οὐδὲν ὠφελήσει)."

[11]Cf. the references to circumcision (5:2-3 and 6:12-13), total obedience (5:3 and 6:13), division between Jew and Gentile (5:6 and 6:15), opponents (5:8 and 6:12-13), and persecution because of the cross (5:11 and 6:12). Cf. Matera:83 for a similar list, and C. -N. Kim:48; Smit:20 for similar correspondences between 5:7-12 and the *exordium*.

[12]See Cic. *Inv.* II.lv.166 for the advice that a deliberative motivation from honor should underscore the honor and praise that could be obtained, cf. 6:14: "But far be it from me to glory except in the cross of Jesus Christ." This aspect is also emphasized by G. Lyons:174 and Smit:24.

[13]Cf. Stowers:52-53, 92-93, 95, 107, 109. For epistolary parallels, cf. also Berger 1984c:1342, 1344. For its epistolary function, cf. also J. L. White 1984:1746-48.

8.3: Figures of diction and thought

Figures of diction and thought are some of the most basic rhetorical phenomena in a speech or a written text. The function of these figures is to draw the audience into an active perception of the text (Cronjé:214–18, 226). This may be obtained by omissions, additions and repetitions, and changes in syntactical order or in the application of words (Bullinger:x-xi).

Many rhetorical handbooks contain a theory of Style (λέξις) that identifies a considerable number of rhetorical figures. It should be a relatively straightforward process to apply this theory to the interpretation of Galatians, since it only presupposes Paul's awareness of how to use such figures in order to stir the perception of his audience. Such elements would make an impression on the audience regardless of how much competence they would have with the theory itself. By identifying rhetorical figures, I take up an aspect has has been extensively traced by, for example, Bengel and Bullinger in earlier centuries, and recently also by Betz and Cronjé.[14] I have found it fruitful to consider the following figures in Paul's argument:

> *Correctio* in 1:7a; 3:4b?
> *Reduplicatio* in 1:8–9; 3:4b?; 4:9.
> *Expolitio* in 1:8–9; 2:16; 3:2, 5.
> *Expeditio* in 1:11–12.
> συνεκδοχή in 1:8–9.
> διαφορά in 2:17, 19a; 3:4b?; 3:11–12; 4:21.
> μετωνυμία in 3:13a.
> ὑπερβατόν in 5:4, 7–8.
> παρονομασία in 5:2–3, 7–8.
> λιτότης in 5:8a; 5:23b.

In addition, as many scholars have observed, the letter also includes several metaphors. I shall comment on them in due course.

8.4: Inductive and deductive argumentation

In the handbooks we find many distinctions between various types of argumentation. One widespread distinction is the one between artificial and inartificial proofs.[15] The conventional and basic distinction is the one between inductive and deductive reasoning:

---

[14]Bullinger 1898:1080–81 listed rhetorical figures in 68 of 149 verses in Galatians. Such figures are also frequently noted by Bengel 1773. Among modern scholars, Cronjé 1985 and Betz, in his commentary, make some observations about style. The fourth book of *ad Herennium* is an excellent source for this type of Hellenistic rhetoric. My classification of figures will follow this source rather than the more specialized systems of later times.

[15]According to Aristotle, a speaker could utilize two types of evidence in a speech:

Inductive reasoning in rhetoric takes the form of *examples* (παραδείγματα) when one infers "from a number of particular cases that such is the rule" (Arist. *Rhet.* I.ii.9).

Deductive reasoning in rhetoric takes the form of *enthymemes* (ἐνθυμήματα) "when, certain things being posited, something different results by reason of them, alongside of them, from their being true, either universally or in most cases" (ibid).

Any audience in antiquity would be familiar with this distinction.

Examples may be taken from history or be invented. Historical examples, however, are to be preferred (Arist. *Rhet.* II.xx.2,8).[16] Their function is to show that a particular instance has actualized a general principle. According to Cicero, examples ought to be indisputable (Cic. *Inv.* I.xxxii.53), because when one grants the truth of an example, one is ready to approve also the general principle, even if the principle is doubtful in itself (cf. Cic. *Inv.* I.xxxi.51).

Deductive logic works in a different way. It often takes the form of a *syllogism*, which is a complete argument containing a conclusion drawn from premises. Note the following famous example (Mack/Robbins:78–79):

First premise: All men are mortal.
Second premise: Socrates is a man.
Conclusion: Therefore, Socrates is mortal.

We see that the first premise is a general maxim, while the second is a specific premise. The conclusion applies the general maxim to the specific premise.[17]

For our purpose it is important to observe that such syllogisms very often consist of only two parts. Aristotle reflects a widespread custom when he states that if one of the premises "is well known, there is no need to mention it, for the hearer can add it himself" (Arist. *Rhet.* I.ii.13). In our example this would mean that one can omit the indisputable premise that

---

On one hand one could use inartificial proofs (πίστεις ἄτεχνοι), that is, proofs that "were already in existence, such as witnesses, tortures, contracts, and the like" (Arist. *Rhet.* I.ii.2). On the other hand a speaker could invent artificial proofs (πίστεις ἔντεχνοι) which "can be constructed by system and by our own efforts" (ibid). It is in this latter type of evidence (which was regarded as most important) that one had to use examples and deductive arguments, which is the distinction that I find important for Galatians.

[16]Aristotle treats the example in *Rhet.* I.ii.8-9, 19; II.xx and II.xxv.8, 13. A survey of the classical handbooks is found in Martin:119–124. Cf. also Mack/Robbins:60.

[17]According to Cicero, a full deductive argument of this kind consists of five parts: The major premise, proof of the major premise, the minor premise, proof of the minor premise, and the conclusion (Cic. *Inv.* I.xxxiv.57–xxxvii.67). In our example it is unnecessary to prove both the maxim that all men are mortal and the premise that Socrates is a man. We therefore have an abridged argument that consists of three parts (cf. Cic. *Inv.* I.xxxvii.67-xl.75 for a discussion of abridged arguments).

Socrates is a man and simply state: "Socrates is mortal, because all men are mortal."[18]

Another way of arguing deductively is to put an issue into a specific perspective according to the theory of topics (cf. the discussion below). This may be combined with syllogistic reasoning, but it doesn't have to be. Often a specific perspective on the issue would be persuasive in itself, since hearers can draw the conclusion for themselves.

Turning to Gal 3, we seem to find a combination of inductive and deductive reasoning:[19]

Gal 3:1-7 seems to correspond to inductive reasoning. First Paul refers to the experience of the Galatians as an example (3:2-5), and then he adds Abraham as an example (cf. 3:6 with the introductory καθώς). The inference is drawn in 3:7: "So you see that . . . (γινώσκετε ἄρα ὅτι)."

In Gal 3:8-14 we seem to find deductive reasoning, however. In every verse we find conjunctions/particles such as ὅτι, ὥστε, γάρ, δέ, ἵνα (2 or more in 3:8, 10, 11, 14). The five double constructions (assertion + Hebrew Bible text) seem to correspond to enthymemes where one of the parts has been omitted. According to Aristotle, it is common to let a maxim (i.e., a well-known authoritative citation) be one of the premises or the conclusion of an enthymeme (Arist. *Rhet.* II.xxi.2). In a rhetorical setting, it is customary to introduce the conclusion before such a citation and to omit the second premise (Mack/Robbins:79). Therefore it is illuminating to look for abridged syllogisms and other deductive arguments in Gal 3:8-14.[20]

8.5: The theory of topics

The rhetorical handbooks contain long lists of *Topics* which may be utilized in a given part of a speech.[21] These lists are collections of sources for available ways of arguing persuasively, that is, of different perspectives that one may apply to a given case. Most of them are to be regarded as commonplace in the culture, and they therefore give us valuable clues to the implied logic in

---

[18]Cicero refers to those who allow the conclusion to be omitted when it is obvious and also to those who allow either the major or the minor premise to be omitted (Cic. *Inv.* I.xl.72–xli.75). He is also a witness to this custom, although he rejects it as inappropriate.

[19]Both Arist. *Rhet.* II.xx.9 and Cic. *Inv.* I.xli.76 advise a speaker, if possible, to vary the two types of argumentation.

[20]This is similar for Pauline texts in general, cf. Siegert:192–93; Hansen:88–89.

[21]Cf. Martin:107–118 for this theory. Also Wuellner 1978:470–75 focuses this theory for the interpretation of Galatians, but I cannot agree that the topic of quality versus that of quantity is important for ancient rhetoric. In his commentary, H. D. Betz occasionally draws on topics from the handbooks.

argumentation. This mode of arguing deductively may be regarded as the most simple and easiest perceivable to one's disposal, because its point is to play on perspectives that are prevalent and common in the culture. The point of rhetoric is not to argue from logically irresistible truths, but from the probable, that which generally happens — perspectives which the audience is willing to accept.[22]

Aristotle collected large lists of such topics, some suitable for the three kinds of rhetoric, and some that were generally applicable.[23] All important handbooks since his time also include such lists, but their classification differs.[24]

I will frequently compare Paul's argumentation with such topics. The twenty eight General Topics presented by Aristotle in *Rhet.* II.xxiii are always important to consult, because we find a collection of normal, everyday argumentation within the Hellenistic culture whose value for New Testament research cannot be overestimated.

Four of these topics are so widespread that we also find them in abbreviated lists of topics. It seems as if the most widespread modes of arguing a case are stating that a Contrary and an Analogous statement are true and those of substantiating it with Examples and previous Judgments. These topics are found in Arist. *Rhet.* II.xxiii.1, 11, 12, 17. Both *ad Alexandrum* 1422a.25-27 and Arist. *Rhet.* II.xxv.4-7 refer to Contrary, Analogy, and previous Judgment in brief lists. *Ad Herenn.* II.xviii.28; II.xxix.46 refer to Analogy, Example, and previous Judgment, while the late Hermog. *Prog.* 7:10 - 8:14 includes all four.[25] Contrary, Analogy, and Example are also found abbreviated into a sequence of rhetorical figures in *ad Herenn.* IV.xliii.56.

Turning to Gal 3:1-14, we seem to find these proofs utilized:[26] The main Example is Abraham (3:6). The Analogy to righteousness by faith is

---

[22]According to Aristotle a major difference between logical syllogisms and rhetorical enthymemes is that the latter is derived from material which "will be sometimes necessary, but for the most part only generally true . . . . For that which is probable ($\tau\grave{o}$ $\varepsilon\grave{\iota}\kappa\acute{o}\varsigma$) is that which generally happens, not however unreservedly, as some define it, but that which is concerned with things that may be other than they are" (*Rhet.* I.ii.14-15). Cf. also Martin:106.

[23]For deliberative rhetoric, cf. Arist. *Rhet.* I.v-vii; for epideictic rhetoric, I.ix.15-27; for judicial rhetoric, I.xi-xii; and for the 28 generally applicable topics, II.xxiii.

[24]Cicero, for example, structures the topics differently from Aristotle: He distinguishes between topics related to the person and to the case itself, and the latter topics were divided into topics that were coherent with the action, connected to its performance, adjunct to it, or a consequence of it (Cf. Cic. *Inv.* I.xxiv.34-xxx.49).

[25]See Mack/Robbins:51-52, 57-63 for an extensive discussion.

[26]Siegert:55-56, 65-66, 70-76 has demonstrated the presence of these topics in the LXX, which was Paul's scripture. He also regards them as typical for Paul's argumentation (182-90, 210-11, 224-27, 157-64). Cf. also Berger 1984a:45 who has noted the

blessing by faith (3:8-9), which has a Contrary in the curse of Deut 27:26 (3:10). A new Analogy is found in Hab 2:4: life by faith (3:11). All these proofs are taken from the Hebrew Bible, an authority containing previous Judgments.

In addition to these most widespread topics, the chapter on General Topics also includes other perspectives that I find illuminating for the interpretation of Galatians:

> The topic *From the more and less* (ἐκ τοῦ μᾶλλον καὶ ἧττον) consists in claiming that a predicate exists in those cases where it is less probably affirmable, and it must also exist in cases where it is more probably affirmable (cf. II.xxiii.5). This topic seems to be fruitful for the implied logic of 1:8-9.
> *Dilemma* is another topic (cf. II.xxiii.15) which seems to be fruitful for the interpretation of 2:14.
> Another topic consists in *turning upon the opponent what has been said against ourselves* (cf. II.xxiii.7). This topic may be used many times in Galatians, but in 2:17-18 we find an explicit accusation which is turned back on the opponents.
> The topic *Examining together* (ἅμα σκοπεῖν) consists in pointing to an inconsistency between what has been done and what is to be done (cf. II.xxiii.27). This topic may be illuminating for the interpretation of 3:3 and 4:8-9.

Some topics are recommended for use in special parts of a speech. Typical for the *exordium* and the *peroratio* is the method of *Amplification* (αὔξησις), that is, "the principle of using Commonplaces to stir the hearers" (*ad Herenn.* II.xxx.47) or "a passage which results in arousing great hatred against some person, or violent offence at some action" (Cic. *Inv.* I.liii.100).[27] It is well known that Paul diverges from his normal letter form in Galatians. Instead of opening with thanksgiving and praise of his addressees, he replaces the thanksgiving with a rebuke.[28] Paul seems to regard the situation in Galatia as so dangerous that he neglects the widespread advice of capturing the goodwill of his audience by flattering remarks.[29] This feature

---

presence of Example and Previous Judgments in Gal 3, and Hansen:89-90, who has noted the presence of Example.

[27]Although αὔξησις is best suited for epideictic speeches, it is "common to all kinds of Rhetoric, for all men employ extenuation (τῷ μειοῦν) or amplification (καὶ αὔξειν) whether deliberating, praising or blaming, accusing or defending" (Arist. *Rhet.* II.xviii.4). It is found especially in the *exordium* and the *peroratio* of a speech, cf. Martin:153. For an extensive presentation of αὔξησις, cf. Martin:153-58.

[28]For θαυμάζειν as an epistolary formula of rebuke, cf. above sec. 7.2.1. Paul also neglects the opportunity to denote the Galatian churches with Christian epithets in the address of 1:2. Cf. the epithets beloved, called, and holy (Rom 1:7); sanctified, called, and holy (1 Cor 1:2); holy (2 Cor 1:1; Phil 1:1); in God our Father and the Lord Jesus Christ (1 and 2 Thess 1:1).

[29]Cf., for example, *ad Herenn.* I.v.8 and Cic. *Inv.* I.xvi.22.

corresponds to the method of Amplification, and we will compare Paul's way of describing the situation with conventional topics for such purposes.

8.6: *Judicial argumentation: Stasis theory*

According to the rhetorical handbooks, a lawyer should consider various aspects of a given case before he composes his speech.[30] The main step, which occupies the most space in the handbooks, is the determination of the *stasis of a case*. I find parts of stasis theory illuminating for the interpretation of the first section of Galatians.[31]

Stasis theory concerns different modes of handling a judicial case. It was conceptualized by Hermagoras (2nd century BCE) in a no longer extant handbook and rendered with slight modifications in Cicero's *De Inventione* (1st century BCE) and by Hermogenes (2nd century CE).[32] According to this theory, a lawyer could handle a case according to four rational stases: He could treat it as a question of fact, definition, quality, or jurisdiction. The theory also includes four legal stases, which concern disputes about the content of written documents.

According to G. A. Kennedy, we now take up a very difficult part of rhetorical theory, one which should not be used by scholars without extensive reading in the rhetorical sources (18-19, 36). It is therefore important for us to stick to the basic distinctions and not to stray to the refinements that also exist. The theory as such is very simple, however, and we may assume a certain familiarity with it in any Hellenistic audience with some contact with legal pursuits.

8.6.1: *Rational stasis*

The decision about stasis should take its departure from the claims of the parties involved in the situation.[33]

The first possibility is to defend the case (or accuse correspondingly) within the *stasis of Fact* (στοχασμός, *coniectura*). The point of dispute here

---

[30]Cf. Martin:15-28 for the considerations of the case as general or concrete, as having a stasis or being non-systatic, of the *causa*, the *genera causarum*, the *ductus*, and of the case as related to one law or many.

[31]I was encouraged by E. Baasland to study the theory of stasis, cf. his 1988b:76 for a short hint for the importance of the theory.

[32]Martin:28-52 gives a useful presentation of the theory from all relevant handbooks. A useful diachronical presentation is found in Nadeaus's text edition of Hermog. *Stat.*, pp. 370-86. Both *ad Alexandrum* 1442b.33 - 1444a.15 and Arist. *Rhet.* I.xiii.9-19 show that the mode of reasoning is old, but Cicero and *ad Herennium* are the earliest preserved witnesses to the theory as a system. *Ad Herenn.* I.xi.18 acknowledges that the system often included four stases, but renders a modification with three.

[33]Cf. *ad Herenn.* I.xi.18; xvi.26-xvii.27; Cic. *Inv.* I.xiii.18-xiv.19; Martin:28.

is whether or not the accused person actually committed the crime (cf. Cic. *Inv.* I.viii.11; *ad Herenn.* I.xi.18; Martin:30–32).

The second possibility concerns the *stasis of Definition* (ὅρος, *definitio*). According to Cicero, "the controversy about a definition arises when there is agreement as to the fact and the question is by what word that which has been done is to be described" (*Inv.* I.viii.11). This stasis would enable a speaker to define the case in another way than the prosecutors did. If one could define it in a new way, one could also draw on other laws to settle the case, for example, by defining murder as self-defense (cf. also *ad Herenn.* I.xii.21; Martin:32–36).

The *stasis of Quality* (ποιότης, *qualitas*) is the third possible strategy. According to Cicero:

> there is a controversy about the nature or character of an act when there is both agreement as to what has been done and certainty as to how the act should be defined, but there is a question nevertheless about how important it is or of what kind, or in general about its quality, e.g., was it just or unjust, profitable or unprofitable? (*Inv.* I.ix.12; cf. also *ad Herenn.* I.xiv.24 – xv.25; Martin:36–41).

The *stasis of Jurisdiction* (μετάληψις, *translatio*) is a fourth possibility that concerns the juridical basis for the process itself. Cicero explains:

> In the fourth issue which we call the translative there is a controversy when the question arises as to who ought to bring the action or against whom, or in what manner or before what court or under what law or at what time, and in general when there is some argument about changing or invalidating the form of procedure (*Inv.* I.xi.16; cf. also *ad Herenn.* I.xii.22; Martin:42–43).

The defense or the prosecutor in a given case could treat the case according to its fact, its definition, or its quality. In addition one could delay the case by objecting against some part of the procedure itself, or perhaps annul the whole case in this way. Such were the basic choices one faced.

It is not my intention to claim that Paul should have composed a juridical speech according to one or more of these strategies. The connection is rather that Paul knew these conventional modes of argumentation, and that he acknowledged their persuasive force. Thus he might reflect these conventions, although he does not pursue the case before a court.

H. D. Betz classifies Galatians as a speech within the judicial genus. He sees the letter as a self-apology by Paul before the Galatians against accusations made by the opponents concerning him and his Gospel (1975:377). He finds the stasis in 3:1–5, claims that there is agreement on the fact that Paul founded the churches of Galatia, and argues that the challenge for Paul was to prove that he founded them rightfully and legally rather than "in vain" (1979:129). Therefore, Paul treats the case within the stasis of Quality.

This identification of the nature of the Galatian argument raises the question if Paul defended the right of the Galatians to remain uncircumcised.[34] It appears that the *implied readers* were accused of not being circumcised, and the *implied author* persuaded them to remain uncircumcised. Given this situation, the stasis of Fact would be unsuitable.[35] Paul could not deny that the Galatians were uncircumcised when his point was to defend their right to remain so. Therefore, the argument from 2:16 onward deals with the situation from the perspective of the stasis of Definition.[36]

Several possibilities existed for Paul within this stasis:

He could, as in Rom 2:25-29 and in some Jewish texts, try to define a circumcised person in another way than the opponents. He could argue that somebody (outwardly) uncircumcised should be reckoned as (inwardly) circumcised if he keeps the precepts of the law.[37] In this way he could try to make the claims of the opponents void, because the Galatians would have fulfilled their duties by their ethical circumcision. In Galatians, however, I find no trace of this approach.

Another strategy would be to use different words than the opponents to address the case (Martin:33). It seems that Paul has chosen this strategy when he discusses the problem from the perspective of law/works of the law versus faith/hearing by faith (cf. Gal 2:16; 3:2-12). This choice allows Paul to define the problem in such a manner that he can draw on Hebrew Bible texts to support his case. If so, it is a strategy that removes the interpreter from a definition of the real problem in Galatia. In all probability the problem involved more than a claim for circumcision. Our challenge is not to define the details of the problem as it existed, however, but to interpret the manner in which Paul responded. If Paul decided to prosecute the case from

---

[34]This perspective is underscored by C. -N. Kim:49, 53. Note his statement that: "Paulus übernahm in diesen Kampf sozusagen die Rolle des Rechtsanwalts für die Heidenchristen" (294). This does not mean that I deny that Paul also may defend himself against some charges in the letter, cf. the discussion of Gal 1:16b-22 below in sec. 8.7.2.

[35]Contra Kennedy:146-47 who considers the stasis of fact, corresponding to what he regards as the central questions: What Gospel is true? What should the Galatians do?

[36]If so, there is no need for the stasis of quality, contra H. D. Betz above. Also contra Hester 1984:227-28 who uses 2:11-12 as his basis: The disputed question of the *narratio* is the quality of Paul's relations to Jerusalem.

Also Mack:69-70 has briefly identified the issue as one of definition, corresponding to the question: "Who is worthy to receive the inheritance of that divine promise to Abraham?"

[37]Borgen 1980:86-89; 1983a:66-69 demonstrates such argumentation in Rom 2 and by some opponents of Philo (*Migr* 86-93; *Quest in Exod* II.2). McEleney:328-33 refers to further Jewish texts that give dispensation from circumcision.

the perspective of law versus faith, it is this perspective that is of interest to us.[38]

> We also have to discuss whether the Stasis of Jurisdiction may be fruitful for the exegesis:
> When Paul limits the period of the Mosaic law to the era before Christ (cf. Gal 3:15-25), he is very near an objection *a tempore*, that is, to annul the relevance of a law from a temporal point of view.
> When he attacks his opponents by curses and blame (cf. Gal 1:7-9; 5:10b; 6:12-13), he is very near an objection *a persona accusatoris*, that is, against the right of the opponents to pursue a process.

8.6.2: *Hebrew Bible citations and legal stasis*

According to Cicero, after the choice of the rational stasis according to which he would defend his case, a lawyer had to consult the legal stasis if the dispute turns to written documents (Cic. *Inv.* I.xii.17; Martin:46). These four stases concerned disputes connected to interpretation of written documents. Such disputes could be of four kinds: They could be related to the will behind the words in a law, to contradictory laws, to ambiguous expressions, or to reasoning from analogy.[39]

The first of these disputes concerns *Letter and intent* (*scriptum et voluntas*), and it "arises when the framer's intention appears to be at variance with the letter of the text" (*ad Herenn.* I.xi.19). The point was to emphasize the will of the lawgiver and to interpret and employ the law in the light of it. This technique was especially persuasive if one could find words in the laws themselves that revealed this will.

The second dispute concerns *Conflicting laws* (*leges contrariae*): "when one law orders or permits a deed while another forbids it" (*ad Herenn.* I.xi.20). This conflict has to be reconciled, because contradictory statements were irreconcilable with the nature of justice.

The third dispute concerns *Ambiguity* (*ambiguitas*): "when a text presents two or more meanings" (*ad Herenn.* I.xii.20). The point is to argue for

---

[38]We see that the observation by Schmithals 1956b:30 (cf. 1983:29-30) is important: Paul discusses the case at another level than the real problem. It is not due to misinformation, however, but rather as noted by Westerholm 1988:118: "Paul placed the particular issue in the broader context of a discussion of the origin, nature, and function of the Mosaic law as a whole."

[39]Presented in Martin:46-52. Hermagoras taught these as legal questions, while Hermogenes denoted them as legal stases, cf. Nadeau's text edition of Hermog. *Stat.*, pp. 378, 385-86. Cic. *Inv.* I.xiii.17-18 also treats them as disputes separate from the stasis, while *ad Herenn.* I.xi.19 - xiii.23 presents them as subdivisions of what he denotes as the legal stasis. The disputes, however, are the same in spite of different classifications.

Cicero also tabulates a fifth stasis here: Definition (*ibid*). This dispute differs so slightly from Ambiguity that we can understand why the other textbooks do not regard it as a stasis of its own.

the interpretation that seems most natural and corresponds to the intention of the author.

The fourth dispute concerns *Reasoning from Analogy* (*syllogismus*): "when a matter that arises for adjudication lacks a specifically applicable law, but an analogy is sought from other existing laws on the basis of a certain similarity to the matter in question" (*ad Herenn.* I.xiii.23; Martin:31-32).

If Paul plays on conventions from stasis theory in Galatians, these conventions should be evident in his appeals to scripture. The Hebrew Bible is the written law according to which Paul must justify his position. As the following table demonstrates, such is the case in Galatians:[40]

As commonly recognized by Pauline scholars,[41] this table demonstrates a concentration in the use of scripture in Galatians especially, which must be more than accidental:

> The Hebrew Bible is cited more than once in only two sections of the letter, namely in 3:6-16 and 4:21-31, and in eight of the eleven references the citation/paraphrase is consciously introduced with long clauses.
>
> In seven citations we find changes in the text. Gal 3:10, 13 belong to the twelve most adapted citations by Paul, where we find three changes or more (Koch 1986:187).
>
> The use of tradition is very limited: Most of it has been taken from traditions which we have found to be connected in our survey of Jewish texts above: five times Paul uses the Abraham tradition, and twice Deuteronomy. The remaining four citations are also easy to relate to dtr-SH: Two citations from Leviticus that represent the law, and two from the prophets that refer to the future era of restoration.

---

[40]Cf. Koch 1986:22-23 for the list and for the categories and observations of changes in the texts (102-66). He does not include the paraphrase of 4:22-23, but I find it appropriate to include it since Paul's use of scripture is conscious and explicit here.

[41]The most recent treatment in given by Koch 1986 (esp. 33, 48-83, 90, 284-85, 288-89, 299-301 for the observations which follow). Similar observations are also made in Ellis 1957:10-16, 117-25, 139-47.

a) Hebrew Bible citations are found with a certain frequency especially in 2 Cor 8-9, Gal, and Rom.

b) Paul seems to prefer certain Hebrew Bible traditions, especially Isaiah, Psalms, Deuteronomy, Genesis, and the Book of the Twelve Prophets.

c) Hebrew Bible citations very often form important parts of Paul's argumentation.

d) Hebrew Bible citations are especially connected to themes such as the righteousness of God versus the law, and the calling of the church from Jews and Gentiles versus the election of Israel.

e) Paul seems to cite the LXX, but often with conscious changes in the text.

TABLE: HEBREW BIBLE CITATIONS IN GALATIANS.

TEXT	CITATION AND INTRODUCTION	CHANGES
3:6	Gen 15:6 – καθὼς . . .	Change in succession of words
3:8	Gen 12:3/18:8 – προευηγγελίσατο τῷ ᾽Αβραὰμ ὅτι . . .	Mixed Citation Omission
3:10	Deut 27:26/29:19b(?) – γέγραπται γὰρ ὅτι . . .	Mixed Citation Change in Gender Omission
3:11	Hab 2:4 – ὅτι . . .	Omission
3:12	Lev 18:5 – ἀλλ᾽ . . .	Omission Exchange (Paul's formulation)
3:13	Deut 21:23/27:26 – ὅτι γέγραπται . . .	Mixed Citation Omission Addition.
3:16	Gen 13:15, etc. – οὐ λέγει . . . ἀλλ᾽	
4:22-23	Gen 16:15/17:16/21:2, 9 – γέγραπται γὰρ ὅτι . . .	Paraphrase
4:27	Isa 54:1 – γέγραπται γὰρ . . .	
4:30	Gen 21:10 – ἀλλὰ τί λέγει ἡ γραφή	Omission Exchange (Paul's formulation)
5:14	Lev 19:18 – ὁ γὰρ πᾶς νόμος ἐν ἑνὶ λόγῳ πεπλήρωται, ἐν τῷ . . .	

It has not been easy to find constructive comparative texts in Jewish exegetical traditions to Paul's use of scripture.[42] The attempt to relate it to techniques from Hellenistic rhetoric is not a new proposal: D. Daube demonstrated that Hillel's seven rules of interpretation seem to be influenced by Hellenistic rhetoric.[43]   F. Siegert averred that Paul's hermeneutic "liegt ganz im Bereich des hellenistischen common sense" (158-61; esp. 158). He also points especially to juridical methods, but without drawing on the theory of stasis.   Recently J. S. Vos has explicitly introduced the stasis of *legum contrariarum* as a clue to the interpretation of Gal 3:11-12 and Rom 10:5-10.

Undoubtedly, almost every time Paul cites the Hebrew Bible to support his understanding of righteousness, law, and faith, he is in opposition to Jewish exegesis (Koch 1986:299-300).   Thus a Hebrew Bible citation also involves a dispute about its true meaning, and we are virtually every time cast into a discussion relating to the stasis presented above.

Some words about the *inner relation* between the first three disputes are necessary.   Most important is Letter and intent, since a discussion also of Conflicting laws according to Hermogenes is a kind of Letter and intent (*Stat.* 41,4-5; 83,20 - 84,2; Vos:261-62).   When two laws conflict, one must seek to find the intention behind each of them in order to explain their different purposes.   The stasis of Ambiguity, however, is not often appealed to as a basic dispute, since it normally would demand a law where it is possible to draw two different conclusions as a result of where to place the accent or where to separate syllables (*Stat.* 41,15).   It is rather appealed to as a part of the discussion related to the other disputes, especially in questions arising from utterances of the gods (*Stat.* 90,12-15).   We must be especially aware of a conflict where the one party relies on the letter while the other appeals to the intent.   This may involve also conflicting laws and appeals to ambiguities in the text.

It is also necessary to have in view the recommendations for the division of each dispute.   The rhetor is supplied with a list of relevant topics according to which one may pursue a process in each case.   The handbooks give

---

[42]Cf. Koch 1986:190-98, 202-30 for this. A review of research is found *ibid* 1-10. Cf. also Ellis 1957:83-84; Hays 1989:5-14.   The free technique of citations has its parallel only to a certain extent in the Damascus scroll of Qumran.   Paul's exegetical method is not easy to define as allegorical or typological, or similar to rabbinical rules, midrashes, homilies, and pesher commentaries.

[43]Cf. Daube 1949 who repeatedly refers to the legal stasis for the main ideas underlying Hillel's program (246-51), to Analogy for rules 2-4 (251-52), and to Ambiguity for the last rule (257).   The thirteen rules of Ishmael mainly specify Hillel's rules, but add a new rule concerning Conflicting Laws, cf. Strack/Stemberger:31.

A Hellenistic influence in these rules is accepted also by other scholars, cf. Mayer:1196-98; Koch 1986:221; Strack/Stemberger:27; Hansen:204; Hengel 1991:28.

advice about persuasive argumentations which, although they differ from each other, evidence some constant perspectives.[44] Since Paul argues outside a court setting, we have no reason to consider these lists as important for his disposition of the argument.[45] They are important rather by the fact that they reflect the conventional modes of argumentation. It is therefore notable that the topic Intention of the framer of the law is important in all disputes.[46] Once again we see that an appeal to the intention of the lawgiver is of primary importance.

We have a method of analyzing Paul's appeal to the Hebrew Bible both on a macro-level and on a micro-level. On the macro-level we will seek for information in the text of Gal 3 as a whole to see if we find traces of these disputes. On the micro-level we examine each Hebrew Bible citation for evidence whether Paul's changes in the LXX text may indicate how Paul defends his interpretation.[47]

The question is then whether the first audience in Galatia is likely to have perceived a possible employment of the stasis theory at this point. The normal attitude among Paul's readers would probably be to accept his use of the Hebrew Bible without further discussion. If so, an employment of the stasis theory would probably not be observed. In Galatia, however, the audience is likely to read more carefully. They have opponents in their midst who would object to Paul's interpretation at several points. Thus they are inevitably cast into a discussion of the correct intention of the presented texts. The conventional framework for such discussions is set by the stasis theory. The benefit of using the stasis theory is not only that Paul's hermeneutic is explained, but also that it takes place within a framework that is likely also to govern its reception among his audience.

8.7: Gal 1:1 - 4:11: A Rhetorical outline

Before we turn to the detailed exegesis, it may be helpful to outline briefly the Arrangement (*dispositio*) of the letter. The function of such an outline is to establish the main traits of Paul's argument as a preliminary horizon which may illuminate its details.

---

[44]The lists are brief in *ad Herenn.* II.ix.13–xii.18, but more comprehensive in Cicero and Hermogenes, cf. Martin:240–43.

[45]Contra Vos:265–66 who finds the whole argument of Gal 3:9–22 to reflect one broadly used *dispositio* related to Conflicting laws.

[46]We primarily find it as the first general topic after the presentation of the case in Hermog. *Stat.* 82:13–16; 85:5–9, 12–15; 88:18 – 89:10; 91:7–12.

[47]I follow Koch 1986:101, 346–47 in asking for conscious Pauline changes over against the LXX text. Ellis 1957:14–15 also recommends this approach with some modifications. Cf. also Hengel 1991:35–36 (with notes 191 and 192).

8.7.1: Gal 1:1-12: Prescript, rebuke, and transition (exordium)

The letter to the Galatians opens with two sections that correspond to epistolary conventions: Gal 1:1-5 is structured according to customs of prescripts in epistolography, and Gal 1:6-7 is similar to θαυμάζω expressions in letters of rebuke (cf. sec. 7.2.1). We find that these epistolary conventions are broadly extended, however: The prescript is clearly extended by 1:1, 4-5 in a way that only corresponds to Romans among the early letters of Paul. The rebuke in Gal 1:6-7 is followed by curses in 1:8-9. It will also be argued below (cf. sec. 9.1.1) that I find it appropriate to regard Gal 1:10-12 as a transition, being as much a part of the opening section as an introduction to the narrative part of the letter.

The question is now whether these extended epistolary parts and the transition may correspond to the advice for an opening of a speech, an *exordium*. According to the handbooks, an *exordium* should aim at making the audience receptive, well-disposed, and attentive. The main methods in this respect are a discussion of one's own person, the person of the adversaries, that of the audience, and the facts themselves.[48] Although the handbooks also discuss other aspects of an *exordium*,[49] it will suffice in this context to see how these four methods seem to be used to set the scene for the discussion in Galatians.

> The *person of Paul* is treated extensively. His divine authority is underscored in 1:1, 8, 10-12 in a way that presents him as a trustworthy apostle of God.
>
> The *audience* is treated in 1:6-7a, where they are rebuked and depicted as being on the verge of apostasy. This grave description corresponds to the advice of Aristotle: "Hearers pay most attention to things that are important, that concern their own interests, that are astonishing . . . wherefore one should put into their heads that the speech deals with such subjects" (*Rhet.* III.xiv.7).
>
> The *opponents* are dealt with in 1:7b-9, where they are described as false teachers and cursed with a double curse.
>
> The treatment of *the case itself* is more indirectly touched upon: The emphasis on the deliverance and resurrection of Christ (1:1c, 4) underscores that Christ has brought a new age. In 1:6-9 Paul's gospel is opposed to that of the opponents, which is no gospel. Thus it is indicated that competing definitions of the gospel play an important role in the conflict.

---

[48]Cf. Martin:63-64; Arist. *Rhet.* III.xiv.7-8; *ad Herenn.* I.iv.7-v.8; Cic. *Inv.* I.xvi.22-23.

[49]Cf. the distinction made between a *Direct Opening (principium)*, in Greek called the *Prooimion*, and the *Subtle Approach (insinuatio)*, called the *Ephodos* (*ad Herenn.* I.iv.6; cf. Cic. *Inv.* I.xv.20). When choosing among them, one has to consider the case itself, whether it is honorable, discreditable, doubtful, or petty (*ad Herenn.* I.iii.5; I.iv.6; cf. Cic. *Inv.* I.xv.20). I find it too farfetched to apply this to Paul as done by H. D. Betz 1979:44-45 and Lüdemann:48-53, especially when they claim that Paul seems to have mixed the two types of *exordia*.

We see that Gal 1:1-12 seems to function in a similar way as an *exordium* of a speech. It sets the scene for the following discussion by concentrating on four conventional themes. It emphasizes the trustworthiness of Paul and the severe danger of the Galatian churches. The opponents are cursed, and the facts are briefly alluded to.

8.7.2: Gal 1:13 - 2:14: Statement of facts (narratio)

The narrative section in Galatians consists of three episodes: Paul's calling to be an apostle (1:13-24), the Jerusalem Meeting (2:1-10), and the incident at Antioch (2:11-14).[50] One of the crucial problems in scholarship is to relate this narrative section to the argument of the letter as a whole. Attempts have been made to interpret the section as a *narratio*, which is part of either a judicial defense or a deliberative speech.[51] Both approaches I find to contain some truth, but also to be too one-sided. They both underscore the necessity of Paul to establish his own $\hat{\eta}\theta o \varsigma$ in one sense or another.

Some scholars regard 1:13 - 2:21 as a defense for Paul's authority, according to charges found in 1:11-12. I find this approach especially relevant for the passage 1:16b-22. The use of an oath in 1:20 corresponds to the rhetorical custom of using an oath as a proof of a vital argument that cannot be proved by other means (Martin:100; Sampley:480-82). We may also note the wealth of temporal and geographical data in 1:16b-22.[52] According to the handbooks, such data should not be included in a narrative unless it is important for the defense itself.[53] This approach does not explain the whole narrative, however. Such $o\dot{v}$-$\dot{\alpha}\lambda\lambda\dot{\alpha}$ phrases as in 1:11-12 do not necessarily refer to actual charges; they often refer to potential or real misunderstandings (G. Lyons:105-112). In addition it is difficult to explain all the features in the narrative in light of the charges found in 1:11-12.[54]

---

[50]The Jerusalem meeting (2:1-10) and the incident at Antioch (2:11-14) clearly stand out as episodes of their own.

I hold 1:13-24 together in spite of the twofold $\xi\pi\epsilon\iota\tau\alpha$ (1:18, 21), because 1:22-23 clearly links the section by referring to the persecution of 1:13-14 and to the commission to preach the Gospel in 1:16 (cf. Gaventa:316). The twofold $\xi\pi\epsilon\iota\tau\alpha$ may be due to Paul's need to be more accurate because of possible charges against him.

[51]Cf. the discussion above in sec. 7.2.2. R. G. Hall:284-87, on the other hand, regards the section as part of the proof.

[52]We find six geographical names and the following seven temporal indications: $\epsilon\dot{v}\theta\dot{\epsilon}\omega\varsigma$ $o\dot{v}$ . . . $o\dot{v}\delta\dot{\epsilon}$ . . . $\dot{\alpha}\lambda\lambda\dot{\alpha}$ . . . $\kappa\alpha\dot{\iota}$ $\pi\dot{\alpha}\lambda\iota\nu$ (1:16-17); $\xi\pi\epsilon\iota\tau\alpha$ $\mu\epsilon\tau\dot{\alpha}$ $\xi\tau\eta$ $\tau\rho\dot{\iota}\alpha$ . . . $\dot{\eta}\mu\dot{\epsilon}\rho\alpha\varsigma$ $\delta\epsilon\kappa\alpha\pi\dot{\epsilon}\nu\tau\epsilon$ (1:18); $\xi\pi\epsilon\iota\tau\alpha$ (1:21).

[53]Cf., for example, *ad Herennium* concerning the quality of brevity: "In general it is better to pass by not only that which weakens the cause but also that which neither weakens nor helps it" (I.ix.14). For similar advice, see Cic. *Inv.* I.xx.28; Martin:83.

[54]H. D. Betz 1975:365 notes that a *narratio* should be as brief as possible, by "not saying more than occasion demands," but he has not been able to explain why these episodes are occupied with Paul's difficult relations with the apostles.

It is plausible but too one-sided to regard the *narratio* as seeking to emphasize Paul's prototypical behavior in order that the Galatians may follow his example (cf. 4:12: "Brethren, I beseech you, become as I am"). Although such use of autobiography would correspond to well-known customs in antiquity,[55] we may ask why Paul also underscores other aspects of these episodes if this were his only intention.

I find it more fruitful to interpret the narrative from two other angles:

On one hand it is constructive to read it from a reader perspective. According to W. Iser, a reading of a text always involves both retrospection and anticipation.[56] The reading of a sentence is always accompanied by its connection both to the horizon of what has been stated and to the horizon of what one expects to follow.[57] The reading of the *exordium* has established a horizon for the readers of the letter and also created expectations about what will follow.

On the other hand rhetorical handbooks contain advice for an alternative type of narrative. According to *ad Herennium*, "there is a second type which often enters into a speech as a means of winning belief or incriminating our adversary or effecting a transition or setting the stage for something" (I.viii.12; cf. also Cic. *Inv.* I.xix.27; Martin:76). We have seen that the *exordium* has sought to win belief for Paul, incriminated his adversaries, and only alluded to the case itself so it could need a transition to be presented fully.

After reading the *exordium*, it will be part of any reader's horizon that Paul is eager to win his audience's belief in him. As we shall see in chapter 9, this is especially important for a person who dares to issue a double curse

---

Hester 1984 has structured the *narratio* in a way that gives better correspondence to 1:11-12: He claims that 1:11-12 is the stasis, which defines the issue as one of quality, namely of the quality of Paul's meetings in Jerusalem (226-27). Then 1:13-14 and 2:11-14 cannot be regarded as parts of the narrative and are classified as a transition (228-29) and a digression (231-32; a χρεία in his 1986:404-407) respectively.

When he also regards 2:3-5 as an insertion not related to the main issue, then we see even clearer the insufficiency of this approach (1986:398-400).

[55]Cf. G. Lyons:170-76, who refers to customs in autobiography in antiquity (17-73), and Gaventa:313-22, who refers to customs in epistolography (322-26). Also Smiga: 151-58 takes the narrative to form the background for 4:12.

[56]Cf. Iser:177-183. His terms are "Protention und Retention" (181).

[57]Cf. Iser:182: "So spielen im Lesevorgang ständig modifizierte Erwartungen und erneut abgewandelte Erinnerungen ineinander." Cf. also pp. 161-169 for his distinction between Theme and Horizon: The point of current reading is denoted as the Theme, but it is always related to the Horizon of what has been read or is anticipated to follow. When the eye moves towards another Theme, the old theme will become part of the Horizon and still influence the reading.

on his opponents. This horizon is further substantiated and confirmed throughout the narrative:

> In 1:13-24 Paul emphasizes that as a Jew he was one of the most outstanding (1:13-14), that he was called by the grace of God (1:15), that he saw the Son of God and was entrusted a divine commission (1:16), that he immediately showed his loyalty to it (1:17, 21), and that he occasioned praise to God (1:24).
>
> In the next episode it is stated that he was given a revelation to go to Jerusalem (2:2), he did not yield submission to the false brethren (2:5), the apostles perceived the grace that was given to him (2:9), and that he was eager to fulfill the obligation toward Jerusalem (2:10).
>
> In the last episode it is emphasized that he reacted boldly against Peter himself when necessary (2:11, 14).
>
> It is this function of the narrative that the above presented approaches have seen: Paul establishes his ἦθος both by responding to possible charges and by standing forth as an example.

After reading the *exordium* a reader (especially the first readers in Galatia) will have been deeply influenced by the description of the Galatians being on the verge of apostasy. Also this part of the horizon is confirmed in the narrative:

> In the reference to his former life in Judaism, Paul describes a Jewish zeal that led to violent persecution of the Church in order to destroy it (1:13). A zeal for the Jewish law is denoted as a threat to Christian churches.[58]
>
> In the Jerusalem episode, Paul claims that the discussion was so fundamental that it might show that Paul had worked in vain (2:2).[59] The discussion was even decisive for the preservation of the truth of the gospel among the Galatians (2:5).
>
> In the incident at Antioch the withdrawal by Cephas and the others seems trivial at the surface level. Paul, however, again takes it as threatening the truth of the gospel (2:14).
>
> We see that the narrative juxtaposes the crisis in Galatia with crises also in persecuted churches, in Jerusalem, and in Antioch.

The most impressive part of the *exordium* is the double curse on the opponents. It is evident that this attack on the opponents will be an important element in the horizon when one proceeds to the narrative. It is therefore noteworthy that the perspective of incriminating adversaries is substantiated in it:[60]

> It is implicitly present in 1:13-16 when Paul states that his former enmity toward the gospel was radically stopped by divine intervention. His zeal for the law

---

[58]Cf. Hengel 1991:68-86 for the historical realities and theological aspects of this persecution. He observes that πόρθειν is a very strong phrase for persecution (71-72).

[59]Cf. C. -N. Kim:168-79 for an extensive treatment of this verse.

[60]Cf. C. -N. Kim:121, 244-45 for an emphasis on the motif of combat as constitutive for the narrative.

is judged as illegitimate by God himself. The negative descriptions of enemies of the gospel are emphasized more openly in Gal 2:

The party that advocated circumcision in Jerusalem is described as "false brethren secretly brought in, who slipped in to spy out our freedom . . . that they might bring us into bondage" (2:4).[61]

Peter is described in Antioch as condemned (2:11), as acting out of fear (2:12), as a hypocrite together with his fellow Jews (2:13), and as not being straightforward about the truth of the Gospel (2:14).[62]

We have argued that the main strategy of Paul is to defend the case with a new pair of Definitions at a general level, and that this strategy is alluded to in the *exordium* by the opposition between two radically different preachings. The most important function served by the narrative seems to be to prepare the ground for the explicit presentation of this Definition from 2:16 onward.[63]

Among Paul's three examples, it is only the middle one that treats the problem of circumcision, cf. 2:1–10. Both the opening and the concluding sequence broaden the perspective:

In 1:13–14 Paul refers to his life in Judaism (ἀναστροφήν . . . ἐν τῷ Ἰουδαϊσμῷ) and his zeal for the traditions of his fathers (τῶν πατρικῶν μου παραδόσεων). It is therefore a zeal for Jewish traditions as a whole that causes problems for Christians.

It is a similar aspect that is taken up in 2:14: Paul accuses Peter of compelling the Gentiles to live like Jews (ἀναγκάζεις Ἰουδαΐζειν). Thus the narrative ends at the general level where it started.[64] Although the problem in Galatia may seem trivial as in Antioch, it is the relation to the whole Jewish law that is implicitly present. The need for discussing the problem at a general level should therefore be demonstrated.

Also the content of his definitions is presented implicitly in the narrative: Paul was previously zealous for the traditions of the fathers (1:14), but now he preaches faith (1:23).

---

[61]Terms such as παρεισάκτος, παρεισέρχομαι, and κατασκόπειν represent more than "language of political demagoguery" (H. D. Betz 1979:90). They are rather metaphors "of spies or traitors introducing themselves by stealth into the enemy's camp" (Lightfoot:106, cf. also Burton:83).

[62]It is difficult to translate the terms of 2:11, 14, but the accusatory function should be clear enough: Καταγινώσκειν in 2:11 could be taken in the sense of "condemn" (cf. Burton:103; H. D. Betz 1979:106) or "acknowledge," "see through" (cf. Neitzel:145–46). Ὀρθοπόδειν πρός (hap.leg.) in 2:14 could be taken in the sense of "making a straight path toward" (cf. Burton:110; Mussner:144), or "stand firmly footed according to" (cf. Neitzel:146–48).

[63]We may compare the advice in *ad Herennium* to "set forth the judgement rendered by others in an analogous cause, whether that cause be of equal, or less, or greater importance; then we shall gradually approach our own cause and establish the analogy" (I.vi.9). Cf. for similar advice Cic. *Inv.* I.xvii.24.

[64]According to *ad Herenn.* I.ix.14 the opening and the end of a narrative are important, because one should begin the narrative where one needs to begin and carry on forward only to the point one needs to reach. Cf. also Cic. *Inv.* I.xx.28; Martin:82–83.

The interpretation of the narrative in Gal 1–2 has always been a challenge for scholars. I hope that its main functions have been illuminated by a reader-oriented perspective combined with conventions for a transitional *narratio* and the stasis theory. The point has not been to do full justice to all its elements, but rather to illuminate those aspects of it that may be important for our interpretation of 1:6–12 and 2:15–21.

8.7.3: Gal 2:15–21: Definition of the case (A brief speech)

The section 2:15–21 has always been a puzzle to interpreters of Galatians. If Galatians were composed strictly according to the rules for a speech, one would expect to find a proposition (*propositio*) at this place between the narrative and the argumentation.[65] Since the section is argumentative, however, it is better to take it as a transitional speech (Kennedy:148–49). Most scholars do so and discuss whether it was given in Antioch or whether it was formed for this particular place in the letter.[66]

If Paul has inserted a brief speech at this point, we may ask whether it is possible to identify its theme. Since Paul seems to introduce his pair of definitions of the case in 2:16, we may ask if it is modeled upon the conventional pattern for such speeches. The table on the following page compares the guidelines for speeches according to the stasis of Definition given in *ad Herenn.* II.xii.17; Cic. *Inv.* II.xvii.52ff, and Hermog. *Stat.* 59:11ff (cf. also Martin:233–34):

These speeches take their departure in conflicting Definitions of the case. The defendant's Definition of the case is juxtaposed with the plaintiff's Counterdefinition. Then one can draw on other topics both in the sections of proofs and of refutation.

---

[65]This view has been taken by H. D. Betz 1975:367 (cf. also Hansen:68–69, 100–01). A *propositio* contains three parts, however. The two former parts, *enumeration* and *exposition*, are not found here (cf. *ad Herenn.* I.x.17. See also Cic. *Inv.* I.xxii.31 – xxiii.33 with clear illustrations that are far from the wording in Gal 2:15–21). Further: If 2:19–20 is meant by Paul as an extremely brief summary of the argument in Gal 3–4, he has done it in a way that a reader would not be able to perceive!

[66]For this section as a speech from Antioch, cf. Sieffert:115–17; Bligh:176; Lührmann 1978:46–47; Neitzel:143–45. For an address toward the Galatians, cf. Borse 1984:112. Most modern commentaries opt for a combination: Paul formally addresses Cephas, but the content is intended for the Galatians, cf. Oepke:87; Mussner:135; Schlier 1965:87–88. See also Klein 1964:126–27.

TABLE: LISTS OF TOPICS IN THE STASIS OF DEFINITION

Ad Herenn. II.xii.17	Cic. Inv. II. xvii.52 — xviii.	Hermog. Stat. 59:11 — 61:20
		1) Presentation of the case
1) Brief definition	1) Brief definition	2) Definition
		3) Counterdefinition
	2) Lengthy discussion of reasons for support	
		4) Inference
2) Connect our conduct with the definition	3) Connect the act of the accused and the definition	
		5) Intention of the framer of the law
	4) Focus the enormity of the deed	6) Gravity
3) Refute the principle underlying the contrary definition	5) Refute the definition of the opposing counsel	8) Refute one of the counter-propositions
		9) Quality and intention
a: False	a: False	
b: Inexpedient	c: Inexpedient	
c: Disgraceful	b: Dishonorable	
d: Harmful		
	d: Comparison	7) Comparison
e: Refer to department of Law		
	e: Analogy	
	f: Induction	

All handbooks state that one should open with a definition of the case according to one's own strategy. This part of the speech is rendered in greater detail by Hermogenes, who distinguishes three steps: (1) Presentation of the case, (2) Definition, and (3) Counterdefinition. Then the section of proofs follows, which should be lengthy according to Cicero. He refers to two such proofs: (3) The connection of the disputed act with the definition, a topic which is rendered also in *ad Herennium*, and (4) the focusing on the enormity of the deed, a topic which is rendered also by Hermogenes. Again Hermogenes is more detailed. He also advises that one should use (4) Inference — to draw both Definition and Counterdefinition together — and that one should scrutinize (5) the Intention of the framer of the law.

The last part of the speech consists in the refutation of the Counterdefinition or one of the principles underlying it. Both *ad Herennium* and Cicero advise a speaker to emphasize topics such as whether the position of the opponents is false, inexpedient, dishonorable, and so forth. Hermogenes refers instead to topics such as Quality and Intention.

The remaining topics correspond to the general topics rendered above: The topic of Comparison between the definitions corresponds to the argument from Contrary; the reference to departments of laws by *ad Herennium* corresponds roughly to the topic of Previous Judgments; the references to Analogy and Induction by Cicero correspond to Analogy and Example above.

In Gal 2:16 Paul seems to introduce the Definition and Counterdefinition of the Galatian problem: He juxtaposes righteousness by the works of the law with righteousness by faith. If stasis is theory illuminating for the introduction of this contrast, we should also expect that it is followed by arguments in 2:16-21 that correspond to topics as rendered in the lists we have presented. Therefore, the discussion in section 10.2.1 will seek to demonstrate that Paul in fact follows this pattern. This speech takes the place of a *propositio* and introduces Paul's main strategy according to the stasis of Definition. This strategy has only been alluded to and prepared for earlier in the letter. Now it is openly expressed, preparing for the main discussion which follows. This means that our detailed exegesis in chapter 10 has to start with this speech in order to understand 3:8-14 properly.

8.7.4: Gal 3:1 - 4:11: Section of Proofs
The main discussion in the first part of Galatians has five elements: three rounds of arguments (3:6[8]-14, 15-29; 4:1-7) are both preceded (3:1-5[7]) and succeeded (4:8-11) by direct addresses to the Galatians.[67]

---

[67]Cf. for a similar analysis Smit:14-15. This structure also corresponds to changes in the I-you axis, cf. Smiga:183-84.

In this section Paul does not pursue the goal of winning belief. It seems that the narrative has supplied the readers with the necessary information in this respect. The opening and closing sections substantiate the horizon of crisis and near apostasy in Galatia (cf. 3:1, 3-4; 4:9-11). We also find an indirect attack on the opponents in 3:1 ("Who has bewitched you?"), and we have to discuss whether the curse in 3:10 also should be seen in this perspective.

We have discovered that the following perspectives are fruitful for the analysis which will be pursued in chapter 10:

> Paul seems to employ inductive reasoning in 3:1-7 and to change to deductive reasoning from 3:8 onward.
> The theory of topics may explain the logical sequence of some of the arguments.
> The stasis discussion seems to be carried further: The Definition of the case as one concerning faith versus law (cf. 2:16) is clearly present. In 3:2-12 Paul defines those of faith both according to the bestowal of the Spirit (3:2, 5) and the concepts of righteousness (3:6-7), blessing and curse (3:8-10), and life (3:11-12). Those of faith are defined further in 3:26-29 and 4:6-7.
> The stasis discussion also seems to be extended to an exegesis of the Hebrew Bible in light of legal stasis.

8.7.5: The deliberative part of Galatians

As argued above, the *dissuasio* in 5:1-12 and the *peroratio* in 6:11-18 are marked by deliberative argumentation connected to the problem of circumcision (cf. sec. 8.2). The question is now whether 4:12-31 and the parenesis in 5:13 - 6:10 also fit this rhetorical context.

As for the transitional section 4:12-20, we may note that 4:12 presents the first exhortation in the letter (cf. 4:12). The main topics are those of joy (4:15) and friendship (4:13-15), a friendship that the Galatians are on the verge of losing (4:16-20). Both topics are typical for deliberative argumentation.[68]

As for the Sarah-Hagar section (4:21-31), it may be seen as a transition to emphasizing the concept of freedom versus slavery, which will be of central importance in the *dissuasio* (cf. 5:1, 13).[69] Paul takes up a contrast more suitable for a deliberative setting. As he has proved the truth of the

---

[68]For joy and pleasure, cf. *ad Alexandrum* 1421b, 23-31. Although we do not find these arguments in Cicero and *ad Herennium*, the arguments are taken up in earlier handbooks, cf. Martin:169, 173-74. For friendship, cf. Cic. *Inv.* II.lii.157; lvi.168. See also Martin:172-73.

[69]These categories have been presented earlier in the letter. Paul has indicated in 2:4 that circumcision is also a problem of freedom versus slavery. In addition he has referred to life under the law and the στοιχεῖα as a life in slavery (4:1, 3, 7-9). But 4:22 is the first place in the letter where Paul presents it as a pair of contrasts, and it becomes the basis for the following exhortations (cf. 5:1, 13).

faith/law contrast with references to the Hebrew Bible, the section 4:21–31 seems to be a Hebrew Bible proof for the latter.[70]

The section opens in 4:22 by presenting the contrast between the two sons of Abraham: "One by a slave and one by a free (ἕνα ἐκ τῆς παιδίσκης καὶ ἕνα ἐκ τῆς ἐλευθέρας)." The point of the following argumentation is to define these sons in a way that links the son of the slave to the law and the son of the free woman to the promise. Having managed this in 4:23–27, Paul can conclude that the Galatians are "children of promise" (4:28), thus "not children of the slave, but of the free woman" (4:31). Then his *dissuasio* can utilize the aspect of slavery/freedom further.

As for the general parenesis in 5:13 – 6:10, scholars have energetically debated its function in the letter.[71] Its presence causes few problems for our flexible rhetorical approach, since the distinction between general parenesis and deliberation breaks down in epistolography.[72] It is therefore not surprising to find this mixture in Galatians, when we treat it as a letter and not as a speech.

Its connection with the problem of circumcision has been explained persuasively by J. M. G. Barclay: The circumcision problem in Galatia raised questions related to both identity and patterns of behavior. It was no abstract discussion, but it was related to duties which the Galatians should practice. Therefore a rejection of circumcision (and the Sinaitic legislation) naturally also involved positive statements about how to obey the truth (1988:73–74, 216–17).

> P. Borgen 1980 and 1982 has proposed another connection with the problem of circumcision: He finds corresponding expressions between Gal 5:13, 16–17, 24 and texts about the effects of circumcision by Philo in *Migr* 92; *Spec* 1:9, 305; *Quest in Gen* III.52 (Cf. also 1QS v.5 and 1QpHab xi.13 in Qumran). Thus Paul may have taken up concepts which a Jewish audience normally would connect to circumcision as a removal of passions and desires, and he transferred them into a new setting. If Borgen is right, we see yet another reason to regard the parenesis as an integral part of the letter.

For our purpose, the verses that take up themes from the first part of the letter are of most interest: a) the horizon of crisis on the verge of apostasy is underscored here (cf. 4:16–17; 5:4, 7–8); b) the attack on the opponents is

---

[70]Cf. Hansen:150–54. Also Dahl 1973:61, 66 claims that the function of this passage is to form a background for the request in 5:1.

[71]Cf. Merk 1969 for a discussion of the starting point of the parenesis, where he opts for 5:13. Cf. Barclay 1988:9–26 for a survey of different modes of seeing its function in the letter.

[72]Cf. Stowers:52–53, 92–93, 95, 107, 109. For epistolary comparisons, cf. also Berger 1984c:1342, 1344. For its epistolary function, cf. also J. L. White 1984:1746–48.

also carried further (cf. 5:7–10, 12; 6:12–13; and possibly 4:29–30); c) some verses will be treated in section 10.5 below, since they have a content similar to the curse of 3:10. We find them at the opening of the *dissuasio* (5:2–4), at the opening of the *parenesis* (5:14), and in the *peroratio* (6:13, 16).

8.8: Conclusion

As argued above, I find it crucial to emphasize the rhetorical interpretation of the argument of Galatians. This approach has been justified in chapter 7, and its flexibility has been presented in chapter 8. Let me summarize a few important observations made in those two chapters:

> I have found it necessary to argue for some caution in the application of rhetorical criticism, and to propose that the interest should be moved from *genus* and Arrangement toward Invention of Style (cf. sec. 7.3).

> For the identification of the Rhetorical Situation, it is enough to observe that the letter itself presents it as concerning the necessity of circumcision (cf. sec. 8.1).

> The *genus* of Galatians seems to be mixed, with mainly judicial argumentation up to 4:11, and primarily deliberative argumentation from 4:12 onward (cf. sec. 8.2).

> In the interpretation of Galatians, it is important to draw on the theory of rhetorical figures, the distinction between inductive and deductive reasoning, and the general theory of topics (cf. secs. 8.3–5).

> With regard to stasis theory, it seems that Paul argues according to the stasis of Definition from 2:16 onward. It also seems productive to consult the theory of legal stasis as a possible clue to the logic behind Paul's use of Hebrew Bible citations (cf. sec. 8.6).

> Regarding the Arrangement of Galatians, 1:1–12 seems to function as an *exordium* with its four conventional themes. The narrative seems to be a transitional section both keeping alive the horizon created by the *exordium* and also preparing for the discussion from 2:16 onward (cf. sec. 8.7). We may therefore pass by the narrative in our exegesis below, but certainly not the discussion from 2:16 onward.

With these insights we should be well prepared for a detailed discussion of the argument in Gal 1:6–12 and 2:16 – 3:14.

CHAPTER 9

9.0: THE ANATHEMAS OF GAL 1:8-9 IN CONTEXT

As argued above (cf. sec. 8.7.1) Paul's letter to the Galatians opens with three parts that function as an *exordium* for the letter: (a) 1:1-5: prescript; (b) 1:6-9: rebuke; (c) 1:10-12: transition. Since the anathemas close the rebuke (1:8-9 in 1:6-9) and precede the transition (1:10-12), these two parts will attract our attention in this chapter. After a brief discussion of the structure of the text (cf. sec. 9.1), we will interpret the anathemas in their context (cf. sec. 9.2). Then we will turn to the pragmatic aspects of the anathemas, drawing on conventional expectations about the illocutionary force of curses and asking what we may predict concerning their force and probable effects in Galatia (cf. sec. 9.3). Finally we will seek to substantiate our interpretation with an excursus on the other anathema texts in Paul (cf. sec. 9.4).

9.1: Structure of Gal 1:6-12

9.1.1: Gal 1:10-12 as a transitional unit
The classification of 1:10-12 within the argument of Galatians has long been difficult for scholars to settle. In the following I will argue that these verses belong to the *exordium* as a transition.

The verses 1:10-12 seem to belong together in some important respects: They are all connected to each other by a γάρ in 1:11 and 1:12. There appears to be a relation also between the content of the verses: Paul seems to refute objections (factual or invented) both in the questions of 1:10 and the denials of 1:11-12. We also find a γάρ in 1:10 and 1:13, however, and the section thus seems to be related both to the preceding rebuke and the following narrative.[1]

The section has further clear links to 1:1-9: The questions in 1:10a seem to arise naturally out of Paul's shocking anathemas.[2] It is also significant that 1:10b-12 seems to be linked to 1:1:

---

[1] In 1:11 there is strong textual evidence for δέ instead of γάρ. The connective effect is the same, however, whether we have four occurrences of γάρ or if one of them is δέ. Cf. G. Lyons:136-38 for this connective effect.

[2] This is noted by many scholars. Some relate 1:10 to the rebuke, cf. Sieffert:36; Zahn:53; Burton:31-32; Schlier 1965:41-42; Borse 1984:51-52; Rohde:46-47. Other scholars argue that 1:10 opens a new section, but note the connection, cf. Becker:15; Ridderbos:55-56. Cf. sec. 9.2.3 below for the interpretation.

1:1: ἀπόστολος	1:10b: Χριστοῦ δοῦλος
1:1: οὐκ ἀπ᾽ ἀνθρώπων οὐδὲ δι᾽ ἀνθρώπου	1:11-12a: οὐκ . . . κατὰ ἄνθρωπον οὐδὲ . . . παρὰ ἀνθρώπου οὔτε ἐδιδάχθην
1:1: ἀλλὰ διὰ Ἰησοῦ Χριστοῦ	1:12b: ἀλλὰ δι᾽ ἀποκαλύψεως Ἰησοῦ Χριστοῦ.

In this way 1:1 and the transition form an *inclusio* to the whole *exordium*.

On the other hand, γνωρίζω γὰρ ὑμῖν, ἀδελφοί, an expression which introduces a new section at other places (cf. 1 Cor 15:1 and 2 Cor 8:1), introduces 1:11-12.[3] Also the content seems to prepare for the succeeding *narratio*,[4] which refutes the charges charges against Paul (factual or invented).

Taken together, these observations lead to the conclusion that 1:10-12 is a transitional unit between 1:6-9 and the narrative from 1:13 onward.[5] In our semantic field analysis above (cf. sec. 2.3.1) we could therefore concentrate on the field of 1:6-9. In the interpretation of the anathemas in their context, however, we have to give due attention also to the content of these verses.

9.1.2: Structure of 1:6-12

The structure of the rebuke and the transition may be tabulated as on the next page:

Accusations precede and refutations succed the two anathemas in 1:8-9. The anathemas themselves have a similar structure: introductions (cf. Intr 1 and 2); similar protases (cf. Pro 1 and 2); and identical apodoses (cf. Apo 1 and 2).

---

[3]According to J. L. White 1971:93-94 this "Disclosure Formula" belongs to the stock formulas belonging to the introductory sections of a letter. It should therefore not be taken as an opening of the narrative section of Galatians (97), but rather as a preparation for it (H. D. Betz 1979:56).

[4]Many scholars take 1:11-12 as thematic verses that govern the narrative, cf. Sieffert:39; Burton:35; Mussner:77; Borse 1984:53. H. D. Betz 1979:62 regards only 1:12 as such a thesis. Although I agree about the connection, I have above (sec. 8.3.2) criticized constructing too close a connection between these verses and the narrative.

[5]Cf. for similar judgments Mussner:62; Ebeling:84; G. Lyons:131. Smit:9-10 sees 1:10-12 as a part of the *exordium*, and Lüdemann:52-54 regards 1:10 as belonging to the *exordium* and 1:11-12 as a transition.

It has also been proposed that 1:13-14 could be related to this opening (cf. J. L. White 1971:94-97 who regards ἠκούσατε γάρ as belonging to the formulas of an opening section), or that the transition could be made briefer (for 1:10-11 as a transition, cf. Oepke:53; H. D. Betz 1979:46; for 1:10 cf. Borse 1984:52).

TABLE: The Structure of Gal 1:6-12

Accusations (1:6-7)

	⁶Θαυμάζω
Acc Gal	ὅτι οὕτως ταχέως μετατίθεσθε
	ἀπὸ τοῦ καλέσαντος ὑμᾶς ἐν χάριτι [Χριστοῦ]
	εἰς ἕτερον εὐαγγέλιον,
Corr	⁷ὃ οὐκ ἔστιν ἄλλο·
Acc Opp 1	εἰ μή τινές εἰσιν οἱ ταράσσοντες ὑμᾶς
Acc Opp 2	καὶ θέλοντες μεταστρέψαι τὸ εὐαγγέλιον τοῦ Χριστοῦ.

Anathemas (1:8-9)

Intr 1	⁸ἀλλὰ καὶ
Pro 1	ἐὰν ἡμεῖς ἢ ἄγγελος ἐξ οὐρανοῦ
	εὐαγγελίζηται [ὑμῖν] παρ᾽ ὃ εὐηγγελισάμεθα ὑμῖν,
Apo 1	ἀνάθεμα ἔστω.
Intr 2	⁹ὡς προειρήκαμεν, καὶ ἄρτι πάλιν λέγω,
Pro 2	εἴ τις
	ὑμᾶς εὐαγγελίζεται παρ᾽ ὃ παρελάβετε,
Apo 2	ἀνάθεμα ἔστω.

Refutations (1:10-12)

Ques 1	¹⁰Ἄρτι γὰρ ἀνθρώπους πείθω ἢ τὸν θεόν;
Ques 2	ἢ ζητῶ ἀνθρώποις ἀρέσκειν;
Con Cl	εἰ ἔτι ἀνθρώποις ἤρεσκον,
	Χριστοῦ δοῦλος οὐκ ἂν ἤμην.
Intr	¹¹Γνωρίζω γὰρ ὑμῖν, ἀδελφοί,
Den 1	τὸ εὐαγγέλιον τὸ εὐαγγελισθὲν ὑπ᾽ ἐμοῦ
	ὅτι οὐκ ἔστιν κατὰ ἄνθρωπον·
Den 2	¹²οὐδὲ γὰρ ἐγὼ παρὰ ἀνθρώπου παρέλαβον αὐτό,
Den 3	οὔτε ἐδιδάχθην,
Assert	ἀλλὰ δι᾽ ἀποκαλύψεως Ἰησοῦ Χριστοῦ.

Prior to the anathemas we find accusations against both the Galatians and the opponents. Paul accuses the Galatians (1:6, cf. Acc Gal) with a correction attached to it (1:7a, cf. Corr), and he poses two accusations against the opponents (1:7b, cf. Acc Opp 1 and 2).

After the anathemas we find two units of refutations. In 1:10 we find refutations concerning Paul's person. They are formed as questions (cf. Ques 1 and 2) and as a conditional clause (cf. Con Cl). In 1:11-12 we find refutations concerning Paul's Gospel introduced by a Disclosure Formula (cf. Intr). They are formed as three denials (cf. Den 1, 2 and 3) and one concluding assertion (cf. Assert).

In this way all four themes belonging to an *exordium* are present in the section: We find a treatment of the persons of the addressees (1:6), the opponents (1:7, 9), the speaker himself (1:8, 10-11), and indirectly also the subject itself (1:6-9, 11-12; cf. *ad Herenn.* I.iv.8 and Cic. Inv. I.xvi.22).

9.2: Accusations, anathemas and refutations in 1:6–12

9.2.1: Accusations (1:6–7)

a: Accusations of apostasy (1:6–7a)

In 1:6–7a Paul accuses the Galatians of being on the verge of apostasy, a charge — as investigated above in part I — frequently related to covenant traditions like the deuteronomistic traditions. It is therefore significant for our purpose that the anathemas of 1:8–9 are found in this context.

Paul begins by utilizing an expression of surprise: "I am astonished that you are so quickly deserting . . . ." Both the epistolary formula Θαυμάζειν and the expression οὕτως ταχέως serve an amplifying purpose. It is not certain that Paul really is surprised (contra, e.g., Mussner:53), or that he really regards the development in Galatia as swift (contra, e.g., Mussner:53–54; Rohde:38–39).[6] Whatever the case, the expressions serve a specific rhetorical purpose (H. D. Betz 1979:46–48; Bullinger:923): Paul amplifies the seriousness by denoting the situation as unexpected and as a swift apostasy.[7]

The accusation of apostasy is formed in this way: "You are . . . deserting him who called you (μετατίθεσθε ἀπὸ τοῦ καλέσαντος ὑμᾶς) . . . ." The term μετατίθεσθαι is found in political language (Oepke:48; H. D. Betz 1979:47), but also in connections denoting apostasy from the Jewish law. In the active sense we have found it in the Deut 27–30 tradition in Philo, (Post 88 refers to the accursed man "who removes the boundaries of the good").[8] In the middle voice it means "turn from/apostasize from" (cf. 2 Macc 7:24: ". . . if he would turn from [μεταθέμενον ἀπό] the ways of his fathers"; Burton 19–20). Paul surprises his readers by denoting their state as an ongoing apostasy from God.[9]

Paul refers to the alternative teaching in the following way: ". . . to a different gospel (εἰς ἕτερον εὐαγγέλιον) — not that there is another gospel (ὃ οὐκ ἔστιν ἄλλο)." We may note a possible play upon the difference in mean-

---

[6]Also contra proposals that Paul is referring to a brief period since his last visit (= so soon), cf. Oepke:47; Borse 1984:46.

[7]Similar Amplifications are conventional, cf. the second and third topic of Amplification in ad Herenn. II.xxx.48 and Cic. Inv. I.liii.101: One can show who is affected by the act (it is most dreadful when it affects all as in Galatia), and one can point to the evil which will come as a result.

[8]The text is treated above sec. 4.1.2b. Cf. also Hos 5:10.

[9]See especially Ebeling:62–64. When Paul uses καλεῖν in this way, he always refers to God as the one who calls, cf. Mussner:54. The present tense of the verb indicates that the process is still in progress, cf. Burton:18–19; Mussner:54; H. D. Betz 1979:47. The passive construction may be taken to excuse the Galatians, since it implies that they are removed by others, cf. Luther 26:46–47.

ing between ἕτερον and ἄλλο here. Although most scholars reject such a play on words — since these words seem to be used synonymously in the New Testament[10] — 1 Cor 15:39-41 proves that Paul still is able to draw on the different nuances.[11] Paul first accuses the Galatians of turning to a gospel of a different kind (= ἕτερον), that is, a Gospel of another class or quality. Similar accusations are repeatedly found in apostasy traditions concerning Israel turning to other Gods (ἕτεροι θεοί).[12] Paul then corrects himself: He denies that numerically (cf. ἄλλο) any gospel outside his Gospel exists, so that apostasy from it is apostasy from the Gospel as such (H. D. Betz 1979:49). Regardless of how the first audience perceived the wordplay, they would certainly perceive the figure of *correctio*, and thus they could be drawn into a reflection about the illegitimacy of the teaching of the opponents.[13]

This opening of the letter is certainly an unexpected deviation from common conventions, which rather should predict a thanksgiving in an epistolary setting and flattery of the audience in a speech setting. Such deviation makes an impression on the audience (Iser:145-55), since they are challenged to reflect about their situation within a new perspective. We may safely assume that they have not, at least, considered an acceptance of circumcision (and other claims of the law?) to be equal to apostasy.

b: Accusations of seduction (1:7b)

While the accusations against the Galatians counter the most widespread guidelines for an *exordium*, accusations against the opponents conform neatly to them.[14] In 1:7b Paul discredits his opponents by two negative descriptions:

First he refers to the opponents as "some who trouble you (οἱ ταράσσοντες ὑμᾶς)." Ταράσσειν is a very general term which may denote disturbances of many kinds (cf. 5:10 and Acts 15:24; Schlier 1965:38;

---

[10]Cf. *BDR* par 306,4; Oepke:49-50; Rohde:41; J. K. Elliott:140-41; C. -N. Kim:35-37.

[11]In 1 Cor 15:39-41 Paul uses ἄλλος in 15:39, 41 for numerical non-identity, but ἕτερον in 15:40 for difference in kind. Cf. Burton:420-22; Sieffert:31-32; Bruce:80-81.

[12]Cf. in Deut 27-30: Deut 28:14, 36, 64; 29:25; 30:17. Cf. further Josh 24:2; Judg 2:12; 2 Kgs 22:17, etc. These Gods were not considered to be of the same class as Yahweh, cf. Burton:421.

[13]For 1:7a as *correctio*, cf. H. D. Betz 1979:49; Bullinger:910 and *ad Herenn.* IV.xxvi.36 where it is stated: "This figure makes an impression upon the hearer, for the idea when expressed by an ordinary word seems rather feebly stated, but after the speaker's own amendment it is made more striking by means of the more appropriate expression." Cf. also Cronjé:222 for this effect.

[14]According to the handbooks, a speaker can secure good-will if he can bring his opponents into hatred, unpopularity, or contempt, cf. H. D. Betz 1979:44-45 and *ad Herenn.* I.v.8; Cic. *Inv.* I.xvi.22.

Rohde:42). It often denotes the destructive work of political agitators (H. D. Betz 1979:49), and it may take the meaning of "raising seditions among you" (Lightfoot:77).

Second Paul states that the opponents "want to pervert the gospel of Christ ($\theta \acute{\epsilon} \lambda o \nu \tau \epsilon \varsigma \ \mu \epsilon \tau \alpha \sigma \tau \rho \acute{\epsilon} \psi \alpha \iota \ \tau \grave{o} \ \epsilon \grave{v} \alpha \gamma \gamma \acute{\epsilon} \lambda \iota o \nu \ \tau o \hat{v} \ X \rho \iota \sigma \tau o \hat{v}$)." $M \epsilon \tau \alpha \sigma \tau \rho \acute{\epsilon} \phi \epsilon \iota \nu$ means "to change from one state to another," and in a negative context like this it means "to pervert" (Burton:25; Schlier 1965:39).[15] It seems obvious that the opponents themselves never openly intended to pervert the Galatians, nor was it a hidden strategy of theirs. Again we have an instance of Amplification: Paul points to a consequence of their teaching, and by presenting it as their intention, he amplifies their activity as especially cruel (similar Bligh:84–86).[16]

There is another amplification implicit in the last statement. When Paul refers to the apostasy as an apostasy from God, he defines the seduction as a seduction from the gospel of Christ rather than simply from his own teaching. In this way the discourse depicts both the Galatians and the opponents as opposing God and Christ themselves!

The charge against the opponents is connected to 1:6-7a in an ambiguous way. It may be taken as an adversarial statement, or as an exception to the statement in 1:7a.[17] The latter possibility gives it an ironic twist: Paul states in 1:7a that there is no other gospel, but he presents one exception in 1:7b: There may exist another "gospel" in the preaching of the opponents, but there it is a perversion of the Gospel of Christ (Lightfoot:76)!

c: Apostasy and seduction in the rest of Galatians (3:1-5; 4:8-11; 5:4, 7-8)

The perception that Gal 1:6-7 contains accusations of apostasy and seduction is confirmed by the fact that Paul elsewhere in the letter makes similar accusations. As soon as a person reads the *exordium*, these accusations become part of the horizon that influences further reading.[18] It is notable that Paul substantiates their importance both in the opening and the closing sec-

---

[15]Also here H. D. Betz 1979:50 points to a background in political language, denoting revolutionary activities.

[16]Such Amplification is conventional, cf. *ad Herenn.* II.xxx.49 and Cic. *Inv.* I.liii.102: According to their seventh topic, a speaker may focus on the cruelty of the deed which is utterly at variance with law and equity.

[17]The most common possibility is to take $\epsilon \grave{\iota} \ \mu \acute{\eta}$ as introducing an exception (cf. Lightfoot:76; Bruce:82; H. D. Betz 1979:49; *BDR* par 376,1), but it may also be equivalent with $\grave{\alpha} \lambda \lambda \grave{\alpha}$ introducing an adversative statement (cf. Oepke:50; Mussner:57; *BDR* par 448,8).

[18]Cf. Iser:161-69, 177–83 and the presentation above in sec. 8.7.2 for the relation between Theme and Horizon as an effective literary device.

tions of the *argumentatio* (cf. 3:1, 3–4; 4:8–11) and in the *dissuasio* (cf. 5:4, 7–8).[19]

In 3:1–5 Paul alludes to these themes discreetly in several ways. Most allusions have the form of questions and openly challenge the audience to reflect about their own situation:

In 3:1, 3 Paul twice addresses the Galatians as "foolish (ἀνόητοι)." This corresponds to commonplace insults in rebukes, but it may also accuse the Galatians of not being able to understand the Scriptures in a proper way in relation to the Gospel.[20]

In 3:3 he asks ironically: "Are you now ending with the flesh (νῦν σαρκὶ ἐπιτελεῖσθε)?" He then accuses them of choosing the opposite to life in the Spirit, which is yet another allusion to apostasy. The ambiguous meaning of σάρξ may underscore this aspect, if we take it as denoting the sphere of sin and corruption (H. D. Betz 1979:133; Rohde:133). Perhaps also ἐπιτελεῖσθε is ambiguous; in addition to the notion of being fulfilled by the flesh, it may also imply that they end with the flesh (Ebeling:221).

In 3:4 Paul asks: "Did you experience so many things in vain? — if it really is in vain (εἴ γε καὶ εἰκῇ)." Here it is the term εἰκῇ that alludes to apostasy (cf. 1 Cor 15:2: ". . . by which you are saved . . . unless you believed in vain [εἰκῇ ἐπιστεύσατε])."

> The last clause in 3:4b is ambiguous. Many commentators take it to be an expression of hope as the RSV translation suggests. In this case it must be taken as a *correctio*,[21] where the point is to leave the door open for the hope that the Galatians have not come so far in their development yet.[22] It may also be taken as a *reduplicatio*, however, a rhetorical figure where one word is repeated for the purpose of Amplification (*ad Herenn.* IV.xxviii.38). Then it is better to take it as a threat: "If so, it really was in vain!"[23] Perhaps this ambiguity is intended by Paul: The audience becomes bewildered by the statement; does Paul see any hope or does he not? In this way they are drawn into a reflection about their mutual relationship.

Paul alludes to the theme of seduction in 3:1 when he asks: "Who has bewitched you (τίς ὑμᾶς ἐβάσκανεν)?" Many commentators take this

---

[19]Also Smiga:110–14, 131–41 holds these sections together, and he denotes them as "You-rebukes." We find indirect allusions to apostasy also in the narrative, cf. above sec. 8.7.2.

[20]Schlier 1965:119; H. D. Betz 1979:130; Rohde:128–29

[21] Cf. Bullinger:911; Bengel:736; Luther 26:218–19.

[22]Cf. Sieffert:145–46; Lightfoot:135–36; Burton:149, 151; Mussner:210; Bruce:150.

[23]Cf. Oepke:101; H. D. Betz 1979:135; Borse 1984:124; Rohde:134; and especially Ridderbos:115–16 who emphasizes the notion of perdition and curse in the last clause. Perhaps also a *diaphora* is involved here, that is, a figure where a repetition of the same word changes its meaning the last time, cf. *ad Herenn.* IV.xiv.21. In this context it could imply that εἰκῇ has connotations of eternal judgment in the repetition.

expression figuratively as a sarcastic remark,[24] which may designate the activity of the opponents as "leading astray."[25] Since βασκαίνειν is the technical term in the classical Mediterranean world for "bewitch," it is more probable that Paul goes even further, implying the work of a demonic power behind their preaching.[26]

While 3:1–4 alludes discreetly to the theme of apostasy, the section 4:8–11 underscores it even more than 1:6–7:

In 4:8–9 Paul compares past and present according to a conventional perspective:[27] On one hand he describes the conversion of the Galatians from their pagan past to a Christian belief (cf. 4:8–9a). Their present danger consists in acting in a way contrary to this conversion. Paul invites the Galatians to reflect upon this inconsistency by asking a question: "How can you turn back again to the weak and beggarly elemental spirits, whose slaves you want to be once more?" (4:9b).

This Amplification of the case is very severe: The Galatians will not only turn back to Judaism, but their action is defined as equal to an apostasy back into paganism.[28] This is underscored by the abnormal use of ἐπι-στρέφειν which is taken from missionary language: Instead of denoting conversion from paganism, Paul lets it denote apostasy back to it.[29] He also indicates this by a Reduplication of the term πάλιν, emphasizing it the second time by connecting it with the almost synonymous term ἄνωθεν.[30] It is clear from 4:10 that it is Jewish obedience to law with its claim for calendar observance that Paul attacks: "You observe days, and months, and seasons, and years!"[31]

---

[24]Cf. Lightfoot:133; Oepke:100; H. D. Betz 1979:131.

[25]Cf. Burton:143–44; Sieffert:136.

[26]Cf. Schlier 1965:119; Mussner:206; Borse 1984:122–23. This accusation will be discussed further in sec. 9.3.4b below.

[27]Cf. the topic *Examining together*, which according to Aristotle is ". . . when something contrary to what has already been done is on the point of being done, consists in examining them together (ἅμα σκοπεῖν)" (Arist. *Rhet.* II.xxiii.27). H. D. Betz 1979:216 rather takes it as a Dilemma.

[28]See especially Rohde:180 for this. It is not necessary for us to enter into the debate of the disputed meaning of στοιχεῖα (Cf. the overview by Mussner:293–97), since Paul's point of setting both the στοιχεῖα, the pagan gods, and Jewish obedience to law on equal footing is clear enough.

[29]Cf. H. D. Betz 1979:216; Rohde:180 and the figure of Metaphor in *ad Herenn.* IV.xxxiv.45.

[30]Cf. for this rhetorical figure *ad Herenn.* IV.xxviii.38 and Bullinger:264–65. Also Burton:232 has made similar observations.

[31]Cf. Zahn:209–11; Lightfoot:171; Sieffert:238–39; Burton:233–34; Oepke:139; Bruce:205–206; Rohde:181–82. The wording is very close to Gen 1:14, a verse which is often connected to calendar observance in Jewish texts, cf. Lührmann 1980. Some phrases do not smoothly fit this reference, however, cf. the discussion of καιροί and παρατηρεῖν in Lührmann 1980:430–31. Paul may therefore use general descriptions

In 4:11 Paul amplifies the seriousness by a conventional *appeal to pity*: He describes himself as bewildered and resigned, since his whole missionary work seems to have been in vain (εἰκῇ, cf. 3:4).[32]

Also in the *dissuasio* we find these themes. In 5:4, 7-8 they are openly expressed in a way that causes few exegetical problems. The theme of apostasy occurs in 5:4, where Paul warns the Galatians about the consequences of circumcision: "You are severed from Christ (κατηργήθητε ἀπὸ Χριστοῦ), you who would be justified by the law; you have fallen away from grace (τῆς χάριτος ἐξεπέσατε)." Paul both opens and closes the verse with references to apostasy. The effect is underscored by a transposition of words so the synonymous verbs are placed first and last in the sentence.[33]

The theme of seduction occurs in 5:7-8. Again we find a transposition of words, this time with similar words ending the first clause and starting the next: "Who hindered you from obeying the truth (πείθεσθαι)? This persuasion (ἡ πεισμονή) is not from him who called you." The opponents are first accused of hindering obedience toward the truth, a clear act of seduction. Then Paul draws on *Paronomasia* and introduces the ambiguous word πεισμονή.[34] Although this term may design "obedience," it is clear in this context that Paul takes it to denote a negative "persuasion."[35] The question is an obvious Understatement:[36] When the persuasion is not from God (= the one who called, cf. 1:6), the audience is invited to reflect about its real source, and Paul may very well imply that it is demonic (cf. 3:1).[37]

To conclude: The themes of apostasy and seduction do not only surround the anathemas of 1:8-9, but 3:1-4; 4:8-11, and 5:4, 7-8 all give

---

which also may include pagan superstition (cf. Lührmann 1980:431, 443; Duncan:137; Mussner:298-303; H. D. Betz 1979:218), and thus also in this subtle way denote Judaism as a kind of paganism (cf. for this polemical effect Duncan:137; Barclay 1988:63-64).

[32]Cf. for conventional appeals to pity Cic. *Inv.* I.lv.106 - lvi.109. Gal 4:11 seems to correspond to his sixth and tenth pieces of advice: One can show that one is in distress contrary to all expectation, or one can reveal one's helplessness and weakness.

[33]Cf. the rhetorical figure Hyperbaton in *ad Herenn.* IV.xxxii.44. As in Gal 1:6, Paul does not regard this apostasy as having been fulfilled, cf. his confidence in 5:10a: "I have confidence in the Lord that you will take no other view than mine."

[34]Cf. the similarity between πείθειν and πεισμονή which is noted also by Lightfoot:205; Oepke:159-60; Bligh:429; Schlier 1965:236; Rohde:220. The rhetorical figure is presented in *ad Herenn.* IV.xxi.29-xxii.30. Bengel:748 regards the terms as so identical that he classifies the figure as *diaphora*, a figure where a similar change of meaning is utilized.

[35]Cf. H. D. Betz 1979:265. The ambiguity of πεισμονή (which I take in the active sense as most scholars do) is discussed by Sieffert:290-92; Burton:283.

[36]Cf. *ad Herenn.* IV.xxxviii.50 for the figure λιτότης.

[37]Cf. Luther 27:33-35; H. D. Betz 1979:265; Schlier 1965:236; Mussner:356; Bruce:234; Duncan:158. Bengel:748 implies the evil influence of the opponents.

evidence that they constitute Paul's Amplification of the situation throughout the letter. The first audience is not given any chance to forget how serious Paul perceives their situation to be.

9.2.2: A double anathema (1:8–9)

The change from *ἐάν-eventualis* to *εἴ-realis* between 1:8 and 1:9, shows that only the last verse utters the factual curse. Nevertheless it is appropriate to understand it as a double anathema, since the reduplication in 1:8–9 is important for the perception of its authority.

a: Rhetorical constructions in 1:8–9

A close look at the rhetoric of the double anathema will reveal that it is bound to be perceived as a powerful curse by the audience in Galatia. This is due both to its reduplication, its implied logic, and its authority.

The figure of *expolitio* with *reduplicatio* is most striking for an audience.[38] It is introduced solemnly the second time: "As we have said before, so now I say again." Thus it is clear to everyone that the anathema is more than an emotional outburst; it is composed of carefully constructed sentences in order to serve a specific aim (Bengel:730). With reduplication Paul underscores both the current crime and its sanction: a) It is most impressive in the apodosis, when Paul ends both clauses with an identical "let him be accursed (ἀνάθεμα ἔστω)!"; b) It is also present in the protasis, denoting the crime; "preach to you a gospel contrary to . . ." (Bullinger:271). Paul twice refers to the cursed action with the term εὐαγγελίζεσθαι, he twice refers to a preaching among you (ὑμῖν[39] and ὑμᾶς), and he twice defines this preaching as "contrary to (παρ' ὅ)" his gospel. Thus the discourse underscores the theme of seduction from 1:7b. Paul defines the false teaching as contrary to his own teaching by the preposition παρά — which may indicate that it is diametrically opposed to his Gospel (Oepke:51), but it may

---

[38]According to *ad Herenn.* IV.xlii.54: "Refining (*expolitio*) consists in dwelling on the same topic and yet seeming to say something ever new." When this is done by repetition, one should "not repeat the same thing precisely — for that, to be sure, would weary the hearer and not refine the idea — but with changes." Cf. also *reduplicatio*, which is "the repetition of one or more words for the purpose of Amplification . . . . The reiteration of the same word makes a deep impression upon the hearer and inflicts a major wound upon the opposition — as if a weapon should repeatedly pierce the same part of the body" (*ad Herenn.* IV.xxviii.38).

[39]The first ὑμῖν in 1:8 is text-critically uncertain. There are strong arguments for including it, however, cf. the editions of Nestlé and UBS (which include it in brackets) and Metzger:590. If deleted, a reference to the preaching "to you" is present anyhow in the last part of the protasis of 1:8.

also indicate that it goes beyond it.[40] It may therefore not appear as a false Gospel to the Galatians, but it is, quite definitely, judged to be so by Paul.

The figure of *expolitio* is also characterized by a repetition with changes of words: a) The hypothetical ἐάν clause in 1:8 is followed by an εἴ clause in 1:9 which introduces the real case;[41] b) The relation between the Galatians and the Gospel is climactically described: In 1:8 Paul writes that the Gospel has been preached among them (εὐηγγελισάμεθα ὑμῖν), and in 1:9 he writes that they have also received it (παρελάβετε). The seduction is thus not only against a Gospel they have heard about, but against a Gospel they have received as the true one;[42] c) Lastly Paul also changes the subjects of the act of seduction. In the hypothetical 1:8 he refers to his own missionary team and to an angel from heaven, but 1:9 only refers to the impersonal τις. This change is the most important for the implied logic of the double anathema.

First we may underscore that the change of subjects between 1:8 and 1:9 conforms to the conventional topic *From the more and less* (ἐκ τοῦ μᾶλλον καὶ ἧττον).[43] The greater examples are rendered in 1:8: Paul first puts himself and his co-workers under the anathema.[44] Such a move demonstrates that Paul himself is bound by the same obligation that he wants to impose on others (Mussner:60). Paul next issues the anathema against an angel from heaven. This move is also striking, since Paul must have strong confidence in his Gospel in order to dare to curse an angel.[45] The implied logic between

---

[40]Cf. the careful discussion of παρά by Burton:27-28: "The translation 'other than' is not quite accurate, because it suggests any variation whatever from Paul's message. 'Contrary to' slightly exaggerates this idea of contrariety, suggesting direct contradiction. 'Not in accordance with' or 'at variance with' seems to come nearest to expressing the idea of the Greek." Cf. Schlier 1965:40; Bruce:83; Rohde:43.

[41]Cf. Schlier 1965:40; Mussner:59, 61; H. D. Betz 1979:50, 52. See also Rohde:42, 45 who distinguishes between the unreal possibility and the real case, and H. D. Betz 1979:54 who takes the second anathema to actualize the first.

[42]Cf. Luther 26:56; Mussner:61-62; Ebeling:82-83 for an emphasis on this aspect.

[43]Cf. Sieffert:34 and Arist. *Rhet.* II.xxiii.4 for this topic. Also Ebeling:82 regards 1:8 as "alle andere Möglichkeiten überbietener." Cf. further Wiles:127 and also Bullinger:427 for the reference to an angel as a hyperbolical Hypothesis.

[44]For ἡμεῖς referring also to Paul's co-workers, cf. Sieffert:34; Lightfoot:77; H. D. Betz 1979:52. It is common to take the plural as a plural of the author, however, cf. Oepke:51; Schlier 1965:39; Rohde:45, a difference of no importance to our interpretation.

[45]The presence of the angel has caused many problems for interpreters of Galatians. Most scholars note its rhetorical function, cf. Oepke:52; Burton:26; Borse 1984:49; U. B. Müller:198. It is possible (but hardly probable) that Paul may allude to a claim by the opponents of having received angelic inspiration, cf. H. D. Betz 1979:53; Ellis 1974:138.

Paul does not refer to the angel as Satan in disguise as in 2 Cor 11:3, 13-15, contra Neyrey:86, 89, 96-97. It is improbable that Paul shifts from a hypothetical anathema on himself to a "witchcraft accusation" in the same sentence. It is true that ἄγγελος is an ambiguous figure, and this is probably why Paul denotes it as an angel ἐξ οὐρανοῦ, in order to underscore the fact that he uses it in a positive way.

1:8 and 1:9 thus seems to be: If Paul regards the seduction as so dangerous that he will even uphold the anathema in the former two examples, he will certainly also impose it on the opponents in Galatia ($\tau\iota\varsigma$ in 1:9, cf. $\tau\iota\nu\acute{\epsilon}\varsigma$ in 1:7).[46] It also seems that the rhetorical figure of *Synecdoche* is implied here.[47] By referring to the examples of himself/his co-workers on the one end, and to an angel from heaven on the other, the whole field of possible seduction is implied. The effect is that all seducers are included in the anathema, an effect that is underscored by the general $\tau\iota\varsigma$ in 1:9.[48]

Second we may underscore that the change of subjects also concerns the authority behind the curse. This authority is emphasized in 1:9a when it is stated that "As we have said before, so now I say again." We may note that Paul includes a "we" in the sentence, thus implying that the curse is sanctioned by a larger group. We may also note the prefix $\pi\rho o$- in the verb. This may indicate that the curse is amplified not only as a repetition of 1:8,[49] but also as corresponding to a warning given on an earlier occasion.[50]

More important for the authority are the subjects in 1:8, however: a) When Paul includes himself in the anathema, this seems to be equal to a promissory oath.[51] The implication is that the curse has a higher authority than himself; b) When he also dares to curse an angel, it is clear to everyone that the authority behind this anathema must be God himself, who is the only one who stands above the angels and who might make a curse effective on heavenly beings; c) The implication of this is that the factual curse on the opponents in 1:9 is a curse sanctioned by God!

We may safely assume that not all of these rhetorical features will be perceived by everyone in the audience. It is more probable that different persons will perceive different aspects, but they will all certainly be deeply impressed by the divine authority of the double anathema.

---

[46]It is not explicitly stated in 1:9 that the opponents are hit by the curse, but this is clear by its relation to 1:7 and by Paul's use of impersonal pronouns to denote the opponents elsewhere in the letter.

[47]Cf. *ad Herenn.* IV.xxxiii.44 for this figure which "occurs when the whole is known from a small part or a part from the whole."

[48]Cf. Luther 26:56; Sieffert:34; Ebeling:82 for similar observations.

[49]Contra Bengel:730; Schlier 1965:40; Bruce:84; Behnisch:246.

[50]It is especially the $\mathring{\alpha}\rho\tau\iota$ $\pi\acute{\alpha}\lambda\iota\nu$ that indicates such temporal distance. Cf. for this view Sieffert:35; Zahn:51; Lightfoot:78; Oepke:52; Burton:29; Bligh:90; Mussner:61; H. D. Betz 1979:53–54; Rohde:44–45.

[51]Cf. Bligh:87–88. Luther 26:55 observes that Paul curses himself first in order to be able to reprove others more freely and severely. We may also refer to Josephus' reference in *Vita* 101: "He ended with oaths and horrible imprecations, by which he thought to gain credit for the statements in his letter." It is natural to take this as a reference to the effect that self-imprecations may have.

b: The impact of deuteronomistic traditions on 1:8-9

According to Iser, any reading of a text involves a tension between foreground and background (155-61). Authors select particular elements from a tradition which they make present in the text itself, knowing that those who read the text also will infer the background from which these elements have been selected, if it is familiar to them. The question is now whether the double anathema is connected to such a background which may become activated among the first readers of the letter together with the anathema itself.

'Aνάθεμα as a curse is found only in Jewish tradition. The only known exception is a pagan curse table from Megara, but also this table seems to reveal Jewish influence (cf. the discussion above sec. 6.2.2). The possible background must therefore be sought in Jewish tradition. In part I of this study we compared the semantic field of 1:6-9 to the semantic fields of Jewish texts of curse and חרם/ἀνάθεμα. The discussion in sec. 6.3 led us to consider the Deut 27-30 tradition combined with Deut 13 as a probable background for the double anathema.[52]

Such a proposal is not without problems:

> a) The form of Gal 1:8-9 is found in curse texts from the Deut 27-30 tradition, but there we do not find the ἀνάθεμα term.
> b) The term is present in Deut 13, but there the sanction on the seducers is the death penalty and not a curse.
> c) The semantic similarities are not so obvious as one could wish.

On the other hand we can argue:

> a) If one looks for Jewish curse texts with such divine authority that even angels may be cursed, there is no real alternative to covenantal curses.
> b) If one looks for severe legislation against false teachers in the Hebrew Bible, there is no real alternative to Deut 13.
> c) We may argue that the difference between Deut 27-30 texts using curse terms, while Gal 1:8-9 employs ἀνάθεμα, is not important, since these traditions seem to have converged at the time of Paul (cf. sec. 6.2.2).
> d) We may further argue that the difference between the death penalty — which is underscored in Deut 13 — and anathema/curse is of minor importance, since the death penalty in the course of time often was replaced by curse and excommunication as a preparation for the judgment of God (cf. sec. 6.3.5).
> e) A combination between Deut 27-30 and Deut 13 is explicitly found also in Josephus (*Ant* 4:309-10).

If we summarize the details in the semantic correspondence between Gal 1:6-9 and covenantal curses/Deut 13, we may underscore the text like this (spaced underlining for correspondences that are not so explicit):

---

[52]Cf. H. D. Betz 1979:51 who draws on 1QS ii.5-17, and Mussner:60 who draws on Deut 27:15-26; 29:19-20. For a reference to Deut 13, cf. Sandnes:70-73.

⁶Θαυμάζω ὅτι οὕτως ταχέως <u>μετατίθεσθε ἀπὸ τοῦ καλέσαντος</u>
<u>ὑμᾶς</u> ἐν χάριτι [Χριστοῦ] <u>εἰς ἕτερον</u> εὐαγγέλιον,
⁷ὃ οὐκ ἔστιν ἄλλο·
  εἰ μή τινές εἰσιν οἱ ταράσσοντες ὑμᾶς
  καὶ θέλοντες μεταστρέψαι τὸ εὐαγγέλιον τοῦ Χριστοῦ.
⁸ἀλλὰ καὶ
  <u>ἐὰν ἡμεῖς ἢ ἄγγελος ἐξ οὐρανοῦ</u>
  εὐαγγελίζηται [<u>ὑμῖν</u>] <u>παρ' ὃ</u> εὐηγγελισάμεθα <u>ὑμῖν</u>,
  <u>ἀνάθεμα ἔστω.</u>
⁹ὡς προειρήκαμεν, καὶ ἄρτι πάλιν λέγω,
  <u>εἴ τις ὑμᾶς</u> εὐαγγελίζεται <u>παρ' ὃ</u> παρελάβετε,
  <u>ἀνάθεμα ἔστω.</u>

If we leave aside the introductory formulas of 1:6a and 1:9a, and the amplification of the accusation in 1:7, we have one accusation in 1:6b and two anathemas in 1:8, 9b with the following correspondences (cf. the arguments above sec. 6.3):

The accusation μετατίθεσθε ἀπὸ τοῦ καλέσαντος ὑμᾶς in 1:6 corresponds to the crime in Deut 13, which is one of πλάνειν ἀπὸ κυρίου τοῦ θεοῦ (13:5), of ζήτειν ἀποστῆσαι ἀπὸ κυρίου τοῦ θεοῦ (13:10), and of ἀφιστῆναι πάντας (13:13). Paul uses a synonymous verb and has paraphrased the reference to God. Further, the general theme of apostasy is primarily connected with the covenantal curse tradition.

The reference εἰς ἕτερον εὐαγγέλιον in 1:6 corresponds to the apostasy in Deut 13, which is described as one of serving θεοῖς ἑτέροις (13:2, 6, 13).

The casuistic εἰ/ἐάν form with the second person plural is only found in Deut 27–30 texts, as are the majority of legal curses in any form. It is also found in Deut 13:2 ("arises among you," cf. 13:15). This correspondence may be accidental, however, since Paul also in 1:6 and 1:11 has similar references to ὑμᾶς/ὑμῖν.

We find a similar use of παρά to define the crime, compare παράνομοι in Deut 13:13 (LXX) with παρ' ὃ εὐηγγελισάμεθα in Gal 1:8 and a similar expression in 1:9.

Metonymous expressions similar to ἀνάθεμα εἶναι are typical marks of the Deut 27–30 tradition.

The element of curse in self-imprecations and curses on angelic beings also lead to covenantal curses. It is only these curses which carry such authority that they are used to bind oneself together with the whole people, and which also in Qumran occasionally are used to curse heavenly beings.

We may further note that the structure of Gal 1:8–9 seems to be similar to the structure of Deut 27:15–26: The Hebrew Bible text consists of 11 curses on different major crimes. The point is to cover the whole field of morality with representative examples,[53] a feature similar to the rhetorical figure of *Synecdoche*. This aim is underscored by the general curse on any lawbreaker that concludes the text.

It is possible to object against this list of correspondences that it is not specific enough to persuade, and that it has not been possible to demonstrate precise enough correspondences with Jewish texts belonging to a well-defined

---

[53] Cf. sec. 4.1.2a above for Deut 27:15–26.

tradition. The correspondences are more general and presuppose a general fusion of the Deut 27–30 and Deut 13 traditions. On the other hand we may point to the small number of חרם/ἀνάθεμα texts from the post-Hebrew Bible period as part of an explanation. It is further notable that all remaining elements of Gal 1:6b, 8, 9b refer to the Gospel (cf. χάρις [Χριστοῦ] in 1:6; εὐαγγέλιον/εὐαγγελίζεσθαι in 1:6b, 8, 9b, and παραλαμβάνειν in 1:9b). Thus it may make sense that Paul has alluded to deuteronomistic traditions, but changed them at one important point, substituting the law with the gospel.

The double anathema claims to carry divine authority by its hypothetical inclusion of angels from heaven. Its severity is therefore to be taken for granted whether a background in deuteronomistic traditions is perceived or not. If one looks for a scriptural basis for such a curse and such a reaction against false teachers, however, no real alternative to covenantal curses and the law of Deut 13 seems to exist.

Once this connection is made among the readers of the letter, however, one problem becomes important: Paul deviates radically from Jewish tradition by substituting the gospel for the law.[54] The function of the Hebrew Bible traditions is to guard the law, while Paul makes it guard the gospel of Christ. Although such deviation is radical and unconventional, a construction of an analogy to deuteronomistic texts is rather conventional:

In a Jewish setting we find many examples of such analogies: Analogies to the curses of Deut 27–30 have been found in Jer 11:3; 17:5; Mal 1:14; *2 Enoch* 52; *Bib. Ant.* 26:5, and the liturgical curses in Qumran (cf. secs. 4.1.2cd). As for Deut 13, the chapter itself is constructed of three analogies: 11QTemple 54–55 demonstrates that also the analogous law of Deut 17:2–7 is connected to Deut 13; different renderings of the law were found in CD 12:2–3, in Philo (*Spec Leg* I:315–18), and in Josephus (*Ant* 4:309–10; cf. sec. 6.3.6).

In ancient rhetoric this would correspond to the *stasis of Reasoning from Analogy* (*syllogismus*; cf. sec. 8.6.2 above): When a case arises that lacks a specifically applicable law, an analogy is established from other existing laws on the basis of certain similarities. An employment of this stasis would explain why Paul would find it important to allude to deuteronomistic traditions, because they would be his legal basis. It would also explain why Paul made his innovations, because he transferred the deuteronomistic traditions to a case where it has not been employed before.

The unexpected feature of the double anathema is thus not the allusion to deuteronomistic traditions, but rather its deviations from certain vital ele-

---

[54]For deviation as a literary technique, cf. Iser:145–55 and the observations above for Gal 1:6–7.

ments therein: Paul utters curses not on lawbreakers, but on persons who preach obedience toward the law. This deviation is considerable, and it will cause bewilderment among the audience about its legitimacy. We will return to this point below (cf. sec. 9.3.3), when we consider the pragmatic aspect of the text.

9.2.3: Refutations (1:10–12)

It is common to regard 1:10–12 as containing refutations, and most scholars see these verses as Paul's defense against factual charges from the opponents. It is not necessary to imply such charges, however, since it is a rhetorical custom also to rebut invented charges in order to emphasize one's own character.[55] The verses are in fact easier to interpret if we regard them as connected to the double anathema. This does not mean that I deny that charges may have existed, but rather that I do not regard this possibility as important for an interpretation.

1:10a: The first question of 1:10 is a *crux interpretum* which is much easier to comprehend in connection with 1:9: "For am I now (ἄρτι) persuading men or God (ἀνθρώπους πείθω ἢ τὸν θεόν)?"[56] The ἄρτι refers to the preceding verses,[57] and thus it refers to a double objection that may arise naturally out of the anathemas.[58] If the legitimacy of the anathemas is questionable, it is natural to ask if Paul issues them in order to persuade by illegitimate means.

When Paul actualizes Hebrew Bible inspired curses contrary to their Hebrew Bible intention, does he himself act as a seducer, as a person who seeks to persuade men by illegitimate means?[59] Just as Paul in 1:8 included himself in the anathema, in 1:10a he turns also the accusation of seduction toward himself. Paul clearly implies the answer to be negative, but we should not too hastily assume that his first audience immediately would do the same.

When Paul puts his opponents under a curse, does he act as a religious

---

[55]Cf. G. Lyons:105–12 and examples from Cynic philosophers in Malherbe 1970: 214–17.

[56]Translation by H. D. Betz 1979:44.

[57]Cf. Bengel:730; Lightfoot:79; Burton:30; Oepke:53; Mussner:63; G. Lyons:145. It is not necessary to imply charges that have been formerly raised against Paul, but which are refuted now.

[58]A similar interpretation is found in Brown:49; H. D. Betz 1979:54–55; Ebeling:86–88; Lüdemann:51; cf. also Schlier 1965:41–42; Becker:15; C. -N. Kim:42–44; Lategan:176. The connections to 1:8–9 are not underscored in the same way by these scholars, however.

[59]For πείθειν in this negative sense as a current topic in antiquity, cf. H. D. Betz 1979:54–55 and Lüdemann:51.

charlatan who tries to persuade God by magic, spells, and the like?[60] Again Paul implies a negative answer, since his curse does not stem from the personal sphere of magical sorcery, but rather conforms with the will of God. Paul's first audience, however, might still hesitate in their judgment. Thus 1:10a underscores the legitimacy of the anathemas. Paul challenges his audience to regard him neither as a seducer nor as a sorcerer, but rather to give due attention to his curses![61]

1:10b: The next charge which Paul takes up is the accusation of being a flatterer: "Or am I trying to please men (ἢ ζητῶ ἀνθρώποις ἀρέσκειν)?"[62] After the anathemas of 1:8-9 it seems impossible to accuse Paul of acting as a flatterer. Paul refutes this charge by emphasizing its unreal consequence: "If I were still pleasing men, I should not be a servant of Christ."[63] Thus his use of anathemas is implicitly defended: He has acted out of motives quite different from the pleasing of human beings——rather by obedience as a servant of Christ.

1:11-12: In 1:8-9 Paul cursed those who perverted the Gospel as preached by him. This makes it necessary not only to establish the *ethos* of Paul as in 1:10, but also to underscore the authority of the Gospel. Paul now

---

[60]Cf. H. D. Betz 1979:54-55 and Lüdemann:51 for this as a current topic in antiquity. Also Bruce:85 interprets the expression in this way.

[61]The problem with this interpretation is that it seems forced to use the term πείθειν for such magical compulsion of God. This has led several scholars to take πείθειν to mean to "seek favor of," cf. the RSV translation: "Am I now seeking the favor of men, or of God?" (cf. Sieffert:36-37; Burton:30-31; Rohde:46-47). The implied answers are "no" and "yes" respectively.

Another solution is to regard the question as a ζεῦγμα, a figure where one verb is connected to two phrases, but only applies to one of them. Thus we have to imply another verb in the second clause, for example, that the verb ἀρέσκειν is anticipated: Am I now persuading men or seeking favor of God? (cf. BDR par 479,2 for this figure, and Oepke:53-54; Mussner:63 for this solution). Borse 1984:51 rather implies verbs such as "obey" or "serve" in the second part of the question). Again the implied answer is "yes" the last time.

It is not forced to relate πείθειν to a magical compulsion of God, however. This is clearly demonstrated in Josephus even for the concept of curse. In *Ant* 4:123 he refers to the following statement by Balaam: He wants to offer sacrifices "if perchance I may persuade God (εἰ πείσαι τὸν θεόν) to suffer me to bind these people under a curse."

[62]For this figure in antiquity, cf. again H. D. Betz 1979:55 and Lüdemann:51-52.

This charge may be factual, since Paul in the next clause uses ἔτι ("If I were still"). We may imply a charge from the opponents here, cf. Burton 33-34; Mussner:64; Borgen 1982:41. On the other hand the ἔτι may stand in contrast to Paul's past as a Pharisee (cf. Burton:33-34; Mussner:64; H. D. Betz 1979:56; G. Lyons:147-48), or only denote a theological contrast (cf. Oepke:54).

[63]It is a *modus tollens*-argument: Since Paul is sure that the second clause is false, he uses this antecedent to refute the truth of the εἰ-clause, cf. for such logic R. A. Young:41-42. See also G. Lyons:143.

takes up "the gospel which was preached by me (τὸ εὐαγγέλιον τὸ εὐαγγελισθὲν ὑπ' ἐμοῦ)," and he underscores its reliability by the rhetorical figure *expeditio*. Paul wants to highlight that it "is not man's gospel" (1:11b). According to this figure he then eliminates two human sources for it, in order to underscore its divine origin:[64] "For I did not receive it from man, nor was I taught it, but it came to me through a revelation of Jesus Christ" (1:12).[65]

To sum up: We have now seen how 1:10–12 functions as a transitional unit between the *exordium* and the *narratio*. In these verses Paul underscores the legitimacy of his curses both by defending his own *ethos* and by emphasizing the divine origin of the Gospel. Thus, it seems that the double anathema is of major importance to him, and it is time to reflect upon its pragmatic aspects.

9.3: Force and effects of the double anathema

According to a distinction in the Speech Act Theory presented above in section 1.4, every utterance involves both meaning, illocutionary force, and intended effects. Some utterances may be classified as performatives in the sense that they are part of an institutional procedure. In such cases their illocutionary force is closely bound to their specific setting. Other utterances are not part of such institutional frames. The double anathema belongs to this latter group, since we do not know of any such institutional framework that may explain its force. In these cases we have to consult social conventions connected to the utterance on a broad scale in order to determine their illocutionary force.

Up until now we have only interpreted the meaning of the double anathema. Its illocutionary force is also important to consider, since by this curse Paul urges his audience actually to regard the opponents as cursed persons. By the solemn curse he puts before the audience a serious challenge: They must not overlook the implicit demand radically to change their perception of the teachers. Before we can pursue this pragmatic aspect further, however, we need to review some basic features regarding the function of curses in the cultural environment of Paul and the Galatian churches.

---

[64]Cf. for this figure *ad Herenn*. IV.xxix.40: It "occurs when we have enumerated the several ways by which something could have been brought about, and all are then discarded except the one on which we are insisting." Also C. -N. Kim:55–67 takes 1:12 as a contrast-statement in order to emphasize 1:12b. Cf. *ibid* 67–120 for an extensive discussion of the content of 1:12b.

[65]The same figure is also employed above in 1:1. Bullinger:333 has also noted that Paul plays upon the synonymity between *receive* and *teach*.

9.3.1: Curse and conventions in Greek and Jewish culture

According to W. Speyer, the concept of curse and blessing functions in similar ways in different cultures. For this reason, similarities may throw mutual light on each other (1163). He has collected a substantial amount of material concerning curse in Greek and Roman culture (1174–1228) which, according to Little (184), is the most extensive presentation of this material. Although Speyer observes that the magical worldview was challenged by a more rational and scientific approach from the 4th century BCE onward, magical belief seems to have been important for ordinary people during the entire Hellenistic period. This holds true especially for Asia Minor, which is the region that is primarily of interest to us (1222–28).[66] Curses also function in a similar manner as in Jewish covenantal traditions: It is common to draw on curses as sanctions for securing important taboos of the community, sacred laws, or important moral norms. We also find that religious communities of different kinds frequently secured their special laws by curses (1180, 1204–7; cf. also Wiefel:229–31). In our brief review of conventional expectations connected to curses, we may therefore note the correspondence between Greek and Jewish culture and then substantiate it with observations in our Jewish material from different periods.[67]

First, we find that the *belief in the power of curses* was strong in both cultures. In Greek culture, curses were even portrayed as demonic beings with a life of their own (Speyer:1196; Hempel:75–76). This belief could go so far that it caused a fear of uttering the curse: Thus self-imprecations could take the form of conditional blessings (Hempel:34).

We also find this conviction in Jewish literature.[68] An illustrative example is the curse on the rebuilder of Jericho which Joshua laid down in Josh 6:26. When Hiel of Bethel rebuilt Jericho, this curse at once became effective (cf. 1 Kgs 16:34). The same thought underlies the curses of Deut 27:15–26: Once a man becomes guilty of one of these crimes, the curse becomes effective on him. The curse is especially effective when uttered from a parent, a prophet, or a particularly spiritual man (cf. the example of Balaam in Num 22–24).[69]

---

[66]During the time of persecutions in Antiquity, Christians were often accused of being cursed and treated as such, cf. Speyer:1217–22, 1227–28. This clearly indicates that the concept of curse was current during the whole period, including at the time of Paul.

[67]In addition to Speyer, I will also utilize observations from Greek material in Hempel 1925. It is Pedersen 1914 and Hempel 1925 who have collected the most evidence of this pragmatic aspect from Hebrew Bible texts, while Hunzinger 1954 and Horbury 1985 have made important observations concerning rabbinic texts.

[68]Cf. Pedersen 1914:87–88 for the following. See also Hempel:26–27.

[69]Cf. Pedersen 1914:93; 1926:442; Scharbert 1958a:6; Hempel:77–80.

After the curse is uttered, it has to find its victim, and it hits the one who deserves it (Pedersen 1914:89). We may compare Gen 27:13, where Rebekah utters an oath that the curse may come upon her if Isaac curses Jacob. We may also compare Sir 21:27, where it is stated that an illegitimate curse will fall back on the one who utters it: "When an ungodly man curses his adversary, he curses his own soul."

Evidence for this efficacy is also found in later texts. In *T. Judah* 11:4 a pronunciation of a curse causes death. In *Lives Proph.* 22:13 it is stated that when Elisha cursed his servant, he became a leper. In Qumran we find a prescription that a man who utters a curse when he should not do it commits a crime so serious that he has to be expelled (1QS vii.1-2).[70] In the Talmud, we find that *bMak.* 11a even testifies that some Rabbis could argue that the curse of a sage, though uttered without cause, would take effect.

Second, curses were regarded as an *evil, poisonous substance which occupies humans*, destroys them from inside, and makes them a threat to their environments. In short: Curse is a negation of life.[71] In Greek culture it is attested that an accursed person is regarded as a threat against his environment, and that all persons or things that are connected to him also come under the curse (Speyer:1181; Hempel:30-31, 35).

Many Jewish texts describe the curse as penetrating into the body. In Num 5:27 the effects of the curse water on the guilty woman are that "her body shall swell, and her thigh shall fall away, and the woman shall become an execration among her people." Ps 109:18 can say that the curse may "soak into his body like water, like oil into his bones." Therefore both Num 5:21, 27 and Deut 21:23 can identify people as a curse in a metonymic way.[72] In Deut 28:21 it is stated that "the Lord will make the pestilence cleave to you until he has consumed you off the land" (cf. further for bodily sickness 28:22, 28, 35, 59b-61, 65).

This aspect is also found in many intertestamental texts. Philo states that curses will "linger and waste both soul and body" (*Praem* 136, cf. also the vivid descriptions of *Praem* 143-46, 151), he connects curse and pollution (*Spec* 2:50), and he describes the effect of the curse water of Num 5 in this

---

[70]Cf. Forkman:46. Lohse translates: "Und wenn er einen Fluch ausgesprochen hat (קלל), etwa weil er durch eine Notlage verängstigt war, oder welchen Anlass er auch haben mag, und er liest im Buch oder spricht den Segensspruch (ברך), so soll man ihn ausschliessen." The translation in *DSSE*: "If any man has uttered the (Most) Venerable Name even though frivolously" seems to be too free in relation to the curse-blessing terminology.

[71]Pedersen 1914:64, 71-72. Cf. also his 1926:437, 442-43.

[72]This metonymic use of curse denotes more than Scharbert seems to allow, cf. his 1958a:12 and *TWAT* 1:283: The woman and man have become a curse, not only partakers in a fate so horrifying that later they will become referred to in curse formulas.

way: One lays oneself open to every curse, and "the signs of their fulfilment thou wilt exhibit in thy body" (*Spec* 3:61).

A cursed man is a danger to his surroundings, since the curse is believed to radiate from the man or from the place where it is settled.[73] According to Deut 21:23 the body of the cursed man must not remain all night upon the tree, since "you shall not defile the land." According to Deut 29:18 the presence of an accursed man within the people "would lead to the sweeping away of moist and dry alike." Both Achan (cf. Josh 6:18; 7:11-12 with the חרם term) and Jonathan (cf. 1 Sam 14:24-46 with the ארר term) are examples of cursed men who were thought to bring the curse also to their fellow countrymen.

Philo states that the effects of curses will be that "whole families will waste away . . . cities will be suddenly left stripped of inhabitants" (*Praem* 133). He states that when Canaan was laid under a curse, he became "a source of misery for his successors" (*Virt* 202). In *3 Apoc. Bar.* 4:8 it is stated that when God cursed the wine, "he did not permit Adam to touch it." Josephus reports of the return of Antipater that "no one came near him or greeted him . . . . On the contrary, they did not restrain themselves from receiving him with curses" (Ant 17:88).

Also the rabbinic traditions bear witness to this view of curse. According to *bMoᶜed Qat.* 17a the חרם enters the body like a curse, "it penetrates the two hundred and forty eight joints (on one's body)" (Horbury:35-36). A banned person is therefore treated like a leper according to special rules, which according to *bMoᶜed Qat.* 16a entails that all should keep a distance of at least eight feet from him (Hunzinger 1954:49-50; *TRE* 5:163).

Third, we find that the normal reaction against an accursed person is *expulsion from the community*. It is important to drive him away from one's midst. In Greek culture a ban is more frequent than the death sentence, since death was seen rather as caused by the expulsion and curse, as a penalty effectuated by the gods (Speyer:1179, 1181, 1184-88).[74]

Also in Jewish culture the normal reaction is to expel the accursed person from society and therefore to surrender the sinner over to the sphere of misfortune and death (Pedersen 1914:65-66, 78-79; Hempel:30, 36). This feature is reflected in the curses of Gen 3:14 and 4:11, where we find the construction "Cursed are you from (ארור מן) . . . ."[75] The fate of such a cursed and expelled men is described in Jer 17:6: "He is like a shrub in the

---

[73]Cf. Pedersen 1914:73-75 for the following. See also Hempel:29-31.

[74]For the *homo sacer* as an outlaw in Roman jurisdiction, cf. Speyer:1183-84. Cf. further Hempel:30.

[75]Cf. Pedersen 1914:68; Scharbert 1958a:5-6; *TWAT* 1:440-41; Schottroff:58-59.

desert . . . . He shall dwell in the parched places of the wilderness, and in an uninhabited salt land. "

In Deut 29:20 the terminology of expulsion is connected to the curse: "And the Lord would single him out (בדל/LXX: διαστελεῖ) from all the tribes of Israel for calamity, in accordance with all the curses . . . ." As noted above, Ezra 10:8 seems to demonstrate that this verse has been connected to Deut 23:2-9 in a way that authorized excommunication of cursed persons in post-exilic Judaism.[76]

In Qumran the clearest example is CD 20:6-8: "But when his deeds are revealed, according to the interpretation of the Law in which the men of perfect holiness walk, let no man defer to him with regard to money or work, for all the Holy Ones of the Most High have cursed him."[77] Compare also 1QS ii.16, where the curse includes the threat to be "cut off from the midst of all the sons of light." Josephus combines ban and curse in *Ant* 7:208; 18:287, and he parallels the curse on Cain with his expulsion (*Ant* 1:58; cf. *Jub.* 4:4).

In the rabbinic period, *bMo'ed Qat.* 16a, 17a depicts the ban as a curse.[78] At the time of Paul the Jewish ban seems to have been practiced as a form of partial exclusion from society: The banned person had to appear as a mourner and as leprous, all contact with other persons had to take place at the distance of eight feet, and certain restrictions concerning contact with other people were also observed.[79] The aim of these measures was to isolate the banned person from normal contact with his fellow Jews.

To sum up: Both in Greek and Jewish culture we find corresponding conventions connected to curse: belief in curse as an effective power when uttered, the effect that the cursed man is possessed by evil and consequently a threat to his surroundings, and a normal reaction of total or partial expulsion.

9.3.2: Pauline curse and conventions

Before we turn to the pragmatic aspects of Gal 1, we have to ask the critical question whether conventions like the ones presented above are likely to be part of Paul's perspective.

a: The relationship between Gal 1:8-9 and Rom 12:14; 3:14

An interpretation of Gal 1:8-9 as an act of effective cursing seems to counter Paul's own exhortation in Rom 12:14: "Bless those who persecute

---

[76]Cf. above sec. 6.3.5 and Horbury:17, 19-20, 30.

[77]Lohse holds the manuscripts A₁ and B separate from each other and tabulates the verses in CD 20:6-8. In *DSSE*, however, our passage is incorporated into column VIII of manuscript A₁.

[78]Cf. the presentation above in sec. 6.2.2. See also Horbury:34-38; Hunzinger 1954:46.

[79]Cf. Hunzinger 1954:47-51; *TRE* 5:163; Forkman:100-105.

you, bless and do not curse them." This appears to be a contradiction, and there have been many attempts to overcome it. Rhode observes (46) that Paul places himself under the curse in Gal 1:8, not only other persons as in Rom 12:14. In addition, he observes (44) that the curse is not placed on any specific persons, so they are given the opportunity to repent and escape it. Behnisch emphasizes (250-51) that the curse in Gal 1:9-9 is laid on persons belonging to the church, and not on outsiders as in Rom 12:14. The most convincing explanation has been extensively argued by W. Wiefel: Rom 12:14 refers to quite a different setting, namely the use of curse for self-protection, either as a sacred means to protect one's own right, or as a means of evil retribution.[80] As noted above, the semantic field of this curse text is different from the semantic field of Galatians (cf. sec. 2.2.1), an observation that corroborates a connection to some other situation. In Rom 12:14, the issue is a persecuted group.[81] This is very different from the context of an authoritative covenantal curse.

Rom 3:14 also refers to a prohibited form of cursing: "Their mouth is full of curses and bitterness." The reference is found in a chain of Hebrew Bible citations (3:10-18) aimed at demonstrating that "all men, both Jews and Greeks, are under the power of sin" (3:9; cf. 3:19). Like in Rom 12:14, the kind of curse to which it refers concerns evil retribution. Note the synonyms to the curses: On one hand the act of cursing is paralleled with evil use of the tongue (cf. 3:13), and on the other hand with the shedding of blood and causing of ruin and misery (3:15-16). Rom 3:13-14 refers to sins from the mouth, and 3:15-16 applies to sins in deeds.[82] The cursing in the context of these verses, then, has a function very different from curse in the context of covenantal tradition.

To conclude: I see no contradiction between Paul's prohibition of cursing in Rom 12:14 and 3:14, and his use of a curse in Gal 1:8-9. In the former texts, Paul prohibits the practice of using curses for evil retribution when the purpose is self-protection. In Gal 1:8-9, in contrast, Paul draws on the dynamics of authoritative covenantal tradition to secure the truth of the Gospel of Christ.

---

[80]Cf. the broad description of this form of curse in Greek culture and Judaism by Wiefel:212-22. Cf. also Speyer:1211-17. A similar observation is made by Ebeling:76, 78.

[81]Cf. Wiefel:221-22. Cf. also Michel 1978:386; Schlier 1977:379 who compare it with the Jewish custom of cursing one's enemies.

Paul probably alludes to a Jesus tradition in this verse (cf. Wilckens 1982:22-23; Dunn 1988a:745 together with most scholars, contrary to Sauer who regards Rom 12:14 as the starting point of the tradition). Luke 6:27-28 and Matt 5:44 also contain similar exhortations within a context of persecution and enmity.

[82]Cf. Michel 1978:143; Koch 1986:179.

b: The curse ceremony of 1 Cor 5

It is not enough to argue that Paul does not oppose the authoritative use of curses. We also have to ask if he in fact has employed it in places other than Galatians. A survey of his remaining anathemas will be given below (cf. sec. 9.4), because at this stage it should suffice to draw on 1 Cor 5.

In 1 Cor 5:4–5 Paul declares that an expulsion of a fornicator shall take place within the assembly in a way that involves the concept of curse.[83] The process has thus come further than in Gal 1:8–9: Paul has "already pronounced judgment (ἤδη κέκρικα)" (5:3). His prescriptions are easy to connect with conventional expectations as presented above:

The reaction of *expulsion* is the dominant perspective of 1 Cor 5 (Wiles:148). The section opens with the admonition: "Let him who has done this be removed from among you (ἀρθῇ ἐκ μέσου ὑμῶν)" (5:2). It closes by citing the Hebrew Bible for the same purpose: "Drive out (ἐξάρατε) the wicked person from among you" (5:13).[84] In addition, it is stated twice that they should not associate (συναναμίγνυσθαι) with such guilty brethren (5:9, 11), not even eat with them (5:11b). The expulsion thus had severe consequences of social isolation.

In 5:5 Paul wants the congregation to *deliver the offender over to the destructive effects of the curse*: "You are to deliver this man to Satan for the destruction of the flesh, that his spirit may be saved in the day of the Lord Jesus."[85] The man is driven from the sphere of blessing over to the sphere of evil and corruption. The curse is considered to work by itself, and Paul may think of material losses, illnesses, and finally death.[86] Since Paul here employs the theological contrast σάρξ/πνεῦμα, it is probably not possible to determine precisely in what way he regards the corruption and salvation to take place.[87]

---

[83]Cf. Weiss:129–31; Brun:106–7; Lietzmann 1949:23; Wiefel:224; Forkman:143–44; Wiles:142–50; Conzelmann:97; Lang:72.

[84]This phrase occurs several places in the LXX, cf. Deut 17:7; 19:19; 21:21; 22:21, 24; 24:7, and Paul's only variation is that he changes the 2nd person singular imperative to 2nd person plural (cf. Koch 1986:18, 102).

[85]This translation involves difficult syntactical problems, cf. the alternative connections of phrases listed by Forkman:141–43; Conzelmann:97. They are of no importance for our purpose, however, since all possibilities emphasize the same aspect: The expulsion is not just an earthly matter, but also the living Lord takes part in it.

[86]Cf. Weiss:131; Barrett 1968:126; Forkman:144, 146; Wiles:148–49; Lang:72. A few scholars immediately relate it to death (cf. Brun:107; Lietzmann 1949:23; Käsemann 1954:252; Wiefel:224–25; Conzelmann:97) which seems too specific, while the proposal that it is only σάρξ as the sinful nature in man that is destroyed (cf. Grosheide:123; Fee:209–13) seems to weaken the severity of the curse too much.

[87]Cf. especially Thiselton for the idea that Paul expresses himself vaguely, posing as much a theological evaluation of the sinner as a concrete description of his fate. Also Forkman:146 is reserved, since he regards the σάρξ-πνεῦμα contrast as baptism language.

In 5:6b we find *the proverb of a little leaven* that ferments the whole lump of dough. Since Paul focuses on persons in 5:4–5, 7, it is natural to take the reference to leaven as an allusion to the cursed person possessed by an evil substance.[88]

To sum up: The above discussion has substantiated that corresponding conventional expectations of the effect of curse are found both in Greek and Jewish culture, and, not surprisingly, in Paul. It should therefore be safe to interpret the pragmatic aspect of the double anathema within this framework.

9.3.3: Force and effects in Galatia

a: The double anathema as a challenge

It is important to distinguish between the illocutionary force of the double anathema and its probable effects, which are normally denoted as perlocutions.[89] All the conventions reviewed above concern perlocutionary effects of curse, and there is sufficient reason to hesitate in applying them too hastily to the Galatian situation: Although Paul aims at these perlocutions, it is by no means certain that they will take effect in Galatia.[90]

It is only the illocutionary force that can be applied to the situation with absolute certainty: The double anathema challenges the Galatian audience to regard the opponents as cursed persons.[91] Such a curse cannot be overlooked

---

The proposal by Collins 1980 is also worth consideration: She connects $\sigma\acute{\alpha}\rho\xi$ to the destruction of the offender, while the salvation of the $\pi\nu\varepsilon\widehat{\upsilon}\mu\alpha$ concerns the perseverance of holiness in the church when the offender has been expelled.

[88]Also Weiss:133–34; Barrett 1968:127–28 and Fee:215 take the leaven to denote the person. This is also considered by Grosheide:124. In 5:8 the leaven is explicitly denoted as "the leaven of malice and evil."

The most natural alternative interpretation is to take it as a reference to sin and uncleanness (Lang:73). It has also been suggested that it could be related, for example, to the old man according to baptismal language (Forkman:148) or to the sin of glorying mentioned in the same verse (Grosheide:124).

[89]Cf. Austin:94–103, 121 for this distinction. It is clearly stated by J. Lyons:731: "By the illocutionary force of an utterance is to be understood its status as a promise, a threat, a request, a statement, an exhortation, etc. By its perlocutionary effect is meant its effect upon the beliefs, attitudes or behaviour of the addressee and, in certain cases, its consequential effect upon some state-of-affairs within the control of the addressee." He warns that the intended perlocutionary effect is generally confused with illocutionary force.

[90]Cf. Austin:105–6 who distinguishes between the attempt to perform a speech act and the successful achievement of it.

[91]Such a challenge is clearly implied by the legal form: When the audience both acknowledges the legitimacy of the curse and also subsumes the opponents under it, they should certainly also make it effective.

We may also test 1:8–9 according to the rules indicating illocutionary force which R. A. Young:37–38 has adopted from J. R. Searle:

  a) The Propositional Content Rule: Paul relates the double anathema to a future

once it has been uttered. The primary pragmatic aspect of the curse is that it puts before the Galatian churches a very serious choice: Either to accept the double anathema as a carrier of divine authority, and thus to isolate the opponents, or to reject it as false, and thus to question the authority of Paul himself. The curse claims to carry divine authority, and therefore it demands to be accepted as such.[92] The only alternative is to reject it as false. Thus the situation cannot be as it was before in Galatia: Once the curse has been uttered, the churches are forced to choose between the authority of Paul and his opponents.

The double anathema is therefore more than a parenetic threat,[93] more than a solemn declaration of the border that no Christian must pass (contra Ebeling:81), and more than a petition to God to fulfill the curse (contra Burton:28). Scholars who claim that it implies an immediate deliverance over to the wrath of God,[94] however, proceed too quickly in their interpretation. They overlook the main purpose of the double anathema: to compel the Galatians to make a radical choice.

b: Probable effects of acceptance

Paul's probable intended effect is, of course, that the Galatians should be persuaded to accept the legitimacy of the anathemas. Then he can reckon with some effects in Galatia which will be completed within the frame of the conventions reviewed above.

The Galatians are urged to regard the opponents as cursed persons, that is, persons standing under the judgment of God, delivered unto the sphere of evil and corruption (Rohde:44). Such persons are to be regarded also as unclean persons, persons possessed by evil and are consequently dangerous

---

action to be taken in Galatia.

  b) The Preparatory Rules: Paul believes that the Galatians can regard the opponents as cursed, and also that they will not do it unless he persuades them.

  c) The Sincerity Rule: Paul wants the opponents to be cursed.

  d) The Essential Rule: The double anathema may be taken as an attempt to make the Galatians act.

  We see then, that although 1:8-9 is not formed as an explicit request to curse the opponents, it fulfills the expectations of an implicit attempt to obtain the same result.

  [92]Cf. Asmussen:46-47: "Um fluchen zu können, muss man bei Gott stehen, muss man Mund Gottes sein, muss man um seinetwillen reden." Blessing and curse is "ein wirkliches Wort . . . . Aussage und Anrede, welche von uns ein Ja oder Nein fordern. Die letzte Wort der Ausschliesslichkeit wird aufgenommen oder abgelehnt, wie ein Geschenk, dass man dankbar hinnimmt oder zurückstösst."

  [93]Contra Bornkamm:125; Käsemann 1954:249-50; Hunzinger *TRE* V:165.

  [94]Cf. H. D. Betz 1979:54; Rohde:44; Behnisch:246. Cf. also U. B. Müller:199-200 who speaks of a curse wish that begins the actual judgment.

for their surroundings. The audience is therefore urged to change their interaction with the opponents accordingly. We find no indications in the letter of
how such a decision should be made, or of how it should be announced. It
may or may not take a form analogous to 1 Cor 5. The important matter is
that it will inevitably separate the Galatians and the opponents from each
other (Becker:13; Hansen:86-87). As a result, they will, in some way or
other, be isolated from the churches, so that it will become impossible to pursue their missionary efforts further.[95]

The effects on the opponents are more difficult to predict. We cannot
exclude the possibility that at least some of them could be persuaded to
repent. If not, some possibilities may be considered:

> If they (or some of them) are native people, an expulsion would have the
> grievous effect of social isolation.
>
> If they (or some of them) came from the outside, however, the consequences
> could be quite different: They could return to their home churches, perhaps as
> heroes, since they had pursued their preaching as long as it was possible for them to
> do so. But when treated as cursed persons, their chances of influence would vanish.
>
> An effective curse should cause sickness and death of its victim. We may
> assume that the Galatians would be interested in learning the eventual fate of the
> opponents. The opponents themselves, however, would regard the anathemas as
> illegitimate, and would probably not fear that any physical harm would take effect.

c: Probable effects of rejection

We have to consider seriously the possibility that the Galatian churches
might reject the legitimacy of Paul's double anathema.[96] This possibility is
the only chance for the opponents to survive as teachers in Galatia. We
should not hesitate to assume that they would persuade the Galatians to
respond in this way. The critical point is Paul's deviation from the conventional application of covenant curses:[97] Instead of cursing lawbreakers, Paul

---

[95]It is therefore adequate to connect the anathema with excommunication in some
way, cf. Luther 26:56; Asmussen:46-47; Brown:46-48; Bligh:91; H. D. Betz 1979:54;
Borse 1984:50; Bornhäuser; Wiles:128-29. The main objection to this interpretation has
been that it is impossible to apply it to an angel from heaven, cf. Gal 1:8. It is not: If
this hypothetical possibility should materialize, it is the duty of Christians to avoid any
contact with such angelic or demonic messengers.

[96]Cf. Austin:14-18 for a classification of conditions that must be met if institutional
performatives are to be successful. The typology is more extensive for the failure of ritual
performatives in Grimes:110-16. He complains that scholars have not given enough
attention to the fact that performatives often fail (109-110).

According to Austin:36-37 it is important for institutional performatives that "the procedure must be executed by all participants completely." We have noted in Deut 27:15-
26 how each curse is sanctioned by a response from the audience: "Amen." Similar
responses are found in liturgical curses such as 1QS ii; 4Q 286-87, cf. also *Jub.* 4:5;
33:12.

[97]According to Austin:31 a similar problem exists for performatives in an institutional
setting. Commonly one faces cases where the first condition of accepted conventional

transforms the curses to hit those who were zealous for the law. This point is critical for whether or not the Galatians hear the possible allusions to Deuteronomy. If they do not hear them, the opponents might themselves present the biblical texts as the divinely authorized pronouncements. In fact both covenantal curses and Deut 13 seem to fit better with the theology of the opponents than with the position of Paul. If they hear the deuteronomistic resonances, the opponents might stress Paul's deviation as illegitimate.

Two powerful modes of persuasion would thus stand before the Galatians. They would confront a difficult choice. Would they accept Paul's version in the letter, or would they succumb to the persuasive tactics of the opponents after Paul's letter was read to them? If they reject Paul's anathema, this would have serious consequences for Paul himself. The Galatians would consider him to be a false curser, and they would most likely think that the consequences of his curse would fall back on himself. At the very least they would think that he had made himself vulnerable to the deuteronomistic curses.[98] The probable effects of rejection of the legitimacy of Paul's anathemas would therefore be a schism between himself and the congregations:

> On one hand the Galatians would know that Paul regards them as apostates (cf. 1:6-7; 4:8-11; 5:4) under the curse (cf. 3:10). Also the Galatians would fall under the anathemas of 1:8-9 since they would begin to propagate the same teaching. As a consequence they would know that Paul would not regard them as belonging to his missionary field any longer.
> On the other hand they would also regard Paul as a cursed person, a fact that would inevitably make them break contact with him.
> We may also consider another damaging possibility: The various churches could decide differently in this matter: Some could accept the legitimacy and some reject it. The consequence could be an unhappy schism with serious consequences for mutual relations between neighboring congregations.

In 4:16-17 Paul touches on the danger of enmity between himself and the Galatian churches, and the verses may therefore be connected to the probable effects of the rejection of Paul's authority.

> In 4:16 Paul writes: "Have I then become your enemy by telling you the truth (ὥστε ἐχθρὸς ὑμῶν γέγονα ἀληθεύων ὑμῖν)?" The term *enemy* can be taken to express both the active sense of Paul being hostile to the Galatians, and passively to

---

procedure may be challenged. He asserts that it may be uncertain how far an accepted conventional "procedure extends — which cases it covers or which varieties it could be made to cover . . . . There will always occur difficult or marginal cases where nothing in the previous history of a conventional procedure will decide conclusively whether such a procedure is or is not correctly applied to such a case."

[98]Cf. Baasland 1984a:140-47 for many possibilities in the deuteronomistic traditions of regarding Paul as a cursed person.

express that the Galatians reject Paul.[99] Although it is uncertain whether this enmity is already present or anticipated, and whether the double anathema is seen as a major cause for it or not, the possibility of enmity is clearly reflected.[100]

In 4:17 Paul writes: "they want to shut you out (ἐκκλεῖσαι ὑμᾶς)." This expression is probably not to be taken to refer to the Galatians becoming severed from Christ and grace,[101] but rather to denote the isolation of the Galatians from the Pauline missionary field.[102]

It is by no means certain that the last word is said between Paul and the Galatians if they reject his legitimacy, however. The possibility would still exist that the opponents, in contrast to Paul, could suffer a fate which persuaded the Galatians that they had made the wrong decision.

To conclude: The double anathema puts before the Galatian congregations a difficult choice. Once uttered the curse demands serious attention. It is impossible for them to have normal relations to both parties after this curse. Paul's intention is to isolate the opponents from the Galatian churches, and his persuasion is found in the letter to the Galatians. The opponents would fight for the opposite reaction — that the audience reject Paul's implicit demand and thus instead terminate their contact with Paul.

9.3.4: The double anathema in context

If this double anathema is important for Paul in Galatians, we should expect him to use the same means as above for the accusation of apostasy, namely to allude to this horizon at several other places in the letter, in order to constantly remind his readers about it. Such allusions seem to be present in 3:1 and 4:29-30, and clear references are present in 3:10 and 5:7-12.

---

[99]Cf. the discussions by Sieffert:251; Burton:244.

[100]It is possible that this enmity has already manifested itself in some form, cf. the perfect tense (γέγονα). If so it could have been caused by curses and threats similar to 1:9 given on a previous occasion, cf. Sieffert:251, Lightfoot:176; Burton:244-46; Oepke:144; Ridderbos:168. It is also possible that Paul puts himself in a future state when using the perfect tense, describing the possible consequence of the letter itself with its severe attacks, cf. Zahn:218-19; Borse 1984:153 and to some extent also Bligh:386.

Other possibilities are as follows: The enmity may have been caused by the opponents and not by Paul's own expressions (cf. Schlier 1965:212; Becker:53; Bruce:211; Rohde:187-88); Paul may refer to an inconceivable possibility (cf. Mussner:309-10), or Paul only refers to alienated friendship according to the friendship *topos* (cf. H. D. Betz 1979:228-29).

[101]So Lightfoot:177; Burton:246; Becker:53; Bligh:388; Bruce:211-12.

[102]Cf. Bengel:743; Sieffert:253; Oepke:144; Ridderbos:168; Mussner:310-11; Borse 1984:156; Rohde:188.

a: The anathema and Gal 3:8-14

In our context it is the connection to 3:10 which is of most interest, a connection which may be present at several levels. The most obvious connection between the verses corresponds to the move between *theme and horizon* (Iser:161-69). A reader who has been deeply shocked by the double anathema in 1:8-9 will inevitably connect it with the curse in 3:10 during the reading process. The texts will be brought together both because they are curses, and also because the crimes seem to be similar in both verses: To preach against the Gospel (1:8-9) may be equated with a life based on the works of the law (3:10a).

From a rhetorical point of view both verses seem to serve the function of *incriminating the opponents*. The rhetorical handbooks advise a speaker to disparage his opponents in the *exordium* of a speech. According to *ad Herenn*. I.v.8 one can "secure goodwill by bringing them into hatred, unpopularity, or contempt. We shall force hatred (*odium*, cf. ἔχθρα or μῖσος) upon them by adducing some base, highhanded, treacherous, cruel, impudent, malicious, or shameful act of theirs."[103] The anathemas may therefore be seen as an extreme measure to bring Paul's opponents into hatred, and 3:10 may serve a similar function.

A more specific connection is found in the *deuteronomistic traditions*. It is obvious that Paul treats deuteronomistic traditions in Gal 3:10-14, since he twice cites from Deuteronomy. If he has alluded to these traditions already in 1:6-9, a connection may be proposed as follows: In 1:6-9 Paul alludes to covenantal curses and the law of Deut 13 with a major deviation from conventional use. In order to persuade his audience, however, such deviation needs a broader discussion as a legitimizing basis, a discussion which is present in 3:8-14.

An even more specific connection is found if the double anathema is perceived in the light of the *stasis of Reasoning from Analogy*. Then Paul would reflect a legal discussion according to rhetorical conventions. If similar reflections from judicial rhetoric are found also in 3:8-14, the possibility that the latter text includes the juridical basis for the double anathema is considerably strengthened.

At this point the various possibilities are only cataloged. The next chapter will reject or confirm the validity of each of these proposals.

b: The anathema and Gal 3:1; 4:29-30; 5:7-12

In 3:1 Paul ironically asks the Galatians: "Who has bewitched you?" Since βασκαίνειν is the technical term in the classical Mediterranean world

---

[103]Cf. similar advice by Cic. *Inv*. I.xvi.22. Also Aristotle knows about this technique, cf. *Rhet*. III.xv.7.

for *bewitch* (e. g., with an evil eye), it is quite possible that some of the audience would perceive it as an implicit *witchcraft accusation*, or more specifically as an *evil eye accusation*.[104] Thus it may indirectly denote his opponents as possessed by Satan, and as being under evil influence. If so, it is inevitable that the Galatians by a retrospective move would combine it with expectations connected to the double anathema.

In 4:29-30 the Hagar-Sarah section is extended in a surprising way. Paul emphasizes the contrast between the sons of the slave and of the free woman by means of an allusion to Gen 21:9 and a citation of Gen 21:10: "But as at that time he who was born according to the flesh persecuted him who was born according to the Spirit, so it is now. But what does scripture say? 'Cast out ($\check{\varepsilon}\kappa\beta\alpha\lambda\varepsilon$) the slave and her son, for the son of the slave shall not inherit with the son of the free woman.'" We see that Paul denotes a Jewish group as persecutors of the church[105] and also as worthy of expulsion from it. It is difficult to find the precise intention of these verses, however.

Although I follow the majority of scholars in relating the section to the relationship between Jews and Christians in general,[106] it is peculiar that Paul includes the request "Cast out the slave and her son" in the citation.[107] It might be that once again we find an implicit allusion to the proper way of dealing with the opponents: The first part of Gen 21:10 is an exhortation; perhaps we cannot overhear the illocutionary force of such a demand. Paul's intention could not be to demand the expulsion of Jews generally from the

---

[104]Luther 26:189-94 took it in this way without questions, cf. also Bengel:735. Cf. more specifically Neyrey:72-73, 75, 86 for an implicit "witchcraft-accusation," and J. H. Elliott for an implicit "evil eye accusation." According to Neyrey:97-99, the ultimate function of such accusations is normally to cause expulsion of the witch.

[105]It is clear that Paul wants to emphasize the persecution, since neither the MT nor the LXX indicate it in Gen 21:9 (the MT has צחק = *laugh, joke*, or perhaps *mock*; the LXX has παίζω = *dance, play*, cf. Baasland 1984a:135). Paul deliberately chooses to follow a special Jewish tradition which emphasizes persecution at this place, cf. references in *Str-B* III, 575-76; Mussner:329-30, and most commentaries.

[106]A few scholars take Paul to denote the opponents as persecutors (cf. Zahn:242; Burton:266; Mussner:330-31). Most scholars, though, understand 4:29 as a proof from experience that substantiates Paul's harsh distinction between Jews and Christians (cf. Oepke:152; H. D. Betz 1979:249; Rohde:204. See further Sieffert:279; Schlier 1965: 227; Bruce:224; Borse 1984:175). This distinction is then proved by a citation of Gen 21:10 in Gal 4:30, since it is clearly stated in the last part of that citation that the son of the slave will not inherit salvation (cf. Sieffert:279; Lightfoot:184; Burton:267; Oepke:152; Schlier 1965:227; Borse 1984:176-77). Paul's changes in the text point to this aspect of the citation as the one most important to him: He omits ταῦτα and exchanges the son of Isaac into "the son of the free woman." This makes the citation suitable for Paul's argument here, cf. Koch 1986:121, 150.

[107]This part of the citation is rendered without changes according to the LXX, so we have no indications of its importance.

churches of Galatia, but rather the expulsion of his opponents.[108] Again, Paul seems to allude to the effects of the curse.

It is in 5:7–12 that Paul comes closest to describing his opponents as cursed persons. This section has many similarities with the *exordium* (Smit:20), and it is part of the important *dissuasio* of the letter (cf. sec. 8.2). When Paul seems to renew his attacks on the opponents as cursed persons here, it is an indication of how important this strategy is.

I have commented on the Understatement in 5:7–8 above (cf. sec. 9.2.1c). When Paul says that this negative persuasion is not from God, he invites the audience to consider its real source, which may be demonic. Again we might see a possible allusion to the status of cursed persons as in 3:1.

In 5:9 Paul cites a proverb: "A little yeast leavens the whole lump." The proverb is not clearly attached to any object, so it is up to the audience to make the connection themselves (H. D. Betz 1979:266). Although it is common to take the yeast as a reference to the teaching of the opponents,[109] it seems more natural to relate it to the people themselves, since the context clearly gives attention to them (cf. 5:7–8, 10b, 12).[110] Thus we once again find a reference which might be related to the pollution and corruption that possess the opponents and also threaten the Galatians.[111]

In 5:10a we find an epistolary confidence formula (H. D. Betz 1979:266–67; Hansen:49–50): "I have confidence in the Lord that you will take no other view than mine." The formula is usually understood as indicating Paul's hope that the Galatian Christians would remain loyal Paulinists in general.[112] It is present in a context which seems to incriminate the opponents as cursed persons, however. Paul's confidence may therefore also include an anticipated acceptance of the double curse: If the Galatians will take no other view than Paul, they also have to approve the anathema of 1:9, and thus will regard the opponents as possessed by evil (cf. 5:9) and worthy of God's judgment (cf. 5:10b).[113]

---

[108]Cf. Zahn:243; Mussner:332 and especially Hansen:145–46. Cf. also H. D. Betz 1979:251; Rohde:205; Neyrey:83.

[109]Cf. Matt 16:6 and Oepke:160; Schlier 1965:237; Mussner:356; Bruce:235; Rohde:221.

[110]Cf. Bengel:748; Zahn:254; Sieffert:292; Lightfoot:206; Borse 1984:185–86; Hansen:146. Also Schlier 1965:237 considers this as a possible reference.

[111]For yeast as a symbol of evil, pollution, and corruption, cf. Lightfoot:206; Bruce: 235; Neyrey:88.

[112]Cf., for example, Oepke:160; Schlier 1965:238; Mussner:358; H. D. Betz 1979:267.

[113]Also Zahn:254 relates 5:10a to Paul's confidence that the Galatians will reject the opponents. A connection between 5:10a and 5:9 is also advocated by Sieffert:293; Burton:284; Rohde:222, but they instead emphasize the teaching rather than the opponents themselves.

In 5:10b we find a curse on the opponents that clearly relates to 1:8–9.[114] Paul turns them over to the judgment of God, quite in accordance with the concept of curse: "He who is troubling you will bear his judgment, whoever he is."[115]

In 5:12 Paul writes ironically: "I wish those who unsettle you would mutilate themselves!" The joke is probably more than a caricature of the ritual of circumcision (contra H. D. Betz 1979:270), and there exists several possible interpretations which all allude to the concept of curse:

> There may be a connection to mutilation in pagan religions. Thus Paul, as in 4:8–11, ironically compares an acceptance of circumcision with an apostasy into paganism,[116] and the unclean characters of the opponents become more visible.
>
> The reference may also be connected with Deut 23:1–2, where mutilated persons are denied entrance to the assembly of the Lord.[117] The point is that mutilation makes one permanently unclean,[118] and thus it would be an external evidence of their inner corruption as cursed persons.
>
> It may also be that Paul refers to the כרת penalty from the Hebrew Bible here, since ἀποκόπτειν often is the LXX translation of this root. Then the verse more openly alludes to the expulsion of the opponents.[119]

To sum up: The main reference to the double anathema has not been commented upon yet. It is found in 3:10, where the scriptural foundation of 1:8–9 seems to be secured. I have noted, however, that conventional motifs related to cursed persons are clearly alluded to in the important *dissuasio* of the letter (cf. 5:7–12), and, together with the possible allusions in 3:1 and 4:30, they seem to keep alive the importance of the anathema in the perception of the audience.

I admit that many of the interpretations above are only possibilities offered by the text. An audience who has been shocked by the opening double anathema, however, would be more receptive to such allusions than modern readers who are not offered a similar difficult choice, and who in addition may not be familiar with curses at all.

---

[114]Cf. for this connection Luther 27:40; Becker:63; H. D. Betz 1979:267; Lührmann 1978:82.

[115]The singular is taken as generic by most commentaries. The reference is not exclusively to the final judgment (contra Sieffert:294), but it is open and thus may include present fulfillment.

[116]Cf. Oepke:163–64. Further Burton:289; Mussner:363; Rohde:224.

[117]Cf. Burton:289; Mussner:363–64.

[118]Cf. Neyrey:83. Since we also find the notion of expulsion in Deut 23:2–9 (cf. Horbury:19–20), we might find a slight allusion to expulsion even here, as noted by Burton:289; Neyrey:83; Hansen:146.

[119]Bengel:748 finds the figure of Metonomy here, (cf. *ad Herenn.* IV.xxxii.43). Paul refers to the cutting away of the foreskin, but takes it to represent the expulsion of the opponents themselves. Cf. also Luther 27:45–46; Brown:279–81.

9.4: *Excursus: Anathema in other Pauline texts*

Paul uses the term ἀνάθεμα also in Rom 9:3; 1 Cor 12:3, and 16:22. It is the aim of this excursus to demonstrate that a covenantal background and an illocutionary force like the one presented above is fitting also for these texts.

a: 1 Cor 16:22

In 1 Cor 16:21-24 we find the final greeting of 1 Corinthians written with Paul's own hand. This greeting includes a brief curse which is formally nearly identical with Gal 1:8-9: "If any one has no love for the Lord, let him be accursed (εἴ τις οὐ φιλεῖ τὸν κύριον, ἤτω ἀνάθεμα). Our Lord, come!" (16:22). I have noted above that it is common to let this formula become an argument for regarding the anathemas as belonging to Christian "sacred laws" (cf. sec. 1.3.1).

The theory of Paul taking up "sacred laws" involves two important elements, both the legal form and the eucharistic allusions:

> The *legal form* has been investigated by E. Käsemann 1954. He connects the two anathemas of Gal 1:8-9 and 1 Cor 16:22 with the *ius talionis* clauses of 1 Cor 3:17; 14:38, and sees them as examples of "sacred law." The common feature is that the clauses have protases like casuistic laws, and that the apodoses do not refer to a human execution, but to the eschatological judgment of God on the last day. The former refer to it by issuing curses which are withdrawn from human administration, the latter by referring to God's eschatological judgment in an *ius talionis* form. Käsemann finds such clauses also in Mark 8:38; Matt 10:32-33; 16:27; Rev 22:18-19, and he argues that 1 Cor 5:3-8 describes this kind of procedure. According to Käsemann, these clauses belong to a very early stage of the development of Christianity, at a time when small congregations had no need for juridical regulations, since a prophet guided by the Holy Spirit provided the leadership.
>
> K. Berger has criticized this theory from a form-critical point of view. He finds that the "sacred laws" do not correspond to prophetic clauses, but rather to clauses from wisdom tradition: They seem to be part of a teaching about the connection between "Tat und Ergehen" (1970:14-32, 40).[120] Berger does not treat the anathemas of 1 Cor 16:22 and Gal 1:8-9, however. It is possible, therefore, to interpret them at least as examples of "sacred law" from the liturgy of the eucharist.[121] The question is, however, whether we should stick to such an explanation of the anathemas if we do not find other clear examples of such "sacred laws."

---

[120]Berger finds wisdom parallels both for the clauses where the verb of the protasis and of the apodosis corresponded to each other (cf. 1 Cor 3:17; 14:38; Rev 22:18-19), and for the clauses without such correspondence, whether the apodosis was future or present. In his 1972 article, he argues that some of the clauses with a future apodosis belonged to the "Initialkatechese innerhalb der Heidenmission," and that some with a present apodosis represented "'Unterscheidungskriterien' zwischen Gerechten und Ungerechten, d.h. . . . eine bestimmte Form der Unterweisung" (330).

[121]Cf. Berger 1972:327-30. U. B. Müller:178-85 accepts Berger's critique of Käsemann, but he argues that 1 Cor 16:22 shows that the curse had a place as "sacred law" within the eucharistic liturgy, and Gal 1:8-9 shows that this curse could be adapted

The *eucharistic aspect* has been investigated by G. Bornkamm: He claims that several elements in 1 Cor 16:20–23 are taken from eucharistic liturgy: The holy kiss (16:20), the μαράνα θά (16:22), and the blessing (16:23). Therefore the ἀνάθεμα, too, could belong to this liturgy. He then finds eucharistic and legal elements combined in *Did.* 10:6; 9:5 and Rev 22:14–21 together with indications also in other texts. These observations are taken by Bornkamm to substantiate his thesis of ἀνάθεμα as a formula of "sacred law" belonging to the eucharistic liturgy.

The problem with this theory is that no one has been able to find explicit evidence for the use of anathema or curse in the liturgy. The closest example is *Did.* 10:6: "If any man be holy, let him come! If any man be not, let him repent: Maran atha, Amen." It is a long way from finding such parenthetical expression in the liturgy to implying that also a curse could be part of it!

Although we find broad acceptance of this theory in current research,[122] we have to conclude that neither its legal nor its eucharistic aspect has been proved. Even if we should accept the eucharistic background, however, the traditio-historical question would still remain: Which traditions had any influence upon the eucharistic curse?

If we instead look to the covenantal traditions considered above for Gal 1:8–9, it is possible to detect both a covenantal function and covenantal language:

The *function* of the anathema is to use a curse to underscore the divine nature of the teaching in the entire letter.[123] Just as in 16:21 Paul's signature authenticates the whole letter, so in 16:22 the curse emphasizes the necessity of obedience to his instructions. Standing at the conclusion of Paul's instructions, the curse functions like Deut 27:26, and it shares as well with Deut 27:26 a quality of being general rather than specific in its focus.[124]

The covenantal *terminology* is found primarily in the curse term within a casuistic clause (cf. the discussion above for Gal 1:8–9). It is also found in the verb "to love" (φιλεῖν), however, since the first commandment often is

---

into a warning against false teachers (197–212).

[122]A broad discussion is found by Klauck:351–63. Cf. also among others: Becker:12–13; Bligh:91; Barrett 1968:397–98; Wiefel:226–29; Stuhlmacher 1968:69; Wiles: 117–19, 151–52; Conzelmann:300; Synofzik:38; C. Wolff:229; Behnisch:247–48; Lang: 249.

[123]Cf. Fee:837–38 for the following. See also Doskocil:55–56.

[124]It refers to the general τις, and it covers all types of disobedience by the general claim to have "love for the Lord." As in Deut 27–28 we also find a combination with a blessing in 16:23: "The grace of the Lord Jesus be with you."

The outcry μαράνα θά fits as smoothly into this interpretation as into the eucharistic one: In a similar way as the repeated "Amen" of Deut 27:15–26, it seems to give additional force to the curse. It is Paul's conviction that when the Lord comes, he will judge according to it, cf. Brun:106; Moule; Barrett 1968:398.

referred to as a claim to love the Lord (cf. Deut 6:5), a feature also echoed by curse texts such as Deut 30:6, 16, 20. We may especially cite Deut 30:19-20: "I have set before you life and death, blessing and curse; therefore choose life, that you and your descendants may live, loving the Lord your God . . . ."[125]

We may note a similar *deviation* from the covenant traditions here as in Gal 1:8-9: Paul requires love for the Lord, that is, love for Christ. Thus he uses the curse to underscore the divine nature of another covenant than the sinaitic one, namely the Gospel and the ethical instructions founded on it.

The *illocutionary force* is present also in this anathema: It is most natural to take it as a general warning for the readers of the letter, that if they fulfill the condition in the protasis, the curse will become effective. Thus its function is to urge obedience to Christ. The letter contains many judgment passages, however (cf. 3:16-17; 5:3-5; 11:27; 14:38), so a reader could also relate the anathema to them (Wiles:151, 153). In this case the anathema enforces the seriousness of these passages. The most concrete judgment passage is 1 Cor 5 which has been treated above, and the anathema in 16:22 may also function as a renewed demand to take action against this offender.

b: 1 Cor 12:3

In 1 Cor 12:1 Paul opens a discussion of the spiritual gifts (περὶ δε τῶν πνευματικῶν), a theme discussed at length from 12:4 onward. Between the superscription and the discussion, however, we find two verses which have been a *crux interpretum* for scholars:

> You know that when you were heathen, you were led astray to dumb idols, however you may have been moved. Therefore I want you to understand that no one speak-

---

[125]The objection that we here find ἀγαπᾶν and not φιλεῖν carries little weight, since Hellenistic Judaism also is influenced from the terminology of the Greek φιλία institution. According to Greek ideals, the closest fellowship between men was the total commitment to one's friends (φίλοι). This was regarded as an exemplary relationship between humans, and terminologically it was transformed also to denote the exemplary relationship between humans and God(s).

The influence of this concept in Hellenistic Judaism is found, for example, in late wisdom tradition: Wis 7:14: "Those who get it (=wisdom), obtain friendship with God (πρὸς θεὸν ἐστείλαντο φιλίαν)." The interchangeability of the two verbs is demonstrated in Prov 8:17 where wisdom says: "I love (ἀγαπῶ) those who love me (ἐμὲ φιλοῦντας)." From Christian tradition we may refer to John 21:15-17 where both verbs are used to denote Peter's love for Christ. Therefore a connection to the first commandment could be expressed both with ἀγαπᾶν and φιλεῖν, and with reference to either God or Christ. Paul prefers ἀγαπᾶν, but in this verse he has taken up another tradition which uses φιλεῖν. For the interchangeability between these verbs, cf. also Spicq:201, 204; Barrett 1968:396-97.

ing by the Spirit of God ever says "Jesus be cursed! (᾽Ανάθεμα ᾽Ιησοῦς)" and no one can say "Jesus is Lord" except by the Holy Spirit (12:2-3).

The logic in these verses is inductive (cf. sec. 8.4 above). From a particular instance of pagan worship (12:2), a general principle is found which also is applied to the particular instance of confessing Christ (12:3; cf. the opening διὸ γνωρίζω ὑμῖν). There is no indication that Paul's concern is on the ecstatic experiences in both cases.[126] Instead the instance of pagan worship, which the Corinthians know very well (cf. οἴδατε), reveals the general principle that people are led to do it under the influence of supernatural powers (cf. the duplication of ἄγειν and ἀπάγειν).[127] Then Paul can conclude in 12:3 that confessions such as "Jesus is cursed" and "Jesus is Lord" are also caused by supernatural influence. Only the latter is caused by the Spirit of God, the former consequently by demonic spirits.[128]

The confession: "Jesus is cursed" is a *crux interpretum* in modern research. Of the many proposals for interpretation,[129] the ones that refer to

---

[126]It is common to regard 12:2-3 as a comparison between ecstatic experiences from the pagan past of the Corinthians and their present spiritual experiences, see, for example, Weiss:295–96; Conzelmann:204–6; C. Wolff:98–99; Lang:163. But no word in 12:2 refers explicitly to ecstasy, and neither do the confessions in 12:3 bear any mark of having been uttered under ecstasy.

[127]Also Bassler:417 and E. Baasland 1988b:81 see a similar connection between the verses. There is no explicit reference to demonic powers in the verse, but the passive ὡς ἂν ἤγεσθε implicitly demands this kind of subject.

[128]Paul uses the figure of Understatement (λιτότης): By stating that no one speaks so by the Spirit of God, he certainly implies that they do it under demonic influence. Cf. 12:1 for the same figure: When Paul writes "I do not want you to be uninformed," it is an understatement for his aim to give them precise information, cf. Baasland 1988b:80.

[129]Many scholars refuse to look for historical realities behind this curse. They rather regard it as a rhetorical antithesis to the baptismal formula, created *ad hoc* by Paul at this point (cf. Holtz 1971:375–76; Conzelmann:204; C. Wolff:101; Lang:163–64). It seems difficult to understand, however, why Paul should create a powerful curse in such a case. Another way of escaping the historical problem is to regard the curse as a copyist's error (cf. Albright/Mann:273 who claim that the copyist may have misunderstood it to be from ἀνα ἄθε μαραν ἄθα ᾽Ιησοῦς both here and in 16:22). Such solutions should only be considered when all others have failed.

A real background for the curse has been sought in many different contexts:

a) A background in *pagan worship* seems attractive, since it would carry the thought of 12:2 further, but it faces the problem that ἀνάθεμα seems to reflect Jewish usage, cf. Fee:579–81.

b) The proposal that Christians became compelled to utter this curse under *pressure from Roman emperor-cult* (cf. Cullmann:219–20) faces the problem that such official persecutions are unknown at this early stage.

c) Some have argued that this curse may have been uttered *within the Christian assembly*: The speakers may have been Christian Gnostics cursing the earthly Jesus (cf. Schmithals 1956a:45–50; Brox and the critique by Pearson); they may have been Christians under charismatic ecstasies (cf. Weiss:295; Barrett 1968:280); they may have been Christians mentally imbalanced (cf. Brun:122–24); or Christians who rightly confess that *deuteronomistic traditions* seem to be most well grounded:[130]

> The curse may be applied to Jesus by Jews from Deut 21:23 since he died on a cross.[131]
>
> The anathema may also be applied to Jesus by Jews since he may have been sentenced to death as a seducer according to the law of Deut 13.[132]
>
> The anathema on Jesus may have been connected to the process of excommunicating Christian leaders from the Synagogue. According to J. D. M. Derrett, a Christian leader could be persecuted by "a warning, a flogging, and ultimately, excommunication if he did not abjure by cursing Jesus."[133]

It is not necessary to choose between these proposals, because they all point to the same background for the anathema, namely that Jews activated deuteronomistic traditions in order to condemn Jesus as a seducer and/or as an apostate. Paul's point is that his readers should connect the curse with the practice of the Jewish synagogue. Thus 12:2 functions as an exposure of pagan worship, and 12:3 thus functions as an exposure of the Jewish Synagogue: Since the Jews regard Jesus as cursed, they demonstrate that they, as the pagans, are not moved by the Spirit of God (Schlatter:331).[134]

The *illocutionary force* is also present in this confession: A person who openly confesses Jesus as anathema urges both himself and his audience to regard Jesus as a cursed person. He thus insists that one should have nothing to do with Jesus and sees this verdict as justified by God through Jesus' death on the cross.

Christ has become a curse for us (cf. Gal 3:13), but fail to honor his resurrection (cf. van Unnik 1973a). The main problem with all these proposals is that they cannot be substantiated by other texts.

[130]1 Cor 12:2 may allude to deuteronomistic curse traditions. According to Maly:85–86 we find similar expressions in Deut 28:36, cf. ἀπάγειν, ἔθνη, and the last phrase: "and there you shall serve other gods, of wood and stone." This link may give evidence to the fact that Paul alludes to deuteronomistic traditions in his description of both pagans (12:2) and Jews (12:3a).

[131]Cf. Schlatter:333; Jeremias:134–35; Maly:94–95; Bassler:418. We have touched on this theory above (cf. sec. 1.3.2b), and we will return to it below (cf. sec. 10.4.1).

[132]Cf. above sec. 6.3.6b and Strobel:81–94; O. Betz 1982.

[133]Derrett 1975:544, citation 548–49. Cf. also his valuable discussion of the cultural probability for such persecutions (545–50).

[134]Another question concerns the reason for Paul to open his discussion of the spiritual gifts in this way. It is difficult for us to be definite at this point, but it seems clear that many of Paul's opponents, perhaps also in Corinth, had strong sympathies for Jewish teaching. They may have been perceived as especially spiritual, and Paul may have felt it necessary to expose such people, if not as possessed by demons themselves, at least as having connections with a demonically inspired people (cf. Ellis 1974, especially 132–33). But if we were to pursue this question further, we ought to consider the whole discussion of Paul's opponents in Corinth, a discussion that would go far beyond the scope of this excursus.

c: Rom 9:3

With Rom 9:1-5 Paul enters the discussion of God's faithfulness toward Israel and their disobedience with a brief *exordium* (Siegert:123). It is in the middle of this opening section that we find the last anathema clause in Paul: "For I could wish that I myself were accursed and cut off from Christ (ἀνάθεμα εἶναι αὐτὸς ἐγὼ ἀπὸ τοῦ Χριστοῦ) for the sake of my brethren."

Just as in Galatians, Paul now enters a difficult discussion where he could expect a skeptical audience,[135] by concentrating on the persons involved, and by only indirectly touching the issue itself. Hence Paul is concerned both about establishing his own ἦθος (9:1-3) and demonstrating his high esteem for the Jewish nation (9:3-5). The curse is located in the overlap between these themes.

In his ἦθος description Paul deliberately uses double expressions[136] in a way that conforms with the rhetorical figure *interpretatio*.[137] In this way Paul secures his ἦθος by underscoring both his trustworthiness (9:1) and his deep affection bordering on pain for the Jewish people (9:2).

In this context 9:3 must be interpreted as Paul's willingness to give the utmost personal sacrifice for the benefit of the Jews.[138] Also here we find a double expression of *interpretatio*: Paul is willing to become accursed (ἀνάθεμα εἶναι), that is, to become cut off from Christ (ἀπὸ τοῦ Χριστοῦ; Dunn 1988a:522). We see how smoothly a deuteronomistic background fits a synonymity between ἀνάθεμα and expulsion.[139] Also the list of prerogatives for

---

[135]Perhaps he knew about rumors that he had turned his back on his own people, cf. Wilckens 1980:189-90; Siegert:121; Räisänen 1987:2895; Dunn 1988a:530-31, but also the critique by Cranfield 1979:453-54. To argue that Paul has been cursed by some opponents, however (cf. Brun:127-28), is probably to make the rumors too specific.

[136]See especially Dunn 1988a:522. Paul asserts twice that he speaks the truth (9:1a: ἀλήθειαν λέγω/οὐ ψεύδομαι), he invokes two witnesses for it (9:1b: τῆς συνειδήσεώς μου/ἐν πνεύματι ἁγίῳ), he speaks twice of his great sorrow (9:2: λύπη . . . μεγάλη/ ἀδιάλειπτος ὀδύνη), and he denotes the Jewish people with a double expression (9:3b: τῶν ἀδελφῶν μου/τῶν συγγενῶν μου).

[137]*Interpretatio* "is the figure which does not duplicate the same word by repeating it, but replaces the word that has been used by another of the same meaning" (*ad Herenn.* IV.xxviii.38). The point of expressing oneself in this way is to make a deep impression on the hearer, cf. *ad Herenn.* IV.xxviii.38: "The hearer cannot but be impressed when the force of the first expression is renewed by the explanatory synonym."

[138]The word ηὐχόμην is open to many interpretations: It may be translated *wish* or *pray*, and it may be taken to introduce both a real offer before God or an unattainable prayer/wish. Cf. discussions by Cranfield 1979:454-57 who opts for the latter alternatives, Michel 1951:96-98 who opts for the former, and Dunn 1988a:524, 532 who leaves it open.

[139]Ἀπό denotes separation, cf. *BDR* par 211,2 and Cranfield 1979:458. Michel 1978:294 regards ἀπὸ τοῦ Χριστοῦ as a ban formula. The concern is for the fate in the final salvation, cf. Michel 1978:294; Stählin:135; Cranfield 1979:457-58. Käsemann 1974:246 points to a cultic procedure and draws an analogy to the sacred laws of eucharist also, but this theory has been criticized above for 1 Cor 16:22.

Israel in 9:4–5 may be seen as covenantal expressions.[140] Again we note the deviation from the conventional use: The curse is not connected to a covenantal relationship to Yahweh, but to Paul's salvific relationship to Christ.

The *illocutionary force* of an anathema makes a strong impression on the readers of the letter. It corresponds to the rhetorical strategy of stirring emotions (πάθος) in the audience (Siegert:121; cf. Martin:158–66): By placing himself hypothetically under a curse, Paul activates strong emotions and obtains the contrary effect than the one of being despised by his readers. By connecting this curse to a hypothetical effect of atonement,[141] he strengthens his ἦθος both by standing forth as innocent in such a respect, and also by his willingness to sacrifice whatever may be necessary (Schlier 1977:285; Dunn 1988a:532).

To conclude: The discussion of the remaining Pauline anathemas seems to have substantiated the fruitfulness of an approach which connects them to covenantal curses. It has also demonstrated that the illocutionary force is

---

The expression ἀπὸ τοῦ Χριστοῦ has its parallel in 8:35: "Who shall separate us from the love of Christ (ἀπὸ τῆς ἀγάπης τοῦ Χριστοῦ)?" Paul immediately gives a list of trials which could be taken as a proof for separation from Christ, and it is illuminating that we find the same expressions in lists of covenantal curses (cf. Münderlein:138–40; Hartman 1980:116; Hodgson:70–71): Tribulation (θλῖψις) and distress (στενοχωρία), cf. Deut 28:53, 55, 57; famine (λιμός), and nakedness (γυμνότης), cf. Deut 28:48; sword (μάχαιρα), cf. Lev 26:8, 25, 33; persecution (διωγμός), cf. Lev 26:7–8, 17, 36. As for peril (κίδυνος) we do not find the term in these curse lists, but there are certainly numerous examples of different dangers! Again we find that the expression ἀπὸ τοῦ Χριστοῦ is paralleled with references to covenantal curses, but this time Paul's point is that Christians should not regard the evils in this way.

Most scholars take this list as referring to tribulations experienced by Christians as witnessed in Paul's tribulation-lists (cf. 2 Cor 6:4–5; 11:26–27; 12:10 and Michel 1978: 283; Käsemann 1974:238; Cranfield 1975:440; Schlier 1977:279; Wilckens 1980:175; Dunn 1988a:498, 505), and they fail to recognize the link also to covenantal curses.

[140]Cf. Hartman 1980:107, 112–13. They may even be taken as blessings of Israel, cf. Dunn 1988a:522, 535; Käsemann 1974:246.

These blessings belong to Israel, but according to 9:3 the nation is now in a state which places them in need of salvation, cf. Wilckens 1980:186; Siegert:122. Perhaps Paul even presupposes that the Jews are under the curse (cf. Stählin:135; Schlier 1977:286; Räisänen 1987:2896), but such a judgment does not belong to the primary message in the verse (cf. Dunn 1988a:524–25). It is not difficult to imply the dtr-SH behind these verses, where Paul alludes to Israel's blessings, punishment, and redemption.

[141]Almost every commentary draws on the example of Moses in Exod 32:32 to explain this feature: Moses showed his willingness to be cut off from the salvific relationship to God in order to save the people of Israel. This may be substantiated by references to contemporary rabbinic traditions that a man could atone for the sufferings of another (cf. *Str-B* II,275–76, 279–82; III,261; Michel 1951:98; Schlier 1977:286) or by a reference to the fate of Achan, who suffered destruction in order to avert the anger of Yahweh from Israel (van Unnik 1973:118–19; Dunn 1988a:531).

important when the term is employed. The main benefit of this approach is that all anathema texts in Paul have been linked in a new way. There is also a link to Gal 3:13: Paul's hypothetical offer to be cursed for the benefit of others in Rom 9:3 has, according to Paul, become reality with Jesus (Stählin:135). With this connection in mind, it is time for us to give attention to the argument of Gal 3.

CHAPTER 10

10: THE CURSES OF GAL 3:10, 13 IN CONTEXT

In this chapter our primary interest is to interpret Paul's antithesis between the blessed and cursed in 3:8-10 and his sequence of curse and blessing in 3:13-14 (cf. secs. 10.3 and 10.4). We also have to interpret these verses in their context — the arguments leading up to the first blessing and curse (cf. sec. 10.2), verses 3:11-12 which come between the curses (cf. sec. 10.3.4), and the verses from the succeeding argumentation with a content similar to the curses (cf. sec. 10.5). First, however, it is important to discuss the structure of 2:14b - 3:14 (cf. sec. 10.1).

10.1: Structure of 2:14b - 3:14

The challenge created by this difficult section of the letter which occupies our interest is, to a large part, created by its brevity. It seems to involve so many "silent points" that frequently bewilder modern scholars.[1] A first step in an attempt to uncover its logic should be a preliminary overview of its structure.

In section 8.7.3 above we argued that Gal 2:15-21 has to be regarded as a speech which introduces the problem to be discussed in a manner that seems to reflect the legal stasis of Definition. I find it natural to connect 2:14b to this speech also, since it, whether it belongs to the speech or not, introduces a problem that actualizes its argumentation.

At the forefront of scholarly debate, however, stands the structure of 3:1-14. The main problem may be posed in this way: Following after the speech in 2:15-21 and the section of questions and rebuke in 3:1-5, where do we find the transition to Paul's main argumentation? Most scholars regard Gal 3:1-5 as a unit separated from 3:6-14.[2] If we follow our observation

---

[1]Cf. the different proposals for interpreting the curses which were reviewed above (sec. 1.3.2). H. D. Betz 1979:137 states that "Paul's way of arguing appears arbitrary in the highest degree," and Mussner:223 states that "seine Gedankenführung ist dabei teilweise recht sprunghaft." Cf. also Siegert:2-3 for similar judgments.

[2]The decisive argument is drawn from content rather than grammar: Paul in 3:1-5 refers to experience, but in 3:6-14 he refers to Scripture, cf. Schlier 1965:127; H. D. Betz 1979:129-30; Mussner:205 (he includes 3:6-18 in the latter section). Some argue that also the verses about Abraham (3:6-9) form a section of their own, resulting in three subsections, cf. Burton:lxxiii, Ridderbos:10. Others, however, have seen a close connection between 3:5 and 3:6: Bruce:153 therefore holds together 3:1-6, regarding 3:6 as a transitional verse, and Bligh:xiii divides between 3:1-4 and 3:5-14.

above in section 8.4, however, we may underscore that 3:1–7 contains inductive reasoning, while Paul shifts to deductive reasoning from 3:8 onward: In 3:1–5 Paul refers to experience, in 3:6 to a parallel in Scripture, and in 3:7 he spells out the general principle which may be drawn from these examples (similar Baasland 1984a:144). Thus it seems to be warranted to go against a broad consensus among scholars. The references to Abraham in 3:6–9 do not represent a series of statements in one unit of argumentation. Rather, 3:6 is part of an inductive unit of argumentation in 3:1–7, and 3:8–9 is part of a deductive argument at the beginning of 3:8–14.

A closer look at 3:8–14 shows that these verses have a different structure than 3:1–7. While the opening verses are structured around five questions (3:1–5) and one comparison (καθώς 3:6), 3:8–14 is structured around five Hebrew Bible citations (cf. the following table; similar Ebeling:228–32).

TABLE: The structure of Gal 3:8–14
(in=introduction; HB=Hebrew Bible citation; con=conclusion)

A in	⁸προϊδοῦσα δὲ ἡ γραφὴ
A	ὅτι ἐκ πίστεως δικαιοῖ τὰ ἔθνη ὁ θεὸς
A in	προευηγγελίσατο τῷ Ἀβραὰμ ὅτι
A HB	Ἐνευλογηθήσονται ἐν σοὶ πάντα τὰ ἔθνη.
A con	⁹ὥστε οἱ ἐκ πίστεως εὐλογοῦνται σὺν τῷ πιστῷ Ἀβραάμ.
B	¹⁰ὅσοι γὰρ ἐξ ἔργων νόμου εἰσὶν ὑπὸ κατάραν εἰσίν·
B in	γέγραπται γὰρ ὅτι
B HB	Ἐπικατάρατος πᾶς ὃς οὐκ ἐμμένει πᾶσιν τοῖς γεγραμμένοις ἐν τῷ βιβλίῳ τοῦ νόμου τοῦ ποιῆσαι αὐτά.
C	¹¹ὅτι δὲ ἐν νόμῳ οὐδεὶς δικαιοῦται παρὰ τῷ θεῷ δῆλον,
C in	ὅτι
C HB	Ὁ δίκαιος ἐκ πίστεως ζήσεται·
D	¹²ὁ δὲ νόμος οὐκ ἔστιν ἐκ πίστεως,
D in	ἀλλ'
D HB	Ὁ ποιήσας αὐτὰ ζήσεται ἐν αὐτοῖς.
E	¹³Χριστὸς ἡμᾶς ἐξηγόρασεν ἐκ τῆς κατάρας τοῦ νόμου γενόμενος ὑπὲρ ἡμῶν κατάρα,
E in	ὅτι γέγραπται,
E HB	Ἐπικατάρατος πᾶς ὁ κρεμάμενος ἐπὶ ξύλου,
E con1	¹⁴ἵνα εἰς τὰ ἔθνη ἡ εὐλογία τοῦ Ἀβραὰμ γένηται ἐν Χριστῷ Ἰησοῦ,
E con2	ἵνα τὴν ἐπαγγελίαν τοῦ πνεύματος λάβωμεν διὰ τῆς πίστεως.

Gal 3:8-14 repeats the same structure five times: After an assertion, there is a statement that introduces a Hebrew Bible citation:

> In **3:8** the assertion that God would justify the Gentiles by faith (A) precedes an introduction (A in) to a proof by means of a mixed citation of Gen 12:3 and 18:18 (A HB).
> In **3:10** the assertion that all who rely on the works of the law are under a curse (B) precedes an introduction (B in) to a proof by means of a citation of Deut 27:26 (B HB).
> In **3:11** the assertion that no man is justified before God by the law (C) precedes a brief introduction (C in) to a proof by means of a citation of Hab 2:4 (C HB).
> In **3:12** the assertion that the law does not rest on faith (D) precedes a brief introduction (D in) to a proof by means of a citation of Lev 18:5 (D HB).
> In **3:13** the assertion that Christ redeemed us by becoming a curse for us (E) precedes an introduction (E in) to a proof by means of a citation of Deut 21:23 (E HB).
> At two points this structure is expanded with further conclusions: In 3:9 the first assertion proved by the Hebrew Bible is expanded with a conclusion (A con), while 3:14 seems to link up the whole argument by means of two conclusions (E con 1 and 2).

The most controversial part of my analysis will be that I connect 3:8-9 with 3:10. As I have gone against the general consensus of relating 3:8-9 to an Abraham section in 3:6-9, I will also go against the general consensus of distinguishing it from 3:10-12. In my view there are many arguments for regarding 3:8-10 as a section of its own treating the antithesis of curse and blessing:

a) We have above in section 4.2 demonstrated that such antitheses are rather conventional in Jewish tradition.

b) The shift from inductive to deductive logic makes a connection between 3:6-7 and 3:8-9 improbable.

c) There is also a shift between 3:10 and 3:11-12: While Paul's own assertions in 3:8-10 are positive, they become denials in 3:11-12 (cf. οὐδείς in 3:11a and οὐκ ἔστιν in 3:12a). This makes it natural to assume that Paul changes to refutations in 3:11-12.

d) When we juxtapose 3:8-9 and 3:10, we recognize a chiastic structure in the verses. After an introduction (3:8a), we find the following elements:

3:8b: A Blessing-HB maxim.
3:9: A Blessing definition: ὥστε οἱ ἐκ πίστεως εὐλογοῦνται
3:10a: A Curse definition: ὅσοι γὰρ ἐξ ἔργων νόμου εἰσίν, ὑπὸ κατάραν εἰσίν
3:10b: A Curse-HB maxim.

I have noted that the structure in 3:8-9 differed somewhat from the rest of the passage in 3:8-14. This may indicate that Paul deliberately wanted to connect the parts of the antithesis as closely as possible to each other, since one Hebrew Bible proof precedes the assertion about blessing and another follows the assertion about a curse.

Finally we may refer to Arist. *Rhet.* II.xxiii.1, where Aristotle presents an argument from the Contrary as the first of his general topics. The point is to demonstrate that a contrary position also has an opposite predicate, "for instance, self-control is good, for (γάρ) lack of self-control is harmful." This is exactly what Paul does in 3:9-10. He proves that those of faith are blessed, and then he turns to those of works of the law, and proves that they are cursed. Paul also utilizes a connecting γάρ, as does Aristotle.

On the basis of these arguments, I regard the structure of 3:8-14 to be: Antithesis of blessing and curse (3:8-10), refutations (3:11-12), and sequence of curse and blessing (3:13-14).

10.2: *The argument leading up to Gal 3:8-14*

10.2.1: *The speech of Gal 2:14b-21*
The speech in Gal 2:14b-21 is important to discuss for several reasons:

a) It addresses a problem that is similar to the Galatian one. It may thus introduce types of argumentation that will be relevant also from 3:1 onward.

b) It contains many disputed passages. Our interpretation of chapter 3 will be strengthened if the topics suitable for a speech according to the stasis of Definition make it easier to recognize its logical pattern (cf. sec. 8.7.3 above for these topics).

c) It is relevant with regard to the interpretation of the curses in 3:10, 13. In 2:16 Paul introduces those definitions of the case on which he draws in 3:8-10. Further we find arguments very similar to the actual curses in 2:18-19.

a: *Dilemma and Definitions (2:14b-16)*
A speech according to the stasis of Definition should open with a Presentation of the case followed by the Definition and the Counterdefinition. In 2:14b the case is presented in the form of a Dilemma (2:14b; cf. Cic. *Inv.* I.xxix.45), and then two pairs of Definitions follow that may be applied to it (2:15-16a; cf. H. D. Betz 1979:115). In 2:16b we find a proof for the Definition according to the topic *Connect our Conduct*, and in 2:16c we find a refutation of a Counterdefinition. It is notable that the incident in Antioch with its Dilemma constitutes the Presentation of the case. This means that the whole speech has to be interpreted in light of this incident, whether or not we regard the speech as originating from that occasion.

2:14b: The Dilemma is presented to Cephas as follows: "If you, though a Jew, live like a Gentile and not like a Jew, how can you compel the

Gentiles to live like Jews?" The natural connection for the first part of the dilemma is 2:12: Cephas ate with the Gentiles in Antioch before the arrival of men from James. This meant living like a Gentile according to the kosher laws, which is a questionable praxis from a Jewish standpoint. The second part comes somewhat as a surprise, however, since we have not heard of any demand on Gentiles to live like Jews in Antioch (cf. H. D. Betz 1979:112). This move seems to correspond with the topic *From the Consequence* (ἐκ τοῦ ἀκολουθοῦντος). Instead of accusing Cephas for his return to Jewish rites, Paul accuses him of an unacceptable consequence that it will have.[3] Thus the dilemma is clear enough: When he ate with Gentiles, he came under pressure from the men from James. When he withdraw, however, he acted in a way that ran counter to his convictions. Sooner or later this would lead to demands on Gentile Christians also to lead a Jewish life.

2:15: The first pair of Definitions comes in 2:15: "We ourselves, who are Jews by birth and not Gentile sinners."[4] These Definitions correspond to Jewish theology which divides humanity into Jews and Gentiles,[5] a worldview according to which also Jewish Christians would define themselves.[6] If these were the only Definitions to be applied, it would be right to "compel the Gentiles to live like Jews" in order to be justified.

2:16a: While the first pair of Definitions is given at birth (φύσει), the second pair is embraced by Jewish Christians as a theological conviction (εἰδότες [δέ]).[7] As Christians, they have been challenged to define themselves according to another pair of Definitions: The first is that "a man is justified through faith in Jesus Christ," which we will denote as Paul's *Definition* of the case. The other, which we will denote as the *Counterdefinition*, states that "a man is justified by works of the law" (cf. also 2:21). This

---

[3]Cf. Arist. *Rhet.* II.xxiii.14: "Again, since in most human affairs the same thing is accompanied by some bad or good result, another topic consists in employing the consequence to exhort or dissuade, accuse or defend, praise or blame." A Dilemma may be seen as a double version of this topic, cf. Arist. *Rhet.* II.xxiii.15. It is thus unnecessary (as H. D. Betz 1979:112) to assume a *post factum* argument by Paul here, since it is a common topic.

For discussions of the possible historical realities behind this consequence and the incident as a whole, cf. Dunn 1983a and Holtz 1986.

[4]Since the classical punctuation makes sense, I see no reason to adopt the more complex proposal of Neitzel:15-27, to punctuate before ἁμαρτωλοί instead of after it.

[5]The word ἁμαρτωλοί denotes Gentiles as sinners in the respect that they do not possess the Torah and thus cannot achieve righteousness, cf. H. D. Betz 1979:115; Mussner:168; Rengstorf:324-26, 328.

[6]The use of *we* is inclusive of all Jewish Christians, Cephas and Paul included, cf. H. D. Betz 1979:115; Mussner:167; Schlier 1965:88; Bruce:137. Paul, however, seems to state this in a concessive clause, cf. Mussner:167; Oepke:90; Burton:119.

[7]Cf. H. D. Betz 1979:116. Paul seems to presuppose that he still argues on common ground, cf. Betz 1979:115; Bruce:139; Borse 1984:112.

means that whereas Jews would argue that there is no important difference between the two Definitions,[8] Paul has to separate them from each other as opposing principles: "A man is not justified by works of the law but (ἐὰν μή)[9] through faith in Jesus Christ."

It is important to note that these definitions are far more than abstract formulations; they both refer to very concrete ways of living:

It is debated whether ἔργα νόμου, which seems to be a reformulation by Paul,[10] refers to Judaism as legalism,[11] or to an emphasis on laws that mark out Israel *per se* according to "covenantal nomism."[12] Since Paul introduces the Definition as suitable for a discussion of the Law on a general level, however, it is better to take it as referring to deeds demanded by the sinaitic legislation.[13] The reference is thus made to a very concrete way of living in obedience to kosher laws and other laws that mark out Jews as a sociological group of its own.

The debate whether πίστις Χριστοῦ should be taken as a subjective[14] or an objective genitive is certainly to be solved in favor of the latter: The opposition between the Definitions demands that both of them refer to human actions.[15] A. von Dobbeler has shown that this term also refers to a quite specific way of life: πίστις refers to more than the individual relationship between one person and God, and it includes more than an intellectual act. It denotes the act of participation in the salvific work of Christ, which con-

---

[8]Cf. Mussner:170-71 for many texts that demonstrate the unity between faith and obedience in Jewish theology. Cf. also the interpretation of 3:12 below.

[9]I take ἐὰν μή in an adversative sense just as εἰ μή in 1:7, cf. Oepke:90; H. D. Betz 1979:117. This counters its usual sense of "except" (cf. *BDR* par 376,1) which may introduce a qualifying definition as Dunn 1983b:112-13 proposes. Cf. for this reading the critique by Räisänen 1985:547.

[10]Cf. though some similar phrases in a letter from Qumran, referred to by Hengel 1991:50-51.

[11]Cf. Bruce:137-38; Burton:120.

[12]Cf. Tyson 1973; Dunn 1983b:107-11; Heiligenthal. Cf. also Hamerton-Kelly 1990b:57-58, 62-64 for the violence that an emphasis on national identity causes.

[13]Cf. Westerholm 1988:116-21, who argues that Paul never perceives the law in terms of legalism. He also states that although it was laws that mark out Israel *per se* which caused problems in Galatia, Paul has chosen to discuss it on a more general level. The proposal of Gaston:100-106 that ἔργα νόμου is a genitive *auctoris*, referring to the works which the law itself performs, is also refuted by Westerholm.

[14]Cf. Howard:57-58; Williams 1980:272-76; 1987b; Hooker. Hays 1983:141-42, 155-70, 200-202, 231-32 even interprets several passages with only the word πίστις referring primarily to the faith of Christ. Cf. Hultgren for further references and critique.

[15]The verbal use of *to believe* in 2:16b demands that Christ is the object of faith in 2:16b, and we have no reason to imply a shift from another sense in 2:16a. Cf. Bruce:138-39; Burton:121; H. D. Betz 1979:117-18; Hultgren. If there is an ambiguity here (cf. Bligh:203-204; Hooker:340-41), the notion of Christ's faith resides only in the background.

stitutes both the citizenship in the salvific nearness to God, and also the inclusion in the pneumatic community of believers (95–96). Faith is thus an interpersonal act that eradicates the division between Jews and Gentiles (166–70). Thus πίστις may also become a sociological mark of identification; compare the expression οἰκείους τῆς πίστεως in Gal 6:10, where οἰκεῖος refers to the organizing structure of Christian communities, and πίστις to faith as its common principle (251–73).[16] Thus πίστις is a mark of identity that delimits Christianity from Judaism (244–51): While a Jewish way of life has νόμος as its basic principle and is marked by obedience toward it, the Christian way of life has the Christ event as its basis and is marked by faith in its salvific force. This faith is mainly a phenomenon of entrance into the community, but it also includes strength for preservation and a way of life pleasing to God (171–242).

It is also important to see how these Definitions function in Paul's argumentation: If Paul is able to argue convincingly that they are opposed to each other and able to prove that righteousness is given by faith, then a claim for kosher laws and circumcision is invalidated! Therefore this definition of the case is immediately supported with two proofs where the Definitions are repeated:[17]

2:16b: The first proof connects the experience of the Christians to the Definition:[18] "We have believed in Christ Jesus, in order to be justified by faith in Christ." Paul emphasizes that they have acted in accordance with the Definition (ἐπιστεύσαμεν) in order to conform to it (ἵνα + Definition).

2:16c: The second proof is a *Refutation of the Counterdefinition* with a maxim: "and not by works of the law, because by works of the law shall no one (πᾶσα σάρξ) be justified." The logic may be reconstructed as a syllogism where the conclusion comes first, and the main presupposition follows in the form of a general maxim:[19]

General maxim: By works of the law shall no flesh be justified.
(Specific premise: We are flesh.)
Conclusion: (We shall) not (be justified) by works of the law.

---

[16]Dobbeler:251–73 also demonstrates that it was common to organize religious groups in an οἶκος, and that there also exists other examples of such groups with πίστις as an important mark of identification (e. g., a private cult in Philadelphia).

[17]Cf. the figure *expolitio* with *reduplicatio* by *ad Herenn.* IV.xlii.54 and in Gal 1:8–9. Here Paul dwells on the same Definitions, but changes the topics so that he each time introduces new perspectives.

[18]Cf. the topic of *Connecting our Conduct with the Definition*, which according to *ad Herennium* and Cicero is a topic suitable for speeches of Definition (see sec. 8.7.3 above).

[19] Cf. above sec. 8.4 for this kind of deductive reasoning.

The specific premise is omitted, because it is self-evident. Paul also implies the verb *justify* in the conclusion, since it is present earlier in the clause. The general maxim is well chosen: It conforms to the fact that Jewish Christians actually did not manage to keep the whole law (Wilckens 1974:89–91). It also conforms to Ps 143:2, although in the present context it is not introduced clearly as a Previous Judgment from Scripture.[20]

Thus Paul has presented his definition of the case. He plays a Jewish way of life off against the Christian mark of identity: πίστις. From a Jewish-Christian point of view, this is so unexpected that Paul has to present many arguments for it to be persuasive. Paul does this in the rest of the speech, but above all in Gal 3.

b: Refutation of a Counterobjection (2:17–18)

Gal 2:17–18 contain the most disputed verses in this speech. They are most naturally interpreted together as Paul's refutation of a Counterobjection (2:17) by turning it back on the opponents (2:18).[21] It is also natural to imply a connection between these two verses and the two parts of the Dilemma in 2:14b:

2:17: The two premises "But if, in our endeavour to be justified in Christ, we ourselves were found to be sinners" correspond to the conduct of Cephas in Antioch, where he "though a Jew, live[d] like a Gentile and not like a Jew." This means that both premises are accepted by Paul,[22] and that the term *sinners* (ἁμαρτωλοί) refers to the fact that Jews were placed on a par with the Gentiles (cf. 2:15).[23] The statement therefore points to a consequence of Paul's emphasis on justification by faith: It nullifies the relevance of the distinction between Jews and Gentiles (cf. 5:6; 6:15).

---

[20]Cf. Sieffert:121; Mussner:174–75; Koch 1986:18; Rohde:112. Most scholars, however, understand it as a Hebrew Bible citation with ὅτι as a citation formula, cf., for example, Zahn:123–24; Lightfoot:115–16; Burton:123–24; Oepke:91; Schlier 1965:94–95; H. D. Betz 1979:118–19; Bruce:140; Borse 1984:114. Some first readers would probably recognize it as a Hebrew Bible citation, but this is not necessary for its persuasive effect.

[21]It is common to see the verses together, but some scholars differ at this point, cf. Klein 1964:141, 146–47; Lambrecht:491–95. An *e contrario* function of 2:18 is noted by Burton:130; Klein 1964:144; Ebeling:181.

[22]Cf. the discussion whether Paul only denies the conclusion in 2:17c or also the middle premise. Μὴ γένοιτο always denies only the conclusion, cf. the instructive discussion in Burton:125, 127–30 and the formal argument by Oepke:92. For the conviction that also the premise "we were found to be sinners" is false in Paul's opinion, cf. Mussner:177; H. D. Betz 1979:119.

[23]Cf. Lightfoot:116–17; Oepke:92; Schlier 1965:95; Becker:30; Bruce:140–41; Hansen:104–105. On the other hand both Burton:129–30 and Mussner:176 take it to refer to the concrete conduct of Cephas in 2:14b. Neitzel:30–39 instead connects the sin with Peter's withdrawal from table fellowship in 2:12b.

The Counterobjection draws a conclusion from these premises which Paul presents in a question[24] that he denies: ". . . is Christ then an agent of sin? Certainly not!" Paul once again takes up the term of sin (ἁμαρτία versus ἁμαρτωλοί). We seem to have an instance of the rhetorical figure *diaphora* "which occurs when the same word is used first in one function, and then in another" (*ad Herenn.* IV.xiv.21). Paul recognizes that Jewish Christians have become sinners as the Gentiles, that is, that the division between Jews and Gentiles has been invalidated. He denies, however, that Christ has promoted sin in a qualified sense.[25]

2:18: In the next verse Paul turns the accusation of sin back on his opponents:[26] "If I[27] build up again those things which I tore down, then I prove myself a transgressor." The premise of this verse corresponds to the withdrawal of Cephas in 2:14b: When he withdrew from table-fellowship with Gentiles, he reinstated the principle of the law that he had torn down.[28]

It has been disputed whether the transgression is connected to the tearing down[29] or to the rebuilding of the law.[30] Since the main verb in the clause is οἰκοδομεῖν, the latter interpretation is most probable. Thus Paul judges the attitude of those Jewish Christians who, as Cephas, want to uphold the distinction between Jews and Gentiles. This is seen by Paul as identical to an attempt to reinstate the law, and it is judged as transgression. The reason for this judgment is not given explicitly but is easy to imply from 2:16: A reinstitution of the law is regarded as a recourse to the Counterdefinition ἐξ ἔργων νόμου, which has been proved to be false.[31]

---

[24]ἆρα is taken as an interrogative particle since μὴ γένοιτο is always found after such particles, cf. Burton:126; Mussner:176. It may be illative, but still within a question, cf. Lambrecht:489–90, but not a causal particle as Borse 1984:115 proposes.

[25]Cf. Burton:126; Duncan:67–68; Oepke:93; Lambrecht:491; Ebeling:180–81; Hansen:105. Paul may also allude to a claim that Christ increases the sin/number of sinners, cf. Bruce:141; Suhl:3108-9.

[26]Cf. this topic in Arist. *Rhet.* II.xxiii.7.

[27]The change to 1st person singular from 2:18 onward has aroused much attention. It is probably a rhetorical feature by means of which Paul uses himself as an example, cf. Mussner:177–78; Oepke:93. It may also indicate that Paul now turns to arguments where there is no common ground between him and his adversaries, cf. H. D. Betz 1979:121.

[28]Contrary to Zahn:129–32, who takes the verse as an *irrealis* concerning Paul's attitude. Cf. *Str-B* III:537–38; Mussner:178 for καταλύειν/οἰκοδομεῖν as rabbinic expressions concerning the law.

[29]The reinstitution of the law makes one regard the former dispensations from it as sinful, cf. Oepke:94; Mussner:179; Borse 1984:116; Rohde:114–15.

[30]The reinstitution of the law is sinful because it draws man back to the law which makes him a sinner, cf. Mundle; Burton:131–33; Klein 1964:144; Wilckens 1974:93; Schlier 1965:97–98.

[31]Cf. for a similar position Duncan 68–69; Bruce:142; Neitzel:136–37; Hansen:106.

The curse of Gal 3:10 will supplement this argument with a further proof: The accusation of being transgressors will be sharpened into a curse on those ἐξ ἔργων νόμου, and it will be proved by a Hebrew Bible citation.

c: Further arguments (2:19-21)

After the refutation, Paul continues by stating four theses in support of his Definition (2:19-20), which is followed by a brief, concluding Refutation (2:21).[32]

2:19a: The first thesis uses the term νόμος twice, and this has caused much discussion: "For I through the law (διὰ νόμου) died to the law (νόμῳ) that I might live to God." Again we seem to face an instance of *diaphora* where Paul explicitly plays on the ambiguity of νόμος as in 4:21: "Tell me, you who desire to be under law (νόμος = the mosaic commandments), do you not hear the law (νόμος = the Pentateuch)?"[33] If this is accepted, the meaning of the clause would be: I through what is written in the Pentateuch/Scripture, died to the claims of the mosaic commandments.[34]

This move conforms to the topic *Intention of the framer of the law*.[35] Its point is to demonstrate that one's own Definition corresponds to the intention of the lawgiver. Paul thus states that it was the law itself (=Pentateuch) which proclaimed freedom from the law (=mosaic commandments), but he does not state the reason for this.

I find that the direction of the argument is indicated in the second thesis of 2:19b: "I have been crucified with Christ." This thesis indicates that the intention of the Pentateuch with regard to the law is connected to the cross of Christ. We will see that the curse of 3:13 will supply this argument with a proof: The intention of the Pentateuch is revealed in Deut 21:23. This curse hit Christ with the intention of redeeming from the curse of the law.

---

[32]Cf. H. D. Betz 1979:121-22, 126. These statements do not prelude the discussion of Gal 3-4; they are rather to be connected to the preceding parts of the actual speech.

[33]For this interpretation of 4:21, cf. Burton:252; Mussner:317-18; H. D. Betz 1979:241; Bruce:215. Cf. Räisänen 1986a:144-47 for analogies to this play on the word νόμος by Paul and other Greek authors, and Westerholm 1988:106-109 for the ambiguity of νόμος referring both to the Pentateuch and the sinaitic legislation.

[34]Cf. Bligh:211-12; Räisänen 1983:58. Also Lightfoot:118 and Burton:133 consider this interpretation as possible, although they do not choose it. For διὰ νόμου + Gen. denoting the mediator, cf. *BDR* par 223,3. Neitzel:137-42 is also close to this interpretation, although he interprets the first νόμος as the law of Christ (cf. Bengel:735; Luther 26:155-56, 161-64). Cf. his references to similar views among the Fathers (139).

It is most common to let νόμος refer to legalism both times, and thus to interpret Paul as referring to a struggle with the unattainable demands of the law which makes one die to the law, cf. Zahn:133; Lightfoot:118; Burton:132-34; Duncan:70; Mussner:179-80; Rohde:115-16.

[35]This topic is common in most judicial speeches, cf. above in secs. 8.6.2 and 8.7.3.

Christians thus die to the law when they participate in this event of salvation,[36] an act which Paul elsewhere connects to baptism.[37]

2:20a: The third thesis states that "it is no longer I who live, but Christ who lives in me." The important aspect for our purpose is not the tenor of the "mystical" language here,[38] but the function of the thesis over against the charge that Christ is the servant of sin: When Christ himself lives through a Christian, there is no reason to fear that a Christian will live as a qualified sinner (similar Rohde:116-17).

2:20b: The fourth thesis takes up Paul's Definition of the case and carries it even further: ". . . and the life I now live in the flesh I live by faith ($\dot{\varepsilon}\nu$ $\pi\iota\sigma\tau\varepsilon\iota$) in the Son of God, who loved me and gave himself for me." The Definition is now rendered with $\dot{\varepsilon}\nu$ $\pi\iota\sigma\tau\varepsilon\iota$, thus indicating that faith is not only a means of salvation, but also a sphere in which the new life is lived (Burton:138-39). This move substantiates the interpretation of $\pi\iota\sigma\tau\iota\varsigma$ as an identity marker of a Christian way of life.

2:21: Paul ends this speech with a brief Refutation: "I do not nullify the grace of God." Paul may be taking up an objection from Jewish Christians,[39] or he may anticipate the objection that he overturns God's grace against the Jewish race. Regardless of the origin of such an objection, it is implicitly turned back on his opponents:[40] ". . . for if justification were through the law, then Christ died to no purpose."

We may underscore the way this verse gets back to the fundamentals of the controversy: Paul contrasts the law with the death of Christ. The opposing definitions which Paul has presented are thus rooted in opposing divine acts.

To sum up: We have seen that the arguments in 2:14b-21 conform well to the outline for speeches according to the stasis of Definition.[41] Although this speech is addressed to a situation other than the Galatian one, it serves its

---

[36]Cf. similar thoughts in Sieffert:130-31; Oepke:95; Bligh:213; Schlier 1965:100-101; Lührmann 1978:45; Cosgrove 1988:139-40; Hansen:107-8.

[37]Cf. for baptismal language in this verse Schlier 1965:99-100; Mussner:180-81; Bruce 144.

[38]Cf. for this Oepke:95-96; H. D. Betz 1979:124.

[39]Cf. Burton:140; Schlier 1965:104; Rohde:117.

[40]Cf. again (as in 2:18) the topic of turning against the opponents what has been said (or here: what may be expected to be said) against ourselves in Arist. *Rhet.* II.xxiii.7. See also H. D. Betz 1979:126-27.

[41]There is a Presentation of the case in the form of a Dilemma (2:14b), two pairs of Definitions where the last pair is separated from each other (2:15-16a), a proof for the Definition according to the topic Connect our conduct with the Definition (2:16b), and a refutation of the Counterdefinition with a syllogism (2:16c). Then there is a refutation of a Counterobjection (2:17-18) before the Definition is substantiated with a brief reference to the Intention of the framer of the law (2:19).

transitional purpose well by preparing for the argumentation of Gal 3:   Paul introduces the pair of Definitions that he will take up again (2:16 versus 3:2, 5, 8-10), and he poses brief arguments that he will discuss more thoroughly in the section of curse and blessing (2:18-19 versus 3:10, 13).

We have seen how Paul has contrasted two fundamental divine gifts: The law versus the death of Christ (2:21).   From these contrasting fundamentals, two ways of being justified have been derived: By works of the law or by faith in Christ (2:16).   Further two different ways of life are described in the speech: A life as a transgressor (2:18) or a life ἐν πίστει where Christ lives in the Christian (2:20).   Thus we face two opposing ways of life, which are contrasted both with regard to origin, to their identity markers, and to their consequences in everyday life.

10.2.2:   The inductive arguments of Gal 3:1-7

Paul opens chapter 3 with a direct address to the Galatians, clearly indicating that he is making a shift over to a new set of arguments. In 2:1-4 we find many elements that remind us of letters of rebuke (cf. above sec. 7.2.1). Paul also seems to recapitulate briefly the content of his *exordium:*[42] rebukes of the Galatians, an attack on the opponents, and an emphasis on the importance of the cross of Christ.[43]   For our purpose it is important to note the inductive arguments in this section, one from experience (3:2.5), and one from the Example of Abraham (3:6).

a: The argument from experience (3:2, 5)
The inductive argument from experience is introduced in 3:2.[44]   It includes both the *Definition* with a minor variation ("by hearing with faith") and the *Counterdefinition* ("by works of the law") from 2:16.[45]   It forms an

---

[42]I follow H. D. Betz 1979:128-29 in taking this section as a part of the argumentation, and not Berger 1984a:44, who proposes a new *exordium* (3:1-2) and narrative (3:3-5).

[43] For rebukes, compare the expression: "O foolish Galatians" (3:1a, 3a) and other questions of rebuke (3:3-4) with 1:6-7a. They are treated above in sec. 9.2.1. For the attack, compare the accusation: "Who has bewitched you?" (3:1a) with 1:7b-9. It is treated above in sec. 9.2.1. For the cross of Christ, compare 3:1b with 1:4.

[44]Cf. Paul's introduction: τοῦτο μόνον θέλω μαθεῖν ἀφ᾽ ὑμῶν, which may be translated literally as "this only I want to learn from you." Paul thus wants to learn something from experience. The inductive mode is also indicated by the fact that Paul wants to subsume a concrete experience under a general principle. Cf. also H. D. Betz 1979:129.

[45]From topics suitable for speeches belonging to the stasis of Definition, we may note that it also corresponds to the topic of Connecting the act of the accused with the Definition, cf. 2:16b. Paul addresses the Galatians not only as eyewitnesses in general, as H. D. Betz 1979:129-30 proposes, but the main point is that he connects their experience to the Definition.

Analogy to 2:16, by shifting the focus from righteousness by faith to the bestowal of the Spirit by faith. This analogy is connected to righteousness as effect to cause: In our Jewish curse texts we have noted that blessings as the bestowal of the Spirit frequently are promised to those that are righteous.[46]

The argument has the form of a *Question*, and thus it openly challenges the audience to reflect about their situation.[47] The proof is strong[48] because it refers to an experience which was very difficult to explain within the boundaries of Jewish theology: *The bestowal of the Spirit on uncircumcised Gentiles.* Within Jewish tradition the Spirit is promised to the Jewish nation in the new era of blessing.

> We know from Acts that such an incident was a very strong argument for the law-free Gentile Mission (cf. Acts 10:44–48; 11:18; 15:8). In Jewish tradition the bestowal of the Spirit was a sign of the new era of blessing, but it was only promised to obedient Jews.[49]
>
> It is first and foremost Joel 2:28–32 that predicts the bestowal of the Spirit in the new era within an address to Israel, calling them to penitence "with all their heart" (2:12). The Gentiles are in view only as an object of judgment (3:2–15). When this text is fulfilled at Pentecost in Acts 2, the Spirit is poured out upon circumcised Jews. Also Isa 44:3–4 predicts that the Spirit will fall upon the seed of Israel.
>
> Further, the Spirit is predicted as part of Israel's restoration in Ezek 11:19 and 36:26–27. In these texts the bestowal of the Spirit in the new era is explicitly given in order to enable obedience to law. In the dtr-SH texts which we presented above in chapter 3, the Spirit was mentioned only in *Jub.* 1:23–24 and 1QS iv.21–22. In both places it is given in order to enable new obedience to law.

---

[46]In appendix 1 it is easy to see how frequently the theme of righteousness is within curse texts, and usually righteousness is demanded as a cause for giving the blessing. Cf. also Dobbeler:58. This move from the cause (=righteousness) to the effect (=bestowal of the Spirit) corresponds to a conventional topic, cf. Arist. *Rhet.* II.xxiii.25.

[47]It is probably not a question where the answer is self-evident, at least not to the opponents, contrary to H. D. Betz 1979:132; Lategan:176 and most commentaries. Rather it seems to be posed as a proof, which according to Aristotle is well chosen if it ascribes contradictions or paradoxes to his opponents. In addition to such instances that demand a reply for further reasoning, Aristotle recommends questions: ". . . when it is intended to show that the opponent either contradicts himself or puts forward a paradox. Further, when the opponent can do nothing else but answer the question by a sophistical solution . . . 'Partly yes, and partly no'" (Arist. *Rhet.* III.xviii.4). Cf. for the use of questions also Martin:133–35.

[48]The expression τοῦτο μόνον indicates that the question is well chosen as a strong argument, cf. Bengel:735; Sieffert:139; Burton:147; Schlier 1965:121; Cosgrove 1988: 41–42.

[49]Cf. Sjöberg:384–85 for references to Palestinian Judaism and rabbinic literature, and Cosgrove 1988:96–97, 100–101 for references to Pseudepigrapha and Qumran. Cf. also Hartman 1980:109; Barclay 1988:84–85; Dobbeler:50–54.

Although the bestowal of the Spirit upon uncircumcised Gentiles in Galatia may have been difficult to explain for the opponents, the Galatians had experienced it as an indisputable fact. If they had to choose between the opposing Definitions, they certainly had to opt for πίστις.

3:3: In the next verse the argument is stretched a bit further: "Having begun with the Spirit, are you now ending with flesh?" Such a move, which seeks to discover a contradiction between past and present, is conventional.[50] Thus Paul accuses the Galatians of having begun according to the principle of faith, but of considering a change for its opposite. Instead of the Definition/ Counterdefinition Paul here opposes the Spirit and the flesh, thus giving the question an ironic flavor: Nobody will normally proceed from the Spirit to the flesh.[51]

3:5: In 3:5 the question of 3:2 is repeated according to the figure *expolitio* with *reduplicatio*.[52] Paul repeats one part of the clause word by word ("by works of the law or by hearing with faith") while making slight changes in the other part: While he focused the initial reception of the Spirit in 3:2, he focuses the current work of the Spirit in 3:5. Thus it becomes even more inexpedient for the Galatians to consider circumcision: Not only had they begun according to the principle of faith, but God has also worked among them according to it up to the present.

Again we may note how the principle of faith is part of a far-reaching act of participation: It is rooted in the act of Christ on the cross (3:1), the proclamation of the Gospel was accompanied by signs of the Spirit (3:2), and πίστις is also the mark of a life that enables a Christian to live in a pneumatic community (3:5).[53]

---

[50]It corresponds to the topic Examining together, which according to Aristotle ". . . when something contrary to what has already been done is on the point of being done, consists in examining them together (ἄμα σκοπεῖν)" (*Rhet.* II.xxiii.27). Cf. for this topic also Gal 4:8–9 in sec. 9.2.1c above.

It is probably not a Dilemma as H. D. Betz 1979:133 proposes, but he is right in finding the figure of antithesis here. Paul may allude to the teaching of his opponents as some sort of perfecting the teaching of Paul, cf. Oepke:101; Schlier 1965:123–24.

[51]Sieffert:141; H. D. Betz 1979:133. The irony is present regardless of the interpretation of σάρξ, either as alluding to the rite of circumcision (H. D. Betz 1979:134), to the human nature in its weakness (Bruce:149), or to flesh as an agency of salvation (Burton:148).

Perhaps also the term ἐπιτελεῖν is ambiguous: It may design both to fulfill and to terminate, cf. Ebeling:221.

[52]Cf. the anathemas 1:8–9; 2:16 and *ad Herenn.* IV.xlii.54 for this figure of thought.

[53]Cf. Dobbeler:9–43 where he argues that it was conventional in the Hellenistic world to demand legitimizing elements in order to believe in a message. Those elements could both be authorizations behind the message, and signs and wonders performed by its preachers. Cf. for the importance of signs the Moses tradition in a Jewish setting and 2 Cor 12:12; Rom 15:18–19 in a Christian setting.

There is more to be discussed in the questions 3:2, 5, however. If we compare them to the expressions of 2:16, we find that Paul renders the Counterdefinition in the same way (ἐξ ἔργων νόμου), but that he *changes the Definition slightly*: While in 2:16 he renders it as "faith in Christ," here he renders it as "hearing with faith (ἀκοὴ πίστεως)." This phrase is so ambiguous that it may encompass all the above noted aspects of πίστις:

> We may prefer the passive sense of ἀκοή and thus translate the genitive as "message/proclamation of faith."[54] In this case faith is connected to its basis in the message about Christ.
> We may also take ἀκοή in the active sense, since the opposition to the Counterdefinition makes it natural to imply a human response. Then we come to the classical interpretation "hearing with faith,"[55] and the focus is on faith as the human response by conversion.
> Lastly ἀκοή may also be understood in the sense of obedience, ὑπακοή. A connection between ἀκοή and ὑπακοή is made in Rom 10:14-17, cf. also the genitive constructions between ὑπακοή and πίστις in Rom 1:5; 16:26. This would correspond to such deuteronomistic texts as Deut 28:1, where Moses summons Israel both to hear God's voice in obedience (ἀκοῇ εἰσακούσητε) and to do his commandments (φυλάσσειν καὶ ποιεῖν). See also Deut 30:12-13, where it is stated twice that one can hear (ἀκουεῖν) and do (ποιεῖν) the law.[56] This last alternative connects faith to the obedient life of a Christian.
> Thus we see how the ambiguous phrase ἀκοὴ πίστεως underscores the complexity of the πίστις concept which A. von Dobbeler has analyzed in Paul. Faith is regarded as a mark of identity for Christians which is rooted in the message about Christ, which marks the conversion experience, and which also is shown in the obedient life in the community.

b: The Example of Abraham (3:6-7)

Abraham is introduced as a similar Example with the expression καθώς.[57] This example is extremely well chosen: It illustrates the general principle of faith (cf. the questions of 3:2, 5), and it also connects faith to righteousness (cf. 2:16a). It thus functions as a Contrary to the syllogism of

---

[54]Cf. Sieffert:140-41; H. D. Betz 1979:133 and the extensive discussion by Hays 1983:143-49. Mostly the genitive is taken as an objective, but it may also be taken as a qualitative, cf. Oepke:100-101; Schlier:121-22.

[55]Cf. Zahn:140-41; Lightfoot:135; Ridderbos:113; Rohde:131; Williams 1989; Hansen:110-11. The genitive is understood as a subjective.

[56]Philo cites Deut 28:1 in *Praem* 79 and comments on it by separating the two phrases: It is important "not merely to hear (ἀκοῆς) them, but to carry them out by your life and conduct (διὰ τῶν τοῦ βίου πράξεων ἐπιτελῆτε)." By separating the expressions, Philo can underscore that it is necessary both to hear and to do the law. Like Philo, Paul may in Gal 3:2, 5 separate the concept of doing from that of hearing, but unlike him he may relate only the first of them to the law.

[57]Thus I regard καθώς not mainly as a citation formula as H. D. Betz 1979:140, but rather as introducing a real comparison, cf. Mussner:213; Koch 1986:106; Williams 1987a:92-95; Hays 1989:108.

2:16c: While 2:16c proved that no flesh could be justified before God through the works of the law, Gen 15:6 proves the contrary position, namely that a man can be justified by faith.

The main power of this proof is not that it consists in a Hebrew Bible citation, but that it is an appeal to an authoritative Example (παράδειγμα) from History.[58] It was customary in Jewish tradition to refer to a certain paradigmatic conduct by Abraham that one ought to imitate, and to assert that God supplied him with (salvific) benefits because of this.[59]

Such references to heroes of the past were widespread in Hellenistic culture.[60] The most important Examples are those which served as models for identification and commitment within a nation.[61] In Jewish tradition this resulted in many references to heroes of the past, among which Sir 44:1 – 50:24 is a well-known example. In Christian tradition we may refer to Hebrews 11 with its many references to the heroes of faith.[62]

It is notable that Paul does not supply his readers with a long list of Examples, but both in Galatians and in Romans he concentrates on the figure of Abraham. This is probably not only due to the fact that Abraham was regarded as the founder of the Jewish race, but also because he came before the period of the law and thus could serve as a hero of identification independent of obedience to the Torah.

The Example itself is a *Quotation* from Gen 15:6 which corresponds exactly to the LXX, the name of Abraham at the beginning being the only alteration (Koch 1986:106). When Paul plays the faith of Abraham off against obedience to the law, he counters Jewish tradition.[63] The Hebrew Bible citation thus involves an Ambiguity: Faith is the ambiguous term that

---

[58]Cf. Ridderbos:118; Luz:180–82, 279–80; Hansen:89–90, 112 who indicate the same. Wieser:42–43, 79–81 denotes this as the "Bewährungsmodell" in Paul. This is contrary to Howard:54–55 who argues that Christians are connected to Abraham through the History of Salvation.

[59]Cf. Berger *TRE* 1:373–74 for this use which he distinguishes from the soteriological function of Abraham (376). Abraham served as an Example both for Jews and Proselytes (373). Cf. also Wieser:160–71 for Jewish material which he characterizes as the motif of "Bewährung," and for material concerning Abraham and the Gentiles (171–75). See also Dobbeler:132.

[60]Cf. Baasland 1986:198. He refers to Alewell (5–35) for the theory and for its frequency in Roman literature (54–91, 100–118). Any audience would expect that such examples were to be used by a speaker (cf. 91).

[61]Cf. Alewell:33, 96–99 for the preference for well-known and domestic examples.

[62]Cf. also the letter of James, where the παράδειγμα of Abraham, Rahab, the prophets, Job, and Elijah are considered as people who have shown their fidelity not only in words, but also in deed, cf. Baasland 1988a:3666.

[63]Cf. the Jewish material in *Str-B* III:187–201; Mussner:218; Wieser:161–65; Dobbeler:116–25. The Jewish tradition is also found in Jas 2:20–26, cf. Hahn:92–97.

Paul employs in a new way.[64] Since the argument is so brief, Paul seems to presuppose that the Galatians will accept that the faith of Abraham is faith in his sense of the word.[65]

c: The general principle of faith

Paul draws the conclusion of his inductive proofs in 3:7: "So you see that (γινώσκετε[66] ἄρα ὅτι) it is men of faith who are the sons of Abraham." The logic is that both the bestowal of the Spirit in Galatia and the example of Abraham substantiate the same general principle, namely the principle of faith.[67]

Paul introduces a new phrase in the conclusion: Those of faith are "sons of Abraham (υἱοὶ . . . 'Αβραάμ)." This is a standard phrase for Jewish national identity. It is not that Jews relied on such sonship only in terms of descent; they also emphasized that a Jew had to imitate Abraham to be regarded as his son.[68] Thus Abraham became a hero who should promote identification and commitment to the law in the Jewish nation.

In a similar way Paul also speaks of the Christian community as a group in this verse. They are "sons of Abraham," and they belong to a group where faith is the marker of identity: οἱ ἐκ πίστεως. This group should imitate Abraham in his paradigmatic attitude of faith.

---

[64]Cf. above sec. 8.6.2 for the stasis of Ambiguity (and legal stasis in general) as a fruitful approach to interpret the Hebrew Bible citations.

[65]The argumentation is broader in Rom 4:3, where Paul defends his interpretation by means of a contextual argument: In Rom 4:18–22 Paul states that Abraham believed in the promise of God which was given in Gen 15:5, and that faith therefore must be interpreted as faith in God's promise. Paul is therefore able to defend his reinterpretation of faith with a move corresponding to the topic What precedes or follows, a topic which draws on the near context for illuminating observations, cf. Cic. Inv. II.xl.117: ". . . it must be shown that from what precedes or follows in the document the doubtful point becomes plain." Thus Gen 15:6 must be interpreted in light of Gen 15:5. It is this topic that has influenced the 7th rule of Hillel, cf. Daube:257. Cf. Rohde:136 for a similar observation on Paul's argument.

[66]Whether γινῶσκετε is to be taken as indicative or imperative is of no importance for our purpose, cf. the presentation of positions by Sieffert:148; H. D. Betz 1979:141. It is important to note that it draws a conclusion from 3:6 (cf. Mussner:216; Rohde:137) and does not introduce a thesis that follows from the discussion of 3:8–14 (cf. H. D. Betz 1979:141).

[67]Cf. Williams 1987a:95; Hansen:111; pace Howard:55–57. Although Howard also sees the connection between 3:2–5 and 3:6, he plays down the role of faith and finds the correspondence between God who "supplies" in 3:5 and God who "reckons" in 3:6. It is unnecessary for us to guess in such a way, however, because 3:7 spells out explicitly what the point of comparison is.

[68]Cf. for Jewish references Mussner:217–18; Berger TRE 1:377; Wieser:160–61. Whether this is a stock phrase from the opponents (cf. the long discussion in Burton:156–59) is not important to discuss for our purpose. Also Bligh:243–44 notices the importance of the imitation motif.

To conclude: Paul's first two arguments in Gal 3 are inductive. The first proof connects the experience of the Galatians with Paul's definition of the case, and the second refers to the Example of Abraham. In both of these instances Paul seeks to persuade that God justifies by the principle of faith.

10.3: Curse and blessing in antithesis: Gal 3:8–12

10.3.1: Conflict of laws in Gal 3:15–29

We have seen how the argument from 2:16 onward has been presented in a way similar to the stasis of Definition from Hellenistic rhetoric. It is easy to see that also the section 3:8–14 is influenced by it, since the Definitions are juxtaposed also here: faith versus law/works of the law in 3:8–10, 11, 12.

In addition, another rhetorical element is present, however, which will become clearly explicit from 3:15 onward. This element is the employment of the Hellenistic legal stasis (cf. above sec. 8.6.2).

At the center of Gal 3 we find the opposition between the Abraham promise and the Sinai legislation in 3:15–18. It is presented as a conflict between two legal documents, and according to J. Vos we seem to be cast into a legal discussion similar to the stasis of *Conflicting laws* (265).

According to *ad Herennium*, "When two laws conflict, we must first see whether they have been superseded or restricted" (*ad Herenn.* II.x.15). Paul's discussion seems to reflect this custom of arguing in a twofold way: On one hand he emphasizes that the promise has not been superseded by the law (3:17–18). On the other hand he emphasizes that the Sinai covenant has been restricted by having a minor role (3:19–22; Vos:266). It has also been superseded by the coming of faith (3:23–25).

This Conflict of Laws is also discussed with a concern for the *Intention* of the lawgiver. Paul asks why the Sinai covenant was given (3:19a) and answers with a χάριν phrase (3:19b). As in Hellenistic rhetoric, his presupposition is that there must be an intent that does not contradict the promise (3:21). Here we also find conclusions with ὥστε (3:24) and ἵνα (3:22, 24).

Finally, we also find a clear example of *Ambiguity* in 3:16. When Paul discusses the promise of Gen 13:15 (cf. Gen 17:8; 24:7), he emphasizes the point that it is given in the singular and not in the plural. This demonstrates an ambiguity in the text, whether it should be taken to relate to a group or to a specific person.[69]

---

[69]For references to Jewish exegesis of σπέρμα and also to possible predecessors of Paul's individual exegesis of the term, cf. Mussner:238–40; H. D. Betz 1979:157; Hansen:207–8. For Jewish texts that discuss singular versus plural, cf. Schlier 1965:145; Bruce:172–73.

We thus find that a combination of Conflict of laws and Letter and intent is involved in the argument from Gal 3:15 onward at a macro level, and also that at least one of the minor arguments involves Ambiguity. It seems reasonable that Paul should supply his stasis of Definition argument with an emphasis on the stasis of Conflicting laws. Both he and his audience know that a demand for works of the law is rooted in Scripture and that it is more well-founded than the demand for faith. A conflict between Paul's argument and other scriptural passages must have been present in the mind of the first audience. What becomes explicitly treated from 3:15 onward may also be important as a more or less implicit element of the argument in 3:8–14.

As for 3:8–10 we have argued in section 10.1 that it contains blessing and curse in an antithesis. Our survey of the Jewish texts above in chapters 3–4 has shown that many of them, especially from the Deut 27–30 tradition, contain similar antithetic constructions. The content of Paul's antithesis, however, seems to oppose the conventional Jewish antithesis in a radical way.[70]

10.3.2: *The blessing on those of faith (3:8–9)*

It is conventional and well-founded to take these verses as a realized blessing:

a) In 3:9 it is spoken in the present passive tense, which may be taken as a divine passive.

b) The condition is fulfilled as 3:2, 5 demonstrate: The Galatians both have and are acting out of faith.

c) The presence of the Spirit is also a sign that the audience has been blessed by God (cf. 3:2, 5).

a: The syllogistic logic in 3:8–9

If Paul has changed from inductive to deductive logic, it should be possible to put his implied logic in a syllogistic form, whether Paul has meant it as a syllogism or not. In 3:8 it is easy to find a general premise and a conclusion, as well as to reconstruct a specific premise that fits into the argument:[71]

> *General premise*: In thee (=Abraham) shall all the nations be blessed (3:8b).
> *Specific premise*: Those who are men of faith are in Abraham (=3:7).
> *Conclusion*: Those who are men of faith are blessed (3:9a; cf. 3:8a: God would justify the Gentiles by faith).

---

[70]Lührmann 1978:56–59 is closest to this reading by his indications that Paul redefines the concept of blessing and curse in these verses. Cf. also Bring on 3:10; Hartman 1980:110–11; Ebeling:229, 234, 238.

[71]Cf. Thuruthumaly:96; Mack:70; Hübner 1984a:17.

It is unnecessary for Paul to spell out the specific premise in 3:8, since he has argued it already in 3:7.[72] It is so important, however, that it, together with the conclusion, is alluded to also in 3:9.

The *General premise* is taken from the Hebrew Bible and thus has the force of a Previous Judgment. It states that blessing for Gentiles is given "in thee" (i. e., in Abraham). The *Specific premise* specifies this condition by stating that one has to have faith in order to be in Abraham, that is to be a son of Abraham. Also this premise is based on a Previous Judgment from Scripture, as the logic of 3:6-7 has demonstrated. When we take these premises together, we see in the *Conclusion* that blessing for the Gentiles is given to those who have the same faith as Abraham. They "are blessed with Abraham who had faith (σὺν τῷ πιστῷ Ἀβραάμ)."[73]

b: Ambiguities in Gen 12:3

In Gen 12:3 we find two important ambiguities on which Paul seems to draw. The first ambiguity has been presented above (cf. sec. 5.2), where we noted that many Jewish texts relate Gen 12:3 to the era of restoration. Although it is a promise to Abraham, Jews have read it as especially relevant for the conditions in the new era. Paul seems to follow this tradition, as indicated by the two verbs with the prefix προ.

As for the second ambiguity, Paul involves himself in a dispute about the expression "in thee (ἐν σοί)." Jewish tradition also emphasized this phrase, but took it to refer to the obedience of Abraham.[74] The implied logic is indicated both by the changes in the citation itself and by its context.

It is important to note that Paul gives a mixed citation from Gen 12:3; 18:18 (cf. 22:18; 26:4; Koch 1986:162-63). He thus prefers the expression "all the nations (πάντα τὰ ἔθνη)" from the latter text(s) to the expression "all the families of the earth" (Gen 12:3). Therefore he favors the saying that most clearly relates to the inclusion of Gentile Christians.[75] By such mixing of scriptural passages, Paul demonstrates that he seeks to explain the

---

[72]As argued above sec. 8.4, it is conventional in a rhetorical setting to introduce the conclusion before a citation and to omit the specific premise, if it is well-known.

[73]It is thus the paradigmatic attitude of Abraham that is most important to Paul here (as in Jewish tradition), cf. Berger *TRE* 1:373-76. The adjective πίστος in 3:9b is taken to mean *believing* rather than *faithful* or *trustworthy*, cf. Bruce:157; Burton:162.

It is possible that Paul on a secondary level may also imply the Semitic notion of *corporate personality* here: Abraham embodied his seed when he was blessed, cf. Mussner: 222; Berger *TRE* 1:375.

[74]Cf. the references in *Str-B* III:539; Mussner:220-21.

[75]This preference is seen by many scholars, cf., for example, Bruce:156; H. D. Betz 1979:142; Koch 1986:163; Hansen:115.

Ambiguity in light of the original intention of God. He thus combines the stasis of Ambiguity with the stasis of Letter and intent.[76]

We also find other clear indications that Paul seeks for God's initial will: First he also combines this mixed citation with Gen 15:6 (cf. 3:6 which is the implied specific premise in 3:8). Second he introduces the whole argument with the following: "And the Scripture, foreseeing ($\pi\rho o\ddot{\imath}\delta o\hat{\upsilon}\sigma\alpha$) that God would justify the Gentiles by faith, preached the gospel beforehand ($\pi\rho o$-$\varepsilon\upsilon\eta\gamma\gamma\varepsilon\lambda\acute{\imath}\sigma\alpha\tau o$) to Abraham."[77] Paul refers to Scripture as a subject of its own that both foresees and preaches beforehand the principle of faith, which is consequently in accordance with the intention of God.[78] Thus the text includes three different indications of the logic involved: Two verbs with $\pi\rho o$ as a prefix, mixed citation, and connection between Gen 12:3 and 15:6. It should be safe to conclude that Paul thus argues about the original intention of God with regard to the blessing.

10.3.3: The curse on those of the law (3:10)

a: The curse as a realized curse

It is common also to regard the curse of 3:10 as a realized curse.[79] This view may be substantiated by several observations:

We find a reduplication of $\varepsilon\iota\sigma\iota\nu$ in the present tense in 3:10a. Although this is different from 3:9, the difference rather forces the curse to be taken as a realized entity in the present.

The expression $\upsilon\pi\grave{o}$ $\kappa\alpha\tau\acute{\alpha}\rho\alpha\nu$ is special. If the antithesis to 3:9 is accurate, we should expect $\kappa\alpha\tau\alpha\rho\hat{\alpha}\sigma\theta\alpha\iota$ in the present passive tense here. The question is then whether the phrase $\upsilon\pi\grave{o}$ $\kappa\alpha\tau\acute{\alpha}\rho\alpha\nu$ $\varepsilon\iota\sigma\acute{\iota}\nu$ is weaker than such a formulation. The three occurrences of the expression in Jewish texts show that this is not the case.

---

[76]Another way of explaining it is to say that Paul works within the topic Intention of the framer of the law. Cicero states about this topic that one shall "examine the whole document which contains the ambiguity in question in all its parts, to see if any thing is apposite to our interpretation . . . . For it is easy to estimate what it is likely that the writer intended from the complete context . . . ." (Cic. *Inv.* II.xl.117).

[77]There is a causal relation between these expressions: Because the Scripture saw beforehand, it preached the Gospel beforehand, cf. Mussner:220.

[78]Cf. similar expressions in Gal 3:22; 4:21, 30. *Str-B* III:538 referred to such expressions in rabbinic literature. Klein 1964:149 regards such phrases as juridical and concerning the intention of a law. Cf. also Hays 1989:105 who takes them to express "God's ultimate purpose."

[79]Cf. Stanley:497–501 and Braswell:75–77 for a new emphasis on 3:10 as a "threat." Stanley:509–11 shows that tendencies in this direction also are found by some other scholars, though they balance it with the traditional view.

In Jewish material we found expressions similar to ὑπὸ κατάραν only in 3 texts. It is least explicit in *1 Enoch* 98:4, where it is stated that those who commit sin "shall come under a great curse." In Josephus, however, the context also supplies us with information about the effect of the curses:

In *Ant* 4:123 he reports that Balaam wants to "bind these people under a curse," and in its context this is intended to cause the defeat of the Jewish army before Balak.

In *Ant* 18:287 Petronius fears that he will be "put under the ban of a curse for all time to come," a fear that is substantiated by the fact that he sees the power of God as a real one, cf. 285–86, 288.

All these texts speak about curse as a future (possible) reality. It is notable, however, that they employ the verb in a futuristic sense (cf. "shall come under" [*1 Enoch* 98:4]; "if perchance I may" [*Ant* 4:123]; "he would be put under the ban" [*Ant* 18:287]); and not in the present tense as in Gal 3:10. I therefore take the verb εἰσιν in 3:10 to underscore the curse as a present reality.

We have also noted that curses in the ἐπικατάρατος ὅς form as in 3:10b often are placed in a juridical setting (cf. above sec. 4.1), where they are perceived as judgments succeeded by divine and/or human punishment.

The question is then whether the condition in 3:10a has been fulfilled or not. The curse is on those "who rely on works of the law (ἐξ ἔργων νόμου)." This phrase is found also in the preceding verses 2:16; 3:2, 5, where it refers to the Counterdefinition. Since Paul accuses the opponents of representing such an attitude, adherents of this principle are present in Galatia.

It is also noteworthy that 3:10 opens with the correlative pronoun ὅσοι. When it is used in this absolute sense, it often has the meaning "as many as" = "all" (= πάντες οἱ).[80] But the word normally refers to something that is at issue in the context.[81] It is noteworthy that the other three occurrences of this pronoun in the letter refer to groups in Galatia.[82] It is also a fact that the opponents are referred to by means of impersonal pronouns elsewhere in the letter.[83]

---

[80]Cf. *BDR* par 304,1 and Schlier 1965:132; Mussner:223.

[81]Cf. *BDR* par 304,3. Cf. Rom 2:12 where the double ὅσοι refers to Jews and Gentiles in the context, and Rom 8:14 where it refers to those led by the Spirit in the context.

[82]In 3:27 the Galatian Christians are addressed with ὅσοι in a 2nd person plural: "For as many of you (ὅσοι γάρ) as were baptized into Christ . . . ."
In 6:16 Paul blesses "all who (ὅσοι) walk by this rule." As an effective blessing it is meant for the actual readers of the letter.
In 6:12 Paul refers to his opponents with this pronoun: "It is those who want to (ὅσοι θέλουσιν) make a good showing in the flesh."

[83]Cf. above sec. 8.1. Stanley:498 argues that ὅσοι indicates an element of uncertainty or potentiality. This may also be correct and would correspond to Paul's way of referring to the opponents throughout the letter. It may also be true that the pronoun may include the Galatians: If they accept the false teaching, they would of course come into the same position as the opponents, and thus come under the same curse.

It thus seems clear that the condition for the curse is fulfilled in Galatia. Paul's opponents are posing a claim for circumcision on the Galatians, and they are therefore ἐξ ἔργων νόμου. Just like the double anathema in 1:8-9, this curse is also issued with an eye especially on them.[84] With regard to the reason for this curse on the opponents, the problems of interpretation are very difficult and they have caused much confusion in the research (cf. the review above in sec. 1.3.2a).

b: 3:10 as an abbreviated syllogism
Also the logic in 3:10 may be put in a syllogistic form, but unlike 3:8-9 it is difficult to identify the omitted specific premise:

> *General premise*: "Cursed be every one who does not abide by all things written in the book of the law, and do them" (3:10b).
> (*Specific premise*: ???)
> *Conclusion*: All who rely on the works of the law are under a curse (3:10a).

The context does not provide us with immediate clues for reconstruction of the omitted premise. It is also amazing that an affirmative statement is proved by a negative one.[85] Furthermore, since this is a rhetorical enthymeme, it is by no means certain that the logic from the premises to the conclusion is very precise. Therefore many scholars have suggested that Paul does not emphasize all the phrases in the Hebrew Bible citation:

> Those supporting the qualitative interpretation emphasize the last part of the citation: Paul curses those who keep law because it is wrong to "do" the law (ποιεῖν), that is, to use it as a means of salvation (cf. Schlier 1965:132-34; Fuller:32-35).
> H. D. Betz emphasizes the other part of the citation: The curse hits those "not abiding in everything which is written . . . ." It is clear from 3:19 that the Jews did not live up to this: Since the law was given to produce sins, all Jews became transgressors (1979:146).
> E. P. Sanders has suggested that Paul has chosen this Hebrew Bible citation because it is the only one that combines curse and νόμος; the other expressions are of no importance (1983:21; cf. also Hays 1983:206-7).

---

[84]H. D. Betz 1979:144 also sees that the curse includes the Galatian opponents and must be connected with Gal 1:8-9, but he does not discuss the implications of this observation. Also Ridderbos:123-24 claims that Paul's eye is on his opponents here. Hansen:119-20 also connects it to the opponents. He claims that the implied logic corresponds to the topic From the More to the Less: If the opponents themselves are under the curse because they do not keep the law, how much more will the Galatians come under the curse!

[85]Cf. the observation by Luther 26:252. In our Jewish material it is only Neh 10:30 that seems to connect curse and keeping of law, but there it underscores the necessity of obedience: ". . . and enter into a curse and an oath to walk in God's law . . . ."

G. Howard argues that the important phrase is πᾶς. Since the curse hits both Jews and Gentiles, its point is not to demand obedience, but to reveal the suppressing force of the law in general (60–62).

J. P. Braswell argues that the omitted premise is that the Jewish people (= ἐξ ἔργων νόμου) are under the Torah. Since 3:10b states that the Torah threatens a curse, 3:10a thus concludes that as many as are of works of the law are under a curse (76).

Other scholars state that Deut 27:26 is not able to prove 3:10a. It is only when it is supplied with the arguments of 3:11–12 that Paul has fulfilled the argument (Koch 1986:265–68. Cf. Cosgrove 1988:53–54, 61; Thuruthumaly:106; Barrett 1985:26; Mack:70).

The omitted premise may be reconstructed in a way that makes it most naturally a bridge between the parts of the argument. It may be constructed with its first part as similar to the first part of the conclusion as possible, and the second part as similar to the Hebrew Bible citation as possible:

(*Specific premise*: All who rely on the works of the law do not abide by all things written in the book of the law and do them.)

The problem with this reconstruction is that it is ambiguous. If we remember that it is especially the opponents that are hit by the curse, at least two interpretations stand forth as especially persuasive.

c: An empirical meaning: A curse on those who in practice do not keep the law

It is important to have in mind the distinction in Aristotle between logical and rhetorical enthymemes (cf. sec. 8.5 above). This means that it is not necessary for Paul to argue in a way that is logically, necessarily true. He does not have to imply a fundamental maxim which states that it is necessarily impossible for any human to fulfill the law.[86]

Since it is part of a rhetorical syllogism, it is enough that it is "for the most part only generally true . . . . For that which is probable (τὸ εἰκός) is that which generally happens" (Arist. *Rhet.* I.ii.14–15). It is thus enough for Paul to imply that people do not in fact seem to keep the law. Whether this is caused by necessity or not is a question which may be left unanswered. I therefore find it most natural to take the curse as an empirical fact rather than as a fundamental principle.[87] Such an empirical fact also seems to be implied

---

[86]Most scholars lean in this direction, cf., for example, Sieffert:152; Zahn:150–51; Lightfoot:137–38; Lietzmann 1923:18; Oepke:105; Becker:36; Mussner:224–26; Ridderbos:123–24; Rohde:141; Brun:71; Schoeps:176–77; Räisänen 1983:94–95; Hübner 1984a:18–19; Donaldson:104.

[87]Räisänen 1983:96 also speaks of an empirical fact, but he does not underscore the fact that it is different from a fundamental maxim. Other scholars who seem to lean in a direction similar to this are Burton:164–65; Wilckens 1974:92, 94; Sanders 1978:104 (in an earlier article where he combines it with the interpretation presented above); Wester-

above in 2:16c, and Paul will relate law to sin in 3:19-22.[88]

With this interpretation the curse makes perfectly good sense for the first audience in Galatia. Paul refers in 6:13 to the fact that the opponents themselves do not keep the law. We have thus no reason to expect that they are perceived as exceptions from this general experience of human sin. The question is, though, if it is possible to press the interpretation further in order to detect a specific area where their breaking of law is especially striking.

> Before I turn to my own proposal, let me review another proposal that seems attractive, although it suffers from the weakness that it is difficult to find indications for it in the context: The opponents may be hit by this curse because their zeal for the law made them adherents of religious violence rather than of the commandment of love.
>
> E. Baasland has pointed to the frequency of the theme of persecution in Galatians (1984a:135-40): Terms for persecution are found in at least five places in the letter ($\delta\iota\omega\kappa\epsilon\iota\nu$ in 1:13, 23; 4:29; 5:11; 6:12; $\pi\acute{o}\rho\theta\epsilon\iota\nu$ in 1:13, 23).[89] In each case there is reference to the persecution of Christians, the former two even refer to Paul's own past as a persecutor of the Church. We have reason to ask if this theme is prominent because Paul related it to the opponents in some way.
>
> This suspicion gains strength when we find Paul describing his opponents as zealous for the Galatians in a bad manner (4:17: $\zeta\eta\lambda o\hat{v}\sigma\iota\nu$ $\hat{v}\mu\hat{a}\varsigma$ $o\hat{v}$ $\kappa\alpha\lambda\hat{\omega}\varsigma$). Since this term occurs three times in 4:18-19, we have reason to ask if it at least in the first occurrence may have the more technical meaning of denoting the opponents as "zealots for the law."[90] Therefore we may have reasons to follow R. G. Hamerton-Kelly in his proposal that the opponents represented an obedience to law inspired by the violent archetypal zealot Phineas the priest (Num 25:11, cf. Ps 106:30-31):[91] Thus they were cursed "because they have chosen to live within a violent interpretation of the law. In that state they do not perform the real intention of the law, which is love of neighbour, and this is clear from their zeal to exclude the Gentiles who do not accept their interpretation" (1990a:102-12; citation 111-12).

---

holm 1988:162.

Such an interpretation is also confirmed by the historical lessons from Jewish history. It has been demonstrated time and time again that the law failed to lead the nation into blessing, cf. Bligh:257-60. Noth 1938 argues that such historical experience corresponds to the original meaning of the curse, because it has been added to the text by deuteronomistic editors who had seen the curse fulfilled in the history of Israel.

[88]The reference in 3:19-22 indicates that Paul is not very far from implying the fundamental maxim about the impossibility of keeping the law. The argument of 3:10 may therefore easily be stretched in this direction.

[89]For the question whether $\pi\acute{a}\sigma\chi\epsilon\iota\nu$ in 3:4 also could relate to such persecutions, cf. Baasland 1984a:139-40.

[90]Cf. Hamerton-Kelly 1990a:105 and the rhetorical figure *diaphora*.

[91]For the prominence of this tradition at the time of Paul, cf. Hengel 1976:151-234. Cf. also his 1991:84 where he observes that Deut 27:26 might be taken to motivate such persecution.

d: An extended meaning: A curse on those who do not practice faith

In the Jewish material presented above in part I, we found curse and blessing in explicit antitheses 64 times. In about half of these texts it is not only curse and blessing terminology that constitutes the antithesis, but also descriptions of the deeds involved. It is noteworthy that in these cases the cursed deeds are always the opposite of the blessed deeds. Therefore it belongs to conventional expectations that cursed actions should be the opposite of blessed actions.[92]

When we apply this conventional expectation to Gal 3:8-10, it should be expected that since the blessed are those who have faith like Abraham, the cursed should be those who disobey this claim for faith. The question is therefore whether Deut 27:26 also can be taken as requiring faith. If so, Paul would use the text in a way contrary to Jewish tradition, and we are cast into a stasis dispute concerning its meaning.

It is natural to look for a stasis dispute behind Paul's use of Deut 27:26, since this citation belongs to the most radically changed citations in the Pauline letters. It is a mixed citation that displays a change in gender as well as omission.[93]

The omission of ἄνθρωπος from Deut 27:26 supports our hesitation to take the curse as a fundamental maxim intended to be generalized for all people. The change in gender in the last word (αὐτά instead of αὐτούς) is caused by the insertion of phrases similar to Deut 28:58, 61; 29:19, 20 (cf. also 29:26; 30:10): Instead of citing "all the words of this law (πᾶσιν τοῖς λόγοις νόμου τούτου)" from Deut 27:26, Paul instead chooses the expression

---

[92]Among the Deut 27-30 texts we find 16 such antitheses:

a) if you obey the commandments . . . if you do not obey (Deut 11:27-28: cf. also 28:1-2, 15-16; 30:15-18);

b) the man who trusts in man . . . who trusts in the Lord (Jer 17:5, 7);

c) fornication and impurity . . . worship God (*Jub.* 20:6, 9);

d) achieve the good . . . does not do the good (*T. Naph.* 8:4, 6);

e) fulfill the laws . . . lawbreakers and transgressors (*Praem* 126);

f) men of God/walk perfectly in all ways . . . men of Satan/guilty wickedness (1QSii.2.4);

g) zealous/not disobedient . . . transgressors (*Ant* 4:306-7);

h) 7 pairs of antithetical descriptions in *2 Enoch* 52.

In the Gen 12:3 formula we find the antithesis between the blessing versus the cursing of Israel 13 times. Other references:

a) wicked . . . righteous (Prov 3:33; cf. also *1 Enoch* 41:8);

b) God for his holy purpose . . . Satan for his sinful (1QM xiii.2, 4);

c) acquit the wicked . . . rebuke the wicked (Prov 24:24-25).

[93]Cf. Koch 1986:111, 120, 163-65, 187. This is contrary to H. D. Betz 1979:145 who asserts that Paul's text may have contained what he quoted, or he may have quoted from memory.

"all things written in the book of the law (πᾶσιν τοῖς γεγραμμένοις ἐν τῷ βιβλίῳ τοῦ νόμου)."

Thus we find the same strategy as above: In 3:8-9 Paul holds together different verses from the Abraham tradition, and here he holds together different verses from Deut 27-30. Since we hold 3:8-10 together as a unity, we may also ask whether the introductory phrases of the foreseeing and preaching beforehand of the Scripture also may apply to the curse. Taken together, these observations indicate that Paul also here seeks for the Intention of the framer of the law.

It is noteworthy that Jewish tradition also could discuss this verse according to a dispute of *Ambiguity*:

Deut 27:26 exhorts obedience to the whole Law: "Cursed be he who does not confirm the words of this law by doing them." In a similar way curses were frequently used to exhort covenantal obedience toward the whole Torah. Repeatedly we find explicit references to the obligation to keep the commandments.[94]

The LXX has inserted the term *all* (ἐν πᾶσιν τοῖς λόγοις) into the verse, and is followed by the Samaritan Targum and in Rabbinic Scriptures such as *Lev. Rab.* XXV:1 and *ySota* 7:21ᵈ,6 (cf. *Str-B* III:541). Deut 27:26 is also referred to as a general curse in distinction to the others in Deut 27:15-25 that are seen as particular, cf. *bSota* 37a and *Num. Rab.* IX:47.

Two points seem to be debated, however, namely the meaning of יקם (=to confirm) and the persons addressed. While it is clear in the MT and LXX that every Jew should confirm the law by doing it, this is not so obvious to rabbinic scholars: *ySota* 7:21ᵈ,6 discusses the matter:[95] According to Schimeon b. Jaqim (c. 270 CE) the curse addresses the leader of the Synagogue, that he confirm the reading of the Scripture; according to R. Schimeon b. Chalaphta (c. 190 CE) it addresses judges in lower courts; according to Schemuel (d. 254 CE) it tells the Rabbis that they should control obedience; and according to R. Tanchum b. Chijja (c. 300 CE) it tells every man to support students of the Torah. *Lev. Rab.* XXV:1 goes even further: If a man has not learned the Torah, he will escape this curse if he administers charity or maintains scholars and protests against wrongdoing (cf. also *Eccl. Rab.* VII:12,1). We thus find a tendency among some rabbis to weaken the curse.[96]

On the other hand, *4 Ezra* demonstrates that a demand to fulfill the whole law could also be sharpened: This book does not discuss Deut 27:26, but it includes its Contrary in the form of a blessing: "Blessed are those who are alive and keep your commandments" (7:45). In the shadow of the fall of Jerusalem in 70 CE, the author strives to find a hope for Israel in the future (*OTP* 1:520-21). He is aware of the sinful nature of humanity, that "all who have been born are involved in iniquities, and are full of sins and burdened with transgressions" (7:68; cf. 7:48). If God does not show mercy "not one of ten-thousandth of mankind could have life . . . . There

---

[94]From the Deut 27-30 curses, cf. especially: Deut 11:27-28; 28:1-2, 15, 45; 30:16; Jer 11:3-4; 26:4; 44:23; Dan 9:11; Neh 10:29; *1 Enoch* 5:4; *T. Naph.* 8:7; *Praem* 126, 162; *Ant* 4:302, 306.

[95]Text in *Str-B* III:542. Cf. also Sanders 1978:122-23.

[96]Cf. Lövy:417-22 for supplementing references and the conclusion that the rabbis also struggled with the problem of human sin in these considerations.

would probably be left only very few of the innumerable multitude" (7:138-39). The angel demands total obedience, however: "that they might keep the Law of the Lawgiver perfectly" (7:89). He even asserts that the multitude must perish if not perfected (9:22) and that even Israel who has "received the Law and sinned will perish" (9:36). This is a very strict interpretation of the demand for obedience to law, which is not common in Jewish theology (Sanders 1977:409-18, especially 416).

The curse of Deut 27:26 demands obedience to the law. We see that its content may be open to discussion: It may be weakened — as some rabbinic interpretations — and it may be sharpened — as in *4 Ezra*.

In my view, Paul's changes in the text indicate his perception of the Ambiguity of Deut 27:26:[97] When Paul inserts phrases from other places in Deut 27-30, he makes an omission in the text:[98]

Deut 27:26: τοῖς λόγοις   τοῦ νόμου τούτου

Gal 3:10: τοῖς γεγραμμένοις   ἐν τῷ βιβλίῳ τοῦ νόμου

Deut 28:58: τὰ γεγραμμένοις   ἐν τῷ βιβλίῳ   τούτῳ
Deut 28:61: τὴν μὴ γεγραμμένην ἐν τῷ βιβλίῳ τοῦ νόμου τούτου
Deut 29:19: αἱ γεγραμμέναι   ἐν τῷ βιβλίῳ τοῦ νόμου τούτου
Deut 29:20: τὰς γεγραμμένας   ἐν τῷ βιβλίῳ τοῦ νόμου τούτου
        = Identical with 29:26: 30:10.

Paul omits the word τούτου which limits the intention of the phrases to the Deuteronomic law corpus. This means it is possible also here to interpret νόμος in a wider sense including the whole Pentateuch (cf. Gal 2:19). This is further indicated by Paul's preference for the expression "written in the book." Although some scholars take this to denote all the laws of the Pentateuch,[99] I take it in the same way as 4:21-22. After Paul asks in 4:21: "do you not hear the law (νόμος)?" he paraphrases the Hagar/Sarah story, introducing it with "For it is written (γέγραπται γάρ) . . . ."

Clearly the Pentateuch includes more than legal requirements in our sense; it also includes narrative parts and promises and the like. Paul has in fact cited one of these in 3:8: the blessing of those who have a faith like Abraham's. Thus the Pentateuch contains a claim for faith, and those who do

---

[97]If Paul draws on the Ambiguity of the curse, it would of course have been possible for him to interpret the curse as a fundamental maxim. He could regard it as a prophecy laid down in the law to bear witness to the impossibility of fulfilling it. The problem with this interpretation is that we do not find any hints of its adequacy in the context.

[98]When Schlier 1965:132; Koch 1986:165 state that Paul wants to emphasize γράμμα as an opposition to πνεῦμα as in 2 Cor 3:6-7, they fail to reflect on the omission of τούτου.

[99]Mussner:223-24; Borse 1984:128 take Paul's change in this way.

not practice this faith do not "abide by all things written."[100]

It is important to remember what we have said about "works of the law" and "faith" as markers of identity above (cf. 2:16). The point at issue is not faith as a personal, intellectual belief. It is rather faith as a constituting element and mark for the Christian community, as an interpersonal act that overturns the division between Jews and Gentiles. In this perspective it makes sense that persons who claim obedience toward the law cannot at the same time also practice faith as the mark of identity. It is impossible to include the Gentiles both on the basis of the Sinai covenant *and* on the basis of the Abraham promise as interpreted by Paul. Two principles have to be played off against each other, and Paul seems to have been able to let even the curse of Deut 27:26 substantiate his case.

The main victims of this curse are not Jews in general, although it has implications that affect them too. The curse is issued against the opponents in a way that supplements the double anathema in 1:8-9: In 1:9 Paul curses those "preaching to you a gospel contrary to the one which you received." There the curse was issued without a discussion of its legitimacy. The substantiation from Scripture follows in 3:10: They are cursed not only by Paul, but also by Deut 27:26 itself, because they do not include Gentiles by faith, that is: They "do not abide by all things written in the book of the law." The curse in 3:10 thus functions as a proof for the legitimacy of the double anathema.

The meaning is also similar to that of 2:18: There Paul accused those who rebuilt the law of being transgressors. We found that such rebuilding of the law made Cephas withdraw from table-fellowship with Gentiles (cf. 2:12, 14b) and thus to uphold the distinction between Jews and Gentiles. This accusation is sharpened and proved here: They are not only transgressors, but also cursed. It is not only Paul who judges this attitude, but also Scripture in Deut 27:26, because it is contrary to the promise of Gen 12:3.

---

[100]In addition to the sense of νόμος, there are two further ambiguous points in Deut 27:26: First it may be debated which claims are included in the phrase "the words of the law (τοῖς λόγοις τοῦ νόμου)." Paul chooses expressions that make it easier to relate the phrase also to the promise made to Abraham. Second it may be debated what sense "doing" (ποιεῖν) connotes. Paul takes it to refer to more than obedience to the precepts of the law, namely also to obedience to the promise of inclusion of the Gentiles by faith.

This interpretation is not so startling as it may seem. We find some modern scholars who lean in a similar direction,[101] but most forcefully a similar interpretation was advocated by M. Luther in his 1535 lectures on Galatians.[102] I argue for this interpretation — in spite of the inevitable objections from some scholars — for several reasons:

a) The antithesis makes it natural to expect faith to be contrasted with disobedience toward faith.

b) Such a contrast is also natural when faith is interpreted as a marker of identity for Christian communities, which cannot be reconciled with Torah obedience as a marker of identity.

c) Paul's changes in the citation make it natural to assume that he seeks for the Intention of God in the curse (cf. also the verbs with the prefix $\pi\rho o$ in 3:8 and the Jewish tradition that discusses its Ambiguity).

d) The changes (omission of $\tau o\acute{u}\tau o\upsilon$ and inclusion of $\grave{\epsilon}\nu$ $\tau\tilde{\omega}$ $\beta\iota\beta\lambda\acute{\iota}\omega$) make the formulation more open concerning what is written in the whole Pentateuch.

e) Paul plays on the double meaning of $\nu\acute{o}\mu o\varsigma$ in 4:21 as an introduction to the Hagar-Sarah story. Thus he might do the same in 3:8-10, where Gen 12:3 is cited.

f) The connections to 1:8-9 and 2:18 become clearer with this interpretation.

10.3.4: The antithesis as an implicit Conflict of laws

Regardless of whether or not we accept the extended meaning of Deut 27:26, Paul has shaped an antithesis of curse and blessing that deviates considerably from conventional antitheses as found in the Deut 27-30 tradition. The first readers of the letter will therefore inevitably recall also its deuteronomistic counterpart, with the result that they are cast into the problem of Conflict of laws.[103] What becomes explicit from 3:15 onward (cf. sec. 10.3.1 above) is implicitly present already here:

---

[101]Dunn 1985:534-35 states that the curse hits the Jews because they have chosen a false set of priorities, by emphasizing national identity at the cost of "faith and love from the heart." He is followed by Hamerton-Kelly 1990a:111-12.

Bring on 3:10, 12 is even closer, when he states that to refuse Gentiles righteousness through faith alone is not to remain faithful to all that is written in the law. His main emphasis, however, that the intention of Deut 27:26 is to predict the fulfillment of the law by Christ, presses the text too far.

Cf. also Braswell:78-79 who utilizes the same wordplay on $\nu\acute{o}\mu o\varsigma$ to state that the Torah includes the paradigmatic Abrahamic "law of faith."

[102]Luther has both an empirical interpretation of the curse (cf. 26:254, 257, 260, 286), and also an extended interpretation where emphasis is laid on the disobedience toward God's claim for faith (cf. 26:248, 251-55, and 257-68). He states that "They rush into Scripture without any judgment and take hold of only one part of it, namely, the Law . . . . Therefore those who neglect or despise the promise and then grasp hold of the Law in order to be justified through it are under a curse" (254-55).

[103]Cf. Iser:155-161 for the foreground-background relation (a reader will also imply the background of a usage if this background is familiar to him) and for the literary effect of deviation (145-55). The normal Jewish way to include faith in an antithesis is found in 1QM xiii.3: "Blessed be all those who < serve > Him in righteousness and who know Him by faith (באמונה)." This blessing is contrasted with a curse on sinners, wicked, ungodly, and unclean (cf. xiii.4-5).

While Deut 28 blesses the obedient nation, Paul has found another bless-ing in Gen 12:3 on those of faith. The choice of Abraham's blessing instead of blessings from Deut 28 is easy to explain. First we have seen that Jewish texts also have combined these traditions (cf. above sec. 5.2.4). Second Paul may have deliberately concentrated on Hebrew Bible texts prior to the covenant from Sinai, in order to defend his interpretation as corresponding to the Intention of the framer of the law. In 3:15–18 this priority of the promise will be emphasized.

While Deut 27–28 curses disobedient Jews, Paul is bold enough to find a deeper level even in the curse of Deut 27:26 that may be played off against it: On one hand Deut 27:26 curses the opponents based on the empirical fact that nobody has been able to keep the law. On the other hand it may even curse the opponents because they do not practice faith as the main mark of identity for the Christian church. In both cases Deut 27:26 is taken as a prophetic element that undermines the sinaitic covenant.

With this antithesis Paul has supplied his argumentation from 2:16 onward with a new Analogy and Contrary:[104] From discussing righteousness (2:16–21; 3:6) and the Spirit (3:2–5) he has now proceeded to a discussion of blessing and curse. The Previous Judgments from Ps 143 (cf. 2:16c) and Gen 15 (cf. 3:6) are now supplied with authoritative statements also from Gen 12 and Deut 27. Paul has also supplied the double anathema with a scriptural foundation: If it is legitimate to redefine the antithesis of curse and blessing in the way done here, Paul can certainly also construct an Analogy to covenantal curses and Deut 13 as done in 1:8–9!

We thus see that all the possibilities for a connection between the double anathema and 3:10 proposed above in sec. 9.3.4a may be upheld:

A connection corresponding to Theme and Horizon and corresponding to the function of incriminating the opponents has been substantiated, since Gal 3:10 also has the opponents especially in view. This connection is valid even if one does not accept the extended interpretation of 3:10.

The extended interpretation of 3:10 makes it legitimize the deviation from covenantal curses in 1:8–9, since even Deut 27:26 itself can be taken to curse those that do not practice faith.

We have noted an extensive use of legal stasis in 3:8–10. Paul argues similarly to both the stasis of Ambiguity, Letter and intent, and Conflicting laws. Thus it may even be probable that he in 1:8–9 employs the form of covenantal curses and the law of Deut 13 according to the stasis of Reasoning from Analogy in order to construct a new curse for a new situation.

---

[104]Cf. Borse 1984:128; Thuruthumaly:96, 104 for 3:8–9 as an Analogy. Schenk:43–44 overemphasizes this analogy when he claims that righteousness and blessing are synon-ymous in this context. For 3:10 as a Contrary to 3:8–9, cf. Luther 26:248; Bengel:737; Sieffert:152; Burton:163; Oepke:105; Ridderbos:122; Rohde:140; Thuruthumaly:105.

10.3.5: *The brief refutations of Gal 3:11-12*

a: *3:11-12 as Refutations*

Some scholars have observed that it is possible to reconstruct the logic of 3:11-12 syllogistically. In these verses we find both premises and the conclusion:[105]

> *Major premise*: He who is just by faith will live (3:11b).
> *Minor premise*: But the law does not enjoin faith (3:12a).
> *Conclusion*: Therefore no one is justified by the law (3:11a).

More important is the fact that Paul now moves on to *Refutations*, since both verses open with a denial (οὐδείς in 3:11, οὐκ ἔστιν in 3:12).[106] It will be quite in order with refutations here. Paul has just redefined the concept of blessing and curse in a way so radical that he has certainly provoked objections of many kinds. By taking up some of them at this point, the truth of his redefinition will be confirmed even further. It is conventional to refute both the Counterdefinition and an underlying principle for the Counterdefinition.[107] According to Aristotle this may be done rather briefly by use of objections from an Analogy, a Contrary, and Previous Judgments (*Rhet.* II.xxiii.30; II.xxv.1, 3).

3:11: As noted above in connection with 2:16a, the Counterdefinition would be similar to "a man is justified by works of the law." This would correspond to the traditional meaning of the concept of blessing and curse. It is such a Counterdefinition that is denied in 3:11a: "Now it is evident that no man is justified before God by the law."[108]

The objection follows in 3:11b as a Previous Judgment from Hab 2:4: ". . . for 'He who through faith is righteous shall live.'"[109] This objection

---

[105]Cf. Sieffert:154; Bligh:262–63; Cosgrove 1978:147; Stanley:503.

[106]Cf. Berger 1984a:45 for the same proposal. Cf. also Stanley:502, 505 who states that Paul in these verses denies the positive potentiality of the law.

[107]Cf. the topics for speeches according to the stasis of Definition above in sec. 8.7.3. Cf. further Cic. *Inv.* I.xlii.79 and Martin:124–29.

[108]Paul replaces ἐξ ἔργων νόμου by the briefer phrase ἐν νόμῳ. The reference, however, is the same, cf. H. D. Betz 1979:146; Bruce:161.

Like most commentators (cf., for example, Oepke:105–6; Burton:166) I take the construction "ὅτι . . . δῆλον, ὅτι" to be equivalent to "ὅτι . . . (ἐστίν) δῆλον, ὅτι," reading (ἐστίν) δῆλον as the main sentence, the first ὅτι as introducing its subject, and the second introducing its argument: "It is evident that . . . for."

[109]I consider the debate about whether ἐκ πίστεως qualifies ὁ δίκαιος or ζήσεται to be of minor importance. A survey of the positions is found in Cavallin:33–38. He argues convincingly for the traditional interpretation (38–43). It suits the context of Galatians best to regard ἐκ πίστεως ζήσεται as a formal contrast to ζήσεται ἐν αὐτοῖς. But regardless of grammar, there will be a contrast between faith and law anyhow. I therefore cite the RSV translation, although I am not fully convinced of its correctness.

forms a Contrary to the Counterdefinition. Further it is an Analogy to 3:8-9, since it carries further the blessing terminology with the term "to live (ζήσεται)."[110]

3:12: In the next verse Paul refutes what seems to be a premise behind the Counterdefinition. In his whole argumentation Paul has consistently separated faith from the law. A typical Jewish objection against this would be to claim that faith and law have to be seen together.[111] It is exactly such an objection that Paul denies in 3:12a: "but the law does not rest on faith."[112]

The objection itself is a Previous Judgment from Lev 18:5. Also here we find the theme of life: "He who does them, shall live by them." Paul thus emphasizes that the law itself prescribes doing of the law,[113] which is a principle opposite to faith.

b: Conflict of laws between Hab 2:4 and Lev 18:5

Once again Paul cites the Hebrew Bible in a way that conflicts with Jewish exegesis: Jews would normally not read Hab 2:4 or Lev 18:5 as separating faith and obedience from each other as opposite principles.[114] Again Paul's changes in the text may indicate which stasis he utilizes:

Hab 2:4: ὁ δὲ δίκαιος	ἐκ πίστεώς μου	ζήσεται
Gal 3:11: ὁ δίκαιος	ἐκ πίστεως	ζήσεται
Gal 3:12: ὁ ποιήσας αὐτὰ	ζήσεται	ἐν αὐτοῖς
Lev 18:5: ἃ ποιήσας ἄνθρωπος	ζήσεται	ἐν αὐτοῖς

By changing the opening words of Lev 18:5, Paul gets a clearer contrast: While it opened with a relative pronoun in the LXX, Paul makes it open with the same article as the verse from Hab 2:4. The common denominator of the verses is the term "to live." The other parts of the citations differ from each other, however. They prescribe two different ways of obtaining life: Hab

---

[110]Life is used equivalent with blessing in Deut 30:15-20; *1 Enoch* 5:8; by Josephus in *Ant* 4:122, and by Philo in *Praem* 110; *Leg* 3:107-8. Cf. also Isa 65:20; *Bib. Ant.* 3:10; Ps. Sol. 3:12.

[111]Cf. Burton:167; Dunn 1985:535. Similar to our observation above for Gen 15:6, Jewish tradition has also combined the two concepts in Hab 2:4: 1QpHab 8:1-3 interprets the faith in Hab 2:4 as obedience, cf. H. D. Betz 1979:139, 147. Cf. also *Str-B* III:542-44 for rabbinical references.

[112]The phrase οὐκ ἔστιν ἐκ is taken to refer to faith as the source viz. basis, cf., for example, Lightfoot:139. Οὐκ ἔστιν may also be an interpretative expression ("is not the equivalent of"), cf. H. D. Betz 1979:147.

[113]For this as a reference to Jewish obedience to law, cf. H. D. Betz 1979:148. Similar Jewish expressions are listed in Mussner:229-30, while rabbinic interpretations of Lev 18:5 are found in *Str-B* III:277-78.

[114]Cf. Dobbeler:125-31 for a review of the reception of Hab 2:4 in Judaism.

2:4 prescribes faith, while Lev 18:5 "to live by them," is a reference to Jewish obedience to law. This conscious juxtaposition generates the question of whether Paul sees this legal dispute as one of *Conflict of Laws*.[115]

If this is the case, how can Hab 2:4 be defended as the most important principle? Do we find any indication that one of the verses has been restricted or superseded? It may be of importance that it is only Hab 2:4 which is found in an eschatological context,[116] not Lev 18:5.[117] Thus it is Hab 2:4 which can be defended as the most important principle,[118] while Lev 18:5 represents the superseded and restricted one.[119] This interpretation implies that the term ζήσεται is ambiguous: It is only Hab 2:4 which refers to life as a blessing in the new era; Lev 18:5 uses the term in a weaker sense.[120]

Paul's redefinition of blessing and curse has thus been substantiated by two citations from the Hebrew Bible. Once again Paul thus demonstrates that Scripture requires faith. In Hab 2:4 Paul omits μου from the LXX. This means that he adopts it to his Definition of the case.[121]

While the conflict of laws was an implicit element in the logic of 3:8-10, it is more explicit in 3:11-12, where two opposing laws are consciously juxtaposed. In addition we find some indications of a temporal perspective which may be applied to the laws in order to solve the apparent conflict. This temporal argument has not yet been brought openly into focus, however, and the time is more than ripe for doing it.

---

[115]Cf. Vos:265-67. A similar interpretation based on the 13th middah of Ishmael is found by Schoeps:177-78. Cf. also Dahl 1977:162-64 who refers to Hillel's method for resolving such a dilemma.

[116]Cf. Ellis 1957:121 and the explicit references to the endtime in Hab 2:2-3, which are made even clearer in the LXX.

Both Hanson:42-45 and Hays 1983:151-57 give priority to a christological interpretation of the citation: Christ is the Righteous One who shall live by faith! Although it is possible that Paul was aware of such an interpretation of the verse, he has not drawn on this potential in 3:11. For a christological interpretation, cf. also Cosgrove 1988:55-58.

[117]The Hebrew Bible context gives no indication of an eschatological meaning. I am therefore not convinced by the proposal of Bring *ad loc.* and Reicke:249-50, that this verse must be interpreted christologically: They emphasize that ὁ ποιήσας αὐτά is aorist and therefore refers to something fulfilled, namely that Christ fulfilled the law totally, cf. Rom 8:3-4.

[118]Cf. Cic. *Inv.* II.xlix.145: "In the first place, then, one should compare the laws by considering which one deals with the most important matters (*ad maiores*)."

[119]Cf. *ad Herenn.* II.x.15: "When two laws conflict, we must first see whether they have been superseded or restricted."

[120]Cf. again the rhetorical figure of *diaphora* which we found in 2:17, 19. Cf. also Gal 3:21 which implies that the mosaic law was never given to bring life.

[121]Cf. an extensive treatment of all textual variants by Koch 1985. For this explanation of the Pauline change, cf. Koch: 1985:83-84; 1986:127-28; Fitzmyer 1981:452-53.

10.4: The sequence of curse and blessing in Gal 3:13-14

The argument of 3:13-14 is connected to the preceding verses as an *Asyndeton* (Bengel:737), that is, a rhetorical figure where conjunctions are suppressed in order to obtain animation, great force, and concision (cf. *ad Herenn.* IV.xxx.41). In spite of this emphasis, the verse has created many interpretive difficulties for scholars. We have at least one certain point of departure, however, namely the last half of the verse, which clearly has the form of an abbreviated syllogism. We will begin at that point, and try to uncover the implied logic step by step.

10.4.1: The syllogism of 3:13b

In 3:13b we have an abbreviated syllogism where the conclusion precedes the general premise, and the specific premise is omitted: ". . . having become a curse for us — for it is written, 'Cursed be every one who hangs on a tree.'" The logic may be reconstructed as follows:

> *General premise*: Cursed be every one who hangs on a tree.
> (*Specific premise*: Christ was hanged on a tree.)
> *Conclusion*: Christ has become a curse.

The logic is clear, but very risky: We know from later sources that the curse of Deut 21:23 was used by Jews in their anti-Christian polemic as evidence that Jesus could not be the Messiah, since be became cursed by God.[122] If Paul knew this kind of polemic, this verse would bear witness to his ability to turn such a major offense into a positive proof for the gospel.[123] This explanation is not productive for our purpose, however. It is more important

---

[122]Cf. Jeremias:134-35 for a presentation of the evidence, which is found in different sources:

a) In the Fathers we find that Deut 21:23 is explicitly used as a decisive argument against believing in Christ in Justin's *Dial.* 32:1; 89:1 - 90:1.

b) In the New Testament itself, we find indirect references to a similar polemic: Many places it is said that the Jews blasphemed or forced Christians to blaspheme (1 Tim 1:13; Acts 26:11; 13:45; 18:6); this could be a reference to a use of Deut 21:23 against Jesus. We may also take the ἀνάθεμα Ἰησοῦ of 1 Cor 12:3 as a possible reference to this Jewish polemic.

c) The evidence from the pre-Christian era is 4QpNah i.6-8, but Kuhn:33-34 instead refers to 11QTemple 64:6-13.

[123]Cf. for an emphasis on this explanation, for example, Duncan:98; Becker:38; Bligh:268-69; Beker:182; S. Kim:273-74; Räisänen 1983:249; Barrett 1985:30, 86; Hengel 1991:83-84.

Another strategy would be to let Jesus escape Deut 21:23 by defining the verse in a way that does not affect the Christ, cf. van Unnik 1979:484-85 for this approach by Tertullian and Didascalia Apostolorum.

to understand the function of the positive proof than its possible background in Jewish polemic.

Paul clearly connects Deut 21:23 to Christ. He states that Christ "became a curse *for us* (ὑπὲρ ἡμῶν)," a feature which indicates that he interprets the curse in a positive way. Thus he departs from Jewish tradition, and once again we seem to face an instance of Paul exploiting the *Ambiguity* of a Hebrew Bible citation.

10.4.2: The ambiguity of Deut 21:23

If Paul plays upon Ambiguity in the interpretation of Deut 21:23, he has several predecessors in Jewish theology. The law of Deut 21:22-23 deals with a man who has "committed a crime punishable by death" and orders that he shall be hanged on a tree after the execution. We find different opinions, however, whether the curse refers to blasphemy or whether it can possibly refer to crucifixion.

The various texts have been presented by M. Wilcox and M. J. Bernstein,[124] and in the following summary I will supplement their discussion with a few texts from Philo:

> In the MT there is an *ambiguity* with regard to the curse: קללת אלהים. The problem is whether the phrase means *cursing God* (= objective genitive) or *being cursed by God* (= subjective genitive). The ambiguity is preserved by Aquila and Theodotion who translate it as κατάρα θεοῦ. The subjective genitive is chosen by the LXX, 11QTemple 64:12, Philo in *Post* 26, and *Tg. Neofiti*. They understand the verse as cursing all persons hung upon a tree and do not restrict it to blasphemers. We may note, however, that 11QTemple 64:12 seems to state that it is an accursed person who is hanged, not that the curse is a result of being hanged upon a tree. The objective genitive we find in Symmachus, *Tg. Pseudo-Jonathan*, *mSanh.* 6:4, and in Josephus in *Ant* 4:202. This allows for two possibilities: On one hand Deut 21:23 may be related to a person who has blasphemed Yahweh (cf., for example, *Ant* 4:202); on the other hand it may denote a hanged person as a blasphemy toward God (cf., for example, Rabbi Meir in *bSanh.* 46b). We thus see that when Paul chooses the subjective genitive, he represents "one of a number of approaches to this text which existed in an exegetically pluralistic world" (Bernstein:45).
>
> Some texts also draw on an *ambiguity in the designation of the punishment*, to be "hanged" (תלוי). The term does not refer to crucifixion, but to the hanging of the corpse of a person who has been stoned. The verse thus does not refer to the execution itself, but to the treatment of a corpse after an execution. On the other hand we find Deut 21:23 referring to crucifixion in 11QTemple 64:6-13,[125] the

---

[124]Wilcox:86-90 treats the two first ambiguities, while Bernstein only treats the first, but in a more extensive way.

[125]It is, however, debated whether תלה refers to crucifixion or to hanging as a form of strangulation, cf. the discussion in Fitzmyer 1978:504-07. Like Fitzmyer (cf. also O. Betz 1982:607-8), I regard it as most probable that it refers to crucifixion, since the term does so in 4QpNah i.8. But even if Baumgarten should be right in relating it to strangulation, the scroll takes Deut 21:23 in a new way, since it refers to hanging as causing the

Peshitta to Deut 21:22, possibly also 4QpNah i.7-8,[126] and in Philo in *Spec* 3:152.[127]

A *third ambiguity is exploited by Philo*, who manages to connect Deut 21:23 with the curses of Deut 28. In a discussion of the nature of the apostate Jew in *Post* 23-27, Philo connects the curse of Deut 28:66 with Deut 21:23 because of the common term *hanging* (תלוי). Philo states that "he that forsakes Him, inasmuch as he approaches the unresting creation is, as we might expect, carried about" (23). He is thus hit by the curse of Deut 28:66: "your life shall hang (κρεμαμένη) in doubt before you" (24). Because the apostate is thus hanging without any firm foothold, he is also hit by Deut 21:23: "he that hangeth (κρεμάμενον) on a tree is cursed of God" (26). Here Philo allegorizes the wood to designate the body. To hang on a tree is therefore to fasten the mind "on the body, which Nature wrought as a receptacle and abode of pleasures."[128]

To sum up: The curse in Deut 21:23 has been open to many interpretations in Jewish theology. Some see it as denoting the blasphemer or blasphemy, others as denoting all who are sentenced to death, some as referring to impalement after execution, others to execution by crucifixion. Philo even treats it allegorically to denote a man hanging on his body with its desires and pleasures. I have found no evidence, however, that the verse has been interpreted in a positive way.

As usual, we will seek to reconstruct Paul's way of arguing from his changes in the text and from the context. Paul changes the LXX text in three ways: It is a mixed citation where Paul omits the reference to God and adds an article (Koch 1986:124-25, 132, 165-66, 187):

Gal 3:13:	ἐπικατάρατος		πᾶς ὁ κρεμάμενος ἐπὶ ξύλου
Deut 21:23:	κεκατηραμένος	ὑπὸ θεοῦ	πᾶς κρεμάμενος ἐπὶ ξύλου
Deut 27:26:	ἐπικατάρατος		πᾶς . . . .

The addition of the article is probably stylistic (Koch 1986:132). More important is the omission of the reference to a curse by God (ὑπὸ θεοῦ).

---

death of the sentenced person: "you shall hang him also on the tree and he shall die" (64:10-11).

[126] 4QpNah i.7-8 clearly refers to crucifixion, but it is rather uncertain whether it may be regarded as a textual variant to Deut 21:23. Wilcox:88 is skeptical, while Jeremias:134-35 and Fitzmyer 1978:501-2 defend that possibility.

[127] Cf. Bruce:164-65: Philo cites Deut 21:23 rather freely, and "he replaces κρεμάννυμι with ἀνασκολοπίζω, 'impale,' 'crucify.' Elsewhere (*Post. C.* 61; *Som.* 2.213) he associates ἀνασκολοπίζω by 'nailing up' (προσηλόω), indicating that he has crucifixion in mind rather than impalement."

[128] Cf. R. Williamson:194-97 for a brief commentary on the section. In *Post* 26 Philo thus does not treat Deut 21:23 concerning a man sentenced to a death penalty, but he relates it to the inner ethical vices of any lawbreaker. He is also able to uphold the verse in its common meaning, however, cf. *Spec* 3:152 where he treats the hanging as an additional penalty on the murderer.

Thus Paul seems to treat Deut 21:23 as a Scriptural curse, but not as denoting Christ as cursed and rejected by God. This seems to open a possibility both that Christ is cursed according to Deut 21:23, and that this corresponds to the will of God.[129]

The most important change, however, is that Paul has mixed the citation with Deut 27:26, by taking up the formula ἐπικατάρατος πᾶς.[130] This connection indicates that Paul again is searching for the *Intention of the framer of the law*, by reading together passages from the whole document in order to find its true meaning (cf. 3:8, 10 above). Paul finds the intention by interpreting Deut 21:23 in light of Deut 27-30. We have just seen that Philo could work in a similar way in *Post* 23-27. In Philo it is explicitly stated that he aims at disclosing the real intention of Scripture: "It is for this reason that it is written (διὰ τοῦτο . . . γέγραπται; 24)" and "This is why the lawgiver says in another place (οὗ χάριν ἐν ἑτέροις; 26)."

The connection to Deut 27-30 is not surprising in the context. This tradition has just been brought to mind in 3:8-10, and it is therefore natural for Paul to allude to it again.

10.4.3: The impact of the Deut 27-30 tradition on 3:13-14

T. L. Donaldson has proposed that one should read 3:13-14 against the background of Jewish texts which treat the eschatological inclusion of the Gentiles (99-100, 105-6). Our semantic field analysis has pointed more precisely to a combination of texts from the Deut 27-30 tradition and the Abraham tradition as most adequate:[131]

> We found expressions similar to κατάρα τοῦ νόμου and γίνομαι κατάρα almost exclusively in Deut 27-30 texts (cf. above secs. 2.2.2 and 5.1; Mussner:233).
> We found the sequence of curse and blessing also mainly in Deut 27-30 texts (cf. above sec. 2.2.2, ch. 3 and sec. 5.3).
> Lastly we found the theme of blessing of the Gentiles both in the Deut 27-30 and in the Abraham tradition (cf. above secs. 2.2.2 and 5.2).

Now this possible connection has been even more substantiated, both by Paul's mixing of citations in 3:13 and by his activation of the Deut 27-30

---

[129]Although they differ in their inferences, it is common among scholars to make the observation that this omission makes Deut 21:23 christologically applicable for Paul, cf. Sieffert:161; Mussner:233; Rohde:144; Koch 1986:124-25.

[130]Cf. Baasland 1984a:144-45 who also emphasizes that 3:13 is turned into a general curse and contrasted with 3:10. See also Caneday:196-98, 204. We have seen above in chapter 4 that a form identical to Deut 27:26 is found almost only in the Deut 27-30 tradition. It is therefore clear that even if he does not take up Deut 27:26 specifically, he certainly takes up a form from the Deut 27-30 tradition.

[131]Cf. Hays 1989:109 for a brief assertion of the same.

tradition in 3:8–10. He has just reshaped the curse-blessing antithesis with the help of Abraham texts, an antithesis which is closely linked to the historical sequence of curse and blessing known as the deuteronomistic scheme of history (=dtr-SH, cf. ch. 3 above). A reader would therefore not be surprised if Paul also reshapes the latter part of the tradition in 3:13–14.

The implied logic is easy to reconstruct in a syllogistic way, although 3:13–14 formally do not contain a syllogism. It is clear that 3:14 must contain the conclusion in such logic, since we here find two ἵνα clauses. If 3:13 is a premise in a syllogistic logic, it is probably the Specific premise, since it emphasizes the redemptive work of one person. If a premise is omitted here, it then seems to be the General premise. Its content most probably has to include a reference to a release from the curse (cf. 3:13a) which is followed by a period of blessing (cf. 3:14):

> (*General premise*: Those that are redeemed from the curse will be blessed).
> *Specific premise*: We were redeemed by Christ from the curse of the law (3:13).
> *Conclusion*: Therefore we will be blessed (3:14).

Paul, indeed, may have omitted such a general premise. The audience may easily bring the deuteronomistic background to mind themselves, since it is both widespread and often connected to antitheses as 3:8–10.[132]

The *omitted General premise* that makes the whole logic understandable. The historical sequence of curse and blessing (3:13–14) is pictured against a background of a christianized dtr-SH. The *Specific premise* is the critical point of the logic: It is disputable that Christ should become the turning point of the ages, so Paul has to prove it with Hebrew Bible citation. The *Conclusion* in 3:14 is an extended variation of the brief syllogistic reconstruction above. It is divided into two ἵνα clauses,[133] which function as a conclusion to the syllogistic logic of 3:13–14 *and* as a conclusion to the whole discussion 3:1–14. The clauses may be tabulated as follows (similar Borse 1984:131):

(Conclusion:	We . . .	will be blessed).	
3:14a:	that upon the Gentiles . . .	. . . the blessing of Abraham might come . . .	in Christ Jesus.
3:14b:	that we . . .	. . . might receive the promise of the Spirit . . .	through faith.

---

[132]Cf. again Iser:155–61 and the relation between foreground and background.

[133]Whether the last ἵνα clause is dependent of the first (cf. H. D. Betz 1979:152), or they are parallel to each other (cf. Rohde:145), the second clause must be interpreted as a more specific interpretation of the first (cf. Burton:177; Bruce:167).

We see that both clauses include the elements which belong to the conclusion of the syllogistic logic. Gal 3:14a refers especially to the Gentiles and the blessing of Abraham, and thus also links up with the argument of 3:8-9. Gal 3:14b refers especially to the bestowal of the Spirit by faith, and thus also links up with the argument of 3:2-5. While 3:14a emphasizes the objective ground (=blessing in Christ), 3:14b concentrates on its subjective acquirement (Spirit through faith; Dobbeler:58).

Again we face an implicit *Conflict of laws*. According to such deuteronomistic texts as Deut 30, it is the law which is the objective ground that is held up for the people at the turn of the eras (cf. Deut 30:10-13). The subjective response is obedience to the law in practical life (cf. Deut 30:2, 8, 10, 14, 16). Again we see that obedience toward the law is exchanged by faith in Christ.

We have thus found a fruitful, deuteronomistic background for the interpretation of the curses in 3:13. Paul proves that Christ has become the turning point of the ages by a reference to the Ambiguity of Deut 21:23: This curse has been understood as a curse on criminals, but Paul has now discovered a deeper meaning in it. God has laid it down in the Scripture, not for the purpose of cursing criminals, but with the intention of preaching Christ beforehand (cf. the expression above 3:8). Thus Deut 21:23 is a hidden prophecy in Scripture about the way Christ would redeem from the curse and inaugurate the new era (similar Caneday:188-91, 204-5).

Deut 21:23 suits such a purpose very well: It is the only law in the deuteronomic law corpus that has a curse as a sanction. It may thus easily be drawn together with the curses of Deut 27. It is also the only deuteronomic law that denotes individual persons as cursed in a metonymic way (cf. above sec. 5.1.3). It may thus easily be drawn together with the other metonymic expressions of Israel as cursed in the Deut 27-30 tradition.

In this light our interpretation of Gal 2:19 above has been substantiated further: In 2:19 Paul states that Christians have died to the mosaic law in a way prescribed by the Pentateuch and related to the cross of Christ. In 3:13 Paul proves this argument, by presenting a scriptural passage that predicts the redemption by Christ on the cross.

> This reading of Deut 21:23 as a prophecy about Christ is not as arbitrary as it may seem. We find an illuminating parallel to it if we turn to Justin (2nd Century CE).
>
> Justin's discussion of Deut 21:23 is found in *Dial.* 89-96. It is the Jew Trypho who introduces the problem in 89 (cf. also 32): He accepts that the Scriptures announce that Christ had to suffer, but he wishes "to learn if you can prove it to us whether it was by the suffering cursed in the law."

Justin's answer seems to contain three different approaches, where the two latter work in a way similar to Paul's (Skarsaune:216–20, 238):[134] One refers to the will of the Father and the other treats Deut 21:23 as a prophecy.

The second argument in *Dial.* 95 is similar to Paul's, and Justin follows Paul's words in Gal 3 very closely (tables in Skarsaune:118–19). This argument states that "the Father of all wished His Christ for the whole human family to take upon Him the curses of all."

The third argument seems to be an afterthought: Deut 21:23 may also be taken as a prophecy about Jews cursing Jesus and the Christians: ". . . God foretold that which would be done by you all . . . ."

Although none of these arguments corresponds exactly to our interpretation of Paul, it is important for us to see *the hermeneutical principle at work*, which is explicitly stated in 90,1 (cf. also 92,1; van Unnik 1979:489–98): ". . . what the prophets said and did they veiled by parables and types, as you admitted to us; so that it was not easy for all to understand the most < of what they said >, since they concealed the truth by these means, that those who are eager to find out and learn it might do so with much labor." It is a discussion of Deut 21:23 which actualizes this prophetical principle which seeks for the concealed intention of the text.[135]

10.4.4: *Redemption as expiation*

So far we have been able to uncover the implied logic of 3:13–14 as a whole. The function of Christ as the inaugurator of the new era has been revealed, and also the function of Deut 21:23 as a hidden prophecy. We have not explained, however, how Christ could be understood to redeem by being a curse for us. Some proposals for this connection have been presented above in sec. 1.3.2b. I see many reasons for following H. Merklein in relating this part of the argument to traditions about expiation.

Merklein observes that dtr-SH texts like Deut 30:1–10 and *1 Enoch* 93 expect the future salvation to be given by divine intervention (16–20).[136] He further

---

[134]The first argument in *Dial.* 91–94 (which may be a reflection from Justin's source) indicates that Deut 21:23 did not hit Jesus. It refers to the fact that Moses broke one of the commandments when he made the image of the serpent, but was reckoned as blameless. In a similar way, the law will be suspended at the realization of this typology when Jesus is nailed on the cross.

[135]Luther 26:290–91 sees the same hermeneutical principle in this verse: "These are the adorable mysteries of Scripture, the true cabala, which even Moses disclosed rather obscurely in a few places."

[136]In our survey above (cf. ch. 3) we have emphasized the importance of conversion to the law in this respect. We also find many references to divine intervention, however. It is expected that Yahweh will:

a) Restore your fortunes, gather you again (cf. Deut 30:3–4; Jer 29:14; Ezek 16:53; Bar 2:34; *Ant* 4:314);

b) Create new heavens and a new earth (Isa 65:17);

c) Bring back, build up, plant, give a heart that knows the Lord (Jer 24:6–7);

d) Open the windows of heaven, pour down blessing (Mal 3:10; *1 Enoch* 11:1);

e) Reveal peace, transplant them, build my sanctuary, dwell with them (*Jub.* 1:15–17);

f) Cut off foreskin of their heart, create a holy spirit, purify (*Jub.* 1:23);

observes that apocalyptic traditions, the Priestly source of the Pentateuch, and the Qumran texts are occupied with the sinfulness of humankind and underscore the necessity of expiation as a solution to this plight (18–23).[137] Merklein also observes that Gal 3:13 contains the concept of substitution, which may be related to the suffering servant of Isa 53 (24–25).[138] Above all it may be related to the concept of cultic expiation in Lev 4–5; 16–17, since we find there a similar identity between the sinner and the dying sacrificial animal: The rites of the laying on of hands and sprinkling of blood seem to presuppose a transference of identity that is a real analogy to the denotation of Jesus as κατάρα (26–30).[139]

There are many reasons for regarding this connection as illuminating for Gal 3:13:

a) It *corresponds to the overall argument* that the death of Jesus fulfilled the intention of God laid down in Scripture.[140]

b) It illuminates the use of *the ὑπὲρ ἡμῶν formula*,[141] which seems to be

---

g) Heal his servants, show mercy (*Jub.* 23:30–31).

Outside the Deut 27–30 texts we find some other deuteronomistically influenced passages: Make a feast, destroy the covering of the peoples, swallow up death, wipe away tears, take away reproach (Isa 25:6–8); bring the dead to life (*Bib. Ant.* 3:10); show mercy again (*Tob* 13:9). In addition some Balaam texts underscore that it was God who turned the curse into a blessing (Deut 23:5; Neh 13:2; *Deter* 71; *Migr* 115). Thus an emphasis on a divine act of redemption by the turn of the eras has a natural place in dtr-SH texts.

[137]In our material we even find this emphasis connected to dtr-SH: In CD iii.18 the survey of Israel's sins and punishment leads to this redemptive act: God "forgave them their sins (כפר בצד צונם) and pardoned their wickedness."

[138]This connection is also found by, for example, Luther 26:278; Hofius 1983a:285.

O. Betz 1990a:205–6 takes the ἐπικατάρατος to correspond to מקולל in Hebrew (cf. 11QTemple 64:12) and understands Paul to have connected it with מחולל in Isa 53:5. It is unlikely that this specific connection would have been perceived by the Galatian audience, but we cannot rule out the possibility that it may have been an important connection to Paul.

[139]Merklein draws on Gese 1983 (cf. especially 95–98 for the rites) and Janowski (cf. especially 198–247 for the rites). Merklein does not claim that Gal 3:13 contains cultic language, but that this concept is the only real analogy to Paul's expressions (29). Also Hofius 1983b:32–37, 40–41 makes the same connection. Such an identity between sinner and Christ is also emphasized by Luther 26:277, 280, esp. 288.

[140]The law has not been exposed as false, *pace*, for example, Duncan:101; Rohde:144–45; Beker:261. It has rather got its prize; it has reached its goal by the fulfillment of Deut 21:23. Cf. for a position like this Oepke:109; Brown:131–32, 134–35; Büchsel:126; Schoeps:180; O. Betz 1990b:134, 185.

Also Ridderbos:126–27 points to a fulfillment, but he rather points to Exod 21:30 that demands ransom money for a forfeited life. Cf. also Burton:169–71 who speaks about a fulfillment of God's intention which he (wrongly) distinguishes from the intention of the law.

[141]Scholars vigorously debate whether "we" refers to Christians generally or to Jewish Christians only, cf. the overview of positions by Donaldson:94 (notes 2 and 3). It is difficult to follow him in his proposal that there is a necessary step between the cross and the liberation of the Gentiles, namely the liberation of Jewish Christians (95–97). See Caneday:203–4 and Braswell:74–75, 88–89 for recent publications that follow Donaldson.

connected with the concept of expiation.[142]

c) It explains how the death of Jesus could be related to *redemption with the term* ἐξαγοράζειν. This is an intensive expression of the verb ἀγοράζειν (= "to buy"; Büchsel:126-28). It is found in the New Testament also in Col 4:5 and Eph 5:16 with time as an object, but only in Gal 3:13; 4:5 as denoting the redemption by Christ. It is probably implied in this expression that Christ has paid the proper price when redeeming us from the curse.[143]

d) It takes *the illocutionary force of the curse seriously*: It was the execution of the curse with all its power of destruction and death which brought salvation.

e) It fits well into a *reader perspective*, since the concept is probably well-known to the Galatian audience. This may be deduced from the fact that it seems to play a central role in Paul's preaching, cf. 2 Cor 5:21; Rom 3:25-26; 8:3 (Merklein:32-34). It may also be deduced from the fact that expiation also in Hellenistic culture is regarded as the most appropriate means of eliminating the power of curses (Speyer:1190-91).[144]

These observations differ from those of N. A. Dahl and M. Wilcox who argue for a "midrash" on Gen 22 lying behind the section.[145] Their main arguments are as follows:

The link word between Gal 3:13 and Gen 22 is the term "tree = wood" (ξύλου). It is found in Gen 22:6a, 7b, 9, where especially the latter reference is interesting: Abraham binds Isaac and puts him "upon the altar, on top of the wood (ἐπάνω τῶν ξύλων)" (Wilcox:95-96).[146]

If this were important to Paul, we should expect it to be indicated more explicitly than by a slight change of pronouns. It is more credulous to follow Westerholm 1988:194-95 in his proposal that Paul includes the Gentiles through an unconscious generalization.

[142]Cf. 2 Cor 5:21 and Schlier 1965:139-40; Mussner:231-32; Stuhlmacher 1977: 455-60: Merklein:29.

[143]Cf. Rohde:143-44; Oepke:109 and the use of ἀγοράζειν for the redemption of Christ (the price is explicitly mentioned in 1 Cor 6:20; 7:23; Apoc 5:9, but not in 2 Pet 2:1; Apoc 14:3-4).

An allusion to the purchase of slaves to freedom (cf. Büchsel:124-26) is hard to find, since the term is not related to such purchases (cf. Mussner:232). On the other hand the term has probably not lost all of its connotations of purchase (cf. Bruce:166). For its connection to expiation, cf. Merklein:29-30.

[144]Speyer claims that "Das Opferwesen ist grossenteils aus dem Gedanken der Sühneleistung für fluchwürdige Verbrechen entstanden" (1190).

[145]Cf. the presentation above in sec. 1.3.2b. The other Hebrew Bible allusions that were presented there have even fewer points of contact with Gal 3:13, and so they need no further discussion.

[146]Dahl 1974:154 rather sees the link in the motif of "a ram caught in a thicket" (Gen 22:13) which corresponds to a man hanging upon a tree. This link is more imprecise, however.

Gal 3:14a may be seen as a paraphrase of Gen 22:18, where the expression "the blessing of Abraham" is taken from Gen 28:4, and the expression "in Christ Jesus" substitutes "by your descendants" (Dahl 1974:153).

These connections are also supported by the mixed citation in 3:8 that may include Gen 22:18. Note also that Deut 21:23b recalls the promise to Abraham, and that Gal 3:16 takes Christ as the singular seed of Abraham (Wilcox:95-97).

A serious problem with this proposal, however, is that the relevance of these observations cannot be proved. Since the word ξύλου does not belong to Paul's changes in the text, we cannot argue that it is important to him as a linkword. Since the "paraphrase" in Gal 3:14 contains so many expressions that do not correspond to Gen 22:18, it is difficult to uphold it as such. Further the mixed citation in Gal 3:8 emphasizes other aspects than the Isaac parallel, and Paul does not utilize the recalling of the promise to Abraham in Deut 21:23b.

The major objection to this proposal, however, is that if Paul does allude to Gen 22 here, he would relate it to a tradition that interprets the faith of Abraham in terms of obedience, and this would counter his interpretation of faith above in 3:6.[147]

10.4.5: Gal 3:13-14 as a temporal argument

The main argumentative force of 3:13-14 is its temporal aspect: The Christ event has brought the turn of the eras. This argument is of major importance in the letter as a whole, since Paul opens by stating this point (1:4) and treats it broadly in 3:15-25 which follows (cf. sec. 10.3.1 above). It is such a temporal argument which may legitimate Paul's conscious redefinition of the main mark of identity for the people of God, which again and again has caused Conflict of laws in his interpretation of the Hebrew Bible.

The kernel of this argument is that Christ has brought a new era where the mosaic legislation has been superseded.[148] This opens the way for a hermeneutic that may explain the legitimacy of both Definitions and of both types of Conflicting laws:

On one hand the principle of the "works of the law" is acknowledged as corresponding to the will of God, namely in the old and superseded era: This was so because the ultimate will of God had not been revealed yet. It was not possible to see other meanings in the texts than the traditional Jewish ones.

In the old era covenantal curses and Deut 13 should be applied according to their Jewish interpretation.

In the old era the antithesis of blessing and curse would correspond to its conventional reception among Jews.

In the old era Lev 18:5 was the main principle to which both the example of Abraham and Hab 2:4 should be harmonized.

---

[147]Cf. Hahn:98-100, 107 who claims that Paul wants to dissolve Gen 15:6 from its traditional connection to Gen 22.

[148]Cf. Brown:134-36; Braswell:74-75, 88-89 for similar interpretations. Cf. also the structure of Paul's thought set up by Westerholm 1988:153-54.

In the old era the covenantal curses were a constant threat to the Jewish nation and its members who broke the law.[149] Thus the curses of the law created a social reality, with expulsion of apostates and lawbreakers. Further they defined Gentiles as outsiders since they did not keep the law. The curses also created history when the whole nation became the object of God's punishment.

On the other hand the emphasis should now be laid on the principle of faith, since Christ has inaugurated the new era. In 3:13a Paul claims that Christ has "redeemed us from the curse of the law (ἐκ τῆς κατάρας τοῦ νόμου)." The period of covenantal curses (as also the period of the law; cf. 4:5) has come to an end. In light of this epoch-making Christ event, it is possible to read the Scriptures in a way that reveals the initial will of God:

Now Paul can, as in 2:19, claim that the law has brought an end to the law, and that the cross of Christ is the the focal point.

Now Paul can, as in 3:6, take Abraham as the prototype for faith in distinction to a Jewish way of life.

Now Paul can, as in 3:8-10, interpret both the Abraham blessing and the curse in a new way, with the result that the blessing is for those of faith, and the curse is for those of the law.

Now Paul can, as in 3:11-12, play Hab 2:4 off against Lev 18:5.

Now he even can, as in 1:8-9, issue covenantal curses on another basis than the law.

Paul shares the general conviction that there are no contradictions in the legislation. Every contradiction is apparent and can be reconciled (Martin: 48; Vos:260). From a Jewish perspective one could argue that a strong position should base its arguments on clear words such as Lev 18:5 and harmonize the faith references to it.[150] Paul, on the other hand, utilizes the temporal argument for another strong strategy, namely to argue that the mosaic law has been superseded and restricted (cf. *ad Herenn.* II.x.15). The mosaic law has had its time, but now the time has come for the fulfillment of the initial will of God.[151]

Such a temporal argument is so strong that it may even be categorized as a legal objection of its own. According to the stasis of Jurisdiction, one could delay or annul a case by objecting against various aspects of a lawsuit. One such aspect is time, and the corresponding objection is denoted *a tempore* (cf. Martin:43 and above sec. 8.6.1). Its point is to object that the pursuit is being attempted at the wrong time. So in Galatia: Since the opponents appear after the Christ event, they have come too late for a claim for circumcision to be legitimate.

---

[149]When Bligh:265-66; H. D. Betz 1979:149 propose that Paul here comes close to denoting the law itself as a curse, they are pressing the phrase too far. Paul instead uses it in a similar way as Jewish tradition prior to him.

[150]Cf. Cic. *Inv.* II.xlix.147: ". . . what is plainly stated seems to be stronger and more binding." To rely on ambiguities in the text is to maintain a weaker position.

[151]Thus this matter is also the most important, cf. the topic in Cic. *Inv.* II.xlix.145.

When we recognize the importance of this argument, new light is also thrown upon the sequence of arguments in 3:8-14. By posing them in this order, Paul displays an implicit description of the History of Salvation: Abraham represents a period of blessing (3:8-9), then the mosaic law represents a period of curse (3:10-12), before Christ has inaugurated the new era of blessing for both Jews and Gentiles (Luz:149; Ebeling:233-34).

10.5: Relations to the following argumentation in the letter

The fruitfulness of our new interpretation of the curse and blessing motif in Galatians may be further substantiated if it fits easily into the succeeding argumentation of the letter. We have already shown that there are connections between 3:8-14, the anathemas in 1:8-9, and the arguments of 2:18-19. In this section I will discuss the relation to other verses in the area of content, namely 3:19, 21-22, 25-26; 4:4-5 in the *argumentatio*, 5:2-4 in the *dissuasio*, 5:14; 6:2 in the *parenesis*, and 6:13, 16 in the *peroratio*.

10.5.1: The relation between 3:10 and 3:19, 21-22

From 3:19 onward Paul relativizes the law in relation to fulfillment in Christ (Merklein:70). Here we find descriptions of the function of the law which are similar to the curse in 3:10.

In 3:19 Paul states that the law is divine,[152] but that it is "added because of transgressions." The phrase τῶν παραβάσεων χάριν is ambiguous from a reader perspective (Merklein:69), and it is probably not important to scrutinize its "exact" meaning. The preposition χάριν is an indication that Paul is seeking the initial intention of God (Vos:264). It is not advisable to press it beyond the everyday experience that the issuing of commands creates temptations to disobey them.[153]   Thus this expression corresponds to the empirical interpretation of the curse in 3:10, since it stresses the sins in everyone's daily life. Paul immediately extends his expression, however: "till the offspring should come to whom the promise had been made." Thus Paul immediately proceeds by stating that a fulfillment by faith has always

---

[152]It is farfetched to press the phrase "ordained by angels" to denote that the law was given by hostile angelic powers, cf. the discussion by Westerholm 1988:176-79.

[153]Cf. Westerholm 1988:186. The preposition χάριν may denote the cause, that is, the law was given because of sins in order to prevent them or to restrain them. This interpretation seems too weak, cf. Gal 3:22. Most scholars therefore understand it as denoting the purpose. This purpose may be that of revealing sin (cf. Mussner:245-46; Merklein:69), or it may be that of creating a temptation to sin. To take this purpose as one of producing sin in a qualified sense (cf. Schlier 1965:152-54; Bruce:175) is probably to press the expression too far. Cf. Räisänen 1983:140-41 for a broader presentation of positions in the research.

been intended by God, and a broader reference that suits the extended interpretation of 3:10 is also given.

In 3:21-22 Paul discusses the relationship between the law and the
promises. These verses must be seen together, since he presents an opposing
thesis in 3:21 and his own in 3:22. When in 3:21 he presents the hypothetical
possibility that "a law had been given which could make alive," it is clearly
implied that it is to be rejected.[154] It is not implied, however, that the law
was given with the opposite purpose of giving life. Gal 3:22 rather shows
that it was given for another and temporal purpose: On one hand it was given
to consign all things to sin, that is, to demonstrate and deepen the bondage of
humanity to sin.[155] Again we find a description of the law that fits the empirical interpretation of 3:10. On the other hand Paul also this time extends his
description to include the promise of faith (cf. 3:22b). Again he supplies his
description of the law with a wider frame that also suits the extended meaning
of 3:10.

To conclude: Both in 3:19 and 3:21-22 the function of the law is described within a narrower and a broader perspective: On one hand the law
should reveal or give temptations to sin; on the other hand God's purpose has
always aimed at the primacy of faith. In this way both the empirical and the
extended interpretation of 3:10 fit the argument.

10.5.2: The relation between 3:13-14 and 3:25-26; 4:4-5

In the extensive presentation of the temporal argument in 3:15 - 4:7 we
find two texts which, like Gal 3:13-14, give attention to the transition
between the eras, namely 3:25-26 and 4:4-5.[156]

In 3:25 this transition is described with the phrase "we are no longer
under a custodian." The function of a custodian has been much debated
recently. It is an open metaphor, which is probably to be taken as denoting a
confining guardianship, rather than emphasizing the constraining, pedagogical, or protective function of the law.[157] Be this as it may, the main emphasis

---

[154]Paul uses a *modus tollens* argument: Since he is sure that the consequence is false
(righteousness is not given by the law), he uses this false antecedent to refute also the
thought that the law can make alive. Cf. for such logic R. A. Young:41-42.

Thus our interpretation of 3:12 is supported: We have to take the reference to life by
the law in a weaker sense also in that verse.

[155]Cf. Westerholm 1988:196; Bruce:180. Cf. Merklein:74 for the interpretation that
the law should reveal the sinner as such and thus reveal humanity as a collection of sinners.

[156]Cf. Hays 1983:118, 229 for parallel tabulations of these texts. Also Smiga:183-84
holds them together.

[157]Cf. N. H. Young, esp. 170-73. See also Belleville:59-60. Cf. for a constraining
purpose Schlier 1965:168-70; H. D. Betz 1979:177-78; Rohde:161-62; for a pedagogical
Burton:200; Lull 1986; for a protective Gordon 1989:153-54.

is clearly on its temporal function, since the task of a custodian has been fulfilled when the child becomes mature.[158] As in Gal 3:13-14 the temporal function of the law corresponds to the intention of God. Just as in 3:8, the Scripture becomes the acting subject also in 3:22a.[159] The period of the law has reached its goal with the coming of Christ (cf. the expression in 3:24: "our custodian until Christ came [παιδαγωγὸς ἡμῶν . . . εἰς Χριστόν])."[160]

The meaning of 4:5: "to redeem those[161] who were under the law" is very similar. Here Paul uses the same verb as in 3:13 (ἐξαγοράζειν). Whereas in 3:13 Christ redeemed from the curse by becoming a curse, here he redeems those under the law by being born under the law himself (cf. 4:4b). The expressions are thus analogous, this latter one more general than the former (Ridderbos:156; Rohde:172).

An interpretive clue is found in 4:1-2, which forms an Analogy from human jurisdiction, which 4:4-5 applies to the redemption. Here Paul states that an heir "is under guardians and trustees (ὑπὸ ἐπιτρόπους ἐστὶν καὶ οἰκονόμους) until the date set by the father (ἄχρι τῆς προθεσμίας τοῦ πατρός)." Although this example does not fit smoothly into Roman or Hellenistic jurisdiction,[162] the function of these tutors and supervisors is to administer the property of the heir for a limited period. Again the temporal aspect is the most important one. Paul also refers explicitly to the fact that this conforms with the intention of the father, who has limited the period beforehand. Against this background the redemption by Christ is equivalent to the termination of the period of "guardians and trustees," and God consequently sent his Son "when the time had fully come" (4:4a).

To conclude: Our interpretation of 3:13-14 has thus been substantiated by 3:24-25 and 4:1-5. Both of these sections emphasize the temporal aspect of the mosaic law, which Christ has brought to an end. This has taken place according to God's intention and according to the purpose of the law itself, not as a rejection or invalidation of it.

10.5.3: The relation between 3:10-13 and 5:2-4

I have argued above (cf. sec. 8.2) that the section 5:1-12 conforms to a *dissuasio* in a deliberative speech. The double expression in 5:2-3,[163] may

---

[158]Cf. N. H. Young:168-69, 174; Gordon 1989:151-52; Westerholm 1988:195-96.

[159]Cf. Belleville:56; Lull 1986:486.

[160]Εἰς is taken in a temporal sense, cf. H. D. Betz 1979:178; Bruce:183.

[161]As in 3:13-14, the pronoun probably denotes both Jewish and Gentile Christians (cf. Burton:219; Rohde:172) and not only Jewish Christians (cf. H. D. Betz 1979:208).

[162]Cf. the different discussions by Burton:212-15; Oepke:127-28; H. D. Betz 1979: 203-204; Belleville:62-63.

[163]Gal 5:2 and 5:3 seem to have been constructed in close connection with each other: Both open with a solemn address, where 5:3 is connected to 5:2 with πάλιν (cf. Lightfoot:203; Oepke:156; Bruce:229; Rohde:215. Other scholars take it to refer to

both be taken as general deliberative warnings,[164] but they may also be connected more specifically to the curses in 3:10, 13:

In 5:2 Paul warns that Christ will be of no advantage if they receive circumcision. Seen in the light of 3:13 this means that they will have no share in the redemption from the curse of the law.[165] This is underscored by 5:4: "You are severed from Christ . . . you have fallen away from grace."[166] The result is thus that the covenantal curses become effective.[167] We thus see that the mosaic law has only been outdated for those in Christ. It is thus not only a question of living in the era of fulfillment, one must also partake in the sphere of blessing which is restricted to Christ and faith.

In 5:3 Paul warns "every man who receives circumcision that he is bound to keep the whole law." This statement is often connected with the curse in 3:10, whether it is taken in the fundamental or empirical way, and thus Paul warns the Galatians of the impossible task they take upon themselves by adherence to the law.[168]

The grammar is ambiguous, however: We find no conditional relation, so the duty is not explicitly presented as a consequence of accepting the rite.[169] The metaphor of *debtor* is also ambiguous: Although it is often taken

---

Paul's preaching from an earlier occasion, cf. Zahn:247; Burton:274-75; Mussner:347), both warn against accepting circumcision, and we find a play on words between the verses on the *paronomasia* of "be of advantage" (ὠφελήσει 5:2b) and debtor (ὀφειλέτης 5:3b) (cf. Lührmann 1978:81; Howard:16. For this rhetorical figure, cf. *ad Herenn.* IV.xxi.29).

[164]Gal 5:2-3 may be taken as arguments within the topics Disadvantageous and Laborious: Paul dissuades his audience by pointing to a disadvantage of receiving circumcision, namely that "Christ will be of no advantage to you" (5:2), and he points to a laborious task they would take on themselves by this acceptance, namely to be "bound to keep the whole law" (Cf. Burton:274; Sanders 1983:27-29). In the current situation it would be enough for the audience to perceive the verses in this way, since they will be taken as strong warnings against circumcision.

[165]The future tense of the verb refers to the consequence by an eventual acceptance of circumcision (Burton:273; Rohde:215). It is hardly an eschatological future (*pace* Mussner:346).

[166]According to Mussner:349, Paul does not use the future tense here, but the proleptical aorist, which denotes what will happen when they accept the rite.

[167]Relations between 5:4 and curse are seen by H. D. Betz 1979:261; Mussner:349. Cf. also Schlier 1965:232.

[168]Cf. Sieffert:284; Becker:61; Borse 1984:180; Lührmann 1978:81; Rohde:215-16; Schoeps:177; Räisänen 1983:95. Cf. Bligh:421 for such a connection when 3:10 has been interpreted as an empirical truth. Also Schlier 1965:232, who prefers a qualitative interpretation, connects 5:3 to the curse of 3:10.

[169]Contrary to Schlier 1965:232; H. D. Betz 1979:259; who draw on Rom 2:25 in this respect. The participle hardly has a conditional meaning as Mussner:347 argues. Paul states the warning with special regard to "every man who receives circumcision."

negatively, it may also be taken as denoting a positive, juridical duty.[170] Thus it is even possible to take the warning as a reminder of the extended interpretation of 3:10: Like the opponents, the Galatians also have a duty to "keep the whole law." They need to hear this especially, however, since their acceptance of circumcision will bring them into violation of the principle of faith. Thus by accepting the rite, they will not keep the law according to its intention, because the law itself (=Pentateuch) teaches faith as the principle of the new era.[171]

To conclude: It is not mandatory for Paul's audience to relate his warnings in 5:2–4 to the curses in 3:10, 13. But if they do, 5:2 and 5:4 will supplement the interpretation of 3:13, and the ambiguous expression in 5:3 may fit both the empirical and the extended interpretation of 3:10.

10.5.4: The relation between 3:10, 14b and 5:14; 6:2

In his interpretation of the curse in 3:10, Luther includes the perspective that a Christian could fulfill the law by a life in the Spirit (26:255, 260). It is notable that 3:8–14 ends with an emphasis on the Spirit, and that the whole argument of 3:1 – 4:7 both opens and ends with such references (cf. 3:2, 5 and 4:6).[172] We have seen above (cf. Gal 3:2 in sec. 10.2.2a) that Jewish tradition perceives the function of the Spirit in the new era to produce new obedience. It is therefore significant that when Paul comes to the parenetic part of the letter, he refers to the new life, saying that one should "walk in the Spirit ($\pi\nu\epsilon\dot{\upsilon}\mu\alpha\tau\iota$ $\pi\epsilon\rho\iota\pi\alpha\tau\epsilon\hat{\iota}\nu/\sigma\tau\upsilon\iota\chi\epsilon\hat{\iota}\nu$)" (5:16, 25). There are many indications that this pneumatic life is regarded as the fulfillment of the law in some way or another:

---

[170]It is often taken for granted that the metaphor of the debtor underscores the notion of slavery from Gal 5:1 (cf. Bruce:231; Borse 1984:179–80; Howard:16). Elsewhere, however, Paul uses this term for the positive responsibilities that Christians have, cf. Rom 1:14; 8:12; 15:27 (cf. also Tiedtke/Link:666–668). Thus the metaphor may rather impose a juridical duty on the Galatians (cf. Dahl 1967:143–44).

[171]Also Luther 27:12 seems to have observed this grammatical possibility. He states that there are two possible interpretations, and the most simple is that it warns: "even in the very act of circumcision he does not receive circumcision, and even in the fulfilling of the Law he does not fulfill it but transgress it." Luther takes this grammatical possibility in a different way (as a negative experience that one becomes more bound and enslaved by the Law by observing it, cf. 12–15), but he at least notes the same grammatical possibility as utilized above.

[172]Thus an emphasis on the Spirit is very clear, but probably not to such an extent as Williams 1988 argues, namely that all references to promises in Gal 3–4 refer to the promise of the Spirit. Also Schenk:45 overstates the case when he regards Spirit and blessing as synonymous in 3:14. What is true is that among the blessings bestowed on Christians, Paul underscores the importance of the Spirit at vital places in his argument.

The effects of the Spirit are denoted as "fruit (καρπός)" (5:22a), a metaphor which in Jewish tradition may denote the obedience to law of the new era (Barclay 1988:121).

The first fruit of the Spirit is love (5:22). In 5:5-6 Paul combines both this love and the Spirit with faith (cf. the expressions ". . . through the Spirit, by faith [πνεύματι ἐκ πίστεως]" [5:5] and "faith working through love [πίστις δι' ἀγάπας ἐνεργομένη]" [5:6]). It is thus not faith alone which is the principle of the new era, but faith combined with the Spirit and its first fruit, love. Again we see how faith is connected to a far-reaching act of participation in Christian life (Dobbeler:67).

Against the fruits of the Spirit "there is no law (οὐκ ἔστιν νόμος)" (5:23b). This expression is probably an example of *Understatement*: Instead of claiming that these fruits fulfill the law, Paul more modestly states that no law (including the law of God) would judge them.[173]

The main reference to a fulfillment of the law is found in 5:14, however: "For the whole law is fulfilled in one word, 'You shall love your neighbor as yourself.'" Paul cites Lev 19:18 according to the LXX without changes in the text. His introduction to the citation, however, seems to indicate that he searches for the *Intention of the framer of the law*.[174] He states that love is a fulfillment (πληροῦν instead of ποιεῖν in 5:3) of the law as an entity (ὁ . . . πᾶς νόμος instead of ὅλον τὸν νόμον in 5:3). According to S. Westerholm "πληροῦν is specially suited . . . for use by an author who claims to have superior insight into what is required to satisfy the 'true' intention of the law-giver or the 'real' demand of the law" (1986:234).[175] The same term is employed in 6:2, where Paul exhorts one to "fulfill the law of Christ (ἀναπληρώσετε τὸν νόμον τοῦ Χριστοῦ)."

There are many "silent points" involved in this argument. On one hand the term πληροῦν is ambiguous, and it does not indicate very precisely in what way the law is fulfilled.[176] On the other hand the relation between the law in 5:14 and the law of Christ in 6:2 is not made explicit: Does Paul speak of the mosaic law having been restored/redefined in some way or another by Christ?[177] Or does he rather regard the law of Christ as something quite new, but with a content that corresponds to the good parts of the super-

---

[173]Cf. Burton:318. Cf. *ad Herenn.* IV.xxxviii.50 for the figure λιτότης. This verse is thus a counterpart to 5:14 and not to 5:18. For other interpretations cf. Barclay 1988: 122-25.

[174]Cf. Wischmeyer for a broad traditio-historical background for Paul's reinterpretation of Lev 19:18. A stasis dispute about the true meaning of this verse is involved since Jews would not play it off against national laws as Paul does, cf. Barclay 1988:135-36.

[175]Cf. also Westerholm 1988:203-205. See also Dobbeler:68 for a brief assertion.

[176]For an emphasis on this ambiguity in πληροῦν cf. Westerholm 1986:235; Barclay 1988:140-41. Also Sanders 1983:97-98 argues that Paul expresses himself rather loosely.

[177]Cf., for example, Barclay 1988:126-35; O. Betz 1990b:152-54, 178, 183-84, 195-96.

seded mosaic law?[178] Regardless of how Paul perceives the accurate relation between the law of Christ and the mosaic law, it is clear that his emphasis on the Spirit is no accidental feature. It is the Spirit who enables Christians to fulfill the law, not only by faith, but also by love, and thus to satisfy the demand of Deut 27:26.[179]

10.5.5: The relation between 3:8-10 and 6:13, 16

In 6:13 Paul attacks the opponents in a way that has often been connected with the interpretation of Gal 3:10: "For even those who receive circumcision do not themselves keep the law, but they desire to have you circumcised (οὐδὲ γὰρ οἱ περιτεμνόμενοι αὐτοὶ νόμον φυλάσσουσιν ἀλλὰ θέλουσιν ὑμᾶς περιτέμνεσθαι)." The content of this charge seems to correspond neatly to our empirical interpretation of 3:10: They do not keep it, because nobody does! Grammatically, however, the charge is very open, and there is no indication in the text of what its content may be (cf. H. D. Betz 1979:316-17). Since it is both preceded and succeeded by references to circumcision, it is possible to interpret it as if it is the claim for circumcision that constitutes disobedience toward the law.[180] Thus even the extended interpretation of 3:10 may be related to this verse.

Finally, in 6:16 Paul restates his redefinition of the blessing: "Peace and mercy be upon all who walk by this rule, upon the Israel of God." The first part of this blessing is clearly conditional. The blessing is only for those who adhere to Paul's rule (κανών) which is rendered in 6:15: "For neither circumcision counts for anything, nor uncircumcision, but a new creation." Again we see that Paul blesses those who regard nationalistic commandments as superseded. It is more difficult to grasp the meaning of the last part of the blessing: "upon the Israel of God (καὶ ἐπὶ τὸν Ἰσραὴλ τοῦ θεοῦ)." Scholarly opinion is divided here, but regardless of the interpretation one chooses, this part of the blessing also contains an implicit redefinition.

> Most scholars tend to suggest that Paul has carried his redefinition even further than elsewhere in his letters: Paul transfers the name *Israel* to the new church of both Jews and Gentiles.[181] This interpretation would correspond smoothly to our emphasis on Paul's redefinition of the blessed: Paul not only redefines blessing and curse, but he is even ready to draw the consequence concerning who has the right to

---

[178]Cf., for example, Westerholm 1988:208-18; Hofius 1983a:281-86; Merklein:103-106.

[179]Cf. also Bring ad 3:10; Hübner 1984a:40-41.

[180]Cf. Barrett 1985:87. This causal relation is not explicit in the grammatical structure, but the grammar does not argue against it either. Also Luther 27:131-32 contends that one does not keep the law by the act of circumcision.

[181]Lightfoot:224-25; Sieffert:345-46; Oepke:204-5; Ridderbos:227; Schlier 1965: 283; Borse 1984:223-24; Rohde:278; Dahl 1950; Wiles:133-34.

be denoted as the true Israel.[182] There are certain important problems that make this reading difficult, however: The most common way to take καί is to make it introduce a new group; Paul does not elsewhere denote the church as *Israel*, and neither do other known Christian texts before 160 CE.[183]

If καί introduces a new group, some scholars have proposed that it will have to be Jewish Christianity.[184] H. D. Betz has proposed an identification of them that makes good sense: Paul blesses Jewish Christians loyal to his Gospel, and so excludes false brethren like those in 2:4-5 and the cursed opponents as in 1:8-9.[185]

The most plausible interpretation though, is to regard it as a blessing of the Jewish nation in an eschatological perspective: Paul has a strong hope for salvation of the whole of Israel, and thus it will be natural for him to bless the nation in an afterthought, and hope for the salvation of as many of his kinsmen as possible (cf. Rom 9:1-5; 11:25-32).[186] Paul thus still sticks to his redefinition, since it is an anticipated future conversion of Israel to which he refers.

When Paul activates his attacks on the opponents and his redefinition of the blessed at the very end of his letter, it seems plausible that some in his audience would recall the curses of 1:8-9 and 3:10. Thus the importance of the double anathema once again seems to have been substantiated.

To sum up: The fruitfulness of our interpretation of 3:8-14 has been tested also in its relations to the rest of the letter: It corresponds to key verses both in the *argumentatio* (3:19, 21-22, 25-26; 4:4-5), the *dissuasio* (5:2-4), the parenesis (5:14), and the postscript (6:13, 16). The reinterpretation of curse and blessing is thus more than minor arguments in the letter. It is rather organically related both to its main theme and to most of its main parts.

---

[182]Cf. Wiles:116, 129, 134 for this as an intended counterpart to the curse of 1:8-9.

[183]Cf. Johnson:56-60 for a critique. Καί is mostly taken as explicative/epexegetic, but some refer instead to Jewish prayers where this copula introduces a statement of the whole after a statement of a part (cf. Oepke:205; Schlier 1965:283).

[184]Cf. Zahn:283-84; Schenk 1950.

[185]Cf. H. D. Betz 1979:322-23.

[186]Cf. Burton:357-58; Mussner:416-17; Bruce:274-75; Johnson and especially Richardson:74-84.

CHAPTER 11

11.0: FINAL SUMMARY AND CONCLUSION

In his theological-ecclesiastical reflections on Galatians, H. Asmussen makes these statements regarding the double anathema: "Eine Kirche, die nicht fluchen kann, kann auch nicht segnen . . . . Sie wird Kirche der Moralathleten und der harmlosen Kaffeetanten" (46). Such a statement is challenging for several reasons.

It is challenging if it is applied to the practice of church discipline today. In our western churches we live in a culture where curses have lost their force, and where churches have developed other modes of church discipline that function in legal ways that satisfy their needs. This volume will therefore not advocate a renewal of curses in modern church life. The statement of Asmussen can only be endorsed when the term "fluchen" is taken as a metaphor.

The statement is also challenging as a description of Pauline mission in the first century CE. It is rather unusual to interpret curses as a powerful means of communication as is done in this study. Can we imagine that Paul, the author of the hymn to love in 1 Cor 13, could issue curses on his opponents in a way advocated here? In a time when Jewish-Christian dialogue has created a climate where controversies between religions are played down, this would certainly be improper to claim. The present author, however, sees no way of escaping this and other aspects of the often hostile and sharp controversies between Judaism and Christianity in the course of history.

It is important to note that it is Paul as a Jew who issues the anathema on opponents as fellow Jews. Seen from such a perspective his language is not more strident than the prophets often were toward their fellow countrymen in their preaching. In addition the curse is not issued upon Jews in general, but is used as an inner ecclesiastical medium between an apostle and other Christian missionaries. Thus there should be no basis for anti-Semitic reactions if Paul's anathema is understood in its proper context.

11.1: An outline of the argument

From our double observation that there is, on one hand, a new relative consensus concerning curse in Hebrew Bible research (cf. sec. 1.2), and that, on the other hand, scholarly opinions with regard to curses in Galatians differ in many respects (cf. sec. 1.3), we set before ourselves three tasks: To investigate Paul's Galatian curses from the perspective of their syntactic, semantic, and pragmatic aspects (cf. sec. 1.4).

The priority has been given to an analysis of Paul's argument on a *syntactic level*. This analysis has been carried out without presuppositions concerning the historical conditions in Galatia (cf. sec. 7.1), but rather by employing the method of rhetorical criticism (cf. secs. 1.4.1; 7.2 and 7.3). Since this method is used in various ways by scholars, I found it necessary to argue for a rather flexible approach that concentrates on the most widespread and conventional rhetorical patterns:

> The approach should be flexible enough to allow Galatians to be a letter with both judicial and deliberative rhetoric (cf. sec. 8.2), and with an Arrangement that does not conform exactly to the patterns of the handbooks (cf. sec. 8.7).
> It should concentrate on simple rhetorical effects as figures of diction and thought, as the difference between inductive and deductive logic and as the theory of topics (cf. secs. 8.3 – 8.5).
> It should also be flexible enough to bring in some aspects in a more detailed way than what has been done to date, if it seems to prove fruitful and relative, such as the stasis theory from judicial rhetoric (cf. sec. 8.6).

We have found that the double anathema in 1:8-9 is present in an exordium that amplifies the situation in Galatia as one of apostasy and seduction (cf. 1:6-7 in sec. 9.2.1). It is followed by verses that defend the $\hat{\eta}\theta o\varsigma$ of Paul, who has dared to issue such a curse (cf. 1:10-12 in sec. 9.2.3). The double anathema itself is presented in a way that claims divine authority (cf. sec. 9.2.2a). We found its *semantic* counterparts in Jewish tradition to be a combination of covenantal curses and the law against seducers from Deut 13 (cf. sec.9.2.2b).

At this point we had to rely on the semantic analysis (cf. sec. 1.4.2) that was carried out in chapters 2 and 6 (cf. also tables in the appendices).

> We found that an anathema would have been perceived as a curse at the time of Paul, since חרם/$\dot{\alpha}\nu\dot{\alpha}\theta\varepsilon\mu\alpha$ seems to have developed into curse at this time (cf. sec. 6.2).
> Gal 1:6-9 further shared many features with curses from the Deut 27–30 tradition and with חרם/$\dot{\alpha}\nu\dot{\alpha}\theta\varepsilon\mu\alpha$ texts with deuteronomistic influence: Although the correspondence was ambiguous concerning the structure of present accusations and curse and the feature of curse on seducers, it was quite unambiguous concerning the form, expressions similar to $\dot{\alpha}\nu\dot{\alpha}\theta\varepsilon\mu\alpha$ $\varepsilon\tilde{i}\nu\alpha\iota$, explicit curses in self-imprecations, curse on angelic beings, and the theme of apostasy (cf. secs. 6.3.1 – 6.3.5).
> The law of Deut 13 attracted special attention, however, because it is the only pentateuchal law that orders the death penalty for seducers, and that also has the חרם term, a form like Gal 1:8-9, and the theme of apostasy (cf. sec. 6.3.6).

The semantic correspondences were not indisputable, however, so the conclusion was a tentative one. On the other hand, $\dot{\alpha}\nu\dot{\alpha}\theta\varepsilon\mu\alpha$ is a Jewish and not a

Greek curse term, and there are no other suitable candidates for curses with divine sanction and laws against seducers in Jewish tradition. A covenantal background also fits the remaining ἀνάθεμα texts in Paul (cf. sec. 9.4).

The *pragmatic* aspects of such curse was analyzed utilizing the distinction in Speech Act Theory between locution, illocution, and perlocution of an utterance (cf. sec. 1.4.3). Since a curse is perceived as a powerful word in the culture of Paul (cf. secs. 9.3.1 and 9.3.2), it will inevitably have an *illocutionary force* on the readers of the letter. This force consists in a demand to regard the opponents as persons cursed by God. Therefore, the Galatian churches are given a difficult choice. They cannot ignore this demand when the curses have been uttered. They have to choose between the authority of Paul and the authority of the opponents. In the former case they will have to regard the opponents as seducers; in the latter case they will have to regard Paul as a false curser, who is hit himself by curses which he illegitimately speaks against others. After the reading of the letter, the Galatian churches cannot go on keeping close contact with both parties of the conflict (cf. sec. 9.3.3a).

As a powerful word the curse also aims at certain *perlocutionary effects*. These effects are not easy to predict with certainty, but they will take place within the conventional expectations set by the cultural context.

> With regard to curses in Jewish and Greek culture and in Paul in 1 Cor 5, we found these effects to be fear of the cursed persons, since they are polluted by evil and under the judgment of God. This would lead to isolation or expulsion in some way or another (cf. secs. 9.3.1 and 9.3.2). In the case of Galatians, these consequences will affect either the opponents or Paul, depending on whether or not they accept the legitimacy of Paul's double anathema (cf. sec. 9.3.3bc).

The Galatian choice is thus more comprehensive than seen by previous scholars. The letter challenges its first audience not only to choose between two opposing gospels, but also between Paul and his opponents as persons. Person and message are seen as a unity. The Galatians should thus not only reject a certain teaching, but also turn away from the persons who preach it.

When we see this pragmatic function of curse in Galatians, we understand that it is a shockingly powerful element in the letter. This insight also throws new light on the semantic and syntactic levels: It is important for Paul that his curses carry the most powerful authority, hence his use of the covenantal curse tradition. It is an allusion to covenantal traditions with a major deviation, however: The curse is issued on those who claim obedience toward the law instead of lawbreakers. Hence Paul has to return to a discussion of the legitimacy of such deviation if he wants to persuade his audience. Such legitimizing discussion is found in 3:8–14.

We have found the curse-blessing section 3:8-14 to be present in a context of judicial argumentation that develops in a way similar to parts of *stasis theory* in Hellenistic rhetoric: The speech of 2:14b-21 corresponds to the way an argument is presented according to the stasis of Definition: Paul defends *faith* as the marker of identity for Christian communities in contrast to *works of the law* (cf. secs. 8.7.3 and 10.2.1). This strategy is in 3:1-7 supplied with inductive proofs such as the reception of the Spirit and the example of Abraham (cf. sec. 10.2.2), and it explicitly shifts over to an argument according to the stasis of Conflict of laws from 3:15 onward (cf. sec. 10.3.1). The curse and blessing motif itself is present as an antithesis in 3:8-10 and a sequence in 3:13-14 (cf. secs. 2.2.1c and 10.1). The *semantic* counterparts to this structure in Jewish tradition we found to be the covenantal curse tradition based on Deut 27- 30.

The semantic correspondences were more evident here than in 1:8-9 (cf. chs. 2-5 and the appendices):

> In thirteen texts from the Deut 27-30 tradition we found that almost all the texts contain the combination of curse and blessing both in antithesis and sequence; one third of the terms contain a form similar to Gal 3:10, half of them utilize expressions like κατάρα τοῦ νόμου and γίνομαι κατάρα; half of the texts contain the theme of life; and one fourth of the texts refer to blessing for Gentiles. Thus texts like *1 Enoch* 1-11; 91-5; *Jub.* 1; 20; 23; *T. Levi* 10-18; *T. Naph.* 3-4; 8; *Praem* 126-72; 1QS i-iv; CD i-viii; and *Ant* 4:302-14 (cf. also Isa 65; Jer 17.24-44; Malachi) seem to be very close parallels to Paul's exposition (cf. ch. 3).

Also outside these texts a deuteronomistic relation was found for most semantic features:

> A form similar to Gal 3:10 was found primarily in deuteronomistically influenced texts (cf. sec. 4.1).
>
> Expressions similar to κατάρα τοῦ νόμου and γίνομαι κατάρα were almost exclusively found in this tradition (cf. sec. 5.1) as well as texts with curse and blessing in sequence (cf. sec. 5.3).
>
> The feature of curse and blessing in antithesis, however, was much more ambiguous, but it is important to note that antithetic constructions were conventional (cf. sec. 4.2).
>
> The feature of blessing to the Gentiles seems to be found especially in the Abraham tradition (cf. sec. 5.2).
>
> We thus concluded that Gal 3:8-14 seems to relate clearly to the Deut 27-30 tradition, and it also seems to combine it with Abraham traditions (cf. sec. 6.4).

Again it is striking how Paul deviates from the conventional application of these traditions. His antithesis forms an implicit Conflict of laws with conventional deuteronomistic antitheses: Instead of blessing those obedient to Torah, Paul picks up the Abraham blessing for those of faith. Instead of cursing the lawbreakers, Paul takes the curse of Deut 27:26 to fall on those who advocate works of the law as a marker of identity for the people of God (cf. sec. 10.3.4). We found that Paul utilized judicial strategies for this reinterpretation: He drew on Ambiguities in the text and searched for the hidden, initial Intention of God (cf. secs. 10.3.2b, 10.3.3d and 10.4.2).

Two specific interpretations may be emphasized as especially challenging:

> The curse of Deut 27:26 is interpreted in a way that makes it hit those who do not practice faith as the mark of identity for the Christian church (cf. sec. 10.3.3d). Paul gives this controversial proposal as an additional aspect to its empirical meaning as a curse on those who in practice do not keep the law (cf. sec. 10.3.3c).
>
> The curse on Christ in 3:13 is understood to reflect that the Christ-event is the turning point of the ages in a deuteronomistic view of history (cf. sec. 10.4.3). It is thus a temporal argument which may explain why it is legitimate in the new era to reinterpret Hebrew Bible texts so fundamentally as done here (cf. sec. 10.4.5).

While Paul only alluded to deuteronomistic traditions in 1:8-9, he more openly reinterprets them in 3:8-14. Thus the relations between these curse sections may be seen at several levels:

> Both the double anathema and the curse of 3:10 serve the function of incriminating the opponents of Paul. Thus 3:10 is a curse that reinforces the illocutionary force of 1:8-9 (cf. sec. 10.3.3a).
>
> The interpretation of 3:10 as hitting those who do not practice faith makes it legitimize the deviation from covenantal curses in 1:8-9 (cf. secs. 9.3.4a and 10.3.4).
>
> The extensive use of legal stasis in 3:8-10 makes it probable that Paul in 1:8-9 employs the form of covenantal curses and the law of Deut 13 according to the stasis of Reasoning from Analogy, in order to construct a new curse for a new situation (cf. secs. 9.3.4a and 10.3.4).

Paul's shocking anathema in 1:9 has thus been confirmed by an extensive redefinition of deuteronomistic traditions: Both the antithesis and the dtr-SH have been reshaped in a way that substantiates the legitimacy of the anathema. Thus Paul knows what he is doing when he forces the Galatians to choose between himself and the opponents. He knows that his exposition of the scriptures is so firmly established in the Christ-event and in Hebrew Bible texts that he has a good chance of convincing the churches of Galatia.

Thus a fresh interpretation of the Galatian curses has been presented. Its fruitfulness has been applied briefly also to remaining curse texts by Paul (cf. secs. 9.3.2 and 9.4) and to other related parts of the letter (cf. secs. 9.3.4b and 10.5).

11.2: The Galatian Choice

The theme of this monograph is connected to several broader contexts that should elicit further research. Above all it is connected to the curse theme in other New Testament texts (cf. above sec. 1.1), to the interpretation of Galatians at a broader scale, to Pauline theology in general, and to the application of the method of rhetorical criticism. At this stage I only want to push the discussion further with regard to one important question: The challenge of reconstructing the history of mission in the early Church. I have consciously refused to involve such reconstruction in the exegesis of the text (cf. above sec. 7.1). Now that I have reached a conclusion, I find it appropriate to draw some inferences about our knowledge concerning early Christian mission.

Paul's letter to the Galatians bears witness to the fact that early Christianity ran into a conflict which concerned several related items:

a) It was a *conflict with Gentile converts* where Jewish Christians differed considerably in their approach. Already in Judaism itself we find different opinions with regard to the inclusion of Gentiles into the people of God. This diversity also caused problems for early Christian mission.

b) It was also a *conflict of how to perceive the work of Christ*. Should the effects of his death and resurrection be harmonized with a Jewish concern for the Law and national identity? Or should it rather be taken as a decisive turning point that created a new basis for the inclusion of Gentiles?

c) It was a *conflict concerning the interpretation of Hebrew Bible* as the main authority for Christians. Should it be interpreted in harmony with Jewish conventions, or should the Christ-event be understood as throwing new light on the text of the Scripture in a way that causes a deeper understanding of its initial Intention?

d) Above all it was a *conflict of the mark of identity for the Christian movement*. Should Christians also cling to obedience of the Mosaic commandments as an outer sign for their adherence to the people of God? Or should this old mark of distinction be exchanged for a concern of faith in Christ as a new act of participation, as an interpersonal act that overturned the division between Jews and Gentiles? It was thus a conflict moving at a deep emotional level with major consequences for everyday life, both for Jews and Gentiles.

Paul's letter to the Galatians gives evidence in many ways that this conflict was perceived as a very serious one:

a) The *employment of rhetorical skills* on a broad spectrum testify that it was perceived by Paul as urgent to succeed in his persuasion of the audience.

b) More specifically the *employment of judicial modes of argumentation* gave the conflict an unmistakable flavor of a lawsuit.

c) Further, the various changes Paul makes in the LXX quotations demonstrate that his *serious involvement with Scripture* was carried out in detail.

d) Paul even was courageous enough to *involve covenant traditions with divine authority*. These traditions — which were applied to exhort obedience toward the law in a forceful way — he found necessary to use for the sake of amplifying obedience toward the gospel of Christ.

e) Paul amplifies the conflict in a way that made it a question of *apostasy* from God and of being led astray by *false teachers* (cf. 1:6–7).

f) He even amplifies the conflict to such extent that he *cursed his opponents*. There is no compromise; the Galatians have to choose one of the positions and reject the other. Message and preachers were regarded as a unity. When one of the teachings was rejected, also its defenders had to leave the scene in Galatia.

The letter to the Galatians testifies that in the early Church there were conflicts where an apostle established an authoritative position of leadership by treating *compromise as impossible*. One of the conflicts concerns the circumcision of Gentiles. The opponents who lost in the long run apparently would not tolerate that Gentiles remain uncircumcised, while Paul would by no means accept the imposition of circumcision on Gentiles. Circumcision was important, because it concerned a primary mark of identity for the Christian movement: Should they present themselves as a sect within Judaism, or should they act in a way that included Gentiles on a par with Jews? According to Paul it involved nothing more than the question of how to be "straightforward about the truth of the gospel" (Gal 2:14a). To reject Paul's position was, according to him, to turn to a different gospel which is no gospel but is "to pervert the gospel of Christ" (Gal 1:7).

We do not know whether or not Paul succeeded in persuading the Galatians. Perhaps we may take the preservation of the letter as an indication that he did, since the Galatians would probably not preserve the letter of a false curser. Be this as it may. What is important to note is the severity which Paul employs in his defense of the Gospel. We should not follow him in his actual use of curses, especially since their force seems to be lost in our culture. On the other hand we are reminded of the nature of the Gospel: Since it is holy and divine, church leaders should defend it from perversion with utmost seriousness. Such seriousness is likely, in certain situations, to involve the rejection of persons who preach a radically different Gospel.

APPENDIX 1

TABLES FOR THE SEMANTIC FIELD ANALYSIS

As argued above in ch. 2, the semantic elements from Gal 1:6–9 and 3:8–14 (cf. secs. 2.2 and 2.3 for the categories) have been compared with Jewish curse and חרם/ἀνάθεμα texts (cf. sec. 2.1 for their distribution in various groups). The Jewish texts with the identification of semantic elements are presented fully in Appendix 2. This appendix gives an abbreviated overview over the findings.

The texts are presented in the same *order* in each group: First we present texts from the Hebrew Bible (HB), then the Apocrypha, the Pseudepigrapha, Philo, Qumran, and lastly Josephus. The HB texts are presented in their canonical order according to MT, while the other texts are presented in alphabetical order.

ABBREVIATIONS

TERMS is the column for tabulating:
- the various terms in curse texts:
  a = אלה
  b = ארר
  c = קלל
  d = (ἐπ)άρα(σθαι)
  e = (ἐπι)κατάρα(σθαι)
  f = Other

- the various terms in ban texts:
  ch = *chrm*/חרם
  s = substantive, v = verb
  a = ἀνάθεμα
  s = substantive, v = verb

3:8–14 is the column for indicating a structure similar to Gal 3:8–14:

  CU/BL = Curse and blessing in antithesis
  CU-BL = Curse and blessing in sequence

  (x) = Theme present without curse or blessing term

3:10 is the column for tabulating similarities with the curse of Gal 3:10:

  Form = Formal similarities with Gal 3:10:
      F = Curse with curse condition as relative clause (sometimes with nomen) or as participial phrase
      f^* = Curse with curse reason
      f = Curse with 3rd/2nd person pronoun, proper name or nomen

  LB = Lawbreaking theme connected with curse
  LK = Lawkeeping theme connected with curse
  HK = Expressions like ὑπὸ κατάραν

3:13f is the column for tabulating similarities with Gal 3:13:

BG = Blessing to Gentiles
(x) = Theme present without blessing terminology

KN = Expressions like κατάρα τοῦ νόμου
GK = Expressions like γίνομαι κατάραν

Two other features are also placed here, although they are as related to 3:10 as to 3:13:

RI = Terms for righteousness
LS = Terms for Life and/or Spirit
　　　L = life, *S* = Spirit

1:8f is the column for indicating similarities with Gal 1:8-9:

AC+CU = Structure of present accusation and curse/anathema
　　　The present accusation:
　　　　　　　– must be present in the context, not in curse conditions
　　　　　　　– must concern present, not anticipated or general wrongdoings

Form similar to Gal 1:8-9:
　　　f* = Legal form with εἰ/ἐάν
　　　f = Other legal form similar to Gal 1:8-9

AE = Expressions like ἀνάθεμα εἶναι

OBJ = Object of curse/ban:
　　　SE = Seducer
　　　SI = Self-imprecation
　　　AN = Angelic being

AP = Terms for apostasy/idolatry (a wide and not very precise category)

CURSES RELATED TO DEUT 27-30:

	Terms	3:8-14			3:10				3:13f					1:8f				
		CU	BL	CU-BL	FORM	LB	LK	HK	BG	KN	GK	RI	LS	AC+CU	FORM	AE	OBJ	AP
ut 11:26-29	c e	x	x			x									f*			x
ut 27-30	abcde	x	x	x(x)	12F	x				x			L	x	f*		SI	x
					6f													
sh 8:34	c e	x	x															
Kings 22:19	c e										x			(x)				x
a 65:20	c ef	(x)	x	x x									L					
c 11:3	b e	x	(x)		F	x								(x)				x
c 17:5f	b e	x	x		F									(x)				x
c 24:5-10	c e	x	(x)	(x x)							x							
c 25:17f	c										x							
c 26:6	c e					x					x			x	f*			
c 29:18	a			x(x)		x					x			x				
c 42:18-20	a cd										x			x				x
c 44:8-12,22	a cde					x					x			x				x
ek 16:57-60	a			x(x)		x			(x)					x				x
ch 5:2f	a d					x												
ch 8:12f	c e			x x					(x)		x							
1:14-2:2	b e	x	(x)		F	x								x	f*		SE	
3:8f	b f			x x		x								x				
3:65f	a f			(x x)														
9:11f	a e			x(x)		x				x								x
10:30	a de							x									SI	
hr 34:24f	a									x				x				x
1:19f;3:8	d			x(x)		x				x	x							x
. Ant. 26:5					F	x									f		SI	
n 5:4-7	e	x	x	x(x)		x			(x)	x		x	L	x				
n 102:3-5	e	x	(x)	x(x)								x						
noch 52		x	x		7F	x												
. 1:15f				x x						x		x						
. 4:4f					F	x											SI	
. 20:6		x	x			x			x	x								
. 23:29f				(x)x								x						
. 33:11f					F	x											SI	
evi 10;14;16	e	x	(x)	x(x)		x			(x)	x				x			SE	x
aph 3:5-4:5	e			x(x)		x			(x)			x						x
aph 8:3-7	e	x	x			x			(x)			x						
a 73	de	x	x															
es 177	de	x	x															
es 250	d																	x
3:36	e																	x
3:107f	de				2F	x							L					
t 23-26	de																	x
t 84,88	de				F	x						x						
em 126-72	d	x	x	x(x)	6f	x			(x)			x	x	x				x
ii.4-18	abc	x	x	(x x)	F,2f*	x				x		x					SI	x
v.12	a					x				x								

	Terms	3:8-14 CU/BL:CU-BL	3:10 FORM:LB LK HK	3:13f BG :KN GK :RI LS	1:8f AC+CU :FORM AE :OBJ AP
CD i.14-17	a	(x x): x(x)	: x	: x : x	: :SE
CD xv.1-5	a	:	: x	: x :	: :SI
CD xx.6-8	b	:	: x	: :	: :
1Q22 i.8-10	c	:	: x	: :	: : x
4Q 280-82	b	:	F,2f* x	: :	: :AN
4Q 286-87	b	:	F,4f* x	: :	: :AN
		:	:	: :	: :
Ant 4:302-7	e	x x :(x x)	: x	: :	: :
Ant 5:69f	d	:	:	: :	: :
Bell 5:401	e	x x :	: x	: :	: :

2: CURSES RELATED TO GEN/NUM

Primal curses	Terms	3:8-14 CU/BL:CU-BL	3:10 FORM:LB LK HK	3:13f BG :KN GK :RI LS	1:8f AC+CU :FORM AE :OBJ AP
Gen 3:14,17	b e	:	2f* : x	: :	: :SE
Gen 4:11-12	b e	:	f* : x	: :	x : :
Gen 5:29	b e	:	:	: :	: :
Gen 8:21	c e	:	:	: :	: :
Gen 9:24-26	b e	x x :	f :	: :	: :
		:	:	: :	: :
Wis 12:11	e	:	: x	: :	: :
		:	:	: :	: :
A+E, Vita 3		:	:	: :	: :
A+E, Vita 37-44		:	: x	: :	: :
A+E, Apoc 10	e	:	: x	: :	:
A+E, Apoc 24,26	e	:	2f* : x	: :	: :SE
3 Apoc. Bar. 4	e	: x x	:	(x): :	: :SE
Bib. Ant. 3:9f		: x(x)	:	: : L	: :
Jub. 3:23,25		:	: x	: :	: :
Jub. 7:10		x x :	f :	: :	: :
Jub. 9:14		:	: x	: :	: :SI
Jub. 10:29-32		:	f : x	: :	x : :SI
		:	:	: :	: :
Agric 20f	e	:	f* : x	: : x	: :
Agric 107	d	:	:	: :	: :
Cher 52	d	:	: x	: :	: :
Deter 96-103	de	:	f : x	: :	: : x
Deter 121f	e	:	:	: : x	: :
Heres 260	e	:	:	: : x	: :
Heres 296	d	:	: x	: :	x : :
Leg 2:61f	e	:	: x	: :	: :
Leg 3:65-75	e	:	f* : x	: :	: :SE
Leg 3:104-113	de	x(x):	f*,f:	: :	: :SE
Leg 3:222	e	:	f* : x	: :	: :
Leg 3:246f	e	:	f : x	: :	: :
Praem 72	d	:	: x	: :	: :
Sobr 30-51	de	:	2f : x	: :. x	: :
Virt 202	d	:	: x	: :	: :
Ant 1:58	d	:	: x	: :	: :
Ant 1:142	de	x x :	:	: :	: :

Gen 12-formula

	Terms	3:8-14 CU/BL:CU-BL	3:10 FORM:LB LK HK	3:13f BG :KN GK :RI LS	1:8f AC+CU :FORM AE :OBJ AP
Gen 12:2f	bc e	x x :	:	x : :	: :
Gen 27:28f	b e	x x :	F :	x : :	: :
Num 24:9	b e	x x :	F :	x : :	: :
		:	:	: :	: :
Job 13:13-15	e	x x :(x x)	F :	x : : x	. : :
		:	:	: :	: :
Jub. 12:23		x x :	:	x : :	: :
Jub. 25:21f		x x :	:	x : : x	: :
Jub. 26:23f		x x :	:	x : :	: :
Jub. 31:17		x x :	:	x : :	: :
Jub. 31:20		x x :	:	x : : x	: :
T. Levi 4:6	e	x x :	:	x : :	: :
		:	:	: :	: :
Migr 1	e	x x :	:	x : :	: :
Migr 109f	e	x x :	:	x : : x	: :
Mos 1:291	e	x x :	:	x : :	: :

Balaam-episode

	Terms	3:8-14 CU/BL:CU-BL	3:10 FORM:LB LK HK	3:13f BG :KN GK :RI LS	1:8f AC+CU :FORM AE :OBJ AP
Num 22-24	b def	x x :	:	: : x	: :
Deut 23:5f	c e	: x x	:	: :	: :
Josh 24:9f	cd	x x :	:	: :	: :
Neh 13:2	c e	: x x	:	: :	: :
		:	:	: :	: :
Bib. Ant. 18		x x :	:	x : :	: :
		:	:	: :	: :
Conf 64f,72	de	:	:	: :	: :
Conf 159	e	x x :	:	: :	: :
Peter 71	de	: x x	:	: :	: :
Migr 113-18	de	x x : x x	:	: :	x : : x
Mos 1:263-305	de	x x :	: x	: :	: :
		:	:	: :	: :
Ant 4:104-26,57	de	x x :	: x	: : L	: :

: CURSES RELATED TO DIVINE LAWS

(Mostly general, but some specific references: a = adultery, i = idolatry, m = murder, mi = mixed marriages.)

	Terms	3:8-14 CU/BL:CU-BL	3:10 FORM:LB LK HK	3:13f BG :KN GK :RI LS	1:8f AC+CU :FORM AE :OBJ AP
Gen 49:6f	b e	:	f* : x	: :	: :
Num 5:18-27	ab de	:	: x	: x :	: f :SI
Deut 21:22f	c e	:	: x	: x :	: :
Judg 9:56f	c e	:	: x	: :	x : :
2 Kings 9:34	b e	:	:	: :	: :
Isa 24:5f	a d	: x(x)	: x	(x): :	x : :
Jer 23:10	a	:	: x	: :	: :
Jer 29:21-23	c e	:	: x	: :	x : :
Ps 37:21f	c e	x x :	:	: : x	: :
Ps 119:21	b e	x x :	f : x	: :	: :
Job 5:3	f	:	:	: :	: :
Job 24:13,18	c e	:	: x	: :	: :
Prov 3:33	b e	x x :	:	: : x	: :
Neh 13:23,25	c e	:	: x	: :	x : :
		:	:	: :	: :

	Terms	3:8-14		3:10		3:13f			1:8f		
		CU/BL	CU-BL	FORM	LB LK HK	BG	KN GK	RI LS	AC+CU	FORM AE	OBJ AP
a Sir 23:22,26	e				x						
Sir 41:8-10	e				x						x
Wis 3:10,12f	e	x x		f				x			x
i Wis 14:6-8	e	x x		f*				x			x
							f				
1 En 22:10f	e				x						
1 En 27:1f	e	x x			x						
1 En 41:8		x x			x			x			
1 En 59:1f		x x									
1 En 97:10	e	x(x)			x				x		
1 En 98:4	e	x(x)			x x				x		
mi Jub. 30:14f					x						
m 4Macc 2:18-20	e			f	x						
Prop. 1:9	d				x						
Ps Sol 3:9-11	e	(x x)			x			x L			
Ps Sol 4:12ff	d	x x			x						
mi TJud 11:3-5	e				x				x		
Abr 40	d				x						
Conf 196	d	x(x)			x						x
Congr 57	d	x(x)			x						x
Decal 87	d	x(x)									
Post 81	d	x(x)			x						
Post 159	d				x						
Post 176	d				x						
Sobr 67	d				x						
Spec 1:188	d				x						
a Spec 2:50	d				x						
a Spec 3:61	d				x						
Spec 4:91	d				x						
CD xii.20-22	b				x						
1QM xiii.1-6	b f	x x		4f*	x			x			AN
4QPs37 iii	c	x x			x						
11Q Tem 64:12	c				x						
m Ant 7:39	d				x				x		
m Ant 18.346	d				x				x		
m Bell 1:480	d				x						
m Bell 4:360f	d				x						

4:   CURSES IN SOCIAL RELATIONS

Oaths	Terms	3:8-14		3:10		3:13f			1:8f		
		CU/BL	CU-BL	FORM	LB LK HK	BG	KN GK	RI LS	AC+CU	FORM AE	OBJ AP
Gen 24:40f	a d f										
Gen 26:28f	a d										
Josh 6:26	b e			F							
Judg 5:23f	b e	x x		f*							
Judg 21:18	b e			F							
1Sam 14:24.28	ab de			2F							
Ezek 17:13-21	a d f		x(x)		x	(x)			(x)		x
Hos 4:2f	a d				x						
Hos 10:4	a										
1 EnFragmSyn	e										SI
4QTest 21-24	b			F	x						SE
Ant 5:31	d										
Ant 6:117-128	d				x					f	
Ant 6:276	d										SI
Bell 1:260	e								x		

Unknown thief

	Terms	3:8-14 CU/BL:CU-BL	3:10 FORM:LB LK HK	3:13f BG :KN GK :RI LS	1:8f AC+CU :FORM AE :OBJ AP
Lev 5:1	a f	:	: x	: :	: :
Judg 17:2	a d	x x :	: x	: :	: :
Prov 29:24	a f	:	: x	: :	: :
		:	. :	: :	: :
CD ix.10-12	a	:	: x	: :	: :

Parent-child

	Terms	3:8-14 CU/BL:CU-BL	3:10 FORM:LB LK HK	3:13f BG :KN GK :RI LS	1:8f AC+CU :FORM AE :OBJ AP
Gen 27:12f	c e	x x :	:	: :	: :
Exod 21:17	c f	:	:	: :	: :
Lev 20:9	c f	':	:	: :	: :
Prov 20:20	c f	:	:	: :	: :
Prov 30:11	c e	x x :	:	: :	: :
		:	:	: :	: :
Sir 3:9,16	e	x x :	:	: :	: : x

Ruler-people

	Terms	3:8-14 CU/BL:CU-BL	3:10 FORM:LB LK HK	3:13f BG :KN GK :RI LS	1:8f AC+CU :FORM AE :OBJ AP
Exod 22:27	b f	:	:	: :	: :
Judg 9:27f	c e	:	:	: :	: :
1 Sam 26:19	b e	:	:	x :	: : x
2 Sam 16:5-13	c e	:	: x	x :	: :
2 Sam 19:22	c e	:	:	: :	: :
1 Kings 2:8	c e	:	:	: :	: :
Isa 8:21	c f	:	:	: :	: :
Eccl 10:20	c e	:	:	: :	: :
		:	:	: :	: :
Ant 7:208	d	:	: x	: :	: :
Ant 17:88	d	:	: x	: :	: :

Rich-poor

	Terms	3:8-14 CU/BL:CU-BL	3:10 FORM:LB LK HK	3:13f BG :KN GK :RI LS	1:8f AC+CU :FORM AE :OBJ AP
Prov 11:26	f	x x :	:	: :	: :
Prov 28:27	b f	x(x):	:	: :	: :
Eccl 10:20	c e	:	:	: :	: :
		:	:	: :	: :
Sir 4:5f	e	:	:	: :	: :
Sir 29:6	e	:	:	: :	: :
Sir 34:24	e	:	:	: :	: :
		:	:	: :	: :
Bell 6:203	e	:	:	: :	: :

Jews-Gentiles

	Terms	3:8-14 CU/BL:CU-BL	3:10 FORM:LB LK HK	3:13f BG :KN GK :RI LS	1:8f AC+CU :FORM AE :OBJ AP
Josh 9:22-24	b e	:	f* :	: :	x : :
1 Sam 17:43	c e	:	:	: :	: :
Jer 49:13	c e	:	:	x :	: :
		:	:	: :	: :
2 Macc 12:35	e	:	:	: :	: :
		:	:	: :	: :
Jub. 24:29,32f		:	:	: x	: :
		:	:	: :	: :
Ant 6:186	d	:	:	: :	: :
Ant 18:287	d	:	: x	: :	: f :
Ap 1:203f	e	:	:	: :	: :
Bell 7:112f	d	:	:	: :	: :

Other relations	Terms	3:8-14 CU/BL	CU-BL	3:10 FORM	LB	LK	HK	3:13f BG	KN	GK	RI	LS	1:8f AC+CU	FORM	AE	OBJ	AP
Lev 19:14	c f																
Prov 24:24	ef	x	x														
Prov 27:14	c e	x	x														
Prov 30:10	c e																
Eccl 7:20-22	c e										x						
Sir 28:13	e	x	(x)		x												

5:   OTHER CURSE TEXTS

	Terms	3:8-14 CU/BL	CU-BL	3:10 FORM	LB	LK	HK	3:13f BG	KN	GK	RI	LS	1:8f AC+CU	FORM	AE	OBJ	AP
Lev 24:11-23	c e																
1 Sam 3:13	c f																
2 Kings 2:23f	c e																
Jer 15:10	c e																
Jer 20:14f	b e			2f*													
Jer 48:10	b e			2F													
Ps 10:7	a d				x												
Ps 59:13	a d				x												
Ps 62:5	c e	x	x														
Ps 109:17ff,28	c e	x	x		x												
Job 3:1,7f	bc ef																
Job 31:30	a e																
Prov 26:2	cd																
Ep Jer 66	e	x	x														
Sir 21:27	e																x
Sir 23:14	e																
Sir 33:12	e	x	x														
Ep Arist 311	d																
MartIsa 5:9																	
Prop. 22:7,13	e																
T. Benj. 6:5	e																
T. Job 13:4f	e																
Conf 44,51	de				x												
Decal 74f	e																
Migr 111	e																
Mos 2:196-204	de				x												x
Prob 137	d	x	(x)														
Somn 2:237	d																
Spec 2:129	d																
1QS vii.1	c	x	x														
11Q Tem 60:18	a																x
Ant 2:12	d																
Ant 4:50	d				x												
Ant 9:64	d																
Ant 14:22	d										x						
Ant 17:3	d																
Bell 3:297	e																
Bell 6:46	d																
Bell 6:98	e																
Bell 6:306f	e	x	x														
Vita 101	d															SI	

6: חרם/ANATHEMA TEXTS

	Ch	a	3:8-14 CU/BL	:CU-BL	3:10 FORM:LB	LK	HK	3:13f BG	:KN	GK	:RI	LS	1:8f AC+CU	:FORM	AE	:OBJ	AP
Exod 22:19	v			:	:				:		:			: f		:	x
Lev 27:29	sv	v		:	:				:		:			: f	(x)	:	
Num 21:2f	v	v		:	:				:		:			:		:	
Deut 2:34; 3:6	v			:	:				:		:			:		:	
7:1f,25f	sv	s		:	:				:		:			:	x	:	x
13:13-18	sv	sv		:(x x)	:				:		:			: f*		:SE	x
20:16-18	sv	sv		:	:				:		:			: f		:SE	x
Josh 2:10	v			:	:				:		:			:		:	
6:17-21	sv	sv		:	:				:		:			:	(x)	:	
7:1,11-15	s	s		:	: x				:		:		x	:	x	:	
8:25f	v			:	:				:		:			:		:	
10:1,28-40	v			:	:				:		:			:		:	
11:10-21	v			:	:				:		:			:		:	
22:20	s	s		:	: x				:		:			:		:	
Judg 1:17	sv	sv		:	:				:		:			:		:	
21:9-11	v	v		:	:				:		:			:		:	
1 Sam 15:2-21	sv	v		:	: x				:		:			:		:	
1 Kgs 9:20f	v			:	:				:		:			:		:	
20:42	s			:	:				:		:			:	(x)	:	
2 Kgs 19:10f	v	v		:	:				:		:			:		:	
Isa 34:2,5	sv			:	:				:		:			:	(x)	:	
37:11	v			:	:				:		:			:		:	
43:27f	s			: x x	: x				:		:	S	x	:	(x)	:	
Jer 25:8f	v			:	: x				:		:		x	:		:	
50:21,26	v			:	:				:		:			:		:	
51:3	v			:	:				:		:			:		:	
Zech 14:11	s	s		: x(x)	:			x	:		:			:		:	
Mal 3:22f	s			: x(x)	:				:		:			:		:	
Dan 11:44	v	v		:	:				:		:			:		:	
Ezra 10:7f	v	v		:	:				:		:			: f		:	
1 Chr 2:7	s	s		:	: x				:		:			:		:	
1 Chr 4:41	v	v		:	:				:		:			:		:	
2 Chr 20:23	v			:	:				:		:			:		:	
32:14	v			:	:				:		:			:		:	
1 Macc 5:4f		v		:	:				:		:			:		:	
Sir 16:9	s			:	:				:		:			:	(x)	:	
39:30	v			:	:				:		:			:		:	
46:6	s			:	:				:		:			:	(x)	:	
				:	:				:		:			:		:	
2 Ap. Bar 62:3				:	:				:		:			:		:	x
Bib. Ant. 21:3				:	:				:		:			:		:	
26:2				:	:				:		:			:		:	x
29:3				:	:				:		:			:		:	x
1 En 6:4-6		v		:	:				:		:			:		:SI,AN	
1 En 95:4				:	: x				:		:			:		:	
1 En.Fragm.Syn.		v		:	:				:		:			:		:SI	
				:	:				:		:			:		:	
CD ix.1	v			:	:				:		:			: f		:	
1QM ix.6f	s			:	:				:		:			:		:	
xviii.5	v			:	:				:		:			:		:	
11QTem 2:10f	s			:	:				:		:			:	x	:	x
55:2-11	s			:	:				:		:			: f		:SE	x
62:13-16	sv			:	:				:		:			: f		:SE	x

APPENDIX 2

TEXTS FOR THE SEMANTIC FIELD ANALYSIS[1]

1: CURSES RELATED TO DEUTERONOMY 27-30

Deut 11:26-29: (3:8-14: CU/BL) (3:10: LB) (1:8f: f*, AP)

²⁶Behold, I set before you this day a *blessing* and a *curse* (קללה, κατάραν): ²⁷the *blessing* if you obey the commandments of the Lord your God, which I command you this day, ²⁸and the *curse* (קללה, κατάρας), if you (=f*) do not obey the commandments of the Lord your God, but turn aside from the way which I command you this day (=LB), to go after other gods which you have not known (=AP). ²⁹And when the Lord your God brings you into the land which you are entering to take possession of it, you shall set the *blessing* on Mount Gerizim and the *curse* (קללה, κατάραν) on Mount Ebal.

Deut 27-30: (3:8-14: CU/BL, CU-(BL)) (3:10: F, f, LB) (3:13f: KN, L) (1:8f: AC+CU, f*, SI, AP)

27 ¹²When you have passed over the Jordan, these shall stand upon Mount Gerizim to *bless* the people: Simeon, Levi, Judah, Issachar, Joseph, and Benjamin. ¹³And these shall stand upon Mount Ebal for the *curse*: (קללה, κατάρας) Reuben, Gad, Asher, Zebulun, Dan, and Naphtali.

¹⁵'*Cursed* (=F; ארור, ἐπικατάρατος) be the man who makes a graven or molten image, an abomination to the Lord, a thing made by the hands of a craftsman, and sets it up in secret (=AP).' And all the people shall answer and say, 'Amen' (=SI).

¹⁶'*Cursed* be he who dishonors his father and his mother.' And all the people shall say, 'Amen.'

¹⁷'*Cursed* be he who removes his neighbor's landmark.' And all the people shall say, 'Amen.'

¹⁸'*Cursed* be he who misleads a blind man on the road.' And all the people shall say, 'Amen.'

¹⁹'*Cursed* be he who perverts the justice due to the sojourner, the fatherless, and the widow.' And all the people shall say, 'Amen.'

²⁰'*Cursed* be he who lies with his father's wife, because he has uncovered her who is his father's.' And all the people shall say, 'Amen.'

²¹'*Cursed* be he who lies with any kind of beast.' And all the people shall say, 'Amen.'

²²'*Cursed* be he who lies with his sister, whether the daughter of his father or the daugther of his mother.' And all the people shall say, 'Amen.'

²³'*Cursed* be he who lies with his mother-in-law.' And all the people shall say, 'Amen.'

²⁴'*Cursed* be he who slays his neighbor in secret.' And all the people shall say, 'Amen.'

²⁵'*Cursed* be he who takes a bribe to slay an innocent person.' And all the people shall say, 'Amen.'

²⁶'*Cursed* be he who does not confirm the words of this law by doing them.' And all the people shall say, 'Amen.'

---

[1]Cf. appendix 1 for presentation and abbreviations.

28 ²And all these *blessings* shall come upon you and overtake you, if you obey the voice of the Lord your God. ³*Blessed* shall you be . . . .

¹⁵But if you (=f*) will not obey the voice of the Lord your God, or be careful to do all his commandments and his statutes which I command you this day (=LB), then all these *curses* (קללה, κατάραι) shall come upon you and overtake you.

¹⁶*Cursed* (=f; ארור, ἐπικατάρατος) shall you be in the city, and *cursed* shall you be in the field. ¹⁷*Cursed* shall be your basket and your kneading-trough. ¹⁸*Cursed* shall be the fruit of your body, and the fruit of your ground, the increase of your cattle, and the young of your flock. ¹⁹*Cursed* shall you be when you come in, and *cursed* shall you be when you go out. ²⁰The Lord will send upon you *curses,* (מארה, --) confusion, and frustration, in all that you undertake to do, until you are destroyed and perish quickly, on account of the evil of your doings, because you have forsaken me (=AP).

⁴⁵All these *curses* (קללה, κατάραι) shall come upon you and pursue you and overtake you, till you are destroyed, because you did not obey the voice of the Lord your God, to keep his commandments and his statutes which he commanded you (=LB).

29 . . . ¹¹that you may enter into the *sworn covenant* (=KN, SI; ברית + אלה, διαθήκη + ἀραῖς) of the Lord your God which the Lord your God makes with you this day . . . .

¹³Nor is it with you only that I make this *sworn covenant* . . . .

¹⁷Beware lest there be among you a man or woman or family or tribe, whose heart turns away this day from the Lord our God to go and serve the gods of those nations (=AP); lest there be among you a root bearing poisonous and bitter fruit, ¹⁸one who, when he hears the words of this *sworn covenant* (אלה, ἀρᾶς), *blesses* himself in his heart, saying, 'I shall be safe, though I walk in the stubbornness of my heart.' This would lead to the sweeping away of moist and dry alike. ¹⁹The Lord would not pardon him, but rather the anger of the Lord and his jealousy would smoke against that man, and the *curses* (אלה, ἀραί) written in this book (=KN) would settle upon him, and the Lord would blot out his name from under heaven. ²⁰And the Lord would single him out from all the tribes of Israel for calamity, in accordance with all the *curses* (אלה, ἀράς) of the covenant written in this book of the law (=KN).

²⁴ 'Because they forsook the covenant . . . ²⁵and went and served other gods and worshiped them (=AC) . . . ²⁶therefore the anger of the Lord was kindled against this land, bringing upon it all the *curses* (קללה, κατάρας) written in this book (=KN).

30 ¹And when all these things come upon you, the *blessing* and the *curse* (קללה, κατάρα), which I have set before you . . . ³Then the Lord your God will restore your fortunes, and have compassion upon you, and he will gather you again from all the peoples (=(BL)) . . . .

⁷And the Lord your God will put all these *curses* (אלה, ἀράς) upon your foes and enemies who persecuted you.

¹⁹I call heaven and earth to witness against you this day, that I have set before you life (=L) and death, *blessing* and *curse* (קלל, κατάραν); therefore choose life (=L), that you and your descendants may live (=L).

Josh 8:34: (3:8-14: CU/BL)

³⁴And afterward he (=Joshua) read all the words of the law, the *blessing* and the *curse* (קללה, (9:2e) κατάρας), according to all that is written in the book of the law.

2 Kings 22:17, 19: (3:13f: GK) (1:8f: AC, AP)

¹⁷Because they have forsaken me and have burned incense to other gods (AC, AP) . . . ¹⁹because your heart was penitent, and you humbled yourself before the Lord, when

you heard how I spoke against this place, and against its inhabitants, that they should become a desolation and a *curse* (=GK; קְלָלָה, κατάραν).

Isa 65:15-16, 20, 23: (3:8-14: (CU)/BL, (CU)-BL) (3:13f: L)
   ¹⁵You shall leave your name to my chosen for a *curse* (שְׁנַע, πλησμονήν), and the
Lord God will slay you; but his servants he will call by a different name.   ¹⁶So that he
who *blesses* himself in the land shall *bless* himself by the God of truth . . . .
   ²⁰No more shall there be in it an infant that lives but a few days, or an old man who
does not fill out his days (=L), for the child shall die a hundred years old, and the sinner
a hundred years old shall be *accursed* (קְלָל, ἐπικατάρατος) . . . ²³ . . . for they shall be
the offspring of the *blessed* of the Lord.

Jer 11:3-4, 10-11: (3:8-14: CU/(BL)) (3:10: F, LB) (1:8f: (AC+CU), AP)
   ³Thus says the Lord, the God of Israel: *Cursed* (=F; אָרוּר, ἐπικατάρατος) be the
man who does not heed the words of this covenant (=LB), ⁴which I commanded your
fathers when I brought them out of the land of Egypt, from the iron furnace, saying,
Listen to my voice, and do all that I command you. So shall you be my people and I will
be your God (=(BL)).
   ¹⁰They have turned back to the iniquities of their forefathers, who refused to hear
my words; they have gone after other gods to serve them (=AC; AP) . . . . ¹¹Therefore,
thus says the Lord, Behold, I am bringing evil upon them which they cannot escape
(=(CU)) . . . .

Jer 17:1-8: (3:8-14: CU/BL) (3:10: F) (1:8f: (AC+CU), AP)
   ¹"The sin of Judah is written with a pen of iron . . . ²while their children remember
their altars and their Asherim, beside every green tree, and on the high hills (=AC; AP)
. . . ³ . . .Your wealth and your treasures I will give for spoil . . . ⁴ . . . and I will make
you serve your enemies in a land which you do not know (=(CU)) . . . .
   ⁵Thus says the Lord: "*Cursed* (=F; אָרוּר, ἐπικατάρατος) is the man who trusts in
man and makes flesh his arm, whose heart turns away from the Lord (=AP). ⁶He is like
a shrub in the desert, and shall not see any good come. He shall dwell in the parched
places of the wilderness, in an uninhabited salt land.
   ⁷*Blessed* is the man who trusts in the Lord, whose trust is the Lord. ⁸He is like a
tree planted by water . . . ."

Jer 24:5-10: (3:8-10: CU/(BL), (CU-BL)) (3:13f: GK)
   ⁵"Thus says the Lord, the God of Israel: Like these good figs, so I will regard as
good the exiles from Judah, whom I have sent away from this place to the land of the
Chaldeans (=(CU)). ⁶I will set my eyes upon them for good, and I will bring them back
to this land (=(BL)) . . . ."
   ⁸"But thus says the Lord: Like the bad figs which are so bad they cannot be eaten,
so will I treat Zedekiah the king of Judah . . . . ⁹I will make them a horror to all the
kingdoms of the earth, to be a reproach, a byword, a taunt, and a *curse* (=GK; קְלָלָה,
κατάραν) in all the places where I shall drive them. ¹⁰And I will send sword, famine and
pestilence upon them, until they shall be utterly destroyed from the land which I gave to
them and their fathers".

Jer 25:17-18: (3:13f: GK)
   ¹⁷So I took the cup from the Lord's hand, and made all the nations to whom the
Lord sent me drink it; ¹⁸Jerusalem and the cities of Judah, its kings and princes, to make
them a desolation and a waste, a hissing and a *curse* (=GK; קְלָל, (32:18) --), as at this
day.

Jer 26:4-6: (3:10: LB) (3:13f: GK) (1:8f: AC+CU, f*)

⁴Thus says the Lord: If you (=f*) will not listen to me, to walk in my law which I have set before you, ⁵and to heed the words of my servants the prophets whom I send to you urgently, though you have not heeded (=AC; LB), ⁶then I will make this house like Shiloh, and I will make this city a *curse* (=GK; קללה, (33:6) κατάραν) for all the nations of the earth.

Jer 29:14-15, 18-19: (3:8-14: CU-(BL)) (3:10: LB) (3:13f: GK) (1:8f: AC+CU)

¹⁴ . . . I will restore your fortunes and gather you from all the nations and all the places where I have driven you (=(BL)) . . . .

¹⁵"Because you have said, 'The Lord has raised up prophets for us in Babylon,' (=AC) . . . ¹⁸I will pursue them with sword, famine, and pestilence, and I will make them a horror to all the kingdoms of the earth, to be a *curse* (=GK; אלה, --), a terror, a hissing, and a reproach among all the nations where I have driven them, ¹⁹because they did not heed my words (=LB), says the Lord . . . .

Jer 42:18-20: (3:13f: GK) (1:8f: AC+CU, AP)

¹⁸ . . . You shall become an *execration* (= GK; אלה, (49:18) ἄβατον), a horror, a *curse* (=GK; קללה, ἀράν) and a taunt. You shall see this place no more. ¹⁹The Lord has said to you, O remnant of Judah, 'Do not go to Egypt.' Know for a certainty that I have warned you this day ²⁰that you have gone astray (=AC; AP) . . . ²¹ . . . but you have not obeyed the voice of the Lord your God in anything that he has sent me to tell you (=AC).

Jer 44:8-9, 12, 22-23: (3:10: LB) (3:13f: GK) (1:8f: AC+CU, AP)

⁸Why do you provoke me to anger with the works of your hands, burning incense to other gods (=AC; AP) in the land of Egypt where you have come to live, that you may be cut off and become a *curse* (=GK; קללה, (51:8) κατάραν) and a taunt among all the nations of the earth? ⁹Have you forgotten the wickedness of your fathers (=LB) . . . .

¹² . . . they shall die by the sword and by famine, and they shall become an *execration* (=GK; אלה, (51:12) ὀνειδισμόν), a horror, a *curse* (=GK; קללה, κατάραν), and a taunt.

²²The Lord could no longer bear your evil doings and the abominations which you committed (=AC; LB); therefore your land has become a desolation and a waste and a *curse* (=GK; קללה, (51:22) ἀράν) without inhabitant, as it is this day. ²³It is because you burned incense (=AP), and because you sinned against the Lord and did not obey the voice of the Lord or walk in his law and in his statutes and in his testimonies (=AC; LB), that this evil has befallen you, as at this day.

Ezek 16:53, 57-60: (3:8-14: CU-(BL)) (3:10: LB) (3:13f: (BG)) (1:8f: AC+CU, AP)

⁵³I will restore their fortunes (=(BL)), both the fortunes of Sodom . . . and the fortunes of Samaria (=BG) . . . and I will restore your own fortunes in the midst of them.

⁵⁷Now you have become like her an object of reproach for the daughters of Edom and all her neighbours, and for the daughters of the Philistines, those round about who despise you. ⁵⁸You bear the penalty of your lewdness and your abominations (=AC; AP), says the Lord. ⁵⁹Yea, thus says the Lord God: I will deal with you as you have done, who have despised the *oath* (אלה, --) in breaking the covenant (=LB), ⁶⁰yet I will remember my covenant with you in the days of your youth, and I will establish with you an everlasting covenant (=(BL)).

Zech 5:2-3: (3:10: LB)

²And he said to me, "What do you see?" I answered, "I see a flying scroll; its length is twenty cubits, and its breadth ten cubits." ³Then he said to me, "This is the *curse*

(אלה, ἀρά) that goes out over the face of the whole land, for every one who steals (=LB) shall be cut off henceforth according to it, and everyone who swears falsely (=LB) shall be cut off henceforth according to it."

Zech 8:12 - 13:22: (3:8-12: CU-BL) (3:13f: GK, (BG))
12 . . . I will cause the remnant of this people to possess all these things. 13And as you have been a byword of *cursing* (= GK; קללה, κατάρα) among the nations, O house of Judah and house of Israel, so will I save you and you shall be a *blessing*.
22Many people and strong nations shall come to seek the Lord of hosts in Jerusalem, and to entreat the favor of the Lord (=(BG)).

Mal 1:14 - 2:8: (3:8-14; CU/(BL) (3:10: F, LB) (1:8f: AC+CU, f*, SE)
14*Cursed* (=F; ארור, ἐπικατάρατος) be the cheat who has a male in his flock, and vows it, and yet sacrifices to the Lord what is blemished (=LB) . . . .
2 1And now, O priests, this command is for you. 2If you (=f*) will not listen, if you will not lay it to heart to give glory to my name (=LB), says the Lord of hosts, then I will send the *curse* (מארה, κατάραν) upon you and I will *curse* (ארר, ἐπικαταράσομαι) your *blessings*; indeed I have already *cursed* (ארר, καταράσομαι) them, because you do not lay it to heart (=LB).
5My covenant with him (=Levi) was a covenant of life and peace (=(BL)), and I gave them to him, that he might fear; and he feared me . . . .
8But you have turned aside from the way; you have caused many to stumble by your instruction (=AC; SE).

Mal 3:8-12: (3:8-14: CU-BL) (3:10: LB) (1:8f: AC+CU)
8Will man rob God? Yet you are robbing me. But you say, 'How are we robbing thee?' In your tithes and offerings. 9You are *cursed* (ארר, ἀποβλέπετε) with a *curse* (מארה, ἀποβλέποντες), for you are robbing me, the whole nation of you (=AC; LB).
10Bring the full tithes into the storehouse . . . pour down for you an overflowing *blessing* . . . .
12 Then all nations will call you *blessed* . . . .

Lam 3:65-66: (3:8-12: (CU-BL))
65Thou wilt give them dullness of heart; thy *curse* (תאלה, μόχθον) will be on them. 66Thou wilt pursue them in anger and destroy them, from under thy heavens, O Lord (=(BL); (CU) in 3:43-54).

Dan 9:11 - 12:17: (3:8-12: CU-(BL)) (3:10: LB) (3:13f: KN) (1:8f: AP)
11All Israel has transgressed the law and turned aside, refusing to obey thy voice (=LB, AP). And the *curse* (אלה, κατάρα) and oath which are written in the law of Moses (=KN) the servant of God have been poured out upon us, because we have sinned against him (=LB). 12He has confirmed his words . . . by bringing upon us a great calamity.
17 . . . Oh Lord, cause thy face to shine upon thy sanctuary, which is desolate (=(BL)).

Neh 10:28-29: (3:10: LK) (1:8f: SI)
28 . . . all who have separated themselves from the peoples of the lands to the law of God . . . 29join with their brethren, their nobles, and enter into a *curse* (אלה, (II Esdr 20:30) κατηράσαντο + ἀρᾷ) and an oath (=SI) to walk in God's law which was given by Moses the servant of God, and to observe and do all the commandments of the Lord our Lord and his ordinances and his statutes (=LK).

2 Chr 34:24-25: (3:13f: KN) (1:8f: AC+CU, AP)

²⁴Thus says the Lord, Behold, I will bring evil upon this place and upon its inhabitants, all the *curses* (אלה, --) that are written in the book (=KN) which was read before the king of Judah. ²⁵Because they have forsaken me and have burned incense to other gods (=AC; AP) . . . .

Bar 1:19-20; 2:34-35; 3:8: (3:8-14: CU-(BL)) (3:10: LB) (3:13f: KN, GK) (1:8f: AP)

¹⁹From the day when the Lord brought our fathers out of the land of Egypt until today, we have been disobedient to the Lord our God, and we have been negligent, in not heeding his voice (=LB). ²⁰So to this day there have clung to us the calamities and the *curse* (ἀρά) which the Lord declared through Moses his servant (=KN) . . . .

2 ³⁴I will bring them again into the land . . . and I will increase them (=(BL)) . . . .

3 ⁸Behold, we are today in our exile where thou hast scattered us, to be reproached and *cursed* (=GK; ἀράν) and punished for all the iniquities of our fathers (=LB) who forsook the Lord our God (=AP).

Bib. Ant. 26:5: (3:10: F, LB) (1:8f: SI)

⁵ . . . (Kenaz) said to them, "Behold you have seen all the wonders that God has revealed to us until this day. And behold, when we were seeking out all those who planned evil deeds craftily against the Lord and against Israel (=LB), God revealed them to us according to their works. And now, *cursed* (=F) be the man who would plot to do such things among you, brothers." And all the people answered, "Amen, amen" (=SI). And when this had been said, he burned all those men in the fire and everything that had been found with them except the precious stones.

1 Enoch 1:1 - 2:8; 5:4-8: (3:8-14: CU/BL) (3:10: LB) (3:13f: GK, RI, L) (1:8f: AC+CU)

¹The *blessing* of Enoch, with which he *blessed* the elect and the righteous (=RI) who would be present on the day of tribulation at (the time of) the removal of all the ungodly ones.

⁸ . . . They shall all belong to God, and they shall prosper and be *blessed*; and the light of God shall shine unto them.

5 ⁴But as for you, you have not been longsuffering and you have not done the commandments of the Lord, but you have transgressed and spoken slanderously grave and harsh words with your impure mouths against his greatness (=AC; LB). Oh you hard-hearted, may you not find peace! ⁵Therefore, you shall *curse* (καταράσεσθε) your days, and the years of your life shall perish and multiply in *eternal execration* (κατάραν αἰώνων) and there will not be any mercy unto you. ⁶In those days, you shall make your names an *eternal execration* (=GK; κατάραν αἰώνιον) unto all the righteous (=RI); and the sinners shall *curse* (καταράσονται) you continually — you together with the sinners. ⁷But to the elect there shall be light, joy, and peace, and they shall inherit the earth (=(BL)). To you, wicked ones, on the contrary, there will be a *curse* (κατάρα). ⁸And then wisdom shall be given to the elect. And they shall all live (=L) . . . .

(Cf. sequence of curse and blessing in chs. 6–11; blessing for Gentiles in 10:21.)

1 Enoch 102:3-5; 103:3: (3:8-14: CU/(BL), CU-(BL)) (3:13f: RI)

³ . . . You sinners, you are *accursed* (ἐπικατάρατοι) forever; there is no peace for you! ⁴But you, souls of the righteous, fear not; and be hopeful, you souls that died in righteousness (=RI, (BL))! ⁵Be not sad because your souls have gone down into Sheol in sorrow; or (because) your flesh fared not well the earthly existence in accordance with

your goodness; indeed the time you happened to be in existence was (a time of) sinners, a time of *curse* and a time of plague.

103 ³For all good things, and joy and honor (=(BL)) are prepared for and written down for the souls of those who died in righteousness (=RI).

2 Enoch 52: (3:8-14: CU/BL) (3:10: F, LB)

¹*Happy* is he who opens his heart for praise, and praises the Lord. ²*Cursed* (=F) is he who opens his heart to insults, and to slander against his neighbor (=LB).

³*Happy* is he who opens his lips, both *blessing* and praising the Lord. ⁴*Cursed* is he who opens his lips for *cursing* and blasphemy, before the face of the Lord.

⁵*Happy* — is he who glorifies all the works of the Lord. ⁶*Cursed* is he who insults the creatures of the Lord. ⁷*Happy* is he who organizes the works of his hand, so as to raise them up. ⁸*Cursed* — who looks to obliterate works of others.

⁹*Happy* is he who preserves the foundations of the fathers, where they have been made sure. ¹⁰*Cursed* is he who destroys the rules and restrictions of his fathers.

¹¹*Happy* is he who establishes peace. ¹²*Cursed* is he who strikes down those who are in peace.

¹³*Happy* is he who speaks peace, and he possesses peace. ¹⁴*Cursed* is he who speaks peace, but there is no peace in his heart.

¹⁵All this will make itself known in the scales in the book on the great judgement day.

Jub. 1:15-16: (3:8-14: CU-BL) (3:13f: GK, RI)

¹⁵And afterward they will turn to me from among the nations with all their heart and with all their soul and with all their might. And I shall gather them from the midst of all the nations. And they will seek me so that I might be found by them. When they seek me with all their heart and with all their soul, I shall reveal to them an abundance of peace in righteousness (=RI). ¹⁶And with all my heart and with all my soul I shall transplant them as a righteous plant (=RI). And they will be a *blessing* and not a *curse* (=GK).

Jub. 4:4-5: (3:10: F, LB) (1:8f: SI)

⁴And the Lord rebuked Cain on account of Abel because he killed him (=LB). And he made him a fugitive on the earth because of the blood of his brother. And he *cursed* him on the earth. ⁵And therefore it is written in the heavenly tablets, "*Cursed* is (=F) one who strikes his fellow with malice (=LB)." And all who have seen and heard shall say "so be it" (=SI). And the man who saw and did not report (it) shall be *cursed* like him.

Jub. 20:6-10: (3:8-14: CU/BL) (3:10: LB) (3:13f: GK, BG)

⁶(Abraham said:) And you guard yourself from all fornication and impurity, and from all corruption of sin (=LB), so that you might not make your name a *curse* (=GK), and all your life a hissing, and all your sons a destruction by the sword. And you will be *cursed* like Sodom, and all your remnant like the sons of Gomorrah.

⁹But worship the Most High God . . . .

¹⁰And you will become a *blessing* upon the earth; and all the nations of the earth will desire you . . . so that they might be *blessed* just as I am (BG).

Jub. 23:29-30: (3:8-14: (CU)-BL) (3:13f: RI)

²⁹ . . . all of their days will be days of *blessing* and healing. ³⁰And then the Lord will heal his servants, and they will rise up and see great peace. And they will drive out their enemies, and the righteous ones (=RI) will see and give praise, and rejoice forever and ever with joy, and they will see all of their judgments and all of their *curses* among their enemies.

Jub. 33:11-13: (3:10: F, LB) (1:8f: SI)

[11]And there shall be no defilement before our God among the people whom he has chosen for himself as a possession. [12]And again it is written a second time: "Let anyone who lies with his father's wife be *cursed* (=F) because he has uncovered his father's shame (=LB)." And all the holy ones of the Lord said, "So be it, so be it" (=SI). [13]And you, Moses, command the children of Israel and let them keep this word because it is a judgment worthy of death.

T. Levi 10:3-4: (3:10: LB) (3:13f: GK) (1:8f: AC+CU)

[3]And you shall act lawlessly in Israel (=LB), with the result that Jerusalem cannot bear the presence of your wickedness, but the curtain of the Temple will be torn, so that it will no longer conceal your shameful behavior (=AC; LB). [4]You shall be scattered as captives among the nations, where you will be a disgrace and a *curse* (=GK; κατάραν).

T. Levi 13:3; 4:4: (3:8-14: CU/(BL)) (1:8f: AC+CU, SE, AP)

[3]For every one who knows the Law of God shall be honored wherever he goes (=(BL)) . . . .

14 [4]For what will all the nations do if you become darkened with impiety (=AP)? You will bring down a *curse* (κατάραν) on our nation, because you want to destroy the light of the Law which was granted to you for the enlightenment of every man, teaching commandments which are opposed to God's just ordinances (=AC; SE).

T. Levi 16:5: (3:8-14: CU-(BL)) (3:13: GK)

[5]You shall have no place that is clean, but you will be a *curse* (GK; κατάραν) and a dispersion among the nations until he will again have regard for you, and will take you back in compassion (=(BL)). (Cf. blessing for Gentiles in 18:9f.)

T. Naph. 3:5-4:5: (3:8-14: CU-(BL)) (3:10: LB) (3:13f: BG), RI) (1:8f: AP)

[5]Likewise the Watchers departed from nature's order; the Lord pronounced a *curse* (κατηράσατο) on them at the Flood. On their account he ordered that the earth be without dweller or produce. 4 [1]I say these things, my children, because I have read in the writing of holy Enoch that you also will stray from the Lord (=AP), living in accord with every wickedness of the gentiles and committing every lawlessness of Sodom (=LB). [2]The Lord will impose captivity upon you; you shall serve your enemies there and you will be engulfed in hardship and difficulty until the Lord will wear you all out (=(CU)). [3]And after you have been decimated and reduced in number, you will return and acknowledge the Lord your God. [4]And it shall happen that when they come into the land of their fathers (=(BL)), they will again neglect the Lord and act impiously (=LB), [5]and the Lord will disperse them over the face of the whole earth (=(CU)) until the mercy of the Lord comes (=(BL)), a man who effects righteousness (=RI), and he will work mercy on all who are far and near (=(BG)).

T. Naph. 8:3-6: (3:8-14: CU/BL) (3:10: LB) (3:13f: BG), RI)

[3]Through his kingly power God will appear to save the race of Israel (=(BL)), and to assemble the righteous (=RI) from among the nations (=(BG)).

[4]If you achieve the good, my children, men and angels will *bless* you; and God will be glorified through you among the gentiles . . . .

[6]The one who does not do the good (=LB), men and angels will *curse* (καταράσονται), and God will be dishonoured among the gentiles because of him; . . .

Fuga 73: (3:8-14: CU/BL)

In adherence to the same principle he ascribes the *blessing* of the good and the *cursing* (καταρᾶσθαι) of the guilty to different persons. Both, it is true, receive praise, but *blessing* those worthy of *blessing* enjoys the prerogative which belong to eulogies, while the laying of *curses* (ἀράς) on the evil occupies but a second place. Therefore . . . he set the six best over the *blessing*, . . . and the other six over the *cursing* (κατάρας) . . . .

Heres 177: (3:8-14: CU/BL)

Once more, does not Moses take two mountains, that is symbolically two kinds, and again distinguishes between them according to proportional equality, assign one to those who *bless*, the other to those who *curse* (καταρωμένοις)? Then he places upon them the twelve patriarchs to show to those who need warning, that *curses* (ἀραί) are equal in number to *blessings* and (if we may say so without offence) of equal value.

Heres 250: (1:8f: AP)

The first form (=of ecstasy) is mentioned in the *curses* (ἀραῖς) described in Deuteronomy, where he says that madness and loss of sight and "ecstasy" of mind will overtake the impious (=AP), so that they shall differ in nought from blind men groping at noonday as in deep darkness.

Leg 3:36: (1:8f: AP)

In keeping with this the sacred word pronounces a *curse* (καταρᾶται) on one setting up in secret a graven or molten image (AP), the work of the hands of the craftsman. For why, O mind, does thou hoard and treasure in thyself those wrong opinions . . . . Why dost thou not rather bring them forth into the open . . . ?

Leg 3:107-8: (3:10: F, LB) (3:13f: L)

[107] . . . "*Accursed* (=F; ἐπικατάρατον)", says Moses in the *Curses* (ἀραῖς), "is he who removes his neighbour's landmarks (=LB)": — for God set as a landmark and law for the soul virtue, the tree of life (=L). This is removed by the man who has fixed as landmark in its stead wickedness, the tree of death.

[108] "*Cursed* (=F; ἐπικατάρατος) again is he who causes a blind man to go astray in the way," "and he that smiteth his neighbour craftily (=LB)." And these also are acts of pleasure, the utterly godless one . . . .

Post 23-26: (1:8f: AP)

[23] . . . He therefore that draws night to God longs for stability, but he that forsakes Him (=AP), inasmuch as he approaches the unresting creation is, as we might expect, carried about. [24]It is for this reason that it is written in the *Curses* (ἀραῖς) "He shall not cause thee to rest, and there shall be no standing for the sole of thy feet," and a little later "thy life shall be hanging before thine eyes."

[25] . . . And, as the [26]lawgiver said, his whole life is hanging, with no firm foothold, but always swept off its feet by interests drawing and dragging him in opposite directions. This is why the lawgiver says in another place that "he that hangeth on a tree is *cursed* (κεκατηραμένον) of God."

Post 84, 88: (3:10: F, LB) (3:13f: RI)

[84]Moses, full of indignation at such people, pronounces a *curse* (καταρᾶται) on them saying, "*Cursed* (=F; ἐπικατάρατος) is he who shifts his neighbor's boundaries (=LB)." What he describes as "near" and "hard by" like a neighbor is the good thing.

[88] . . . Thus the man who removes the boundaries of the good and beautiful both is *accursed* (ἐπάρατος) and is pronounced to be so with justice (=RI).

Praem 126–72: (3:8–14: CU/BL, CU-(BL)) (3:10: f, LB) (3:13f: RI) (1:8f: AC+CU, AP)

[126]These are the *blessings* invoked upon good men, men who fulfil the laws by their deeds, which *blessings* will be accomplished by the gift of the bounteous God, who glorifies and rewards moral excellence because of its likeness to Himself. We must now investigate the *curses* (ἀράς) delivered against the lawbreakers and transgressors (=LB).

[127]The first *curse* (ἀράν) which he describes as the lightest of their evils is poverty and dearth and lack of necessaries and conditions of absolute destitution.

[134]Always the weaker will supply an evil and *accursed* (ἐπάρατοι) meal to the stronger.

[141]*Cursed* (=f; ἐπάρατοι) will they be in their cities and villages, *cursed* in their houses and farm buildings. *Cursed* will be the field and all the seed dropped therein, *cursed* the fertile parts of the uplands and every kind of cultivated tree. *Cursed* their heeds of cattle, barren without hope or increase, *cursed* all their fruits, blasted at the very height of their ripening.

[142] . . . For these are the wages of impiety (=AP) and disobedience (=LB).

[154]But they have closed their eyes to the whole of this law (=AC, LB) . . . . [157]For this they themselves will receive the full measure of *curses* (ἀράς) and penalties named above, but the land . . . disburdened of the heavy weight of its impious inhabitants (=AP) . . . full of tranquility and peace and justice (=RI), she will renew her youth and bloom and take her rest calm and serene (=(BL)) . . . .

[162]I have now described without any reservation the curses (ἀράς) and penalties which they will deservedly suffer who disregard the holy laws (=LB) of justice (=RI) and piety, who have been seduced by the polytheistic creeds which finally lead to atheism (=AP) and have forgotten the teaching of their race and of their fathers (=LB), . . .

[169]Everything will suddenly be reversed, God will turn the *curses* (ἀράς) against the enemies of these penitents, the enemies who rejoiced in the misfortunes of the nation . . . . (Cf. blessing for Gentiles in 171f.)

1QS i.24–ii.18: (CU/BL, (CU-BL)) (3:10: F, f*, LB) (3:13f: KN, RI) (1:8f: SI, AP)

[24] "We have strayed, [25]we have <disobeyed>! We and our fathers before us have sinned and done wickedly (=LB) in walking [26]<counter to the precepts> of truth and righteousness (=RI). <And God has> judged us and our fathers also (=(CU)); ii [1]but He has bestowed His bountiful mercy on us from everlasting to everlasting" (=(BL)).

And the Priests shall *bless* all [2]the men of the lot of God who walk perfectly in all His ways . . . .

[4] . . . And the Levites shall *curse* (קלל) all the men [5]of the lot of Satan, saying: 'Be *cursed* (=f*; ארור) because of all your guilty wickedness! May he [6]deliver you up for torture at the hands of the vengeful Avengers! May he visit you with destruction by the hand of all the Wreakers of Revenge! [7]Be *cursed* (=f*; ארור) without mercy because of the darkness of your deeds! Be damned [8]in the shadowy place of everlasting fire! May God not heed when you call on Him, nor pardon you by blotting out your sin! [9]May He raise His angry face towards you for vengeance! May there be no "Peace" for you in the mouth of those who hold fast to the Fathers!' [10]And after the *blessing* and the *cursing* (קלל), all those entering the Covenant shall say, 'Amen, Amen!' (=SI).

[11]And the Priests and Levites shall continue, saying: '*Cursed* (=F; ארור) be the man who enters this Covenant while walking among the idols of his heart (=AP), [12]who sets up before himself his stumbling-block of sin so that he may backslide! [13]Hearing the words of this Covenant, he *blesses* himself in his heart and says, "Peace be with me, [14]even though I walk in the stubbornness of my heart," whereas his spirit, parched <for lack of truth> and watered <with lies>, shall be destroyed without [15]pardon. God's

wrath and His zeal for His precepts shall consume him in everlasting destruction. All
¹⁶the *curses* (אלה) of the Covenant (=KN) shall cling to him and God will set him apart
for evil. He shall be cut off from the midst of all the sons of light, and because he has
turned aside ¹⁷from God on account of his idols (=AP) and his stumbling block of sin, his
lot shall be among those who are *cursed* (ארר) for ever.' ¹⁸And after them, all those
entering the Covenant shall answer and say, 'Amen, Amen!' (=SI).

1QS v.12-13: (3:10: LB) (3:13f: KN)
    . . . and matters revealed they have treated with insolence (=LB). Therefore Wrath
shall rise up to condemn, and Vengeance shall be executed by the *curses* (אלה) of the
Covenant (=KN), and great chastisements of eternal destruction shall be visited upon
them, leaving no remnant.

CD i.14-17; ii.4-6 iii.18-19: (3:8-14: (CU/BL), CU-(BL)) (3:10: LB) (3:13f: KN,
    RI) (1:8f: SE)
    ¹⁴ . . . when the Scoffer arose who shed over Israel the ¹⁵waters of lies (=SE). He
caused them to wander in a pathless wilderness, laying low the everlasting heights,
abolishing ¹⁶the ways of righteousness (=RI) and removing the boundary with which the
forefathers had marked out their inheritance (=LB), that he might call down ¹⁷on them the
curses (אלה) of the Covenant (=KN) and deliver them up to the avenging sword of the
Covenant.
    ii ⁴ . . . Patience and much forgiveness (=(BL)) are with Him ⁵towards those who
turn from transgression; but power, might, and great flaming wrath ⁶by the hand of all the
Angels of Destruction (=(CU)) towards those who depart from the way and abhor the
Precept.
    iii ¹⁸ . . . But God, in His wonderful mysteries, forgave them their sin and pardoned
their wickedness; ¹⁹and He built them a sure house in Israel (=(BL)).

CD xv.1-5: (3:10: LB) (3:13f: KN) (1:8f: SI)
    <He shall not> ¹swear by (the Name), nor by Aleph and Lamed (Elohim), nor by
Aleph and Dalet (Adonai), but a binding oath ²by the *curses* (אלה) of the Covenant
(=KN) . . . .
    ³ . . . But if he has sworn an oath (=SI) by the *curses* (אלה) of the Covenant
(=KN) before ⁴the judges and has transgressed it (=LB), then he is guilty and shall con-
fess and make restitution; but he shall not be burdened ⁵with a capital sin.

CD xx.6-8: (Cf col VIII in *DSSE*) (3:10: LB)
    ⁶But when his deeds are revealed (=LB), according to the interpretation of the Law
in which ⁷the men of perfect holiness walk, let no man defer to him with regard to money
or work, ⁸for all the Holy Ones of the Most High have *cursed* (ארר) him.

1Q22 i.8-10: (3:10: LB) (1:8: AP)
    . . . <They will serve> ⁸false gods which shall be for them a snare and a pitfall
(=AP). <They will sin against the> holy <days>, and against the Sabbath and the
Covenant, <and against the commandments> which ⁹I command you to keep this day
(=LB). <Therefore I will smite> them with a mighty <blow> in the midst of the land
<which they> ¹⁰cross the Jordan <to possess>. And when all the *curses* (קללה) come
upon them and catch up with them to destroy them and blot them out . . . .

4Q 280-82: (3:10: F, f*, LB) (1:8f: AN)
    < . . . And they shall continue saying: Be *cur>sed* (=f*, AN; ארור), Melkiresha,
in all the thou<ghts of your guilty inclination. May> God <deliver you up> for tor-

ture at the hands of the vengeful Avengers. May God not heed <when> you call on Him. <May he raise His angry face> towards you. May there by no (greeting of) 'Peace' for you in the mouth of all those who hold fast to the Father<s. May you be *cursed*> (=f*)> with no remnant, and damned without escape.

Cursed (=F; ארור) be those who practi<se their wicked designs> and <es>tablish in their heart your (evil) devices, plotting against the Covenant of God (=LB) . . . .

4Q 286–87: (3:10: F, f*, LB) (1:8f: AN)

Afterwards <they> shall damn Satan and all his guilty lot. They shall answer and say, *Cursed* (=f*, AN; ארור) be <S>atan in his hostile design, and damned in his guilty dominion. *Cursed* be all the spirits of his <lo>t in their wicked design, and damned in their thoughts of unclean impurity. For they are the lot of darkness and their visitation is for eternal destruction. Amen. Amen.

Cursed be the Wicke<d One in all . . .> of his dominions, and may all the sons of Satan be damned in all the works of their service until their annihilation <for ever, Amen, amen.>

And <they shall continue to say: Be *cursed*, Ang>el of Perdition and Spir<it of Dest>ruction, in all the thoughts of your g<uilty> inclination <and all your abomina>ble <plots> and <your> wicked design, <and> may you be <da>mned . . . . Amen, Am<en>.

<*Cursed* (=F; ארור) be a>ll those who practi<se> their <wicked designs> and establish <in their heart> your (evil) devices, <plotting against God>d'<s Covenant> . . . to exchange the judgemen<ts of truth for folly.> (=LB).

Ant 4:302, 306–7, 312–14: (3:8–14: CU/BL, (CU-BL)) (3:10: LB)

[302] . . . On the following days . . . he gave them *blessings* with *curses* (καταρας) upon such as should not live in accordance with the laws but should transgress the ordinances that were therein (=LB).

[306]And first those on Mount Gerizim were to invoke the best of *blessings* upon such as were zealous for the worship of God and for the observance of the laws and were not disobedient to the words of Moses . . . .

[307]Thereafter, in the same order, they should *imprecate curses* (καταρας) upon future transgressors (=LB), mutually responding in corroboration of the pronouncements. These *blessings* and *curses* (καταρας) he put on record himself, to the end that their lesson never be abolished by time . . . .

[312]Moses foretold . . . that, if they transgressed His rites, they would experience afflictions [313]of such sort that their land would be filled with the arms of enemies, their cities razed (=(CU)).

[314]"Howbeit," said he, "God who created you will restore those cities to your citizens and the temple too (=(BL)) . . . .

Ant 5:69–70:

[69]Proceeding thence to Sikima, with all the people, he erected an altar at the spot foreordained by Moses, and, dividing his army, posted one half of it on mount Gerizim and the other half on Hebel, whereon also stood the altar, along with the Levites and the priests. [70] After sacrificing and pronouncing *imprecations* (ἀράς), which they also left graven upon the altar, they returned to Shiloh.

Bell 5:401: (3:8–14: CU/BL) (3:10: LB)

[401]But as for you, what have you done that is *blessed* by the lawgiver, what deed

that he has *cursed* (κατηραμένων) have you left undone? How much more impious are you (=LB) than those who have been defeated in the past!

2: CURSES RELATED TO GEN/NUM

Primal curses

Gen 3:13–14.17: (3:10: f*, LB) (1:8f: SE)

¹³ . . . The woman said, "The serpent beguiled me, and I ate" (=SE). ¹⁴The Lord God said to the serpent, "Because you have done this (=LB), *cursed* (f*; ארור, ἐπικατάρατος) are you above all the cattle . . . ."

¹⁷And to Adam he said, "Because you have listened to the voice of your wife, and have eaten of the tree of which I commanded you, 'You shall not eat of it' (LB), *cursed* (f*; ארור, ἐπικατάρατος) is the ground because of you . . . ."

Gen 4:10–12: (3:10; f*, LB) (1:8f: AC+CU)

¹⁰And the Lord said, "What have you done? The voice of your brother's blood is crying to me from the ground (=AC; LB). ¹¹And now you are *cursed* (=f*; ארור, ἐπικατάρατος) from the ground, which has opened its mouth to receive your brother's blood from your hand (=LB). ¹²When you till the ground, it shall no longer yield to you its strength; you shall be a fugitive and a wanderer on the earth."

Gen 5:29:

²⁹ . . . (Lamech said) "Out of the ground which the Lord has *cursed* (ארר, κατηράσατο) this one shall bring us relief from our work and from the toil of our hands."

Gen 8:21:

²¹ . . . (The Lord said) "I will never again *curse* (קלל, καταράσασθαι) the ground because of man, for the imagination of man's heart is evil from his youth; neither will I ever again destroy every living creature as I have done."

Gen 9:24–26: (3:8–14: CU/BL) (3:10: f)

²⁴When Noah awoke from his wine and knew what his youngest son had done to him, ²⁵he said, "*Cursed* (=f; ארור, ἐπικατάρατος) be Canaan; a slave of slaves shall he be to his brothers." ²⁶He also said, "*Blessed* by the Lord my God be Shem; and let Canaan be his slave . . . ."

Wis 12:10–11: (3:10: LB)

¹⁰ . . . though thou wast not unaware that their origin was evil, and their wickedness inborn (=LB), and that their way of thinking would never change. ¹¹For they (=Canaanites) were an *accursed* (κατηραμένον) race from the beginning, and it was not through fear of any one that thou didst leave them unpunished for their sins.

Adam and Eve, Vita 3:

Adam answered, "Do not wish to speak such words lest the Lord God bring on us some further *curse*."

Adam and Eve, Vita 37, 39, 44: (3:10: LB)

³⁷ . . . And Eve said to the serpent in a loud voice, "*Cursed* beast! How is it that you were not afraid to throw yourself at the image of God, but have dared to attack it?

And how were your teeth made strong? . . ."

³⁹Then Seth said to the beast, "May the Lord God rebuke you. Stop; be quiet; close your mouth, *cursed* enemy of the truth, chaotic destroyer . . . .

⁴⁴ . . . And Adam said to Eve, What have you done? You have brought upon us a great wound, transgression and sin in all our generations (=LB) . . . and they shall *curse* us, saying, "Our parents who were from the beginning have brought upon us all evils."

Adam and Eve, Apoc. 10: (3:10: LB)
And Seth and Eve went into the regions of Paradise. As they were going, Eve saw her son and a wild beast attacking him. And Eve wept, saying, "Woe is me! For when I come to the day of resurrection, all who have sinned will *curse* (καταράσονται) me, saying that Eve did not keep the command of God (=LB)."

Adam and Eve, Apoc. 24, 26: (3:10: f*, LB) (1:8f: SE)
²⁴God said to Adam, 'Because you transgressed my commandment and listened to your wife (LB), *cursed* (=f*) (ἐπικατάρατος) is the ground in your labors . . . because you did not keep my commandment (LB).'

²⁶"And after he had told me these things, he spoke to the serpent in great wrath, saying to him, 'Since you have done this and become an ungrateful vessel, so far as to lead astray the careless of heart (=AC; SE), *accursed* (=f*; ἐπικατάρατος) are you beyond all wild beasts . . . .'"

3 Apoc. Bar. 4:8-9, 15: (3:8-14: CU-BL) (3:13f: (BG)) (1:8f: SE)
⁸And I said, "I pray you, show me which is the tree which caused Adam to stray (=SE)." And the angel said, "It is the vine which the angel Samaèl planted by which the Lord God became angered, and he *cursed* (ἐκατηράσατο) him and his plantling. For this reason he did not permit Adam to touch it. And because of this the devil became envious, and tricked him by means of his vine." ⁹And I Baruch said, "And since the vine became the cause of such evil (=SE) and was *cursed* (κατάρας) by God and (was) the destruction of the first formed, how is it now of such great use?"

¹⁵And God sent the angel Sarasael, and he said to him, "Rise, Noah, plant the sprig, for the Lord says this: 'Its bitterness will be changed into sweetness, and its *curse* (κατάρα) will become a *blessing*, and its fruit will become the blood of God, and just as the race of men have been condemned through it, so through Jesus Christ Emmanuel in it (they) will receive a calling and entrance into Paradise'" (=(BG)).

Bib. Ant. 3:9-10: (3:8-14: CU-(BL)) (3:13f: L)
⁹And God said, "I will never again *curse* the earth on man's account, for the tendency of man's heart is foolish from his youth; and so I will never destroy all living creatures at one time as I have done. But when those inhabiting the earth sin, I will judge them by famine or by sword or by fire or by death (=(CU)) . . . .

¹⁰But when the years appointed for the world have been fulfilled, then the light will cease and the darkness will fade away. And I will bring the dead to life (=L) . . . and there will be another earth and another heaven, an everlasting dwelling place (=(BL))."

Jub. 3:23, 25: (3:10: LB)
²³And the Lord *cursed* the serpent and he was angry with it forever. And he was angry with the woman also because she had listened to the voice of the serpent and had eaten.

²⁵And to Adam he said, "Because you listened to the voice of your wife and you ate from that tree from which I commanded you that you should not eat (LB), the land shall be *cursed* because of you."

Jub. 7:10, 13: (3:8-14: CU/BL) (3:10: f)

¹⁰And Noah woke up from his wine, and knew everything which his youngest son had done to him. And he *cursed* his son and said, "*Cursed* (=f) is Canaan, let him be an enslaved servant of his brothers." ¹¹And he *blessed* Shem, and said . . . .

¹³And Ham knew that his father *cursed* his youngest son, and it was disgusting to him that he *cursed* his son. And he separated from his father, he and his sons with him: Cush and Mizraim and Put and Canaan.

Jub. 9:14-15: (3:10: LB) (1:8f: SI)

¹⁴And thus the sons of Noah divided for their children before Noah, their father. And he made them all swear an oath to *curse* each and every one who desired to seize a portion which did not come in his lot. ¹⁵And they all said, "So be it and so let it be to them and to their sons forever (=SI) . . . on account of all the evil of the pollution of their errors which have filled the earth with sin and pollution and fornification and transgression (=LB)."

Jub. 10:29-32: (3:10: f, LB) (1:8f: AC+CU, SI)

²⁹But Canaan saw that the land of Lebanon as far as the river of Egypt was very good. And he did not go into the land of his inheritance . . . .

³⁰And Ham, his father, and Cush and Mizraim, his brothers, said to him, "You have dwelt in a land which is not yours nor did it come forth for us by lot. Do not do this, because if you do this, you and your children will fall in the land and be *cursed* with sedition because by sedition you have dwelt and by sedition (=AC; LB) your children will fall and you will be uprooted forever.

³²You are *cursed* (=f) and you will be *cursed* more than all the sons of Noah by the *curse* which we swore with an oath (=SI) before the holy judge and before Noah, our father."

Agric 20-21: (3:10: f*, LB) (3:13f: RI)

²⁰ . . . Moses, the allwise, ascribes to the righteous man (=RI) soul-husbandry . . . whereas to the unrighteous man he ascribes that working on the ground . . . ²¹For he says, "Cain was one working on the ground," and, a little later, when he is discovered to have incurred the pollution of fraticide (=LB), it is said: "*Cursed* (=f*; ἐπικατάρατος) art thou from the ground which hath opened her mouth to receive thy brother's blood . . . ."

Agric 107:

Eve's serpent is represented by the lawgiver as thirsting for man's blood, for he says in the *curses* (ἀραῖς) pronounced on it, "He shall lie in wait for thy head, and thou shalt lie in wait for his heel . . . ."

Cher 52: (3:10: LB)

. . . Why then, soul of man . . . dost thou . . . embrace outward sense, which unmans and defiles thee (=LB)? For this thou shalt bring forth that thing of ruin and confusion, Cain, the fratricide (=LB), the *accursed* (ἐπάρατον), the possession which is no possession.

Deter 96-103: (3:10: f, LB) (1:8f: AP)

⁹⁶On Cain, who rejects repentance, He proceeds, owing to the enormity of his guilt, to lay *curses* (ἀράς) most appropriate to the murder of a brother (=LB). And first He says to him "Now also art thou *accursed* (=f; ἐπικατάρατος) from the earth", showing that it is not now for the first time, when he has perpetrated the treacherous deed (=LB),

that he is abominable and *accursed* (ἐπάρατος), but that he was so before also when he plotted the murder, since the purpose is as important as the completed act . . . .

[98]Now He says that the mind will be *accursed* (κατάρατον) not from anything else than from the earth; for the earthly part of each one of us is discovered to be accountable for our most dire misfortunes . . . .

[100]The manner in which the mind becomes *accursed* (καταρᾶτοι) from the earth is indicated by the words, "which opened its mouth to receive thy brother's blood . . . ."

[103] . . . So we see that God cannot but *curse* (καταρᾶται) the godless and impious Cain (=AP), because, opening wide the inner chambers of his complex being, he stood agape for all outward things . . . .

Deter 121-22: (3:13f: RI)
[121] . . . "Noah" means righteous (=RI), and it is said of him, "This man shall cause us to rest from our works and from the pains of our hands and from the earth which God hath *cursed* (κατηράσατο) . . . ."

[122] . . . But the crowning purport of righteousness (=RI) is to give us full rest "from the earth which the Lord God hath *cursed* (κατηράσατο)." By this is meant wickedness . . . .

Heres 260: (3:13f: RI)
. . . Noah was just (=RI). Is he not in the same breath shown as a prophet? Were not the curses (κατάρας) which he called down on subsequent generations, the prayers which he made on their behalf, all of which the actual event confirmed, uttered by him under divine possession?

Heres 296: (3:10: LB) (1:8f: AC+CU)
"The mind of man," says Moses, "is carefully intent upon wickedness from youth." The *curse is heaviest* (ἐπαρατοτάτη) on this "generation," to use the figurative term for the literal "age," in which the body is in its bloom and the soul inflated, when the smouldering passions are being fanned into a flame (=AC; LB) . . . .

Leg 2:61-62: (3:10: LB)
[61]But if, in addition to designing the bad deed, it goes on to carry out its design and do the thing, the unrighteous act (=LB) has been spread out of doors as well. [62]It is in accordance with this that a *curse* (καταρᾶται) is pronounced on Canaan, because he reported abroad the change of the soul.

Leg 3:65-75: (3:10: f*, LB) (1:8f: SE)
[65]"And the Lord God said to the serpent, 'Because thou hast done this (LB), *cursed* (=f*; ἐπικατάρατος) art thou from among all cattle and from among all the beasts of the earth . . . .' For what reason does he *curse* (καταρᾶται) the serpent without giving it opportunity to defend itself . . . ?"

[66] . . . When, then, the woman said "the serpent beguiled me" (=SE), what was there to prevent His inquiring here too from the serpent, whether he beguiled her, instead of prejudging the case and pronouncing the *curse* (καταρᾶσθαι) without listening to any defence?

[68] . . . Quite appropriately therefore does God pronounce the *curse* (καταρᾶται) without giving pleasure an opportunity of defending herself, since she has in her no seed from which virtue might spring, but is always and everywhere guilty and foul.

[75]Thou seest that God both *curses* (καταρᾶται) the serpent without allowing him to defend himself — for he is pleasure — and slays Er without bringing an open charge against him; for he is the body.

Leg 3:104-113: (3:8-14: CU/(BL)) (3:10: f*,f) (1:8f: SE)

[104]Seeing then that we have found two natures created, undergoing moulding, and chiselled into full relief by God's hands, the one essentially hurtful, blameworthy and *accursed* (κατάρατον), the other beneficial and praiseworthy (=(BL)) . . . .

[107]"And the Lord God said to the serpent, *Cursed* (f; ἐπικατάρατος) art thou from among all cattle and from among all the beasts of the earth." Just as joy, being a good condition of the soul, deserves prayer, so pleasure, the passion par excellence, deserves *cursing* (κατάρας); it shifts the standards of the soul and renders it a lover of passion instead of a lover of virtue (=SE).

[111]*Accursed* (=f*; ἐπικατάρατος) on these grounds is pleasure. Let us see how appropriate the *curses* (καταρᾶται) are which he pronounces upon it. He says that it is *cursed* (ἐπάρατον) from all cattle. Our irrational faculty of sense-perception, then, is of the cattle kind, and each of our senses *curses* (καταρᾶται) pleasure as a most deadly enemy . . . .

[112] . . . How, then, should not sense rightly lay *curses* (ἀράς) on pleasure that maims it? [113]It is *cursed* (ἐπικατάρατος) also beyond all the wild beasts. By these I mean the passions of the soul, for by these the mind is wounded and destroyed.

Leg 3:222: (3:10: f*, LB)

. . . "To Adam God said, 'Because thou hast listened to the voice of thy wife, and hast eaten of the tree, of which I commanded thee not to eat (of it thou hast eaten) (LB), *cursed* (f*; ἐπικατάρατος) is the ground in respect of thy labours.'" Most profitless is it that Mind should listen to Sense-perception, and not Sense-perception to Mind . . . .

Leg 3,246-47: (3:10: f, LB)

[246]The words "and thou didst eat of the tree of which alone I commanded thee not to eat" are equivalent to "thou didst consent to wickedness (=LB), which it is thy duty to keep off with all thy might": because of this *"cursed"* (=f; ἐπικατάρατος) — not "art thou" but "is the earth in thy works." What then was the reason of this? The serpent, we saw, was pleasure, an irrational elation of soul. She is *accursed* (καταρᾶτοι) on her own account . . . . Adam is the neutral mind, which now proves better, now worse. For in so far as he is mind, his nature is neither bad nor good, but under the influence of virtue and vice it is his wont to shift towards good or bad. [247]It is then just as we would expect, that he is not *accursed* (καταρᾶτοι) on his own account, inasmuch as he is neither wickedness nor conduct with wickedness for its rule, but the earth is *accursed* (καταρᾶτοι) in his works.

Praem 72: (3:10: LB)

For he says that he laid a *curse* (ἀπὰν ἐπηράσατο) upon the fratricide (=Cain)(=LB) that he should ever "groan and tremble."

Sobr 30-51: (3:10: 2f, LB) (3:13f: RI)

[30]To resume. When the just man (=Noah)(=RI) has returned to soberness and knows "what his younger son has done to him, he utters *curses* (ἀράς) stern and deep . . . ."

[31]But who is it that he *curses* (καταρᾶται)? [32]It was Noah's son Ham, who from idle curiosity wished to see his father naked, and laughed at what he saw and proclaimed aloud what it was right to leave untold. But it is Canaan who is charged with another's misdeeds (=LB) and reaps the *curses* (ἀράς). For it is said, "*Cursed* (=f; ἐπικατάρατος) be Canaan; a servant, a bondman shall he be to his brethren."

[47]It is natural enough, then, that the just man (=RI) should appear to lay *curses* (ἀράς) on the grandson Canaan. I say "appear," because virtually he does *curse*

(καταρᾶται) his son in *cursing* (--) Canaan, since when Ham has been moved to sin, he himself becomes Canaan, for it is a single subject, wickedness, which is presented in two different aspects, rest and motion.

⁵¹. . . Let us now observe the form which the *curses* (ἀράς) take. "*Cursed* (=f; ἐπικατάρατος)," he says, "is Canaan, a bondman shall he be to his brethren . . . ."

Virt 202: (3:10: LB)

Yet of the three sons born to him (=Noah) . . . one ventured to pour reproach upon the author of his preservation. He held up to scorn and laughter some lapse into which his father had fallen involuntarily (=LB) . . . . He then had no profit from the glories of his birth, laid under a *curse* (ἐπάρατος) and a source of misery for his successors, a worthy fate for one who had no thought for the honour due to parents (=LB).

Ant 1:58: (3:10: LB)

God, however, exempted him from the penalty merited by the murder (=LB), Cain having offered a sacrifice and therewith supplicated Him not to visit him too severely in His wrath; but He made him *accursed* (ἐπάρατον) and threatened to punish his posterity in the seventh generation, and expelled him from that land with his wife.

Ant 1:142: (3:8-14: CU/BL)

Noah, on learning what had passed, invoked a *blessing* on his other sons, but *cursed* (κατηράσατο) not Ham himself, because of his nearness of kin, but his posterity. The other descendants of Ham escaped the *curse* (ἀράν), but divine vengeance pursued the children of Chananaeus.

Gen 12 formula

Gen 12:2-3: (3:8-14: CU/BL) (3:13f: BG)

²And I will make of you a great nation, and I will *bless* you, and make your name great, so that you will be a *blessing*. ³I will *bless* those who *bless* you (=BG), and him who *curses* (קלל, καταρωμένους) you I will *curse* (ארר, καταράσομαι); and by you all the families of the earth shall *bless* themselves (=BG).

Gen 27:28-29: (3:8-14: CU/BL) (3:10: F) (3:13f: BG)

²⁸May God give you of the dew of heaven, and of the fatness of the earth, and plenty of grain and wine. ²⁹Let peoples serve you, and nations bow down to you. Be Lord over your brothers, and may your mother's sons bow down to you. *Cursed* (=F; ארור, ἐπικατάρατος) be every one who *curses* (ארר, καταρώμενος) you, and *blessed* be every one who *blesses* you (=BG).

Num 24:9: (3:8-14: CU/BL) (3:10: F) (3:13f: BG)

⁹ . . . *Blessed* be every one who *blesses* you (=BG), and *cursed* (=F; ארור, καταρώμενοι) be every one who *curses* (ארר, κεκατήρανται) you."

Tob 13:10.13-15: (3:8-14: CU/BL; (CU-BL)) (3:10: F) (3:13f: BG, RI)

¹⁰O Jerusalem, the holy city, he will afflict you for the deeds of your sons (=(CU)), but again he will show mercy (=(BL)) to the sons of the righteous (=RI).

¹³Many nations will come from afar to the name of the lord God (=BG) . . . .

¹⁴*Cursed* (=F; ἐπικατάρατοι) are all who hate you; *blessed* for ever will be all who

love you (=BG). ¹⁵Rejoice and be glad for the sons of the righteous (=RI) . . . .

Jub. 12:23: (3:8–14: CU/BL) (3:13f: BG)

And I shall *bless* you and I shall make your name great, and you will be *blessed* in the land and all the nations of the earth will *bless* themselves by you (=BG). And whoever *blesses* you I shall *bless* (=BG), and whoever *curses* you I shall *curse*.

Jub. 25:21–22: (3:8–14: CU/BL) (3:13f: BG, RI)

²¹(Rebecca said to Jacob:) May your name and your seed stand for all ages; and may God Most High be their God. And may the God of Righteousness (=RI) dwell with them; and with them his sanctuary be built in all ages. ²²The one who *blesses* you will be *blessed* (=BG), and all flesh which *curses* you falsely will be *cursed*.

Jub. 26:23–24: (3:8–14: CU/BL) (3:13f: BG)

²³(Isaac said to Jacob:) May the Lord give and multiply to you from the dew of heaven and from the dew of earth, and an abundance of wheat and oil may he multiply for you. May nations serve you, and the people bow down to you.

²⁴ . . . And may all of the *blessings* with which the Lord *blessed* me and *blessed* Abraham my father, belong to you and to your seed forever. May the one who *curses* you be *cursed*, and the one who *blesses* you be *blessed* (=BG).

Jub. 31:17: (3:8–14: CU/BL) (3:13f: BG)

And all who hate you will fall before you, and all your enemies will be uprooted and perish, and whoever *blesses* you will be *blessed* (=BG), and any nation which *curses* you will be *cursed*.

Jub. 31:20: (3:8–14: CU/BL) (3:13f: BG, RI)

And on the day when you sit on your righteous throne of honor (=RI), there will be great peace for all the seed of the beloved's sons (=(BL)). Whoever *blesses* you will be *blessed* (=BG), and all who hate you and afflict you and *curse* you will be uprooted and destroyed from the earth and they shall be *cursed*.

T. Levi 4:6: (3:8–14: CU/BL) (3:13f: BG)

Because those who *bless* him shall be *blessed* (=BG), and those who *curse* (καταρώμενοι) him shall be destroyed.

Migr 1: (3:8–14: CU/BL) (3:13f: BG)

"And the Lord said unto Abraham, Depart out of thy land . . . into the land which I shall show thee; and I will make thee a great nation . . . . And I will *bless* them that *bless* thee (=BG), and them that *curse* (καταρωμένους) thee I will *curse* (κατάρας), and in thee shall all the tribes of the earth be *blessed* (=BG)."

Migr 109–10: (3:8–14: CU/BL) (3:13f: BG, RI)

¹⁰⁹These are the prizes which He bestows upon him who is to become wise. Let us see next those which He accords to others too for the wise man's sake. "I will *bless*," He says, "those that *bless* thee (=BG), and those that *curse* (καταρωμένους) thee I will *curse* (καταράσομαι)." ¹¹⁰That these promises as well as the others are made to show honour to the righteous man (=RI) is clear to everybody . . . .

Mos 1:291: (3:8–14: CU/BL) (3:13f: BG)

²⁹¹Therefore, it shall eat up many nations of its enemies . . . . Worthy of *benediction* are those who *bless* thee (=BG), worthy of *cursing* (κατάρας) those who *curse* (καταρώμωνοι) thee."

The Balaam Episode

Num 22:5 – 24:10: (3:8–14: CU/BL) (3:13f: RI)

22 ⁵ . . . (Balak's messengers said) "Behold, a people has come out of Egypt; they cover the face of the earth, and they are dwelling opposite me. ⁶Come now, *curse* (ארר, ἄρασαι) this people for me, since they are too mighty for me; perhaps I shall be able to defeat them and drive them from the land; for I know that he whom you *bless* is *blessed* and he whom you *curse* (ארר, καταράσῃ) is *cursed* (ארר, κεκατήρανται).

¹⁰ . . . (Balaam to God) "Balak . . . has sent me saying, ¹¹'Behold, a people has come out of Egypt, and it covers the face of the earth; now, come, *curse* (קבב, ἄρασαι) them for me; perhaps I shall be able to fight against them and drive them out.'" ¹²God said to Balaam: "You shall not go with them; you shall not *curse* (ארר, καταράσῃ) the people, for they are *blessed*."

¹⁷ . . . "Come, *curse* (קבב, ἐπικατάρασαι) this people for me.

23 ⁷And Balaam took up his discourse, and said, "From Aram Balak has brought me, the king of Moab from the eastern mountains: 'Come, *curse* (ארר, ἄρασαι) Jacob for me, and come, *denounce* (זעם, ἐπικατάρασαι) Israel!' ⁸How can I *curse* (קבב, ἀράσωμαι) whom God has not *cursed*? (קבב, καταρᾶται) How can I *denounce* (זעם, καταράσωμαι) whom the Lord has not *denounced*? (זעם, καταρᾶται) . . .

¹⁰ . . . Let me die the death of the righteous (=RI), and let my end be like his!" ¹¹And Balak said to Balaam, "What have you done to me? I took you to *curse* (קבב, κατάρασιν) my enemies, and behold, you have done nothing but *bless* them. ¹²And he answered, "Must I not take heed to speak what the Lord puts in my mouth?" ¹³And Balak said to him, "Come with me to another place . . . then *curse* (קבב, κατάρασαι) them for me from there."

²⁵And Balak said to Balaam, "Neither *curse* (קבב, κατάραις καταράσῃ) them at all, nor *bless* them at all . . . .

²⁷ . . . Come now, I will take you to another place; perhaps it will please God that you may *curse* (קבב, καταρᾶσαι) them for me from there."

24 ¹⁰ . . . and Balak said to Balaam, "I called you to *curse* (קבב, καταρᾶσθαι) my enemies, and behold, you have *blessed* them these three times."

Deut 23:5–6: (3:8–14; CU-BL)

⁵ . . . they hired against you Balaam the son of Beor from Pethor of Mesopotamia, to *curse* (קלל, καταράσασθαι) you. ⁶Nevertheless the Lord your God would not hearken to Balaam; but the Lord your God turned the *curse* (קללה, κατάρας) into a *blessing* for you, because the Lord your God loved you.

Josh 24:9–10: (3:8–14: CU/BL)

⁹Then Balak . . . sent and invited Balaam the son of Beor to *curse* (קלל, ἀράσασθαι) you, ¹⁰but I would not listen to Balaam, therefore he *blessed* you; so I delivered you out of his hand.

Neh 13:2–3: (3:8–14: CU-BL)

² . . . they . . . hired Balaam against them to *curse* (קלל, (II Esdr 23:2) καταράσασθαι) them — yet our God turned the *curse* (קללה, κατάραν) into a *blessing*.

[3]When the people heard the law they separated from Israel all those of foreign descent.

Bib. Ant. 18: (3:8–14: CU/BL) (3:13f: BG)

[2]Now Balak was king of Moab . . . he sent to Balaam . . . and commanded him, saying: "Behold I know that in the reign of my father Zippor, when the Amorites fought him, You *cursed* them and they were handed over before him. And now, come and *curse* this people, because they are too many for us, and I will do you great honor."

[6] . . . (God to Balaam) "And do you propose to go forth with them to *curse* whom I have chosen? But if you *curse* them, who will then be there to *bless* you (=BG)?

[12] . . . (Balaam said:) "And the wise and understanding will remember my words that, when I *cursed*, I perished, but though I *blessed*, I was not *blessed*.

Conf 64–65, 72:

[64]Of the worst kind of rising we have an example in the description of him who wished to *curse* (καταράσασθαι) one who was praised by God. For he too is represented as dwelling at the "rising," and this rising though it bears the same name as the other is in direct conflict with it. [65]"Balak," we read, "sent for me from Mesopotamia from the mountains of rising saying, 'Come hither, *curse* (ἄρασαι) for me him who God does not *curse* (ἀρᾶται).'"

[72] . . . He says, "Come hither, *curse* (ἄρασαι) me Jacob, and come hither, send thy *curses* (ἐπικατάρασαι) upon Israel," and that is equivalent to "Put an end to them both, the soul's sight and the soul's hearing, that it may neither see nor hear any true and genuine exellence." For Israel is the type of seeing, and Jacob of hearing.

Conf 159: (3:8–14: CU/BL)

We have a parallel in Balaam, that dealer in auguries and prodigies and in the vanity of unfounded conjectures, for the name Balaam is by interpretation "vain." The lawbook declares that he *cursed* (καταράσασθαι) the Man of Vision, though in words he uttered prayers of *blessing* . . . .

Deter 71: (3:8–14: CU-BL)

It was so with Balaam also. He was a sophist, an empty conglomeration of incompatible and discordant notions. It was his desire to do harm to the godly one by laying *curses* (ἀράς) upon him. But he could not, for God turned his *curses* (κατάρας) into a *blessing*, in order that He might at once convict the unrighteous one of his villainy, and at the same time make good his own love for virtue.

Migr 113–18: (3:8–14: CU/BL, CU-BL) (1:8f: AC+CU, AP)

[113]Accordingly, that empty one, Balaam, though he sang loftiest hymns to God . . . and poured out thousand eulogies on him whose eyes were open, even Israel, has been adjudged impious (=AP) and *accursed* (ἐπάρατος) even by the wise lawgiver, and held to be an utterer not of *blessings* but of *curses* (καταρᾶσθαι) (=AC). [114]For Moses says that as the hired confederate of Israel's enemies he became an evil prophet of evil things, nursing in his soul direst *curses* (ἀράς) on the race beloved by God . . . .

[115]Evidence of this is afforded by the oracles relating to the matter; for it says "God did not give Balaam leave to *curse* (καταράσασθαι) thee, but turned his *curses* (κατάρας) into *blessing* . . . ."

[117]Let no treatment, then, that is marked by prayers and *blessings* on the one hand, or by abusing and *cursing* (κατάρας) on the other hand, be referred to the way it finds vent in speech, but rather to the intention; . . .

[118]This is Moses' first lesson; he tells us what befalls others for the virtuous man's sake, whenever they consent to visit him with blame or praise, with prayers or *imprecations* (κατάρας).

Mos 1:263-305: (3:8-14: CU/BL) (3:10: LB)

[263] . . . and (Balak) thought that, if the power of the Hebrews was invincible in battle, he might be able to overthrow it by *imprecations* (ἀραῖς) of some kind.

[278]"From Mesopotamia hath Balak called me, a far journey from the East, that he may avenge him on the Hebrews through my *cursing* (ἀραῖς). But I, how shall I *curse* (ἀράσομαι) them whom God hath not *cursed* (καταράτοις) . . . . But I shall not be able to harm the people, which shall dwell alone, not reckoned among other nations . . . .

[280] . . . "Are you not ashamed", he (=Balak) cried, "that, summoned to *curse* (κατάραις) the enemy, you have prayed for them?"

[283]" . . . As for me, I was summoned to *bless*, not to *curse* (κατάραις) . . . ."

[285] . . . Balak said: "Sirrah, do not either *curse* (ἀράς) or *bless*, for the silence which avoids danger is better than words which displease." And . . . he led the seer away to another place from which he showed him a part of the Hebrew host and begged him to *curse* (καταρᾶσθαι) them. [286]Here the seer proved himself to be even worse than the king . . . partly because he was dominated by the worst of vices, conceit (=LB), partly because in his heart he longed to *curse* (καταρᾶσθαι), even if he were prevented from doing so with his voice.

[292]Greatly incensed by this, the king said: "Thou wast summoned to *curse* (ἀραῖς) the enemy, and has now trice invoked *blessings* on them . . . ."

[305] . . . In the plotting he (=Balak) had been served by the soothsayer, who, he hoped, would be able by his *curses* (ἀραῖς) to destroy the power of the Hebrews.

Ant 4:104-126, 157: (3:8-14: CU/BL) (3:10: HK) (3:13f: L)

[104]And these, forasmuch as there was a certain Balaam . . . sent, along with the ambassadors of Balak, some of their own notables to entreat the seer to come and deliver *curses* (ἀράς) for the extermination of the Israelites.

[106]For that army, which they invited him to come and *curse* (καταρασόμενον), was in favour with God . . . .

[118] . . . having come, in fact, to *curse* (ἐπὶ κατάρα) his enemies, he was now belauding those very persons and pronouncing them the most *blessed* of men.

[122] . . . the *blessings* for which God has designed their race; it is He who, in His gracious favour to them and His zeal to confer on them a life of felicity (=L) and everlasting renown.

[123](Balaam said) "Come, let us erect yet other altars, and offer sacrifices like unto the first, if perchance I may persuade God to suffer me to bind these people under a *curse* (=HK; ἀραῖς)." [124]Balak consenting thereto, twice did the seer offer sacrifice, but failed to obtain the Deity's consent to *imprecations* (ἀράς) upon the Israelites.

[126]Balak, furious because the Israelites had not been *cursed* (καταράτους), dismissed Balaam, dignifying him with no reward.

[157]This Balaam, in fact, who had been summoned by the Midianites to *curse* (ἐπαράσηται) the Hebrews . . . .

3: CURSE RELATED TO DIVINE LAWS

Gen 49:6-7: (3:10: f*, LB)

[6] . . . in their anger they slay men, and in their wantonness they hamstring oxen (=LB). *Cursed* (=f*; ארור, ἐπικατάρατος) be their anger, for it is fierce; and their

wrath, for it is cruel! I will divide them in Jacob and scatter them in Israel.

Num 5:18-27: (3:10: LB) (3:13f: GK) (1:8f: f, SI)
    [18] . . . And in his hands the priest shall have the water of bitterness that brings the *curse* (ארר, ἐπικαταρωμένου) [19]Then the priest shall make her take an oath, saying 'If no man has lain with you, and if you have not turned aside to uncleanness . . . be free from this water of bitterness that brings the *curse* (ארר, ἐπικαταρωμένου). [20]But if you have gone astray . . . and if you have defiled yourself (=LB) . . .'
    [21] . . . then (let the priest make the woman take the oath of the *curse* (אלה, ἀράς), and say to the woman) 'the Lord make you an *execration* (=GK; אלה, ἀρᾷ) and an oath among your people, when the Lord makes your thigh fall away and your body swell; [22]may this water that brings the *curse* (ארר, ἐπικαταρώμενον) pass into your bowels and make your body swell and your thigh fall away.' And the woman shall say, 'Amen, Amen' (=SI). [23]Then the priest shall write these *curses* (אלה, ἀράς) in a book . . . [24]and he shall make the woman drink the water of bitterness that brings the *curse* (ארר, ἐπικαταρωμένου), and the water of bitterness that brings the *curse* shall enter into her and cause bitter pain . . . .
    [27] . . . then, if she (=f) has defiled herself and has acted unfaithfully against her husband (=LB), the water that brings the *curse* (ארר, ἐπικαταρώμενον) shall enter into her and cause bitter pain, and her body shall swell, and her thigh shall fall away, and the woman shall become an *execration* (=GK; אלה, ἀράν) among her people.

Deut 21:22-23: (3:10: LB) (3:13f: GK)
    [22]And if a man has committed a crime punishable by death (=LB) and he is put to death, and you hang him on a tree, [23]his body shall not remain all night upon the tree, but you shall bury him the same day, for a hanged man is *accursed* (=GK; קלל, κεκατηραμένος) by God . . . ."

Judg 9:56-57: (3:10: LB) (1:8f: AC+CU)
    [56]Thus God requited the crime of Abimelech, which he committed against his father in killing his seventy brothers (=AC; LB); [57]and God also made all the wickedness of the men of Shechem (=AC, LB) fall back upon their heads, and upon them came the *curse* (קללה, κατάρα) of Jotham the son of Jerubbaal.

2 Kings 9:34:
    Then he (=Jehu) went in and ate and drank; and he said, "See now to this *cursed* (ארר, κατηραμένην) woman, and bury her; for she is a king's daughter."

Isa 24:5-6; 25:6: (3:8-14: CU-(BL)) (3:10: LB) (3:13f: (BG)) (1:8f: AC+CU)
    [5]The earth lies polluted under its inhabitants; for they have transgressed the laws, violated the statutes, broken the everlasting covenant (=AC; LB). [6]Therefore a *curse* (אלה, ἀρά) devours the earth, and its inhabitants suffer for their guilt; therefore the inhabitants of the earth are scorched, and few men are left.
    25 [6]On this mountain the Lord of hosts will make for all peoples a feast of fat things, a feast of wine on the lees (=(BL), BG).

Jer 23:10: (3:10: LB)
    For the land is full of adulterers (=LB); because of the *curse* (אלה, --) the land mourns, and the pastures of the wilderness are dried up. Their course is evil, and their might is not right.

Jer 29:21-23: (3:10: LB) (1:8f: AC+CU)

²¹Thus says the Lord of hosts, the God of Israel, concerning Ahab . . . and Zedekiah . . . who are prophesying a lie to you in my name (=AC; LB): Behold, I will deliver them into the hand of Nebuchadrezzar king of Babylon, and he shall slay them before your eyes. ²²Because of them this *curse* (קְלָלָה, (36:22) κατάραν) shall be used by all the exiles from Judah in Babylon . . . ²³because they have committed folly in Israel, they have committed adultery with their neighbours' wives, and they have spoken in my name lying words which I did not command them (=AC; LB).

Ps 37:21-22: (3:8-14: CU/BL) (3:13f: RI)

²¹The wicked borrows, and cannot pay back, but the righteous (=RI) is generous and gives; ²²for those *blessed* by the Lord shall possess the land, but those *cursed* (קְלָל, (36:22) καταρώμενοι) by him shall be cut off.

Ps 119:1, 21: (3:8-14: CU/BL) (3:10: f, LB)

¹*Blessed* are those whose way is blameless, who walk in the law of the Lord! ²¹Thou dost rebuke the insolent, *accursed* (f; אָרוּר, (118:21) ἐπικατάρατοι) ones, who wander from thy commandments (=LB).

Job 5:3:

I have seen the fool taking root, but suddenly I *cursed* (קָנַב, --) his dwelling.

Job 24:13, 18: (3:10; LB)

¹³There are those who rebel against the light, who are not acquainted with its ways, and do not stay in its paths (=LB). ¹⁸You say, 'They are swiftly carried away upon the face of the waters; their portion is *cursed* (קְלָל, καταραθείη) in the land; no treader turns toward their vineyards . . . .'

Prov 3:33: (3:8-14: CU/BL) (3:13f: RI)

The Lord's *curse* (אָרַר, κατάρα) is on the house of the wicked, but he *blesses* the abode of the righteous (=RI).

Neh 13:23, 25: ((3:10: LB) (1:8f: AC+CU)

²³In those days I also saw the Jews who had married women of Ashdod, Ammon and Moab (=AC; LB) . . . . ²⁵And I contended with them and *cursed* (קְלָל, (II Esdr 23:25) κατηρασάμην) them and beat some of them and pulled out their hair.

Sir 23:22, 26: (3:10: LB)

²²So it is with a woman who leaves her husband and provides an heir by a stranger (=LB) . . . . ²⁶She will leave her memory for a *curse* (κατάραν), and her disgrace will not be blotted out.

Sir 41:8-10: (3:10: LB) (1:8f: AP)

⁸Woe to you, ungodly men (=AP), who have forsaken the law of the Most High God (=LB)! ⁹When you are born, you are born to a *curse* (κατάραν); and when you die, a *curse* (κατάραν) is your lot. ¹⁰Whatever is from the dust returns to dust; so the ungodly go from *curse* (κατάρας) to destruction.

Wis 3:10, 12-13: (3:8-14: CU/BL) (3:10: f) (3:13f: RI) (1:8f: AP)

¹⁰But the ungodly (=AP) will be punished as their reasoning deserves, who disregarded the righteous man (=RI), and rebelled against the Lord (=AP);

¹²Their wives are foolish, and their children evil; their offspring are *accursed* (=f; ἐπικατάρατος) ¹³for *blessed* is the barren woman who is undefiled, who has not entered into a sinful union; she will have fruit when God examines souls.

Wis 14:7-9: (3:8-14: CU/BL) (3:10: f*) (3:13f: RI) (1:8f: AP)

⁷For *blessed* is the wood by which righteousness (=RI) comes. ⁸But the idol made with hands is *accursed* (=f*; ἐπικατάρατον), and so is he who made it; because he did the work, and the perishable thing was named a god (=AP). ⁹For equally hateful to God are the ungodly man and his ungodliness (=AP).

---

1 Enoch 22:10-11: (3:10: LB)

¹⁰In like manner, the sinners (=LB) are set apart when they die and are buried in the earth and judgment has not been executed upon them in their lifetime, ¹¹upon this great pain, until the great day of judgment - and to those who *curse* (τῶν κατηραμένων) (there will be) *plague* and pain forever, and the retribution of their spirits.

1 Enoch 27:1-2: (3:8-14: CU/BL) (3:10: LB)

¹At that moment, I said, "For what purpose does this *blessed* land, entirely filled with trees, (have) in its midst this *accursed* (κεκατηραμένη) valley?" ²Then, Uriel, one of the holy angels, who was with me, answered me and said to me, "This *accursed* valley is for those *accursed* forever; here will gather together all (those) *accursed* ones, those who speak with their mouth unbecoming words against the Lord and utter hard words concerning his glory" (=LB).

1 Enoch 41:8: (3:8-14: CU/BL) (3:10: LB) (3:13f: RI)

Surely the many changes of the sun have (both) a *blessing* and a *curse*, and the course of the moon's path is light to the righteous (on the one hand) (=RI) and darkness to the sinners (on the other) (=LB).

1 Enoch 59:1-2: (3:8-14: CU/BL)

¹In those days, my eyes saw the mysteries of lightnings, and of lights, and their judgments; they flash lights for a *blessing* or a *curse*, according to the will of the Lord of the Spirits. ²And there I (also) saw the secrets of the thunder and the secrets of (how when) it resounds in the heights of heaven its voice is heard (in) the earthly dwellings. He showed me whether the sound of the thunder is for peace and *blessing* or for a *curse*, according to the word of the Lord of the Spirits.

1 Enoch 97:10: (3:8-14: CU/(BL)) (3:10: LB) (1:8f: AC+CU)

. . . For your wealth shall not endure but it shall take off from you quickly for you have acquired it all unjustly (=AC; LB), and you shall be given over to a great *curse* (κατάραν). (Cf. the blessings for the righteous in 96:1-3)

1 Enoch 98:4: (3:8-14: CU/(BL)) (3:10: LB, HK)

I have sworn unto you sinners: In the same manner that a mountain has never turned into a servant, nor shall a hill (ever) become a maidservant of a woman; likewise, neither has sin been exported into the world. It is the people who have themselves invented it. And those who commit it (=LB) shall come under a great *curse* (=HK; κατάραν). (Cf. the blessings for the righteous in 99:10)

Jub. 30:14-15: (3:10: LB)

¹⁴And Israel will not be cleansed from this defilement if there is in it a woman from the daughters of gentiles or one who has given any of his daughters to a man who is from any of the gentiles (=LB). ¹⁵For there will be plague upon plague and *curse* upon *curse*, and every judgement, and plague, and *curse* will come.

4 Macc. 2:18-20: (3:10: f, LB)

¹⁸For the temperate mind, as I have said, has the power to triumph over the passions, to transform some of them and quell others. ¹⁹How else did our surpassingly wise father Jacob blame Simeon and Levi and their friends for slaughtering the whole tribe of the Schechemites (=LB) without any appeal to reason, and declare, 'Accursed (=f; ἐπικατάρατος) be their rage?' ²⁰Surely if reason could not control anger, he would not have spoken in this way.

Prop. 1:9: (3:10: LB)

And because Hezekiah showed the gentiles the secrets of David and Solomon and defiled the bones of the place of his fathers (=LB), God *swore* (ἐπηράσατο) that his offspring should be enslaved to his enemies, and God made him sterile from that day.

Ps. Sol. 3:9-12: (3:8-14: (CU/BL)) (3:10: LB) (3:13f: RI, L)

⁹The sinner stumbles and *curses* (καταρᾶται) his life, the day of his birth, and his mother's pains. ¹⁰He adds sin upon sin in his life (=LB); he falls — his fall is serious — and he will not get up. ¹¹The destruction of the sinner is forever, and he will not be remembered when (God) looks after the righteous (=RI). ¹²This is the share of sinners forever, but those who fear the Lord shall rise up to eternal life, (=(BL), L), and their life shall be in the Lord's light, and it shall never end.

Ps. Sol. 4:12-15, 23: (3:8-14: CU/BL) (3:10: LB)

¹²He is satiated with lawless actions at one (place), and (then) his eyes are on another house to destroy it with agitating words (=LB), ¹³With all this his soul, like Hades, is not satisfied. ¹⁴Lord, let his part be in disgrace before you; may he go out groaning and return *cursing* (ἐν ἀρᾷ) ¹⁵Lord, may his life be in pain and poverty and anxiety . . . .

²³*Blessed* are those who fear God in their innocence . . . .

T. Judah 11:3-5: (3:10: LB) (1:8f: AC+CU)

³While I was absent, she went off and brought from Canaan a wife for Shelom (=AC; LB). ⁴When I realized what she had done, I pronounced a *curse* (κατηρασάμην) on her in the anguish of my soul, ⁵and she died in her wickedness, together with her children.

Abr 40: (3:10: LB)

That time bore its harvest of iniquities, and every country and nation and city and household and every private individual was filled with evil practices (=LB) . . . leaving nothing undone which could lead to a guilty and *accursed* (ἐπάρατον) life.

Conf 196: (3:8-14: CU/(BL)) (3:10: LB) (1:8f: AP)

But God the Master-planter wills to sow noble living throughout the All (=(BL)), and to disperse and banish from the Commonwealth of the world the impiety which He holds *accursed* (ἐπάρατον). Thus the evil ways which hate virtue may at least cease to build the city of vice (=LB) and the tower of godlessness (=AP).

Congr 56–57: (3:8–14: CU/(BL)) (3:10: LB) (1:8f: AP)

⁵⁶The mind which truly loves God, that has the vision of Him, He "plants in," as a branch of goodly birth (=(BL)) . . . .

⁵⁷On the other hand he (=God) banishes the unjust and godless souls from himself to the furthest bounds, and disperses them to the place of pleasures and lusts and injustices. That place is most fitly called the place of the impious (=AP), but it is not that mythical place of the impious in Hades. For the true Hades is the life of the bad, a life of damnation and blood-guiltiness (=LB), the victim of every *curse* (ἀραῖς).

Decal 87: (3:8–14: CU/(BL))

For every soul has for its birthfellow and housemate a monitor whose way is to admit nothing that calls for censure . . . . And if he has the strength to persuade it, he rejoices and makes peace (=(BL)). But if he cannot, he makes war to the bitter end, never leaving it alone by day or night, but plying it with stabs and deadly wounds until he breaks the thread of its miserable and *ill-starred* (ἐπάρατον) life.

Post 80–81: (3:8–14: CU/(BL)) (3:10: LB)

⁸⁰Now, if a man brings a correct and unerring judgement to bear only on ends that are good, I for my part set this man down as happy (=(BL)) . . . .

⁸¹But if a man has used a natural aptness and readiness not only for good and worthy ends, but also for their opposites (=LB), treating as alike things widely different, let him be deemed unhappy. Certainly the words in the Babel passage are of the nature of a *curse* (ἀράς), where we read "nothing shall be wanting to them, which they purpose to do."

Post 159: (3:10: LB)

. . . the bodily "good things," and yet all these are shared with others by men abominable (=LB) and *accursed* (ἐπάρατον); whereas, had they been good things, no bad man would have had part in any of them.

Post 176: (3:10: LB)

. . . when he has become fairly soaked, and is under the fumes of his debauch, they (=evil intentions) will become pregnant, and there will be guilt in their travailing (=LB), and a *curse* (ἐπαράτοις) upon their offspring.

Sobr 67: (3:10: LB)

. . . nor think that health or wealth or the like, which are shared by the most wicked (=LB) and *abominable* (ἐπαρατοτάτων) of men, are true goods.

Spec 1:188: (3:10: LB)

The one (=kid) on whom the lot fell was to be sacrificed to God, the other was to be sent out into a trackless and desolate wilderness bearing on its back the *curses* (ἀράς) which had lain upon the transgressors (=LB) who have now been purified by conversion to the better life and through their new obedience have washed away their old dis-obedience to the law (=LB).

Spec 2:50: (3:10: LB)

He not only attacks in his fury the marriage-beds of others, but even plays the pederast and forces the male type of nature to debase and convert itself into the feminine form (=LB), just to indulge a polluted and *accursed* (ἐπαράτῳ) passion.

Spec 3:61: (3:10: LB)

But if thou hast set at naught thy husband and eagerly gratified thy new desires

(=LB), . . . be well assured that thou hast laid thyself open to every *curse* (ἀραῖς), and the signs of their fulfilment thou wilt exhibit in thy body.

Spec 4:91: (3:10: LB)
    And when it (=desire) takes hold of the region of the belly, it produces gourmands, insatiable, debauched, eagerly pursuing a loose and dissolute life (=LB) . . . all this finally resulting in an unhappy and *accursed* (ἐπάρατον) life which is more painful than any death.

CD xii.20–22:
    20...And these are the precepts 21in which the Master shall walk in his commerce with all the living in accordance with the statute proper to every age. And in accordance with this statute 22shall the seed of Israel walk and they shall not be *cursed* (ארר).

1QM xiii.1–6: (3:8–14: CU/BL) (3:10: f*, LB) (3:13f: RI) (1:8f: AN)
    1(The High Priest) shall come, and his brethren the Priests and the Levites, and all the elders of the army shall be with him; and standing, they shall *bless* the God of Israel and all His works of truth, and shall *execrate* (זעם) 2Satan there and all the spirits of his company. Speaking, they shall say:
    Blessed be the God of Israel for all His holy purpose and for His works of truth! *Blessed* be 3all those who <serve> Him in righteousness (=RI) and who know Him by faith!
    4*Cursed* (=f*; ארור) be Satan for his sinful purpose and may he be *execrated* (זעם) for his wicked rule! *Cursed* (AN; ארור) be all the spirits of his company for their ungodly purpose 5and may they be *execrated* (זעם) for all their service of uncleanness (=LB)! Truly they are the company of Darkness, but the company of God is one of <eternal> light.

4QpPs37 iii.9–13: (3:8–14: CU/BL) (3:10: LB)
    9. . . Truly, those whom He <*blesses* shall possess> the land, but those whom he *curses* (קלל) <shall be cut off>.
    10Interpreted, this concerns the congregation of the Poor, who <shall possess> the whole world as an inheritance . . .
    11. . . <But those who> 12shall be cut off, they are the violent <of the nation and> the wicked of Israel (=LB); they shall be cut off and blotted out 13for ever.

11Q Temple 64:9–12: (3:10: LB)
    9. . . If a man is guilty of a capital crime (=LB) and flees 10(abroad) to the nations, and *curses* (קלל) his people, the children of Israel, you shall hang him also on the tree, 11 and he shall die. But his body shall not stay overnight on the tree. Indeed you shall bury him on the same day. For 12he who is hanged on the tree is *accursed* (קלל) of God and men.

Ant 7:39: (3:10: LB) (1:8f: AC+CU)
    He (=David) also called down terrible *curses* (ἀράς) upon the man who had murdered him (=Abenner) (=LB) and declared his whole house and his accomplices liable to the penalties for having caused his death (=AC, LB); for he was concerned that he himself should not seem to have brought this about in violation of the sworn pledges which he had given Abenner.

Ant 18:346: (3:10: LB) (1:8f: AC+CU)
...In fact, he (=Anilaeus) even put to death a man of highest rank because he had
spoken too frankly (=LB). He, fixing his mind on loyalty to the laws and on vengeance
against his slayer, pronounced a *curse* (ἐπηράσατο) on Anilaeus himself and Asinaeus and
all their companions, to suffer a similar end at the hands of their enemies — the brothers
because they had been the leaders in transgressing the laws (=AC; LB), the others
because they failed to come to his rescue when they saw how he was treated for
championing the Law.

Bell 1:480: (3:10: LB)
Another calumny came simultaneously to inflame the king's (=Herod's) wrath. He
was told that the young princes had their mother's name perpetually on their lips, *cursing*
(ἐπαρωμένους) him while they bemoaned her (=LB, cf. that Herod killed her).

Bell 4:360-62: (3:10: LB)
360 . . . and then proceeded to murder him (=LB). 361In his dying moments Niger
imprecated (ἐπηράσατο) upon their heads the vengeance of the Romans, famine and
pestilence to add to the horrors of war, and, to crown all, internecine strife; 362all which
curses (--) upon the wretches were ratified by God . . . .

4: CURSES IN SOCIAL RELATIONS

Oaths

Gen 24:40-41:
40But he (=Isaac) said to me, ". . . you shall take a wife for my son from my
kindred and from my father's house; 41then you will be free from my *oath* (אלה, τῆς
ἀρᾶς), when you come to my kindred; and if they will not give her to you, you will be
free from my *oath* (אלה, ὁρκισμοῦ)."

Gen 26:28-29:
28They said, "We see plainly that the Lord is with you; so we say, let there be an
oath (אלה, ἀρά) between you and us . . . .
29. . . You are now the *blessed* of the Lord."

Josh 6:26: (3:10: F)
Joshua laid an oath upon them at that time, saying, "*Cursed* (=F; ארור,
ἐπικατάρατος) before the Lord be the man that rises up and rebuilds this city, Jericho.
At the cost of his first-born shall he lay its foundation, And at the cost of his youngest son
shall he set up its gates."

Judg 5:23-24: (3:8-14: CU/BL) (3:10:f*)
23*Curse* (=f*; ארר, καταράσασθε) Meroz, says the angel of the Lord, *curse* (ארר +
ארור, καταράσει καταράσασθε) bitterly its inhabitants, because they came not to the help
of the Lord, to the help of the Lord against the mighty. 24Most *blessed* of women be Jael
. . . .

Judg 21:17-18: (3:10: F)
17And they said, "There must be an inheritance for the survivors of Benjamin, that a
tribe be not blotted out from Israel. 18Yet we cannot give them wives of our daughters."
For the people of Israel had sworn, "*Cursed* (=F; ארור, ἐπικατάρατος) be he who gives a
wife to Benjamin."

1 Sam 14:24, 28: (3:10: F)

²⁴Saul laid an *oath* (אלה, ἀρᾶται) on the people, saying: "*Cursed* (=F; ארור, ἐπικατάρατος) be the man who eats food until it is evening and I am avenged on my enemies."

²⁸Then one of the people said, "Your father strictly charged the people with an oath, saying, '*Cursed* (=F; ארור, ἐπικατάρατος) be the man who eats food this day.'"

Ezek 17:13-23: (3:8-14: CU-(BL)) (3:10: LB) (3:13: (BG)) (1:8f: AC+CU, AP)

¹³And he (=the king of Babylon) took one of seed royal and made a covenant with him, putting him under *oath* (אלה, ἀρᾷ) . . . .

¹⁶As I live, says the Lord God, surely in the place where the king dwells who made him king, whose *oath* (אלה, ἀράν) he despised, and whose covenant with him he broke, in Babylon he shall die . . . .

¹⁸Because he despised the *oath* (אלה, ὁρκωμοσίαν) and broke the covenant, because he gave his hand and yet did all these things, he shall not escape.

¹⁹Therefore thus says the Lord God: As I live, surely my *oath* (אלה, ὁρκωμοσίαν) which he despised, and my covenant which he broke (=LB) I will requite upon his head. ²⁰I will spread my net over him, and he shall be taken in my snare . . . for the treason he has committed against me (=AC; AP).

. . . ²³on the mountain height of Israel will I plant it, that it might bring forth boughs and bear fruit, and become a noble cedar (=(BL)); and under it will dwell all kinds of beasts, in the shade of its branches birds of every sort will nest (=(BG)).

Hos 4:2-3: (3:10: LB)

²There is *swearing* (אלה, ἀρά) lying, killing, stealing, and committing adultery; they break all bounds and murder follows murder (=LB). ³Therefore the land mourns, and all who dwell in it languish . . . .

Hos 10:4:

They utter mere words; with empty *oaths* (אלה, --) they make covenants; so judgment springs up like poisonous weeds in the furrows of the field.

---

1 Enoch Fragment from Syncellos 1-2: (tr. Uhlig) (1:8f: SI)

¹Und wegen des Berges aber, auf dem sie schwuren und sich gegenseitig durch *Verwünschungen* verplichteten (=SI), dass sie bis in die Ewigkeit nicht davon ablassen würden: ²Kälte und Schnee und Reif und Tau sollen nicht auf ihn herabkommen, nur der *Fluch* (κατάραν) soll auf ihn herabkommen, bis zum Tag des grossen Gerichtes.

4QTest 21-24: (3:10: F, LB) (1:8f: SE)

²¹When Joshua had finished offering praise and thanksgiving, ²²he said: *Cursed* (=F; ארור) be the man who rebuilds this city!   May he lay its foundation ²³on his first-born, and set its gate upon his youngest son.   Behold, an *accursed* (ארור) man, a man of Satan, ²⁴has risen to become a fowler's net to his people, and a cause of destruction to all his neighbours (=SE).   And <his brother> arose ²⁵<and ruled>, both being instruments of violence (=LB).

Ant 5:31:

As for the city . . . he (=Joshua) pronounced *imprecations* (ἀράς), that if he laid foundations of walls he should be bereft of his firstborn and if he completed the walls he should lose the youngest of his sons. Nor was this *curse* (ἀράς) unregarded by the Deity, but in the sequel we shall recount the calamity which it entailed.

Ant 6:117–128: (3:10: LB) (1:8f: f)
[117]For, in his (=Saul's) desire to avenge himself and to exact punishment from the Philistines, he invoked a *curse* (ἐπαρᾶται) upon the Hebrews, that should any man (=f) desist from slaughtering the foe and take food, before oncoming night should stay them from carnage and the pursuit of the enemy, he should be *accursed* (ἐπάρατος) . . . [118]. . . Saul's son, not having heard his father's *curse* (ἀράς) nor the people's approbation thereof, broke off a piece of a honeycomb and began to eat it. [119]But learning, as he did so, how his father under a dire *curse* (ἀράς) had forbidden any man to taste aught before sundown, he ceased to eat but said that his father's interdict was not right . . . .
[126]Being asked by his father wherein he had gone astray and of what wrong or unholy act in all his life he was conscious (=LB), "Of nothing, father," said he, "save that yesterday, all ignorant of that *imprecation* (ἀράν) and oath of thine, while in pursuit of the enemy, I tasted a honeycomb."
[128]Thereupon all the people were moved to grief and sympathy and they swore that they would not suffer Jonathan, the author of that victory, to die. Thus then did they snatch him from his father's *curse* (ἀράς), and themselves offered prayers for the young man to God, that He would grant him absolution from his sin.

Ant 6:276: (1:8f: SI)
Then, having renewed his (=Jonathan's) oaths of life-long mutual affection and fidelity, and having called God to witness the *curses* (ἐπηράσατο) which he invoked upon himself should he violate their covenant and change to the contrary (=SI) . . . .

Bell 1:260: (1:8f: AC+CU)
. . . Immediately after, certain Parthians who had been left behind, with orders to do so, arrested Phasael and Hyrcanus, the prisoners *cursing* (καταρωμένους) them bitterly for their perjury and breach of faith (=AC).

Unknown Thief

Lev 5:1: (3:10: LB)
If any one sins in that he hears a public *adjuration* (אלה, ὁρκισμοῦ) to testify and though he is a witness, whether he has seen or come to know the matter, yet does not speak (=LB), he shall bear his iniquity.

Judg 17:2: (3:8–14: CU/BL) (3:10: LB)
And he (=Micah) said to his mother, "The eleven hundred pieces of silver which were taken from you (=LB), about which you uttered a *curse* (אלה, (B)ἠράσω (A)ἐξώρκισας), and also spoke it in my ears, behold, the silver is with me; I took it." And his mother said, "*Blessed* be my son by the Lord."

Prov 29:24: (3:10: LB)
The partner of a thief (=LB) hates his own life; he hears the *curse* (אלה, ὅρκου), but discloses nothing.

CD ix.10–12: (3:10: LB)
[10]. . . When anything is lost, [11]and it is not known who has stolen it from the prop-

erty of the camp in which it was stolen (=LB), its owner shall ¹²pronounce a *curse* (אלה), and any man who, on hearing (it), knows but does not tell, shall himself be guilty.

Parent-Child

Gen 27:12–13: (3:8–14: CU/BL)
(Jacob said) ". . . ¹²Perhaps my father will feel me, and I shall seem to be mocking him, and bring a *curse* (קללה, κατάραν) upon myself and not a *blessing*." ¹³His mother said to him, "Upon me be your *curse* (קללה, κατάρα) my son; only obey my word, and go, fetch them to me."

Exod 21:17:
Whoever *curses* (קלל, κακολογῶν) his father or his mother shall be put to death.

Lev 20:9:
For every one who *curses* (קלל, κακῶς εἴπῃ) his father or his mother shall be put to death; he has *cursed* (קלל, κακῶς εἶπεν) his father or his mother, his blood is upon him.

Prov 20:20:
If one *curses* (קלל, (20:9a) κακολογοῦντος) his father or his mother, his lamp will be put out in the utter darkness.

Prov 30:11: (3:8–14: CU/BL)
There are those who *curse* (קלל, καταρᾶται) their fathers and do not *bless* their mothers.

Sir 3:9, 16: (3:8–14: CU/BL) (1:8f: AP)
⁹For a father's *blessing* strengthens the houses of the children, but a mother's *curse* (κατάρα) uproots their foundations.
¹⁶Whoever forsakes his father is like a blasphemer (=AP), and whoever angers his mother is *cursed* (κεκατηραμένος) by the Lord.

Ruler-People

Exod 22:27:
You shall not *revile* (קלל, κακολογήσεις) God, nor *curse* (ארר, κακῶς ἐρεῖς) a ruler of your people.

Judg 9:27–28:
²⁷. . . (they) ate and drank and *reviled* (קלל, κατηρῶντο) Abimelech. ²⁸ And Gaal the son of Ebel said: "Who is Abimelech, and who are we of Shechem, that we should serve him?"

1 Sam 26:19: (1:8f: AC+CU, AP)
(David said) . . . If it is the Lord who has stirred you up against me, may he accept an offering, but if it is men, may they be *cursed* (ארר, ἐπικατάρατοι) before the Lord, for they have driven me out this day that I should have no share in the heritage of the Lord (=AC), saying, 'Go, serve other gods' (=AP) . . . ."

2 Sam 16:5-13: (3:10: LB) (1:8f: AC+CU)
⁵When King David came to Bahurim, there came out a man . . . and as he came he *cursed* (קלל, καταράσθαι) continually . . . . ⁷And Shimei said as he *cursed*, "Begone, begone, you man of blood (=AC; LB), you worthless fellow! ⁸The Lord has avenged upon you all the blood of the house of Saul (=AC; LB) . . . ." ⁹Then Abishai the son of Zeruiah said to the king, "Why should this dead dog *curse* my lord the king? . . . ¹⁰But the king said, ". . . If he is *cursing* because the Lord has said to him '*Curse* David,' who then shall say 'Why have you done so?'. . . ¹²It may be that the Lord will look upon my affliction, and that the Lord will repay me with good for this *cursing* of me today." ¹³So David and his men went on the road, while Shimei went along on the hillside opposite him and *cursed* as he went, and threw stones at him and flung dust.

2 Sam 19:22:
Abishai . . . answered, "Shall not Shimei be put to death for this, because he *cursed* (קלל, κατηράσατο) the Lord's anointed?"

1 Kings 2:8:
(David said) And there is also with you Shimei . . . who *cursed* (קלל, κατηράσατο) me with a grievous *curse* (קללה, κατάραν) on the day when I went to Mahanaim.

Isa 8:21:
They will pass through the land, greatly distressed and hungry; and when they are hungry, they will be enraged and will *curse* (קלל, κακῶς ἐρεῦτε) their king and their God.

Eccl 10:20:
Even in your thought, do not *curse* (קלל, καταράσῃ) the king, nor in your bedchamber *curse* the rich; for a bird of the air will carry your voice, or some winged creature tell the matter.

Ant 7:208: (3:10: LB)
He (=Samuis) also bade him (=David) leave the country as one under a ban and *accursed* (ἐπάρατον); and he gave thanks to God for having deprived David of his kingdom and for having exacted punishment of him, through his own son, for the crimes which he had committed against his master (=LB).

Ant 17:88: (3:10: LB)
But Antipater could now foresee the evil fate in store of him, for no one came near him or greeted him with good wishes and words of favourable omen, as they had done on his departure. On the contrary, they did not restrain themselves from receiving him with *curses* (ἀραῖς), thinking that he was there to pay the penalty for his crimes against his brothers (=LB).

Rich-Poor

Prov 11:26: (3:8-14: CU/BL)
The people *curse* (קבב, --) him who holds back grain, but a *blessing* is on the head of him who sells it.

Prov 28:27: (3:8–14: CU/(BL))
He who gives to the poor will not want (=(BL)), but he who hides his eyes will get many a *curse* (ארר, ἀπορίᾳ).

Eccl 10:20:
Even in your thought, do not *curse* the king, nor in your bedchamber *curse* (קלל, καταράσῃ) the rich; for a bird of the air will carry your voice, or some winged creature tell the matter.

Sir 4:5–6:
⁵Do not avert your eye from the needy, nor give a man occasion to *curse* (καταράσασθαι) you; ⁶for if in bitterness of soul he calls down a *curse* (καταρωμένου) upon you, his Creator will hear his prayer.

Sir 29:6:
If the lender exerts pressure, he will hardly get back half, and will regard this as a windfall. If he does not, the borrower has robbed him of his money, and he has needlessly made him his enemy; he will repay him with *curses* (κατάρας) and reproaches, and instead of glory will repay him with dishonor.

Sir 34:24:
When one prays and another *curses* ((31, 29) καταρώμενος), to whose voice will the Lord listen?

Bell 6:203:
With deep indignation in her heart, the poor woman constantly abused and *cursed* (καταρωμένη) these extortioners and so incensed them against her.

Jews-Gentiles

Josh 9:22–24: (3:10: f*) (1:8f: AC+CU)
²²Joshua summoned them (=Gibeonites), and he said to them, "Why did you deceive us, saying, 'We are very far from you,' when you dwell among us? (=AC) ²³Now therefore you are *cursed* (f*; ארור, ἐπικατάρατοι), and some of you shall always be slaves, hewers of wood and drawers of water for the house of my God."

1 Sam 17:43:
. . . And the Philistine *cursed* (קלל, κατηράσατο) David by his gods.

Jer 49:13: (3:13f: GK)
For I have sworn by myself, says the Lord, that Bozrah shall become a horror, a taunt, a waste, and a *curse* (=GK; קללה, (30:7) κατάρασιν); and all her cities shall be perpetual wastes."

---

2 Macc 12:35:
. . . wishing to take the *accursed* (κατάρατον) man (=Gorgias of Idumea) alive
. . . .

Jub. 24:27-29, 32-33: (3:13f: RI)

²⁷And Isaac knew on that day that under pressure he swore an oath to them to make peace with them. ²⁸And Isaac *cursed* the Philistines on that day, and he said, "*Cursed* be the Philistines for the day of wrath and anger from among all the nations. May the Lord make them as scorn and a *curse* and (the object of) wrath and anger at the hands of the sinners, the nations, and in the hands of the Kittim. ²⁹. . . may the righteous people (=RI) uproot them from beneath the sky with judgement . . . ."

³². . . And neither name nor seed will be left for them in all the earth, because they shall walk in an eternal *curse*. ³³And thus it is written and engraved concerning him in the heavenly tablets to be done to him in the day of judgment so that they might be uprooted from the earth.

Ant 6:186:

. . . This roused Goliath's anger, and he called down *curses* (ἀράς) upon him in his god's name and threatened to give his flesh to the beasts of earth and the birds of heaven to rend asunder.

Ant 18:287: (3:10: HK) (1:8f: f)

. . . For if he (=f) should slay them — and they would certainly not give up their accustomed manner of worship without war — he would be deprived of their revenue and would be put under the ban of the *curse* (=HK; ἀράς) for all time to come.

Ap 1:203-4:

²⁰³. . . The Jew, without saying a word, drew his bow, shot and struck the bird, and killed it. ²⁰⁴The seer and some others were indignant, and heaped *curses* (κατᾰρωμένων) upon him.

Bell 7:112-13:

¹¹²On his way he (=Titus) visited Jerusalem, and contrasting the sorry scene of desolation before his eyes with the former splendour of the city . . . .

¹¹³. . . heaping *curses* (ἐπαρώμενος) upon the criminal authors of the revolt, who had brought this chastisement upon it . . . .

Other Relations

Lev 19:14:

You shall not *curse* (קלל, κακῶς ἐρεῖς) the deaf or put a stumbling block before the blind, but you shall fear your God: I am the Lord.

Prov 24:24-25: (3:8-14: CU/BL)

²⁴He who says to the wicked, "You are innocent," will be *cursed* (קנב, ἐπικατάρατος) by peoples, abhorred by nations; ²⁵but those who rebuke the wicked will have delight, and a good *blessing* will be upon him.

Prov 27:14: (3:8-14: CU/BL)

He who *blesses* his neighbor with a loud voice, rising early in the morning, will be counted as *cursing* (קללה, καταρωμένου).

Prov 30:10:
Do not slander a servant to his master, lest he *curse* (קלל, καταράσηται) you, and you be held guilty.

Eccl 7:20–22: (3:13f: RI)
²⁰Surely there is not a righteous man (=RI) on earth who does good and never sins. ²¹Do not give heed to all the things that men say, lest you hear your servant *cursing* (קלל, καταρωμένου) you; ²²your heart knows that many times you have yourself *cursed* (קלל, κατηράσω) others.

Sir 28:13, 19: (3:8–14: CU/(BL)) (3:10: LB)
¹³*Curse* (καταράσασθε) the whisperer and the deceiver (=LB), for he has destroyed many who were at peace.
¹⁹Happy (=(BL)) is the man who is protected from it, who has not been exposed to its anger . . . .

5: OTHER CURSE TEXTS

Lev 24:11–23:
¹¹and the Israelite woman's son blasphemed the Name, and *cursed* (קלל, κατηράσατο).
¹⁴And the Lord said to Moses, "Bring out of the camp him who *cursed* (קלל, καταρασάμενον); and let all who heard him lay their hands upon his head, and let all the congregation stone him. ¹⁵And say to the people of Israel, Whoever *curses* (קלל, καταράσηται) his God shall bear his sin..."
²³So Moses spoke to the people of Israel; and they brought him who had *cursed* (קלל, καταρασάμενον) out of the camp, and stoned him with stones.

1 Sam 3:13:
(The Lord said) . . . And I tell him that I am about to punish his house for ever, for the iniquity which he knew, because his sons were *blaspheming* (קלל, κακολογοῦντες) God, and he did not restrain them.

2 Kings 2:23–24:
²³He (=Elisha) went up from there to Bethel; and while he was going up on the way, some small boys came out of the city and jeered at him, saying, "Go up you bald-head! Go up, you baldhead!" ²⁴And he turned around, and when he saw them, he *cursed* (קלל, κατηράσατο) them in the name of the Lord. And two she-bears came out of the woods and tore forty-two of the boys.

Jer 15:10:
Woe is me, my mother, that you bore me, a man of strife and contention to the whole land! I have not lent, nor have I borrowed, yet all of them *curse* (קלל, καταρωμένοις) me.

Jer 20:14–15: (3:10: f*)
¹⁴*Cursed* (=f*; ארור, ἐπικατάρατος) be the day on which I was born! The day when my mother bore me, let it not be *blessed*! ¹⁵*Cursed* (=f*; ארור, ἐπικατάρατος) be the man who brought the news to my father, "A son is born to you," making him very glad.

Jer 48:10: (3:10: F)

Cursed (=F; אָרוּר, (31:10) ἐπικατάρατος) is he who does the work of the Lord with slackness; and *cursed* (=F; אָרוּר, --) is he who keeps back his sword from bloodshed.

Ps 10:7: (3:10: LB)

His mouth is filled with *cursing* (אָלָה, (9:28) ἀράς) and deceit and oppression; under his tongue are mischief and iniquity (=LB).

Ps 59:13-14: (3:10: LB)

¹³For the sin of their mouths, the words of their lips, let them be trapped in their pride. For the *cursing* (אָלָה, (58:13) ἀράς) and lies which they utter (=LB), ¹⁴consume them in wrath, consume them till they are no more, that men may know that God rules over Jacob to the ends of the earth.

Ps 62:5: (3:8-14: CU/BL)

They take pleasure in falsehood. They *bless* him with their mouths, but inwardly they *curse* (קָלַל, (61:5) κατηρῶντο).

Ps 109:17-19, 28: (3:8-14:CU/BL) (3:10: LB)

¹⁷For he did not remember to show kindness but pursued the poor and needy and the brokenhearted to their death (=LB). ¹⁸He loved to *curse* (קְלָלָה, (108:17) κατάραν); let *curses* (--, --) come on him! He did not like *blessing*; may it be far from him! ¹⁹He clothed himself with *cursing* (קְלָלָה, (108:18) κατάραν) as his coat, may it soak into his body like water, like oil into his bones!

²⁸Let them *curse* (קָלַל, (108:28) καταράσονται), but do thou *bless*.

Job 3:1, 7-8:

¹After this Job opened his mouth and *cursed* (קָלַל, κατηράσατο) the day of his birth.

⁷Yea, let that night be barren; let no joyful cry be heard in it. ⁸Let those *curse* (קָנַב, καταράσαιτο) it who *curse* (אָרַר, καταρώμενος) the day, who are skilled to rouse up Leviathan.

Job 31:30:

I have not let my mouth sin by asking for his life with a *curse* (אָלָה, κατάραν);

Prov 26:2:

Like a sparrow in its flitting, like a swallow in its flying, a *curse* (קְלָלָה, ἀρά) that is causeless does not alight.

Ep Jer 66: (3:8-14: CU/BL)

For they (=the gods) can neither *curse* (καταράσωνται) nor *bless* kings.

Sir 21:27: (1:8f: AP)

When an ungodly man (=AP) *curses* (καταρᾶσθαι) his adversary, he *curses* (καταρᾶται) his own soul.

Sir 23:14:

Remember your father and mother when you sit among great men; lest you be forgetful in their presence, and be deemed a fool on account of your habits; then you will wish that you had never been born, and you will *curse* (καταράσῃ) the day of your birth.

Sir 33:12: (3:8–14: CU/BL)

[12]Some of them he *blessed* and exalted, and some of them he made holy and brought near to himself; but some of them he *cursed* (κατηράσατο) and brought low, and he turned them out of their place.

Ep. Arist. 311:

There was general approval of what they said, and they commanded that a *curse* (διαράσασθαι) should be laid, as was their custom, on anyone who should alter the version by any addition or change to any part of the written text, or any deletion either. This was a good step taken, to ensure that the words were preserved completely and permanently in perpetuity.

Mart. Isa. 5:9:

And Isaiah answered (the false prophet Belkira) and said, "If it is within my power to say, '*Condemned* and *cursed* be you, and all your hosts, and all your house . . . .'"

Prop. 22:7, 13:

[7]When children treated him disrespectfully, he (=Elisha) *cursed* (κατηράσατο) them, and two bears came out and tore to pieces forty-two of them.

[13]When his servant, named Gehazi, went to Naaman secretly, against his wishes, and asked for silver, and later upon returning denied it, Elisha rebuked and *cursed* (κατηράσατο) him, and he became a leper.

T. Benj. 6:5:

The good set of mind does not talk from both sides of its mouth; Praises and *curses* (κατάρας), abuse and honor, calm and strife, hypocrisy and truth, poverty and wealth, but it has one disposition, uncontaminated and pure, toward all men.

T. Job 13:4–5:

[4]And my servants, who prepared the meals for the widows and the poor, grew tired and [5]would *curse* (κατηρῶντο) me in contempt . . . .

Conf 44, 47, 51: (3:10: LB)

[44]The truth of my words is attested . . . by a chorister of the prophetic company (=Jeremiah), who possessed by divine inspiration spoke thus: ". . . I did not owe, nor did they owe to me, nor did my strength fail from their *curses* (καταρῶν)."

[47]Men plunder, rob, kidnap, spoil, sack, outrage, maltreat, violate (=LB) . . . .

[51]"Nor did my strength fail from the *curses* (ἀρῶν) which they laid upon me," but with all my might and main I clung to the divine truths . . . .

Decal 74–75:

[74]Pray you therefore that you may be made like your images and thus enjoy supreme happiness . . . . [75]As a matter of fact I expect that such advice would be received with indignation as savouring of *imprecations* (κατάραις) rather than of prayers . . . .

Migr 111:

Do you not see the toadies who by day and night batter to pieces and wear out the ears of those on whom they fawn, not content with just assenting to everything they say, but spinning out long speeches and declaiming and many a time uttering prayers with their voice, but never ceasing to *curse* (καταρώμενοι) with their heart?

Mos 2:196–204: (3:10: LB) (1:8f: AP)

[196]And, lo, this half-bred person, having a quarrel with someone of the nation that has vision and knowledge, losing in his anger all control over himself, and also urged by fondness for Egyptian atheism, extended his impiety from earth to heaven (=AP), and with his soul and tongue and all the organism of speech alike *accursed* (ἐπαράτῳ), foul, abominable, in the superabundance of his manifold wickedness *cursed* (καταρασάμενος) Him.

[198]And yet even reviling is a lesser sin compared with *cursing* (κατάρας) . . . .
[199]Answer me, thou man, Does anyone *curse* (καταρᾶται) God? Then what other god does he call on to make good the *curse* (ἀράς), or is it clear that he invokes the help of God against Himself?

[203]And so on this occasion the following law was promulgated: Whoever *curses* (καταράσηται) God, let him bear the guilt of his sin, but he that nameth the name of the Lord (=LB) let him die. [204]. . . Thou hast held the naming to be worse than the *cursing* (καταρᾶσθαι).

Prob 137: (3:8–14: CU/(BL))

And this doctrine that freedom is glorious and honourable (=(BL)), slavery *execrable* (ἐπάρατον) and disgraceful, is attested by cities and nations . . . .

Somn 2:237:

What then could make the wicked mind, fit subject for every manner of *curse* (ἀραῖς), think that he could stand alone, when he is carried to and fro as in a flood . . . .

Spec 2:129:

Parents pray that they may leave behind them alive the children they have begotten to succeed to their name, race and property, and the *imprecations* (ἀραῖς) of their implacable enemies are just the opposite, that the sons and daughters may die before their parents.

1QS vii.1: (Trans. Lohse) (3:8–14: CU/BL)

[1]Und wenn er einen *Fluch* (קלל) ausgesprochen hat, etwa weil er durch eine Notlage verängstigt war, oder welchen Anlass er auch haben mag, — und er liest im Buch oder spricht den *Segensspruch*, so soll man ihn ausschliessen, [2]und er soll nicht wieder in den Rat der Gemeinschaft zurückkehren.

11QTemple 60:17–20: (1:8f: AP)

[17]. . . There shall be found among you none who makes his son or daughter pass [18]through fire, nor an augur or a soothsayer, a diviner or a sorcerer, one who *casts spells* (אלה) or a medium, [19]or wizards or necromancers. For they are an abomination before me, all who practise [20]such things (=AP).

Ant 2:12:

But they (=Joseph's brothers), understanding that the vision predicted for him power and majesty and a destined supremacy over themselves, revealed nothing of this to Joseph, as though the dream were unintelligible to them; they uttered *prayers* (ἀράς), however, that nothing of what they augured might ever come to pass and continued to hate him yet the more.

Ant 4:50: (3:10: LB)

(Moses said) But if the accusations which they have made against me be true, then mayest thou keep these men free from all harm, and that destruction which I have *imprecated* (ἐπηρασάμην) on them, bring thou upon me . . . save thou this multitude that followeth thy commandments, preserving them unscathed and exempt from the punishment of them that have sinned (=LB).

Ant 9:64:

Now, when a certain woman cried out, "Have pity, my lord," he (=Joram) was angered, thinking that she was about to beg for food or the like, and called down God's *curse* (ἐπηράσατο) upon her, saying that he had neither threshing-floor nor wine-press from which he might give her something at her entreaty.

Ant 14:22: (3:13f: RI)

Now there was a certain Onias, who, being a righteous man (=RI) and dear to God . . . was taken to the camp of the Jews and was asked to place a *curse* (ἀράς) on Aristobulus and his fellow-rebels, just as he had, by his prayers, put an end to the rainless period.

Ant 17:3:

. . . for he (=Antipater) made it appear that he had denounced his brothers for the sake of assuring Herod's safety and not through enmity toward them and earlier toward his father. Such was the *accursed* (ἀραί) madness that drove him on.

Bell 3:297:

Cursing (καταρώμενοι), in their dying moments, not the Romans but their own people, in the end they all perished, to the number of twelve thousand.

Bell 6:46:

(Titus said) "I refrain on this occasion from an encomium on the warrior's death and the immortality reserved for those who fall in the frenzy of battle, but for any who think otherwise the worst I could wish (ἐπαρασαίμην) is that they may die in peace of disease, soul and body alike condemned to the tomb . . . ."

Bell 6:98:

His words (=Josephus' appeal) were received by the people in dejection and silence; but the tyrant, after many invectives and *imprecations* (καταρασάμενος) upon Josephus, ended by saying that he "could never fear capture, since the city was God's."

Bell 6:306-7: (3:8-14: CU/BL)

[306]During the whole period up to the outbreak of war he (=Jesus, son of Ananias) neither approached nor was seen talking to any of the citizens, but daily, like a prayer that he had conned, repeated his lament, "Woe to Jerusalem!" [307]He neither *cursed* (κατηρᾶτο) any of those who beat him from day to day, nor *blessed* those who offered him food: to all men that melancholy presage was his only reply.

Vita 101: (1:8f: SI)

. . . He (=John) ended with oaths and horrible *imprecations* (=SI; ἀράς), by which he thought to gain credit for the statements in his letter.

6: חרם/ἀνάθεμα TEXTS

(In this part the following abbreviations will appear: Hiph. = Hiphil; hoph. = hophal; sub. = substantive.)

Exod 22:19: (1:8f: f, AP)
Whoever sacrifices to any god (=f; AP), save to the Lord only, shall be *utterly destroyed* (hoph.; ὀλεθρευθήσεται).

Lev 27:28-29: (1:8f: f, AE)
²⁸But no *devoted* (sub.; ἀνάθεμα) thing that a man *devotes* (hiph.; ἀναθῇ) to the Lord, of anything that he has, whether of man or beast, or of his inherited field, shall be sold or redeemed; every *devoted* (sub.; ἀνάθεμα) thing is most holy to the Lord.
²⁹No one *devoted* (=f; AE; sub., --), who is to be utterly *destroyed* (hoph.; ἀνατεθῇ) from among men, shall be ransomed; he shall be put to death.

Num 21:2-3:
²And Israel vowed a vow to the Lord, and said, "If thou wilt indeed give this people into my hand, then I will *utterly destroy* (hiph.; ἀναθεματιῶ) their cities." ³And the Lord hearkened to the voice of Israel, and gave over the Canaanites; and they *utterly destroyed* (hiph.; ἀνεθεμάτισεν) them and their cities; so the name of the place was called Hormah (ἀνάθεμα).

Deut 2:34:
And we captured all his (=Sihon's) cities at that time and *utterly destroyed* (hiph.; ἐξωλεθρεύσαμεν) every city, men, women, and children; we left none remaining; . . .

Deut 3:6:
And we *utterly destroyed* (hiph.; ἐξωλεθρεύσαμεν) them (=Og's cities), as we did to Sihon the king of Heshbon, *destroying* (hiph.; ἐξωλεθρεύσαμεν) every city, men, women, and children.

Deut 7:1f, 25f: (1:8f: AE, AP)
¹When the Lord your God brings you into the land which you are entering to take possession of it, and clears away many nations before you, the Hittites, the Girgashites, the Amorites, the Canaanites, the Perizzites, the Hivites, and the Jebusites, seven nations greater and mightier than yourselves, ²and when the Lord your God gives them over to you, and you defeat them; then you must *utterly destroy* (sub. + hiph.; ἀφανισμῷ ἀφανιεῖς) them; you shall make no covenant with them, and show no mercy to them.
²⁵The graven images of their gods you shall burn with fire; you shall not covet the silver or the gold that is on them, or take it for yourselves, lest you be ensnared by it; for it is an abomination to the Lord your God. ²⁶And you shall not bring an abominable thing into your house (=AP), and become *accursed* (=AE; sub.; ἀνάθεμα) like it; you shall utterly detest and abhor it; for it is an *accursed* (sub.; ἀνάθεμα) thing.

Deut 13:13-18: (3:8-14: (CU-BL)) (1:8f: f*, SE, AP)
¹³If you hear (=f*) in one of your cities, which the Lord your God gives you to dwell there, ¹⁴that certain base fellows have gone out among you and have drawn away the inhabitants of the city (=SE), saying, 'Let us go and serve other gods,' which you have not known (=AP) . . . . ¹⁶you shall surely put the inhabitants of that city to the sword, *destroying it utterly* (hiph.; ἀναθέματι ἀναθεματιεῖτε), all who are in it and its cattle, with the edge of the sword. ¹⁷You shall gather all its spoil into the midst of its open

square, and burn the city and all its spoil with fire, as a whole burnt offering to the Lord your God; it shall be a heap for ever, it shall not be built again. [18]None of the *devoted things* (sub.; ἀναθέματος) shall cleave to your hand; that the Lord may turn from the fierceness of his anger (=(CU)), and show you mercy, and have compassion on you, and multiply you (=(BL)), as he swore to your fathers.

Deut 20:16-18: (1:8f: f, SE, AP)

[16]But in the cities of these peoples that the Lord your God gives you for an inheritance, you shall save alive nothing that breathes, [17]but you shall *utterly destroy* (=f; sub. + hiph.; ἀναθέματι ἀναθεματιεῖτε) them, the Hittites and the Amorites, the Canaanites and the Perizzites, the Hivites and the Jebusites, as the Lord your God has commanded; [18]that they may not teach you to do (=SE) according to all their abominable practices which they have done in service of their gods (=AP), and so to sin against the Lord your God.

Josh 2:10:

(Rahab said:) For we have heard how the Lord dried up the water of the Red Sea before you when you came out of Egypt, and what you did to the two kings of the Amorites that were beyond the Jordan, to Sihon and Og, whom you *utterly destroyed* (hiph.; ἐξωλεθρεύσατε).

Josh 6:17-18, 21: (1:8f: (AE))

[17]And the city and all that is within it shall be *devoted* (sub.; ἀνάθεμα) to the Lord for *destruction*; only Rahab the harlot and all who are with her in her house shall live, because she hid the messengers that we sent. [18]But you, keep yourselves from the things *devoted to destruction* (sub.; ἀναθέματος), lest when you have *devoted* (hiph.; ἐνθυμηθέντες?) them you take any of the *devoted* (sub.; ἀναθέματος) things and make the camp of Israel a thing for *destruction* (=(AE); sub.; ἀνάθεμα), and bring trouble upon it. [21]Then they *utterly destroyed* (hiph.; ἀνεθεμάτισεν) all in the city, both men and women, young and old, oxen, sheep, and asses, with the edge of the sword.

Josh 7:1, 11-15: (3:10: LB) (1:8f: AC+CU, AE)

[1]But the people of Israel broke faith (=LB) in regard to the *devoted things* (sub.; ἀναθέματος); for Achan the son of Carmi, son of Zabdi, son of Zerah, of the tribe of Judah, took some of the *devoted things* (sub.; ἀναθέματος); and the anger of the Lord burned against the people of Israel. [10]The Lord said to Joshua, "Arise, why have you thus fallen upon your face? [11]Israel has sinned; they have transgressed my covenant which I commanded them (=AC; LB); they have taken some of the *devoted things* (sub.; ἀναθέματος); they have stolen, and lied (=AC; LB), and put them among their own stuff. [12]Therefore the people of Israel cannot stand before their enemies; they turn their backs before their enemies, because they have become a *thing for destruction* (=AE; sub.; ἀνάθεμα). I will be with you no more, unless you *destroy the devoted things* (sub.; ἀνάθεμα) from among you. [13]Up, sanctify the people, and say, 'Sanctify yourselves for tomorrow; for thus says the Lord, God of Israel, "There are *devoted things* (sub.; ἀνάθεμα) in the midst of you, O Israel; you cannot stand before your enemies, until you take away the *devoted things* (sub.; ἀνάθεμα) from among you." [15]And he who is taken with the *devoted things* (sub., --) shall be burned with fire, he and all that he has, because he has transgressed the covenant of the Lord (=LB), and because he has done a shameful thing in Israel.'"

Josh 8:25-26:
²⁵And all who fell that day, both men and women, were twelve thousand, all the people of Ai. ²⁶For Joshua did not draw back his hand, with which he stretched out the javelin, until he had *utterly destroyed* (hiph., --) all the inhabitants of Ai.

Josh 10:1, 28-40:
¹When Adonizedek king of Jerusalem heard how Joshua had taken Ai, and had *utterly destroyed* (hiph.; ἐξωλέθρευσεν) it, doing to Ai and its king as he had done to Jericho and its king . . . .

²⁸And Joshua took Makkedah on that day, and smote it and its king with the edge of the sword; he *utterly destroyed* (hiph.; ἐξωλέθρευσαν) every person in it, he left none remaining;

³⁴And Joshua passed on with all Israel from Lachish to Eglon; and they laid siege to it, and assaulted it; ³⁵and they took it on that day, and smote it with the edge of the sword; and every person in it he *utterly destroyed* (hiph.; ἐφόνευσαν) that day, as he had done to Lachish.

³⁶Then Joshua went up with all Israel from Eglon to Hebron; and they assaulted it, ³⁷and took it, and smote it with the edge of the sword, and its king and its towns, and every person in it; he left none remaining, as he had done to Eglon, and *utterly destroyed* (hiph.; ἐξωλέθρευσαν) it with every person in it.

³⁸Then Joshua, with all Israel, turned back to Debir and assaulted it, ³⁹and he took it with its king and all its towns; and they smote them with the edge of the sword, and *utterly destroyed* (hiph.; ἐξωλέθρευσαν) every person in it; he left none remaining; as he had done to Hebron and to Libnah and its king, so he did to Debir and to its king.

⁴⁰So Joshua defeated the whole land, the hill country and the Negeb and the lowland and the slopes, and all their kings; he left none remaining, but *utterly destroyed* (hiph.; ἐξωλέθρευσεν) all that breathed, as the Lord God of Israel commanded.

Josh 11:10-12, 20-21:
¹⁰And Joshua turned back at that time, and took Hazor, and smote its king with the edge of the sword . . . . ¹¹And they put to the sword all who were in it, *utterly destroying* (hiph.; ἐξωλέθρευσαν) them; there was none left that breathed, and he burned Hazor with fire. ¹²And all the cities of those kings, and all their kings, Joshua took, and smote them with the edge of the sword, *utterly destroying* (hiph.; ἐξωλέθρευσαν) them, as Moses the servant of the Lord had commanded.

²⁰For it was the Lord's doing to harden their hearts that they should come against Israel in battle, in order that they should be *utterly destroyed* (hiph.; ἐξολεθρευθῶσιν), and should receive no mercy but be exterminated, as the Lord commanded Moses. ²¹And Joshua came at that time, and wiped out the Anakim from the hill country, from Hebron, from Debir, from Anab, and from all the hill country of Judah, and from all the hill country of Israel; Joshua *utterly destroyed* (hiph.; ἐξωλέθρευσεν) them with their cities.

Josh 22:20: (3:10: LB)
Did not Achan the son of Zerah break faith (=LB) in the matter of the *devoted things* (sub.; ἀναθέματος), and wrath fell upon all the congregation of Israel? And he did not perish alone for his iniquity.

Judg 1:17:
And Judah went with Simeon his brother, and they defeated the Canaanites who inhabited Zephath, and *utterly destroyed* (hiph., (A)ἀνεθεμάτισαν . . . καὶ ἐξωλέθρευσαν/ (B)ἐξωλέθρευσαν) it. So the name of the city was called Hormah ((A)Ἐξολέθρευσις/ (B)ἀνάθεμα).

Judg 21:9-11:
⁹For when the people were mustered, behold, not one of the inhabitants of Jabesh-gilead was there. ¹⁰So the congregation sent thither twelve thousand of their bravest men, and commanded them, "Go and smite the inhabitants of Jabesh-gilead with the edge of the sword; also the women and the little ones. ¹¹This is what you shall do; every male and every woman that has lain with a male you shall *utterly destroy*" (hiph.; ἀναθεματιεῖτε).

1 Sam 15:2-21: (3:10: LB)
²Thus says the Lord of hosts, "I will punish what Amalek did to Israel in opposing them on the way, when they came up out of Egypt. ³Now go and smite Amalek, and *utterly destroy* (hiph.; ἐξολέθρευσις . . . και ἀναθεματιεῖς) all that they have; do not spare them, but kill both man and woman, infant and suckling, ox and sheep, camel and ass."
⁸And he (=Saul) took Agag the king of the Amalekites alive, and *utterly destroyed* (hiph.; ἀπέκτεινεν) all the people with the edge of the sword. ⁹But Saul and the people spared Agag, and the best of the sheep and of the oxen and of the fatlings, and the lambs, and all that was good, and would not *utterly destroy* (hiph.; ἐξολεθρεῦσαι) them; all that was despised and worthless they *utterly destroyed* (hiph.; ἐξωλέθρευσαν).
¹⁵Saul said, "They have brought them from the Amalekites; for the people spared the best of the sheep and of the oxen, to sacrifice to the Lord your God; and the rest we have *utterly destroyed* (hiph.; ἐξωλέθρευσα)."
¹⁸(Samuel said:) And the Lord sent you on a mission, and said, "Go, *utterly destroy* (hiph.; ἐξολέθρευσον) the sinners, the Amalekites, and fight against them until they are consumed." ¹⁹Why then did you not obey the voice of the Lord (=LB)? Why did you swoop on the spoil, and do what was evil in the sight of the Lord?" ²⁰And Saul said to Samuel, "I have obeyed the voice of the Lord, I have gone on the mission on which the Lord sent me, I have brought Agag the king of Amalek, and I have *utterly destroyed* (hiph.; ἐξωλέθρευσα) the Amalekites. ²¹But the people took of the spoil, sheep and oxen, the best of the things *devoted to destruction* (sub.; ἐξολεθρεύματος), to sacrifice to the Lord your God in Gilgal."

1 Kgs 9:20-21:
²⁰All the people who were left of the Amorites, the Hittites, the Perizzites, the Hivites, and the Jebusites, who were not of the people of Israel — ²¹their descendants who were left after them in the land, whom the people of Israel were unable to *destroy utterly* (hiph.; ἐξολεθρεῦσαι) — these Solomon made a forced levy of slaves, and so they are to this day.

1 Kgs 20:42: (1:8f: (AE))
And he (=the prophet) said to him (=Ahab), "Thus says the Lord, 'Because you have let go out of your hand the man whom I had *devoted to destruction* ((AE); sub.; (21:42) ὀλέθριον), therefore your life shall go for his life, and your people for his people.'"

2 Kgs 19:10-11:
¹⁰"Thus shall you speak to Hezekiah king of Judah: 'Do not let your God on whom you rely deceive you by promising that Jerusalem will not be given into the hand of the king of Assyria. ¹¹Behold, you have heard what the kings of Assyria have done to all lands, *destroying them utterly* (hiph.; ἀναθεματίσαι). And shall you be delivered?'"

Isa 34:2, 5: (1:8f: (AE))
²For the Lord is enraged against all the nations, and furious against all their host, he

has *doomed* (hiph.; ἀπολέσαι) them, has given them over for slaughter . . . .

⁵For my sword has drunk its fill in the heavens; behold it descends for judgement upon Edom, upon the people I have *doomed* ((AE); sub.; ἀπωλείας).

Isa 37:11:
Behold, you have heard what the kings of Assyria have done to all lands, *destroying them utterly* (hiph.; ἀπώλεσαν). And shall you be delivered?

Isa 43:27 – 44:3: (3:8-14: CU-BL) (3:10: LB) (3:13f: S) (1:8f: AC+CU, (AE))
²⁷Your first father sinned, and your mediators transgressed against me (=AC; LB). ²⁸Therefore, I profaned the princes of the sanctuary, I delivered Jacob to *utter destruction* ((AE); sub.; ἀπολέσαι) and Israel to reviling.

44 ¹"But now, hear, O Jacob my servant, Israel whom I have chosen . . . . ³For I will pour water on the thirsty land, and streams on the dry ground; I will pour my Spirit (=S) upon your descendants; and my *blessing* on your offspring.

Jer 25:8-9: (3:10: LB) (1:8f: AC+CU)
⁸Therefore thus says the Lord of hosts: Because you have not obeyed my words (=AC; LB), ⁹behold, I will send for all the tribes of the north . . . and I will bring them against this land and its inhabitants, and against all these nations round about; I will *utterly destroy* (hiph.; ἐξερημώσω) them, and make them a horror, a hissing, and an everlasting reproach.

Jer 50:21, 26:
²¹Go up against the land of Merathaim, and against the inhabitants of Pekod. Slay, and *utterly destroy* (hiph.; (27:21) ἀφάνισον?) after them, says the Lord, and do all that I have commanded you.

²⁶Come against her from every quarter; open her granaries; pile her up like heaps of grain, and *destroy her utterly* (hiph., (27:26) ἐξολεθρεύσατε); let nothing be left of her.

Jer 51:3:
Let not the archer bend his (=Babylon's) bow, and let him not stand up in his coat of mail. Spare not her young men; *utterly destroy* (hiph.; (28:3) ἀφανίσατε) all her host.

Zech 14:11: (3:8-14: CU-(BL))
And it (=the land) shall be inhabited, for there shall be no more *curse* (sub.; ἀνάθεμα); Jerusalem shall dwell in security (=(BL)). (Cf. blessing for Gentiles in 14:16f.)

Mal 3:22-23: (3:8-14: CU-(BL))
²²Behold, I will send you Elijah the prophet before the great and terrible day of the Lord comes. ²³And he will turn the hearts of fathers to their children and the hearts of children to their fathers (=(BL)), lest I come and smite the land with a *curse* (sub.; ἄρδην).

Dan 11:44:
But tidings from the east and the north shall alarm him, and he shall go forth with great fury to exterminate and *utterly destroy* (hiph., ἀποκτεῖναι/ἀναθεματίσαι) many.

Ezra 10:7-8: (1:8f: f)
⁷And a proclamation was made throughout Judah and Jerusalem to all the returned exiles that they should assemble at Jerusalem, ⁸and that if any one (=f) did not come

within three days, by order of the officials and the elders all his property should be *for-feited* (hoph., (Ezra II 10:8) ἀναθεματισθήσεται), and he himself banned from the congregation of the exiles.

1 Chr 2:7: (3:10: LB)
The sons of Carmi: Achar, the troubler of Israel, who transgressed (=LB) in the matter of the *devoted thing* (sub.; ἀνάθεμα).

1 Chr 4:41:
These, registered by name, came in the days of Hezekiah, king of Judah, and destroyed their tents and the Meunim who were found there, and *exterminated* (hiph.; ἀνεθεμάτισαν) them to this day . . . .

2 Chr 20:23:
For the men of Ammon and Moab rose against the inhabitants of Mount Seir, *destroying them utterly* (hiph.; ἐξολεθρεῦσαι), and when they had made an end of the inhabitants of Seir, they all helped to destroy one another.

2 Chr 32:14:
(Sennacherib to Hezekiah:) Who among all the gods of those nations which my fathers *utterly destroyed* (hiph.; ἐξωλέθρευσαν) was able to deliver his people from my hand, that your god should be able to deliver you from my hand?

---

1 Macc 5:4-5:
⁴He (=Judas) also remembered the wickedness of the sons of Baean, who were a trap and a snare to the people and ambushed them on the highways. ⁵They were shut up by him in their towers; and he encamped against them, *vowed their complete destruction* (ἀναθεμάτισεν), and burned with fire their towers and all who were in them.

Sir 16:9: (trans. Sauer) (1:8f: (AE))
Und nicht verschonte er ein Volk, das dem *Bann* verfallen war ((AE); גוי חרם, ἔθνος ἀπωλείας), und das hinweggerafft wurde in seiner Schuld.

Sir 39:30: (trans. Sauer)
Reissende Tiere, Skorpione und Ottern, und das Schwert der Rache, mit dem *Bann* zu belegen (hiph.; εἰς ὄλεθρον) die Bösen; alle diese sind für ihren Zweck erschaffen worden, und sie liegen im Vorrat bereit und warten auf die Zeit, zu der sie aufgeboten werden.

Sir 46:6: (trans. Sauer) (1:8f: (AE))
<Und er schleuderte sie> auf <ein feindliches Volk>, und am <Berghang vernichtete er Feinde>, um einem jeden Volke, das dem *Bann* verfallen war ((AE); חרם גוי, --), zu erkennen zu geben, dass der Herr acht hat auf ihre Kriege, und auch deshalb, weil er vollkommen in der Nachfolge Gottes stand . . . .

---

2 Apoc. Bar. 62:1-3: (1:8f: AP)
¹And the seventh black waters you have seen; that is the perversion of the ideas of Jeroboam who planned to make two golden calves (=AP), ²and all the iniquities accomplished by the kings who succeeded him, ³and the *curse* of Jezebel, and the idolatry which Israel practised at that time (=AP) . . . .

Bib. Ant. 21:3:

Are not these the words that I spoke before you, Lord, When Achan stole from the things under *ban* and the people were delivered up before you . . . .

Bib. Ant. 26:2: (1:8f: AP)

And Kenaz said, "Should we burn those precious stones in the fire or consecrate them to you, because we do not have any like those?" And God said to him, "If God in his own name takes anything from the things under the *ban*, what will man do? And so now you will take those precious stones and everything that has been found in the book; and when you have arranged for the men, you will place the stones apart with the books, because the fire cannot burn them up, and afterward I will show you how to destroy them. But the men and everything else that has been found, you will burn in the fire. And when all the people have been gathered together, you will say to them, 'So it will be done to every man whose heart has turned from his God'" (=AP).

Bib. Ant. 29:3: (1:8f: AP)

Now in those days Zebul established a treasury for the Lord and said to the people: "Behold if anyone wishes to consecrate gold and silver to the Lord, let him bring it to the treasury of the Lord in Shiloh; only do not let anyone who has anything belonging to idols (=AP) wish to consecrate it to the treasuries of the Lord, because the Lord does not want the abominations of the things under the *ban* lest you disturb the assembly of the Lord . . . ."

1 Enoch 6:4-6: (1:8f: SI, AN)

⁴But they all (=the angels) responded to him, "Let us all swear an oath and bind everyone among us by a *curse* (=SI, AN; ἀναθεματίσωμεν) not to abandon this suggestion but to do the deed." ⁵Then they all swore together and bound one another by (the *curse* (ἀνεθεμάτισαν)). ⁶And they were altogether two hundred; and they descended into Ardos, which is the summit of Hermon. And they called the mount Armon, for they swore and bound one another by *curse* (=SI, AN).

1 Enoch 95:4: (3:10: LB)

Woe unto you who pronounce *anathemas* so that they may be neutralized! (Salutary) remedy is far from you, on account of your sins (=LB).

1 Enoch Fragment from Syncellos 1-2: (tr. Uhlig) (1:8f: SI)

¹Und wegen des Berges aber, auf dem sie schwuren und sich gegenseitig durch *Verwünschungen* (ἀνεθεμέτισαν) verplichteten (=SI), dass sie bis in die Ewigkeit nicht davon ablassen würden: ²Kälte und Schnee und Reif und Tau sollen nicht auf ihn herabkommen, nur der *Fluch* soll auf ihn herabkommen, bis zum Tag des grossen Gerichtes.

CD ix.1: (1:8f: f)

Every man who (=f) vows another to *destruction* (hiph.) by the laws of the Gentiles shall himself be put to death.

1QM ix.6-7:

⁶The priests shall sound for them the trumpets of Pursuit, and they shall deploy against all the enemy in a pursuit to destruction; and the horsemen ⁷shall thrust them back on the flanks of the battle until they are *utterly destroyed* (sub.).

1QM xviii.3-5:

³. . . the Priests shall blow ⁴<the six trumpets> of the Reminder and all the battle

formations shall rally to them and shall divide against all the < camp of the> Kittim ⁵to *destroy them utterly* (hiph.).

11QTemple 2:9–11: (1:8f: AE, AP)
    ⁹. . . You must <not> br<ing any abominable idol> into your house (=AP) ¹⁰<and come> *under the ban* (=AE; sub.) together with it.   You shall de<test and abominate it>, ¹¹for it is *under the ban* (sub.).

11QTemple 55:2–11: (1:8f: f, SE, AP)
    ²If (=f) in on<e of your cities in which I> give you to dw<ell> you hear this said: ‘³Men, <s>ons of <Beli>al have arisen in your midst and have led astray all the inhabitants ⁴of their city (=SE) saying, "Let us go and worship gods whom you have not known!" (=AP) . . .
    ⁶. . . you shall surely put all the inhabitants of that city to the sword . . . .
    ⁸. . . and assemble all the booty in ⁹(the city) square and shall burn it with fire . . . .
    ¹⁰. . . Nothing ¹¹from that which has been placed under the *ban* (sub.) shall cleave to your hand . . . .

11QTemple 62:13–16: (1:8f: f; SE, AP)
    ¹³But in the cities of the peoples which I give you as an inheritance, you shall not leave alive ¹⁴any creature.   Indeed you shall *utterly exterminate* (=f; hiph. + sub.) the Hittites, the Amorites, the Canaanites, ¹⁵the Hivites the Jebusites, the Girgashites and the Perizzites, as I have commanded you, that ¹⁶they may not teach you (=SE) to practise all the abominations that they have performed to their gods (=AP).

BIBLIOGRAPHY

1: SOURCES

The Bible

MT: *Biblia Hebraica.* Ed. Rudolf Kittel. Stuttgart: Württembergische Bibelanstalt, 1973 (=1937).
LXX: *Septuaginta I-II.* Ed. Alfred Ralphs. Stuttgart: Deutsche Bibelstiftung, 1935.
Novum Testamentum Graece. Ed. Kurt Aland, M. Black, C. M. Martini, B. M. Metzger, A. Wikgren. Stuttgart: Deutsche Bibelstiftung, 1979[26].
RSV: *The Holy Bible, Revised Standard Version.* Division of Education of the National Council of Churches, 1952.

Ancient Near Eastern Sources

ANET: *Ancient Near Eastern Texts Relating to the Old Testament.* Ed. James B. Pritchard. Princeton: Princeton University Press, 1969[3] (with sup.).

Jewish sources

APOT: *The Apocrypha and Pseudepigrapha of the Old Testament in English I-II.* Ed. Robert H. Charles. Oxford: Clarendon, 1913.
OTP 1: *The Old Testament Pseudepigrapha. 1: Apocalyptic Literature and Testaments.* Ed. James H. Charlesworth. New York: Doubleday, 1983.
OTP 2: *The Old Testament Pseudepigrapha. II: Expansions of the "Old Testament" and Legends, Wisdom and Philosophical Literature, Prayers, Psalms and Odes, Fragments of lost Judeo-Hellenistic Works.* Ed. James H. Charlesworth. New York: Doubleday, 1985.
The Oxford Annotated Apocrypha of the Old Testament RSV. Expanded ed. by Bruce M. Metzger. New York: Oxford University Press, 1977.
Jesus Sirach. JSHRZ III,5. Ed. Georg Sauer. Gütersloh: Gütersloher, 1981.
The Greek Versions of The Testaments of the Twelve Patriarchs. Ed. Robert H. Charles. Darmstadt, 1960[2] (=1908).
Apocalypsis Henochi Graece. PVTG 3. Ed. M. Black. Leiden: Brill, 1970:1-44.
Das Äthiopische Henochsbuch. JSHRZ V,6. Ed. Siegbert Uhlig. Gütersloh: Gütersloher, 1984.
Testamentum Iobi. PVTG 2. Ed. S. Brock. Leiden: Brill, 1967:1-59.
Apocalypsis Baruchi graece. PVTG 2. Ed. J. -C. Picard. Leiden: Brill, 1967:61-96.
"Apocalypsis Mosis." Pp. 1-23 in *Apocalypses Apocryphae.* Ed. K. von Tischendorf; photoprint from the Leipzig edition, 1866. Hildesheim: G. Olms, 1966.
Das Buch der Jubiläen. JSHRZ II,3. Ed. Klaus Berger. Gütersloh: Gütersloher, 1981.

Die Texte aus Qumran, Hebräisch und Deutsch. Ed. and trans. Eduard Lohse. München: Kösel, 1981[3].
Die Texte vom Toten Meer I-II. Ed. Johann Maier. München - Basel: Reinhardt, 1960.
DSSE: *The Dead Sea Scrolls in English.* Ed. Geza Vermes. Third edition, revised and augmented. London: Penguin Books, 1987.
The Temple Scroll. JSOTSup 34. Ed. Johann Maier. Sheffield: JSOT Press, 1985 (also

available: *Die Tempelrolle vom Toten Meer.* München: Reinhardt, 1978).
The Temple Scroll. Vol II: Text and Commentary. Ed. Yigael Yadin. Jerusalem: The
Israel Exploration Society, 1983.
Discoveries in the Judaean Desert I: Qumran Cave 1. Ed. D. Barthélemy, J. T. Milik.
Oxford: Clarendon, 1955.
The Zadokite Documents. Ed. Chaim Rabin. With translation and notes. Revised edi-
tion. Oxford: Clarendon, 1958².

Philo I-X. LCL. Ed. and trans. F. H. Colson, G. H. Whitaker. London: Heinemann;
Cambridge: Harvard University Press, 1929–1962.

Josephus I-X. LCL. Ed. and trans. J. Thackeray, R. Marcus, A. Wikgren, L. H. Feld-
man. London: Heinemann; Cambridge: Harvard University Press, 1926–1965.

The Mishnah. Trans. Herbert Danby. Oxford: Oxford University Press, 1933.
The Babylonian Talmud I-XVIII. Ed. Isidore Epstein. London: Soncino, 1935–1952.
Str-B: Kommentar zum Neuen Testament aus Talmud und Midrasch I-IV. Ed. Hermann
L. Strack, Paul Billerbeck. München: Beck, 1922–1928.
Sanhedrin-Makkôt (IV Seder, Neziqin. 4 u 5 Traktat) from *Die Mischna. Text,
Übersetzung und ausfürliche Erklärung.* Ed. Samuel Krauss. Giessen: Töpelmann,
1933.

Greek and Latin sources

ad Alexan.: Rhetorica ad Alexandrum. LCL. Ed. H. Rackham. In the volume with
Aristotle: Problems II. London: Heinemann; Cambridge: Harvard University
Press, 1937.
ad Herenn.: (Cicero) ad C. Herennium. LCL 403. Ed. Harry Caplan. Cambridge:
Harvard University Press; London: Heinemann, 1989⁶.
Arist. Rhet.: Aristotle: The 'Art' of Rhetoric. LCL 193. Ed. John H. Freese. Cam-
bridge: Harvard University Press - London: Heinemann, 1982⁷.
Cic. Inv.: Cicero: De Inventione. LCL 386. Ed. H. M. Hubbell. In the volume with
De Optimo Genere Oratorum, Topica. London: Heinemann - Cambridge: Harvard
University Press, 1976⁴.
Hermog. *Prog.:* "ΕΡΜΟΓΕΝΟΤΣ ΠΡΟΓΤΜΝΑΣΜΑΤΑ. " Pp. 1–27 in *Hermogenes.
Opera.* Rhetores Graeci VI. Ed. Hugo Rabe. Leipzig: Teubner, 1913. Transla-
tion: Pp. 23–38 in Baldwin, C. S: *Medieval Rhetoric and Poetic.* New York:
Macmillan, 1928.
Hermog. *Stat.:* "ΕΡΜΟΓΕΝΟΤΣ ΤΕΧΝΗΣ ΡΗΤΟΡΙΚΗΣ. ΠΕΡΙ ΤΩΝ ΣΤΑΣΕΩΝ. "
Pp. 28–92 in *Hermogenes. Opera.* Rhetores Graeci VI. Ed. Hugo Rabe. Leipzig:
Teubner, 1913. Ray Nadeau: "Hermogenes' *On Stases:* A Translation with an
Introduction and Notes." *Speech Monographs* 31 (1964):361–424.

Early Christian Sources:

The Apostolic Fathers I-II. LCL 24–25. Ed. and trans. Kirsopp Lake. Cambridge: Har-
vard University Press; London: Heinemann, 1975–1970 (=1912–1913).
The Ante-Nicene Fathers. Volume I: The Apostolic Fathers - Justin Martyr - Irenaeus.
Ed. A. Roberts, J. Donaldson. American reprint. Grand Rapids: Eerdmans, 1967.

2: WORKS OF REFERENCE

Bauer, Walter: *Wörterbuch zu den Schriften des Neuen Testaments und der übrigen urchristlichen Literatur.* Berlin, New York: De Gruyter, 1971.
Gesenius, Wilhelm: *Hebräisches und Aramäishes Handwörterbuch über das Alte Testament.* Berlin, Göttingen, Heidelberg: Springer, 1962[17].

Barthélemy, Dominique and O. Rickenbacher: *Konkordanz zum Hebräischen Sirach.* Göttingen: Vandenhoeck & Ruprecht, 1973.
Borgen, Peder and R. Skarsten: *Complete KWIC-Concordance of Philo's Writings.* Magnetic tape. Trondheim and Bergen, 1973.
Computer-Konkordanz zum Novum Testamentum Graece. Berlin, New York: De Gruyter, 1980.
Denis, Albert-Marie: *Concordance Grecque des Pseudépigraphes d'Ancien Testament.* Louvain-la-Neuve: Institute Orientaliste, 1987.
Hatch, Edwin and Henry A. Redpath: *A Concordance to the Septuagint and the Other Greek Versions of the Old Testament (including the Apocryphal Books).* Graz: Akademische Druck- u. Verlagsanstalt, 1954.
Kuhn, Karl G: *Konkordanz zu den Qumrantexten.* Göttingen: Vandenhoeck & Ruprecht, 1960 (cf also "Nachträge zur 'Konkordanz zu den Qumrantexten.'" *RevQ* 4 (1963): 163–234).
Lisowsky, Gerhard: *Konkordanz zum Hebräischen Alten Testament.* Stuttgart: Württembergische Bibelanstalt, 1958.
Mayer, Günter: *Index Philoneus.* Berlin - New York: De Gruyter, 1974.
Rengstorf, Karl H. ed.: *A Complete Concordance of Flavius Josephus I-IV.* Leiden: Brill, 1973-1983.
Schmoller, Alfred: *Handkonkordanz zum Griechischen Neuen Testament.* Stuttgart: Württembergische Bibelanstalt, 1973[15].

BDR: Blass, Friedrich, A. Debrunner and F. Rehkopf: *Grammatik des neutestamentlichen Griechisch.* Göttingen: Vandenhoeck & Ruprecht, 1984[16].

NIDNTT: *The New International Dictionary of New Testament Theology I-III.* Ed. Colin Brown. Exeter: Paternoster, 1975-1978.
RAC: *Reallexikon für Antike und Christentum. Sachwörterbuch zur Auseinandersetzung des Christentums mit der Antiken Welt, I ff.* Ed. Theodor Klauser. Stuttgart: Hiersemann, 1950ff.
TDOT: *Theological Dictionary of the Old Testament I ff.* Ed. G. Johannes Botterweck, Helmer Ringgren. Michigan: Eerdmans, 1974ff.
THAT: *Theologisches Handwörterbuch zum Alten Testament I-II.* Ed. Ernst Jenni, Claus Westermann. München - Zürich: Kaiser, 1971-1976.
TDNT: *Theological Dictionary of the New Testament I-IX.* Ed. Gerhard Kittel, G. Friedrich. Grand Rapids: Eerdmans, 1964-1974.
TRE: *Theologische Realenzyklopädie, I ff.* Eds. Gerhard Krause, Gerhard Müller. Berlin - New York: De Gruyter, 1977ff.
TWAT: *Theologisches Wörterbuch zum Alten Testament I ff.* Ed. G. Johannes Botterweck, Helmer Ringgren. Stuttgart - Berlin - Köln - Mainz: Kohlhammer, 1970ff.

ANRW: *Aufstieg und Niedergang der römischen Welt. Geschichte und Kultur Roms im Spiegel der neueren Forschung.* Ed. Hildegard Temporini, Wolfgang Haase. Berlin - New York: De Gruyter, 1972-.

3: SECONDARY LITERATURE

ALBRIGHT, W. F and C. S. MANN
  1969   "Two texts in 1. Corinthians." *NTS* 16:271-76.
ALEWELL, Karl
  1913   *Über das rhetorische "paradeigma." Theorie, Beispielsammlungen, Verwendung in der römischen Literatur der Kaiserzeit.* Leipzig: Hoffmann.
ALT, Albrecht
  1934   "Die Ursprünge des israelitischen Rechts." Pp. 278-332 in *Kleine Schriften zur Geschichte des Volkes Israel I.* München: Beck, 1953.
ASMUSSEN, Hans
  1935   *Theologisch-kirchliche Erwägungen zum Galaterbrief.* München: Kaiser.
ATTRIDGE, Harold W.
  1984   "Josephus and His Works." Pp. 185-232 in *Jewish Writings of the Second Temple Period.* Ed. Michael E. Stone. Assen: Van Gorcum; Philadelphia: Fortress.
AUNE, David E.
  1981   "Galatians: A Commentary on Paul's Letter to the Churches of Galatia, by Hans Dieter Betz." *RelSRev* 7:323-28.
AUSTIN, John L.
  1975   *How to Do Things with Words. The William James Lectures delivered at Harward University in 1955.* Cambridge: Clarendon.
BAASLAND, Ernst
  1984a   "Persecution: A Neglected Feature in the Letter to the Galatians." *ST* 38:135-50.
  1986   "Zum Beispiel der Beispielerzälungen. Zur Formenlehre der Gleichnisse und zur Methodik der Gleichnisauslegung." *NT* 28:193-219.
  1988a   "Literarische Form, Thematik und geschichtliche Einordnung des Jakobusbriefes." Pp. 3646-84 in *ANRW* II, 25.5.
  1988b   "Die peri-Formel und die Argumentation(ssituation) des Paulus." *ST* 42:69-87.
BALTZER, Klaus
  1971   *The Covenant Formulary in Old Testament, Jewish, and Early Christian Writings.* Oxford: Blackwell (trans. from: *Das Bundesformular.* WMANT 4. Neukirchen-Vluyn: Neukirchener, 1964²).
BARCLAY, John M. G.
  1987   "Mirror-Reading a Polemical Letter: Galatians as a Test Case." *JSNT* 31:73-93.
  1988   *Obeying the Truth: A study of Paul's Ethics in Galatians.* Studies of the New Testament and Its World. Edinburgh: T. & T. Clark.
BARRETT, C. Kingsley
  1968   *A Commentary on the First Epistle to the Corintians.* Black NT Commentaries. London: Black.
  1985   *Freedom and Obligation. A Study of the Epistle to the Galatians.* London: SPCK.
BASSLER, Jouette M.
  1982   "1 Cor 12:3 — Curse and Confession in Context." *JBL* 101:415-18.

BAUMGARTEN, Joseph M.
1972   "Does *tlh* in the Temple Scroll Refer to Crucifixion?" *JBL* 91:472-81.
BAUR, Ferdinand C.
1866   *Paulus, der Apostel Jesu Christi. I.* Second edition. Leipzig:Fues.
BECKER, Jürgen
1976   "Der Brief and die Galater." Pp. 1-85 in *Die Briefe an die Galater,
         Epheser, Philipper, Kolosser, Thessalonicher und Philemon.* NTD 8. 14th
         edition. Göttingen: Vandenhoeck & Ruprecht.
BEGG, Christopher T.
1986   "The Function of Josh 7,1 - 8,29 in the Deuteronomistic History." *Bib*
         67:320-34.
BEHM, Johannes
TDNT   1:354f., art. "ἀνάθεμα, ἀνάθημα, κατάθεμα."
BEHNISCH, Martin
1984   "Fluch und Evangelium. Galater 1,9 als ein Aspekt paulinischer
         Theologie." *Berliner Theologische Zeitschrift* 1:241-54.
BEKER, J. Christian
1980   *Paul the Apostle. The Triumph of God in Life and Thought.* Edinburgh:
         T. & T. Clark.
BELLEFONTAINE, E.
1975   "The Curses of Deuteronomy 27: Their Relationship to the Prohibitives."
         Pp. 49-61 in FS John L. McKenzie: *No Famine in the Land.* Ed. James
         W. Flanagan, A. W. Robinson. Missoula: Scholars.
BELLEVILLE, Linda L.
1986   "'Under Law.' Structural Analysis and the Pauline Concept of Law in
         Galatians 3.21 - 4.11." *JSNT* 26:53-78.
BENGEL, Johann A.
1773   *Gnomon Novi Testamenti.* Stuttgart: Steinkopf, 1887[8] (= 1773[3]).
BERGER, Klaus
1970   "Zu den sogenannten Sätzen Heiligen Rechts." *NTS* 17:10-40
1972   "Die sog. "Sätze heiligen Rechts" im N.T. Ihre Funktion und ihr Sitz im
         Leben." *TZ* 28:305-30.
1980   "Die impliziten Gegner. Zur Methode des Erschliessens von 'Gegnern' in
         neutestamentlichen Texten." Pp. 373-400 in FS G. Bornkamm: *Kirche.*
         Tübingen: Mohr.
1984a   *Exegese des Neuen Testaments. Neue Wege wom Text zur Auslegung.* UTB
         658. Heidelberg: Quelle & Meyer, 1984[2].
1984b   *Formgeschichte des Neuen Testaments.* Heidelberg: Quelle & Meyer.
1984c   "Hellenistische Gattungen im Neuen Testament." Pp. 1031-1432 in *ANRW*
         II, 25.2.
TRE   1:372-82, art. "Abraham II. Im Frühjudentum und Neuen Testament."
BERNSTEIN, Moshe J.
1983   "כי קללת אלהים תלוי" (Deut 21:23): A Study in Early Jewish Exegesis."
         JQR 74:21-45.
BETZ, Hans D.
1974   "Spirit, Freedom and Law: Paul's Message to the Galatian Churches."
         SEÅ 39:145-60.
1975   "The Literary Composition and Function of Paul's Letter to the Galatians."
         NTS 21:353-79.
1979   *Galatians. A Commentary on Paul's Letter to the Churches in Galatia.*
         Hermeneia. Philadelphia: Fortress.

BETZ, Otto
1982   "Probleme des Prozesses Jesu." Pp. 565-647 in *ANRW* II, 25.1.
1990a   "Die Übersetzungen von Jes 53 (LXX, Targum) und die Theologia Crucis
            des Paulus." Pp. 197-216 in *Jesus. Der Herr der Kirche.* Aufsätze zur
            biblischen Theologie II. WUNT 52. Tübingen: Mohr/Siebeck.
1990b   "Der fleischliche Mensch und das geistliche Gesetz. Zum biblischen
            Hintergrund der paulinischen Gesetzeslehre." Pp. 129-96 in *Jesus. Der
            Herr der Kirche.* Aufsätze zur biblischen Theologie II. WUNT 52.
            Tübingen: Mohr/Siebeck.
TRE   5:716-22, art. "Beschneidung. II. Altes Testament, Frühjudentum und
            Neues Testament."
BJERKELUND, Carl J.
1967   *PARAKALÔ. Form, Funktion und Sinn des parakalô-Sätze in den paulinis-
            chen Briefen.* Bibliotheca Theologica Norvegica 1. Oslo:
            Universitetsforlaget.
BLACK, Matthew
1985   *The Book of Enoch or 1 Enoch. A New English Edition with Commentary
            and Textual Notes.* SVTP VII. Leiden: Brill.
BLANK, Sheldon H.
1950   "The Curse, Blasphemy, the Spell and the Oath." *HUCA* 23:73-95.
BLIDSTEIN, Gerald J.
1974   "'*Atimia*': A Greek Parallel to Ezra 10,8 and to Post-Biblical Exclusion
            from the Community." *VT* 24:357-60.
BLIGH, John
1969   *Galatians. A Discussion of St. Paul's Epistle.* Householder Commentaries
            1. London: St. Paul.
BORGEN, Peder
1980   "Observations on the Theme 'Paul and Philo.'" Pp. 85-102 in Sigfred
            Pedersen ed. *Die Paulinische Literatur und Theologie.* Aarhus: Aros;
            Göttingen: Vandenhoeck & Ruprecht (also available in Borgen 1983b:15-
            32; 1987:61-71).
1982   "Paul preaches circumcision and pleases men." Pp. 37-46 in FS C. K.
            Barrett: *Paul and Paulinism.* Ed. Morna D. Hooker, S. G. Wilson.
            London: SPCK (also available in Borgen 1983b, 33-42).
1983a   "The Early Church and the Hellenistic Synagogue." *ST* 37:55-78 (Also
            available in his 1983b, 75-97; 1987, 207-32).
1983b   *Paul preaches Circumcision and pleases Men.* Relieff 8. Trondheim:
            Tapir.
1984a   "Philo of Alexandria. A critical and synthetical survey of research since
            World War II." Pp. 98-154 in *ANRW* II, 21.1.
1984b   "Philo of Alexandria." Pp. 233-82 in *Jewish Writings of the Second
            Temple Period. Apocrypha, Pseudepigrapha, Qumran Sectarian Writings,
            Philo, Josephus.* Ed. Michael E. Stone. Assen: Van Gorcum; Philadel-
            phia: Fortress (also available in Borgen 1987a:17-59).
1985   "The Cross-National Church for Jews and Greeks. Observations on Paul's
            Letter to the Galatians." Pp. 225-48 in FS H. L. Jansen: *The Many and
            the One.* Relieff 15. Ed. P. Borgen. Trondheim: Tapir (cf. also Borgen
            1987:255-72).
1987   *Philo, John and Paul. New Perspectives on Judaism and Early
            Christianity.* Brown Judaic Studies 131. Atlanta: Scholars.
1992   "'There shall come forth a man.' Reflections on Messianic ideas in Philo."
            Pp. 341-61 in *The Messiah.* Ed. J. Charlesworth. Minneapolis: Fortress.

BORNHÄUSER, Karl
1932   "Anathema esto! (Gal 1,8 u 9; 1 Kor 16,22)." *Die Reformation* 26:82–83.
BORNKAMM, Günther
1952   "Das Anathema in der urchristlichen Abendmahlsliturgie." Pp. 123–32 in *Das Ende des Gesetzes. Paulusstudien. Gesammelte Aufsätze I.* BEvT 16. München: Kaiser, 1961³.
BORSE, Udo
1972   *Der Standort des Galaterbriefes.* BBB 41. Bonn: Hanstein.
1984   *Der Brief an die Galater.* RNT. Regensburg: Pustet.
BRASWELL, Joseph P.
1991   "'The Blessing of Abraham' versus 'the Curse of the Law': Another Look at Gal 3:10–13." *WTJ* 53:73–91.
BREKELMANS, C.
THAT   1:635–39, art. "חרם."
BRICHTO, H. C.
1963   *The problem of "curse" in the Hebrew Bible.* JBLMS 13. Philadelphia: Society of Biblical Literature.
BRING, Ragnar
1958   *Pauli brev till Galaterna.* Tolkning av Nya Testamentet VIII. Stockholm: Svenska kyrkans diakonistyrelses bokförlag (also available: *Commentary on Galatians.* Philadelphia: Muhlenberg, 1961).
BRINSMEAD, Bernhard H.
1982   *Galatians — Dialogical Response to Opponents.* SBLDS 65. Chico: Scholars.
BROWN, J.
1957   *An Exposition of the Epistle of Paul the Apostle to the Galatians.* Evansville.
BROX, Norbert
1968   "ΑΝΑΘΕΜΑ ΙΗΣΟΥΣ (1 Kor 12,3)." *BZ* 12:103–11.
BRUCE, Frederick F.
1982   *The Epistle of Paul to the Galatians. A Commentary on the Greek Text.* The New International Greek Testament Commentary. Exeter: Paternoster.
BRUN, Lyder
1932   *Segen und Fluch im Urchristentum.* Norske Vitenskapsakademi i Oslo, Skrifter II, Hist.-Filos. klasse, 1932,1. Oslo.
BÜCHSEL, Friedrich
TDNT   1:124–28, art. "ἀγοράζω, ἐξαγοράζω."
BULLINGER, E. W.
1898   *Figures of Speech Used in the Bible.* Explained and Illustrated. London: Eyre & Spottiswoode; New York: E. & J. B. Young & Co.
BURGMANN, Hans
1980   "Antichrist — Antimessias. Der Makkabäer Simon?" *Judaica* 36:152–74.
BURTON, Ernest de Witt
1980   *A Critical and Exegetical Commentary on The Epistle to the Galatians.* ICC. First imprint, 1920. Edinburgh: T. & T. Clark.
BUTLER, Trent C.
1983   *Joshua.* Word Biblical Commentary 7. Waco: Word.
CANEDAY, Ardel
1989   "Redeemed From the Curse of the Law. The Use of Deut 21:22–23 in Gal 3:13." *Trinity Journal* 10:185–209.

CAVALLIN, H. C. C.
1978   "'The Righteous Shall Live by Faith.' A Decisive Argument for the Traditional Interpretation." *ST* 32:33–43.
CLASSEN, Carl J.
1991   "Paulus und die antike Rhetorik." *ZNW* 82:1–33.
COLLINS, Adela Y.
1973   "The Function of 'Excommunication' in Paul." *HTR* 73:251–63.
CONZELMANN, Hans
1975   *1 Corinthians. A Commentary on the First Epistle to the Corinthians.* Hermeneia. Philadelphia: Fortress.
COSGROVE, Charles H.
1978   "The Mosaic Law Preaches Faith: A Study in Galatians 3." *WTJ* 41:146–64.
1988   *The Cross and the Spirit. A Study in the Argument and Theology of Galatians.* Macon: Mercer.
COUGHENOUR, R. A.
1978   "The Woe-Oracles in Ethiopic Enoch." *JJS* 9:192–97.
CRANFIELD, C. E. B.
1975   *A Critical and Exegetical Commentary on the Epistle to the Romans. Vol I.* ICC. Edinburgh: T. & T. Clark.
1979   *A Critical and Exegetical Commentary on the Epistle to the Romans. Vol II.* ICC. Edinburgh: T. & T. Clark.
CRAWLEY, Alfred E.
1911   "Cursing and blessing." Pp. 367–74 in *Encyclopædia of Religion and Ethics. Vol 4.* Ed. J. Hastings. Edinburgh: T. & T. Clark; New York: Scribner's Sons.
CRONJÉ, J. van W.
1985   "Defamiliarization in the letter to the Galatians." Pp. 214–227 in FS Bruce M. Metzger: *A South African Perspective on the New Testament.* Ed. J. H. Petzer, P. J. Hartin. Leiden: Brill.
CROWNFIELD, Frederick C.
1945   "The Singular Problem of the Dual Galatians." *JBL* 64:491–500.
CULLMANN, Oscar
1963   *The Christology of The New Testament.* The New Testament Library. Second edition. London: SCM 1963.
DAHL, Nils A.
1950   "Zur Auslegung von Gal 6,16." *Judaica* 6:161–70.
1967   "Evangelium og plikt." Pp. 142–54 in FS Regin Prenter: *Festskrift til Regin Prenter.* Ed. Gustaf Wingren, A. M. Aagaard. København: Gyldendal.
1973   "Paul's Letter to the Galatians. Epistolary Genre, Content and Structure." Unpublished paper. Yale.
1974   "The Atonement - An Adequate Reward for the Akedah?" Pp. 146–60 in *The Crucified Messiah and Other Essays.* Minneapolis: Augsburg.
1977   "Contradictions in Scripture." Pp. 159–77 in *Studies in Paul.* Minneapolis: Augsburg (also avaliable: "Widersprüche in der Bibel, ein altes hermeneu tisches Problem." *ST* 25:1–19.
DAUBE, David
1949   "Rabbinic Methods of Interpretation and Hellenistic Rhetoric." *HUCA* 22:239–64.
DAVENPORT, Gene L.
1971   *The Eschatology of the Book of Jubilees.* SPB 20. Leiden: Brill.

DEISSMANN, Adolf
1901 "Anathema." *ZNW* 2:342.
1924 *Licht vom Osten.* Tübingen: Mohr/Siebeck.
DERRETT, J. Duncan M.
1975 "Cursing Jesus (1 Cor. 12.3): The Jews as Religious 'Persecutors.'" *NTS* 21:544–54.
1983 "'Bechuqey hagoyim.' Damascus Document ix.1 Again." *RevQ* 11:409–15.
DOBBELER, Axel von
1987 *Glaube als Teilhabe.* WUNT II, 22. Tübingen: Mohr.
DÖLLER, Johann
1913 "Der Bann (חרם) im Alten Testament und im späteren Judentum." *ZKT* 37:1–24.
DONALDSON, T. L.
1986 "The 'Curse of the Law' and the Inclusion of the Gentiles: Galatians 3,13–14." *NTS* 32:94–112.
DOSKOCIL, Walter
1958 *Der Bann in der Urkirche. Eine rechtsgeschichtliche Untersuchung.* Münchener Theologische Studien 3,11. München: Zink.
DUNCAN, George S.
1934 *The Epistle of Paul to the Galatians.* MNTC. London: Hodder & Stoughton.
DUNN, James D. G.
1983a "The Incident at Antioch (Gal 2:11–18)." *JSNT* 18:3–57.
1983b "The New Perspective on Paul." *BJRL* 65:95–122.
1985 "Works of the Law and the Curse of the Law (Galatians 3.10–14)." *NTS* 31:523–42.
1988a *Romans 1–8.* Word Biblical Commentary 38A. Dallas: Word.
Romans 9–16. Word Biblical Commentary 38B. Dallas: Word.
1988b "The Theology of Galatians." Pp. 1–16 in *SBL 1988 Seminar Papers.* SBLSPS 27. Atlanta: Scholars.
EBELING, Gerhard.
1981 *Die Wahrheit des Evangeliums. Eine Lesehilfe zum Galaterbrief.* Tübingen: Mohr/Siebeck (also available: *The Truth of the Gospel. An Exposition of Galatians.* Philadelphia: Fortress, 1985).
ECKERT, Jost
1971 *Die urchristliche Verkündigung im Streit zwischen Paulus und seinen Gegnern nach dem Galaterbrief.* Biblische Untersuchungen 6. Regensburg: Pustet.
EGGER, Wilhelm
1987 *Methodenlehre zum Neuen Testament. Einführung in linguistische und historisch-kritische Methoden.* Freiburg, Basel, Wien: Herder.
ELLIOTT, John H.
1990 "Paul, Galatians, and the Evil Eye." *CurTM* 17:262–73.
ELLIOTT, James K
1969 "The Use of ἕτερος in the New Testament." *ZNW* 60:140–41.
ELLIS, E. Earle
1957 *Paul's Use of the Old Testament.* Revised, 1981. Grand Rapids: Baker.
1974 "Spiritual Gifts in the Pauline Community." *NTS* 20:128–44.
1975a "Paul and His Opponents: Trends in the Research." Pp. 264–98 in FS Morton Smith: *Christianity, Judaism and other Greco-Roman Cults.* SJLA 12,1. Ed. Jacob Neusner. Leiden: Brill.

1975b   "'Weisheit' und 'Erkenntnis' im 1. Korintherbrief." Pp. 109–28 in FS W.
         G. Kümmel: *Jesus und Paulus.* Ed. E. Earle Ellis, E. Grässer.
         Göttingen: Vandenhoeck & Ruprecht.
EVANS-PRITCHARD, E. E.
1956   *Nuer Religion.* Oxford: Clarendon.
FEE, Gordon D.
1987   *The First Epistle to the Corinthians.* NICNT. Grand Rapids: Eerdmans.
FENSHAM, F. C.
1962   "Malediction and Benediction in Ancient Near Eastern Vassal-Treaties and
         the Old Testament." *ZAW* 74:1–9.
1963   "Common Trends in Curses of the Near Eastern Treaties and kudurruIns-
         criptions compared with Maledictions of Amos and Isaiah." *ZAW* 75:155–
         75.
FINNIGAN, R.
1969   "How to Do Things with Words: Performative Utterances among the
         Limba of Sierra Leone." *Man* (New Ser.) 4:537–52.
FISCHER, Ulrich
1978   *Eschatologie und Jenseitserwartung im hellenistischen Diasporajudentum.*
         BZNW 44. Berlin - New York: De Gruyter.
FITZMYER, Joseph A.
1978   "Crucifixion in Ancient Palestine, Qumran Literature and the New Testa-
         ment." *CBQ* 40:493–513.
1981   "Habakkuk 2:3–4 and the New Testament." Pp. 447–55 in FS Henri
         Cazelles: *De la Tôrah au Messie.* Ed. Maurice Carrez, J. Doré, P. Grelot.
         Paris: Desclee.
FORKMAN, Göran
1972   *The Limits of the Religious Community. Expulsion from the Religious Com-
         munity within the Qumran Sect, within Rabbinic Judaism and within Primi-
         tive Christianity.* ConBNT 5. Lund: Gleerup.
FOWLER, Robert M.
1985   "Who Is 'the Reader' in Reader Response Criticism?" *Semeia* 31:5–23.
FRANKENA, R.
1965   "The Vassal-Treaties of Esarhaddon and the Dating of Deuteronomy." *OTS*
         14:122–54.
FULLER, Daniel P.
1975   "Paul and 'the Works of the Law.'" *WTJ* 38:28–42.
GASTON, Lloyd
1987   *Paul and the Torah.* Vancouver: University of British Columbia Press.
GAVENTA, Beverly R.
1986   "Galatians 1 and 2: Autobiography as Paradigm." *NT* 28:309–26.
GESE, Hartmut
1967   "Der Dekalog als Ganzheit betrachtet." *ZTK* 64:121–38 (also available pp.
         63–80 in *Vom Sinai zum Zion. Alttestamentliche Beiträge zur biblischen
         Theologie.* BEvT 64. München: Kaiser, 1974).
1983   "Die Sühne." Pp. 85–106 in *Zur biblischen Theologie. Alttestamentliche
         Vorträge.* Tübingen: Mohr.
GLAZIER-McDONALD, Beth
1987   *Malachi. The Divine Messenger.* SBLDS 98. Atlanta: Scholars.
GOLDSTEIN, Jonathan A.
1976   *1 Maccabees. A New Translation with Introduction and Commentary.* AB
         41. New York: Doubleday.

GOPPELT, Leonhard
1939   *Typos. Die typologische Deutung des Alten Testaments im Neuen.* Darm-
        stadt: Wissenschaftliche Buchgesellschaft, 1981.
GORDON, T. David
1987   "The Problem at Galatia." *Int* 41:32–43.
1989   "A Note on Paidagôgos in Galatians 3.24–25." *NTS* 35:150–54.
GRIMES, Ronald L.
1988   "Infelicitous Performances and Ritual Criticism." *Semeia* 41:103–22.
GROSHEIDE, F. W.
1953   *Commentary on the First Epistle to the Corinthians.* NICNT. Grand
        Rapids: Eerdmans.
GROSS, H.
1987   *Tobit. Judit.* Die Neue Echter Bibel. Kommentar zum Alten Testament
        mit der Einheitsübersetzung. Würzburg: Echter Verlag.
GUNTHER, John J.
1973   St Paul's Opponents and Their Background. A Study of Apocalyptic and
        Jewish Sectarian Teachings. NovTSup 35. Leiden: Brill.
HAHN, F.
1971   "Genesis 15,6 im Neuen Testament." Pp. 90–107 in FS G. von Rad:
        Probleme biblischer Theologie. Ed. Hans W. Wolff. München: Kaiser.
HALL, Jerome
1985   "Paul, the Lawyer, on Law." *Journal of Law and Religion* 3:331–79.
HALL, Robert G.
1987   "The Rhetorical Outline for Galatians. A Reconsideration." *JBL* 106:277–
        87.
HAMERTON-KELLY, R. G.
1990a   "Sacred Violence and the Curse of the Law (Galatians 3.13): The Death of
        Christ as a Sacrificial Travesty." *NTS* 36:98–118.
1990b   "Sacred Violence and 'Works of Law.' 'Is Christ Then an Agent of Sin'
        (Galatians 2:17)." *CBQ* 52:55–75.
HANSEN, G. Walter
1989   *Abraham in Galatians. Epistolary and Rhetorical Contexts.* JSNTSup 29.
        Sheffield: Sheffield Academic Press.
HANSON, Anthony T.
1974   *Studies in Paul's Technique and Theology.* London: SPCK.
HARTMAN, Lars
1979   *Asking for a Meaning: A Study of 1 Enoch 1–5.* ConBNT 12. Lund:
        Gleerup.
1980   "Bundesideologie in und hinter einigen paulinischen Texten." Pp. 103–18
        in *Die Paulinische Literatur und Theologie.* Teologiske studier 7. Ed.
        Sigfred Pedersen. Århus: Aros; Göttingen: Vandenhoeck & Ruprecht.
HAWKINS, John G.
1971   "The Opponents of Paul in Galatia." Unpublished diss. Yale University.
HAYS, Richard B.
1983   *The Faith of Jesus Christ. An Investigation of the Narrative Substructure of
        Galatians 3:1 - 4:11.* SBLDS 56. Chico: Scholars.
1989   *Echoes of Scripture in the Letters of Paul.* New Haven, London: Yale.
HEILIGENTHAL, Roman
1984   "Soziologische Implikationen der Paulinischen Rechtfertigungslehre im
        Galaterbrief am Beispiel der 'Werke des Gesetzes.' Beobachtungen zur
        Identitätsfindung einer frühchristlichen Gemeinde." *Kairos* 26:38–53.

HELLHOLM, David
1980   *Das Visionenbuch des Hermas als Apokalypse. Formgeschichtliche und texttheoretische Studien zu einer literarischen Gattung, I.* ConBNT 13:1. Lund: Gleerup.

HEMER, Colin J.
1989   *The Book of Acts in the Setting of Hellenistic History.* WUNT 49. Tübingen: Mohr/Siebeck.

HEMPEL, Johannes
1925   "Die israelitischen Anschauungen von Segen und Fluch im Lichte altorientalischer Parallelen." *ZDMG* 79:20–110 (also available pp. 30–113 in *Apoxysmata. Vorarbeiten zu einer Religionsgeschichte und Theologie des Alten Testaments.* BZAW 81. Berlin: Töpelmann, 1961).

HENGEL, Martin
1976   *Die Zeloten. Untersuchungen zur jüdischen Freiheitsbewegung in der Zeit von Herodes I. bis 70 n. Chr.* AGJU 1. Leiden: Brill (verbesserte und erweiterte auflage) (also available: *The Zealots.* Edinburgh: T. & T. Clark 1989).
1989   *The 'Hellenization' of Judaea in the First Century after Christ.* London: SCM; Philadelphia: Trinity.
1991   *The Pre-Christian Paul.* London, New York: SCM.

HESTER, James D.
1984   "The Rhetorical Structure of Galatians 1:11 – 2:14." *JBL* 103:223–33.
1986   "The Use and Influence of Rhetoric in Galatians 2:1–14." *TZ* 42:386–408.

HILLERS, D. R.
1964   *Treaty-Curses and the Old Testament Prophets.* BibOr 16. Rome: Pontifical Biblical Institute.

HIRSCH, Emanuel
1930   "Zwei Fragen zu Galater 6." *ZNW* 29:192–97.

HODGSON, Robert
1983   "Paul the Apostle and First Century Tribulation Lists." *ZNW* 74:59–80

HOFIUS, Otfried
1983a   "Das Gesetz des Mose und das Gesetz Christi." *ZTK* 80:262–86 (also available in Hofius 1989:50–74).
1983b   "Sühne und Versöhnung. Zum paulinischen Verständnis des Kreuzestodes Jesu," pp. 25–46 in Maas, W., ed.: *Versuche, das Leiden und Sterben Jesu zu verstehen.* Schriftenreihe der katholischen Akademie der Erzdiözese Freiburg. München: Schnell & Steiner (also available in Hofius 1989:33–49).
1989   *Paulusstudien.* WUNT 51. Tübingen: Mohr/Siebeck.

HOFMANN, K.
RAC   1:427–30, art. "Anathema."

HOLLADAY, William L.
1986   *Jeremiah 1. A Commentary on the Book of the Prophet Jeremiah Chapters 1–25.* Hermeneia. Philadelphia: Fortress.
1989   *Jeremiah 2. A Commentary on the Book of the Prophet Jeremiah Chapters 26–52.* Hermeneia. Minneapolis: Fortress.

HOLLANDER, Harm W. and Marius de JONGE
1985   *The Testaments of the Twelve Patriarchs. A Commentary.* SVTP 8. Leiden: Brill.

HOLTZ, Traugott
1971   "Das Kennzeichen des Geistes (1 Kor. xii.1–3)." *NTS* 18:365–76.
1986   "Der Antiochenische Zwischenfall (Galater 2.11–14)." *NTS* 32:344–61.

HOOKER, Morna D.
1989   "'ΠΙΣΤΙΣ ΧΡΙΣΤΟΥ.'" *NTS* 35:321–42.
HORBURY, William
1985   "Extirpation and excommunication." *VT* 35:13–38.
HORST, Friedrich
1930   *Das Privilegrecht Jahwehs. Rechtgeschichtliche Untersuchungen zum Deuteronomium.* FRLANT 45 (NF 28). Göttingen: Vandenhoeck & Ruprecht (also avaliable in Horst 1961:17–154).
1957   "Der Eid im Alten Testament." *EvT* 17:366–84 (also available in Horst 1961:292–314).
1961   *Gottes Recht. Gesammelte Studien zum Recht im Alten Testament.* TBü 12. München: Kaiser.
HOWARD, George
1979   *Paul: Crisis in Galatia. A Study in Early Christian Theology.* SNTSMS 35. Cambridge: Cambridge University Press.
HÜBNER, Hans
1973   "Gal 3,10 und die Herkunft des Paulus." *KD* 19:215–31.
1984a   *Law in Paul's Thought. Studies of the New Testament and Its World.* Edinburgh: T. & T. Clark (cf. also *Das Gesetz bei Paulus: Ein Beitrag zum Werden der paulinischen Theologie.* FRLANT 119. Göttingen: Vandenhoeck & Ruprecht, 1978).
1984b   "Der Galaterbrief und das Verhältnis von antiker Rhetorik und Epistolographie." *TLZ* 109:241–50.
TRE   12:5–14, art. "Galaterbrief."
HULTGREN, Arland J.
1980   "The πίστις χριστοῦ Formulation in Paul." *NT* 22:248–63.
HUNZINGER, Claus-Hunno
1954   "Die jüdische Bannpraxis im neutestamentlichen Zeitalter." Unpublished diss. Göttingen (typewritten).
TRE   5:161–67, art. "Bann. II: Frühjudentum und Neues Testament."
ISER, Wolfgang
1990   *Der Akt des Lesens. Theorie ästhetischer Wirkung.* UTB 636. München: Fink (=1984²: durchgesehene und verbesserte Auflage; also available: *The Act of Reading. A Theory of Aesthetic Response.* Baltimore: Johns Hopkins University Press, 1978).
JANOWSKI, Bernd
1982   *Sühne als Heilsgeschehen. Studien zur Sühnetheologie der Priesterschrift and zur Wurzel KPR im Alten Orient und im Alten Testament.* WMANT 55. Neukirchen-Vluyn: Neukirchener.
JEREMIAS, Gert
1963   *Der Lehrer der Gerechtigkeit.* SUNT 2. Göttingen: Vandenhoeck & Ruprecht.
JERVELL, Jacob
1969   "Ein Interpolator interpretiert. Zu der christlichen Bearbeitung der Testamente der zwölf Patriarchen." Pp. 30–61 in *Studien zu den Testamenten der Zwölf Patriarchen.* Ed. W. Eltester. Berlin: Töpelmann.
JEWETT, Robert
1970   "The Agitators and the Galatian Congregation." *NTS* 17:198–212.
JOHNSON Jr., S. Lewis
1987   "Paul and 'The Israel of God.'" *Mishkan* 6-7:49–65.
de JONGE, Marius
1975   *The Testaments of the Twelve Patriarchs. A Study of their Text, Composi-*

tion and Origin. Van Gorcum's theologische Bibliotheek 25. Assen: Van Gorcum.

1980   "The Main Issues in the Study of the Testaments of the Twelve Patriarchs." *NTS* 26:508–24.

1986   "The Future of Israel in the Testaments of the Twelve Patriarchs." *JSJ* 17:196–211.

KANG, Sa-Moon
1989   *Divine War in the Old Testament and in the Ancient Near East*. BZAW 177. Berlin - New York: De Gruyter.

KÄSEMANN, Ernst
1954   "Sätze heiligen Rechts im Neuen Testament." *NTS* 1:248–60.
1974   *An die Römer*. HNT 8a. Tübingen: Mohr/Siebeck 19742.

KEE, Howard C.
1978   "The Ethical Dimensions of the Testaments of the XII as a Clue to Provenance." *NTS* 24:259–70.

KENNEDY, George A.
1984   *New Testament Interpretation through Rhetorical Criticism*. Studies in Religion. Chapel Hill, London: University of North Carolina Press.

KIM, C. -N.
1984   "Der Kampf des Paulus für das Evangelium in Galatien." Unpublished diss. Mainz.

KIM, Seyoon
1981   *The Origin of Paul's Gospel*. Michigan: Eerdmans 1982 (first publ. WUNT II, 4. Tübingen: Mohr/Siebeck, 1981).

KISS, Igor
1964   "Der Begriff 'Fluch' in Neuen Testament." *Communio Viatorum* 7:87–92.

KLAUCK, Hans-Josef
1982   *Herrenmahl und hellenistischer Kult. Eine religionsgeschichtliche Untersuchung zum ersten Korinterbrief*. NTA NF 15. Münster: Aschendorf.

KLEIN, G.
1918   *Studien über Paulus*. Beiträge zur Religionswissenschaft 3. Stockholm.

KLEIN, Günter
1964   "Individualgeschichte und Weltgeschichte bei Paulus. Eine Interpretation ihres Verhältnisses im Galaterbrief." *EvT* 24:126–65 (Also available pp. 180–224 in *Rekonstruktion und Interpretation. Gesammelte Aufsätze zum Neuen Testament*. BEvT 50. München: Kaiser, 1969).

KNIERIM, R.
THAT   1:920–22, art. "מצל - treulos sein."

KOCH, Dietrich-Alex
1985   "Der Text von Hab 2,4b in der Septuaginta und im Neuen Testament." *ZNW* 76:68–85.

1986   *Die Schrift als Zeuge des Evangeliums: Untersuchungen zur Verwendung und zum Verständnis der Schrift bei Paulus*. BHT 69. Tübingen: Mohr/Siebeck.

KÖSTER, Helmut
1968   "ΓΝΩΜΑΙ ΔΙΑΦΟΡΟΙ. Ursprung und Wesen der Mannigfaltigkeit in der Geschichte des frühen Christentums." *ZTK* 65:160–203 (in English: *HThR* 58:279–318).

KRATZ, Corinne A.
1989   "Genres of power: A comparative analysis of Okiek blessings, curses and oaths." *Man* (New Ser.) 24:636–56.

KRAUS, Hans-Joachim
1978   *Psalmen. 2. Teilband. Psalmen 60–150.* BKAT XV/2. Grundlegend
           überarbeitete und veränderte Auflage. Neukirchen-Vluyn: Neukirchener,
           1978⁵.
KUHN, Heinz-Wolfgang
1975   "Jesus als Gekreuzigter in der frühchristlichen Verkündigung bis zur Mitte
           des 2. Jahrhunderts." *ZTK* 72:1–46.
LAMBRECHT, Jan
1978   "The Line of Thought in Gal 2.14b-21." *NTS* 24:484–95.
LANG, Friedrich
1986   *Die Briefe an die Korinther.* NTD 7. Göttingen: Vandenhoeck &
           Ruprecht.
LATEGAN, Bernard C.
1989   "Levels of Reader Instructions in the Text of Galatians." *Semeia* 48:171–
           84.
LEHMANN, Manfred R.
1969   "Biblical Oaths." *ZAW* 81:74–92.
LICHTENBERGER, Hermann
1980   *Studien zum Menschenbild in Texten der Qumrangemeinde.* SUNT 15.
           Göttingen: Vandenhoeck & Ruprecht.
LIEDKE, Gerhard
1971   *Gestalt un Bezeichnung alttestamentlicher Rechtssätze.* WMANT 39.
           Neukirchen-Vluyn: Neukirchener.
LIETZMANN, Hans
1923   *An die Galater.* HNT 10. Tübingen: Mohr/Siebeck.
1949   *An die Korinther I/II.* HNT 9. Tübingen: Mohr/Siebeck.
LIGHTFOOT, Joseph B.
1876   *St. Paul's Epistle to the Galatians.* Fifth edition. London: MacMillan,
           1876.
LITTLE, Lester K.
1987   "Cursing." Pp. 182–85 in *The Encyclopedia of Religion, Vol 4.* Ed. Mir-
           cea Eliade. New York - London: MacMillan.
LOHSE, Eduard (ed.)
1981   *Die Texte aus Qumran, Hebräisch und Deutsch.* Third edition. München:
           Kösel.
LOHFINK, Norbert
1962   "Der Bundesschluss im Land Moab." *BZ* (Neue Folge) 6:32–56.
TDOT   5:180–99, art. "הרם."
LÖVY, M.
1903   "Die Paulinische Lehre vom Gesetz." *MGWJ* 47:417–33.
LÜBBE, J.
1986   "A Reinterpretation of 4Q Testimonia." *RevQ* 12:187–97.
LÜDEMANN, Gerd
1984   *Paul, Apostle to the Gentiles. Studies in Chronology.* London: SCM (also
           available: *Paulus der Heidenapostel I: Studien zur Chronologie.*
           FRLANT 123. Göttingen: Vandenhoeck & Ruprecht, 1980).
LÜHRMANN, Dieter
1978   *Der Brief an die Galater.* Zürcher Bibelkommentare NT 7. Zürich:
           Theologischer Verlag.
1980   "Tage, Monate, Jahreszeiten, Jahre (Gal 4,10)." Pp. 428–45 in FS C.
           Westermann: *Werden und Wirken des Alten Testaments.* Göttingen:
           Vandenhoeck & Ruprecht; Neukirchen-Vluyn: Neukirchener.

LULL, David J.
1980   *The Spirit in Galatia. Paul's Interpretation of "pneuma" as Divine Power.* SBLDS 49. Chico: Scholars.
1986   "'The Law Was Our Pedagogue.' A Study in Galatians 3,19–25." *JBL* 105:481–98.

LUNDBLOM, Jack R.
1985   "The Double Curse in Jeremiah 20:14–18." *JBL* 104:589–600.

LÜTGERT, Wilhelm
1919   *Gesetz und Geist. Eine Untersuchung zur Vorgeschichte des Galaterbriefes.* BFCT 22/6. Gütersloh: Bertelsmann.

LUTHER, Martin
1535   *Lectures on Galatians 1535. Luther's Works, Vols. 26–27.* Ed. Jaroslav Pelikan. Saint Louis: Concordia, 1963–64.

LUZ, Ulrich
1968   *Das Geschichtsverständnis des Paulus.* BEvT 49. München: Kaiser.

LYONS, George
1985   *Pauline Autobiography. Toward a New Understanding.* SBLDS 73. Atlanta: Scholars.

LYONS, John
1977   *Semantics I/II.* Cambridge: Cambridge University Press.

MACK, Burton L.
1990   *Rhetoric and the New Testament.* Guides to Biblical Scholarship. NT-series. Minneapolis: Fortress.

MACK, Burton L. and Vernon K. ROBBINS
1989   *Patterns of Persuasion in the Gospels.* Foundations & Facets. Literary Facets. Sonoma: Polebridge.

MALHERBE, Abraham J.
1970   "'Gentle as a Nurse.' The Cynic Background to 1 Thess ii." *NT* 12:203–17.
1977   "Ancient Epistolary Theorists." *Ohio Journal of Religious Studies* 5,2:3–77 (also available as SBLSBS 19. Atlanta: Scholars, 1988).

MALY, K.
1966   "1 Kor 12,1–3, eine Regel zur Unterscheidung der Geister?" *BZ* 10:82–95.

MARROU, Henri-Irénée
1957   *Geschichte der Erziehung im klassischen Altertum.* Freiburg, München: Alber.

MARTIN, Josef
1974   *Antike Rhetorik. Technik und Methode.* Handbuch der Altertumswissenschaft 2.3. München: Beck.

MARXSEN, Willi
1964   *Einleitung in das Neue Testament. Eine Einfürung in ihre Probleme.* Gütersloh: Gütersloher.

MATERA, Frank J.
1988   "The Culmination of Paul's Argument to the Galatians: Gal 5.1 – 6.17." *JSNT* 32:79–91.

MAYER, Günter
RAC   6:1194–1211, art. "Exegese II (Judentum)."

MAYES, Andrew D. H.
1979   *Deuteronomy.* NCB. London: Marshall, Morgan & Scott.
1981   "Deuteronomy 4 and the Literary Criticism of Deuteronomy." *JBL* 100:23–51.

McBRIDE, S. Dean
1987   "Polity of the Covenant People. The Book of Deuteronomy." *Int* 41:229–44.
TRE   8:530–43, art. "Deuteronomium."
McCARTHY, Dennis J.
1978   *Treaty and Covenant.* AnBib 21a. New rewritten edition. Rome: Pontifical Biblical Institute.
McELENEY, Neil J.
1974   "Conversion, Circumcision and the Law." *NTS* 20:319–41.
McKENZIE, Steven L. and Howard N. WALLACE
1983   "Covenant Themes in Malachi." *CBQ* 45:549–63.
McKNIGHT, Edgar V.
1988   *Post-Modern Use of the Bible. The Emergence of Reader-Oriented Criticism.* Nashville: Abingdon.
MERK, Otto
1969   "Der Beginn der Paränese im Galaterbrief." *ZNW* 60:83–104.
MERKLEIN, Helmut
1987   "Die Bedeutung des Kreuzestodes Christi für die paulinische Gerechtigkeits- und Gesetzesthematik." Pp. 1–106 in *Studien zu Jesus und Paulus.* WUNT 43. Tübingen: Mohr/Siebeck.
METZGER, Bruce M.
1975   *A Textual Commentary on the Greek New Testament.* Corrected edition. London - New York: United Bible Societies.
MICHAELIS, D. W.
1931   "Judaistische Heidenchristen." *ZNW* 30:83–89.
MICHEL, Otto
1951   "Opferbereitschaft für Israel." Pp. 94–100 in *In memoriam E. Lohmeyer.* Ed. W. Schmauch. Stuttgart: Evangelisches Verlagswerk.
1978   *Der Brief an die Römer.* Kritisch-Exegetischer Kommentar über das NT IV. Fifth edition. Göttingen: Vandenhoeck & Ruprecht 1978.
1984   "Die Rettung Israels und die Rolle Roms nach den Reden im 'Bellum Iudaicum.' Analysen und Perspektiven." Pp. 945–76 in *ANRW* II, 21.2.
MILIK, J. T.
1972   "Milkî-tsedeq et Milkî-reshac dans les anciens écrits juifs et chrétiens." *JJS* 23:95–144.
MITCHELL, Christopher W.
1987   *The Meaning of BRK "To Bless" in The Old Testament.* SBLDS 95. Atlanta: Scholars.
MOORE, Michael S.
1990   *The Balaam Traditions: Their Character and Development.* SBLDS 113. Atlanta: Scholars.
MOULE, C. F. D.
1960   "A Reconsideration of the Context of Maranatha." *NTS* 6:307–10.
MOWINCKEL, Sigmund
1924   *Psalmenstudien V. Segen und Fluch im Israels Kult und Psalmdichtung.* Norske vitenskapsakademi i Oslo, Skrifter II, HisFil kl, 1923,3. Kristiania. (also available in *Psalmenstudien III-VI.* Amsterdam: Schippers, 1966).
MÜLLER, Hans-Peter
1969   *Ursprünge und Strukturen alttestamentlicher Eschatologie.* BZAW 109. Berlin: Töpelmann.

MÜLLER, Ulrich B.
1975   *Prophetie und Predigt im Neuen Testament. Formgeschichtliche Untersuchungen zur urchristlichen Prophetie.* SNT 10. Gütersloh: Gütersloher.
MUNCK, Johannes
1954   *Paulus und die Heilsgeschichte.* Acta Jutlandica XXVI,1. Aarhus: Universitetsforlaget (also available: *Paul and the Salvation of Mankind.* Atlanta, 1977).
MÜNDERLEIN, Gerhard
1965   "Interpretation einer Tradition. Bemerkungen zu Röm 8,35f." *KD* 11:136–42.
MUNDLE, Wilhelm
1924   "Zur Auslegung von Gal 2,17.18." *ZNW* 23:152–53.
MURPHY, Frederick J.
1985   *The Structure and Meaning of Second Baruch.* SBLDS 78. Atlanta: Scholars.
1988a   "Retelling the Bible: Idolatry in Pseudo-Philo." *JBL* 107:275–87.
1988b   "The Eternal Covenant in Pseudo-Philo." *JSPseud* 3:43–57.
1988c   "God in Pseudo-Philo." *JSJ* 19:1–18.
MUSSNER, Franz
1974   *Der Galaterbrief.* HTKNT IX. Freiburg-Basel-Wien: Herder.
NEITZEL, Heinz
1983   "Zur Interpretation von Galater 2,11–21." *TQ* 163:15–39, 131–49.
NEUSNER, Jacob
1985   *A History of the Mishnaic Law of Damages. Part V: The Mishnaic System of Damages.* SJLA 35,5. Leiden: Brill.
NEYREY, Jerome H.
1988   "Bewitched in Galatia: Paul and Cultural Anthropology." *CBQ* 50:72–100.
NICKELSBURG, George W. E.
1977   "Apocalyptic and Myth in 1 Enoch 6–11." *JBL* 96:383–405.
1980   "Good and Bad Leaders in Pseudo-Philo's Liber Antiquitatum Biblicarum." Pp. 49–65 in *Ideal Figures in Ancient Judaism. Profiles and Paradigms.* SBLSCS 12. Ed. George W. E. Nickelsburg; J. J. Collins. Chico: Scholars.
1981   *Jewish Literature Between the Bible and the Mishnah. A Historical and Literary Introduction.* London: SCM.
NORDEN, Eduard
1958   *Die Antike Kunstprosa vom VI. Jahrhundert v. Chr. bis in die Zeit der Renaissance. II.* Stuttgart: Teubner, 1958⁵.
NOTH, Martin
1938   "Die mit des Gesetzes Werken umgehen, die sind unter dem Fluch." Pp. 127–45 in *In piam memoriam Alexander von Bulmerincq.* Abhandlungen der Herder-Gesellschaft und des Herder-Instituts zu Riga. VI Band Nr 3. Riga (also available pp. 155–71 in *Gesammelte Studien zum Alten Testament.* TBü 6. München: Kaiser, 1960²).
OEPKE, Albrecht and Joachim ROHDE.
1973   *Der Brief des Paulus an die Galater.* THKNT IX. Veränderte und erweiterte Auflage. Berlin: Evangelische Verlagsanstalt, 1973³.
PAURITSCH, K.
1971   *Die neue Gemeinde: Gott sammelt Ausgestossene und Arme (Jes 56–66). Die Botschaft des Tritojesaja- Buches literar-, form-, gattungskritisch und*

redaktionsgeschichtlich untersucht. AnBib 47. Rome: Biblical Institute Press.

PEARSON, Birger A.
1967   "Did the Gnostics curse Jesus?" *JBL* 86:301–05.

PEDERSEN, Johannes
1914   *Der Eid bei den Semiten in seiner Verhältnis zu verwandten erscheinungen sowie die stellung des Eides im Islam.* Studien zur Geschichte und Kultur des islamischen Orients 3. Strassburg: K. J. Trubner.
1926   *Israel. Its life and culture I-II.* København: Branner.

PETERSEN, David L.
1984   *Haggai and Zechariah 1–8. A Commentary.* OTL. Philadelphia: SCM.

PLÖGER, Josef G.
1967   *Literarkritische, formgeschichtliche und stilkritische Untersuchungen zum Deuteronomium.* BBB 26. Bonn: Hanstein.

PREUSS, Horst D.
1982   *Deuteronomium.* Erträge der Forschung 164. Darmstadt: Wissenschaftliche Buchgesellschaft.

von RAD, Gerhard
1938   "Das formgeschichtliche Problem des Hexateuch." *BWANT* 4. folge, Heft 26. Stuttgart (also available pp. 9–86 in *Gesammelte Studien zum Alten Testament.* TBü 8. München: Kaiser, 1971[4]).
1966   *Deuteronomy. A Commentary.* OTL. London: SCM.

RÄISÄNEN, Heikki.
1983   *Paul and the Law.* WUNT 29. Tübingen: Mohr/Siebeck.
1985   "Galatians 2,16 and Paul's Break with Judaism." *NTS* 31:543–53 (also pp. 168–84 in Räisänen 1986b).
1986a   "Sprachliches zum Spiel des Paulus mit ΝΟΜΟΣ." Pp. 119–47 in Räisänen 1986b.
1986b   *The Torah and Christ. Essays in German and English on the Problem of the Law in Early Christianity.* Publ. of the Finnish Exegetical Society 45. Helsinki: The Finnish Exegetical Society.
1987   "Römer 9–11: Analyse eines geistigen Ringens." Pp. 2891–2939 in *ANRW* II, 25.4.

RAY, B.
1973   "'Performative Utterances' in African Rituals." *HR* 13:16–35.

REICKE, Bo
1985   "Paulus über das Gesetz." *TZ* 41:237–57.

RENDTORFF, Rolf
1961   "Genesis 8,21 und die Urgeschichte des Jahwisten." *KD* 7:69–78.

RENGSTORF, K. H.
TDNT   1:317–33, art. ἁμαρτωλός."

REVENTLOW, Henning G.
1961   *Das Heiligkeitsgesetz. Formgeschichtlich untersucht.* WMANT 6. Neukirchen: Neukirchener.
1962a   *Wächter über Israel. Ezechiel und seine Tradition.* BZAW 82. Berlin: Töpelmann.
1962b   *Das Amt des Propheten bei Amos.* FRLANT 80. Göttingen: Vandenhoeck & Ruprecht.

RICHARDSON, Peter
1969   *Israel in the Apostolic Church.* SNTSMS 10. Cambridge: Cambridge University Press.

RIDDERBOS, Herman N.
1979   *The Epistle of Paul to the Churches of Galatia.* NICNT. Eleventh edition.
          Grand Rapids: Eerdmans.

RIESNER, Rainer
1990   *Die Frühzeit des Paulus. Studien zur Chronologie, Missionsstrategie und
          Theologie des Apostels bis zum ersten Thessalonicher-brief.* Habilitation
          Tübingen (to appear in WUNT. Tübingen: Mohr/Siebeck).

RIMMON-KENAN, Shlomith
1983   *Narrative Fiction: Contemporary Poetics.* London: Methuen.

ROETZEL, Calvin J.
1972   *Judgement in the Community. A Study of the Relationship Between
          Eschatology and Ecclesiology in Paul.* Leiden: Brill.

ROFÉ, Alexander
1985   "The Laws of Warfare in the Book of Deuteronomy: Their Origins, Intent
          and Positivity." *JSOT* 32:23–44.

ROHDE, Joachim
1989   *Der Brief des Paulus an die Galater.* THKNT IX. Berlin: Evangelische
          Verlagsanstalt.

ROPES, James H.
1929   *The Singular Problem of the Epistle to the Galatians.* HTS 14. Cam-
          bridge: Harvard University Press.

RUPRECHT, Eberhard.
1979a   "Vorgegebene Tradition und theologische Gestaltung in Genesis xii 1–3."
          VT 29:171–88.
1979b   "Der traditionsgeschichtliche Hintergrund der einzelnen Elemente von Gen
          xii 2–3." *VT* 29:444–64.

SAMPLEY, J. Paul
1977   "'Before God, I do not lie' (Gal 1,20): Paul's Self-defence in the Light of
          Roman Legal Praxis." *NTS* 23:477–82.

SANDERS, Edward P.
1977   *Paul and Palestinian Judaism. A Comparison of Patterns of Religion.*
          London: SCM.
1978   "On the Question of Fulfilling the Law in Paul and Rabbinic Judaism." Pp.
          103–26 in FS David Daube: *Donum Gentilicium.* Ed. E. Bammel, C. K.
          Barrett, W. D. Davies. Oxford: Clarendon.
1983   *Paul, the Law, and the Jewish People.* Philadelphia: Fortress.

SANDNES, Karl O.
1991   *"Paul — One of the Prophets"? A Contribution to the Apostle's Self-
          Understanding.* WUNT II, 43. Tübingen: Mohr/Siebeck.

SAUER, Jürgen
1985   "Traditionsgeschichtliche Erwägungen zu den synoptischen und paulinis-
          chen Aussagen über Feindesliebe und Wiedervergeltungsverzicht." *ZNW*
          76:1–28.

SCHARBERT, Josef
1958a   "'Fluchen' und 'Segnen' im Alten Testament." *Bib* 39:1–26.
1958b   *Solidarität in Segen und Fluch im Alten Testament und in seiner Umwelt.*
          1. Väterfluch and Vätersegen. BBB 14. Bonn: P. Hanstein.
TWAT   1:279–85, art. "אלה."
TWAT   1:437–51, art. "ארר."
TWAT   7:40–49, art. "קלל."

SCHENK, Wolfgang
1967   *Der Segen im Neuen Testament. Eine begriffsanalytische Studie.*

Theologische Arbeiten XXV. Berlin: Evangelische Verlagsanstalt.

SCHLATTER, Adolf

1934   *Paulus der Bote Jesu. Eine Deutung seiner Briefe an die Korinther.* Stuttgart: Calwer.

SCHLIER, Heinrich

1965   *Der Brief an die Galater.* Kritisch-Exegetischer Kommentar über das NT 7. 4. durchgesehene Aufl. der Neuarbeitung. Göttingen: Vandenhoeck & Ruprecht 1965[13].).

1977   *Der Römerbrief.* HTKNT VI. Freiburg - Basel - Wien: Herder.

SCHMITHALS, Walter

1956a   *Die Gnosis in Korinth. Eine Untersuchung zu den Korintherbriefen.* FRLANT, Neue Folge 48. Göttingen: Vandenhoeck & Ruprecht.

1956b   "Die Häretiker in Galatien." *ZNW* 47:25-67.

1983   "Judaisten in Galatien?" *ZNW* 74:27-58.

SCHMITT, Armin

1986   *Das Buch der Weisheit. Ein Kommentar.* Würzburg: Echter.

SCHOEPS, Hans J.

1961   *Paul: The Theology of the Apostle in the Light of Jewish Religious History.* Trans. H. Knight. Philadelphia: Westminster.

SCHOTTROFF, Willy

1969   *Der altisraelitische Fluchspruch.* WMANT 30. Neukirchen-Vluyn: Neukirchener.

SCHREINER, J.

1962   "Segen für die Völker in der Verheissung an die Väter." *BZ* 6:1-31.

SCHRENK, G.

1950   "Der Segenswunsch nach der Kampfepistel." *Judaica* 6:170-90.

SCHULZ, Hermann

1969   *Das Todesrecht im Alten Testament. Studien zur Rechtsform der Mot-Jumat-Sätze.* BZAW 114. Berlin: Töpelmann.

SCHÜRER, Emil

1979   *The History of the Jewish people in the Age of Jesus Christ (175 BC - AD 135) vol II.* A new English version rev. and ed. by Geza Vermes, F. Millar, M. Black. Edinburgh: T. & T. Clark.

1986   *The History of the Jewish people in the Age of Jesus Christ (175 BC - AD 135) vol III.1.* Also ed. M. Goodman. Edinburgh: T. & T. Clark.

1987   *The History of the Jewish people in the Age of Jesus Christ (175 BC - AD 135) vol III.2.* Edinburgh: T. & T. Clark.

SCHWARTZ, Daniel R.

1983   "Two Pauline Allusions to the Redemptive Mechanism of the Crucifixion." *JBL* 102:259-68.

SCHWEITZER, Albert

1930   *Die Mystik des Apostels Paulus.* Tübingen: Mohr.

SCHWIENHORST-SCHÖNBERGER, Ludger

1990   *Das Bundesbuch (Ex 20,22 - 23,33). Studien zu seiner Entstehung und Theologie.* BZAW 188. Berlin - New York: De Gruyter.

SEKINE, Seizo

1989   *Die Tritojesajanische Sammlung (Jes 56–66) redaktionsgeschichtlich untersucht.* BZAW 175. Berlin - New York: De Gruyter.

SIEFFERT, Friedrich

1880   *Handbuch über den Brief an die Galater.* Kritisch-Exegetischer Kommentar über das NT 7. Göttingen: Vandenhoeck & Ruprecht.

SIEGERT, Folker
1985   *Argumentation bei Paulus, gezeigt an Röm 9-11.* WUNT 34. Tübingen:
        Mohr.
SJÖBERG, Erik
TDNT   6:375-89, art. "πνεῦμα C III: רוח in Palestinian Judaism."
SKARSAUNE, Oskar
1987   *The Proof from Prophecy. A Study in Justin Martyr's Proof-Text Tradition:*
        Text-Type, Provenance, Theological Profile. NovTSup LVI. Leiden:
        Brill.
SLINGERLAND, Dixon
1986   "The Nature of Nomos (Law) within the Testaments of the Twelve
        Patriarchs." *JBL* 105:39-48.
SMIGA, G. M.
1985   "Language, experience, and theology: The argumentation of Galatians 3:6
        - 4:7 in light of the literary form of letter." Unpublished diss. Rome.
SMIT, Joop
1989   "The Letter of Paul to the Galatians: A Deliberative Speech." *NTS* 35:1-
        26.
SMITH, Ralph L.
1984   *Micah-Malachi.* Word Biblical Commentary 32. Waco: Word.
SPEYER, Wolfgang
RAC   7:1161-1288, art. "Fluch."
SPICQ, C.
1956   "Comment comprendre ΦΙΛΕΙΝ dans 1 Cor XVI,22?" *NT* 1:200-04.
STÄHLIN, G.
1962   "Zum Gebrauch von Beteuerungsformeln im Neuen Testament." *NT*
        5:115-43.
STANLEY, Christopher D.
1990   "'Under a Curse': A fresh reading of Galatians 3.10-14." *NTS* 36:481-
        511.
STECK, Odil H.
1967   *Israel und das Gewaltsame Geschick der Propheten. Untersuchungen zur*
        Überlieferung des deuteronomistischen Geshichtsbildes im Alten Testament,
        Spätjudentum und Urchristentum. WMANT 23. Neukirchen-Vluyn:
        Neukrichener.
1971   "Gen 12,1-3 und die Urgeschichte des Jahwisten." Pp. 525-54 in FS G.
        von Rad: *Probleme biblischer Theologie.* Ed. Hans W. Wolff. München:
        Kaiser.
STEGEMANN, Hartmut
1985   "Some Aspects of Eschatology in Texts from the Qumran Community and
        in the Teachings of Jesus." Pp. 408-26 in *Biblical Archaeology Today.*
        Proceedings of the International Congress on Biblical Archaeology, April
        1984. Jerusalem: Israel Exploration Society.
STOWERS, Stanley K.
1986   *Letter Writing in Greco-Roman Antiquity.* Library of Early Christianity 5.
        Philadelphia: Westminster.
STRACK, Hermann L. and Günter STEMBERGER
1982   *Einleitung in Talmud und Midrasch.* Beck'sche Elementarbücher. Völlig
        neu bearb. Auflage. München: Beck 1982[7].
STROBEL, August
1980   *Die Stunde der Wahrheit. Untersuchungen zum Strafverfahren gegen Jesus.*
        WUNT 21. Tübingen: Mohr.

STUHLMACHER, Peter
1968   *Das paulinische Evangelium. I: Vorgeschichte.* FRLANT 95. Göttingen:
          Vandenhoeck & Ruprecht.
1977   "Zur paulinischen Christologie." *ZTK* 74:449-63.
STULMAN, Louis
1986   *The Prose Sermons of the Book of Jeremiah. A Redescription of the Cor-
          respondences with the Deuteronomistic Literature in the Light of Recent
          Text-critical Research.* SBLDS 83. Atlanta: Scholars.
SUHL, Alfred
1987   "Der Galaterbrief - Situation und Argumentation." Pp. 3067-3134 in
          ANRW II, 25.4.
SYNOFZIK, Ernst
1977   *Die Gerichts- und Vergeltungsaussagen bei Paulus. Eine traditionsges-
          chichtliche Untersuchung.* GTA 8. Göttingen: Vandenhoeck & Ruprecht.
THISELTON, Anthony C.
1973   "The Meaning of ΣΑΡΞ in 1 Corinthians 5,5: A Fresh Approach in the
          Light of Logical and Semantic Factors." *SJT* 26:204-28.
THOMPSON, John A.
1977   "Israel's 'Lovers.'" *VT* 27:475-81.
1979   "Israel's 'Haters.'" *VT* 29:200-205.
1980   *The Book of Jeremiah.* NICOT. Grand Rapids: Eerdmans.
THURUTHUMALY, Joseph
1981   *Blessing in St Paul (Eulogein in St Paul).* Pontifical Institute Publications
          35. Kerala: Pontifical Institute of Theology and Philosophy.
TIEDTKE, Erich and Hans-Georg LINK
NIDNTT   2:666-68, art. "ὀφείλω."
TYSON, Joseph B.
1968   "Paul's Opponents in Galatia." *NT* 10:241-54.
1973   "'Works of Law' in Galatians." *JBL* 92:423-31.
TÅNGBERG, K. Arvid
1987   *Die prophetische Mahnrede. Form- und traditionsgeschichtliche Studien
          zum prophetischen Umkehrruf.* FRLANT 143. Göttingen: Vandenhoeck
          & Ruprecht.
van UNNIK, Willem C.
1973a   "Jesus: Anathema or Kyrios (1 Cor 12:3)." Pp. 113-26 in FS C. F. D.
          Moule: *Christ and the Spirit in the New Testament.* Cambridge:
          University Press.
1973b   "Tarsus or Jerusalem, the City of Paul's Youth." Pp. 259-320 in Sparsa
          Collecta. *The collected Essays of W. C. van Unnik, I.* NovTSup 29.
          Leiden: Brill.
1979   "Der Fluch der Gekreuzigten. Deuteronomium 21,23 in der Deutung
          Justinus des Märtyrers." Pp. 483-99 in FS E. Dinkler: *Theologia Crucis
          — Signum Crucis.* Ed. Carl Andresen, G. Klein. Tübingen:
          Mohr/Siebeck.
VASSILYEV, L. M.
1974   "The Theory of Semantic Fields: A Survey." *Linguistics* 137:79-93.
de VAUX, Roland
1965   *Ancient Israel. Its Life and Institutions.* London: Darton, Longman &
          Todd.
VICKERS, Brian
1988   *In Defence of Rhetoric.* Oxford: Clarendon.

VIELHAUER, Philipp
1978   *Geshichte der urchristlichen Literatur. Einleitung in das Neue Testament, die Apokryphen und die Apostolischen Väter.* Second edition. Berlin - New York: De Gruyter.

VOS, J. S.
1992   "Die hermeneutische Antinomie bei Paulus (Galater 3.11-12; Römer 10.5-10)." *NTS* 38:254-70.

VOUGA, Francois
1988   "Zur rhetorischen Gattung des Galaterbriefes." *ZNW* 79:291-92.

WACHOLDER, Ben Zion
1989   "Rules of Testimony in Qumranic Jurisprudence: CD 9 and 11QTorah 64." *JJS* 40:163-74.

WAGNER, Volker
1972   *Rechtssätze in gebundener Sprache und Rechtssatzreihen im israelitischen Recht.* BZAW 127. Berlin - New York: De Gruyter.

WALLIS, G.
1974   "Der Vollbürgereid in Deuteronomium 27;15-26." *HUCA* 45:47-63.

WATSON, Duane F.
1988   "The New Testament and Greco-Roman Rhetoric: A Bibliography." *JETS* 31:465-72.

WEHMEIER, Gerhard
1970   *Der Segen im Alten Testament. Eine semasiologische Untersuchung der Wurzel* ברך. Theologische Dissertationen 6. Basel.

WEINFELD, Moshe
1965   "Traces of Assyrian Treaty Formulae in Deuteronomy." *Bib* 46:417-27.
1972   *Deuteronomy and the Deuteronomic School.* Oxford: Clarendon.
TDOT   1:253-79, art. "ברית."

WEISE, M.
1961   *Kultzeiten und kultischer Bundesschluss in der "Ordensregel" vom Toten Meer.* SPB 3. Leiden: Brill.

WEISS, Johannes
1925   *Der erste Korintherbrief.* Kritisch-exegetischer Kommentar über das Neue Testament. Göttingen: Vandenhoeck & Ruprecht.

WELTEN, Peter
TRE   5:159-61, art. "Bann. I: Altes Testament."

WESTERHOLM, Stephen
1986   "On Fulfilling the Whole Law (Gal 5:14)." *SEÅ* 51-52:229-37.
1988   *Israel's Law and the Church's Faith. Paul and His Recent Interpreters.* Grand Rapids: Eerdmans.

WESTERMANN, Claus
1960   *Grundformen prophetischer Rede.* BEvT 31. München: Kaiser 19714.
1964   "Arten der Erzählung in der Genesis." Pp. 9-91 in *Forschung am Alten Testament. Gesammelte Studien.* TBü 24. München: Kaiser.
1968   *Der Segen in der Bibel und im Handeln der Kirche.* München: Kaiser.
1969   *Isaiah 40-66. A Commentary.* OTL London: SCM 1978³ (also available: Das Buch Jesaia, 40-66. ATD 19. Göttingen: Vandenhoeck & Ruprecht).
1974   *Genesis. 1. Teilband. Genesis 1-11.* BKAT I/1. Neukirchen-Vluyn: Neukirchener.
1981   *Genesis. 2. Teilband. Genesis 12-36.* BKAT I/2. Neukirchen-Vluyn: Neukirchener.

WHITE, Hugh C.
1988   "Introduction: Speech Act Theory and Literary Criticism." *Semeia* 41:1–24.

WHITE, John L.
1971   "Introductory Formulae in the Body of the Pauline Letter." *JBL* 90:91–97.
1984   "New Testament Epistolary Literature in the Framework of Ancient Epistolography." Pp. 1730–56 in *ANRW* II, 25.2.
1986   *Light from Ancient Letters*. Foundations and Facets. Philadelphia: Fortress.

WIEFEL, Wolfgang
1969   "Fluch und Sakralrecht. Religionsgeschichtliche Prolegomena zur Frühentwicklung des Kirchenrechts." *Numen* 16:211–33.

WIESER, Friedrich E.
1987   *Die Abrahamvorstellungen im Neuen Testament*. Europäische Hochschulschriften 23; 317. Bern: Lang.

WILCKENS, Ulrich
1974   "Was heisst bei Paulus: 'Aus Werken des Gesetzes wird kein Mensch gerecht'?" Pp. 77–109 in *Rechtfertigung als Freiheit: Paulusstudien*. Neukirchen-Vluyn: Neukirchener.
1978   *Der Brief and die Römer (Röm 1-5)*. EKKNT VI/1. Zürich - Einsiedeln - Köln: Benziger.
1980   *Der Brief and die Römer (Röm 6-11)*. EKKNT VI/2. Zürich - Einsiedeln - Köln: Benziger.
1982   *Der Brief and die Römer (Röm 12-16)*. EKKNT VI/3. Zürich - Einsiedeln - Köln: Benziger.

WILCOX, Max
1977   "'Upon the Tree' - Deut 21,22–23 in The New Testament." *JBL* 96:85–99.

WILDBERGER, Hans
1989   *Jesaja. 2. Teilband. Jesaja 13-27*. BKAT X/2. Neukirchen-Vluyn: Neukirchener.

WILES, Gordon P.
1974   *Paul's Intercessory Prayers. The Significance of the Intercessory Prayer Passages in the Letters of St. Paul*. SNTSMS 24. London: Cambridge University Press.

WILLIAMS, Sam K.
1980   "The 'Righteousness of God' in Romans." *JBL* 99:241–90.
1987a   "Justification and the Spirit in Galatians." *JSNT* 29:91–100.
1987b   "Again *Pistis Christou*." *CBQ* 49:431–47.
1988   "Promise in Galatians: A Reading of Paul's Reading of Scripture." *JBL* 107:709–20.
1989   "The Hearing of Faith: AKOH ΠΙΣΤΕΩΣ in Galatians 3." *NTS* 35:82–93.

WILLIAMSON, Hugh G. M.
1985   *Ezra, Nehemiah*. Word Biblical Commentary 16. Waco: Word.

WILLIAMSON, Ronald
1989   *Jews in the Hellenistic World: Philo*. Cambridge Commentaries on Writings of the Jewish and Christian World 200 BC to AD 200. Cambridge: Cambridge University Press.

WISCHMEYER, Oda
1986   "Das Gebot der Nächstenliebe bei Paulus." *BZ* 30:161–87.

WOLFF, Christian
1982   *Der erste Brief des Paulus an die Korinther. Zweiter Teil: Auslegung der Kapitel 8-16*. THKNT VII/2. Berlin: Evangelische Verlagsanstalt.

WOLFF, Hans W.
  1961   "Das Kerygma des deuteronomistischen Geschichtswerks." *ZAW* 73:171–
            86 (also available pp. 308–24 in *Gesammelte Studien zum Alten Testament*.
            TBü 22. München: Kaiser, 1964).
  1964   "Das Kerygma des Jahwisten." Pp. 345–73 in *Gesammelte Studien zum
            Alten Testament*. TBü 22. München: Kaiser (also available: EvT 24:73–
            98).
WUELLNER, Wilhelm H.
  1978   "Toposforschung und Torahinterpretation bei Paulus und Jesus." *NTS*
            24:463–83.
  1987   "Where Is Rhetorical Criticism Taking Us?" *CBQ* 49:448–63.
YOUNG, Norman H.
  1987   "Paidagogos: The Social Setting of a Pauline Metaphor." *NT* 29:150–76.
YOUNG, Richard A.
  1989   "A Classification of Conditional Sentences based on Speech Act Theory."
            GTJ 10:29–49.
ZAHN, Th.
  1905   *Der Brief des Paulus an die Galater*. Kommentar zum NT IX. Leipzig:
            Deichert.
ZIMMERLI, Walther
  1969   *Ezechiel. 1. Teilband. Ezechiel 1–24*. BKAT XIII/1. Neukirchen-Vluyn:
            Neukirchener.

INDEX OF PASSAGES

INDEX OF MODERN AUTHORS

INDEX OF SUBJECTS

EMORY STUDIES IN EARLY CHRISTIANITY

Vernon K. Robbins, General Editor
David B. Gowler, Associate Editor

Volumes in this series investigate early Christian literature in the context of Mediterranean literature, religion, society, and culture. The authors use interdisciplinary methods informed by social, rhetorical, literary, and anthropological approaches to move beyond limits within traditional literary-historical investigations. The studies presuppose that Christianity began as a Jewish movement in various geographical, political, economic, and social locations in the Greco-Roman world.

*1.   David B. Gowler, *Host, Guest, Enemy and Friend: Portraits of the Pharisees in Luke and Acts*, 1991.

*2.   H. Wayne Merritt, *In Word and Deed: Moral Integrity in Paul*, 1993.

*3.   Vernon K. Robbins, *New Boundaries in Old Territory: Form and Social Rhetoric in Mark*, 1994. Ed. and introduced by David B. Gowler.

4.   Jan Botha, *Subject to Whose Authority? Multiple Readings of Romans 13*, 1994.

5.   Kjell Arne Morland, *The Rhetoric of Curse in Galatians: Paul Confronts Another Gospel*.

Forthcoming volume:

6.   Eds. Peder Borgen, Vernon K. Robbins, and David B. Gowler, *Recruitment, Conquest, and Conflict: Strategies in Judaism, Early Christianity, and the Greco-Roman World*.

*The first three volumes were published by and are available from Peter Lang Publishing, Inc., 275 Seventh Avenue, 28th Floor, New York, NY 10001-6708; (212) 647-7700; FAX (212) 647-7707; customer service (800) 770-5264, (212) 647-7706.
All subsequent volumes are available through Scholars Press.